Personality Psychology

Personality Psychology
Foundations and Findings

Marianne Miserandino
Arcadia University

PEARSON

Boston   Columbus   Indianapolis   New York   San Francisco   Upper Saddle River
Amsterdam   Cape Town   Dubai   London   Madrid   Milan   Munich   Paris   Montreal   Toronto
Delhi   Mexico City   Sao Paulo   Sydney   Hong Kong   Seoul   Singapore   Taipei   Tokyo

Editorial Director: Craig Campanella
Editor in Chief: Jessica Mosher
Executive Editor: Susan Hartman
Editorial Project Manager: LeeAnn Doherty
Editorial Assistant: Alexandra Mitton
Director of Marketing: Brandy Dawson
Senior Marketing Manager: Nicole Kunzmann
Marketing Assistant: Jessica Warren
Director of Production: Lisa Iarkowski
Managing Editor: Elizabeth Napolitano
Senior Production Project Manager: Roberta Sherman
Manufacturing Manager: Mary Fischer
Manufacturing Buyer: Sherry Lewis

Art Director: Leslie Osher
Cover Designer: Ilze Lemesis
Manager, Visual Research: Martha Shethar
Photo Researcher: Debbie Needleman
Cover Art: Franck Boston/Shutterstock
Media Editor: Michael Halas
Media Project Manager: Pamela Weldin
Supplements Editor: Katherin S. Cebik
Full-Service Project Management: Laserwords Maine
Composition: Laserwords
Printer/Binder: Quad/Versailles
Cover Printer: Lehigh-Phoenix Color/Hagerstown
Text Font: Minion

Library of Congress Cataloging-in-Publication Data

Miserandino, Marianne.
  Personality psychology : foundations and findings / by Marianne Miserandino.
       p. cm.
  ISBN 978-0-205-73887-8 (alk. paper)
  1.   Personality.   I. Title.
  BF698.M556 2011
  155.2—dc23
                                                            2011030719

10 9 8 7 6 5 4 3 2 QUV 15 14 13 12 11

www.pearsonhighered.com

ISBN-10: 0-205-73887-7
ISBN-13: 978-0-205-73887-8

Dedication

To Dimitri, with all my love, except for the chapter on resilience—that is dedicated to my mother, who taught me all I know on the subject and who passed away when that chapter was being written.

BRIEF CONTENTS

CONTENTS

PREFACE

What makes this book different from many of the current textbooks on personality psychology? This book is evidence-based: It focuses on what psychologists have discovered about the human personality.

This mission is directly reflected in the title of the book: *Personality Psychology: Foundations and Findings*. *Foundations* refers to the basic questions and accumulated knowledge in each of the areas of traits, genetics, neuroscience, self and identity, intrapsychic aspects, regulation and motivation, and cognition as it applies to the human personality. *Findings* refers to the cutting-edge research in each of these areas in which personality psychologists are actively engaged every day. By studying both of these parts of the research process, you will have a context for understanding new developments in the field.

In the process of learning about research, I hope you will learn about yourself, the people around you, and how personality psychology applies to your everyday life. But more than that, I hope that this grounding in basic research will help you understand and interpret new discoveries in psychology and related fields as they occur in the future. Although theories may be refined and facts updated, the scientific method of evaluating findings and putting them together to build an understanding of the human personality will outlast every edition of this book.

For Instructors: Approach of This Book

This book reflects personality research as contained in the latest *Handbook of Personality Psychology* (John, Robins, & Pervin, 2008) rather than an overview of the theories or schools of personality psychology. For many years, there has been this unusual split between what personality psychologists do (research), and what students learn in a personality course (theories). I believe that there is a place for both kinds of courses in most schools. I happen to teach in a psychology department that is committed to research, so much so that our majors take four labs in addition to Research Methods and Statistics, and every one of them writes a senior thesis, sometimes involving original research! I've been teaching both social psychology and personality psychology with labs for over 20 years.

Because this book represents the state-of-the-art of the field of personality, you won't see many topics that you would normally see in an undergraduate personality textbook. Notably missing are entire chapters or sections devoted to the major schools of thought including the humanistic and behavioristic schools. The book does cover Sigmund Freud in great depth, but barely mentions Carl Jung, Karen Horney, and Albert Bandura and makes no mention of B. F. Skinner! If you wish, these luminaries can easily be covered in your lectures at the appropriate juncture in the text.

As an instructor, I would encourage you to take a look at this research-based view of personality. From my experience as a teacher, I have a pretty good sense of the kinds of studies that pique students' interests and that they can make sense out of even if they haven't had an entire course in research methods. Of course, you may want to emphasize certain methods and techniques more—or less—than others depending on the needs of your students, just as you may wish to skip entire chapters or sections of chapters. In skipping chapters, I urge you to cover at least one of the chapters in the final section examining the whole person—gender, sexual orientation, or resilience—as these topics build on material covered in the earlier chapters.

Supplements

To help you in this approach, there are a number of supplements to help students master the foundations and findings of personality psychology, and to appreciate research findings in personality psychology today. Pearson Education is pleased to offer the following supplements to qualified adopters:

Instructor's Resource Manual (0-205-85365-X): Designed to make your lectures more effective and save you preparation time, this resource gathers together the most effective activities and strategies for teaching your course. Materials are broken up by chapter and include chapter outlines, key terms, lecture suggestions and discussion topics, and classroom activities. Available for download on the Instructor's Resource Center at www.pearsonhighered.com

Test Bank (0-205-09678-6): Each chapter contains multiple choice, true-false, short answer, and essay questions. Available for download on the Instructor's Resource Center at www.pearsonhighered.com.

MyTest Test Bank (0-205-09678-6): A powerful assessment-generation program that helps instructors easily create and print quizzes and exams. Questions and tests can be authored online, allowing instructors ultimate flexibility and the ability to efficiently manage assessments anytime, anywhere! Instructors can easily access existing questions, edit, create, and store using simple drag-and-drop techniques and Word-like controls. Data on each question provides information on difficulty level and page number of corresponding text discussion. In addition, each question maps to the text's major section and learning objective. For more information, go to www.PearsonMyTest.com.

Standard PowerPoint Presentation (0-205-09674-3): The PowerPoint Presentation is an exciting interactive tool for use in the classroom. Each chapter pairs key concepts with images from the textbook to reinforce student learning. Available for download on the Instructor's Resource Center at www.pearsonhighered.com.

CourseSmart eTextbook (0-205-09677-8): CourseSmart Textbooks Online is an exciting choice for students looking to save money. As an alternative to purchasing the print textbook, students can subscribe to the same content online and save up to 60% off the suggested list price of the print text. With a CourseSmart eTextbook, students can search the text, make notes online, print our reading assignments that incorporate lecture notes, and bookmark important passages for later review. For more information, or to subscribe to the CourseSmart eTextbook, visit www.coursesmart.com.

MySearchLab (0-205-23992-7): MySearchLab is an engaging online experience that personalizes learning for students. Features include the ability to highlight and add notes to the eText online or download changes straight to the iPad. Chapter quizzes and flashcards offer immediate feedback and report directly to the grade book. A wide range of writing, grammar, and research tools and access to a variety of academic journals, census data, Associated Press newsfeeds, and discipline-specific readings help students hone their writing and research skills. www.pearsonhighered.com.

For Students: Key Features

There are a number of unique features to this book to help you get excited about research—likened to getting children to eat vegetables by one early reviewer of this book. First, each chapter begins with an eye-opening study to make you curious about the topic of the chapter.

Second, rather than have an entire chapter devoted to research methods, I have integrated research methods into Chapters 1 through 11 in a special **Research Methods Illustrated** section. In my experience, most method chapters are rather dry because beginners don't have the background yet to understand why a particular method is important. Also, method chapters often seem to be placed at the beginning of a textbook so that just as readers are getting excited about the subject matter and are ready to jump in, they have to wait a bit longer to first learn about methods before they get to the good stuff. By integrating the methods, readers will be able to see right away how a particular method is used rather than having to remember it for later or flip back for a refresher.

For example, in the first chapter you will immediately learn about what makes a true experiment. In Chapter 6—where true experiments are often ethically and practically impossible—you will learn about correlational designs. In Chapter 11, when you might wonder if there is a difference between men and women on personality characteristics, you will learn about a statistic that quantifies how big of a difference it is, on average. In this way, each research method is taught in context and reinforced by the material in a given chapter. Sure, it might take you an entire semester to learn about *all* of the major kinds of research methods used by personality psychologists, but you will learn it in a more meaningful and lasting way. Research Methods Illustrated sections include:

- A True Experiment (Chapter 1)
- Factor Analysis (Chapter 2)
- Triangulation and Types of Data (Chapter 3)
- How to Evaluate a Personality. Is the NEO-PI-R a Good Personality Test? (Chapter 4)
- Qualitative Data and Content Analysis (Chapter 5)
- Correlational Designs I: The Logic of Adoption and Twin Studies (Chapter 6)
- Correlational Designs II: Scatterplots, Correlations, and the Alleged "Voodoo Science" of fMRI Studies (Chapter 7)
- Case Study and Psychobiography (Chapter 8)
- Path Analysis (Chapter 9)
- Field Studies and Natural Manipulations (Chapter 10)
- Effect Size and Meta-Analysis (Chapter 11)

Third, Chapters 1 through 11 include a feature called **Then and Now**. These features present an in-depth view of a research method or paradigm over time. Scientists often devote years of their life to studying a certain area or even to a specific research question. One of the things you will quickly learn about research is that results of experiments give us—not answers, as you might expect—but more questions! Research often progresses by asking more sophisticated questions and using more sophisticated methods to answer the same questions. Sir Isaac Newton reportedly said, "If I have seen further, it is only by standing on the shoulders of giants." These Then and Now features will give you a sense of what a research program looks like and an appreciation for the continuity of research across time. This way you can start to see for yourself how findings fit together and build on each other instead of seeming as if they occur in a vacuum (or happen perfectly the first time).

Fourth, each chapter contains a self-assessment, to help you explore some of the topics on a more personal level. These are nearly all legitimate personality tests that are currently used by personality psychologists in their research. I find that there is no better way to understand a topic than to experience it firsthand, and these personality tests will help

"Traditional scientific method has always been at the very best, 20–20 hindsight. It's good for seeing where you've been. It's good for testing the truth of what you think you know, but it can't tell you where you ought to go."

Robert M. Pirsig

you learn more about yourself in the process. For example, as you learn about Sigmund Freud and the psychoanalytic approach to personality, you can learn about your own adult attachment style that developed out of your early relationships. In Chapter 7 you can see how sensation seeking you are. You even can see how resilient or masculine and feminine you are and how much you know about sexual orientation in the chapters on these topics. Self-assessments include:

- Science or Science Fiction? (Chapter 1)
- The Ten-Item Personality Inventory (Chapter 2)
- The Spiritual Transcendence Scale (Chapter 3)
- The Need for Cognition Scale (Chapter 4)
- The Twenty Statements Test (Chapter 5)
- The Rosenberg Self-Esteem Scale (Chapter 5)
- Genetic and environmental contributions to personality (Chapter 6)
- The Brief Sensation Seeking Scale (Chapter 7)
- Adult Attachment Style (Chapter 8)
- The Need for Relatedness at College Questionnaire (Chapter 9)
- The Life Orientation Test (Chapter 10)
- The Personal Attributes Questionnaire (Chapter 11)
- Myths and misperceptions of sexual orientation (Chapter 12)
- The Ego Resiliency Scale (Chapter 13)

Fifth, all chapters feature a special **The Personality of Everyday Life** box, and include margin exercises titled SEE FOR YOURSELF to help you experience, apply, and ultimately make sense out of the findings discussed in the text.

Sixth, the margin critical thinking questions titled THINK ABOUT IT and **Review Questions** at the end of every chapter help you think critically about the theories and research discussed in the text. Actively getting involved in, questioning, processing, and recalling material, as opposed to passively reading the text, will help you recall the material better.

Seventh, there are *numerous* references in the book (nearly 2,000 of them!). By having each topic thoroughly documented, you will be able to investigate a given topic more deeply on your own. Perhaps you will have the opportunity to write a paper or to design a research project in personality psychology. With each topic fully supported with an extensive number of references, this book will serve as a good resource to get you started on such projects, even after your personality course is over. In particular, I've included many references to personality tests used by researchers with the hope that you can incorporate some of these measures into your own studies.

Finally, the book features three integrative chapters on gender, sexual orientation, and resilience (Chapters 11, 12, and 13, respectively). Each of these chapters builds on material from the previous chapters. For example, psychologists still don't have a good sense of what determines our gender or our sexual orientation. Part of it is physiological and part of it is psychological. Also, part of what makes us resilient has to do with our physiological makeup, our emotional responses, and also our cognitive interpretation of events. By reading one or all of these chapters you will see how the building blocks of personality—outlined in Chapters 2 through 10—can be put together to reach an understanding of the human personality.

There are a few things you will not see in this book. First, I have chosen to focus on healthy personality rather than psychopathology or personality disorders. Like other psychologists, I view mental health as occurring on a continuum (Krueger & Tackett, 2003; Widiger & Smith, 1999), so that the difference between so-called normal personality and abnormal personality is one of degree rather than of kind. After all, at what point does a defense mechanism turn into a delusion? And who's to make that judgment? By giving you a grounding in the building blocks of personality, I help you take it a step further on your own or in your next psychology class and study what happens when something goes awry in the process.

In addition, I have aimed to make this book about the personality of *all* persons, regardless of cultural background. I believe that the building blocks of personality are universal, though they play out against a cultural background. Rather than include a separate chapter on culture, or special highlighted boxes within the text, I have chosen to integrate findings on culture throughout the book. Sometimes the building blocks of personality do not vary by culture, but where they do, I make a point of discussing these departures within the relevant chapter.

By the end of reading this book, I hope that you will be as excited about the state of personality psychology as I am. And that crack about research being like vegetables? I like to think of the following quote from Ralph Waldo Emerson:

> *Do not be too timid and squeamish about your actions. All life is an experiment. The more experiments you make the better. What if they are a little coarse, and you may get your coat soiled or torn? What if you do fail, and get fairly rolled in the dirt once or twice. Up again, you shall never be so afraid of a tumble.*

Let us start this experiment together.

Acknowledgments

As trite as it may sound, this book took a whole village to bring to fruition. I wholeheartedly thank each and every one of you (whether I mention you by name or not), from my former students who challenged me with the words "You can write a better textbook," to my colleagues who read and commented on early drafts both at Arcadia University (Josh Blustein, Steve Robbins, Ned Wolff, Angela Gillem, Maddy Brenner, Dawn Michelle Boothby, Peggy Hickman, Sheryl Smith, and Wes Rose) and elsewhere (Dana Dunn, Moravian University; Ed Deci, University of Rochester), to colleagues who cheered me on and shared their experience and expertise on textbook writing (Barbara Nodine, Les Sdorow). I especially wish to thank my team of editors at Pearson who helped me do the impossible, including Susan Hartman, LeeAnn Doherty, Jeff Marshall, and additional reviewers including: Victor Bissonnette, Berry College; Ronen Cuperman, University of Texas at Arlington; Daneen Deptula, Fitchburg State University; Thomas Holtgraves, Ball State University; Ben Gorvine, Northwestern University; John Kurtz, Villanova; Heather LaCost, Waubonsee Community College; Phil O. McClung, West Virginia University at Parkersburg; Daniel Molden, Northwestern University; Kathryn C. Oleson, Reed College; Richard Osbaldiston, Eastern Kentucky University; Christina L. Scott, Saint Mary's College of California; Matthew Scullin, University of Texas at El Paso; and Chuck Tate, California State University Bakersfield. Thanks also to the students of PY332 during the Spring of 2011 for their comments and critiques of an early draft of this book; Dottie Ettinger and the student workers in the Psychology Department; Interlibrary Loan Magician Jay Slott, Michelle Realle, and the student workers in the Arcadia University Landman Library; and Provost Michael Berger and Dean John Hoffman, who supported my yearlong study leave from teaching to write a good first draft of the entire book.

On a personal note, I wish to thank my friends and husband who endured my factoids and frustrations over many a meal and online chat session: Suzanne DuPlantis, Reiko Finamore, Troy Finamore, Rick Arras (the master of analogies and metaphors), Adam Levy, Eileen Kim; my family, whose anecdotes, words, and photos occasionally grace these pages; Phil Jones for proofreading; Monique Legaré and my fellow dancers for having patience with missed rehearsals; my personal support team of Jayne Antonowsky, Parviz Hanjani, and Susan Nolte; Dimitrios Diamantaras for reading every last word of this text and his typesetting expertise; and my "crazy nephew" Dominick who made sure I didn't take the whole process too seriously by taking me to Disneyland with his wife Margherita and mother-in-law Rosaria so he could see my and my great-niece Caterina's faces light up while visiting the Magic Kingdom for our very first time.

About the Author

Marianne Miserandino is the 2010 winner of the Robert S. Daniel Teaching Excellence Award, Four-Year Colleges and Universities, from the Society for the Teaching of Psychology (Division 2 of the American Psychological Association). She was also the 2009 Arcadia University Professor of the Year and the 2000 recipient of the Lindback Award for Teaching Excellence. She currently maintains the Personality Pedagogy website for teachers of personality psychology (http://personalitypedagogy.arcadia.edu), for which she received a grant from the Association for Psychological Science (APS) Fund for Teaching and Public Understanding of Psychological Science.

Her commitment to teaching is evidenced by her work as news editor, reviewer, and frequent contributor to the APA journal *Teaching of Psychology.* She designed and conducted a 4-week study abroad program in Vienna, Austria, for the Arcadia University College of Global Studies on the psychology of Sigmund Freud, Alfred Adler, and Viktor Frankl.

Dr. Miserandino received her BA in psychology from the University of Rochester and a PhD in social-personality psychology from Cornell University. Dr. Miserandino came to Arcadia University after a postdoctoral fellowship in human motivation at the University of Rochester and full-time teaching.

She is a Fellow of the American Psychological Association, and a member of the Association for Psychological Science, the Society for Personality and Social Psychology, the Society for the Teaching of Psychology, Sigma XI—The Scientific Research Society, and the Honor Society of Phi Kappa Phi, and has served on the American Psychological Association Division Two Task Force for Minority Issues.

1 WHO AM I? UNDERSTANDING THE BUILDING BLOCKS OF PERSONALITY

Read the **Chapter** on
mysearchlab.com

The summer after my first year in high school, my mom and I spent a few weeks exploring the east end of Long Island. I had always loved the ocean growing up and I looked forward to the chance of spending every day at the beach. Until that summer, I thought I knew all about the ocean, having lived on Long Island my entire life—all 14 years of it—to that point. But that summer I learned that there was so much more to the ocean than I realized.

I was completely amazed at how different the ocean was each day. Some days the ocean would be very calm and we could walk out a long, long way before the water was over our heads. Other days, the ocean was too rough for small children to go into, with water over our heads and waves breaking just a few feet from shore. Some days the water would be very warm but then an overnight storm would churn up deep water delivering ice-cold water to the shore the next day. Even the color of the ocean varied from the light green of the sea foam to the dark forest green almost black of the deep water. I spent a lot of time thinking and daydreaming that summer while looking out to sea and it struck me that the ocean almost seemed to have a personality.

The ocean is a pretty good metaphor for personality. Think about it: The ocean is made up of water, but it is much more than that. There are tides, waves, inversions, salt, seaweed, and marine life; it is vast and deep; and it changes regularly. Could we understand the ocean only by studying water molecules? By exploring only its depths and ignoring the shore? Obviously, there are many different aspects of the ocean and scientists devote their lives to studying just a small part of what makes up the ocean. The ocean is all of these parts and yet it is also more than these parts. So it is with personality.

To understand personality, we need to understand what a person is like. Is she extroverted or introverted? Is he easygoing? Is she open to new ideas? Is he responsible? Would he make a good mate? Would she make a good lab partner? We also need to understand our genetics and physiology, which gives us our physical being and building blocks of neurons, hormones, and brain structures that take in and process information and direct our responses to the world. And we need to consider that there may be parts of the person hidden under the surface, much like how the ocean has tides and a myriad of creatures hidden in its depths. We also need to know how a person copes with the storms of life.

Even then, a person is more than these things, more than the sum of his or her parts. How does a person function in the world? How does a person think of himself or herself and interact with others? How do gender, sexual orientation, and other social identities and personal self-concepts affect a person? How does a person fit into the large social world, much like how the ocean is part of the larger ecosystem of the earth, including fish, birds, sky, and land? And finally, how does a person, like the ocean, change over time and yet remain fundamentally the same?

Two early personality psychologists mused that there are aspects of personality that are universal to all people, that are shared by similar people, and that are completely unique to a single individual (Kluckhohn & Murray, 1948).

Consider that all humans, regardless of culture, have a genetic makeup, a brain, a nervous system, and are born into a social group. To the extent that these forces affect human personality, there will be universals in human personality.

Of course, people do vary, but there is often a rhyme and a reason to their variance. At a basic level, there are people who are more likely to venture forth in the world to meet other people. We call such people extroverts. Other people, introverts, prefer to keep to themselves. We would expect people who behave similarly to share similar personality characteristics, whether it be extraversion or introversion, neuroticism or emotional stability, openness or concreteness, agreeableness or grumpiness, conscientiousness or impulsiveness, for example.

Finally, we could say that another human universal is the desire for actualization (i.e., to be who we are meant to be; to develop and express our individual identity). Though we may share the same mechanisms (genetics, physiology, neurology), some of the same characteristics (introversion-extraversion), and have some of the same experiences in the world (attachment to caregivers, sexual adjustment, trauma, happiness), the way these building blocks of personality come together forms a unique individual: you!

Knowing that people do vary, personality psychologists attempt to study both the ways people are similar and the ways people are different from each other.

The whole is greater than the sum of its parts: Just as the small pictures, like the ones on the left, combine to form the picture of the whole person on the right, personality is made up of building blocks.

In this book, I will share with you some of the building blocks of human personality at all levels, from the micro-level of genes on up to the macro- or meta-level of the social world. I hope to help you put these individual elements together and think across and beyond these individual levels to understand personality functioning.

What Is Personality Psychology?

Personality psychology is the scientific study of what makes us who we are. Using the scientific method of investigation, it is the study of individual differences: for identifying ways in which people are both similar and different, and for explaining how they became that way.

Part of personality is identifying and studying the building blocks or raw materials that make us think and act as we do. Consider the illustrations in the photos on the top of this page. Though the figure on the left is made up of smaller images, the figure as a whole is more than the mere sum of individual images. The same is true for personality. Although we can study the individual elements that make up the human personality, the elements come together to create a whole person in a way that is not reducible to its parts. And an individual's personality is more than the sum of his or her parts. Not only can the individual parts vary among people, but the way they fit together may vary as well.

> "Whenever two people meet there are six present. There is the man as he sees himself, each as the other person sees him, and each man as he really is."
>
> *William James, the father of American psychology*

The Building Blocks of Personality

What are these individual parts that come together to create a whole person? Most psychologists would agree that to understand human personality we need to understand traits, genetics, neuroscience, self and identity, intrapsychic aspects, regulation and motivation, and cognition. Missing from this list are social and environmental forces that impact human personality at all of these levels. For example, environmental forces—including culture, society, and socialization by parents and peers—have a huge impact on our personalities. The impact of the social environment is felt at multiple levels, from our sense of self and identity to the level of our genetics. Rather than viewing social influences as a separate building block, the impact of societal forces runs as a theme throughout all of the foundations. Let's take a closer look at the building blocks of personality.

SEE FOR YOURSELF

How would you describe yourself? The words that come most readily to mind are often trait terms.

Traits.   How do we go about describing human personality and identifying important personality characteristics? The answer is **traits**: a person's typical way of thinking, feeling, and acting, in various situations, at different times. We may be born with a certain physiology that makes us more likely to develop certain characteristics, but there are many other characteristics that we can develop from our socialization (from parents, peers, teachers, society), and from our personal experiences. These traits will be consistent across our lives and will be expressed in all sorts of ways, as you will see in later chapters, from how we shake hands, to the kind of music we prefer, to even how we decorate our living spaces and the careers we choose.

THINK ABOUT IT

What does it mean to say we inherit "potentialities"?

Genetics.   Personality starts with our genetic makeup that we have inherited from each of our birth parents. Over millennia, evolutionary forces have selected behaviors that improve the survival of the species or survival of an individual and an individual's close genetic relatives (Confer et al., 2010). **Genetics** is the study of how genes and environment affect personality and behavior. We know that even though many personality variables have a genetic component, *every one of them* has an environmental component as well. As we shall see in Chapter 6, nature and nurture work together to make us who we are. Whereas we may inherit specific personality characteristics, we also inherit potentialities that may be expressed in our personalities depending on the environment.

Neuroscience.   Our genes encode our physical bodies, including our brain and nervous system. **Neuroscience** is the study of how our brain and nervous system affect personality and behavior through the study of bodily responses, brain structure, brain activity, and biochemical activity. Some of this research suggests that extroversion, neuroticism, and impulsivity are related to physiological and neurological differences which may be present at birth, or develop soon thereafter. Though the environment and our personal experiences can still impact how these characteristics develop, the current evidence suggests that part of who we are—at least in terms of these three characteristics—is built into us by our neurology.

THINK ABOUT IT

Are you born with a self or does a self develop?

Self and Identity.   **Self and Identity** encompasses our own sense of who we are including our self-concept, self-esteem, and social identity. One of the hallmarks of being human is the ability to reflect on ourselves. We have a sense of who we are: our self-concept. And we have an opinion about that: our self-esteem. We may even try to present ourselves in a certain way to others, or we may embrace what others think about us, taking on a social identity. Where scientists once thought that self-reflection was unique to humans, we now know that a few other species share this capacity including dolphins and chimpanzees. Part of what makes up our personality, in addition to our traits, is our sense of self and social identity.

Intrapsychic Foundations of Personality.   With this sense of self, we can look within ourselves (*intra*) to our own conscious and unconscious thoughts and feelings (*psychic*) that also make up our personality (**intrapsychic**). No doubt you've heard of Sigmund Freud, who established an entire theory about our unconscious motivations and the defenses we use to protect ourselves from threatening thoughts and desires.

> "If a man has been his mother's undisputed darling he retains throughout life the triumphant feeling, the confidence in success, which not seldom brings actual success along with it."
> *Sigmund Freud*

One of Freud's biggest contributions to psychology was the realization that physical disorders could have psychological causes, which were often unconscious. He also claimed that our early experiences left an indelible, but unconscious, imprint on our adult personalities. At the same time, Freud was one of the first to suggest that personality could be changed, and he originated a method of psychotherapy to do so. Since Freud's day, science has discounted some aspects of his theory, even as it has supported others (Westen, 1998a). Today, a complete understanding of personality must also take into account our unconscious motivations, including our defense mechanisms and important attachments, starting with our caregivers and continuing with our intimate relationships.

Regulation and Motivation: Self-Determination Theory.   Although Freud believed that people were controlled by unconscious forces, a modern theory of motivation suggests that people can—and do!—regulate themselves consciously and unconsciously. According to self-determination theory (Deci & Ryan, 1985; Ryan & Deci, 2008), when people feel free to choose, are competent at what they do, and are connected to people around them, they will be motivated and self-directed for the task at hand. People differ in the extent to which they feel self-determined and regulate their own motivation. The building block of **regulation and motivation** is concerned with how people adjust their responses to the environment, both consciously and unconsciously.

Cognitive Foundations.   Finally, people differ in how they process information, especially about the causes and impacts of events in their lives, and expectations for what may happen in the future. Specifically, there are individual differences in locus of control, learned helplessness, learned hopelessness, and optimism-pessimism. The **Cognitive foundation** describes how people perceive and think about information about themselves and the world.

Putting It All Together: Integration

Finally, in **Integration** we combine the building blocks of personality into a whole person. When it comes to personality, the whole is greater than the mere sum of the parts. Consider your own personality. You are equipped with a specific package of genes that have provided a certain type of physiological reactivity and brain function, which, along with life experiences have led you to develop a package of character traits. You are able to reflect on who you are, and who the world wants you to be. You may also be vaguely aware of hidden motives and desires, such as whom you feel emotional attachments to. You may also be enthusiastically engaged in certain activities and bored or disengaged from others. You may face the world with optimism (or pessimism), believing that you have an impact on what befalls you (or not!). Is knowing all of this about you enough to say that we really *know* you?

For the most part, all of these topics stand alone. That is, we can understand any one of them without thinking a whole lot about the others (indeed, your instructor might take these chapters in a different order or omit some of them altogether). However, some of the most interesting aspects of the human experience can be understood only by seeing how these blocks build on each other and interact.

Take gender, for example. How much of our gender is genetic or physiological and how much of it is learned or socialized? Is gender identity grounded in our thoughts, beliefs, and cognitions? What impact do our society's beliefs about gender have on us? Do men and women have different personalities? To answer these questions, we need an understanding of genetics, physiology, self, and cognitions. The picture is even more complicated—and fascinating—when it comes to understanding whom we are attracted to. Genetics and neurology interact with cognitions, attachments, and motivations, to determine our sexual orientation.

Or, consider how people cope with stress. Are there differences in physiology that make some people hardier and more resilient to stress? Or is handling stress more an issue of mind over matter? Are some types of people better able to cope with stress and tragedy? To answer these questions, we need to build on our understanding of neurology, cognitions, and personality traits.

> **THINK ABOUT IT**
>
> Do men and women have different personalities? Are these differences inborn or learned?

Who am I? Am I more than the sum of my genetics, neurology, traits, self and identity, intrapsychic motivations, attachments, and cognitions?

Organization of This Book

This book organizes these seven building blocks of personality into five parts, each revolving around a question, and includes a special section on putting it all together:

- *Part I: The Dispositional Foundations of Personality—Who Do You Say That I Am?* In this section, we consider the theories behind personality traits, the practical way traits are expressed in many aspects of our lives, and how best to measure personality. We also take a look at how people reflect on themselves. After reading this section, you will understand how psychologists describe human personality and also how people describe themselves as reflected in their own self-concepts, self-esteem, and social identities. This section includes four chapters: Chapter 2, Personality Traits: A Good Theory; Chapter 3, Personality Traits: Practical Matters; Chapter 4, Personality Assessment; and Chapter 5, Self and Identity.

- *Part II: The Biological Foundations of Personality—What Makes You* You? Here, we focus on how your unique genetic blueprint impacts your personality. In addition, we look at how your unique brain and physiology impact your personality. Together, these chapters describe the biological foundations of personality. The section includes Chapter 6, Genetics, and Chapter 7, The Neuroscience of Personality.

- *Part III: The Intrapsychic, Regulation, and Motivational Foundations of Personality—Who Do You Feel You Are?* Personality psychologists study aspects of our personality at a deep-down, almost gut level that we may not even be aware of. Sigmund Freud was the first, but by no means the last, to theorize that unconscious processes have a big impact on who we are. This section looks at Freudian theory as well as more modern theories of how unconscious processes such as our motivations, desires, and emotional attachments makes us who we are. This section includes two chapters: Chapter 8, Intrapsychic Foundations of Personality, and Chapter 9, Regulation and Motivation: Self-Determination Theory.

- *Part IV: The Cognitive Foundations of Personality—Who Do You Think You Are?* The philosopher René Descartes famously remarked, "I think therefore I am" and psychologists working in this area couldn't agree more. The specific thoughts we have—like the belief that we control what happens to us or whether we are helpless—make us who we are. Knowing what people think they are, like optimists or pessimists for example, tells us a lot, not just about their personalities, but also about their health and well-being and other important life outcomes. This section includes Chapter 10, Cognitive Foundations of Personality.

- *Part V: Integration Across the Building Blocks of Personality—Is the Whole Person Greater Than the Sum of His or Her Parts?* Finally, having a sense of what makes up the human personality, we need to consider how the individual foundations fit together to make a whole person. In the case of personality, the whole is definitely greater than the sum of its parts. That is, to understand the impact of gender and sexual orientation on personality, we need to consider multiple building blocks at the same time. In fact, if you want to know how an individual person functions in the world, adapting to both good times and bad, and in sickness and health, it would take a consideration of all of the building blocks to understand the resilience of the human spirit. This section includes Chapter 11, Gender and Personality; Chapter 12, Sexual Orientation: An Integrative Mini-Chapter; and Chapter 13, Resilience: An Integrative Mini-Chapter.

As we work our way through the building blocks of personality, you will see how personality psychology has attempted to answer these eternal questions using research. I should warn you right now: In the attempt to answer these questions researchers have discovered—more questions! Instead of definitive answers, think of this book as presenting more of the state-of-the-science on these questions.

How Do Psychologists Study Personality?

You might wonder what the difference is between personality psychologists and you sitting around with friends making guesses about the personality of people you see at a party. In a word: research. Research allows us to formulate and test questions about human behavior, to design accurate methods to answer these questions, and to test competing explanations against one another (Dunn, 1999). By conducting research using sound methods, scientists are able to generalize beyond their own findings and add to the collective knowledge about a given phenomenon and, in many cases, apply their results to make the world a better place for individuals and whole societies (Dunn, 1999).

SEE FOR YOURSELF

What do you think causes people to act the way they do? Where do you believe personality comes from?

The Scientific Method

Research rests on the philosophy of empiricism: using direct experience to draw conclusions about the world. Psychological research relies on the **scientific method** which describes how to make and test observations about the world in order to draw conclusions while minimizing error or bias (Dunn, 1999). The scientific method starts with the identification of basic facts about the world. Then, using this collection of facts, scientists build theories. For example, while people watching at a party we might recognize that there are similarities and differences in how people behave, such as how some people laugh more than others. Then, using these facts as a basis, we can reason what other ideas are likely to be true. We might start to notice that people who laugh a lot like to hang out with other people. Is this true? We could do some more controlled observations of people to test our theory. Theories help scientists ask new questions and suggest where to look for answers and what kinds of answers they might find.

Then scientists make predictions and test predictions based on their theories using controlled methods. For example, you might devise an experiment for these laughing partygoers to see if people who laugh respond differently to the experiment than the nonlaughers, or you might administer a series of personality questionnaires to them and see if the laughers all share a common personality trait which is different from the nonlaughers.

Finally, scientists make their results public by publishing them in journals, on the Internet, or by presenting their results at conferences. They do this to seek out independent verification from other researchers. For example, after the party you might do some investigation using a psychological database such as PsycArticles and read about a study that was conducted by other researchers that also found that people behave differently at a party and identified two kinds of people: extroverts and introverts.

THINK ABOUT IT

How do common sense, anecdotal evidence, personal experience, the opinion of experts, and research differ?

Personality hasn't always embraced the experimental method as much as other branches of psychology have (Cronbach, 1957; Eysenck, 1997), but over the last decade or so there has been a tremendous explosion in experimental personality psychology (John et al., 2008). Science progresses along a continuum from casual observations, which may inspire a hunch or guess about human behavior, to controlled experimentation, in which researchers attempt to prove a theory false (Eysenck, 1997; see Figure 1.1). As long as

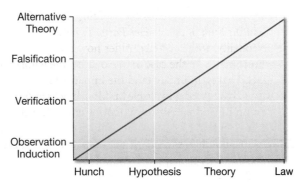

Figure 1.1 Science progresses along a continuum, with methods that become more sophisticated as hunches turn into theory and laws. *Source:* Eysenck (1997, Figure 1, p. 1225). Eysenck, H. J. (1997). Personality and experimental psychology. *Journal of Personality and Social Psychology,* 73(6), 1224–1237.

research evidence supports a theory, that theory will prevail and with more research will reach the status of a law until it is overthrown by an alternative theory that explains the evidence even better. For the most part, personality psychology has many theories, but unfortunately, very few (if any!) actual laws of human behavior.

Observational Studies and Personality Questionnaires

Personality psychologists, like other researchers in psychology, draw on many kinds of methods to explore the human personality (Robins, Fraley, & Krueger, 2007; see Table 1.1). The methods researchers use depend on the kind of questions they are asking. For example, researchers might use an **observational study**, where they observe what people do, to understand a certain phenomenon such as: Do some people talk more than others at a party? Then, based on these observations researchers might make an educated guess or generate a **hypothesis** to explain their findings. Continuing our example, one researcher might hypothesize that extroverted people talk more than introverted people. He might give partygoers a self-report personality questionnaire to see if, indeed, extroverts are doing more of the talking at a party than the introverts are. **Personality questionnaires** are tests in which people answer questions about themselves that identify certain aspects of their personality, like how talkative, outgoing, and sociable they are, all typical traits of an extrovert. Another researcher might hypothesize that extroverts circulate more than introverts. She might give out a personality questionnaire and link people's answers to her observations of how many people each guest talks to and how long each interaction lasts.

Another researcher might present each person with an ambiguous picture and ask him or her to tell a story, administering a projective personality test. Yet another researcher

Table 1.1 Methods and Measures Used in Personality Research

Type of Measure	Mean Frequency	% Ever Used
Self-report scales and questionnaires	6.17	100%
Judgments of self and others	5.07	99
Informant reports	3.68	86
Behavioral observation	3.58	89
Structured interviews	3.15	76
Behavioral responses	3.11	81
Other judgments tasks (e.g., of stimuli)	3.10	79
Narrative/open-ended questionnaires	3.03	74
Reaction time	2.93	61
Experience sampling	2.89	65
Implicit measures	2.76	64
Memory tasks	2.52	62
Autonomic arousal	2.22	57
Judgments of groups/nations/cultures	2.19	43
Hormone levels	1.94	36
Neuroimaging (fMRI, etc.)	1.75	32
Molecular genetics/DNA testing	1.60	26

Note: Prominent personality psychologists ($N = 72$) were asked to rate how often they used each of 17 assessment methods using a scale ranging from 1 (*Not at all*) to 7 (*Very much*), with 4 (*Somewhat*) at the middle. The third column lists the percentage of researchers who have ever used the method in their work.

Source: Robins, Tracy, and Sherman (2007, Table 37.1, p. 676). From R. W. Robins, R. C. Fraley, & R. F. Krueger, eds., *Handbook of Research Methods in Personality Psychology.* Copyright © 2007 by Guilford Press. Reprinted with permission.

could ask guests about their past behavior or the behavior of their parents or siblings. Still another researcher might go so far as to compare the heart rate, hormone levels, or the brain activity of extroverts and introverts to see if differences in their behavior are due to underlying physiological or neurological differences between them. Another researcher might wonder if women are more talkative than men, and if so, how large, on average, is this difference?

Correlational and Experimental Designs

If researchers want to know more about *why* extroverts talk more, this will require different kinds of research. For example, one researcher may want to interview each person at the party or interview their friends, either using set structured questions for each person or by having each person merely tell his or her own story. Analyzing this kind of qualitative data requires different methods than rating scales or questionnaires (see Chapter 5 for more about these methods). Sigmund Freud, the founder of psychoanalysis, built much of his theory on case studies of his patients (we discuss how to conduct a case study when we discuss Freud in Chapter 8).

Still another researcher might investigate whether extroversion and introversion runs in families using a family study. She might even study twins who were separated at birth and adopted by different families to gauge the relative contribution of genetics and environment on extroversion-introversion. She might hypothesize that if extraversion runs in families, then people ought to resemble their birth parents more than their adoptive parents or their twins more than their nontwin siblings.

How do we gauge similarity between children and their parents or between twins? Enter the **correlation coefficient**, indicated by the symbol *r*. A correlation coefficient does just that: It measures the relationship, or *co-relation*, between two variables. Correlations can be positive or negative, depending on the type of relationship the two variables in question have. If two variables increase or decrease at the same time, then they are positively correlated. For example, softball skill and hits at bat are *positively correlated*: Better batters hit the ball more than weaker batters. However, if one variable increases as the other one decreases—or vice versa, decreasing as the other one increases—then the two variables are *negatively correlated*. Golf skill and golf scores are negatively correlated: Better players have *lower* scores.

By convention, correlations are considered high, medium, or low depending on how big they are (see Table 1.2). These numbers should be taken only as a rough guideline, as the size of a correlation doesn't tell us if the relationship is statistically significant, and not merely a fluke. For that, we need to know the sample size and some other information about the sample, so researchers generally report the significance level of any correlations they calculate.

When two variables are related, there are always at least three possible explanations for the findings. First, it's possible that the first variable causes the second. Second, it's possible that the second variable causes the first one. Finally, it's also possible that some third variable causes both of the variables. Because we can't be sure what is causing the relationship we see between two variables we must keep in mind that *correlation* is not the same as *causation*. Knowing that two variables are similar doesn't tell us about *why* they are similar.

Table 1.2 Interpreting Correlations

Negative Correlations	Size	Positive Correlations
.0 to −.3	Small	.0 to .3
−.3 to −.5	Medium	.3 to .5
−.5 to −.9	Large	.5 to .9

Source: From Cohen (1988).

Although a family study would yield some possible answers as to why extroverts talk more (e.g., "It's in their genes" or "They come from a very sociable family"), it wouldn't isolate a specific cause of the talkative behavior that we have observed. To test the theory that one variable *causes* another variable, scientists need to conduct a true experiment (described in the next section). When this is not possible either due to practical or ethical reasons, researchers use correlational studies. In **correlational studies** researchers generally don't manipulate variables, but instead measure two variables to see how they are related.

In personality psychology, in particular, when we want to study how a person with a certain personality behaves, we use a correlational study to measure both personality and behavior. For example, we might give people a personality questionnaire that measures their level of extroversion. Extroverts would score high on this questionnaire whereas introverts would score low. Later, we can see how introverts and extroverts interact with strangers, or differ in physiological arousal, or any other measure that we think would show a difference based on personality. Similarly, we could measure a person's typical level of anxiety and see how he or she reacts to a pop quiz. We would expect people high in anxiety to perform worse than people low in anxiety.

Many studies on the genetics or neuroscience of personality use correlational designs, such as twin or adoption studies. Indeed, when researchers can't manipulate the variable they want to study, they conduct their studies in the "real world" using field studies and natural manipulations, such as studying people coping with job loss, ill health, or natural tragedies, or war (see Chapter 10 for more on these methods). When correlational studies are well designed, replicated, and combined with other kinds of evidence, they are nearly as good as a true experiment in identifying the causes of outcomes (Aronson et al., 1990).

Research Methods Illustrated: A True Experiment

There are many different methods that psychologists use to study human personality and behavior (Revelle, 2007). Researchers could merely observe behavior or they might measure a personality characteristic or they might place people in a controlled situation and see how they react. This latter method, of placing people in a carefully controlled situation and measuring their responses, is called an *experiment*.

In a typical experiment, researchers decide what variable they wish to study. Researchers then design at least two conditions which differ in this variable. In one condition, called the **experimental condition**, participants experience one treatment. In the other, **control condition**, participants experience a different treatment or no treatment at all. Researchers will go to great lengths to ensure that the entire experimental procedure is exactly alike for all participants except for this one difference in the variable being studied.

Then, researchers must use **random assignment** to assign participants to one condition or the other. Random assignment means that every participant in the experiment has an equal chance of experiencing each of the conditions. In the case of two groups, the researcher might flip a coin to decide which treatment a participant will receive.

By having **experimental control**, where all aspects of the experiment are the same except for the variable being studied, and random assignment, where participants have an equal chance of being in any condition, researchers are able to conclude that a difference in reactions of participants must have been due to the variable that was manipulated. This is the logic of a **true experiment** which allows researchers to conclude that what they manipulated *caused* a difference in the outcome they measured (Aronson et al., 1990).

By manipulating one variable, researchers look to see if there was a difference in some response of the participants, which they measure. The variable that researchers manipulate is called the **independent variable** because it is independent of participants' responses. The variable that the researchers measure, the responses of the participants, is called the **dependent variable** because it depends on participants' responses. In fact, many experiments are aptly titled "The effect of _____ on _____" to help readers identify the independent variable (the first blank) and the dependent variable (the second blank) right away.

For example, suppose researchers wanted to see if some cognitive strategies for coping with failure were more effective than others. They might randomly assign participants to one of two treatment conditions: Effective Strategies or Ineffective Strategies. Then, after they learned and practiced these strategies, the researchers could measure how angry, anxious, disappointed, unhappy, and sad they felt afterward. In this experiment, the independent variable, what the researchers manipulated, is type of strategy. The dependent variable, what the researchers measured, is emotion.

If there is a difference in participants' emotions after the experimental treatment, and if the researchers successfully controlled *all other* differences between the groups, then we can conclude that the difference in emotions at the end of the experiment must be due to the treatment during the experiment.

When it comes to research in personality, there are a lot of variables that we cannot manipulate because it is impossible, impractical, or unethical to do so. For example, there is no way to randomly assign people to a certain personality type, like being an extrovert or an introvert. Similarly, it would be wrong to manipulate self-esteem in an experiment by making people in one condition feel bad about themselves. In these cases, researchers either use correlational designs or else researchers see if their manipulation has a different effect on people depending on their personality (Brewer, 2000; Revelle, 2007; Smith, 2000).

This experiment on cognitive strategies for coping with failure was actually part of a more detailed experiment studying the effect of cognitive strategies and personality on emotions after failure (Ng & Diener, 2009). Participants imagined that they failed to get into any of the eight graduate programs to which they had supposedly applied. The researchers manipulated coping strategy, just as described, by randomly assigning all participants to an Effective Strategies condition or an Ineffective Strategies condition.

In the Effective Strategies condition, participants were instructed to reinterpret their failure to see it in a more positive light, to see if they could find something positive in the experience, and to reflect on how they might be able to grow as a person as a result of the event. They were also instructed to think about how they might do something to change or to improve the situation. Participants in the Ineffective Strategies condition were instructed to focus on how upset they were, to admit that they could not deal with what happened, and to think that they should just give up and stop trying to reach their goal of entering graduate school.

The researchers also took into account the personality of the participants by identifying them as being high or low in **Neuroticism**, a personality trait that describes how anxious and vulnerable to negative emotions a person is. Notice that the researchers are unable to randomly assign people to be high or low in Neuroticism, because it is a personality trait. Instead, they merely measured this variable and then assigned people high or low on Neuroticism to conditions, ensuring an equal number of people of both types in each condition.

Finally, they measured how angry, anxious, disappointed, unhappy, and sad they felt afterward, combining these responses into one composite variable of negative emotion. The design of this experiment is a 2 (Coping Strategy) by 2 (Neuroticism) design. There are two **levels**, or groups, within each independent variable: Effective and Ineffective Coping Strategies and High and Low Neuroticism. Note that only one of these variables, Coping Strategy, was actually under experimental control, that is, actually manipulated by the experimenters.

"There are two possible outcomes: If the result confirms the hypothesis, then you've made a measurement. If the result is contrary to the hypothesis, then you've made a discovery."
Enrico Fermi

The true experiment, where participants are randomly assigned to treatment conditions, is one of many methods personality psychologists use to study individuals.

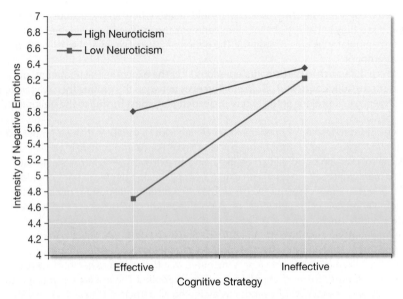

Figure 1.2 Negative emotions experienced by people high and low in Neuroticism who were instructed to use effective or ineffective cognitive strategies to cope with a hypothetical negative event. *Source*: Ng & Diener (2009, Figure 3, p. 459). Reprinted with permission from," Feeling bad? The "power" of positive thinking may not apply to everyone," by Ng, W., & Diener, E. (2009), *Journal of Research in Personality*, 43, 455–463. Permission conveyed through the Copyright Clearance Center.

What did they discover? First, there was a main effect for condition, meaning that the condition that participants were in affected how much negative emotion they reported at the end of the experiment. Participants in the Ineffective Strategies condition reported more negative emotion than participants in the Effective Strategies condition. Second, there was also a main effect for personality, meaning that participants' levels of Neuroticism affected how much negative emotion they reported at the end of the experiment. People high in Neuroticism reported more negative emotion than people low in Neuroticism.

Finally, there was a significant *interaction* between condition and Neuroticism. Whenever we find a significant interaction, it means that one of the main effects is different depending on the level of the other variable. Interaction effects are easiest to see in a graph. Lines that are not parallel to each other suggest an interaction between variables (see Figure 1.2).

Here, the significant interaction between Coping Strategy and Neuroticism suggests that Effective Strategies were effective only for people low in Neuroticism. People low in Neuroticism who used Effective Strategies felt less negative emotions than people low in Neuroticism who used Ineffective Strategies. Essentially, using ineffective strategies made people low in Neuroticism feel like people high in Neuroticism. The conclusion from these results is that the effect of strategy depends on personality, or, as the researchers caution, the power of positive thinking may not work for everyone—it depends on your personality (Ng & Diener, 2009).

Why might be this be the case? Although this is a very good question, it was not the question the researchers sought to answer in this experiment. This question will have to wait for another experiment—or material we shall cover in the chapters ahead!

Types of Data and Personality Assessment

As you can see, there are many ways of answering the seemingly simple question of "Why do some people talk more at a party?" The most accurate answers come from using principles of good research design. As a general rule, we can put more faith in results that come from more than just one study or more than just one method. Even when studying just a single person—that cute, outgoing partygoer telling a joke to a small crowd of admirers—there are many kinds of data we can gather (John & Soto, 2007). We can collect **self-report data** (e.g., questionnaires, interviews), **observation data** from friends or trained observers, **test**

data (e.g., see how they behave in a controlled situation like the laboratory), or even **life data** (e.g., count how many times a person's photo appeared in his or her yearbook or how many campus organizations he or she belongs to). We explore these various kinds of data in more depth in Chapter 3.

> info about people that is publically available such as graduating from college, clubs + organizations, criminal records, marriages + so forth

Of course, a study is only as good as the instruments that a researcher uses. Even a seemingly straightforward personality test is backed by previous experimentation to assure that the questions are understandable and clear, that responders are giving sincere answers (as opposed to answering in bogus or unreliable ways), and that the results of such assessments are valid, reliable, and useful (Smith & Archer, 2008). How can a researcher be sure he or she is using the very best measurements in studies? This topic is so important to personality psychology that we spend an entire chapter discussing the common types of personality tests, the uses of personality tests, and what makes a good personality test, including reliability, validity, generalizability, and response sets.

> "If the only tool you have is a hammer, you tend to see every problem as a nail."
> *Abraham Maslow*

Scientists have a number of tools or methods at their disposal. And like a good carpenter, who chooses the right tool depending on the job at hand, personality psychologists use whatever tool is most appropriate for answering the question they wish to explore. As you learn about each of the building blocks of personality, you will also learn about one of the various methods personality psychologists have used to explore the human personality. Sometimes it is easier to understand a particular method when you can see how it is used by personality psychologists to answer a specific question or to test a specific theory.

The logic of the true experiment requires researchers to control all aspects of the laboratory environment even determining what participants in an experiment will be facing! As you can see, this is an awesome responsibility and one not to be taken lightly. Researchers must adhere to stringent ethical principles and guidelines set out by the American Psychological Association (American Psychological Association, 2002, 2010). These guidelines were put in place to ensure the safety, trust, and welfare of research participants. Let us now turn to a discussion of research ethics.

Then and Now: The Ethics of Research With People

One day in 2004, Paula's world suddenly changed forever. Though she knew she was adopted, the stranger on the other end of the phone gave her the news: You have an identical twin. Identical *strangers* is how Paula and Elyse came to refer to themselves (Schein & Bernstein, 2008). The women discovered that they were both interested in film, had lived in Paris, and were vulnerable to bouts of depression. But what truly disturbed them, is that they and their families, along with five other pairs of identical twins and one set of identical triplets, were unwitting participants in a strange study. The head psychiatrist at the adoption agency *purposely* separated identical twins. But not all identical twins were separated, only those who were born of mothers with a history of disorders like schizophrenia and bipolar disorder. He used the identical twins to conduct his own study of the impact of genetics and environment on

Identical twins Paula Bernstein and Elyse Schein didn't find out until they were adults that they had an identical twin and were unwitting participants in an unethical study in which identical twins who were put up for adoption were purposely separated at birth and adopted by separate families.

the development of mental illnesses, and did so without the knowledge and consent of the birth mothers and the adoptive families. Families thought that the kindly doctor who made regular visits was merely making sure that the children were adjusting well to their adoptive families.

Many adoptive parents said that they would have gladly adopted their child and their child's twin had they known. Many twins were understandably upset to discover—often well into their adult lives—that certain illnesses ran in their biological families, important information that was purposely kept from them and their adoptive families. Finally, although taken from their birth mothers right away, the twins were raised in foster care and not separated from each other until they were 6 to 9 months of age. Many twins reported growing up with a permanent sense of loss or the fantasy that they had a secret twin (Schein & Bernstein, 2008).

Elyse and Paula, like the other participants in this study, were outraged. Because of the pain the study caused and would continue to cause as participants discovered the true circumstances of their birth and adoption, a court order has sealed the documents describing the study and its results until 2066 (Schein & Bernstein, 2008). With horror, the more the facts of their birth came to light, the more their situation reminded Elyse and Paula of the experiments by the Nazi doctor Josef Mengele who conducted inhumane experiments on prisoners in the concentration camps (Lifton, 1986).

Sadly, this study is not the only incident in the history of unethical research that includes the Tuskegee Syphilis study (Reverby, 2009), in which impoverished African American sharecroppers were purposely given syphilis and prevented from obtaining treatment; the Nazi doctors (Lifton, 1986); and studies done on people in prisons, mental hospitals, and orphanages without their consent and often with coercion. Could this twin study be conducted today? The scientific community, including the American Psychological Association (American Psychological Association, 2002, 2010), along with many governments, including the United States (Department of Health and Human Services, 1979), have all agreed to standards of ethical conduct for research with human subjects that protect human participants and prevent studies like these from ever being conducted.

According to the Belmont Report (Department of Health and Human Services, 1979), research with humans must adhere to three principles: respect for persons, beneficence, and justice. The principle of **respect for persons** includes allowing people to choose for themselves whether they wish to participate or not, by giving their consent after they have been informed

THINK ABOUT IT

Does your school have a requirement that students in introductory psychology classes participate in research studies? Is this ethical?

Participants from the Tuskegee Study: From 1932 to public outcry in 1972, the U.S. government carried out an unethical study observing the natural progression of syphilis in humans. The study continued even after penicillin was discovered to be a cure for syphilis in the 1940s.

about the procedures and possible risks of the study. This is called **informed consent.** It also states that the researcher must give extra protection to people who have limited autonomy, or limited physical or mental capacity to give their informed consent.

For example, people who are in jail have limited autonomy and cannot be used for research without extra efforts to ensure that they understand that their participation will not impact their release in any way. Similarly, employees must be assured that their participation will not affect their employment status or their work evaluation. Also, students must be assured that their grades will not be affected by their willingness to participate in a research project or not. Children and people with certain disorders may lack the maturity or the cognitive capacity to evaluate the risks and benefits of participation for themselves, and so parents or legal guardians must give consent for them.

The principle of **beneficence** states that first, and foremost, researchers should do no harm to their participants. This includes using the best research methods and materials, having trained personnel interact with research participants, and minimizing possible harm and maximizing possible benefits of research participation.

Finally, the principle of **justice** suggests that the benefits and the burdens of research participants must be shared equitably among potential research populations. At a basic level, this means that researchers must treat all participants fairly and equally, avoiding samples of convenience, exploitation of vulnerable populations, and by not involving persons from groups unlikely to benefit from the research. For example, researchers should be sure to represent both genders and various ethnic groups in research that would potentially affect them. The principle of justice also states that if research supported by public funds leads to a therapeutic treatment, for example, that treatment must be available to all, not just to those who can afford it.

Justice also suggests that participants should receive some benefit or value for being in the study, either something direct and concrete (e.g., learning experience, monetary reward, treatment for an ailment under study) or more general for society (e.g., understanding personality or finding a cure for cancer).

The Belmont report also led to the **Common Rule** which was adopted by all federal agencies including the National Institutes of Health (NIH) and the National Institute of Mental Health (NIMH), and which is also the rule at all universities, schools, hospitals, and other places where research is conducted. The Common Rule mandates that institutions that conduct research must establish and maintain an **institutional review board (IRB)** to review all research to ensure that it upholds these standards. These boards must include researchers, an ethicist, and members of the community who discuss all research proposals, often making suggestions to ensure that participants' rights are protected. The Common Rule establishes procedures for obtaining informed consent from potential research participants and for explaining all experimental procedures (see Mills, 1976, for an example).

If you have the opportunity to conduct research, you will need to submit a proposal to your school's IRB. Though the questions asked by the IRB on their forms may seem unrelated to research, you can readily see that the questions are all meant to ensure that the principles of respect for persons, beneficence, and justice have all been considered and protected (see Figure 1.3).

Researchers who violate ethical principles face censure from their institution's IRB, as well as from their professional societies, like the American Psychological Association, and from the federal government. Due to these principles and guidelines, it is unlikely that experiments like the twin study could be conducted today. Good researchers must always consider the rights and welfare of their participants in the design and planning of their research studies.

SEE FOR YOURSELF

Does your school have an IRB to review research conducted at your school?

ARCADIA UNIVERSITY IRB Face Sheet

1.	Administration of questionnaires, personality tests, quality of life assessments or other surveys?	☐ Yes ☐ No
	IF YES, ☐ Name and reference of questionnaire provided? ☐ Copy of questionnaire attached?	
2.	Are there any questions of a sensitive nature (e.g., drug/alcohol use/abuse, sexual behavior, sexual orientation)?	☐ Yes ☐ No
3.	Does the research proposal involve the use and disclosure of research subject's medical record information for research purposes?	☐ Yes ☐ No
	3a. **IF YES**, please check the box next to one of the following that is provided with this submission: ☐ Separate authorization for use and disclosure of identifiable health information. ☐ Modified research informed consent document that incorporates HIPAA requirements.	
4.	Are you performing a campus-wide survey of Arcadia faculty, staff and/or students?	☐ Yes ☐ No
	IF YES, attach copy of approval from Committee on Institutional Effectiveness	
5.	Do you or any member of your research group, spouses or any dependent children have any interest (i.e. any property of financial interest including stock in the sponsor company, patents, trademarks, copyrights or licensing, supplemental research grants or consulting arrangements) in the test drug/product, device, research procedure that is the subject of this study? **5a. IF YES, please complete a Conflict of Interest Disclosure Form available through the Arcadia University Grants Office.** Please discuss how these conflicts will be managed during the period of the trial. Include language disclosing such interest in the consent form for the use by research subjects. 5b. In addition, for industry-sponsored trials, please attach the documentation submitted to the sponsor as required by 21CFR54.1, if applicable.	☐ Yes ☐ No
6.	Have the Principal Investigator, Co-PI(s) and faculty advisor taken the on-line CITI Course in the protection of Human Research Subjects? • **IF YES,** attach copy(ies) of certification.	☐ Yes ☐ No
7.	Human subjects or material involved in the proposed activity include any of the following vulnerable subjects *(check all that apply, at least one box must be checked)* ☐ Minors ☐ Pregnant Women ☐ Prisoners ☐ HIV positive subjects ☐ Patients ☐ Arcadia Employees, Staff, Students ☐ Mentally disabled or cognitively impaired subjects ☐ None of the Above **☐ Other (specify):** _____	
8.	is this proposal currently under review, or has it been reviewed and approved by, another institution's IRB? • **IF YES,** include a copy of the approval and if applicable, IRB approval from that institution. If the proposal has not yet been submitted to the other institution, please state an anticipated date of submission and a copy of the other institution's review guidelines.	☐ Yes ☐ No

SAMPLE

_____   _____
Principal Investigator (PI) Signature   Date

_____
Printed Name of PI

_____   _____
Co-Investigator's Signature   Date

_____
Printed Name of Co-Investigator

_____   _____
Co-Investigator's Signature   Date

_____
Printed Name of Co-Investigator

_____   _____
Co-Investigator's Signature   Date

_____
Printed Name of Co-Investigator
* if require additional spaces for signatures please print another copy of this page and append to the first page #2 in the face sheet packet.

Check all attachments that apply (see below for # of copies):

☐ Protocol Summary

☐ Informed Consent/Assent Form Document(s)

☐ Personality tests/inventories/questionnaires

☐ Human Subjects Oriented Training Research Certificate

☐ Conflict of Interest Disclosure Form (If Item #5 checked)

☐ Advertisement(s), recruitment flyers

☐ Copy of grant application (minus appendices) (if applicable)

☐ Copy of HIPAA if 3a is checked

☐ Copy of approval from Committee of Institutional Effectiveness if 4 is checked

☐ Copy of other institutions IRB approval if 8 is checked

February 2010

Figure 1.3 A copy of the form used by the Arcadia University IRB. Note that questions 3 and 7 ensure the principle of autonomy whereas questions 5 and 6 ensure the principle of beneficence. Researchers must address the principle of justice in their narrative describing the procedure of their study which they submit for review to the IRB along with this form. *Source:* Reprinted courtesy of Arcadia University.

Table 1.3 Science or Science Fiction?

1. Most experiments take place in a dark, dank laboratory with scary-looking equipment.
2. The English language contains 17,937 words to describe human personality.
3. Psychologists can judge what people are like based on their residence hall rooms, offices, web pages, and handshakes.
4. Employers can use personality tests to see if potential employees have what it takes to succeed on the job.
5. Dolphins, elephants, and chimpanzees know who they are.
6. Social experiences can change how our genes function.
7. Gamers can control their character in some video games simply by thinking about how they want the character to move.
8. Plastic baby carriers may make it more difficult for parents and children to bond.
9. People who feel competent and who are intrinsically motivated have less dental plaque.
10. College students today feel less in control of their lives than college students of earlier generations.
11. Men are just naturally better than women at certain mathematical tasks such as mental rotation, for example, and no amount of practice or experience can change this fundamental difference.
12. Women with a fluid sexual orientation are capable of experiencing a wider range of erotic experiences and feelings than captured by the labels of lesbian, bisexual, or heterosexual.
13. Experiencing positive emotions such as love, joy, playfulness, wonder, and love make people think more creatively than negative emotions such as sadness, disgust, or anxiety.

Note: All but two of these statements are based on science; the rest are science fiction. To find out which two, keep reading!

Science or Science Fiction? A Brief Introduction to Current Research Findings in Personality Psychology

Now that you know a bit about the methods psychologists use to study personality, it's time to explore their findings. But first, here's a chance for you to see for yourself just how exciting the field of personality psychology is. The field has changed so rapidly over the past decade or so that we might wonder if we are studying science or science fiction. Take a look at Table 1.3. Each of these statements draws on research you will learn about in the coming chapters. Can you tell which is science and which is science fiction?

Chapter Summary

This chapter introduced the topic of personality psychology—the scientific study of what makes us who we are. People vary and personality psychology studies both similarities and differences among people and how they became that way.

Though personality is made up of the building blocks of traits, genetics, neuroscience, self and identity, intrapsychic aspects, regulation and motivation, and cognitions, we are more than the mere sum of these parts. Especially when it comes to understanding gender, sexual orientation, and resilience, for example, these parts work together to make us who we are.

Personality psychologists use many methods to study personality. Using the scientific method, researchers make observations, build theories, and devise and test hypotheses. They may design true experiments, observational studies, correlational studies or administer personality questionnaires (both self-report and projective) to test their hypotheses and theories

✓●⌐**Study** and **Review**
on **mysearchlab.com**
Go online for more resources to help you review.

"Personality is essential. It is in every work of art. When someone walks on stage for a performance and has charisma, everyone is convinced that he has personality. I find that charisma is merely a form of showmanship. Movie stars usually have it. A politician has to have it."

Lukas Foss

about human personality. They may also collect self-report data, observation data, test data, or life data on people. Like a carpenter with a toolbox full of specialized tools, researchers choose the best methods to answer their questions about human personality.

One method personality psychologists use to study people is the true experiment, where researchers have experimental control over the independent variable and randomly assign participants to conditions. If researchers succeeded in controlling all aspects of the experiment except for the one variable under study, then any difference in the dependent variable, or responses of the participants, must have been caused by the independent variable, what the experimenter manipulated. A true experiment is the only research design that allows researchers to draw conclusions about causality. However, there are times when it is impossible, impractical, or unethical to manipulate a variable—such as personality—so that researchers must use alternative methods like correlational designs.

The Belmont Report establishes guidelines researchers must follow for research with human participants. Researchers must apply the principles of respect for persons (including obtaining informed consent and protecting vulnerable populations), beneficence (minimize harm and maximize benefits), and justice (benefits and burdens of research must be shared equitably) while designing their experimental procedures. Researchers must then present their proposed study to an ethical review board, called an institutional review board (IRB), for approval. The IRB will review the proposal specifically making sure that the research upholds these standards. Institutions of the federal government all adhere to these principles, as outlined in the Common Rule, which includes the establishment and oversight of all IRBs throughout the United States.

Review Questions

1. What are some ways in which a single individual is like all others, like some others, and like no others?
2. What is personality psychology? What are the building blocks of personality?
3. How do psychologists study personality? What are some methods and measures used by personality psychologists?
4. What are the four different kinds of data a researcher can collect?
5. When researchers find a difference on some measure between two groups, is there a way to judge how large that difference is?
6. What is a correlation? When are correlational designs used? What is the difference between a correlational design and a true experiment?
7. What is so special about a true experiment? What two characteristics are present in a true experiment? What is an independent variable? What is a dependent variable?
8. According to the research by Ng and Diener (2009), are some coping strategies better than others? Why or why not? Where does personality fit in?
9. What are the three principles that researchers must adhere to in conducting research with human participants? What is an institutional review board?

Key Terms

Personality psychology
Traits
Genetics
Neuroscience
Self and identity
Intrapsychic foundations
Regulation and motivation
Cognitive foundations
Integration
Scientific method
Observational study
Hypothesis

Personality questionnaires
Correlation coefficient
Correlational studies
Experimental condition
Control condition
Random assignment
Experimental control
True experiment
Independent variable
Dependent variable
Neuroticism
Levels

Self-report data
Observation data
Test data
Life data
Respect for persons
Informed consent
Beneficence
Justice
Common Rule
Institutional review board
   (IRB)

2 PERSONALITY TRAITS: A GOOD THEORY

Read the **Chapter** on
mysearchlab.com

"There is nothing so practical as a good theory."

Kurt Lewin

Have you ever tried to judge someone's personality from his or her living space? When I was a brand-new college student, my roommate Kathy was a cheerleader, daughter of the head football coach and little sister of their star quarterback. She was tall, blonde, charming, sociable, flirty, attractive, outgoing, conservative, and slightly daring. We quickly unpacked and set up our room. Then we had the idea of walking down the hallway and introducing ourselves to our new hall-mates. This would both satisfy our curiosity—who were these people we would be living with?—and give us decorating ideas. After all, there's not much one can do with a stark, square, concrete-block room of a dull-pastel color.

We were amazed at the ingenuity with which our peers had transformed these "cell blocks" into cozy and often inviting living spaces: cutesy posters and classic rock album covers on the walls, seashells, massive stereo systems, a snowboard, an open violin case, dressers with elaborate makeup holders and perfume bottles, golden posters for far-away places (Vienna! Venice!), color-coded filing systems, and photos of cool boyfriends. We were amazed at what we could tell about these strangers from their rooms!

As the astute psychology majors that we were, we wondered how much we really learned about our hall-mates. Certainly people decorate their rooms to impress others or to create certain images—and there was a lot of that going around our first year—but at the heart of it all, to what extent does an individual's personality manifest itself in the design and content of a dorm room?

Gosling, Ko, Mannarelli, and Morris (2002) asked this very question in a systematic way. They reasoned that when people live in an environment they leave **behavioral residue** behind. Such physical traces left behind by everyday actions are hints or cues to the personality of the occupant (Gosling et al., 2002). For example, specific items may be left behind either carelessly, like a snowboard that wasn't put away properly, or on purpose to convey a certain image (e.g., "Hey, I'm cool, I'm edgy, I'm a snowboarder!"). Similarly, people may keep mementos from a summer vacation, like seashells, in a prominent place because such items have personal meaning to them or reinforce their own self-views (e.g., "I'm a nature lover"). People may have tidy rooms and organized bookshelves so they can find what they need quickly. All of these are ways we express personalities and leave, perhaps inadvertently, cues for observers (Gosling, 2008).

In this study, anywhere from 1 to 6 observers, ordinary folk with no particular training, visited actual rooms of 83 college student volunteers. These volunteers lived in private houses, apartments, residence halls, co-ops, and Greek-system housing either on or just off campus. The researchers covered names and any photos in the rooms so that observers would not know

What can you tell about the personality of the occupant of this room?

for sure the race or gender of the occupant. The observers then glanced around the rooms and made ratings on a 7-point scale of the extent to which they thought each of 44 descriptions applied to the occupant of the room. Some of the descriptions included:

Anxious, easily upset

Extraverted, enthusiastic

Conventional, uncreative

Critical, quarrelsome

Disorganized, careless

Amazingly enough, there was a great amount of consensus. That is, observers readily agreed on what they thought an occupant was like. Even more amazing, observers were often very accurate in guessing the personality of the occupants. What cues were they using? Sometimes the neatness of a room indicated how conscientious the occupant was. Other times the distinctive look of a space, the presence of unique items, or the variety of books and magazines indicated a creative, open personality. And still other times the researchers couldn't be sure what cues observers used to accurately judge an occupant's extraversion, emotional stability, and agreeableness (see Table 2.1). You can see where you fall on these five factors by taking a short personality test similar to the one used in the study shown in Table 2.2.

Gosling and his colleagues repeated the study looking at people's office spaces and got pretty much the same results. In which space do you think people's personalities shone through the most? If you thought that it would be easier for people to truly express themselves in their bedrooms you'd be right (Gosling et al., 2002). Workplaces tend to constrain how much decoration and personal expression workers can show.

So, my roommate Kathy and I were indeed able to get to know our hall-mates a bit and to identify interesting people on our hallway that we wanted to get to know better. However, we also discovered that our tastes in friends and room decorations were quite different . . . as befitting two very different personalities!

As the opening research study illustrates, there are many ways of describing human personality: charming, sociable, flirty, outgoing, conservative, daring, conventional, uncreative, disorganized, careless, extraverted, enthusiastic, critical, quarrelsome, anxious, easily upset, and some 17,937 others (Allport & Odbert, 1936)! Such descriptors of personality are called traits. In this first chapter on traits, as Kurt Lewin suggested, we start with understanding the theories behind personality traits—including two approaches to studying traits—and the kinds and numbers of traits, and discuss whether there are universal traits that can describe *any* personality. In the next chapter we will study some of the practical applications of trait psychology and, in particular, how traits are expressed in many aspects of our lives, from our handshakes

> **THINK ABOUT IT**
>
> Besides living spaces, where else might we see people express their personalities?

Table 2.1 Cues Observers Use to Determine Personality of Room Occupants

Trait	Consensus	Accuracy	Valid Cues
Neuroticism	.08	.36**	(none)
Extraversion	.31*	.22*	(none)
Openness	.58**	.65**	Distinctiveness of the space, level of decoration, variety of magazines and books
Agreeableness	.20	.20*	(none)
Conscientiousness	.47**	.33**	Organized, neat, uncluttered

Note: Numbers in the table are correlations among observers' ratings. Recall that correlations can be positive or negative. Higher numbers mean that there is a stronger relationship between the variables. Significant effects are noted by asterisks.

* $= p < .05$, ** $= p < .01$.

Source: From Gosling et al. (2002, Tables 4 and 5) Gosling, S. D., Ko, S. J., Mannarelli, T., & Morris, M. E. (2002). A room with a cue: Personality judgments based on offices and bedrooms. *Journal of Personality and Social Psychology*, 82(3), 379–398. Copyright American Psychological Association. Adapted with permission.

Table 2.2 Test Your Own Personality: The Ten-Item Personality Inventory (TIPI)

Here are a number of personality traits that may or may not apply to you. Please write a number next to each statement to indicate the extent to which *you agree or disagree with that statement*. You should rate the extent to which the pair of traits applies to you, even if one characteristic applies more strongly than the other.

Disagree Strongly	Disagree Moderately	Disagree a Little	Neither Agree Nor Disagree	Agree a Little	Agree Moderately	Agree Strongly
1	2	3	4	5	6	7
1._____	Extraverted, enthusiastic					
2._____	Critical, quarrelsome					
3._____	Dependable, self-disciplined					
4._____	Anxious, easily upset					
5._____	Open to new experiences, complex					
6._____	Reserved, quiet					
7._____	Sympathetic, warm					
8._____	Disorganized, careless					
9._____	Calm, emotionally stable					
10._____	Conventional, uncreative					

Note: To score, take the average of your score on the two items listed for each factor. Items marked with an *R* are reversed scored. Extraversion: 1, 6R; Agreeableness: 2R, 7; Conscientiousness: 3, 8R; Emotional Stability: 4R, 9; Openness to experience: 5, 10R. To reverse score, 1 = 7, 2 = 6, 3 = 5, 4 = 4, 5 = 3, 6 = 2, 7 = 1.

Source: Gosling, Rentfrow, and Swann (2003, Appendix A, p. 525). From Gosling, S. D., Rentfrow, P. J., & Swann, W. B. (2003), "A very brief measure of the big-five personality domains," *Journal of Research in Personality*, 37, 504–528. Copyright © 2003 by Academic Press. Reprinted with permission.

to the kind of music we like, to the kind of careers we choose, including how our personality stays consistent, changes, or shows coherence over time.

What Is a Personality Trait?

Traits describe a person's typical style of thinking, feeling, and acting in different kinds of situations and at different times (McCrae & Costa, 1997b). Although we might act differently in specific situations (e.g., a job interview compared to hanging out with a close friend), or at different times (e.g., think of what you were like in high school compared to now), if someone were to follow you around for a while to witness your behavior in many situations and at different times in your life he or she would see some commonalities and consistencies in your reactions (Allport, 1927). These generally persistent ways of acting and reacting are captured by the concept of traits. In contrast, temporary states (such as emotions), attitudes (liberal, conservative), and physical attributes (short, muscular) are not considered personality traits.

Traits are measured over a continuum—that is, in a continuous stretch, from low to high. This means that people who score high on a particular trait, say talkativeness, are more likely to strike up a conversation with a stranger than a person who is low on talkativeness (or high on the trait of "quiet," its opposite). If we were to ask several people from different walks of life "How talkative are you?" we would probably find a normal distribution of responses: Some people would be extremely high or low whereas others would fall somewhere in the middle (see Figure 2.1) on this continuum of talkativeness.

Because traits cannot be directly measured in the same way that, say, height and weight can, psychologists think of traits as hypothetical concepts. That is, psychologists assume traits exist even though we can't see them. For this reason, some psychologists view traits as purely descriptive summaries of behavior without thinking about where they came from or why a person acts that way ("Mario is very sociable; just look at how well he's getting along with everybody").

"Nobody seems to know what a trait is, so it appears to us better to use 'characteristic.'"

Healy, Bronner, and Bowers (1931, p. 311)

SEE FOR YOURSELF

What kind of person are you? List the traits that best describe yourself.

Other psychologists see traits as internal, causal properties ("Well, of course Mario is getting along with everybody; he's a sociable person") and view a trait as a capacity that is present even when the trait is not being directly expressed. Just because you sit quietly in your personality class doesn't mean that you are a quiet person. Just wait until the professor's back is turned and see how many people start to express their talkative natures!

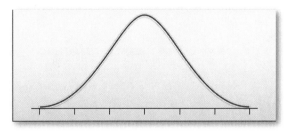

Figure 2.1 Normal Distribution of the Trait of Talkativeness.

Psychologists have long debated the exact number and kinds of traits. In fact, psychologists have even debated how best to study traits. The next section examines two main ways that psychologists have approached the study of traits: through the detailed study of a single individual and through the combined study of numerous people. These approaches have been called idiographic and nomothetic, respectively (Allport, 1937; Allport, 1937/1961). However, because science, by definition, searches for generalized truths, there is an inherent tension between these two approaches to personality that even Allport struggled with (Allport, 1937).

Two Approaches to the Study of Personality Traits

In the **idiographic approach**, the goal is to understand the personality of a single individual with all of his or her quirks or idiosyncrasies and characteristics that make them unique. The psychologist starts with what a single individual thinks is important to know about him or her and seeks to answer the question, "What unique combination of traits best describes this person?" Think about the insights into humankind that we glean from a study of history, the contemplation of a great painting, the power of a moving dramatic performance or a compelling biography. These are examples of idiographic ways of understanding.

By using techniques of good science such as striving for objectivity and minimizing biases, psychologists are able to use case studies and other idiographic methods to study individual personalities (for example, see the Swann, Pelham, & Krull, 1989, and Pelham, 1993, experiments on self-concept).

In the **nomothetic approach**, the goal is to discover universals—concepts that can apply to everyone—by identifying traits that can describe all people or that can be applied to any person. Think about this: According to current estimates the number of people inhabiting planet Earth is over 6.7 billion. Does this mean that we need more than 6.7 billion traits to be able to describe each person? Of course not, but what exactly is the "right" number of traits, and how best should we organize them? This philosophical question started what I like to call The Great Nomothetic Search for Human Universals. The right number of trait terms is a source of some debate, as we will soon see.

Although Allport is often blamed for starting the battle between the idiographic and nomothetic approaches, he is seldom given credit for his brilliant resolution of the conflict. Just as the practice of medicine is essentially idiographic—doctors must diagnose and treat their individual patients—their methods of diagnosis and standards for treatment are based on solid nomothetic sciences of biochemistry,

"A description of one individual without reference to others may be a piece of literature, a biography or a novel. But science? No."
Meyer (1926, p. 217)

"Although the endless variety and colorfulness of human personality intrigue the artist . . . many psychometrists have nevertheless fled from this richness of human nature as from some fearsome [demon]. They have left reality to the novelist."
Cattell (1946, p. 1)

The idiographic approach uses many variables to describe the personality of a single individual in great detail.

The nomothetic approach identifies the few key variables that can describe the personality of many people.

bacteriology, and so on. That is, the idiographic and nomothetic overlap and both contribute to a complete understanding of human personality (Allport, 1937).

Allport cautioned that "individuality cannot be studied by science" (Allport, 1937/1961, p. 8), yet he recognized a place for the study of the individual within psychology:

> *Why should we not start with individual behavior as a source of hunches (as we have in the past), and then seek our generalizations (also as we have in the past), but finally come back to the individual—not for the mechanical application of laws (as we do now), but for a fuller, supplementary, and more accurate assessment than we are now able to give? I suspect that the reason our present assessments are now so often feeble and sometimes even ridiculous, is because we do not take this final step. We stop with our wobbly laws of personality and seldom confront them with the concrete person.* (Allport, 1962, p. 407)

SEE FOR YOURSELF

Can you see which habits and responses make up each of your traits?

Hans Eysenck took up Allport's challenge and found a way of reconciling these two seemingly different approaches to the study of human personality. He realized that one could study both the general (nomothetic) and the specific (idiographic) within a single person and develop a theory of personality from there (Eysenck, 1998). He hypothesized that the human personality is organized into a hierarchy, which we can think of as a pyramid (see Figure 2.2). This pyramid

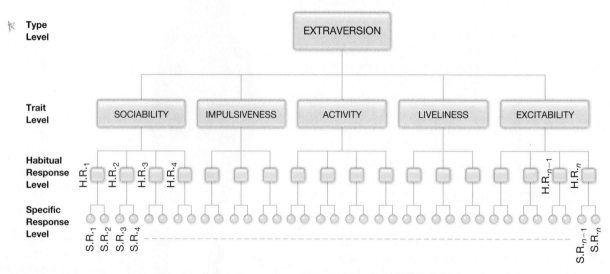

Figure 2.2 The Personality Pyramid: The Hierarchical Organization of Human Personality.
Source: Reprinted with permission from Eysenck, H. J. (1967), The Biological Basis of Personality, (Springfield, IL: Charles C. Thomas). Permission conveyed through the Copyright Clearance Center.

categorizes human personality from the most general level at the top to the most specific level at the bottom. General means a trait is universal or applicable to other people, whereas specific means a trait is more unique to a single individual.

At the very bottom level of the pyramid are specific behaviors including responses, acts, cognitions, or reactions to everyday life (Eysenck, 1990). Because these reactions are observed only once, they may or may not be related to one's personality. However, if the same reaction occurs many times then we might say that the response has become a habit or a typical way of responding. Further, if certain habits occur over time and across situations, then we might say the person is exhibiting a personality trait. Further, if we notice that certain traits tend to occur together in people then we can say that we've identified a personality type, a syndrome (Cattell, 1946), a superfactor, or an "observed constellation of traits" to use Eysenck's words (Eysenck, 1998, p. 36).

According to Eysenck, the lower we go on the pyramid the more idiosyncratic our reactions are. Similarly, the higher we go on the pyramid, the more similar we become to people who may be of a similar personality type. To illustrate how this works, let's imagine a junior engineering major we'll call Lakeisha. Suppose Lakeisha spent Thursday night with her hall-mates watching TV in the lounge. Does this make Lakeisha an extrovert? From one specific *response* we can't draw any conclusions about Lakeisha's personality. After all, there could have been a special show on TV. Now suppose that Lakeisha regularly says "Hi!" to people she passes on campus and often meets up with friends for lunch. We might judge that she has the *habit* of being friendly toward others or seeking the company of others. If she exhibited these habits over time (e.g., during her sophomore year or junior year) and across different situations (e.g., at home, school, a summer internship), then we might say that Lakeisha shows the trait of sociability. If she also demonstrated the traits of impulsiveness, activity, liveliness, and excitability, then we might say that she is an extroverted type and is similar to other extroverted people. Although this example started by studying a single individual—Lakeisha—and ended by drawing conclusions about groups of people, Eysenck cautions that our conclusions must be based experimentally to build a valid scientific theory.

What Do We Know About Personality From the Idiographic Approach?

Studying Individual Personalities: The Idiographic Approach

Imagine a person who describes herself as stubborn, critical, curious, intelligent, funny, and sarcastic. Now compare her to a person who describes herself as caring, quiet, creative, loyal, funny, and loving. Both of these are actual students who responded to the question "What kind of person are you? List the traits that best describe yourself." Such a description, where the psychologist focuses on understanding a specific person and where that person chooses which traits are important to him or her, is an example of the idiographic approach to personality.

Using this approach, Allport identified three different kinds of traits: central traits, secondary traits, and cardinal traits (Allport, 1937). **Central traits** are traits that are of major importance in understanding the person. They are the 5 or 10 traits that people who know you might mention in your letter of recommendation or to someone who doesn't know you when describing you. **Secondary traits** are traits of lesser importance, less consistently displayed or seldom displayed or only slightly revealed so that only a very close friend might notice them (e.g., "shy with new people," "leader like at times").

Finally, an unusual person may have one and only one trait that describes him or her. Such single traits that completely dominate a personality are called **cardinal traits**. These traits are so pervasive and extremely influential that practically every aspect of a person's life is touched by this "ruling passion" or "master sentiment" (Allport, 1937, p. 338). Do you know somebody like this? Even though it is highly unusual in real life to find a one-trait personality, it may not

"The personality of each man is a unique integration, and as such is a datum for psychology, and for psychology only."
Gordon Allport

THINK ABOUT IT

Why is it that cardinal traits seem to occur more often among fictional characters?

be so rare in the world of fictional characters. Just think of Don Juan, Don Quixote, Oscar the Grouch, or any of Snow White's seven little friends! Allport himself noted that the occurrence of a cardinal trait is so unusual in the population that when it does occur we name individual traits after the "celebrity." Notice how the names of actual people like Beau Brummell (the fashionista of early 1800s England), Machiavelli (the manipulative Florentine diplomat), and the Marquis de Sade (don't ask) have entered the English language as trait terms (Allport, 1937, p. 338).

The Idiographic Approach Applied: The Case of Jenny

> "[I]nstead of studying a thousand rats for one hour each or a hundred rats for ten hours each the investigator is more likely to study one rat for a thousand hours. The procedure is . . . appropriate to an enterprise which recognizes individuality."
>
> *B. F. Skinner*

Around 1946 Allport had the unique opportunity to apply the idiographic approach to a real person: "Jenny" (Allport, 1965; Anonymous, 1946). Jenny Gove Masterson was a pseudonym for a woman who wrote a detailed correspondence to two friends over a period of 10 years. Allport edited and published these letters with psychological commentary (Allport, 1965).

Jenny was born in Ireland in 1868 and as a young woman moved to the United States with her husband. Soon, they had a baby and, tragically, her husband passed away leaving Jenny a single mother to fend for herself and baby Ross far away from her native country. To say that Ross became the center of his mother's life was an understatement, and this led to tension between mother and son when Ross was an adult. Jenny wrote to Ross's college roommate, Glenn, and his wife, Isabel, some 10 years after Ross's college years, about the time when their relationship was the most strained. Consider this excerpt from the second letter she wrote to Glenn and Isabel in 1926:

> All during those years and years that I have lived as a hermit socially in order to pay the bills of that contemptible dog, I have never formed any social connection. I never had proper clothes—never had money to spare to entertain, even in a small way. And I would not be a sponge. My whole life has been wasted. (Allport, 1965, p. 11)

The following month, when Jenny was planning on visiting Glenn and Isabel, she sent the following letter:

> My dear Glenn: I enclose a check for fifty ($50) dollars, payable to you. If anything happens to me on my trip East please cash the cheque, and use it for my cremation. If I arrive OK you can let me have the money then. In case of accident, or death, insist on getting my heavy coat—I shall wear it on the trip East. Sewed in the lining of the coat at the bottom hem, left side, is fifty dollars. Five tens. Keep it. I shall have 8 or 10 in my purse, and a $10 bill in a pocket sewed on my corset. (Allport, 1965, p. 17)

As you can see, Jenny was an interesting and articulate woman who wrote with great sincerity and candor. No wonder Allport found these letters a treasure-trove for understanding personality traits. Jenny's personality came out naturally in the letters she wrote. By analyzing her letters, might we be able to identify the traits that made Jenny a unique person? Allport thought so. After editing, Allport enlisted the aid of 36 people who read the letters and described Jenny's traits. They used 198 trait terms, which Allport then arranged in clusters of related words: quarrelsome-suspicious, self-centered, independent-autonomous, dramatic-intense, aesthetic-artistic, aggressive, cynical-morbid, sentimental, and some 13 that remained unclassified.

Allport and others have gone on to analyze Jenny by applying various personality theories, including those of Sigmund Freud and Carl Rogers (Allport, 1965; Baldwin, 1942). Indeed, there are many such cases that illustrate personality functioning through the idiographic method (cf. Barenbaum, 1997; Barry, 2007; Nasby & Read, 1997; Rosenberg, 1989; Simonton, 1999; Swede & Tetlock, 1986; Winter & Carlson, 1988). In fact, others have analyzed *Allport's* personality

THINK ABOUT IT

Would you enjoy having Jenny as a friend?

in his treatment of Jenny: As it turns out, Jenny was writing the letters to him and his wife Ada (Winter, 1997)!

What Do We Know About Personality From the Nomothetic Approach?

Finding Universals: The Nomothetic Approach

Do you remember the two students from my personality class? Between the two of them they used 11 different trait terms to describe themselves. In fact, my whole class of 46 people used 116 different terms to describe themselves. I noted earlier that psychologists who follow the nomothetic approach seek to identify the basic traits that make up the human personality.

Using the idiographic method, Gordon Allport analyzed the letters of "Jenny" and identified sentimental, suspicious, and quarrelsome, among her central traits.

Deciding on the right number of traits, or factors, to account for human personality is like figuring out how many playlists and what labels you need to keep your MP3 collection organized. Some people might organize their individual tracks into playlists by artist, album, genre (e.g., rock, blues, classical), purpose (e.g., working out, driving, studying, relaxing, partying), mood (e.g., angry, melancholy, happy), or even a combination of these. The best way to keep your collection organized depends on your purpose. The same logic applies to traits.

There are at least three different ways to identify the most meaningful and applicable words to describe personality. Researchers typically use a combination of the theoretical approach, the lexical approach, and the measurement approach (sometimes called the questionnaire or assessment tradition; John, Naumann, & Soto, 2008). Once the basic traits have been identified by one of these methods, psychologists use statistical techniques, such as factor analysis, to verify and validate that they have indeed found important traits. These traits can then be applied, or generalized, to other people or populations.

The Theoretical Approach. Sometimes personality psychologists start with a theory or even common wisdom about human personality (Barenbaum & Winter, 2008), referred to as a **theoretical approach** (Barenbaum & Winter, 2008). For example, do you remember Niccolò Machiavelli? Two researchers were so taken by his book of advice to the prince of Florence, *The Prince* (Machiavelli, 1532/1940), that they devised a personality scale to measure Machiavellianism, or manipulativeness (Christie & Geis, 1970; an excerpt from the scale is presented in the chapter on personality assessment). This is how common wisdom can inspire the study of personality traits.

Other times, psychologists start with a theory. Carl Jung hypothesized that people differ in how they evaluate information: either rationally, what he called the thinking function, or through emotions. Jung (1921) spoke of at least two types of personality, *feeling types* and *thinking types*. Sigmund Freud (1915/2000) had a theory that if a child had problems with weaning or toilet training this would affect later adult personality. Perhaps you've heard of an oral personality who is overly dependent or anal personality who is incredibly organized and uptight. These are examples of how psychologists use theory to identify meaningful traits.

"The idiographic pattern is best illuminated by the nomothetic trend."
Saucier and Goldberg (1996, p. 35)

The Lexical Approach.   The **lexical approach** to personality traits explores a particular language and identifies the number of synonyms that describe personality. The reasoning is that if a concept is important to speakers of a language, then that concept will be encoded in their language in multiple ways. People invent terms for salient or useful ideas and these new terms spread and become commonplace in the language. At the same time, useless words drop out. Presumably describing what your loved ones and neighbors are like is very relevant and useful, so crucial individual differences have become encoded in language (Allport, 1937). Now if the same personality trait is found across many different languages, such a trait may qualify as a human universal. In this way an analysis of language, specifically looking for many synonyms and commonalities across languages, may help personality psychologists identify key terms for describing human personality (Goldberg, 1981), whether they be adjectives (Allport & Odbert, 1936) or nouns (Saucier, 2003).

The Measurement Approach.   For the last 60 years or so personality psychologists have been working separately on discovering important aspects of personality and trying to measure personality (Hogan, 1996), called the **measurement approach**. Some psychologists worked within a theoretical tradition, some operationalized their own observations, whereas still others focused on developing the best questionnaires and measurement techniques apart from a theoretical context. For a while it seemed that each researcher devised an original questionnaire to measure what he or she deemed were the most important personality traits (John et al., 2008). The field almost seemed to care more about how accurate their measurements were than about what they were actually measuring (Hogan, 1996)! It needed a taxonomy, or some systematic method of identifying and classifying trait terms that unified them into a coherent body. After all, "the astronomer classifies stars, the chemist elements, the zoologist animals, the botanist plants" (Eysenck, 1991, p. 774).

One way of doing this is to use mathematical and statistical techniques such as *factor analysis* to see if the various trait terms cluster together in some way. For example, Raymond Cattell started with the 4,504 trait terms identified by Allport and Odbert (1936). He reduced these terms to 160 by eliminating similarities in the list. Then he added all traits that had been identified by other psychologists in previous research. Finally, he used an early and crude form of factor analysis—as this was done way before the day of computers—and discovered 16 factors (Cattell, 1946) that formed the basis of his questionnaire: The 16 Personality Factors (16PF; Cattell, Eber, & Tatsuoka, 1970). Ironically, due to some misguided statistical practices of the time, Cattell didn't realize that the 5 factors that are so widely accepted today were staring him right in the face in his own data (Digman, 1996). The Research Methods Illustrated feature explains more about this technique.

Since that time and with the advent of powerful and accessible computers, researchers have been using a combination of these three approaches—theoretical, lexical, and measurement—to identify and organize personality traits. How successful have they been? Read on to find out.

Research Methods Illustrated: Factor Analysis

Imagine that we give a group of participants a questionnaire that lists many different types of music, from soul and funk to heavy metal to country. Participants rate how much they liked each of these genres on a 7-point scale from 1 (*Not at all*) to 7 (*A great deal*).

If people have consistent feelings about any of these types of music then we would expect them to answer the pertinent questions in roughly the same way. For example, say one group of people really enjoy blues and jazz and that their answers to these particular questions are more similar than to questions on how much they like country and religious music. Are there dimensions or aspects of music that are common to blues and jazz but that distinguish this kind of music from country and religious music? From hip-hop? More generally, is there some underlying structure to the answers of our participants? If there is, then do we really need all the separate questions or will fewer questions work just as well?

These are the questions that psychologists try to answer by using factor analysis (Lee & Ashton, 2007). **Factor analysis** is a statistical technique that mathematically identifies a meaningful underlying structure among a set of variables. Suppose some questions are related to each other—but not to other questions; then we can say that we have identified a unique factor in participants' responses to these questions. Depending on what we're studying— say personality or intelligence—it's possible to identify a number of factors that underlie participants' responses.

How do we know that some questions go together? We look at the correlations among all of the questions in our data. Recall that correlations (symbolized by r) represent the strength of a relationship between two variables, with larger numbers indicating that the two variables are highly related. The sign of the r tells us that the two variables are either directly related (positive) or inversely related (negative). The pattern of correlations will tell us which variables go together or correlate with each other and which variables don't seem to fit. Then the computer uses complex matrix algebra to try to re-create this pattern of correlations from a combination of one or more mathematical equations. The result of all this combining and weighting of participants' responses is the formation of factors. A small number of these factors are usually able to re-create the variation among responses in our data set almost as well as all of the original answers themselves.

Each factor can explain a certain amount of variation, called variance, in answers between participants. This is called the **eigenvalue** of the factor. From the eigenvalues, we calculate **factor loadings**, which is an estimate of how strongly each question fits into a given factor. We can interpret factor loadings much like correlations, with higher numbers indicating a stronger correlation between the item and the factor and the positive or negative sign indicating the direction of the relationship. Each factor is defined by the questions with the highest factor loadings. Researchers look at the questions and try to identify what underlying concept the questions are all getting at.

When we do a factor analysis, the first factor that emerges generally accounts for the greatest amount of variation in the data. But because this is mathematically derived rather than inspired by our actual questions, there is no guarantee that the factor makes any sense. At this stage a researcher might move around the factors to find which questions go together the best. This is called rotating the factors and allows us to understand the factors better (kind of like rotating a map to match the direction you are facing to better see where you're going). This doesn't change the number of factors, nor does it change the relationship among the factors, but it does change which questions cluster together. By rotating the factors—and there are a number of mathematical ways of doing this—the combining and weighting of questions that make up that factor shift slightly so that the researcher is better able to see what the underlying factor is.

How do we know how many factors best explain the data? This is where factor analysis is more "art" than "science." Much debate exists on the pros and cons of the various ways of deciding on the right number of factors. Researchers may stop when a new factor doesn't add much, often determined mathematically (e.g., by accepting all eigenvalues greater than 1) or graphically. Often, researchers take a pragmatic approach and keep only the few factors that are actually interpretable. Later factors may capture only measurement error or response bias instead of a meaningful underlying concept.

Once the right numbers have been identified, the researcher must then name the factors. The way to do this is to look at the items that fall together on each factor and see what concept they all appear to be getting at. Take our music taste example from the beginning of this section which was based on an actual experiment. Rentfrow and Gosling (2003) designed the Short Test of Musical Preferences, called the STOMP, in which participants rated how much they liked each of 14 musical genres. The researchers then used factor analysis to see if there was some underlying construct that could explain similarities and differences in participants' musical tastes. The results are shown in Table 2.3. Can you think of an adequate name for each of the factors?

This is how factor analysis is a useful tool for exploring the number and kind of traits contained in the human personality. But note that it does not give the definitive answer to this question (Darlington, 2009). Keep in mind that factor analysis is a useful, but limited statistical method and is only as good as the researcher behind it. At nearly every step of the way, researchers make choices and their choices impact the results. From choosing which questions to ask (and submit to factor analysis), to determining the right number of factors, to interpreting the factors, factor analysis has its shortcomings (Fabrigar, Wegener, MacCallum, & Strahan, 1999). Whereas factor analysis gives *an* answer, it is up to the researchers to make a solid case for their conclusions and to replicate their findings before we can believe it is *the* answer.

Table 2.3 Factor Loadings of the 14 Music Genres on Four Factors

Genre	Factor 1	Factor 2	Factor 3	Factor 4
Blues	**.85**	.01	−.09	.12
Jazz	**.83**	.04	.07	.15
Classical	**.66**	.14	.02	−.13
Folk	**.64**	.09	.15	−.16
Rock	.17	**.85**	−.04	−.07
Alternative	.02	**.80**	.13	.04
Heavy metal	.07	**.75**	−.11	.04
Country	−.06	.05	**.72**	−.03
Soundtracks	.01	.04	**.70**	.17
Religious	.23	−.21	**.64**	−.01
Pop	−.20	.06	**.59**	.45
Rap/hip-hop	−.19	−.12	.17	**.79**
Soul/funk	.39	−.11	.11	**.69**
Electronica/dance	−.02	.15	−.01	**.60**

Note: *N* = 1,704. The highest factor loadings for each dimension are listed in boldface type. The researchers named the factors Reflective and Complex; Intense and Rebellious; Upbeat and Conventional; and Energetic and Rhythmic.

Source: Rentfrow and Gosling, 2003, Table 1, p. 1242 Rentfrow, P. J., & Gosling, S. D. (2003). The do re mi's of everyday life: The structure and personality correlates of music preferences. *Journal of Personality and Social Psychology*, 84(6), 1236–1256. Copyright American Psychological Association. Adapted with permission.

The Great Nomothetic Search for Universal Principles of Personality

How did these three traditions—theoretical, lexical, and measurement—lead to this "most celebrated empirical accomplishment" (McCrae & Costa, 1996, p. 53)? First, recall that Allport and Odbert conducted a lexical analysis and uncovered 4,504 trait terms. From this list of trait terms, Cattell, using factor analysis, identified 16 factors—not realizing the import of only 5 of his factors (Cattell, 1946; Cattell et al., 1970). Others, building on Cattell's statistical work, identified a solution of 5 remarkably similar factors (e.g., Fiske, 1949; Norman, 1963) known as the **Big Five** (Loehlin, 1992). This moniker was not to extol their greatness so much as to emphasize that they are broad factors (John et al., 2008). Each of the Big Five factors describes personality at a high level of abstraction (remember Eysenck's pyramid?) summarizing a large number of more distinct lower level traits.

At the same time, working in the questionnaire approach, researchers found that popular personality tests at the time including the Personality Research Form (Jackson, 1984), the California Q-set (Block, 1961), and even the Myers-Briggs Type Indicator (Myers & McCauley, 1985) all contained 5 factors (Digman, 1996), as do numerous other questionnaires from widely different theoretical traditions (McCrae, 1989).

Finally, others have theorized that for personality traits to be universal they must be rooted in biology (Eysenck, 1990; McCrae & Costa, 1996) or solve evolutionary problems, which these 5 factors appear to do (Buss, 1996).

The remarkable convergence of theory, research, and measurement makes this a particularly exciting time for personality psychologists as the evidence for a **five-factor model** of personality mounts. But there are still plenty of researchers who are not convinced that five is the right number of trait factors and who have proposed their own dimensions or who have identified important traits left out from the five-factor model. However, to fully appreciate the significance of the current five-factor taxonomy—not to mention these alternative models and critiques—we will need to understand earlier models of personality traits.

SEE FOR YOURSELF

How many factors did you use to describe your personality?

Three Superfactors: Eysenck

Psychologist Hans Eysenck spent his lifetime conducting experiments to identify and describe key differences between people. So convinced was he that there were fundamental constitutional differences between people that he first described these personality types in terms of physiological or biological differences between people (Eysenck, 1998). More recent research has proved that Eysenck had the general principle right: His early twin studies support his claim for genetic differences in the three factors, even as the exact physiological mechanisms were unknown to scientists at the time (Eysenck & Eysenck, 1985). He identified three broad dimensions of personality: Psychoticism, Extraversion, and Neuroticism. Eysenck also identified more specific, what he called **narrow traits**, associated with each of these factors (see Table 2.4). Together, these three superfactors form the basis of Eysenck's PEN model of personality (Eysenck, 1952).

the subtraits that make up the each of the three factors of Eysenck's PEN

The first factor, **Psychoticism**, describes how tough-minded or antisocial people are. We can also think about this as impulsivity or disinhibition versus constraint or as undercontrolled versus overcontrolled (Clark & Watson, 2008). People who are high in Psychoticism tend to be selfish and antisocial (Eysenck, 1990; Eysenck & Eysenck, 1985). The narrow traits associated with Psychoticism are aggressive, cold, egocentric, impersonal, impulsive, antisocial, lacking empathy, creative, and tough-minded (Eysenck, 1990; Eysenck & Eysenck, 1985). One writer describes Psychoticism as low agreeableness and low conscientiousness (from the five factors) "with a few other very bad things thrown in" (McAdams, 2009, p. 199). According to Eysenck, a person high in Psychoticism

> *may be cruel and inhumane, lacking in feeling and empathy, and altogether insensitive. . . . He has a liking for odd and unusual things, and a disregard for danger. He likes to make fools of other people and to upset them.* (Eysenck & Eysenck, 1975, pp. 5–6)

Table 2.4 Eysenck's PEN Model: Factors and Narrow Traits

Factors	Narrow Traits
Psychoticism	Aggressive
	Cold
	Egocentric
	Impersonal
	Impulsive
	Antisocial
	Unempathetic
	Creative
	Tough-minded
Extraversion	Sociable
	Lively
	Active
	Assertive
	Sensation-seeking
	Carefree
	Dominant
	Surgent
	Venturesome
Neuroticism	Anxious
	Depressed
	Guilt feelings
	Low self-esteem
	Tense
	Irrational
	Shy
	Moody
	Emotional

Source: From Eysenck (1990, p. 246).

The second factor is **Extraversion** (Eysenck, 1990). Extraversion describes how outgoing people are, both to the social and the physical environments. The narrow traits associated with extraversion are sociable, lively, active, assertive, sensation-seeking, carefree, dominant, surgent, and venturesome (Eysenck, 1990; Eysenck & Eysenck, 1985). In contrast to introverts, extraverts tend to be outgoing and experience many positive feelings such as happiness and joy.

According to Hans Eysenck and Sybil Eysenck in their *Manual of the Eysenck Personality Inventory*:

> *The typical extravert is sociable, likes parties, has many friends, needs to have people to talk to, and does not like reading or studying by himself. He craves excitement, takes chances, often sticks his neck out, acts on the spur of the moment, and is generally an impulsive individual. . . . [H]e is carefree, easygoing, optimistic, and likes to "laugh and be merry". . . . [A]ltogether his feelings are not kept under tight control, and he is not always a reliable person.* (Eysenck & Eysenck, 1975, p. 5)

In contrast, the typical introvert is

> *a quiet, retiring sort of person, introspective, fond of books rather than people. . . . [H]e does not like excitement, takes matters of every day life with proper seriousness. . . . He tends to plan ahead, "looks before he leaps" and distrusts the impulse of the moment. . . . He keeps his feelings under close control . . . [H]e is reliable [and] somewhat pessimistic.* (Eysenck & Eysenck, 1975, p. 5)

The third factor, **Neuroticism**, refers to negative emotionality and emotional reactivity. The narrow traits associated with Neuroticism are anxious, depressed, guilt feelings, low self-esteem, tense, irrational, shy, moody, and emotional (Eysenck, 1990; Eysenck & Eysenck, 1985). People high in Neuroticism tend to be easily upset and vulnerable to negative emotions. In contrast, those low in this trait are even-tempered, calm, relaxed, carefree, unworried, somewhat unemotional, and recover quickly after an upsetting experience.

You can see sample questions from the Eysenck Personality Questionnaire (Eysenck & Eysenck, 1976) used to measure Psychoticism, Extraversion, and Neuroticism in Table 2.5. Eysenck and his colleagues conducted extensive research to demonstrate differences among people high and low in these fundamental factors. Much of his research focused on the physiological differences and genetic evidence for his theory, which we will briefly cover in those chapters.

SEE FOR YOURSELF

Where do your personality traits fall on these three factors?

Table 2.5 Sample Items From an Early Version of the Eysenck Personality Questionnaire

Psychoticism Questions

1. Do you enjoy practical jokes that can sometimes really hurt people?
2. Are there several people who keep trying to avoid you?
3. Do you think people spend too much time safeguarding their future with savings and insurances?

Extraversion Questions

1. Do you have many different hobbies?
2. Do you often take on more activities than you have time for?
3. Would you call yourself happy-go-lucky?

Neuroticism Questions

1. Does your mood often go up and down?
2. Do you ever feel "just miserable" for no reason?
3. Do you worry too long after an embarrassing experience?

Note: Respondents answered *Yes* or *No* to each question.
Source: From Eysenck and Eysenck (1976, pp. 65–68).

For many years Eysenck's theory held an important place in trait theory and inspired numerous experiments. Alas, the prominence of his theory has been eclipsed by the explosion of research on the five-factor model (John et al., 2008). One problem with Eysenck's theory is that many personality psychologists feel that important traits are missing. Eysenck totally disagreed, and claimed that they were looking at different levels in the hierarchy.

Specifically, he believed that other conceptualizations of traits are invalid because they include traits from multiple levels of the hierarchy. For example, Eysenck claimed that Cattell's 16 personality factors are at the third level (the level of traits) and when factor analyzed reduce to Eysenck's three superfactors (Eysenck, 1990). Further, Eysenck was talking about factors at the very top of the hierarchy (the type or superfactor level), but some measures of the five-factor model claim to have identified traits yet instead have mixed habits and responses. When you factor analyze these terms, you get the three superfactors of Psychoticism, Extraversion, and Neuroticism (Eysenck, 1990). Indeed, although Eysenck acknowledged that aspects of the five-factor model overlapped with his theory (e.g., Extraversion and Neuroticism), he countered that the factors of Agreeableness and Conscientiousness were at the level of habits, and therefore not comparable. Finally, he claimed that Openness is more of a cognitive factor and should not be considered a dimension of personality (Eysenck, 1990).

Five Factors: The Big Five and the Five-Factor Model

The five factors that appear to be our best candidates for universal traits are Neuroticism, Extraversion, Openness, Agreeableness and Conscientiousness (John, 1990; John et al., 2008). Because many researchers use slightly different terminology to summarize "their" five factors, even using Roman numerals to identify the factors rather than words, Oliver John and his colleagues (John, 1990, p. 96; John et al., 2008, p. 139) suggested that we think of the five factors using multiple words:

N: Neuroticism, Negative Affectivity, Nervousness (Factor IV)

E: Extraversion, Energy, Enthusiasm (Factor I)

O: Openness, Originality, Open-mindedness (Factor V)

A: Agreeableness, Altruism, Affection (Factor II)

C: Conscientiousness, Control, Constraint (Factor III)

Neuroticism, in contrast to Emotional Stability, refers to how well a person adjusts to the "slings and arrows of daily life." It refers to emotionality, psychological distress, and reactivity. For example, does George worry a lot about what people think of him? Does Ally fall apart under stress? George and Ally would be considered high in Neuroticism. Does Yang stay calm, cool, and collected under pressure? Does James keep his feelings under control? Yang and James are low in Neuroticism, and would be considered high in Emotional Stability. People who are low in Neuroticism are not necessarily high in overall mental health (McCrae & John, 1992)—that would depend on the other factors and perhaps some aspects of personality not captured by a trait model at all. People low in Neuroticism are even-tempered, calm, relaxed, and unruffled (McCrae & John, 1992). One of the best indicators for Neuroticism is agreement with the item "I often feel tense and jittery" from the NEO Personality Inventory—Revised (NEO-PI-R; McCrae, 2007).

According to the NEO-PI-R, each of the five factors are made up of six subscales called **facets**. If we think of Neuroticism as the superfactor, then the facets or narrow traits that make up Neuroticism are anxiety, angry hostility, depression, self-consciousness, impulsiveness (immoderation), and vulnerability to stress (Costa & McCrae, 1992; see Table 2.6).

People who are high in Neuroticism show poorer coping skills in stressful situations, poorer health, and are likely to experience burnout and job changes (John et al., 2008). They are also prone to negative emotions such as fear, sadness, embarrassment, anger, guilt, and disgust (Costa & McCrae, 1992). Emotionally stable people show more commitment to work and great satisfaction with their personal relationships (John et al., 2008). Among undergraduate students at one Swiss university, those who were high on impulsivity—an important facet of Neuroticism—spent more time on the phone, made more cell phone calls in a day, and reported

"Personality psychologists who continue to employ their preferred measure without locating it within the five-factor model can only be likened to geographers who issue reports of new lands but refuse to locate them on a map for others to find."
Ozer and Reise (1994, p. 361)

THINK ABOUT IT

Why are people high in Neuroticism more vulnerable to stress and poor health?

Table 2.6 Facets of Neuroticism

Anxiety
Angry hostility
Depression
Self-consciousness
Impulsiveness
Vulnerability to stress

Source: From Costa and McCrae (1992).

Table 2.7 Facets of Extraversion

Warmth
Gregariousness
Assertiveness
Activity
Excitement-seeking
Positive emotions

Source: From Costa and McCrae (1992).

being more dependent on their cell phones than people who were low in impulsiveness (Billieux, Linden, D'Acremont, Ceschi, & Zermatten, 2006).

Is Dominick full of life and fun to be around? Does Christine enjoy parties with lots of people? Is April more reserved and quiet? Dominick and Christine are more extroverted, whereas April is more introverted. The second factor listed, Extraversion, is contrasted with Introversion and describes how one "surges" or energetically engages with the social world. Extraverted people just *like* other people. They are assertive, active, talkative, and cheerful, enjoy large groups and gatherings, and enjoy excitement (Costa & McCrae, 1992).

The factor of Extraversion is made up of the facets of warmth (friendliness), gregariousness, assertiveness, activity, excitement-seeking, and positive emotions (cheerfulness; Costa & McCrae, 1992; see Table 2.7). Extraversion also refers to energetically seeking out and interacting with others (John & Robins, 1993; McCrae & John, 1992). One of the best indicators of Extraversion is agreement with the item "I am a cheerful, high spirited person" from the NEO-PI-R (McCrae, 2007).

Keep in mind that an energetic, optimistic person who shows enthusiasm and cheerfulness is not necessarily low in anxiety or depression. Anxiety and depression are related to Neuroticism (McCrae & John, 1992). Extraverts are likely to hold leadership positions in groups, have many friends and a greater number of sexual partners, and are more likely to be selected as foreperson of a jury than are Introverts. In contrast, introverts are more likely to experience poorer relationships with parents and peers (John et al., 2008).

The third factor is **Openness** or "Inquiring Intellect" (Digman, 1996; Fiske, 1949). Openness includes the facets of fantasy (imagination), aesthetics (artistic interests), feelings (emotionality), actions (adventurousness), ideas (intellect), and values (psychological liberalism; see Table 2.8). Does Jim have a very active imagination? Does Ellen get completely absorbed in music she is listening to? Jim and Ellen are high in openness. Is Rick pretty well set in his ways? Is Catherine against controversial campus speakers? People high in Openness tend to be imaginative and creative, whereas people low in openness tend to be more conventional, practical, and down-to-earth. People high in Openness tend to go further with their education, to succeed in creative jobs, and to create distinctive work and home environments (John et al., 2008). One of the best indicators of Openness is the experience of chills or goosebumps in response to an aesthetic experience (McCrae, 2007). In sum, a person high in Openness is seen as

Table 2.8 Facets of Openness

Fantasy
Aesthetics
Feelings
Actions
Ideas
Values

Source: From Costa and McCrae (1992).

> *interested in experience for its own sake, eager for variety, tolerant of uncertainty, leading a richer, more complex, less conventional life. By contrast, the closed person is seen as being impoverished in fantasy, insensitive to art and beauty, restricted in affect, behaviorally rigid, bored by ideas, and ideologically dogmatic.* (McCrae, 1990, p. 123)

Openness refers to an appreciation of the life of the mind in such things as ideas, thoughts, fantasies, art, and beauty, and is not the same as intelligence. People can score high in Openness without having a high IQ (McCrae & John, 1992). Similarly, artistic interests are not the same as artistic ability, which is not a personality trait. Openness includes an appreciation of a wide range of feelings in contrast to touchiness or defensiveness, which is part of Neuroticism (McCrae, 1990). Openness refers to an openness to ideas and new things

People high in Openness tend to enjoy the adventurousness of traveling abroad.

rather than an openness to people, which is part of Extraversion. Openness is not the same as excitement-seeking, which is part of Extraversion. People high in Openness like new experiences, not necessarily dangerous or exciting ones.

Having high Openness may sound better or more fun than being low in Openness, but there's no particular psychological benefit to being high or low on this factor (and the same can be said for Extraversion). Rather, the value of creativity or conventionalism depends on the situation, with people at either end found in everyday walks of life (Costa & McCrae, 1992).

Agreeableness refers to the quality of interpersonal relations—that is, how much a person feels for and gets along with others; whether he or she seeks out such enjoyment, as would an extravert, or does not, as would an introvert. Agreeableness can also be thought of as a prosocial or communal orientation to others and is contrasted with antagonism or competitiveness (Costa & McCrae, 1992; Graziano & Eisenberg, 1997; John et al., 2008). People low in Agreeableness show hostility, self-centeredness, spitefulness, indifference, and even jealousy toward others (Digman, 1990). Agreeableness includes the facets of trust (of others), straightforwardness (honesty or morality as opposed to manipulativeness), altruism, compliance (cooperation), modesty, and tender-mindedness (sympathy; see Table 2.9).

Does Ramiro believe that most people are basically well intentioned? Does Betty have great empathy for people in need? Ramiro and Betty would be high in Agreeableness, showing trust in and sympathy for other people, a concern for social harmony, and getting along with others. In contrast, people low in Agreeableness distrust the motives of others and are on the lookout for others who might be trying to take advantage of them. For example, does Jasmine bully or flatter people into getting them to do what she wants? Does Darnell believe that most people will take advantage of you if you let them? Jasmine and Darnell are low in Agreeableness. Some measure of Disagreeableness might be useful in situations requiring tough judgments or "tough love." Some of the most successful U.S. presidents have been low in Agreeableness (Rubenzer, Faschingbauer, & Ones, 2000). Generally, people high in Agreeableness show better performance in work groups than do those low in Agreeableness (John et al., 2008). People low in Agreeableness are often at risk for cardiovascular disease, juvenile delinquency, and interpersonal problems (John et al., 2008). However, Costa and McCrae (1992) noted that the "readiness to fight" is often an advantage in life, and good science demands the skepticism and critical thinking of the person low in Agreeableness.

Finally, **Conscientiousness** refers to an individual's degree of organization, both physical organization, such as the organization of one's office, or mental organization, as in planning ahead and having goals to be achieved. Conscientiousness also includes how we regulate our own impulses such as thinking before acting, delaying gratification, or following norms and rules (John et al., 2008). For example, does Brittany have separate files for each of her

Table 2.9 Facets of Agreeableness

Trust
Straightforwardness
Altruism
Compliance
Modesty
Tender-mindedness

Source: From Costa and McCrae (1992).

Table 2.10 Facets of Conscientiousness

Competence
Order
Dutifulness
Achievement-striving
Self-discipline
Deliberation

Source: From Costa and McCrae (1992).

THINK ABOUT IT

Can people change how agreeable they are?

SEE FOR YOURSELF

Where do your personality traits fall on these five factors?

classes? Does Dimitri put away his video games after he plays with them? If so, Brittany and Dimitri are displaying aspects of Conscientiousness. But consider a person like Charlie who is not dependable and who even cheats at solitaire! Or Lonette, who often does things on the spur of the moment without thinking of the consequences. Both of these people are low in Conscientiousness and might be expected to place short-term pleasures ahead of long-term accomplishments.

Conscientiousness includes the facets of competence (self-efficacy), order, dutifulness, achievement-striving, self-discipline, and deliberation (cautiousness; see Table 2.10). Interestingly, people high in Conscientiousness are rated by their peers and even their spouses as well organized, neat, thorough, and diligent (McCrae & Costa, 1987). They also have higher grade point averages and better on-the-job performance (John et al., 2008). People low in Conscientiousness are more likely to smoke, abuse alcohol and other drugs, show attention deficit disorder, have a poor diet, and not exercise enough. In contrast, people high in Conscientiousness are more likely to adhere to doctor's orders, and—when compared to those low in Conscientiousness—live longer (John et al., 2008)! But don't be so smug if you are high in Conscientiousness; high levels of this trait may also lead to annoying habits such as fastidiousness, compulsive neatness, or workaholic behavior (Costa & McCrae, 1985).

If some of these factors sound familiar, they should: These five are very similar to Eysenck's three factors. That is, both the five-factor model and Eysenck's model identify Neuroticism and Extraversion as two important dimensions of human personality. Further, Eysenck's Psychoticism factor is a combination of Agreeableness and Conscientiousness (Digman, 1996).

A Rose by Any Other Name? Two Models of the Five Factors.   Part of the confusion for the names of the factors is that the factors, especially Openness, look slightly different depending on the method used to identify them. When researchers start with the lexical approach, they get the Big Five of Surgency (Extraversion), Agreeableness, Conscientiousness, Emotional Stability, and Culture (Goldberg, 1990; Norman, 1963). Generally, the phrase *Big Five* refers to this lexical solution. The Big Five factors are identified by Roman numerals that signify the frequency of the factor words in the lexicon. For example, words that refer to lexical factor I, Extraversion, are more

People high in conscientiousness have higher grade point averages than people low in this trait.

common than words of lexical factor V, Openness. Roman numerals also have the advantage of being neutral from a theoretical standpoint (McCrae & John, 1992). However, numbers are less memorable than mnemonics and so the OCEAN labeling has caught on more, especially among students of personality psychology (McCrae & Costa, 1985).

At roughly the same time, Costa and McCrae (1976), using factor analysis, discovered three factors: Anxiety-Adjustment (now called Neuroticism), Introversion-Extraversion, and Openness to experience. They devised an inventory to measure these three factors (the NEO; McCrae & Costa, 1983, 1985), and then persuaded by the strength of the lexical findings, they added scales to measure the factors of Agreeableness and Conscientiousness in 1990 and called their solution the five-factor model (FFM; Costa & McCrae, 1992; Costa, McCrae, & Dye, 1991; Digman, 1996). Indeed, comparing the lexical model with their five-factor model, McCrae and Costa (1985) noted that "the similarities are far more remarkable than the differences" (p. 720). Today, the five factors of the five-factor model—Neuroticism, Extraversion, Openness, Agreeableness, and Conscientiousness—are measured using the revised version of the NEO Personality Inventory (NEO-PI-R; Costa & McCrae, 1992). This ordering of the factors, incidentally, reflects the amount of variance, from largest to smallest, accounted for by each of the five factors.

So, what's the difference between the two models? After all, they seem pretty similar. The major similarity is, of course, a five-factor solution, which is no small feat given all the controversy! Also, the two solutions identify virtually identical factors. One difference is the name of the individual factors. What the Big Five calls Emotional Stability the FFM calls Neuroticism. Both terms refer to the same dimension; the only difference is in direction, or which end of the pole researchers wish to emphasize. Second, the Big Five Culture factor is a narrower view of the FFM factor Openness, which refers to openness to aesthetic or cultural tastes, a wide range of emotions, and a need for variety, and is not limited to creativity and intellectual interests. Yet, both the Big Five and FFM solutions agree that creativity, imagination, and originality are aspects of this factor (Saucier, 1992). Recall that there are fewer words in the English language that describe Openness of personality, so it's no wonder there are disagreements about what this factor represents. Maybe there are some aspects of personality we need questionnaires to measure such as sensitivity to art and beauty (McCrae, 1990).

Other differences are more philosophical and deal with the history behind the two traditions and the empirical usefulness of the models. For example, the Big Five describes personality without attempting to explain where these attributes come from (i.e., they are in our language so they must be important). In contrast, the FFM theorizes, much in the tradition of Eysenck, that the five factors are biological traits (Saucier & Goldberg, 1996). That is, these traits are causal entities that correspond to neuropsychic structures that are in the process of being identified (John & Robins, 1993). Second, because the Big Five is grounded in adjectives, it has been replicated cross-culturally in many different languages. The NEO-PI-R, because it uses sentences, may be more dependent on language and culture and may lose something in the translation (Saucier & Goldberg, 1996). We'll examine cross-cultural evidence for the five-factor solution in the next chapter on traits. For now, we'll use the term *Big Five* when referring to lexically derived factors, *five-factor model* or *FFM* when referring to the questionnaire factors, and *five-factor taxonomy* or *the five factors* when the specific model doesn't matter.

Research on both the Big Five (using adjectival measures) and the FFM (using the NEO-PI-R questionnaire) yield similar results (John & Robins, 1993), giving us even greater faith in a five-factor solution of Neuroticism, Extraversion, Openness, Agreeableness, and Conscientiousness.

Is Five Really the Ultimate Answer to Life, the Universe, and Everything?   Although that sounds like a simple question, the answer is quite complicated. Remember Cattell's claim that 16 was the right number of factors to describe human personality? Eysenck critiqued Cattell's model and noted that direct factor analysis of the 16PF questionnaire recovers 3 factors, remarkably similar to Psychoticism, Extraversion, and Neuroticism (Eysenck, 1991). Interestingly, though similar, this factor analysis failed to find the extreme antisocial aspects of Eysenck's Psychoticism factor. This suggests, according to Eysenck, that the Cattell scales are missing key aspects of personality (Eysenck, 1991). Further, even though one study recovered

"Factor analysis has improved the situation, as has clearer theorizing, but the problem of naming factors is of course still with us."
Hans Eysenck

THINK ABOUT IT

Can you think of traits to describe a person who appreciates art and beauty?

five factors from the responses on the 16PF questionnaire from more than 17,000 people (Krug & Johns, 1986), Eysenck claimed that "it would need a lot of interpretive ingenuity" to make these resemble the Big Five factors of Norman (1963; Eysenck, 1991, p. 778). Instead, the three factors of Psychoticism, Extraversion, and Neuroticism fit the data better (Eysenck, 1991). And on top of it all, Eysenck claims, the 16 factors of Cattell are not even replicable!

Statistically, 16 factors explain more of the variance in personality than 3 factors do, but is the difference theoretically, socially, or practically important (Eysenck, 1991)? It all depends on what your goals are or on what you are trying to predict. We might think of the whole debate as a trade-off of fidelity versus bandwidth (John, 1989). Would you rather have a radio that picks up few stations with fantastic quality of sound or many stations with decent sound? Well, it depends on why you are listening to the radio. When I was a kid, it was incredibly exciting to discover that we could pick up far-away radio stations on our AM transistor radios—one of my classmates claimed that he could hear people talking in French!—never mind that we had to turn up the volume all the way and use a bit of our imaginations. On the other hand, you may be an opera fan who wants to tune in to the Metropolitan Opera Saturday afternoon broadcast to hear your favorite soprano in HD. So, if you are an explorer of personality, like Cattell and the early researchers, then a higher number of factors suits your purpose. If you're trying to find out how people act differently depending on their traits, then a smaller number may be better.

Another way to think of this dilemma of identifying the right number for a taxonomy of personality traits is to consider what happens in a field such as biology with a well-established taxonomy for animals. We can classify the new creature lapping our face at the pound as an animal or as a dog or as a poodle or even as Mr. Bowser, the newest member of your family! The "broadest level of the hierarchy," says John (1989), is to "personality what the categories 'plant' and 'animal' are to the world of natural objects—extremely useful for some initial rough distinctions but of less value for predicting specific behaviors of a particular object" (p. 268).

Researchers have championed anywhere from 1 to 16 factors. We'll consider some of these conceptualizations in turn.

A One-Factor Solution

The smallest number of factors that can account for human personality is, of course, one. Researchers have called this the **general personality factor** or **GPF** (Musek, 2007; Rushton & Irwing, 2008; van der Linden, te Nijenhuis, & Bakker, 2010). The GPF is hypothesized to explain all of human personality in much the same way that g represents a general factor of intelligence underlying all mental abilities (Musek, 2007). This GPF lies at the very top of a hierarchy of personality traits (see Figure 2.3).

What exactly is the GPF? According to Musek (2007) this factor includes all the positive aspects of the five factors: Emotional Stability, Agreeableness, Extraversion, Conscientiousness, and Intellect. Further, the GPF encompasses the two factors of *Alpha* (the emotional stability to get along with others) and *Beta* (the flexibility to deal with change, challenges, and demands) (Musek, 2007). People who are high in GPF are altruistic, sociable, able to handle stress, relaxed, open to experience, dependable, and task-focused (Rushton & Irwing, 2008). Rushton and his colleagues argued that these aspects of personality have been evolutionarily hard-wired as they are necessary for survival (e.g., Rushton, Bons, & Hur, 2008; Rushton & Irwing, 2008).

In one study, participants answered three different measures of the five-factor model and other personality questionnaires (Musek, 2007). When their responses were factor analyzed it turned out that the first factor, the GPF, accounted for 40 to 50% of the variance in participants' responses. The second factor accounted for 17 to 26%. Further, this GPF correlated with measures of well-being and self-esteem. Other researchers found similar evidence for the same GPF using different trait measures (Rushton et al., 2008; Rushton & Irwing, 2008, 2009).

Although this GPF sounds an awful lot like a general "social desirability" factor or a "conformity" factor, Musek (2007) argued that the pattern of results—how this GPF correlates with other personality measures—rules out both of these alternative explanations. However, other researchers believe that a two-factor solution is merely an artifact of the way we measure traits

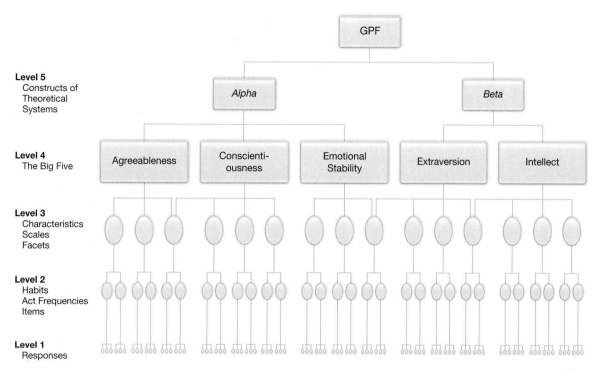

Figure 2.3 The Current Hierarchical Model of Human Personality. *Source:* Adapted from Musek (2007, Figure 2, p. 1225) and Digman (1997, Figure 1, p. 1252). Musek, J. (2007), "A general factor of personality: Evidence for the Big One in the five-factor model," *Journal of Research in Personality,* 41, 1213–1233. Reprinted by permission of Academic Press.

and have evidence that a five- or six-factor solution is superior to a two-factor solution (Ashton, Lee, Goldberg, & de Vries, 2009).

Six- and Seven-Factor Solutions . . . and Beyond!

An alternative to the five-factor taxonomy is the **HEXACO** (or six-factor) **model** (Ashton & Lee, 2005, 2007; Lee & Ashton, 2004). The six factors are Honesty-Humility, Emotionality, Extraversion, Agreeableness, Conscientiousness and Openness to Experience. Five of the factors are very similar to their five-factor counterparts; the major difference is the addition of Honesty-Humility as a separate factor (Ashton & Lee, 2005). This factor emerged out of research in other cultures and languages (e.g., Ashton, Lee, Perugini, et al., 2004; Fung & Ng, 2006) and might be best thought of as a genuineness or trustworthiness factor in English (Ashton, Lee, & Goldberg, 2004). Honesty-Humility includes the facets of sincerity, fairness, greed avoidance, and modesty as contrasted with arrogance and egotism (Lee & Ashton, 2004). Although this sounds similar to Agreeableness, the difference has to do with manipulation and power. For example, a person high in Agreeableness is willing to help another person even when it might be against his or her own self-interest (i.e., altruism). Someone high in Honesty-Humility would not take advantage of another person, especially if that person is disadvantaged in some way (Lee & Ashton, 2004).

However, the HEXACO is not without its critics. For example, McCrae and Costa (2008) suggested that this sixth factor is just a variation of Agreeableness tapping more introverted aspects of Agreeableness, whereas the standard facets of Agreeableness (trust, straightforwardness, altruism, cooperation, modesty, sympathy) tap the more extroverted aspects of getting along with others. They believed that the six-factor model is redundant with the five-factor model and not an improvement on it.

One criticism of five-factor solutions (cf. Saucier, 1997) is that many of them can be traced back to Allport and Odbert (1936), who omitted adjectives that represented temporary states (such as moods) or evaluations (i.e., judgments of character, such as *insignificant, worthy*). When such terms are added back in, the result is a seven-factor solution (Almagor, Tellegen, & Waller, 1995; Benet & Waller, 1995; Benet-Martínez & Waller, 2002). These "Big Seven" factors are very similar to the Big Five, with the two additional factors of Negative Valence and Positive Valence. These additional evaluative dimensions are especially useful for understanding pathology (Durrett & Trull, 2005).

This is one area of current research and debate as researchers try to garner evidence for and against their theories. In sum, John et al. (2008) suggested that five factors is our current best working hypothesis for the organization of human traits. There is much evidence from cross-cultural studies to support this view as well, as we will soon see.

Then and Now: The Four Temperaments and the Five Factors

In ancient Greece, the philosopher Empedocles proposed that all of nature is made up of the four elements of air, earth, fire, and water. Hippocrates, building on this early work, further proposed that humans contained elements of the cosmos, therefore we have within our bodies the corresponding "humors" that affected our temperament or personality. A predominance of blood and one was cheerful and happy; too much yellow bile and one was quick to anger. But it was the Roman physician Galen, around AD 150, who linked these temperaments to diseases and is credited with being the first to recognize a relationship between physiology and personality (see Table 2.11). We might dismiss these ancient personality theories today in favor of empirically based theories, but the wisdom of the ancients is remarkably in line with many modern personality theories.

Because our personality is expressed in our facial expressions, body movements, and gestures, Gordon Allport showed illustrations of these four personality types to participants and found that most people were able to correctly guess which temperament went with each picture (you can try this yourself in Figure 2.4). Allport noted that the four temperaments fit easily into two-factor theories of personality, whether the two factors be speed and intensity of emotional arousal or activity level and a tendency to approach or withdraw from situations (Allport, 1937/1961). Similarly, Hans Eysenck noticed that the four temperaments matched the dimensions of emotional/nonemotional and changeable/unchangeable, two important personality factors identified by the founder of modern experimental psychology, Wilhelm Wundt in the 19th century (Eysenck, 1967). Perhaps you recognized that these dimensions correspond to Neuroticism and Extraversion of both Eysenck and the current five-factor taxonomy (see Figure 2.5).

Today, while researchers have pretty much decided that the five factors—Neuroticism, Extraversion, Openness, Agreeableness, and Conscientiousness—are the major dimensions of human personality; others have suggested that these five are aspects of a two-factor solution, *alpha* and *beta* (Digman, 1997).

Factor ***alpha*** consists of Emotional Stability, Agreeableness, and Conscientiousness whereas Extraversion and Openness to Experience make up ***beta*** (Digman, 1997). Digman (1997) suggested that these two factors represent the major tasks of personality development: socialization and actualization (although he didn't use these labels). By socialization he meant developing according to "society's blueprint" (p. 1250), including learning how to regulate one's own emotions and impulses, living up to expectations, and not being too defensive when interacting with others. By actualization he meant personality growth, or going out into the world being open to new experiences (recall that Surgency is another name for Extraversion) and adapt to them

Table 2.11 The Four Temperaments

Element	Property	Humor	Temperament	Characteristic
Air	Warm and moist	Blood	Sanguine	Hopeful
Earth	Cold and dry	Black bile	Melancholic	Sad
Fire	Warm and dry	Yellow bile	Choleric	Irascible
Water	Cold and moist	Phlegm	Phlegmatic	Apathetic

Source: Adapted from Allport (1937/1961, p. 37). Allport, G. W. (1937/1961). Pattern and growth in personality. New York: Holt, Rinehart and Winston.

(Digman, 1997). Similarly, others have suggested that all humans, regardless of culture, may seek to categorize people as benign versus harmful (socialized) and stimulating versus boring (actualized). They have found evidence for this two-factor solution in Greek samples using Greek trait terms (Saucier, Georgiades, Tsaousis, & Goldberg, 2005).

These two aspects of personality—socialization and actualization—are common themes in many theories of personality. In fact, Wiggins (1968, p. 309) called Extraversion and Anxiety the "Big Two" because they appear in numerous observations, theories, tests, and experimental results of personality psychologists. Although these two factors were replicated by some researchers using various methods (Blackburn, Renwick, Donnelly, & Logan, 2004; DeYoung, 2006; DeYoung, Peterson, & Higgins, 2002; Markon, Krueger, & Watson, 2005), other researchers question these findings (McCrae et al., 2008; Mutch, 2005).

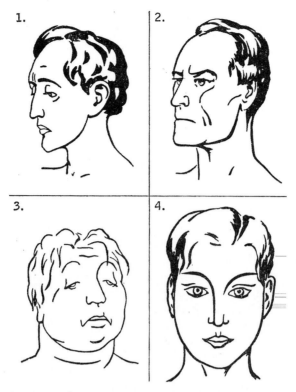

Figure 2.4 Physiognomic Representation of the Four Temperaments: Melancholic, Choleric, Phlegmatic, and Sanguine. *Source:* Allport, G. W. (1937/1961). Pattern and growth in personality. New York: Holt, Rinehart and Winston.

The two factors *alpha* and *beta* are very similar to the dimensions of emotional/nonemotional and changeable/unchangeable first identified as part of the four temperaments of personality over two millennia ago. As Eysenck pointed out, the ancients were not so much trying to devise theories about human personality as they were describing what their "friends, Romans, countrymen" were like. Time—and research—have proven their hunches remarkably accurate. Now if we could only see how they decorated their ancient living spaces!

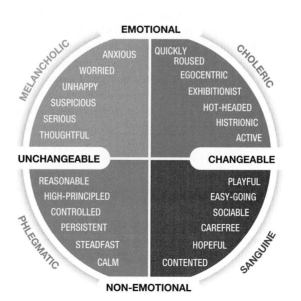

Figure 2.5 Eysenck's Representation of the Four Temperaments in Two Dimensions. *Source:* From Eysenck (1967, p. 35). Reprinted with permission from Eysenck, H. J. (1967), The Biological Basis of Personality, (Springfield, IL: Charles C. Thomas). Permission conveyed through the Copyright Clearance Center.

The Personality of Everyday Life

What can you tell about someone from his or her living space?

People's personalities shine through in many aspects of their daily lives, as we saw in the research study that opened this chapter (Gosling et al., 2002). Now that you know about the various traits that are used to describe personality, you can use this knowledge to understand what people are like based on the physical cues of their surroundings or "native habitat."

First, you must decide if the item or decoration was put there on purpose or if it was just behavioral residue from everyday living. Of course, the person's carelessness tells you something about his or her personality as well!

If an item was put there on purpose, consider the following questions: Is the item expressive of the individual's true personality or was it put there to convey a particular image? One way of telling this is to see if the item is in public view (e.g., a photo on a desk facing outward) or in a place that only the occupant can see (e.g., a photo on a desk facing inward). If it was put there to convey an image, what impression does the owner wish to convey?

If an item is a true expression of the owner's personality, what does it tell us? Recall that people who are high in Conscientiousness tend to have rooms that are more organized, neat, and uncluttered. People who are high in Openness tend to have more decorations in their living space and a greater variety of magazines and books.

As for Extraversion, Neuroticism, and Agreeableness, there are no specific cues you can look for, but perhaps you may be able to take a guess. Recall that for these traits observers were pretty good at guessing the occupants' personality, even though there was little agreement on the specific cues they used to make their judgments.

By applying these findings from the Gosling et al. (2002) study you can be your own Sherlock Holmes!

Chapter Summary

✓•⌐**Study** and **Review**
on **mysearchlab.com**

Go online for more resources to help you review.

In this chapter we defined traits as a person's typical style of thinking, feeling, and acting. Traits can be organized into a hierarchy, moving up from specific responses to habitual responses to traits to a psychological type. Psychologists have studied traits through the idiographic approach, describing a single individual with all of his or her idiosyncrasies, or through the nomothetic approach, describing *any* personality using a set number of key traits.

Within the idiographic approach, individuals may have central and secondary traits or, rarely, a cardinal trait. Allport's analysis of Jenny illustrates the idiographic approach.

Within the nomothetic approach, psychologists might start with a theory to which traits are most useful for describing personality or conduct an analysis of the lexicon to see which descriptions of personality have been coded into language, by statistical and mathematical techniques, or by a combination of any of these approaches. Factor analysis, where numerous traits are reduced to a few meaningful factors, is often used to identify the underlying structure among a set of traits.

Psychologists have debated the right number of factors claiming that 1 to 7 or 16 factors best account for personality. For example, Eysenck identified the three factors of Psychoticism, Extraversion, and Neuroticism. Others have claimed that a single general personality factor explains all of personality, whereas still others identify just two factors of socialization (*alpha*) and actualization (*beta*). Today there is tremendous consensus that the five factors of Neuroticism, Extraversion, Openness, Agreeableness, and Conscientiousness best account for human personality. Some overlap occurs between the theories of Eysenck and the five factors, which, amazingly enough, is similar to ancient conceptualizations of the four temperaments (air, earth, fire, and water).

We opened this chapter with a study that found that observers are able to guess the personality of individuals by observing their living spaces. We saw that people express their personalities by the way they decorate their residence hall rooms, apartment bedrooms, and even offices. In the next chapter, we will consider other ways people express their personalities including music preferences, web pages, and careers and to what extent people change or remain the same—or at least consistent in their personalities—across the life span.

Review Questions

1. What is a trait? Explain how traits are organized into a hierarchy.
2. What is the idiographic approach to the study of traits? Describe Allport's case of "Jenny." How is this an example of the idiographic approach?
3. What is the nomothetic approach? What are the three main ways of identifying the most meaningful and applicable words for describing human personality? What is factor analysis and how is it used in the nomothetic approach?
4. What three factors best account for human personality, according to Eysenck?
5. What are the five factors? What facets make up each factor? What are some important correlates of people high and low in each of the five factors?
6. Is human personality reducible to one factor? Two factors? Six or seven factors? Explain.
7. How is today's view of personality similar to the view of the ancients?
8. What can you tell about a person from their living space?

Key Terms

Behavioral residue
Trait
Idiographic approach
Nomothetic approach
Central traits
Secondary traits
Cardinal traits
Theoretical approach
Lexical approach
Measurement approach

Factor analysis
Eigenvalue
Factor loadings
Big Five
Five-factor model
Narrow traits
Psychoticism
Extraversion
Neuroticism
Facets

Openness
Agreeableness
Conscientiousness
General Personality
    Factor (GPF)
HEXACO model
Alpha
Beta

3 PERSONALITY TRAITS: PRACTICAL MATTERS

Read the Chapter on
mysearchlab.com

"To all such questions about the nature of human nature, trait psychology offers a single yet powerful answer: It varies."

McCrae and Costa (1996, p. 57)

SEE FOR YOURSELF

Next time you meet new people, see if you can predict elements of their personality from their handshakes.

SEE FOR YOURSELF

What kind of person are you? What traits from the five-factor model would you use to describe yourself?

Can you judge someone's personality from his or her handshake? If we express our personalities in our decorating tastes, can something as simple as a handshake also express who we are? Amazingly enough, the answer to these questions is yes—at least when it comes to the five factors of Neuroticism, Extraversion, Openness, Agreeableness, and Conscientiousness.

In one study, participants came to the laboratory for a study on "personality questionnaires" where they were greeted by four experimenters, one at a time (Chaplin, Phillips, Brown, Clanton, & Stein, 2000). Each experimenter shook hands with the participant on arrival and departure, twice in all, for each participant. These experimenters, two men and two women, were trained extensively to rate handshakes on various scales including strength, grip, dryness, temperature, vigor, duration, eye contact, and texture (training took about a month for the experimenters to standardize and validate their judgments). Participants took a version of the Big Five Inventory which measured their personalities on the five factors.

Because a number of the handshake qualities were related to one another, the experimenters created a Firm Handshake Composite from ratings of duration, eye contact, completeness of grip, strength, and vigor. They discovered that men had firmer handshakes than women and that personality for three of the five factors was significantly correlated with this Firm Handshake Composite (Chaplin et al., 2000).

Neurotic participants tended to have a weak handshake, whereas those who were more emotionally stable had a firmer handshake. In addition, extraverts had a firmer handshake than introverts. Interestingly, there was a correlation between handshake and Openness for women only, such that women who had a firmer handshake were more open to experience than women with a softer handshake. Have you ever heard the advice "You never have a second chance to make a first impression"? Well, the authors noted that you might want to take the results of this study to heart, especially if you are nervous and shy on a job interview, graduate school interview, or when meeting business contacts (advice your mother might agree with!).

Our personality is expressed in many aspects of our lives, from our way of interacting with others to the kinds of music we enjoy to the kinds of careers we choose. Indeed, not only do we carry our personality around with us in various situations, but we are who we are across our lifetimes as well. In this chapter we consider whether there are traits left out of the five factors and if this model adequately explains the personality of non-Westerners. Then we take a look at how we express our personalities in various areas of our lives. Finally, we consider how personality develops—both stays consistent and changes—over time and how we maintain a coherent personality over our life spans: all very practical matters for the topic of traits.

What can you tell about the personality of a job candidate from his or her handshake?

What's Missing From the Five Factors?

Take a moment to describe yourself. Do you use standard traits such as sociable, outgoing, fun-loving, and sarcastic? But do you also have responses such as "exhausted," "good time manager," "athletic," "handy," and "beautiful"? Where do these fall on the five factors?

Some critics have claimed that the five factors are complete and can account for even these unusual traits (Saucier & Goldberg, 1998). Others—reanalyzing the same data—take a more liberal view and identify additional factors (Paunonen & Jackson, 2000) illustrating how choosing the right number of factors is more art than science, as we saw in Chapter 2. What is out there beyond the five factors? If we eliminate adjectives that describe physical characteristics (*short, beautiful, heavy*), demographics (*employed, unemployed*), unusual behaviors (*evil, cruel*) and other adjectives not typically used to refer to personality, we have 10 possible candidates (see Table 3.1). Paunonen (2002) even created the Supernumerary Personality Inventory to measure these factors! Just for the record, these clusters also fall outside the six-factor HEXACO model (Lee, Ogunfowora, & Ashton, 2005), discussed in Chapter 2.

Are these parts of personality? Are these traits? Or, are they attitudes, values, or social behaviors? We consider a few of these questions in turn as we take a closer look at three possible traits: intelligence, religiosity, and sexuality.

Is Intelligence a Personality Trait?

Generally, cognitive abilities are not considered personality traits. However, an early personality psychologist, Raymond Cattell, identified ability traits such as memory, mathematical ability, and intelligence (Cattell, 1946). So, is intelligence considered a personality trait today?

Maybe not. First, recall that early studies of the Big Five defined **Openness** as consisting of sophistication, artistic and intellectual interests, and intelligence (Norman, 1963). Psychologists in the lexical tradition thought of this factor as Culture rather than Openness to experience, as we do today. However, other studies find that adjectives such as *intelligent, knowledgeable,* and *cultured* load on a Conscientiousness factor (McCrae & Costa, 1985).

Second, when people rate themselves or a close friend on "intelligence" they are generally thinking of *intelligent, rational* and *logical, clear-minded, mature,* and similar adjectives (Borgatta, 1964). These are personality descriptors that are clearly different from cognitive ability or IQ, which is what we generally think of when we think of intelligence. We seem to think of productive, motivated, hardworking, and well-organized people as having academic intelligence, even though they do not score as such on IQ tests (Sternberg, Conway, Ketron, & Bernstein, 1981). Indeed, when participants rate themselves on intelligence adjectives such as *hardworking, smart,* and *knowledgeable,* these end up loading on a Conscientiousness factor and are not related to measured intelligence (McCrae & Costa, 1985).

Third, there is evidence that there are individual differences in how people perceive and process information about the social world. Some psychologists call this emotional intelligence (Goleman, 1995; Salovey & Mayer, 1994).

> "To say that the five factors are unlikely to be comprehensive in no way denies their profound significance."
> *Buss (1996, p. 204)*

THINK ABOUT IT

When do behaviors become personality traits?

Table 3.1   Adjectival Clusters Beyond the Five Factors

  1. Religious, devout, reverent
  2. Sly, deceptive, manipulative
  3. Honest, ethical, moral
  4. Sexy, sensual, erotic
  5. Thrifty, frugal, miserly
  6. Conservative, traditional, down-to-earth
  7. Masculine-feminine
  8. Egotistical, conceited, snobbish
  9. Humorous, witty, amusing
  10. Risk taking, thrill seeking

Source: Reprinted with permission from Paunonen, S. V., & Jackson, D. N. (2000), "What is beyond the big five? Plenty!," *Journal of Personality*, 68(5), 821–835. Permission conveyed through the Copyright Clearance Center.

Finally, the whole topic of intelligence as an ability in the form of IQ has a long and controversial history in psychology. But because IQ is quite a different concept than traits, this topic is best covered in other psychology classes.

Is Religiosity a Personality Trait?

Think about the following adjectives: *spiritual, prayerful, mystical, worshipful, devout, pious, orthodox, godly, born-again, heretical, irreverent,* and *agnostic* (Saucier & Goldberg, 1998, p. 514). Do you think these form an important dimension of personality beyond the five factors?

Despite the importance of religion in many people's lives, religion has not occupied a central role in psychology, and certainly not in the study of personality (Emmons, Barrett, & Schnitker, 2008). A chapter on the psychology of religion made its debut in only the third edition of the *Handbook of Personality* in 2008 (Emmons et al., 2008). For many people—up to 75% in some polls—spirituality is more than a belief, an attitude, a demographic, a tradition, or a habit: It is a core part of who they are (Emmons et al., 2008).

Whether religiosity is an important dimension of personality beyond the five factors is a source of some debate (cf. Paunonen & Jackson, 2000; Saucier & Goldberg, 1998). For example, Saucier and Goldberg (1998) suggested that religiosity, like many dimensions beyond the five factors, is more appropriately considered a secondary trait, applicable for certain purposes, but not a core aspect of personality. Researchers consistently find correlations between religiosity and Agreeableness, Conscientiousness, and sometimes Openness and Extraversion depending on the aspect of religiosity under study (Emmons et al., 2008). But can religiosity account for personality beyond the five factors?

Consider the concept of **spiritual transcendence**, the ability of individuals to "stand outside of their immediate sense of time and place to view life from a larger, more objective perspective" (Piedmont, 1999, p. 988). According to Piedmont, spiritual transcendence includes a personal search for a greater connection rather than a spiritual encounter with a higher being. The concept of spirituality goes beyond any particular religious tradition, and in fact, Piedmont and his colleagues designed the Spiritual Transcendence Scale (STS) after first meeting with experts from various faiths including Buddhism, Hinduism, Quakerism, Lutheranism, Catholicism, and Judaism (Piedmont, 1999; Piedmont & Leach, 2002). The scale has three facets: Prayer Fulfillment, feelings of joy and contentedness from connection with the transcendent; Universality, seeing humanity as a single interrelated whole such that harming one harms all; and Connectedness, feeling belongingness to and social responsibility and gratitude for, others across generations and across social groups (You can see how you score in spiritual transcendence by taking the short form of the scale in Table 3.2 and finding your score in Table 3.3).

In two different validation samples, Piedmont and colleagues discovered that scores on each of the three transcendence scales were only slightly related to scores on the five factors as measured by both adjectival scales and by scores on the NEO-PI-R. Further, factor analysis yielded six independent factors: five for each of the five factors and one for spiritual transcendence. Together, this suggests that spiritual transcendence is a dimension of personality separate from the five factors of personality (Piedmont, 1999; see also MacDonald, 2000, who came to the same conclusion using his own measure, the Expressions of Spirituality Inventory).

Further, scores on the STS predicted scores on measures of life outcomes beyond the five factors and, in some cases, the effect of spirituality was stronger than the effect of personality! Specifically, spiritual transcendence and personality together predicted scores on locus of control beliefs for health issues, vulnerability to stress, responsiveness to others, perceived social support, prosocial behavior, positive sexual attitudes, and prochoice and prolife attitudes toward abortion (Piedmont, 1999).

This evidence suggests that, indeed, we may think of spirituality as an important part of personality. Whether spirituality, gratitude, ultimate concerns, or some additional aspect of religiosity is best thought of as a trait, dimension, or as some other important part of human personality is still to be determined by researchers (Emmons et al., 2008).

Table 3.2 The Spiritual Transcendence Scale Short Form (STS-R)

Agree or disagree with each of the nine questions below using the following scale:

Strongly Agree = SA

Agree = A

Neutral = N

Disagree = D

Strongly Disagree = SD

1. In the quiet of my prayers and/or meditations, I find a sense of wholeness.	SA A N D SD
2. I have done things in my life because I believed it would please a parent, relative, or friend that had died.	SA A N D SD
3. Although dead, memories and thoughts of some of my relatives continue to influence my current life.	SA A N D SD
4. I find inner strength and/or peace from my prayers and/or meditations.	SA A N D SD
5. I do not have any strong emotional ties to someone who has died.	SA A N D SD
6. There is no higher plane of consciousness or spirituality that binds all people.	SA A N D SD
7. Although individual people may be difficult, I feel an emotional bond with all of humanity.	SA A N D SD
8. My prayers and/or meditations provide me with a sense of emotional support.	SA A N D SD
9. I feel that on a higher level all of us share a common bond.	SA A N D SD

To score, points are assigned to your responses to each item. For items 1, 2, 3, 4, 7, 8, and 9 assign 5 points for each Strongly Agree response, 4 points for each Agree, 3 points for each Neutral, 2 points for each Disagree, and 1 point for each Strongly Disagree. For items 5 and 6, the opposite applies; give 1 point for each Strongly Agree, 2 points for Agree, 3 points for Neutral, 4 points for Disagree, and 5 points for Strongly Disagree. Add your scores for all nine items together. See Table 3.3 for how you compare to others who have taken the test.

Source: STS-R short form copyright © 1999, 2005 by Ralph L. Piedmont, Ph.D. No further copying, distribution, or usage is allowed without the explicit permission of Dr. Piedmont.

Is Sexuality a Personality Trait?

Do you know somebody who is "charming," "flirtatious," or "coy"? Can you account for these aspects of his or her personality within the five factors? There's a good reason for that: Words that described aspects of sexuality or that were more applicable to one gender or the other were purposely excluded from early lexical studies (Buss, 1996). This, according to evolutionary psychologist David Buss, "resulted in the near total omission of the individual differences in sexuality" (p. 203).

Table 3.3 Average Scores on the Spiritual Transcendence Scale by Gender and Age

Gender	Age	Total STS	Prayer Fulfillment (Items 1, 4, 8)	Universality (Items 6, 7, 9)	Connectedness (Items 2, 3, 5)
Women	Up to age 21	29–35	9–12	9–12	10–12
	Ages 21–30	32–38	11–13	11–13	10–13
	Ages 30 and up	35–39	11–14	11–13	10–12
Men	Up to age 21	27–33	8–11	9–11	9–12
	Ages 21–30	23–29	7–11	6–10	8–11
	Ages 30 and up	34–38	13–15	11–13	10–12

This table presents the average range of scores by gender and age group. If your total score falls in this range, then you have an interest in understanding broader, transcendent issues, but also have concerns for immediate needs. You balance both perspectives. If your score is higher than these values, then you have a strong spiritual transcendent orientation. You are concerned with living a life that is in accord with values and meanings that originate with some larger understanding of the purpose of the universe. You tend to see life in terms of "both and" rather than "either or." Individuals whose score is lower than the tabled values are more focused on the tangible realities of daily living. There may be more of a self-oriented focus to life, where personal concerns and issues are of greater concern.

Source: STS-R short form copyright © 1999, 2005 by Ralph L. Piedmont, Ph.D. No further copying, distribution, or usage is allowed without the explicit permission of Dr. Piedmont.

THINK ABOUT IT

Can a person have a personality trait that is expressed in only a few situations?

To rectify this problem, Buss and his colleagues identified all adjectives referring to sexuality from standard dictionary and similar lexical sources (Schmitt & Buss, 2000). Undergraduate students rated themselves on each of these 67 words along with an adjectival measure of the Big Five. When Schmitt and Buss factor-analyzed these responses they found 7 sexuality factors, referred to as the **Sexy Seven:** Sexual Attractiveness (e.g., sexy, stunning, attractive), Relationship Exclusivity (e.g., faithful, monogamous, not promiscuous), Gender Orientation (e.g., feminine, womanly, manly, masculine), Sexual Restraint (e.g., virginal, celibate, chaste), Erotophilic Disposition (e.g., obscene, vulgar, lewd), Emotional Investment (e.g., loving, romantic, compassionate), and Sexual Orientation.

Are these Sexy Seven factors personality traits beyond the Big Five? In an extensive series of tests, Schmitt and Buss discovered that the sexuality factors overlap almost 80% with the five factors, suggesting that they are not really separate factors. For example, when both the Big Five and sexuality adjectives were factor-analyzed together, the result was five factors. Each of these factors included a combination of *both* types of adjectives: Agreeableness and Emotional Investment; Extraversion, Sexual Attractiveness, Erotophilic Disposition, Sexual Restraint; Openness and Sexual Orientation; Neuroticism and Gender Orientation; and Conscientiousness and Relationship Exclusivity. Because sexuality can be accounted for by a combination of factors and facets of the five factors sexuality is not a separate personality trait. Rather, sexuality is—along with musical tastes, room decorating, and handshaking—another way in which we express our traits of Neuroticism, Extraversion, Openness, Agreeableness, and Conscientiousness (Schmitt & Buss, 2000).

Indigenous Personality: Unique Personality Traits?

Although some have claimed that five factors misses important aspects of personality in American culture, the picture is even more complicated when trying to apply the model to other cultures. Because the five-factor taxonomy relies on measures that were validated in mostly American samples, even if they adequately explain personality in another culture, it is possible that we may have missed personality traits that are unique to that culture. For example, consider a person who is polite, generous, responsible, respectful, and has a strong sense of honor. We can readily understand what this means, but can you think of a single word to describe these qualities? If you were Greek, you would immediately recognize this as **philotimo**.

THINK ABOUT IT

In American culture, are philotimo and filial piety traits or behaviors?

How about the qualities of caring for the mental and physical well-being of one's elderly parents, continuing the family line, and bringing honor to one's family and ancestors? For the Chinese, **filial piety** is a very desirable personality trait and is much more than obeying and honoring one's parents. Disappointing a family member is like letting down all of your ancestors—and your future progeny (Ho, 1996; Zhang & Bond, 1998). According to cultural tradition, this trait must be internalized by young people. Filial piety is not captured by the five-factor model alone; indigenous personality traits are necessary to fully explain this construct in Chinese college students (Zhang & Bond, 1998).

Can you think of a person on whom others depend? This person may even have a strong social obligation to take care of others. Whereas this sounds a lot like the relationship between parents and their children to our Western sensibilities, this characteristic of **amae** would seem very natural among Japanese adults. Amae characterizes relationships between people of lower and higher status, such as bosses and workers, in addition to the relationship between parents and children (Doi, 1973).

Although these concepts are readily understandable by an outsider, they are examples of indigenous culture-specific traits (cf. Goldstein, 2000). There is also the Korean concept of *cheong* (human affection; Choi, Kim, & Choi, 1993), the Indian concept of *hishkama karma* (detachment; Sinha, 1993), the Mexican concept of *simpatia* (avoidance of conflict; Triandis, Marin, Lisansky, & Betancourt, 1984), and the Filipino concept of *pakikisama* (going along with others; Enriquez, 1994), among others (Church & Ortiz, 2005). For the most part, these indigenous personality traits lie beyond the five factors.

The Five Factors in Other Cultures

How do we go about applying the five-factor taxonomy to other cultures? Do we take the "transport and test" approach where we translate English measures and see if they apply to people in other cultures? Or, do we start with the lexicon of a particular culture and try to identify indigenous personality traits? There are pros and cons to each of these approaches and the results depend on which method, as well as the specific measures, experimenters employ. Together, this line of research gets us closer to both identifying human universals in personality and understanding the impact of culture on personality. There are five main findings:

1. **Questionnaire measures of the five-factor model reliably replicate across many cultures and languages.** The question-based NEO-PI-R, when translated and then carefully back-translated to ensure that the items are comparable, applies very well across many countries and cultures. So far, the FFM has been tested and validated in over 50 countries including most Western ones as well as Israel, Argentina, Botswana, Ethiopia, Japan, Malta, Peru, South Korea, and Nigeria (McCrae, 2001, 2002; McCrae & Costa, 1997b; McCrae, Terracciano, & 78 Members of the Personality Profiles of Cultures Project, 2005a; McCrae, Terracciano, & 79 Members of the Personality Profiles of Cultures Project, 2005b). In all of these countries, self-ratings and peer ratings converge just as they do in the United States. In addition, five-factor scores correlate impressively with meaningful external criteria on life outcomes such as life satisfaction and getting along with others (Benet-Martínez & Oishi, 2008). In sum, there is "considerable evidence that the FFM dimensions are in fact universally applicable" (McCrae et al., 2005b, p. 408).

2. **Adjectival measures of the Big Five reveal variations of Neuroticism, Extraversion, Agreeableness, and Conscientiousness but not Openness in many different cultures.** The closer a culture is to a Northern European culture, the closer the results are to the Anglo-based Big Five (Saucier & Goldberg, 2001). This held true for 12 languages including German, Polish, Czech, Turkish, Dutch, Italian, Hungarian, Korean, Hebrew, Filipino, Spanish, and Catalonian (Saucier & Goldberg, 2001).

3. **Openness varies across cultures.** Why is this the case? Recall that for the lexical Big Five model Openness is defined as intellect and imagination, but for the five-factor model using sentences (as in the NEO-PI-R) this factor is Openness to Experience. Lexical models find Openness (Norman's V factor) to be language and culture specific. For example, according to Saucier and Goldberg (2001) there were slight variations in which adjectives loaded on the Openness factor in German (*intelligence, competence, talents*), Turkish (*intellect* and *unconventionality*), Hebrew (*sophisticated, sharp, knowledgeable*), Filipino (*intellect, competence, talent*), and Dutch (*intellectual autonomy* vs. *conventionality*).

Because the Openness factor does not consistently appear in other languages it may be that this factor, though it exists cross-culturally, is defined differently in ways unique to a specific culture (Bond, 1994). Indeed, Benet-Martínez and Oishi (2008) suggested that Openness might be unique to Anglo-Saxon cultures. Aspects of Openness, particularly the facets of it such as imagination, emotionality, psychological liberalism, and adventurousness, may tap into Western culture's emphasis on intellectual freedom, emotional expressiveness, and individual uniqueness.

However, consider the item "Sometimes when I am reading poetry or looking at a work of art, I feel a chill or wave of excitement." This is one of the strongest predictors of scores on Openness of the NEO-PI-R in over 40 languages in 51 cultures, not just in Western cultures but also in Brazil, Hong Kong, Japan, Lebanon, and Malaysia (McCrae, 2007). McCrae (2007) explains that this item performs less well as a marker of Openness in African cultures in Botswana, Burkina Faso, Ethiopia, Uganda, and Nigeria, possibly due to measurement problems (e.g., acquiescence, and the fact that the NEO-PI-R was not given in their native language). That this one item seems to embody a more visceral or physiological response leads us to suspect that it may transcend culture and instead capture a human universal. Perhaps the feeling of chills when one is moved is universal, whereas what is likely to give us chills varies by culture.

4. **In some cultures more than five factors are needed to fully describe personality.** In cultures where this happens such as Hungarian and Korean (Saucier & Goldberg, 2001), these

"All people must be responsive to danger, loss, and threat; interact with others to some degree; choose between the risks of exploration and the limitations of familiarity; weigh self against social interest; balance work and play."
McCrae and John (1992, p. 100)

THINK ABOUT IT

Does speaking in another language bring out different aspects of personality? Surprisingly, research suggests that it can!

additional factors tap culture-specific forms of Extraversion or Agreeableness, or aspects of social evaluation (power, morality, attractiveness) that are particularly salient in that culture (Benet-Martínez & Oishi, 2008). Because interpersonal relations are so important, natural languages have developed many terms for getting along with others. No wonder that these traits may fall out on two factors in other languages, but on only one in English (McCrae & Costa, 2008)! In this way Agreeableness and Conscientiousness may tap both universal and culture-specific aspects of personality (Benet-Martínez & Oishi, 2008).

5. We need more research on indigenous personality to truly see which aspects of personality are universal and which are unique to a culture. Although McCrae and Costa (2008) claimed that **indigenous traits**, traits originating in another language and which are unique to a culture, are "interpretable as characteristic adaptations within the Five Factor Theory" (p. 169), others counter that both questionnaire measures and adjectival measures may miss indigenous terms (Benet-Martínez & Oishi, 2008). To remedy this problem, some researchers start with the lexicon of a specific culture and, like Allport and Odbert (1936) did with English, see how many factors best account for personality in these cultures. This kind of research is rare, but it has identified both convergence with the five factors and some culturally unique factors (Benet-Martínez & Oishi, 2008; Cheung & Leung, 1998).

To understand some of these issues—as well as all of these findings on personality traits in other cultures—let's consider some of this research in depth in the next section.

Personality Traits Cross-Culturally: Personality Traits in China

To understand how complicated it can be to test the five factors in other countries, consider current research in a country very different from America: China. China has a collectivistic culture, stemming from roots in Confucianism which emphasizes the fundamental relatedness among individuals (Ho, 1998). When the five-factor model is tested using the NEO-PI-R, the results replicate the FFM for 29 out of the 30 facets (McCrae, Costa, & Yik, 1996). Indeed, Chinese college students scored virtually identical to their American counterparts on this translated version of the NEO-PI-R (McCrae et al., 1996). However, the facet of Actions, part of Openness, did not load on any of the factors. This may indicate problems with the scale, a genuine difference among the Chinese on this dimension, or simply measurement error (McCrae et al., 1996).

Some have wondered if the basic replication of the five-factor model is due to the structure of the questionnaire, the ubiquitous influence of Western culture in the world, or some other explanation (McCrae et al., 1996). A more convincing case for the universality of the five factors would be to start with traditional Chinese values—that is, traits important within Chinese culture—and see how these attributes apply to Chinese personality (McCrae et al., 1996).

Chinese culture emphasizes avoidance of conflict, support of traditions and norms, and a family orientation. How well will the five factors describe Chinese personality?

Cheung et al. (1996) developed the Chinese Personality Assessment Inventory (CPAI) by using a sort of lexical approach by identifying descriptions of Chinese personality from literature, proverbs, surveys, and previous research. This led to the identification of 10 trait clusters unique to the Chinese personality and not covered by Western personality inventories: Harmony (tolerance, contentment), **Ren Qing** (traditional relationship orientation emphasizing give and take and connectedness), Modernization (vs. traditionalism), Thrift (vs. extravagance), **Ah-Q** mentality (defensiveness; named for Ah-Q, a well-known fictional Chinese character depicted in a classic novel), Graciousness (courtesy, kindness, patience, vs. meanness), Veraciousness-Slickness (trustworthiness), Face (reputation, social approval), Family Orientation, and Somatization (expression of distress via physical symptoms). When factor-analyzed, four factors emerged: Dependability (responsibility, practical-mindedness, graciousness), Chinese Tradition (Harmony, Ren Qing, Face), Social Potency (leadership, adventurousness), and Individualism (self-orientation, logical, Ah-Q mentality). These are not quite the five factors we might expect!

However, perhaps focusing solely on traditional Chinese values is too narrow a conceptualization of Chinese personality. What would happen if we factor-analyzed them all together? After all, if Chinese personality is composed of both culturally unique and human universal aspects this would be the way to find them.

Cheung et al. (2001) conducted a follow-up study in which they factor-analyzed responses to the CPAI and the Chinese NEO-PI-R together. They found six factors: five from the five-factor model, as one might expect, plus an indigenous personality factor they called **Interpersonal Relatedness** made up of Harmony, Ren Qing, Ah-Q, and Face. This factor taps the indigenous factors identified in the earlier study, traits that are uniquely encouraged in Chinese culture and not in Anglo-Saxon cultures: instrumentality of relationships, propriety, avoidance of conflict, support of traditions, and compliance with norms (Benet-Martínez & Oishi, 2008).

This six-factor model not only explained the variance among the responses of college students, but it also applied equally well to a sample of nonstudent workers. However, the six-factor model did not apply as well as the traditional five-factor model did to non-Chinese undergraduate students. Here, items from the sixth indigenous factor loaded among the regular five factors. This study supports the existence of a uniquely Chinese personality factor beyond the Western five factors (Cheung et al., 2001).

Perhaps you've noticed that much of the research just reviewed on personality traits, including personality traits in other cultures, is all based on self-report. How can we be sure that we are capturing what people are really like and not what people claim to be like? This is one of many problems with self-report data, but alas, self-report is often the most direct way to find out what a person is like. However, personality psychologists have developed a way to compensate for the weaknesses of any single research method, a topic we take up in the section on *Research Methods Illustrated*.

> **THINK ABOUT IT**
>
> Might we see evidence of this sixth factor in the depiction of people in Chinese art, literature, TV shows, plays, and movies?

Research Methods Illustrated: Triangulation and Types of Data

In ancient times, people would use triangles to measure distance or the height of objects such as the pyramids. Imagine a triangle connecting three points: two on one side of a river and one on the other side. By measuring the angles and applying geometry, they could figure out how far away or high up an object was. This image applies to research in personality. By using different methods we can better understand what a person is like than by using only one method. This process of using multiple methods within a single program of research is called **triangulation** (Brewer, 2000; Campbell & Fiske, 1959). Each method compensates for the weaknesses of the others.

There are four kinds of data that a personality psychologist might collect. The most obvious is to administer personality tests or other self-report questionnaires, called *self-report data* or **S data**. S data include objective personality tests, interviews, narratives, life stories, and survey research (John & Soto, 2007). Even experience sampling procedures, where participants are "beeped" via pagers or cell phones to fill out a questionnaire, are examples of S data. In one study, participants were beeped every 2 hours, on average, to fill out a self-esteem questionnaire and mood measures. Participants who had generally high self-esteem but which fluctuated over the day were angrier and more hostile than participants with stable self-esteem (Kernis, Grannemann, & Barclay, 1989).

We could also place a person in controlled situations that test them to see how they respond. *Test data* or **T data** include information from testing situations (not to be confused with objective or self-report personality tests, which are examples of S data). T data come from experimental procedures or standardized measures that have objective rules for scoring a person's performance. Examples of T data include intelligence tests, task persistence, and reaction times (John & Soto, 2007). The Implicit Association Test (IAT; Greenwald & Farnham, 2000), a computerized reaction-time test, for example, has been used to measure self-esteem. Some projective tests, such as the Thematic Apperception Test (TAT; Morgan & Murray, 1935) or the Rorschach Inkblot Test (Rorschach, 1921), which use standardized stimuli and have explicit scoring guidelines, are also examples of T data.

Instead of relying on only self-reports, we might collect *observation data* or **O data** by watching people in the laboratory or in their daily lives. One can also collect O data by coding behavior from photos or video. Information from knowledgeable informants including friends, spouses, parents, children, teachers, interviewers, and the like are also examples of O data (John & Soto, 2007). Indeed, this is exactly what Costa and McCrae (1992) and others have done to measure the five factors. Another study found that the facial expression of women in their college yearbook photos predicted their marital satisfaction and personal well-being 30 years later (Harker & Keltner, 2001). Observing people's actual behavior, even when it is captured in a photo or a video, gets around the problem of potential bias or memory problems in self-reports (Dunning, Heath, & Suls, 2004).

Finally, we could track down information about a person that is publicly available. *Life data* or **L data** include graduating from college, getting married, getting divorced, moving, in addition to a person's socioeconomic status, memberships in clubs and organizations, number of car accidents, Internet activity, and similar life events (John & Soto, 2007). Researchers have used sources as varied as criminal records to measure antisocial behavior (Caspi, McClay, et al., 2005), counting bottles and cans in garbage containers to measure alcohol consumption (Webb, Campbell, Schwartz, Sechrest, & Grove, 1981), and counting the number of Facebook friends to measure social connectedness (Ellison, Steinfield, & Lampe, 2007).

Together, these four methods of data collection spell out *LOTS*, which should remind us to include *lots* of sources of data in our studies to maximize the validity of our research (John & Soto, 2007). During World War II, the Office of Strategic Services (a forerunner of the CIA) set up a program to select the best candidates for espionage jobs behind enemy lines (Strategic Services, 1948). It collected S data, O data, and T data on the candidates.

Men and women were brought to a special assessment center where they filled out personality questionnaires (S data) and were interviewed (S data) and observed by psychologists who wrote a paragraph describing each candidate's personality (O data). To ensure that the assessment staff would judge the candidates solely on their performance, they had no idea about the background of the candidates (a notable absence of L data).

They even put the candidates through special tests (T data) to see if they could tolerate stress and frustration such as getting their whole group over a large wall, building a wooden structure with recalcitrant workers (who were actually confederates of the assessment staff), staging a mock interrogation, and performing other tasks to see if the candidates could stand up to the emotional

The stress situation: An example of T data. Participants were given 12 minutes to develop a plausible cover story for an imagined crime. They were interviewed by a panel of interrogators who fired questions at them and jumped on any hesitations or inconsistencies in their stories, all while being observed and evaluated by psychologists. (Strategic Services, 1948, facing p. 212).

stress and the intellectual demands of keeping up a false identity while collecting information behind enemy lines.

Using all these kinds of data the assessment team rated each candidate on intelligence, physical ability, motivation, skill, and aspects of personality including emotional stability, leadership, and social relations (a combination of Extraversion and Agreeableness). They hoped to be able to track the actual performance of candidates to see which measures best predicted performance.

Despite the best efforts of the assessment staff—which included many notable psychologists such as Urie Bronfenbrenner, Donald Fiske, Clyde Kluckhohn, Henry Murray, Theodore Newcomb, Edward Tolman, and Kurt Lewin—the government was unwilling to reveal how a particular candidate fared in his or her eventual position due to security issues. The best the assessment team could do was to select promising candidates and to eliminate obviously unsuitable ones.

Although the Assessment Center failed in its original mission to develop a valid selection procedure for selecting spies, it stands today as a fascinating example of how triangulation—the use of multiple methods—can yield a more complete picture of a person.

Expression of Traits in Everyday Life

Our personality traits reveal themselves in lots of ways: body language, taste in decorating and in music, our online presence on the Internet, and also in the careers we choose—even if we happen to be the president of the United States! We can see the influence of traits in numerous ways in our everyday lives.

Personality Traits of Presidents

Do you have what it takes to be a great president? What *does* it take to be a great president? There is a long tradition in personality psychology of studying presidents, along with other famous people, both fictional and real, ever since Sigmund Freud psychoanalyzed the writings and speeches of Woodrow Wilson, the 28th president of the United States (Freud, 1967) and Leonardo Da Vinci (Freud, 1910/1964).

Using the five-factor model, Rubenzer et al. (2000) identified the traits of great presidents. To do this, they enlisted the help of presidential experts: biographers and people who had interacted either professionally or personally with a president. Each expert filled out the NEO-PI-R (Costa & McCrae, 1992) as they thought their target president would. They were instructed to imagine what their subject was like in the 5-year period before he became president. In this way they hoped to get a valid measure of presidents' personalities not confounded by the demands of the job or behavior in office so that each man's personality could be correlated with his later performance as president. The number of raters per president ranged from 1 to 13 with an average of 4.2 raters per president. Where multiple experts rated a single president, their ratings were averaged into a single score.

Compared to the U.S. population at large, presidents tend to be more extraverted, less open to experience, and less agreeable. They score higher than the general population on the facets of achievement striving (Conscientiousness), and emotionality (Openness), but lower on psychological liberalism (Openness), morality (Agreeableness), and modesty (Agreeableness). In the words of Rubenzer et al. (2000):

> [P]residents tends to be hardworking and achievement-minded, willing and able to speak up for their interests, and value the emotional side of life. They tend to trust in the traditional sources of moral authority, yet are willing to bend the truth and to bully or manipulate people to get their own way. They tend to see themselves as just as good as, and maybe better than, other people (p. 407).

Obviously, there is some truth to the stereotype of politicians as devious and bombastic! But what about truly great presidents? How do they compare to the general population? Rubenzer et al. (2000) gathered data from past studies of greatness. Historians often conduct polls assessing the ratings and ranking of the achievements of presidents and their overall historical

THINK ABOUT IT

Why might low Agreeableness be a useful trait for a president?

greatness. Presidents who are rated as truly great tend to be higher in Openness than the average person. This is particularly interesting for, as the authors pointed out, Openness is moderately related to general cognitive ability, suggesting that great presidents are smarter than average. Great presidents are aware of their feelings and are imaginative and more interested in art and beauty (artistic interests) than less successful presidents. They also tend to be willing to question traditional values (psychological liberalism) and open to new ideas and trying new ways of doing things (intellect).

As for the other four factors, there were only small correlations between greatness and personality. Great presidents tend to be slightly more extraverted and conscientious and a little less agreeable than the average person. They are particularly likely to show assertiveness (a facet of Extroversion), perhaps as part of their leadership ability. Although showing sympathy for the less fortunate (Agreeableness), great presidents are no pushovers. They tend to score low on morality and cooperation (Agreeableness). The portrait emerges of a true politician who is not easily led but instead argues, tricks, or even lies when necessary (low in morality). From the Conscientiousness scale, it is no surprise that great presidents score higher in achievement striving and competence. Great presidents set high goals for themselves and the country and are willing to do just about anything to achieve them. Finally, Neuroticism was not related to greatness, so that historically great presidents can be well adjusted or neurotic. However, presidents who felt unable to cope with problems and who were upset by stress (vulnerability) tended to be given low ratings by historians.

Who would you consider to be our greatest president? When historians answer this question, George Washington and Abraham Lincoln rise to the top of nearly every historical poll taken (Rubenzer et al., 2000). What makes these two presidents so special? Figures 3.1 and 3.2 show the distribution of scores of these two great presidents. Whereas Washington's exceptionally high scores in Conscientiousness indicate that he had the traditional virtues of responsibility, dutifulness, self-discipline, as well as leadership (i.e., assertiveness, part of Extraversion) and courage (he scored exceptionally low on vulnerability to stress, part of Neuroticism), he scored low on friendliness (Extraversion) and sympathy (Agreeableness).

In contrast to Washington, Lincoln was higher in Agreeableness and indeed higher than the average president. His scores on Openness and Neuroticism are no surprise given that he suffered from bouts of depression (Rubenzer et al., 2000). He was particularly high in depression, anxiety, and in his awareness of feelings. Although he was high in achievement striving

> **THINK ABOUT IT**
>
> Did the myth of Washington telling the truth about cutting down the cherry tree originate as a way of demonstrating his Conscientiousness trait?

Figure 3.1 Scores of George Washington on the NEO Personality Inventory Compared to the average president. *Source:* Reprinted with permission from Rubenzer, S. J., Faschingbauer, T. R., & Ones, D. S. (2000), "Assessing the U.S. Presidents Using the Revised NEO Personality Inventory," *Assessment*, 7(4), 403–420. Permission conveyed through the Copyright Clearance Center.

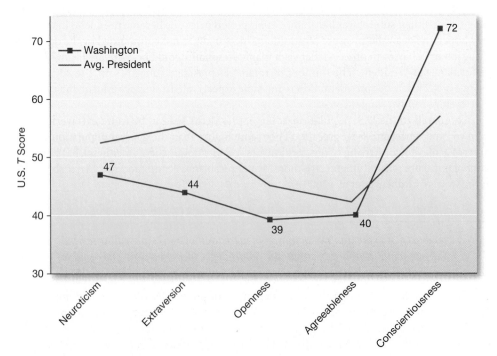

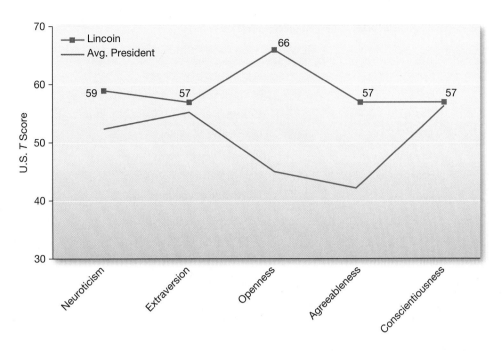

Figure 3.2 Scores of Abraham Lincoln on the NEO Personality Inventory compared to the average president. *Source:* Reprinted with permission from Rubenzer, S. J., Faschingbauer, T. R., & Ones, D. S. (2000), "Assessing the U.S. Presidents Using the Revised NEO Personality Inventory," *Assessment,* 7(4), 403–420. Permission conveyed through the Copyright Clearance Center.

and self-efficacy, he tended to be disorganized (all facets of Conscientiousness). Despite his nickname of "Honest Abe" he was willing to stretch the truth (scoring low on morality) but was generally trusting of others (Agreeableness).

Many of the findings from this study are corroborated by related studies of personality and the presidency using different measures and methods (Kowert, 1996; Rubenzer et al., 2000; cf. Simonton, 1986; Winter, 2005; Young & French, 1996). This discussion about personality and presidents may have you wondering: What about our current president? Well, what do you think? What factors and facets do you think our president is notably high or low on? No doubt the answer to that question is lying in some researcher's filing cabinet awaiting publication in a few years!

Music Preferences and Personality Traits

What's your favorite type of music? Certainly, your choice of music reflects your personal taste, but is it related to your personality? Do people high in Neuroticism enjoy different kinds of music from extraverts? Interesting enough, Cattell wondered about this back in the 1950s and believed that musical choice reflected unconscious motives (Cattell & Anderson, 1953; Cattell & Saunders, 1954).

More recently, Rentfrow and Gosling explored how the personality traits of the five-factor model relate to musical taste (2003). First, they asked over 1,700 college students to take the Short Test of Music Preferences (STOMP). In this test, participants rate how much they enjoy different types of music on a 1 (*Not at all*) to 7 (*A great deal*) scale. The researchers then used factor analysis to identify the major types, or genres, of music (see Table 3.4).

Participants also filled out a series of personality questionnaires including the Big Five Inventory (BFI; John & Srivastava, 1999). The researchers correlated scores on the STOMP with scores on the BFI to see if there was a relationship between the kind of music college students liked and their personality traits.

What did they find? First, there were no gender differences in music preference. Men and women had similar tastes in music according to the STOMP test. Second, chronic mood, like being depressed, had no impact on what music the participants liked. Although college students might choose to listen to various songs depending on mood, overall there was no relationship between mood and the kind of music participants preferred. Finally, different personalities did indeed prefer different kinds of music (see Table 3.5).

THINK ABOUT IT

What can you tell about a person from his or her favorite songs?

Table 3.4 Types of Music and Representative Songs From the Short Test of Music Preferences (STOMP)

Factors	Musical Genres	Representative Songs
Reflective and Complex	Blues	Ray Charles: "Ray's Blues"
	Folk	Bob Dylan: "Blowin' in the Wind"
	Classical	Mozart: "Marriage of Figaro," Overture
	Jazz	Miles Davis: "All Blues"
Intense and Rebellious	Alternative	Nirvana: "Verse Chorus Verse"
	Heavy metal	Marilyn Manson: "Fight Song"
	Rock	Jimi Hendrix: "Voodoo Child"
Upbeat and Conventional	Country	Johnny Cash: "Rusty Cage"
	Religious	Praise Band: "Rock of Ages"
	Pop	Christina Aguilera: "Don't Make Me Love You"
Energetic and Rhythmic	Funk	James Brown: "Superbad Part 1"
	Hip-hop/rap	Tupac Shakur (featuring Snoop Doggy Dogg): "2 of Amerikaz Most Wanted"
	Soul	Aretha Franklin: "Chain of Fools"
	Electronica	DJ Shadow: "What Does Your Soul Look Like"

Source: Rentfrow and Gosling, 2003, Appendix, p. 1255–1256 Rentfrow, P. J., & Gosling, S. D. (2003). The do re mi's of everyday life: The structure and personality correlates of music preferences. *Journal of Personality and Social Psychology*, 84(6), 1236–1256.

As you can see, people who were high in Neuroticism did not like classical, jazz, folk, or blues, what the researchers called Reflective and Complex music. Or, to put it another way, emotionally stable people enjoyed this kind of music, especially those low in angry hostility and vulnerability (this later finding comes from a more detailed study of facets and genres by Zweigenhaft, 2008). Extraverts were particularly fond of the Energetic and Rhythmic music such as hip-hop, funk, soul, and electronica, and Upbeat and Conventional music such as country, religious, and pop, especially if they were high on excitement seeking or positive emotions (see also Dollinger, 1993; Rawlings & Ciancarelli, 1997; Zweigenhaft, 2008). This result makes sense; after all, where might you find a highly extroverted person on a Saturday night? Out clubbing with other extroverts!

What about people who were high in Openness? As you might expect, they liked the more cerebral classical and jazz music, part of the Reflective and Complex genre. This preference was related to scores on openness to fantasy, openness to aesthetics, openness to actions, and

Table 3.5 Correlations Between Five-Factor Traits and Types of Music

Trait	Reflective and Complex	Intense and Rebellious	Upbeat and Conventional	Energetic and Rhythmic
Neuroticism	−.08*	.01	.07	−.01
Extraversion	.01	.00	.24*	.22*
Openness	.44*	.18*	−.14*	.03
Agreeableness	.01	−.04	.23*	.08*
Conscientiousness	−.02	−.04	.15*	.00

Note: Numbers in the table are correlations between traits and liking of music. Recall that correlations can be positive or negative. Higher numbers mean that there is a stronger relationship among the variables. Significant effects are noted by asterisks.

* = $p < .05$.

Source: Rentfrow and Gosling, 2003, Table 3, p. 1250 Rentfrow, P. J., & Gosling, S. D. (2003). The do re mi's of everyday life: The structure and personality correlates of music preferences. *Journal of Personality and Social Psychology*, 84(6), 1236–1256.

openness to ideas (Zweigenhaft, 2008). These people also liked Intense and Rebellious music, especially if they were high on openness to values, but they disdained the Upbeat and Conventional especially if they were high in openness to fantasy, aesthetics, ideas, and values (Zweigenhaft, 2008). Again, it makes sense that people who are open to new ideas and experiences would be attracted to the rebellious and turned off by the conventional, even when it comes to musical preferences (see also Dollinger, 1993; Rawlings & Ciancarelli, 1997). Similarly, they also liked bluegrass, world music, opera, punk, and funk, genres not part of the Rentfrow and Gosling (2003) study (Zweigenhaft, 2008). Finally, people who were high in Conscientiousness showed only a slight preference for the Upbeat and Conventional music, especially for people high in dutifulness or achievement striving (Zweigenhaft, 2008). Interestingly enough, many of these findings were replicated in a sample of college students from the Netherlands (Delsing, TerBogt, Engels, & Meeus, 2008).

Even the way people engage with music seems to be related to personality (Chamorro-Premuzic & Furnham, 2007). People high in Openness, as measured by the NEO Five Factor Inventory (Costa & McCrae, 1992), tended to engage with music in a more intellectual way, concentrating on what they are hearing, enjoying analyzing complex compositions, and admiring the techniques of the musicians. In contrast, people high in Neuroticism, and low in Extraversion and Conscientiousness were more likely to engage with music in a more emotional way, for example, to change or enhance their mood. These people tended to feel emotional after listening to music, whether it be happy, sad, or nostalgic and they often associated specific memories with a particular song.

Do you know somebody who loves to listen to loud music with the bass turned up extra high? McCown, Keiser, Mulhearn, and Williamson (1997) looked at the relationship between preference for exaggerated bass and scores on the Eysenck Personality Inventory. They found that men, more so than women, and people high in Extraversion or Psychoticism enjoyed this music more so than introverts or people low in Psychoticism. The part about extraverts preferring the stimulation of a strong bass should come as no surprise knowing what we do about how introverts need less sensory stimulation than extraverts (see Chapter 7). Personality preferences for this type of music are particularly interesting, because exaggerated bass is a key component in club and rap music. The authors wondered if boosting bass might make less popular forms of music—like classical—more appealing to certain audiences.

What about musicians themselves? If there are personality differences in the kind of music people like to listen to, maybe rock musicians are different from, say, classical musicians. One early study found that pop musicians were slightly higher on Neuroticism and Psychoticism (Wills, 1984) than the average adult. Any ideas how the average self-taught, guitar-playing rocker around age 30 would score on Openness? What about Conscientiousness or Agreeableness? Gillespie and Myors (2000) recruited rock musicians from the metropolitan Sydney, Australia, area for their study. One hundred musicians took the NEO-PI-R (Costa & McCrae, 1992) and answered questions about their musical background. These musicians were high in all six facets of Neuroticism and Openness. Although they were about average in Extraversion, they were especially high in positive emotions and excitement seeking. In contrast, they tended to be low in Agreeableness, especially on the facets of trust, straightforwardness, and compliance, and low in all six facets of Conscientiousness! This is shown graphically in Figure 3.3.

Given how much of our personality we express in the music we like to play as well as listen to, perhaps we should swap our iPod playlists of musical favorites instead of astrology signs when making new friends.

Web Pages and Personality Traits

Living spaces, handshakes, musical preferences—is there any aspect of our behavior that *doesn't* reflect our personality? What about our presence on the Internet, such as usernames and Facebook pages; do these also reflect our personalities? They sure do—of course, they may reflect our true personality or they may reflect managed impressions specifically formulated to impress others (Gosling, 2008).

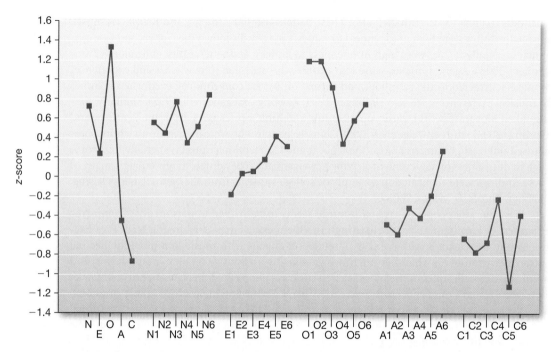

Figure 3.3 Scores of rock musicians on the NEO-PI-R. *Source:* Adapted from Gillespie and Myors (2000, Figure 1, p. 160). Reprinted with permission from Gillespie, W., & Myors, B. (2000), "Personality of rock musicians," *Psychology of Music, 28,* 154–165. Permission conveyed through the Copyright Clearance Center.

One study found a personality difference between people who blog and people who don't (Guadagno, Okdie, & Eno, 2008). Bloggers tend to be higher in Neuroticism and Openness than nonbloggers. In particular, women who are high in Neuroticism are more likely to blog than more emotionally stable women.

Vazire and Gosling (2004) took the idea of online self-expression a bit further and judged people's personalities from their personal web pages. They had trained experts rate 89 randomly selected websites listed in Yahoo!'s personal directory. Then they recruited web page owners to take part in their study. Web page owners rated themselves and their ideal selves on the five factors using the BFI. The researchers also recruited close friends of the owners so they could get an outside opinion of what the owners were really like. They used these ratings to judge the extent to which the web pages reflected what the owners were really like or if the page reflected what the owner wanted people to think they were like.

What can you tell about this person from his web page?

What did they find? First, observers got clear impressions about web page owners. Raters not only agreed with each other, but they also could correctly judge a person's Neuroticism, Openness, and Conscientiousness. Openness was the easiest trait to judge from web pages and was judged the most accurately.

Ratings of Extraversion and Agreeableness, although accurate, were closer to page owners' ideals than to their true selves. After statistically removing the effect of "reality" (i.e., friends' ratings) from owners' ratings, Extraversion and Agreeableness were still judged accurately by observers. That is, raters tended to see a person as extraverted or as agreeable as the person wanted them to see it, rather than the true level of these traits. These results suggest that personal websites reflect both the owners "true" selves with a bit of impression management—of how outgoing and likable one is—thrown in. If these findings have you wondering about what your own web presence says about you, check out the *Personality Of Everyday Life* box below.

Careers and Personality Traits

Do you have what it takes to be a successful astronaut? Would you like to be a clinical psychologist? As you might imagine, there are personality differences among various careers and personality assessment is an important part of personnel selection in many businesses, a point we will take up in the personality assessment Chapter 4. Take the career of astronaut. A successful astronaut must be able to work effectively and smoothly with others in the complex and highly stressful setting of a tiny spacecraft in close quarters far away from loved ones back

The Personality of Everyday Life

What does your online presence say about your personality?

Are you on Facebook? Twitter? Nearly everybody has some sort of an online presence these days, whether it is a personal web page, a blog, a social media account, or a photo on a school or employer's page. The research reviewed in this chapter suggests that our web presence reflects our personality, even without our awareness. What does your presence say about you?

First, consider what impression your e-mail address or username creates. One study found that people low in self-esteem picked usernames such as *emotional_void_82* and *empty_heart,* whereas *kingtony23* and *gorgeouschic* were all high in self-esteem. Similarly, people's perceived competence also shone through—intentionally or unintentionally—in their usernames. Compare *stevethetennisace* and *smartguy* to *spacystacy* and *sloppycrazyandweird* (Gosling, 2008).

Next, how does your page's layout and design as well as content reveal your personality? Recall that observers easily and accurately judged users' levels of Openness, Conscientiousness, and Neuroticism from web pages. Other studies show that bloggers reveal their personalities by their choice of words. People high in Neuroticism use words related to negative emotions, whereas people high in Extroversion use words related to positive emotions. People low in Agreeableness use more swear words than people high in Agreeableness who refer more to community. People high in Conscientiousness write about achievement more so than people low in Conscientiousness (Yarkoni, 2010).

Of course, Facebook profiles are an easy way for people to get to know you (Evans, Gosling, & Carroll, 2008). Visitors are particularly likely to accurately judge personality when users talk about their beliefs, joys, embarrassing moments, proud moments, spirituality, heroes, and when they link to funny videos. Sharing information about least-favorite things is not as helpful in understanding what a person is like.

In sum, are you comfortable with what your online presence says about you? By making yourself aware of the subtle and not-so-subtle ways self-esteem and traits are manifested through online media, you can create a good impression and yet not reveal more than you intend.

on Earth. The National Aeronautics and Space Administration (NASA) must routinely process 2,000 to 4,000 applications to select the less than 1% who will eventually be selected as astronauts (Musson & Helmreich, 2004). What are the characteristics that make up the "right stuff"?

According to research reviewed by Musson and Helmreich (2004), successful astronauts—as well as anybody, both women and men, who must live and work in confined and dangerous settings with others—must be high in independence, achievement striving, and goal orientation (what they call instrumentality); high in interpersonal warmth, sensitivity, and concern for others (expressivity); and low in arrogance, egotism, complaining, nagging, and verbal sniping (interpersonal aggression). In their analysis of the personality traits of aspiring astronauts, these characteristics correlated with high Conscientiousness, high Agreeableness, and low Neuroticism. Applicants who were low in Agreeableness were clearly not cut out for space travel with longer missions and more diverse crews traveling and working in space.

What about professionals, police officers, managers, and sales and semiskilled workers? Which traits are related to success in these occupations? In a meta-analysis of over 117 studies, Barrick and Mount (1991) found that among the five factors, only high Conscientiousness was related to high performance ratings, productivity, training proficiency, low job turnover, and higher salaries. This held true across all of the occupations studied for both men and women including engineers, architects, attorneys, accountants, teachers, doctors, ministers, police officers, clerical workers, farmers, flight attendants, medical assistants, truck drivers, and grocery clerks. In addition, being extraverted was helpful for managers and people in sales; introverts were just as likely as extroverts to be working in any of the other occupations. In addition, Openness and Extraversion were related to job training proficiency.

Rubinstein and Strul (2007) looked for personality differences among doctors, lawyers, clinical psychologists, and artists in Israel using a Hebrew version of the NEO-FFI (McCrae & Costa, 1989). Even though the men and women who volunteered for this study were all Israeli professionals, their results were about what we might expect: Artists were the highest in Openness to Experience, but they were only significantly higher than doctors, who scored the lowest in this trait. Artists and lawyers were the highest in Neuroticism whereas doctors were the most emotionally stable (clinical psychologists fell in between these groups but did not differ significantly from the others). No differences were found among these occupational groups in Conscientiousness, supporting previous findings that high Conscientiousness is related to occupational success regardless of specific job (Barrick & Mount, 1991).

A study of sales personnel at a chain of health clubs in Great Britain echoed these results (Furnham & Fudge, 2008). Sales associates, regardless of gender, were more likely to make their quota of selling memberships if they were high in Conscientiousness and Openness, and low in Agreeableness. The authors surmised that people high in Openness may have a more positive attitude and open mind that helps them succeed at job training (cf. Barrick & Mount, 1991), which may then lead to better on-the-job performance. Contrary to popular opinion, the best salespeople are not necessarily those who are sociable and enjoy the company of others. Rather it is the hardworking, persistent, go-getter—putting in long hours making cold calls, following up with clients—who is most likely to succeed. And being a bit tough, pushy, and dogged (low in Agreeableness) doesn't hurt either!

THINK ABOUT IT

Of the five factors, which one do you think is most closely related to job success?

Does it take special personality traits to be an astronaut?

Personality Development Over the Life Span: Continuity, Change, and Coherence

Think back to what you and your friends were like in junior high. Can you imagine what some of your friends might be like today? Will you be amazed at how much some people have changed? Will some people have not changed at all? Will some people be into different activities and seem like different people, but underneath it all, are really still the same? Of course, we know that everybody matures as they grow and move through adolescence and into young adulthood—or do they?

This mash-up of personality consistency, personality change, and personality coherence is what makes school reunions both fun and scary. The research on personality across the life span reflects the experience of running into old friends: Some people change, some people don't, and some aspects of personality are bound to change because people mature. How can we make sense of all this?

First, when psychologists talk about **development** they refer to both continuity and change in personality (Roberts, Wood, & Caspi, 2008). When we say that personality develops as we grow from childhood into adulthood, we are saying that some aspects of personality stay the same—perhaps how sociable or nervous a person is—whereas some aspects are different: say how much self-esteem a person has or how thrill seeking he or she is. **Continuity** or **consistency** in personality means that the amount of a trait stays about the same. **Personality change** means that the amount of trait is different, either increased or decreased from what it was previously. The difference is often one of degree rather than kind; people generally don't change into something opposite of what they were. That is, an extroverted child is not likely to grow into an introverted adult nor is an anxious, nervous child likely to become a calm, even-tempered adult.

Notice that we can talk about how *traits* change or are consistent in a group of people or we can talk about how a *person* changes or remains consistent over time. People may change or remain consistent compared to what they were like at a previous point in their lives or they may change or remain consistent relative to their peers or some other comparison group.

Even when traits stay the same, we wouldn't expect a trait, say thrill seeking, to look the same in a 6-year-old as in a 16-year-old or a 26-year-old. A sensation-seeking 10-year-old might enjoy exploring the neighborhood on bicycle whereas a sensation-seeking 26-year-old might enjoy extreme sports. This is an example of personality coherence in the trait of sensation seeking.

Personality coherence is when the underlying trait stays the same but the way it is expressed changes (Roberts et al., 2008). We can think of personality coherence as a type of continuity. However, to identify true examples of personality coherence researchers must have a theory for explaining how the two different behaviors are manifestations of the same underlying trait (Caspi & Roberts, 2001).

"Everybody thinks that as you age, you get old. You don't. Inside I still feel like I'm 18. I just don't look it anymore."

An 80-year-old woman to her grown grandson

SEE FOR YOURSELF

In what ways is your personality different from when you were in elementary school?

SEE FOR YOURSELF

In what ways is your personality the same as when you were in elementary school?

SEE FOR YOURSELF

In what ways do you act differently now compared to when you were in elementary school? Can any of these differences be explained by personality coherence?

Are they the same people today (right) as they were 40 years ago when they were in college (left)? Personality remains remarkably consistent across the life span. However, against this backdrop of consistency, personality changes in important ways.

For example, children who show high task persistence in childhood show high achievement orientation in adulthood. You can see that working hard and striving to excel are two aspects of an underlying desire for accomplishment. Shyness also shows personality coherence: Shy children live at home with their parents longer and marry older than their socially bolder peers (Caspi, Elder, & Bem, 1988).

Aggression is another personality variable that shows strong coherence from childhood to adulthood. People who had been rated by their peers as aggressive at age 8 were more likely to commit serious criminal acts by age 30. Men who were rated as aggressive as children were also more likely to engage in physical aggression and abuse their spouses by age 30 (Huesmann, Eron, Lefkowitz, & Walder, 1984; see Figure 3.4).

I love a parade. Personality coherence in Extraversion: Although the activities may change, this extrovert was always a joiner and loved the limelight whether it was Girl Scouts in elementary school or folk dancing as an adult.

The only way to answer the question of how do people develop over their lives is to, well, take a bunch of people and follow them over their lives! This is called a **longitudinal study**. In the last 10 years or so there has been an increase in longitudinal studies and so our knowledge of how people—and traits—change across the life span has increased as well.

A good metaphor to explain how personality changes over time is to picture a harbor filled with different kinds of boats (Roberts, 2010). Some boats might sit lower or higher in the water depending on their shapes, sizes, or cargo. The action of the tide coming in and going out lifts and lowers all the boats in the water at the same time. This action is like general change or **mean-level change** which affects nearly everybody as we grow from infancy to adulthood. The boats are like individual people. Differences between the boats in how

Figure 3.4 Personality coherence in aggressiveness: Mean seriousness of criminal acts committed by age 30 as a function of peer ratings of aggression at age 8. *Source:* From Huesmann et al. (1984, Figure 3, bottom, p. 1125). Huesmann, L. R., Eron, L. D., Lefkowitz, M. M., & Walder, L. O. (1984). Stability of aggression over time and generations. *Developmental Psychology*, 20, 1120–1134.

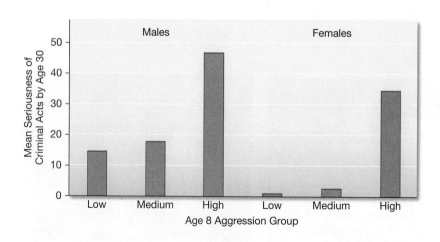

Even though the boats are all different, the tide coming in and going out affects all boats in the same way. Individual people have different personalities, but general change such as maturity, or the aging process, affects us all.

they sit in the water is like **individual change** in personality. Each boat can change in its own unique way due to the actions of the owner who can change the load of a boat so that it rises and falls independently of the other boats.

To understand how personality develops over the life span, we need to understand both general change and individual change. Let's consider three questions about personality development (Roberts, 2010). First, how consistent are people over time? This is a general question about the nature of personality. Second, how much do people change in general? This is a question about general change in personality traits that affect nearly everybody. Third, how and why do individuals develop in their own particular ways? This question looks at individual differences in consistency and change over the life course.

How Consistent Are People Over Time?

Personality is relatively enduring over time; in fact, people become *more* consistent in their traits across the life span (Roberts et al., 2008). Adults are more consistent in their traits than teens who are more consistent than children, a finding verified by many longitudinal studies (Caspi & Silva, 1995). This makes sense; after all, children are still in the process of developing their personalities.

Personality is about as consistent as cognitive ability; more consistent than income, blood pressure, and cholesterol levels; and much more consistent than happiness and self-esteem across a person's lifetime (Roberts, 2010). The peak of consistency is around age 50, a fact that is surprising given that some notable theorists thought that personality was set in childhood or adolescence. Sigmund Freud, for example, believed that personality was set by age 5, and Erik Erikson believed that personality was set by the end of adolescence. Despite popular notions of an adolescent identity crisis or a midlife crisis, people remain consistent in their traits through these times. In fact, there are no periods of particularly dramatic personality change anywhere in the life course (Caspi & Roberts, 2001; Caspi, Roberts, & Shiner, 2005; Roberts et al., 2008).

During this time, and even beyond, the traits of the five factors are the most consistent of all, showing great consistency across all five traits regardless of type of test (self-report, projective tests) or rater (self, observer; Roberts et al., 2008). Traits of the five factors start to become consistent at age 3 and increase in consistency until after age 50. This means that personality is remarkably consistent, despite the turmoil of the teen years or the massive changes that come with starting careers and families in the 20s. These results illustrate the saying "the child is father to the man."

For example, based on a **meta-analysis** (see Chapter 11), a statistical summary of effects from 152 longitudinal studies, Roberts and DelVecchio (2000) came to two conclusions. First, stability increases over the life span, a finding illustrated in Figure 3.5. Second, personality traits measured closer in time tend to be more similar than traits measured further apart in time.

According to reviews and meta-analyses, traits of the five factors show moderate consistency across the life span (Ardelt, 2000; Bazana & Stelmack, 2004; Roberts & DelVecchio, 2000; Schuerger, Zarrella, & Hotz, 1989; see Table 3.6). According to one study, the overall consistency in all five factors across 81 studies suggests that about 29% of the variance in your personality at one point in time can be explained by your personality at another point in time (Bazana & Stelmack, 2004).

William James (1890) observed that "in most of us by the age of thirty, the character has set like plaster, and will never soften again" (p. 121), a view once endorsed by many trait theorists (Costa & McCrae, 1994). However, we now know that this isn't so. Personality change does not stop, nor does it slow down after age 30. Instead, personality shows small gradual changes with age (Srivastava, John, Gosling, & Potter, 2003). Personality is consistent—but not unchanging.

Think about it: If less than a third of your personality stays about the same, then what happens to the other two-thirds? That's where mean-level change and individual change comes in. Even as personality stays consistent, there are subtle changes as we grow and develop, even into adulthood and old age. Psychologists now believe that personality is like an open system that can change throughout life in response to events and environments. Further, once our personalities respond to accommodate these new experiences, we tend to remain at this new level of development for the remainder of our lives. In this way personality change is subtle at any one point in time, but cumulative over the life course (Roberts & Mroczek, 2008).

How Much Do People Change in General?

Here we are asking about **normative change** (Roberts, 2010). Across both cross-sectional and longitudinal studies there are similar changes in personality that, like how an incoming tide affects all the boats in the harbor, affect everybody. The period of greatest normative change occurs in young adulthood between ages 20 and 40. In general, people become more consistent, as we just saw, and better with age.

Specifically, people become more assertive, warm, and self-confident (aspects of Extraversion), agreeable (nice, nurturing), conscientious (responsible, organized, hardworking, rule-oriented), and emotionally stable (calm and relaxed). Openness increases early in life—paralleling being in school—and declines in old age, suggesting that maybe you can't teach an old dog new tricks. Emotional stability increases early in life and remains constant whereas

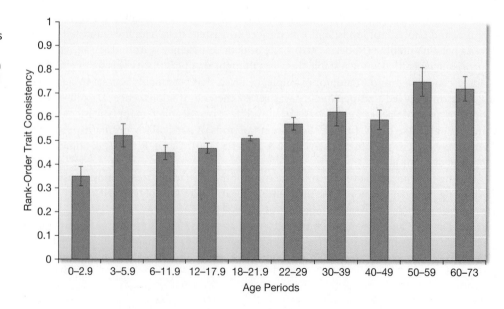

Figure 3.5 Consistency across the life course at various age periods. Personality becomes more consistent with age. *Source:* From Roberts and DelVecchio (2000, Figure 1, p. 15). Roberts, B. W., & DelVecchio, W. F. (2000). The rank-order consistency of person- ality traits from childhood to old age: A quantitative review of longitudinal studies. *Psychological Bulletin*, 126(1), 3–25. Copyright American Psychological Association. Reprinted with permission.

Table 3.6 Average Consistency in Personality Over Time: Stability Coefficients

Trait	Everybody	Women	Men
Neuroticism	.52	.56	.52*
Extraversion	.59	.63	.60*
Openness	.52	.48	.55*
Agreeableness	.48	.51	.46*
Conscientiousness	.50	.50	.50
Overall Personality	.54	.56	.55

Note: Stability coefficients range from 0 to .99, with higher numbers indicating a higher correlation in the trait among various time periods. Average stability in the trait across intervals from as short as less than 3 years to as long as 25 years.

* Significant gender difference in consistency. From a meta-analysis of 81 studies using 95 different samples.

Source: From Bazana and Stelmack (2004).

Agreeableness increases later in life. Agreeableness and Conscientiousness continue to rise into old age (Roberts, Walton, & Viechtbauer, 2006).

In an extensive meta-analysis of 92 longitudinal studies, Roberts, Walton, and Viechtbauer (2006) found evidence for continuity and change in six traits over the life course (see Figure 3.6). They reached three conclusions. First, all six traits showed changes past the age of 30 and indeed four of them—social vitality, Agreeableness, Emotional Stability, and Conscientiousness—showed significant changes in middle or old age. This suggests that personality continues to develop across the life course. Second, contrary to popular belief, young adulthood (ages 20 to 40) and not adolescence appears to be a key period in life when personality traits change the most. Finally, except for Openness and social vitality, which decreased with age suggesting that we experience less positive emotions and sociability, all of the other traits became more positive with age. As we age, we become more self-confident, agreeable, emotionally stable, and conscientious.

This same pattern of results was echoed in a study using a different design. In a cross-sectional study, the researchers compared responses of 132,515 adults aged 21 to 60 who responded to an Internet survey (Srivastava et al., 2003). One interesting difference, however, was that in this study, women but not men were more emotionally stable after age 30; older men had the same level of emotional stability as younger men at age 30. They also found that people were less open in old age. These results also supported the idea that personality continues to change slowly but steadily with age, showing small to moderate systematic changes.

This pattern of older adults showing lower levels of Neuroticism, Openness, and some aspects of Extraversion, and higher levels of Agreeableness and Conscientiousness than college students, also holds for samples outside the United States including Germany, Italy, Portugal, Croatia, and South Korea (McCrae et al., 1999).

Whereas consistency implies that there is a similarity in personality from one age to another, it also suggests that there is a change. One reason why personality changes from childhood to adulthood and from young adulthood to old age is that people mature. Therefore, a certain amount of change in personality is due to **maturation** (Roberts et al., 2008). In particular, we develop higher levels of assertiveness, self-control, responsibility, and emotional stability, especially from age 20 to age 40 (Roberts, Walton, & Viechtbauer, 2006). These changes may be a result of positive experiences in work and personal relationships.

For example, working longer hours or attaining higher status increases aspects of Extraversion (dominance, independence, and self-confidence) and Conscientiousness (self-discipline, competence, and responsibility) in both men and women (Clausen & Gilens, 1990; Elder, 1969; Roberts, 1997; Roberts, Caspi, & Moffitt, 2003). Positive work experiences may also help people become more emotionally stable (Roberts & Chapman, 2000; Scollon & Diener, 2006; Van Aken, Denissen, Branje, Dubas, & Goossens, 2006). For women, higher status at work is also

THINK ABOUT IT

How might maturation affect a person's levels of Neuroticism and Conscientiousness?

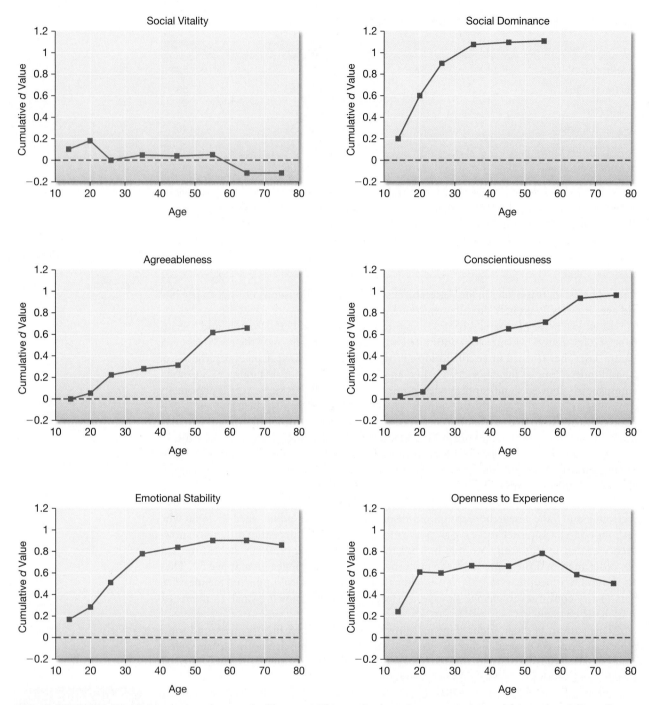

Figure 3.6 Accumulated changes in traits over the life course. The graphs show the average change (*d*) in each trait from the beginning to the end of a decade, added together over the life course. Social dominance and social vitality reflect two different aspects of Extraversion. Social dominance includes dominance, independence, and self-confidence in social situations; social vitality includes sociability, positive affect, gregariousness, and energy level. *Source:* From Roberts, Walton, and Viechtbauer (2006, Figure 2, p. 15).

associated with an increase in masculinity and a decrease in femininity (Kasen, Chen, Sneed, Crawford, & Cohen, 2006).

A stable and happy home life can also change people for the better. In particular, both men and women in fulfilling relationships during their young adult years become less neurotic (Robins, Caspi, & Moffitt, 2002; Roberts & Chapman, 2000; Scollon & Diener, 2006), and more conscientious (Lehnart & Neyer, 2006; Roberts & Bogg, 2004) and agreeable (Lehnart & Neyer, 2006) over time. Even men who married or remarried in late middle age or old age also showed a decrease in Neuroticism with age (women were not studied; Mroczek & Spiro, 2003).

As you can see, all of these normative changes are in the direction of greater maturity and better functioning. The years from a person's 20s to 40s are when most people are busy with the twin concerns of family and career. This is the age when most people seek out a partner and start a family. At the same time, people are choosing and starting careers and their life's work. Young people are also building identities by making commitments to social institutions such as work, marriage, family, and community. These new roles come with expectations, demands, and reinforcements that shape a person into becoming more socially dominant, agreeable, conscientious, and less neurotic (Roberts et al., 2008). Social investment in the conventional roles of adulthood, such as career or family, leads to normative increases in dominance, conscientiousness, and emotional stability in most people. These changes are small over short periods of time, but are quite large over longer periods.

Our personality determines which situations, environments, experiences, or social roles we choose. Once we choose an environment or role, the new situation reinforces these aspects of our personalities. The most common effect of life experiences on personality development is that our choice of environments and roles strengthens the very personality traits that selected them in the first place. Life experiences that elicit behaviors corresponding to a person's disposition are validating and rewarding, often leading to similar behaviors and similar choices in the future.

The saying "life happens while you are busy making other plans" can apply to personality: By making plans and acting on them, we both express and develop our personalities, often without awareness of how we've changed. This type of personality change isn't likely to make headlines or be the topic for a movie-of-the-week, but it is quite powerful nevertheless.

This explains why personality change in adulthood is most often slow and steady, as a result of being exposed to situations of our own choosing and less often as a result of a so-called life-altering experience. Life-altering experiences are actually very rare, and their impact on personality perhaps a bit overblown. In truth, people respond to devastating events with more of their true selves: Individual differences are magnified when people face unpredictable or ambiguous situations without guidelines for how to respond (Caspi & Moffitt, 1993).

How and Why Do Individuals Develop in Their Own Particular Ways?

Have you heard the saying "there's an exception to every rule"? When it comes to normative influences (the tide) on personality (the boats in a harbor) some people do not experience these normative changes. There are individual differences in personality development (Mroczek & Spiro, 2003; Roberts, 1997; Roberts & Mroczek, 2008). Basically, nonnormative experiences make for nonnormative development. For example, women who continued to smoke marijuana into midlife (Roberts & Bogg, 2004) and people who engaged in stealing, fighting, or coming to work drunk (Roberts, Walton, Bogg, & Caspi, 2006) did not increase in Conscientiousness and actually decreased in emotional stability in their adult years. By consciously taking a stand *against* socializing roles—wife, mother, responsible employee—some people exposed themselves to different experiences and missed out on the kinds of personality development that most people go through.

In fact, researchers have identified reliable individual differences in personality change during all stages of life (Roberts et al., 2008): childhood and adolescence (De Fruyt et al., 2006; Pullman, Raudsepp, & Allik, 2006), young adulthood (Donnellan, Conger, & Burzette, 2007; Vaidya, Gray, Haig, & Watson, 2002), middle age (Van Aken et al., 2006), and old age (Steunenberg, Twisk, Beekman, Deeg, & Kerkhof, 2005). These individual differences in personality development are important because personality traits are linked to important outcomes in work, physical health, mental illness, and longevity (Roberts & Mroczek, 2008).

For example, in a study of college students aged 20 to 32 enrolled in an introductory psychology class, participants varied in how much they changed in positive emotions (related to Extraversion) and negative emotions (related to Neuroticism) over the subsequent 2.5 years (Vaidya et al., 2002). Those who had significantly decreased in negative emotions

THINK ABOUT IT

What kinds of situations might impact the personality of people who are about to graduate college?

THINK ABOUT IT

What are nonnormative experiences that might cause people to develop differently from their peers?

had experienced fewer negative events, such as a family member passing away, receiving a failing grade in a course, becoming a regular smoker, or experiencing divorce or separation of their parents, compared to their peers. Those who had significantly increased in positive emotions had experienced more positive events in their lives, such as receiving academic honors or awards, getting promoted at a job, getting engaged, getting accepted into grad school, or getting married, compared to their peers. This study illustrates that we do not merely react to life experiences, but we may internalize them and become changed by them bit by bit until over longer periods of time we become permanently changed by them.

In another study, both men and women who increased in hostility as they developed from college age to about age 40 experienced a range of negative outcomes. People who increased in hostility over their adulthood, compared to those who either maintained or decreased their level of hostility, showed increased obesity, inactivity, social isolation, lower income (women only), worse physical health, greater risk of depression, and the perception that their work and family life was changing for the worse (Siegler et al., 2003).

Similarly, personality change in midlife was associated with successful adaptation to the day-to-day concerns of this periods of life: well-being of family members, work stress, and life satisfaction (Van Aken et al., 2006).

Finally, in a longitudinal study of male veterans aged 43 to 91, those who became more neurotic over time showed a 32% increase in mortality over men whose level of Neuroticism decreased (Mroczek & Spiro, 2007). In fact, the direction of change in neuroticism over the 18 years of the study—whether it was increasing or decreasing—was more important than whether it was high or low to begin with (see Figure 3.7). Among men who were high in Neuroticism, those who were changing to become less neurotic lived longer than men whose neuroticism was increasing.

Where Does Adult Personality Come From?

There is still one big unanswered question: Where does adult personality come from? We know that children have differing **temperaments**, or individual differences, that emerge during the first year of life (Buss & Plomin, 1994). But how and when do these temperaments develop into the five factors of Neuroticism, Extraversion, Openness, Agreeableness, and Conscientiousness? To answer this question, we need longitudinal studies that follow infants from birth to adulthood. Given that researchers have only recently reached consensus on the five-factor model, it will be a good while until we can collect the right evidence to answer this question. However, there is little doubt that childhood temperament does predict to adult personality (Caspi, Roberts, & Shiner, 2005; Caspi & Shiner, 2006; Caspi & Silva, 1995; Digman, 1989; Shiner & Caspi, 2003).

THINK ABOUT IT

Are babies born with a personality? With personality traits? With all five factors?

Figure 3.7 Survival curves for four groups of men according to neuroticism level and change over time, controlling for age, physical health, and depression. *Source:* From Mroczek and Spiro (2007, Figure 1, p. 375). Mroczek, D. K., & Spiro, A. (2007), "Personality change influences mortality in older men," *Psychological Science,* 18(5), 371–376. Reprinted by permission of Blackwell Publishing.

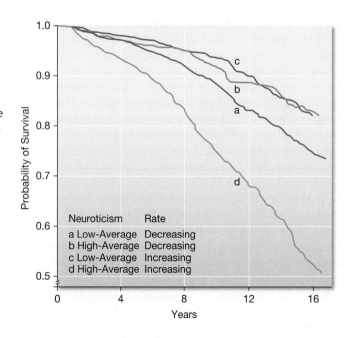

Neuroticism	Rate
a Low-Average	Decreasing
b High-Average	Decreasing
c Low-Average	Increasing
d High-Average	Increasing

For example, in one study researchers identified five temperament groups among a sample of 3-year-old children in New Zealand, based on psychologists' ratings of the child's behavior (Caspi & Silva, 1995). The groups were Well-adjusted, Undercontrolled, Inhibited, Confident, and Reserved. When the children were 18 years old, the five groups showed differences in their personalities. Compared to Well-adjusted children, the Undercontrolled children at age 3 were higher in impulsivity, danger seeking, aggression, and interpersonal alienation at age 18, whereas Inhibited children scored low on these variables. Confident children scored high in impulsivity. Reserved children scored low on dominance. The Well-adjusted group grew up to be, as you might imagine, typical teenagers. By age 3, children have developed individual differences in behavior that are manifested as personality differences by age 18 and last to at least age 26 (Caspi, Harrington, et al., 2003).

Then and Now: The Grant Study of Harvard Graduates

Only a longitudinal study can address the kinds of questions we've been asking about personality in this section. As mentioned earlier, a longitudinal study follows the same group of participants over time—from as short as a few months to as long as many years (Fleeson, 2007; Mroczek, 2007). Currently, only a handful of studies exist that have followed participants for more than 20 years, and far fewer than that have followed children from birth to the end of their lives.

The longest running study is the study of gifted children begun in 1921 by Lewis Terman and slated to continue until the participants are no longer living (Holahan & Sears, 1995; Terman, 1926). Another famous one is the Mills Longitudinal Study of Women, following women from the 1958 and 1960 graduating classes from Mills College, a small, private college in California, to the present, when many of the original participants are in their 70s (Helson, 1967; Helson & Wink, 1992; Roberts & Helson, 1997). These women came of age and lived through some of the most exciting and volatile times of the last century including the civil rights movement and the women's movement. Many of the findings discussed in this section come out of the study of the Mills women (e.g., Roberts & Bogg, 2004; Roberts & Chapman, 2000; Roberts & Helson, 1997).

Perhaps the most famous longitudinal study of all is the Grant Study of Harvard Graduates. The study began in 1938 when Arlie Bock, frustrated that medicine focused on pathology, wanted to find out what combination of physical and mental health led to a successful life (Shenk, 2009). The department store magnate W. T. Grant supported the fledgling research project for the first 10 years, which is why today the study is known as the Grant study. They recruited the most physically and mentally healthy members of the Harvard classes of 1942 to 1944 to volunteer for a lifetime of close scrutiny from a medical, psychological, and social standpoint. They even questioned the men's parents and close family members. The participants received questionnaires every 2 years, physicals every 5 years, and interviews every 15 years. In more recent years participants have been put through MRIs, DNA testing, and even a request that they donate their brains to the study upon their death.

As the men grew into middle age, many of the study participants achieved great success including President John F. Kennedy; former editor of the *Washington Post* Ben Bradlee; four former senate hopefuls; one presidential cabinet member; and one best-selling novelist. At the same time, almost a third of the participants struggled with mental illness by age 50 (Shenk, 2009).

Psychiatrist George Vaillant, who took over the study in 1967, sought not so much to find out what kind of troubles these men faced over a lifetime, but rather how they responded and adapted to what occurred in their lives (Vaillant, 1977, 2002a). For Vaillant, the most inspiring cases were often those where the men had overcome great hardships.

Vaillant studied the kind of defense mechanisms the men used to cope. He identified the classic Freudian defense mechanisms and many others (Vaillant, 1977). Defenses ranged from the most unhealthy such as paranoia or passive aggressiveness, to the healthiest or most mature adaptations such as altruism, humor, and sublimation. Vaillant found that as people matured, their defense mechanisms matured too. Between ages 50 and 75 the men used altruism and humor more frequently and passive aggressiveness and fantasy less frequently. Mature adaptations turned pain and emotional turmoil into occasions for achievement, creativity, and connections with others.

"To be able to study lives in such depth, over so many decades, it was like looking through the Mount Palomar telescope."

George Vaillant as cited in Shenk (2009, p. 38)

Amazingly, the accomplishments of men from the original Grant study can be predicted from their personality during college (Soldz & Vaillant, 1999). Out of the five factors, traits measuring Conscientiousness were the best predictors of the men's lives across a variety of domains including personal adjustment, family relationships, work success, and health behaviors. Conscientious young men grew into successful and better-functioning older men.

However, neuroticism at age 65 was a good indicator of poor adjustment across various domains as a result of, presumably, difficulties in life since college. Neurotic older men had more psychiatric visits, depression, smoking, and use of drugs and alcohol in the course of their lives as compared with more emotionally stable men.

Based on their results, the authors surmise that Extraversion in young adulthood drove career and monetary success, whereas Neuroticism was related to adjustment and the inability to quit smoking in adulthood. Openness was related to adult creativity. Low Openness was related to a more conservative traditional and authoritarian political outlook and to psychiatric usage in adulthood, although this may reflect a greater willingness to explore their inner lives or an experience with psychological distress.

Today, the original Grant study is part of the Harvard Study of Adult Development. Due to the efforts of then-Harvard Law professor Sheldon Glueck, the study was expanded in 1939 to include a control group of nondelinquent boys who were growing up in the inner-city neighborhoods of Boston from 1940 to 1945. In the 1970s Vaillant and his colleagues joined the project, now called the Glueck study, and conducted follow-ups with these men (Vaillant, 1995). At one point, Vaillant even tracked down and interviewed women from the Terman study (Vaillant & Vaillant, 1990)! These additional cohorts were Vaillant's way of broadening his sample so that he could draw conclusions about adult development that were not limited to a sample of upper-class, college-educated, elite men.

A journalist asked Vaillant what he had learned from his research on the Grant study. "That the only thing that really matters in life are your relationships to other people" he replied (Shenk, 2009, p. 46). From the Glueck study he learned that industriousness in childhood, things such as holding a part-time job, taking on chores, or joining sports teams, was a more important predictor of adult mental health than all other factors including family relationships. From the women of the Terman study he learned that whereas social interventions can increase a person's chance of success, they can also destroy human potential (Vaillant, 2002b). Despite having superior intellectual potential and educational advantages, only 5% of the Terman women went on to successful business or professional careers.

At the heart of these findings are biology, environment, personality, and how experiences in our lives affect who we are and what we grow up to be—the kinds of questions that can only be answered with longitudinal studies like the Grant study.

What will you be like at your 40-year high school reunion?

Personality Traits: Theoretical and Practical Conclusions

There you have it: all about traits in a nutshell! From the original lexical studies to modern factor-analytic studies, from the ancients to the cutting-edge research of today, understanding traits is key to understanding people. In particular, the identification of key dimensions of personality—recognized in a simple handshake, as we saw in the opening of this chapter—and their applicability across cultures has inspired lines of research on nomothetic universals, indigenous personality traits, and the numerous ways we express our personality, our traits, in all aspects of our lives.

Of course, there is much more to personality than trait descriptions, as the side quote suggests. (See Block, 1995, 2001, 2010 for an impassioned critique of the five factors in particular.) We might well wonder, for example, how we form an identity or how we are influenced by social roles (McCrae & Costa, 1996). One commentator noted that trait models are essentially "psychology of the stranger" because they describe personality at only a superficial level. In particular, McAdams (1992, p. 229) noted, trait models fall short when it comes to

1. Accounting for personality functioning and personality differences between people beyond the surface level.

2. Adequately describing the richness of persons' lives.

3. Providing a true causal explanation for human behavior rather than circular reasoning ("Raj is outgoing because he's extraverted. We know he's extraverted because he likes to meet new people.").

4. Addressing the social context of human experience—that is, how the ways we interact with others affect who we are.

5. Explaining personality integration and organization within an individual.

Only by studying other aspects of personality—genetics, physiology, identity, motivations, to name only a few—can we come to a complete understanding of human personality.

> "We are fully prepared to admit that personality psychologists have been concerned with many aspects of human nature beyond enduring dispositions . . . and we agree with commentators who note that the five-factor model does not and cannot provide a complete model of personality."
>
> *McCrae and Costa (1996, p. 65)*

Chapter Summary

• •

In this chapter we questioned whether the five-factor model leaves out important traits such as intelligence, religiosity, and sexuality and culture-specific traits such as philotimo, filial piety, and amae. In some cases these traits are indeed an omission (e.g., spiritual transcendence); in other cases these traits are a combination of facets and factors (e.g., sexuality), or abilities (e.g., intelligence). However, the most important question is whether the five factors adequately account for personality in other cultures.

We discovered that there are culture-specific indigenous personality traits that are not accounted for by the five factors (e.g., philotimo in Greece, filial piety in China, amae in Japan). Sentence or questionnaire measures of the five factors replicate across many cultures and languages, but adjectival measures are more sensitive to cultural differences. In particular, Openness varies across cultures and some cultures are best described by more than five factors. Research that combined measures of the five factors with Chinese indigenous trait terms found the five factors plus a unique sixth factor tapping the traditional Chinese values of Harmony, Connectedness, Defensiveness, and Social approval.

People express their traits in many aspects of their everyday lives including handshakes, music preferences, web pages, and careers, including being the president of the United States.

To study individuals in depth, psychologists use multiple methods, called triangulation, in which they use *LOTS* of different methods including L data, O data, T data, and S data to understand personality. They also use longitudinal designs to study people across time. Longitudinal studies such as the Grant Study of Harvard Graduates let us draw conclusions about personality consistency, change, and coherence over the life course.

✓• Study and Review
on **mysearchlab.com**
Go online for more resources to help you review.

Through these studies, we now know that personality is consistent over time, and that consistency increases with age. The traits of the five factors are about as consistent as cognitive abilities are, and show consistency across measures and raters as well as over a lifetime. By age 3 children have developed individual differences in temperament which develop into traits in adulthood.

Against this backdrop of consistency, people do change over the course of a lifetime. In particular, we mature, showing more Agreeableness, Conscientiousness, Emotional Stability, and some aspects of Extraversion (assertive, warm, self-confident) as we enter into old age, but less Openness and other aspects of Extraversion (positive emotions, sociability, and vitality). People's personalities change the most between ages 20 to 40, as they take their place in the adult world of work, family, and community. At the same time, there are individual differences in consistency and change, some related to important health outcomes and well-being.

Traits are but one aspect of human personality, perhaps only scratching the surface of understanding what people are like.

Review Questions

1. What traits may be missing from the five-factor model? Are they traits or abilities or something else? If they are traits, can they be accounted for by some combination of factors and facets of the five-factor model?

2. What are indigenous personality traits? What do we know about universals in human personality and about the impact of culture on personality? How many factors best account for personality in China? How would you describe these factors?

3. What is triangulation? What four kinds of data do psychologists use to understand personality? Give commonly used examples of each.

4. In what ways do we express personality traits in our everyday lives?

5. What is development? What is personality consistency, personality change, and personality coherence?

6. How consistent are people over time? What traits are particularly consistent over the life span?

7. How much do people change in general? What traits are particularly likely to change over the life span?

8. Are there individual differences in personality development? How does adult personality develop out of childhood temperaments?

9. What is a longitudinal study? What are some famous longitudinal studies? What have we learned about human personality from these longitudinal studies?

Key Terms

Openness	Interpersonal Relatedness	Change
Spiritual transcendence	Triangulation	Personality coherence
Sexy Seven	S data	Longitudinal study
Philotimo	T data	Mean-level change
Filial piety	O data	Individual change
Amae	L data	Meta-analysis
Indigenous traits	Development	Normative change
Ren Qing	Continuity	Maturation
Ah-Q	Consistency	Temperaments

4 PERSONALITY ASSESSMENT

Read the Chapter on
mysearchlab.com

Have you ever taken a personality test on the Internet? According to some of these tests, your favorite candy bar, city, ice cream flavor or even the way you eat an Oreo can reveal your hidden personality. What is the difference between legitimate personality tests used by psychologists and the ones you find on the Internet? Amazingly, the need for standards in the measurement of personality had its start at a nightclub in the late 1940s way before the Internet made these sorts of tests so popular.

After a long, hard day of working with clients at a Veterans Hospital psychologist Bertram Forer went to a nightclub for a bit of relaxation (Forer, 1949). He was approached by a man who purported to assess people's personality from a sample of their handwriting. The psychologist declined, and offered to administer the graphologist a Rorschach inkblot test instead. Insulted and hurt by the psychologist's skepticism of his talents, the graphologist said he had "scientific proof" that his method was valid: Clients confirmed the accuracy of his interpretations. The psychologist was not impressed. He replied that a blindfolded psychologist could give at least as good a reading!

Forer went back to his introductory psychology class and conducted a little experiment. Instead of giving students the true results of the personality test he had recently administered, he gave every member of the class the *exact same feedback* (see Table 4.1). He asked students to rate on a 0 (*poor*) to 5 (*perfect*) scale how accurate a description of their personality the feedback was. He found that all but one member of his class thought the description was a perfect or nearly perfect estimation of their true personality.

How is it that different people can believe that the same exact feedback describes them perfectly? The same way that people can believe the feedback from a nightclub graphologist in the 1940s and Oreo-cookie-eating tests on the Internet in the 2010s. These fake personality tests rely on general feedback that can apply to nearly anyone and the public's goodwill to play along with and not question too closely the contents of these tests, rather than scientific evidence. So, how do we know when a personality test is accurate or not? That's where personality assessment comes in.

Personality assessment is the measurement of the individual characteristics of a person. Though there are many types of methods that researchers use to study personality, the most commonly used are personality tests (see Table 4.2). You will see examples of nearly all of these methods as we discuss research findings throughout the text. For example, in Chapter 7 we discuss neuroimaging techniques, hormone levels, and autonomic arousal. In Chapter 5 we discuss open-ended questions and interviews. The principles of good measurement apply to all of these measures and methods.

There are many uses of personality assessment beyond the laboratory. Psychologists may gather and evaluate information about a person from various sources including personality tests, interviews, biographical material, and other people for hiring decisions, job placement, diagnosis, or development of a case study (Wiggins, 2003). In clinical settings, personality assessment may be used to develop models of disorders, design intervention programs, monitor treatments, evaluate treatments, and to make diagnoses (Meyer et al., 2001).

Table 4.1   A Little Something for Everybody?

"You have a great need for other people to like and admire you. You have a tendency to be critical of yourself. You have a great deal of unused capacity which you have not turned to your advantage. While you have some personality weaknesses, you are generally able to compensate for them. Your sexual adjustment has presented problems for you.

Disciplined and self-controlled outside, you tend to be worrisome and insecure inside. At times you have serious doubts as to whether you have made the right decision or done the right thing. You prefer a certain amount of change and variety and become dissatisfied when hemmed in by restrictions and limitations.

You pride yourself as a independent thinker and do not accept others' statements without satisfactory proof. You have found it unwise to be too frank in revealing yourself to others. At times you are extroverted, affable, sociable, while at other times you are introverted, wary, reserved. Some of your aspirations tend to be pretty unrealistic. Security is one of your major goals in life."

Note: How well does this describe your personality? If you are like most people, you will find this an accurate description of your personality. The trouble is, it is so general that it accurately describes nearly *everybody!* The fact that people readily believe such feedback is called the Barnum Effect.

Source: Forer, B. R. (1949), "The fallacy of personal validation: A classroom demonstration of gullibility," *The Journal of Abnormal and Social Psychology,* 44(1), 118–123.

Table 4.2 Assessment Methods and Measures Used in Personality Research

Type of Measure	% of Psychologists Who Reported That They Have Used the Measure
Self-report scales and questionnaires	100%
Judgments of self and others	99
Behavioral observation	89
Informant reports	86
Behavioral responses	81
Other judgment tasks (e.g., of stimuli)	79
Structured interviews	76
Narrative/open-ended questionnaires	74
Experience sampling	65
Implicit measures	64
Memory tasks	62
Reaction time	61
Autonomic arousal	57
Judgments of groups/nations/cultures	43
Hormone levels	36
Neuroimaging (fMRI, etc.)	32
Molecular genetics/DNA testing	26

Note: Prominent personality psychologists ($N = 72$) were asked if they had ever used the method in their work.

Source: Adapted from Robins, Tracy, and Sherman (2007, Table 37.1, p. 676). Reprinted with permission from Robins, R. W., Tracy, J. L., & Sherman, J. W. (2007), "What kinds of methods do personality psychologists use? A survey of journal editors and editorial board members," In R. W. Robins, R. C. Fraley, & R. F. Krueger (Eds.), *Handbook of Research Methods in Personality Psychology,* p. 673–678 (New York, NY: Guilford). Permission conveyed through the Copyright Clearance Center.

In this chapter we consider what makes a good personality test and how people answer personality tests, and see how the results of personality tests have been used by businesses to select the right person for the right job. Along the way, we will take a close look at a few types of personality tests that are used by personality psychologists today.

What Makes a Good Personality Test?

According to standards set up by professional organizations in education and psychology, including the American Psychological Association, the developers of a personality test must demonstrate that the test is valid and reliable, and specify the conditions, populations, and cultures the test applies to (American Educational Research Association, American Psychological Association, &

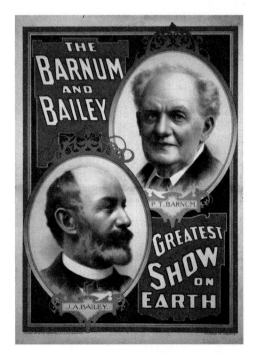

The Barnum Effect, named for famed showman P. T. Barnum, suggests that people falsely believe that invalid personality tests are good personality assessments when they contain "a little something for everybody" like a great circus.

THINK ABOUT IT

Why is peer review an important part of the validation process for personality tests?

National Council on Measurement in Education, 1999). Test developers must also provide theoretical background and research evidence confirming (or disconfirming) that the test is related to certain outcomes. Where possible, developers should make sure that the results obtained are meaningful, and not just due to biased responding on the part of test-takers. Furthermore, this evidence should be published in scientific journals, where it has been reviewed and accepted by other experts in the field (see Clark & Watson, 1995; John & Benet-Martínez, 2000; Simms & Watson, 2007, for how to develop and validate a test).

The biggest difference between a personality test you might find on the Internet ("Does your personality match your favorite animal?" "What eating an Oreo cookie reveals about your personality") and what you find in journals or purchase from a recognized publisher is that legitimate personality tests have reliability, validity, and generalizability, backed by research evidence that is available for public scrutiny.

When we have a good test, we know that we will be able to replicate a certain score (or come close enough, allowing for measurement error) and trust that the test has a particular meaning, which allows us to make inferences about behavior, a construct, or other variables (John & Soto, 2007). When evaluating a test, we should ask ourselves: What does this test measure? Is this test reliable? For what purpose is this test valid? (Smith & Archer, 2008). The answers to these three questions will tell us about the test's reliability, validity, and generalizability.

Test Reliability: Generalizability Across Time, Items, and Raters

Reliability is a prerequisite for validity. We cannot know the correct time with an unreliable watch (Smith & Archer, 2008). A measure must first be consistent in order to be a valid representation of an underlying theoretical construct. **Reliability** is an estimate of how consistent a test is: A good test gives consistent results over time, items, or raters (see Table 4.3).

Reliability describes the extent to which test scores are consistent and reproducible with repeated measurements (Cronbach, Rajaratnam, & Gleser, 1963; John & Soto, 2007). These measurements may be repeated at different times, across multiple items, or using multiple judges or observers. We want to know that a test gives consistent results in all of these situations: across time, across items, and across raters. These are all kinds of reliability (Smith & Archer, 2008).

One way of checking to see if a test has **temporal consistency reliability** is to have respondents take the test a second time to see if their scores are similar (Cronbach, 1947). Of course, when demonstrating **test–retest reliability** we need to be careful that participants are not merely remembering what they originally said in the first test-taking session. We also need to be careful that there are no practice effects, where participants perform better merely because they've seen the test before. To eliminate all of these effects, we want the second test to be far enough removed in time so that there is no memory or practice effects, yet not so much later that our participants have changed in the interim (Campbell & Stanley, 1966).

One way of checking **internal consistency reliability** is to see if different items of the test give similar results. In the early days of psychological testing developers would make up two versions of a test that were comparable and checked to see that the scores on the parallel forms of the test were similar—**parallel-forms reliability** (Cronbach, 1947). Sometimes they would split a test in half and see if test-takers' scores on one half correlated with scores on the other half, to demonstrate **split-half reliability** (Cronbach, 1947). Today, most researchers rely on a statistic called **Cronbach's alpha** (α) (Cronbach, 1951).

Table 4.3 Generalizability Across Time, Items, and Raters

Type of Consistency	Type of Reliability	Facet of Generalizability
Temporal consistency	Test–retest	Across time
Internal consistency	Parallel forms	Across items
	Split-half	
	Cronbach's alpha	
Rater consistency	Interrater reliability	Across raters

Source: Trochim W. M. K. (2006). *Research methods knowledge base,* 3/e. Cincinnati, OH: Atomic Dog Publishing.

Imagine taking the correlation between the scores of two halves of a test. Now imagine calculating the average correlation of all possible halves of the test. That is what Cronbach's alpha reliability estimates: the generalizability of the score from one set of items to another (John & Soto, 2007).

Because an unreliable measure makes it harder to find a true effect, researchers will try to make sure that their measures have an alpha of .70 to .80, and even higher when designing tests that will be used to compare or judge individuals, like IQ tests (Nunnally & Bernstein, 1994). Here, alphas should be greater than .9 and, ideally, at least .95. However, this is not a hard-and-fast rule; it is up to researchers to decide if their measures are good enough depending on the goals of their research (Cortina, 1993; John & Soto, 2007). Good researchers will provide a discussion of their rationale for accepting or rejecting an alpha when they publish their research findings.

To illustrate, suppose a researcher wants to measure Neuroticism. She constructs the scale in Table 4.4. This scale will have a high alpha, but it may lack validity. That is, it may not adequately represent the concept of Neuroticism. Recall that Neuroticism includes the facets of anxiety, angry hostility, depression, self-consciousness, impulsiveness, and vulnerability (Costa & McCrae, 1992). Given the theory behind the scale, we would not expect the scores of the various facets to correlate too highly with each other. However, we would expect high alphas among the eight questions tapping a single facet like anxiety. Of course, we would need to measure more than arachnophobia!

We also want to be sure our measures are reliable across multiple raters (John & Soto, 2007). To check for **interrater reliability** we might have two separate judges rate the personality or behavior of a third person. Researchers will often calculate the average correlation among the scores of all raters or the percentage agreement among raters. If the raters are consistent in their judgments, then these correlations ought to be high. If there is disagreement among raters, it could mean that the construct is ambiguous or too broad, the measure is problematic, or that the raters misunderstand what they are judging. The researcher will need to rethink his or her operationalization of the construct, revise the measure, or work with the raters to clear up any confusion to improve the reliability of their ratings. Again, good researchers will report interrater reliability and how it was achieved in their reports.

For example, consider the study discussed in Chapter 2, where observers tried to judge people's personality based on what their bedrooms looked like (Gosling et al., 2002). Observers rated the personality of occupants using the five factors. Depending on the factor, the average correlation of observers' ratings ranged from a low of .08 for Neuroticism, to a high of .58 for Openness, suggesting that observers were more likely to agree in their judgment of Openness than Neuroticism from the appearance of people's bedrooms.

Test Validity

Validity is the extent to which a test measures what it is supposed to measure (Loevinger, 1957). Because there are many ways to investigate this question—Does the test correlate with other tests? Does it predict behavior? Does it predict some future outcome?—there are many kinds of validity. A test has validity if it is grounded in research evidence, that is, if it correlates with some standard (Loevinger, 1957). The exact standard or the kind of research evidence depends on the specific type of validity a researcher wishes to demonstrate.

SEE FOR YOURSELF

Some professors of very large classes use multiple forms of the same test. What kind of reliability must these tests have?

THINK ABOUT IT

What kinds of questions would measure anxiety? Angry hostility?

"[E]verything that we do as scientists comes back, in the end, to the importance of being valid."
Personality researchers Oliver P. John and Christopher J. Soto (2007, p. 489)

Table 4.4   Redundancy Department: Example of a Scale With High Internal Consistency but With Questionable Validity

I am afraid of spiders
I get anxious around creepy-crawly things
I am not bothered by insects (reverse scored)
Spiders tend to make me nervous

Note: This scale may be a good measure of fear of insects, but not a very good measure of Neuroticism.

Source: John and Soto (2007, p. 471). Reprinted with permission from John, O. P., & Soto, C. J. (2007), "The importance of being valid," as appeared in R. W. Robins & R. C. Fraley (Eds.), *Handbook of Research Methods in Personality Psychology*, p. 461–494 (New York, NY: The Guilford Press). Permission conveyed through the Copyright Clearance Center.

THINK ABOUT IT

Why is face validity insufficient for establishing construct validity?

Every test aims to measure an underlying concept called a construct, which derives from a theory. Therefore, ultimately, every test must have **construct validity** and successfully measure the theoretical concept it was designed to measure (Loevinger, 1957; Simms & Watson, 2007). For example, the Eysenck Personality Inventory is designed to measure Extraversion, Neuroticism, and Impulsivity, three dimensions that Eysenck theorized to be genetic, biological, and determined by our physiology (Eysenck & Eysenck, 1975).

A test has **face validity** when it appears to measure the construct of interest (Cronbach, 1960). For example, you might reasonably figure out that a test that asks about suicide ideation, mood, feelings of sadness, and changes in appetite is measuring feelings of depression. This is an example of a test with high face validity. However, with neuropsychological tests or tests asking about how one interacts with other people it would be harder to see exactly what concept the test is measuring. These are examples of tests with low face validity (Smith & Archer, 2008).

Face validity is not the most convincing type of validity. However, it is useful under two conditions. First, face validity is important for personnel testing, or other situations where the cooperation and motivation of the test-taker can affect the results of a test (Smither, Reilly, Millsap, Perlman, & Stoffey, 1993). When a test has face validity, respondents view the content of a test as fair and relevant to some situation or particular outcome, like job performance (Wiggins, 1973). Test-takers try harder and take a test more seriously if they can see how a test is related to the content of a job (Chan, Schmitt, DeShon, Clause, & Delbridge, 1997). When test items seem obscure to job applicants, they may view the test as busy work or a waste of their time. However, depending on the purpose of the test, test-takers might purposely respond inaccurately, such as presenting themselves as better or worse off than they really are, or to present themselves in a favorable light (Smith & Archer, 2008). Researchers often disguise the content of a test to lessen the possibility that respondents might try to fake their answers, compromising face validity to establish other kinds of validity (Holden & Jackson, 1979).

A second useful condition for face validity is when researchers are developing a new measure of a concept. Often, they will think of items that appear to measure what they want the test to measure. Then they will administer their test to respondents and see which items are actually related to the trait or concept the researcher wants to measure. When it comes to test validity, substance is more important than looks. That is, we need evidence to support the validity of a test. Face validity is not good enough; there must be other kinds of validity for a test to be considered valid.

Criterion validity determines how good a test is, by comparing the results of the test to an external standard like another personality test or some behavioral outcome. For example, a

THINK ABOUT IT

What behavioral outcomes should a test measuring extraversion and introversion correlate with in order to have criterion-related validity?

Which person do you think would score higher on the Need for Cognition Scale if the scale had construct validity?

Table 4.5 The Need for Cognition Scale

1.	I would prefer complex to simple problems.
2.	I like to have the responsibility of handling a situation that requires a lot of thinking.
3.*	Thinking is not my idea of fun.
4.*	I would rather do something that requires little thought than something that is sure to challenge my thinking abilities.
5.*	I try to anticipate and avoid situations where there is a likely chance I will have to think in depth about something.
6.	I find satisfaction in deliberating hard and for long hours.
7.*	I only think as hard as I have to.
8.*	I prefer to think about small, daily projects to long-term ones.
9.*	I like tasks that require little thought once I've learned them.
10.	The idea of relying on thought to make my way to the top appeals to me.
11.	I really enjoy a task that involves coming up with new solutions to problems.
12.*	Learning new ways to think doesn't excite me very much.
13.	I prefer my life to be filled with puzzles that I must solve.
14.	The notion of thinking abstractly is appealing to me.
15.	I would prefer a task that is intellectual, difficult, and important to one that is somewhat important but does not require much thought.
16.*	I feel relief rather than satisfaction after completing a task that required a lot of mental effort.
17.*	It's enough for me that something gets the job done; I don't care how or why it works.
18.	I usually end up deliberating about issues even when they do not affect me personally.

Ratings were made using a -4 to $+4$ Likert scale, in which $+4 =$ *very strong agreement*, $+3 =$ *strong agreement*, $+2 =$ *moderate agreement*, $+1 =$ *slight agreement*, $0 =$ *neither agreement nor disagreement*, $-1 =$ *slight disagreement*, $-2 =$ *moderate disagreement*, $-3 =$ *strong disagreement*, and $-4 =$ *very strong disagreement*. *Indicates reverse scored items.

Source: Cacioppo et al. (1984, Table 1, p. 307). Reprinted with permission from Cacioppo, J. T., Petty, R. E., & Kao, C. F. (1984), "The Efficient Assessment of Need for Cognition," *Journal of Personality Assessment*, 48(3), 306–307. Permission conveyed through the Copyright Clearance Center.

test of extraversion-introversion should distinguish people who seek out the company of others (extraverts) from those that don't (introverts).

Take, for example, the Need for Cognition Scale (Cacioppo & Petty, 1982). This scale measures individual differences in the need for and enjoyment of effortful thinking (see Table 4.5). To establish criterion validity, Cacioppo and Petty (1982) compared two groups of participants assumed to differ in their preferences for heavy thinking: college professors and assembly-line workers. Sure enough, the college professors scored higher on the need for cognition test than the workers, suggesting that the test did indeed capture some important criteria that differed between the two groups, demonstrating criterion validity.

In addition to criterion validity, we might check to see if our test is similar to other tests of the same construct or to tests of related constructs. This establishes **convergent validity** (Campbell & Fiske, 1959). At the same time, we want to be sure that our test is different from tests of constructs that we theorize to be unrelated to the one we are interested in. We might look for **discriminant validity** to be sure that our test taps a different concept entirely (Campbell & Fiske, 1959). To establish construct validity we must demonstrate both what a test measures and what it doesn't measure (John & Soto, 2007); neither type of validity alone is sufficient (Trochim, 2006). Essentially, we want to be sure our test converges with similar constructs and discriminates between dissimilar constructs (Trochim, 2006). For example, the Need for Cognition Scale, as Cacioppo and Petty (1982) hypothesized, correlated with open-mindedness but did not correlate with test anxiety or social desirability, demonstrating convergent and discriminant validity.

At the same time, a test ought to give feedback that is specific to a person or a group of people who share a certain characteristic. A test that gives feedback so general, superficial, or

THINK ABOUT IT

If a high sensation seeker and a low sensation seeker scored differently on a test, what kind of validity would this illustrate?

ambiguous that it could apply to virtually all people lacks predictive validity. Remember the story of Professor Forer, who gave all his students the same personality feedback? He demonstrated that people were quick to trust a test that gave general statements about their personalities.

The fact that people readily believe such feedback is called the **Barnum Effect** (Meehl, 1956; Snyder, Shenkel, & Lowery, 1977) after the circus showman P. T. Barnum, who believed that a good circus had a "little something for everybody." Such tests lack construct validity because they distinguish no one. They give an illusion of accuracy when applied to a single individual (Wiggins, 1973). This is why people think that feedback from a nightclub graphologist, horoscopes, palm readers, and questionable personality tests applies to them.

Many invalid personality tests—especially those circulating on the Internet for fun—provide feedback so general that they can apply to anybody, so that an unthinking reader can easily be taken in. Keep in mind our discussion of validity when you see one of these fake personality tests, and try not to be one of the gullible masses of whom Barnum also said, "There is a sucker born every minute."

Test Generalizability

After designing a reliable measure and validating it, researchers also need to think about the specific uses, settings, and population groups the measure is valid for (John & Soto, 2007). This gets at the third question: For what purpose is this test valid?

Generalizability establishes the boundaries or limitations of a test. We cannot use a test for a use other than what it was intended, nor administer the test to a group of people it was not validated on. For example, the Minnesota Multiphasic Personality Inventory (MMPI; Butcher, Dahlstrom, Graham, Tellegen, & Kaemmer, 1989), the Rorschach inkblot test (Rorschach, 1921), the Beck Depression Inventory (Beck, Steer, & Brown, 1996), and other tests that were designed to diagnose mental disorders cannot be used to determine the fitness of an applicant for work.

Many personality tests specifically note that they are for children or adults but not both. A real challenge for researchers is to establish that their tests are valid for populations other than college students (John & Soto, 2007). Age, gender, race, and cultural background are just some of the population characteristics we must keep in mind when designing, validating, administering, and interpreting tests.

Research Methods Illustrated: Is the NEO-PI-R a Good Personality Test?

Psychologists often use personality tests in their research. As a result, their research will only be as good as the tests they use. Using an unreliable test will make it hard to find a true effect; using an invalid test will render the results useless.

One size fits all? Generalizability establishes the limitations of a test, such as the population for which it is valid.

When researchers publish a personality test, they must conduct validity and reliability analyses and report their findings. For many tests, especially personality and clinical tests, this information is published in the test manual or instruction booklet that comes with the test. Two examples of this are the Minnesota Multiphasic Personality Inventory (MMPI; Butcher et al., 1989) and the NEO Personality Inventory—Revised (NEO-PI-R; Costa & McCrae, 1992). For some tests this information is published in a book or in peer-reviewed journals, as is the case with the Rosenberg Self-Esteem Scale (Rosenberg, 1965), the Crowne-Marlow Social Desirability Scale (Crowne & Marlow, 1960), the Need for Cognition Scale (Cacioppo & Petty, 1982; Cacioppo, Petty, & Kao, 1984), and the Snyder Self-Monitoring Scale (Snyder & Gangestad, 1986).

Now that you understand what makes a good test—reliability, validity, and generalizability—let's evaluate one of the most extensively used personality tests: the NEO-PI-R (Costa & McCrae, 1992).

Does the NEO-PI-R Have Reliability?

To see if the NEO-PI-R is a reliable test, Costa and McCrae (1992) report Cronbach's alpha for each of the factors and facets. The alphas ranged from .56 to .81 for the various facets, which Costa and McCrae find acceptable for scales of only eight items. The internal consistency of the factors is much higher, as you can see in Table 4.6.

To check for test–retest reliability, college students took the NEO-PI-R at two different times, 3 months apart. As you can see in Table 4.6 the correlations were quite high indicating good reliability.

Does the NEO-PI-R Have Validity?

To answer this question, let's first take a look at construct validity. That is, does the NEO-PI-R measure 5 and only 5 factors of personality? Table 4.7 presents the results of a factor analysis of the 30 facet scales from the NEO-PI-R. The factor analysis yielded the 5 factors of Neuroticism, Extraversion, Openness, Agreeableness, and Conscientiousness, as predicted. Together, these factors accounted for 58% of the variance in responses (Costa et al., 1991). As you can see, each facet had the highest loading on the appropriate factor. Some facets also loaded on a second factor. Costa and McCrae (1992) deemed this acceptable because these additional correlations made theoretical sense.

Based on these analyses, it appears that the NEO-PI-R is a good operationalization of the theory behind the test. But does the test have criterion validity? Does it predict to a criterion outside the test? This is where McCrae and Costa have done, and continue to do, a lot of research.

Costa and McCrae (1992) hypothesized that individuals in psychotherapy would score high in Neuroticism and that drug abusers would score low on Agreeableness and Conscientiousness, and indeed they do. In addition, there are significantly high correlations between a person's score on the NEO-PI-R and their friend's or spouse's ratings of their personality (Costa and McCrae, 1992). These two findings demonstrate that the NEO-PI-R has criterion validity.

Costa and McCrae (1992) demonstrated both convergent and discriminant validity by correlating scores on the NEO-PI-R with scores on other personality tests. As expected, scores on Neuroticism and Extraversion correlate with the Neuroticism and Extraversion scales of the Eysenck

Table 4.6 Reliability of the NEO-PI-R

Factor	Alpha	Test–Retest Correlations
Neuroticism	.92	.79
Extraversion	.89	.79
Openness	.87	.80
Agreeableness	.86	.75
Conscientiousness	.90	.83

Source: Adapted from Costa and McCrae (1992, Table 5, p. 44). Costa, P. T., & McCrae, R. R. (1992). Revised NEO personality inventory (NEO-PI-R) and NEO five-factor inventory (NEO-FFI) professional manual. Odessa, FL: Psychological Assessment Resources.

Table 4.7 Factor Structure of the NEO-PI-R

Scale	Factor				
	N	E	O	A	C
Neuroticism Facets					
N1	**.81**	.02	−.01	−.01	−.10
N2	**.63**	−.03	.01	**−.48**	−.08
N3	**.80**	−.10	.02	−.03	−.26
N4	**.73**	−.18	−.09	.04	−.16
N5	**.49**	.35	.02	−.21	−.32
N6	**.70**	−.15	−.09	.04	−.38
Extraversion Facets					
E1	−.12	**.66**	.18	.38	.13
E2	−.18	**.66**	.04	.07	−.03
E3	−.32	**.44**	.23	−.32	.32
E4	.04	**.54**	.16	−.27	**.42**
E5	.00	**.58**	.11	−.38	−.06
E6	−.04	**.74**	.19	.10	.10
Openness Facets					
O1	.18	.18	**.58**	−.14	−.31
O2	.14	.04	**.73**	.17	.14
O3	.37	**.41**	**.50**	−.01	.12
O4	−.19	.22	**.57**	.04	−.04
O5	−.15	−.01	**.75**	−.09	.16
O6	−.13	.08	**.49**	−.07	−.15
Agreeableness Facets					
A1	−.35	.22	.15	**.56**	.03
A2	−.03	−.15	−.11	**.68**	.24
A3	−.06	**.52**	−.05	**.55**	.27
A4	−.16	−.08	.00	**.77**	.01
A5	.19	−.12	−.18	**.59**	−.08
A6	.04	.27	.13	**.62**	.00
Conscientiousness Facets					
C1	**−.41**	.17	.13	.03	**.64**
C2	−.04	.06	−.19	.01	**.70**
C3	−.20	−.04	.01	.29	**.68**
C4	−.09	.23	.15	−.13	**.74**
C5	−.33	.17	−.08	.06	**.75**
C6	−.23	−.28	−.04	.22	**.57**

Note: Significant factor loadings appear in bold print.

Source: Costa and McCrae (1992, Table 5, p. 44). Costa, P.T., & McCrae, R. R. (1992). Revised NEO personality inventory (NEO-PI-R) and NEO five-factor inventory (NEO-FFI) professional manual. Odessa, FL: Psychological Assessment Resources.

Personality Inventory (Eysenck & Eysenck, 1975). Similarly, facet scores on the NEO-PI-R correlate with the appropriate adjective responses from the Adjective Check List (ACL; Gough & Heilbrun, 1983). For example, "friendly" correlated with Warmth and Tender-Mindedness but not with Anxiety or Achievement-Striving. Similarly, "dreamy" correlated with Fantasy, but not any of the other facets of Openness.

Finally, whereas the NEO-PI-R doesn't have special questions or scales to help identify response sets (see the following section), Costa and McCrae (1992) cautioned that if a person has left out more than 40 items, their scores may not be valid.

Does the NEO-PI-R Have Test Generalizability?

As reported in the manual for the NEO-PI-R, the test is valid for use in many populations, including adults and elders, White and non-White respondents, men and women, with high school or college levels of education (Costa & McCrae, 1992). The test is also valid for use in clinical settings, such as drug rehabilitation programs and individual psychotherapy. Many of these uses are described in more detail in the manual. The NEO-PI-R has also been translated into other languages and appears to be valid in other cultures as well (McCrae, 2002). The manual does note that the NEO-PI-R is for adults, so that it would not be appropriate to try to give the test to people younger than 18 (Costa & McCrae, 1992).

As you can see from this brief review of the many studies conducted, the NEO-PI-R does appear to be a valid and reliable test. However, this is merely the beginning of research on the five-factor model of traits. Psychologists may disagree with McCrae and Costa about their theory, the right number of factors, appropriate populations, or the design of their research, but nobody is claiming that the NEO-PI-R is invalid or unreliable. Now that McCrae and Costa have a good measure, it is up to them and other researchers to use this test to explore human personality.

Personality Tests

Now that we've established what makes for a good personality test, let's take a closer look at personality tests. As you can imagine, there are many ways of asking people about their personalities and many different formats respondents can use to tell us. In addition, there is a whole science behind the ways people respond to personality tests, such as identifying whether people are just careless or if they are purposely trying to present themselves in a certain way by their answers. Let us consider the types and formats of personality tests and some of the typical ways people respond to them.

Types and Formats of Personality Tests

Psychologists generally divide personality tests into two kinds: **self-report** and **performance-based**, once called *objective tests* and *projective tests* (Smith & Archer, 2008). In self-report tests respondents answer questions about themselves. Response formats and question styles can vary depending on the purpose of the test and the construct the researcher is trying to measure (Smith & Archer, 2008). Performance-based tests use an unstructured format in which participants must respond to a stimulus in as much detail as they would like, often within certain parameters set by the researcher. Because the stimuli used in these tests are ambiguous, respondents must project their own meanings, significances, patterns, feelings, interpretations, concerns, or worldviews onto the stimulus. These projections of people's private worlds are reflected in their answers (Smith & Archer, 2008).

Self-Report Tests. Self-report personality measures may use a dichotomous two-choice scale (e.g., true–false, yes–no) or a Likert-type rating scale. Likert rating scales might ask participants to rate their agreement (e.g., *strongly disagree* to *strongly agree*), degree (e.g., *very little* to *quite a bit*), similarity (e.g., *uncharacteristic of me* to *characteristic of me*), or frequency (e.g., *never* to *always*) using a scale, such as a 5- or 7-point scale (Simms & Watson, 2007, p. 246). Other possible formats include checklists, forced-choice scales, and visual analog scales (Clark & Watson, 1995; see Figure 4.1).

THINK ABOUT IT

Why were performance-based tests once called projective tests?

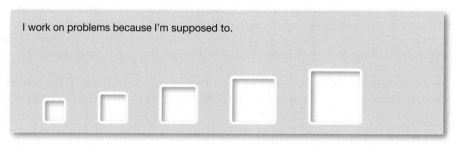

Figure 4.1 Visual analog scale of one item from a test measuring intrinsic and extrinsic motivation in children. The administrators explained verbally to the children that the boxes represented a 1 to 5 Likert scale from *not at all true for me* to *very true for me.* *Source:* Lepper Corpus, and Iyengar (2005, Figure 1, bottom, p. 187). Lepper, M. R., Corpus, J. H., & Iyengar, S. S. (2005). Intrinsic and extrinsic motivational orientations in the classroom: Age differences and academic correlates. *Journal of Educational Psychology, 97*(2), 184–196. Copyright American Psychological Association. Reprinted with permission.

"Responding to questionnaire items is like talking with an anonymous interviewer. People use their item responses to tell an anonymous interviewer who they are and how they would like to be seen."

Psychologists Robert Hogan, Joyce Hogan, and Brent Roberts writing about personality measurement and employment decisions (1996, p. 470)

For example, in the Adjective Check List (ACL; Gough & Heilbrun, 1983), respondents select those adjectives out of 300 that best describe themselves. Based on the number and type of items checked, various scales are scored including achievement, dominance, autonomy, self-confidence, nurturance, and creativity. The Creative Personality scale for the ACL measures creativity in college students (Gough, 1979; see Table 4.8).

Table 4.8 The Creative Personality Scale of the Adjective Check List

Column 1	Column 2
Capable	Affected
Clever	Cautious
Confident	Commonplace
Egotistical	Conservative
Humorous	Conventional
Individualistic	Dissatisfied
Informal	Honest
Insightful	Interests narrow
Intelligent	Mannerly
Interests wide	Sincere
Inventive	Submissive
Original	Suspicious
Reflective	
Resourceful	
Self-confident	
Sexy	
Snobbish	
Unconventional	

Note: Circle those items which best describe yourself. *Scoring:* Give yourself 1 point for every item circled in the first column. Subtract 1 point for every item circled in the second column. Scores can range from −12 to +18. In 1979, Gough reported that in a sample of 1,121 college students, males averaged 5.03, significantly higher than females who scored 3.97. Graduate students in psychology were the most creative group he tested.

Source: Gough, H. G. (1979). A creative personality scale for the adjective checklist. *Journal of Personality and Social Psychology, 37*(8), 1398–1405. Copyright American Psychological Association. Reprinted with permission.

Tests with a **forced-choice format** present respondents with a limited number of choices rather than a rating scale. True–false questions, or instructions to pick which of two statements a respondent thinks best describes himself or herself are examples of forced choices. Personality tests that use a forced-choice format include the Locus of Control Scale (Rotter, 1966), which we will talk about in Chapter 10, and the Machiavellianism Scale (Christie & Geis, 1970; Geis, 1978).

The Machiavellianism Scale is named for Niccolò Machiavelli (1469–1527) who was an astute adviser and diplomat in Florence, Italy, during the Renaissance. He wrote a book, *The Prince,* advising a fictional ruler on how best to acquire and stay in power. Machiavelli believed that most people were too trusting, not very smart, and could readily be taken advantage of for one's own purposes. Personality psychologists Richard Christie and Florence Geis culled statements directly from *The Prince* to design a forced-choice questionnaire to measure Machiavellianism, the extent to which a person believes that other people are easily manipulable (Christie & Geis, 1970).

As you can see in Table 4.9, the items refer to types of interpersonal tactics, views of human nature, and beliefs about morality (Wrightsman, 1991). Originally, the scale was in Likert format, but Christie and Geis devised this forced-choice format to control for the effects of social desirability. Research conducted on this scale suggests that people who are high in Machiavellianism, so-called High Machs are not more hostile, vicious, or vindictive than Low Machs; they just have a cool detachment when dealing with other people, emotional issues, or potentially embarrassing situations.

> "One who deceives will always find those who allow themselves to be deceived."
> *Niccolò Machiavelli*

Table 4.9 Machiavellianism: Sample Questions From the Mach V Attitude Inventory

Please read each of the three statements in each group. Then decide *first* which of the statements is *most true* or comes *the closest* to describing your own beliefs. Circle a plus (+) in the space provided on the answer sheet.

Just decide which of the remaining two statements is *most false* or is the farthest from your own beliefs. Circle the minus (−) in the space provided on the answer sheet.

You will mark *two* statements in each group of three—the one that comes the closest to your own beliefs with a + and the one furthest from your beliefs with a −. The remaining statement should be left unmarked.

		Statement	Most True	Most False
1.	A	It takes more imagination to be a successful criminal than a successful business man.	+	−
	B	The phrase "the road to hell is paved with good intentions" contains a lot of truth.	+	−
	C	Most men forget more easily the death of their father than the loss of their property.	+	−
2.	A	Men are more concerned with the car they drive than with the clothes their wives wear.	+	−
	B	It is very important that imagination and creativity in children be cultivated.	+	−
	C	People suffering from incurable diseases should have the choice of being put painlessly to death.	+	−
3.	A	Never tell anyone the real reason you did something unless it is useful to do so.	+	−
	B	The well-being of the individual is the goal that should be worked for before anything else.	+	−
	C	Once a truly intelligent person makes up his mind about the answer to a problem he rarely continues to think about it.	+	−
4.	A	People are getting so lazy and self-indulgent that it is bad for our country.	+	−
	B	The way to handle people is to tell them what they want to hear.	+	−
	C	It would be a good thing if people were kinder to others less fortunate than themselves.	+	−

Source: Adapted from Geis (1978, Table II-4, pp. 22–25). Geis, F. L. (1978). Machiavellianism. In H. London & J. Exner (Eds.), Dimensions of personality (p. 285–313). New York, NY.: Wiley.

Performance-Based Tests. Performance-based tests such as the Rorschach inkblot test (Rorschach, 1921) and the Thematic Apperception Test (TAT; Morgan & Murray, 1935) are more often used in clinical settings and forensic settings; however, the validity of many performance-based tests is highly controversial (Lilienfeld, Wood, & Garb, 2000). Some scales derived from the Rorschach and the TAT are valid for certain uses, but many other tests are indeed questionable.

There are five categories of projective techniques (Lindzey, 1959; Morgan & Murray, 1935):

reactions to
↦ participants report ambiguous stimuli

1. **Association techniques** (e.g., Word Association Test; Rorschach inkblot test)
2. **Construction techniques** (e.g., Draw-A-Person test; the TAT) *is create a story from a picture of an event in response to an ambiguous stimulus*
3. **Completion techniques** (e.g., sentence-completion tests)
4. **Arrangement or selection of stimuli** (e.g., pick your favorite color, picture, or other stimuli) *move objects around or pick their favorite*
5. **Expression techniques** (e.g., creative doll or puppet play; artwork)

The TAT is used by some personality psychologists to measure motives including the need for affiliation, the need for power, and most often, the need for achievement (McClelland, Atkinson, Clark, & Lowell, 1953). Respondents write a story in response to a picture. The stories are then coded for certain elements indicative of achievement motivation.

For example, take a look at the photo below. A person high in need for achievement might write a story like this:

> *In the picture I believe the little boy that I will call Jimmy has just come home running from school because he has just gotten his first A on a test. He tells his*

Self-report tests are frequently used for job selection and placement.

SEE FOR YOURSELF

Write a story about the photo below. Who is the boy? What is he doing? How did he get here? What will happen next?

This original photo, from 1940, by American photographer Marion Post Wolcott (1910–1990) was modified by Henry Murray for use as one of the cards in the Thematic Apperception Test.

parents how he knows that when he grows up he will be a doctor and can take care of everyone in the town when they get sick. He will be known by everyone and will be the best doctor in the whole world. His father says that he is positive that someday he will be something really amazing. Jimmy now asks his mom and dad, can I do a big boy chore as a reward for doing so good in school? I know I can do it, you just have to give me a chance to try. His parents tell him that the tasks of feeding the animals are still too dangerous for him, that maybe he can do something else. He says that [is] fine and goes out and sits in the barn door just thinking about all the wonderful things that he will accomplish during his lifetime; he even is considering [a] career as an astronaut. This is where you see him in the picture, just anxious to be able to do all the things that he wants and knows he will be able to do.

This story, written by a college student, contains themes such as high standards, unusual achievements, persistence, and an impediment toward success that suggest a high need for achievement (McClelland et al., 1953).

Similarly, the Goodenough-Harris Draw-A-Person (DAP) test may be interpreted according to the presence or absence of certain elements (e.g., size of the eyes may indicate paranoia; absence of a face may indicate depression). Here, the figure drawn is believed to represent the self-image of the respondent (Machover, 1949). Others have developed highly specific scoring guidelines depending on the level of detail of the picture (Koppitz, 1968). The global and sign approaches vary in their validity (Lilienfeld et al., 2000). The photo below depicts a variation of the Draw-A-Person test used by an art therapist working with cancer survivors.

Response Sets

There are pros and cons to both self-report and performance-based tests. Self-report tests can give us access to an amazing amount of information about various aspects of people's thoughts and experiences. Self-report tests are relatively easy to administer and to score. Indeed, self-reports may be the only way to measure certain aspects of personality including well-being, values, and life goals (Paulhus & Vazire, 2007).

However, there are some notable problems with self-reports. People may not be the best judges of their own skill, expertise, or knowledge, often overestimating their performance (Dunning et al., 2004). People may also wish to present themselves in a certain light and answer in a way that, unfortunately, jeopardizes the validity of the test (Paulhus & Vazire, 2007). For example, some people may answer questions to make themselves appear better than they really are by **faking good**, such as appearing more psychologically healthy, more qualified, or more experienced than they really are. Others might make themselves appear worse by **faking bad**, such as appearing unqualified or in need of special treatment. This is more problematic in clinical situations where people are evaluated for a diagnosis or for treatment than in job hiring and assessment (Tett et al., 2006). Luckily, the incidence of deliberate faking among job applicants is rather low (Hough, Eaton, Dunnette, Kamp, & McCloy, 1990).

Some people may portray themselves in an exaggeratedly positive manner where they try to appear more cooperative, likable, or socially appropriate than they really

THINK ABOUT IT

When might a person wish to fake good? When might a person wish to fake bad?

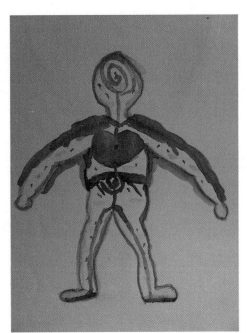

A variation of the Draw-A-Person test. An example of a self-portrait of a 48-year-old woman recovering from cancer depicting where and how she experiences pain and health in her body. She experiences physical pain in her abdomen and feet, psychological pain as anxious thoughts in her head, and responsibilities as a weight on her shoulders. She experiences health when she feels love in her heart.

are, often by not admitting to distasteful, but perfectly human tendencies such as enjoying gossiping or having sexual urges. Psychologists call this **socially desirable responding**. Other people may be accommodating to the point of agreeing with whatever the question is asking, engaging in yea-saying or **acquiescent responding**. On the flip side, others might disagree with almost everything, engaging in nay-saying or **reactant responding** (Paulhus & Vazire, 2007).

Others, may engage in **extreme responding** where they avoid the middle of the scale, choosing the more extreme ends like choosing mostly 1s and 5s on a 5-point scale. Others, may engage in **moderate responding** often choosing the midpoint of the scale in their responses.

Still others may respond in **patterned responding** by making patterns on an answer sheet by marking their answers in a physical pattern like 1-2-3-4-5-4-3-2-1 or circling all 3s down the page. And then there's just plain-old carelessness, where a person might leave out a question, forget to turn a page, or circle an answer on the wrong line throwing off all the answers.

When people have a set way that they tend to respond to self-report questions—either deliberately or unknowingly—psychologists call these **response sets** or **noncontent responding**. Response sets can lead to false results (Cronbach, 1947, 1950). Yea-saying, for example, can artificially inflate scores whereas nay-saying can artificially depress scores. Imagine an anxiety scale that asks about which symptoms a person has experienced in the past week. A person with a high score might truly be an anxious person—or he or she might be a yea-sayer.

Response sets can vary by culture. One study found that Canadian and American high school students showed more extreme responding, compared to Japanese and Chinese students, a tendency that correlated with personal ratings of individualism (Chen, Lee, & Stevenson, 1995). Asian students showed more moderate responding. Despite a relationship between culture and response sets, response sets were not strong enough to account for cultural differences in individualism–collectivism scores. As you might expect, North American participants showed more individualism than participants in the Asian cultures.

Test constructors have devised ways of identifying and minimizing response sets. For example, designers might include the statement "I am happy" and its exact opposite "I am not happy" to catch people engaging in acquiescent or reactant responding. A good way to control both kinds of response sets is to write half the items so that a high rating indicates that the responder has the trait and the other half so that a low rating indicates that the responder has the trait (Paulhus & Vazire, 2007). This reverse scoring of some items prevents a person from getting a high score simply by agreeing or disagreeing with each of the items (Wiggins, 1973).

To identify pattern responding researchers might set up computer programs to catch certain patterns. Sometimes researchers will include extremely rare questions to check for pattern or random responses. For example, it would be highly unlikely for a person to agree that he or she were born in Pago-Pago or that he or she recently had a liver transplant (Paulhus & Vazire, 2007). Although any one of these usual items on an **infrequency scale** could be true, a number of such answers suggests that all of a responder's answers are suspicious. Such scales are often called *lie scales* because they are designed to identify a person who is lying.

To work around the problem of extreme responding the Q-sort test (Block, 1961), for example, forces respondents to limit the number of times each response can be used (Paulhus & Vazire, 2007). The 100 items of this test are listed on small cards. Some of the items include "Is a talkative individual," "Is calm, relaxed in manner," and "Feels a lack of personal meaning in life."

Respondents must sort the cards into 1 of 9 piles, representing a 1 to 9 scale, indicating how characteristic of them each statement is. However, respondents must sort a set number of cards into each pile. For example, respondents can choose only 5 items that are the most characteristics of them (pile 9) and 5 items that are the least characteristic of them (pile 1), and 18 in the middle pile indicating that they are neither characteristic nor uncharacteristic of them (pile 5). This forces participants to use the full scale and avoids many types of response sets including extreme responding, moderate responding, acquiescent responding, or reactant responding.

THINK ABOUT IT

What should a researcher do about noncontent responding of a participant?

THINK ABOUT IT

Why do response sets vary by culture?

THINK ABOUT IT

What should a researcher do about a participant who scores high on a lie scale?

Social desirability responding is a bit harder for researchers to control. Sometimes a forced-choice format, where both statements make a person appear equally good, can make it easier for respondents to answer truthfully rather than choose the one that makes them look better than they are (Paulhus, 1991). Another method is to give participants a scale that measures their tendency for socially desirable responding and then use their scores to statistically control for social desirability in the score of interest (Paulhus, 1991).

One such scale is the Crowne-Marlow Social Desirability Scale (Crowne & Marlow, 1960). As you can see in Table 4.10, most people, if they were completely honest, would have to admit that they have intensely disliked someone or have felt resentful. However, some people have a very hard time admitting that they have these all-too-human feelings. These are the kind of people who would score particularly high in social desirability on the Crowne-Marlow scale and are likely to respond in a socially desirable manner to *any* personality questionnaire.

Another way to control for social desirability is to structure the testing situation to minimize the pressure for participants to look good (Paulhus, 1991). This can be done by assuring respondents of anonymity in their responses, physically separating respondents from each other, or having respondents seal their responses in an envelope to be deposited in a box on their way out of the testing room. Sometimes questions can be phrased to appear reasonable so that a person will feel comfortable giving a true answer.

Finally, other researchers suggest that social desirability responding is merely a type of impression management and needs to be treated as a personality difference and not as a response set to be screened our or controlled for (Uziel, 2010).

THINK ABOUT IT

How might social desirability responding invalidate a participant's responses?

Personality Tests and Selection

The area of psychological assessment has a lot to offer the business world. Personality tests, in particular, can be used to aid in selection, training, and performance (Barrick & Mount, 1991; Borman, Hanson, & Hedge, 1997; Hogan et al., 1996; Rothstein & Goffin, 2006).

When psychologists ask if a test works, they look for reliability and validity data: Does the test give consistent results, and does it predict to a criterion in the real world? Employers need to know the same information, but they ask the question differently. According to Hogan et al. (1996), businesses want to know:

Has this test been used in our industry?

Has it been used for Job X?

Can it identify persons who will perform well in Job X?

Will it work in our unique company? (p. 472)

When applying personality testing to the employment situation, we must be careful. Though our tests are not able to predict if a specific employee will be absent on a specific day, say next Tuesday, for example, we can predict how people with *these* characteristics are likely to behave *on average* when it comes to absenteeism or any work behavior (Barrick & Mount,

Table 4.10 Sample Items From the Crowne-Marlow Social Desirability Scale

1. Before voting I thoroughly investigate the qualifications of all the candidates.
2. I never hesitate to go out of my way to help someone in trouble.
3. *It is sometimes hard for me to go on with my work if I am not encouraged.
4. I have never intensely disliked anyone.
5. *I like to gossip at times.
6. *I sometimes feel resentful when I don't get my way.

Note: Respondents answer *True* or *False* to each item. Items with an * are reverse scored. The full test contains 33 items.

Source: Crowne, D. P., & Marlow, D. (1960). A new scale of social desirability independent of psychopathology. *Journal of Consulting Psychology,* 24(4), 349–354.

Personality tests are an important part of job selection for many industries including foreign service, law enforcement, airlines, and even some medical schools.

THINK ABOUT IT

Is it fair to use personality testing to hire and fire people? Why or why not?

1991; Hogan et al., 1996). For example, Openness to experience is a good predictor of how well a person is likely to respond to training, and Conscientiousness is a good predictor of many indexes of performance, including tardiness and absenteeism (Barrick & Mount, 1991). Friendliness, courteousness, responsiveness, and reliability—Agreeableness, Emotional Stability, and Conscientiousness—predict success in customer service positions (Frei & McDaniel, 1998).

Hiring the right person for the right job can save a business millions of dollars each year. According to one industry expert, the cost of recruiting and training a new worker, including productivity loss, equals about 150% of an employee's annual salary (Gale, 2002). In a company with 1,000 employees with an average turnover rate of 10% (considered low for most industries), if the average salary is $50,000 the annual cost of turnover could exceed $7.5 million a year.

Researchers are actively trying to determine the best combination of personality and skills that can predict important job outcomes (Bartram, 2005; Borman et al., 1997). These may include traditional outcomes such as production, sales, turnover, length of service, absenteeism, accidents, theft, and fit between the person and the organization. But more and more, employers around the world are looking to maximize process-oriented outcomes of their personnel including leading and deciding; supporting and cooperating; interacting and presenting; analyzing and interpreting; creating and conceptualizing; organizing and executing; adapting and coping; and enterprising and performing (Bartram, 2005).

According to a 2001 survey (see Table 4.11) close to a third of employers use some form of psychological assessment as part of the hiring process (Society for Industrial and Organizational

Table 4.11 How Many U.S. Companies Use Employment Tests? Percentage of Employers Who …

Test job applicants in basic literacy and/or math skills	41%
Engage in various forms of job skill testing	68
Use one or more forms of psychological measurement or assessment	29
Use cognitive ability tests	20
Use interest inventories	8
Use some form of managerial assessments	14
Use personality tests	13
Use physical simulations of job tasks	10

Note: Information from a 2001 survey of 1,627 human resource managers who are members of the American Management Association.

Source: Society for Industrial and Organizational Psychology (2010).

Psychology, 2010), including mental and physical ability tests, achievement tests, interest measures, work and personal values measures, and personality questionnaires (U.S. Department of Labor Employment and Training Administration, 2006).

One 2006 study found that roughly 20% of companies in the Fortune 1000 use some form of personality testing (Piotrowski & Armstrong, 2006). Further, some 28.5% of companies screen potential employees for honesty and integrity and 22% for potential for violence. Surveys have also found that businesses use personality testing to improve employee fit and to reduce turnover. Indeed, some businesses reported a decrease in turnover ranging from 20% to as much as 70% after personality testing programs were implemented (Rothstein & Goffin, 2006). According to survey of 3,800 employees from seven companies across a variety of industries and jobs, applicants with a combination of the personality characteristics of adaptability, passion for work, emotional maturity, positive disposition, self-efficacy, and an achievement orientation are 14 times more likely than people without these qualities to be engaged and productive employees (Development Dimensions International Inc., 2005).

The use of preemployment personality testing by businesses is currently on the upswing (Rothstein & Goffin, 2006) due to better theoretical constructs, better testing methods, and the power of personality tests to predict job outcomes above and beyond other selection methods (Ones, Dilchert, Viswesvaran, & Judge, 2007; Rothstein & Goffin, 2006). Personality measures that hold to the principles of good test construction discussed throughout this chapter can help predict job performance and enhance fairness in hiring and personnel decisions (Hogan et al., 1996).

Employers can use personality tests to either screen out marginal applicants or to identify exceptional applicants. In either case, the measures they use—whether it be to identify knowledge, attitudes, job skills, or personality—must have proven criterion validity (Hogan et al., 1996).

Businesses may streamline their hiring process when they have many applicants for a large number of openings and need to fill the positions on a continuous basis. In such cases, employers screen out problematic applicants by using measures that predict accidents, absenteeism, turnover, and other **counterproductive work behaviors** (Hogan et al., 1996). For example, New Horizons Computer Learning Centers of Colorado, a small software training company, screened for applicants who were Internet savvy by instructing them to take a test online. If they were unable to navigate their way around the website, New Horizons learned from experience that such a person was not a good fit for the organization. This allowed its recruiters to spend more face-to-face time with applicants who were most likely to succeed (Gale, 2002).

However, if an organization has only a few applicants for a few openings, its goal is to hire excellent applicants rather than screen out marginal ones. Here, it may use personality tests to identify an applicant with characteristics that match the psychological requirements of the job (Hogan et al., 1996). For example, applicants applying for jobs in sales should be extraverted and ambitious (Deb, 1983; Oda, 1983), whereas people in customer service positions should be friendly, stable, and dependable, scoring high in Agreeableness, Emotional Stability, and Conscientiousness of the five factors (Frei & McDaniel, 1998).

For example, the web giant Google is notorious for its creative recruiting programs aimed at identifying the very best programmers, engineers, and mathematicians. In 2004, mysterious ads appeared in the subway system in Cambridge, Massachusetts; in Harvard Square; and along a California Highway in Silicon Valley. One billboard simply read "the first 10-digit prime found in consecutive digits of *e*.com" (NPR, 2004). The ads themselves were actually for job openings, but because the company name didn't appear anywhere on the signs, people had no idea they were looking at recruitment ads for one of the largest and most prestigious tech places to work. Anybody could try, but only the most qualified people succeeded in solving two mathematical puzzles to find the correct website and password (see the photo on page 96) to view the full advertisements and apply for the jobs (see the photo on page 96).

Integrity Testing

According to one estimate, employee theft costs employers over $100 billion worldwide each year (Sauser, 2007). No wonder that about a third of employers use some form of **integrity testing** (Berry, Sackett, & Wiemann, 2007; Ones, Viswesvaran, & Schmidt, 1993; Sackett,

THINK ABOUT IT

What is criterion validity? Why must employment tests have this in order to be legal?

Congratulations. You've made it to level 2. Go to **www.Linux.org** and enter *Bobsyouruncle* as the login and the answer to this equation as the password.

$$f(1) = 7182818284$$
$$f(2) = 8182845904$$
$$f(3) = 8747135266$$
$$f(4) = 7427466391$$
$$f(5) = \underline{\hspace{2cm}}$$

The mysterious billboard led to yet another mathematical puzzle which finally let to another website . . . *Source:* Vox (2004).

Burris, & Callahan, 1989; Sackett & Wanek, 1996). This is where employers test the honesty of job candidates to see if they are likely to steal or cheat. "Strong ethics are critical for our industry," says a senior human relations specialist at Randolph-Brooks Federal Credit Union. "These tellers are handling other people's money" (Gale, 2002).

There are two kinds of integrity tests: overt integrity tests and personality-based measures (Sackett et al., 1989). In **overt** or **clear purpose integrity tests**, responders understand that the intent of the test is to detect honesty. These tests often have two parts, one that directly assesses attitudes toward dishonest behaviors (e.g., "Do you think it's okay to take home pens or envelopes from the office?" "Under what conditions is it acceptable to steal from an employer?"), and a second part that asks about theft and other illegal activities, such as drug use and gambling (e.g., "How often do you take drugs before going to work?" "How often have you let your car insurance lapse?"). Responses on these kinds of overt tests are easy to distort to create a favorable impression or fake good on (Berry et al., 2007).

A more subtle way of assessing integrity is to use **disguised purpose integrity tests**, like personality tests, to assess characteristics related to a range of behaviors including disciplinary problems, violence on the job, absenteeism, tardiness, drug abuse, and theft. Personality dimensions such as reliability, conscientiousness, adjustment, trustworthiness, and sociability consistently predict these kinds of counterproductive behaviors (Ones et al., 1993).

THINK ABOUT IT

Is it ethical to use disguised purpose integrity tests? Is it more ethical to use overt integrity tests? Why?

Success Stories

Psychologists have studied personality assessment in many types of organizations, including Foreign Service (Thayer, 1973; Wiggins, 1973), law enforcement (Bernstein, 1980; Hargrave & Hiatt, 1989), airlines (Butcher, 1994; Hörmann & Maschke, 1996), and even some medical schools (Hojat, Callahan, & Gonnella, 2004; Lumsden, Bore, Millar, Jack, & Powis, 2005; Tyssen

Congratulations.

Nice work. Well done. Mazel tov. You've made it to Google Labs and we're glad you're here.

One thing we learned while building Google is that it's easier to find what you're looking for if it comes looking for you. What we're looking for are the best engineers in the world. And here you are.

As you can imagine, we get many, many resumes every day, so we developed this little process to increase the signal to noise ratio. We apologize for taking so much of your time just to ask you to consider working with us. We hope you'll feel it was worthwhile when you look at some of the interesting projects we're developing right now. You'll find links to more information about our efforts below, but before you get immersed in machine learning and genetic algorithms, please send your resume to us at problem-solver@google.com.

We're tackling a lot of engineering challenges that may not actually be solvable. If they are, they'll change a lot of things. If they're not, well, it will be fun to try anyway. We could use your big, magnificent brain to help us find out.

Some information about our current projects:

- Why you should work at Google
- Looking for interesting work that matters to millions of people?
- http://labs.google.com

. . . where they were finally rewarded with an invitation to apply for a job at Google. *Source:* Vox (2004).

et al., 2007; Urlings-Strop, Stijnen, Themmen, & Splinter, 2009). Ideally, preemployment testing programs should first develop standards of what a successful employee is like by assessing all employees and identifying those characteristics linked to successful job performance. Once criterion validity for an assessment has been established, then employers can use the test to select future employees. Programs following this model are in place at many restaurants, retailers, grocers, and trucking companies including the grocery chain Albertson's, and retailers such as Neiman Marcus and Target (Cha, 2005).

This is precisely what Outback Steakhouse, known for its fun, friendly, and accommodating atmosphere, did. In an industry with high turnover rates of 200% annually, we might wonder how Outback maintains a turnover rate of only 40 to 60% among its approximately 45,000 employees. The key to Outback's success is hiring the right people, thanks to a customized personality assessment program. First, Outback administered a personality test to all of its servers and identified key personality traits such as sympathy, adaptability, gregariousness, sociability, and meticulousness that characterized the typical Outback server. Then, when hiring new servers, as part of a three-phase interview process applicants take a personality test and those who don't fit this mold, scoring below set cutoffs on certain characteristics like compassion and initiative, are cut from consideration (Gale, 2002).

Even Universal Studios Hollywood Theme Park takes its entertainment business seriously (Cha, 2005). Job applicants take a 50-minute online personality assessment and are classified into groups depending on their scores. Applicants scoring in the green range for customer service have an 83% chance of getting hired whereas those in the yellow range have a 16% chance. Those scoring in the red range have only a 1% chance. Then, Universal interviews all applicants in case the assessment is wrong, but recruiter Nathan Giles explained that this almost never happens. Largely as a result of better hiring decisions, customer service and employee retention are up at Universal and theft and absenteeism are down (Cha, 2005).

However, these preemployment testing programs have many critics. For example, the reliability and validity data of their screening tests are not open to scientific scrutiny. Also, disgruntled rejected applicants have posted answer keys on the Internet compromising the validity of the test. There's even a Facebook page against the company that designs and administers these assessment programs for allegedly dehumanizing the workforce! All of this raises questions about the legality of preemployment testing.

Legal Issues

The U.S. government has established a set of uniform guidelines to ensure that employee selection meets federal laws that prohibit discrimination on the basis of race, color, religion, sex, or national origin (Equal Employment Opportunity Commission, Civil Service Commission, Department of Labor, Department of Justice, 1978). According to these guidelines, assessment tests are legal unless they have a disparate impact on disadvantaged groups. Employers must prove that their assessment predicts to job-related tasks or competencies by establishing construct validity. For example, an employer would have to demonstrate that a higher-level mathematics test predicts job success for engineers in order to use such tests to select employees. This is what Google did before it advertised openings in its corporation with the mysterious billboards.

Personality tests may be used to select employees. This is perfectly legal as long as there is evidence that preemployment personality tests identify personality characteristics that are important for successful performance on the job. For example, successful pilots in a European charter airline company scored lower in aggressiveness (impatient, impulsive, distrustful), neuroticism, empathy (affected by other's misfortune, warm-hearted), and higher in vitality (active in sports, robust, looking for physical challenge) than pilots who were dismissed, reevaluated, downgraded, or experienced some other problem in their 3 years of employment (Hörmann & Maschke, 1996).

Research suggests that preemployment integrity testing is valid, useful, and, according to meta-analyses of 665 measures, predictive of who is likely to engage in counterproductive behavior on the job (Ones et al., 1993, 2007). Integrity tests predict supervisors' ratings of job performance; absenteeism; tardiness; and disciplinary problems on the job such as theft, dismissals for theft, and other illegal activities (Ones et al., 1993). At the very least, such tests alert applicants

THINK ABOUT IT

Do preemployment testing programs dehumanize job applicants? Why or why not?

SEE FOR YOURSELF

Have you ever taken a test as part of a job interview? Was it testing, skills, personality, integrity, or something else?

The Personality of Everyday Life

What can they ask you on a job interview?

How old are you? Are you married? Pregnant? A U.S. citizen? What is your ancestry? Your native language? Do you have any disabilities? Do you take prescription drugs? How much do you smoke or drink? Though you might be tempted to answer *any* question a potential employer throws at you in the context of a job interview, these questions may violate privacy laws, equal opportunity laws, or the Americans with Disabilities Act and are therefore illegal for interviewers to ask. What about personality tests?

For example, according to the Americans with Disabilities Act employers cannot ask about disabilities or conduct a medical exam during the selection process. Under this law, employers cannot use a clinical test, such as a depression inventory or the MMPI that can diagnose a mental illness, to screen applicants. However, they can use nonclinical tests, and indeed many do use tests measuring the five factors or other personality traits.

In contrast to clinical tests, which may carry the stigma of mental health, or medical information, which violate privacy laws, well-constructed personality inventories that describe nonclinical populations can actually help people with disabilities, people from disadvantaged groups, or members of groups likely to be unfairly excluded from hiring based on ethnicity, age, gender, disability, and even other characteristics not protected by law but which are known to affect people's judgments such as attractiveness and weight (Hogan et al., 1996). Because of the anonymity granted by many testing situations people who might not present well in a one-on-one interview may be better able to demonstrate their qualifications on a test.

In addition, people do have a right to privacy on selection tests unless an employer can show a compelling need for personal information—again, establishing criterion validity—about an applicant such as in positions where the safety of the public is at stake. Employers must balance a person's right to privacy with their own need to hire competent people who are not a threat to others (Hogan et al., 1996).

So, what should you do if asked one of these questions or if asked to take an integrity test or a personality test? You might ask the interviewer how a question—or a personality test—bears on the requirements of the job (Reeves, 2009). Often, interviewers are merely trying to establish friendly rapport when they inadvertently hit on an illegal question. As a student of personality psychology, knowing about assessment and personality testing makes you a more astute job candidate.

Tests that explicitly screen for characteristics that are important for success on the job are legal. What kind of personality traits make for a successful server?

that a potential employer cares about theft and dishonesty in its workforce](Wanek, 1999). Because the validity of integrity testing to predict job-relevant counterproductive behavior is well established, such tests are allowable by law.

Hogan et al. (1996) cautioned that although personality assessment—when done correctly—is appropriate, employers should evaluate the results along with other information about the applicant including skills, job experience, and ability to learn. Relying solely on personality tests to make hiring decisions may be misguided. A senior human relations specialist at Randolph-Brooks Federal Credit Union explained that when she interviews a job applicant she will ask them about their marginal answers. Because many applicants are just out of high school, they may not understand appropriate behavior in the workplace. Talking with them may clear up their misconceptions (Gale, 2002).

Then and Now: Personality Assessment and Matchmaking

What qualities go into a good marriage? Back in 1939 psychologist George W. Crane devised the Marital Rating Scale to give couples feedback on their marriage (Joyce & Baker, 2008). Husbands or wives would take this test (see Figure 4.2) and rate the wives' behavior. Wives would then score "merits" and "demerits" depending on what they did or didn't do.

For example, using slang or profanity would earn 5 demerits whereas "reacting with pleasure and delight to marital congress" would earn 10 merits. The number of merits and demerits would be tallied up and the wife would receive a score from "Very Poor (Failures)" to "Very Superior." (Alas, we don't know what happened to the husband's rating chart, if Crane ever developed one.)

Crane started out scientifically enough by interviewing 600 husbands on their wives' qualities. He compiled the 50 most frequently mentioned positive and negative qualities and fashioned them into a questionnaire. However, the weighted scoring of the items came from his own personal biases about which qualities he felt were more important to a successful marriage.

Crane went on to establish the Scientific Marriage Foundation in 1957, where he claimed to have arranged over 5,000 marriages by using principles of psychological testing. Men and women filled out forms that were then matched into compatible pairs by using an early computer.

Gender roles and qualities desired in a mate may have changed since Crane's day—and psychologists today view his questionnaire as dated and humorous—but the principle of using psychological testing to match people is even more popular today. Witness the growth of online dating services including Match.com, ScientificMatch.com, PerfectMatch.com, Chemistry.com, and eHarmony.com, all of which use some form of personality assessment.

For example, eHarmony explicitly matches couples based on similarity of attitudes, beliefs, interests, leisure activities, and personality, including stability, sociability, and desire for closeness, using a questionnaire of over 400 items. In fact, it has created a model to predict couple compatibility using advanced statistics including factor analysis, regression analysis, and discriminant analysis. Its goal is to match couples to maximize their compatibilities and minimize their differences on key attributes (Carter & Snow, 2004). In fact, eHarmony has the only patented online matching system (U.S. Patent No. 6,735,568; Houran, Lange, Rentfrow, & Bruckner, 2004).

"Similarities are like money in the bank," said Neil Clark Warren, the founder of eHarmony. "Differences are like debts you owe. It's all right to have a few differences, as long as you have plenty of equity in your account" (Gottlieb, 2006, p. 60).

In the only study publicly available evaluating online dating sites, coincidentally conducted by eHarmony, married couples matched through eHarmony had higher happiness, optimism, commitment, and overall success of their marriage compared to couples who were not matched by eHarmony (Carter & Snow, 2004).

Although the test used to judge how successful couples were is a valid test—the Dyadic Adjustment Scale (Spanier, 1976)—critics have questioned whether high scores on this

"Because if you don't ask it, you're never gonna know. So we had tons of questions on ability, even more on interest. Just every type of personality aspect that was ever measured, we were measuring it all."

Galen Buckwalter, vice president of Research and Development, eHarmony, as quoted in Gottlieb (2006, p. 60)

MARITAL RATING SCALE
WIFE'S CHART
George W. Crane, Ph. D., M. D.
(Copyright 1939)

In computing the score, check the various items under DEMERITS which fit the wife, and add the total. Each item counts one point unless specifically weighted as in the parentheses. Then check the items under MERITS which apply; now subtract the DEMERIT score from the MERIT score. The result is the wife's raw score. Interpret it according to this table:

RAW SCORES	INTERPRETATION
0 — 24	Very Poor (Failures)
25 — 41	Poor
42 — 58	Average
59 — 75	Superior
76 and up	Very Superior

DEMERITS	MERITS
1. Slow in coming to bed — delays till husband is almost asleep.	1. A good hostess—even to unexpected guests.
2. Doesn't like children. (5)	2. Has meals on time.
3. Fails to sew on buttons or darn socks regularly.	3. Can carry on an interesting conversation.
4. Wears soiled or ragged dresses and aprons around the house.	4. Can play a musical instrument, as piano, violin, etc.
5. Wears red nail polish.	5. Dresses for breakfast.
6. Often late for appointments. (5)	6. Neat housekeeper — tidy and clean.
7. Seams in hose often crooked.	7. Personally puts children to bed.
8. Goes to bed with curlers on her hair or much face cream.	8. Never goes to bed angry, always makes up first. (5)
9. Puts her cold feet on husband at night to warm them.	9. Asks husband's opinions regarding important decisions and purchases.
10. Is a back seat driver.	10. Good sense of humor—jolly and gay.
11. Flirts with other men at parties or in restaurants. (5)	11. Religious — sends children to church or Sunday school and goes herself. (10)
12. Is suspicious and jealous. (5)	12. Lets husband sleep late on Sunday and holidays.

Figure 4.2 The cover page of the Marital Rating Scale. *Source:* Joyce and Baker (2008, Figure 1, p. 144).

particular test actually predict a better marriage. They also question whether the test was validated for this purpose or for the age range of participants (Houran et al., 2004).

Finally, the two comparison groups differed in age, education, income, motivation, and other variables (Houran et al., 2004). For example, the couples who met on eHarmony may have been more motivated to see their relationships succeed; after all, they met through an online dating service that promised exactly this outcome for a hefty fee!

Matchmaker, matchmaker: Even online dating services use personality assessment to make matches.

The lesson to be learned from this story is that principles of good research design and good testing—validity, reliability, and generalization—make the best partnerships. In the words of Warren, "Twelve thousand new people a day taking a 436-item questionnaire! . . . We've got more data than they could collect in a thousand years."

Chapter Summary

In this chapter we learned all about personality tests: what makes a good personality test, kinds of personality tests, format of tests, response sets, and the various uses of personality tests.

The biggest difference between real personality tests and fun personality tests you might find on the Internet is that real personality tests have been empirically tested to have reliability, validity, and limited generalizability. Fake personality tests often use Barnum statements to fool people into thinking that they are accurate measures of personality.

Tests, like any good measurement instrument, such as a watch, must be reliable, giving a consistent measure of an underlying theoretical construct. A reliable test will give consistent results across time (temporal consistency reliability, test–retest reliability), across items (internal consistency reliability: parallel-forms reliability, split-half reliability, Cronbach's alpha), and across raters (interrater reliability).

A valid test has construct validity, meaning that it has operationalized a theory, or predicts to an external standard such as an outcome or behavior (criterion validity). Tests may or may not look like they are measuring a specific construct (face validity), but respondents may be more motivated to answer questions that make sense to them and have face validity.

Scores on personality tests ought to be correlated with other measures of similar tests (convergent validity) but be uncorrelated with measures of unrelated constructs (discriminant validity). Tests, are valid only for the uses, settings, and populations they were validated for. Researchers and people using tests must consider the conditions under which tests are generalizable or not. For example, tests may be applicable for adults or children, or for use within a particular culture.

Using these criteria—construct validity, criterion validity, convergent validity, discriminant validity, test–retest reliability, interrater reliability, Cronbach's alpha, generalizability—the NEO-PI-R appears to be a good measure of the five-factor model of personality.

Personality tests can be self-report (objective) or performance-based (projective). Self-report tests may use a Likert scale, checklists, forced-choice, or visual analog scales. The Creative Personality Scale of the Adjective Check List and the Machiavellianism Scale are two kinds of self-report tests. The Thematic Apperception Test and the Goodenough-Harris Draw-A-Person test are two kinds of performance-based tests.

"If you want to know what Waldo is like, why not just ask him?"
Personality researchers Delroy L. Paulhus and Simine Vazire (2007, p. 224)

✓• Study and Review
on **mysearchlab.com**
Go online for more resources to help you review.

When designing, administering, and scoring personality tests, we must be mindful of response sets or noncontent responding of participants including faking good, faking bad, socially desirable responding, acquiescent responding, reactant responding, extreme responding, moderate responding, patterned responding, and carelessness. Some tests include an infrequency or lie scale to identify people who may be purposely giving misleading answers to a test. The Crowne-Marlow Social Desirability Scale can be used to identify people with a socially desirable response set to statistically control for this tendency in their responses on other personality tests.

Businesses often use personality tests to screen applicants for important characteristics related to success on the job or to eliminate applicants who are likely to show counterproductive work behaviors. Integrity testing, using either clear purpose integrity tests or disguised purpose integrity tests, can be used to screen for honesty in job applicants. Legally, a business must be sure that an assessment program does not have disparate impact on any protected group and predicts to job-related tasks or competencies by demonstrating construct validity, content validity, or criterion validity of the test. Medical tests and clinical tests are disallowed, and other questions that may violate the right to privacy are allowed only when an employer can demonstrate a valid need for personal information.

Although valid and reliable personality assessment is useful and appropriate, employers should evaluate the results along with other information about the applicant including skills, job experience, and ability to learn and not rely on testing alone to select potential employees.

Online dating sites often use personality tests to match people. These services are only as good as the measures they use.

Personality assessment has been around for a long time, and continues to be important in research, work, and, for some, their love lives. If you haven't already, no doubt you will be asked to take a personality test for one of these purposes. Understanding what goes into personality testing will help you perform your best and understand the impact of assessment in your life—and to not be taken in by nightclub graphologists, circus showmen, or Oreo-cookie-eating personality tests. Though P. T. Barnum believed that a sucker might be born every minute, you need not be one of them!

Review Questions

1. What is personality assessment? What makes a good personality test?
2. What is reliability? What are the different kinds of reliability?
3. What is validity? What are the different kinds of validity?
4. What is test generalizability?
5. Is the NEO-PI-R a good personality test? Why or why not?
6. What are self-report tests? Describe various test formats used by personality psychologists including dichotomous, Likert ratings, checklists, forced-choice scales, and visual analog scales, giving examples of each.
7. What are performance-based tests? What are the five categories of projective tests?
8. What are response sets? Describe the common types of response sets. What is an infrequency scale? What is it designed to measure?
9. What is social desirability? How it is measured? What are some strategies for dealing with a social desirable response set?
10. What kind of validity must employers demonstrate to legally use personality tests to screen candidates?
11. What are counterproductive work behaviors? How might an employer screen for these? What is integrity testing? How might an employer test for integrity?
12. What are some of the legal issues surrounding employment testing?

Key Terms

Personality assessment
Reliability
Temporal consistency
  reliability
Test–retest reliability
Internal consistency
  reliability
Parallel-forms reliability
Split-half reliability
Cronbach's alpha
Rater consistency
Interrater reliability
Validity
Construct validity
Face validity
Criterion validity

Convergent validity
Discriminant validity
Barnum Effect
Generalizability
Self-report tests
Performance-based tests
Forced-choice format
Association techniques
Construction techniques
Completion techniques
Arrangement or selection
  of stimuli
Expression techniques
Faking good
Faking bad
Socially desirable responding

Acquiescent responding
Reactant responding
Extreme responding
Moderate responding
Patterned responding
Response sets
Noncontent responding
Infrequency scale
Counterproductive work
  behaviors
Integrity tests
Overt integrity tests
Clear purpose integrity tests
Disguised purpose integrity
  tests

5 SELF AND IDENTITY

Read the **Chapter** on
mysearchlab.com

SEE FOR YOURSELF

Who are you? Give 20 answers to the statement "I am …"

SEE FOR YOURSELF

How many of your answers to the Twenty Statements Test were trait terms? Social categories? What does this say about you?

THINK ABOUT IT

Do animals have a sense of self? How would we know?

The web sitcom series *The Guild* stars Felicia Day as a neurotic woman who is addicted—along with five other misfits—to an online role-playing game. In one episode, the 20-something Zaboo is trying to break free from the control of his overbearing mother, who he fears will become an expert on the Internet and ruin his life there too. He laments "The only place that I can be myself is online." The show raises all sorts of questions about reality and identity, like, who are we on the inside and how do we portray ourselves to others? To the extent that these two aspects of our identity are slightly different, we might well wonder, along with the characters in the show, who is the real me, or even the real *you*?

Let's just start with this most basic question: Who are you? On a blank screen or piece of paper, can you think of 20 answers to this question?

This was the exact task facing college students in a classic study. Most of their responses to this **Twenty Statements Test (TST)** (Kuhn & McPartland, 1954) were of the form "I am …" Students gave anywhere from 1 or 2 responses on up to the full 20, with a median of 17 responses. One interesting finding is that the first attributes people listed defined themselves in terms of social groups or categories to which they belonged, such as "student," "girl," " husband," "from Chicago," "daughter," "pre-med," "Baptist," and "oldest child." Only later did they get into more idiosyncratic trait terms such as "happy," "bored," "pretty good student," "good wife," and "interesting."

Additionally, Kuhn and McPartland (1954) found that members of religious minorities at the State University of Iowa at the time (e.g., Catholic and Jewish) were particularly likely to mention religious affiliation as an aspect of their self-concept and to mention it sooner than members of religious majorities (e.g., Methodist, Presbyterian) or people without a religious affiliation.

This study illustrates that our self-concepts are defined by the social world: how we are similar to others and how we are unique compared to others. In fact, we are constantly discovering, creating, defining, and maintaining who we are—emphasizing either our connections or our uniqueness—and how we feel about ourselves through our interactions with the social world. In this chapter we explore these three aspects of the self: how we define or think about ourselves (our self-concepts), how we evaluate or think *of* ourselves (our self-esteem), and what we show to others (our social identity).

Self-Concept

Think about your 20 answers to the question "Who are you?" Together, these reflect your **self-concept:** the set of ideas and inferences that you hold about yourself, including your traits, social roles, schemas, and relationships (Baumeister, 1997). Part of what makes the self hard to know is that we are hardly unbiased observers. We take center stage in our own lives! In addition, the self may be difficult to know because we are constantly growing and developing as well as revealing different facets of ourselves in different situations. In fact, it is through social interactions that we develop both our self-concepts and our evaluation of ourselves.

How Does the Self-Concept Develop?

Do you have a self? Of course you do, but how did you get it? It should be no surprise to you that we aren't exactly born with a self, but you might wonder, how do we develop one? Do we just grow a self even as we grow taller? Or, do we need to have certain experiences in order to form a self? The answer is a bit of both: We develop a sense of self out of physical development and cognitive maturation along with social experiences.

In the 1970s, many psychologists and biologists supposed that humans were unique in their capacity to reflect on themselves. This ability of being aware of having an experience and of reflecting on oneself—having self-awareness or self-consciousness—is believed to be evidence of having a self-concept. Is it true that this ability is unique to humans?

Chimpanzees and Self-Recognition. Psychologist Gordon Gallup investigated this question in a series of experiments with chimpanzees (Gallup, 1977). He placed a full-length mirror in a room with a chimpanzee and observed how the chimp responded to this mirror stimulation. For the first 1 or 2 days, the chimps acted as if the reflection were another chimp, showing other-directed social responses such as bobbing, vocalizing, and threatening, much the way a chimp would respond when confronting a strange chimp in the wild. However, very soon the chimps started to respond to the reflection in the mirror with *self*-directed responses: grooming places they couldn't normally see (e.g., picking food out of their teeth), entertaining themselves by blowing bubbles or making faces, and so on. But after about 10 days, the chimps grew tired of this sport and adapted to the presence of the mirror. This is when the real test began.

At this point, the mirror was removed, the chimps were anesthetized, and while they were unconscious, bright red paint was placed across the eyebrow ridge of one eye and on the top half of the opposite ear. The researchers used a special paint that was odorless and imperceptible to the touch. Indeed, upon waking, the chimps did not pay any special attention to the newly marked areas. Then the mirror was returned to their chamber. How do you think chimps responded to their own reflections? Would they show other-directed responses (e.g., vocalize at the mirror) or would chimps touch *their own* brow and ear indicating self-recognition?

The man in the mirror: Until about 1 or 2 years of age babies do not recognize the reflection in the mirror as themselves.

As it turned out, chimps spent over 25% more time touching *themselves!* And they spent about twice as much time touching their eyebrows than their ears. However, chimps that did not have the chance to adapt to the mirror did not pay any more attention to the marked areas of their bodies than to the nonmarked areas. This suggests that self-recognition must have been learned during their earlier experience with the mirror.

Gallup and others saw chimps' self-directed behaviors in this **mirror test** as evidence of self-recognition. It is no accident that great apes like chimpanzees and orangutans—humans' closest relatives—show self-recognition. There is no evidence of self-recognition in rhesus monkeys, capuchin monkeys, java monkeys, spider monkeys, mandrill, hamadryas, baboons, stumptail macaques, or two species of gibbons (Gallup, 1977). Self-recognition seems to be more than visual recognition: Baboons could not be trained to recognize themselves even using raisins as rewards. Nor is self-recognition related to mirror use per se. Monkeys are able to use the mirror as a tool to manipulate and find objects but are unable to recognize their own reflections.

Happy, the elephant, at the mirror touching the mark with the tip of her trunk.

Self-recognition in a dolphin.

(Brown, McDowell, & Robinson, 1965). Using similar, or even improved, methods self-recognition has been demonstrated in elephants (Plotnik, de Waal, & Reiss, 2006), dolphins (Reiss & Marino, 2001), whales (Delfour & Marten, 2001), and even magpies (Prior, Schwarz, & Güntürkün, 2008)! The photos on pages 107 and 108 illustrate what this self-recognition in animals might look like.

Now you might think that there is something special about chimps who have spent their entire lives living in a psychology laboratory, but on this count, even chimps raised in the wild show self-recognition on the mirror test (Gallup, 1977). However, chimps who are taken from their mothers soon after birth and raised in isolation without contact with other chimps are *unable* to recognize themselves. In fact, at first they pretty much just sit and stare at their reflection in the mirror, never becoming adapted to it. When they are anesthetized and marked with the red paint they show no change in viewing time, suggesting that they have no idea that it is their own reflection in the mirror.

Gallup and his colleagues suspected that lack of social experience with other chimps somehow prevented proper emotional development including self-recognition. He gave two of these isolated chimps remedial social experience by placing them in a cage with each other for 3 months. When these chimps were placed before the mirror with paint markings, they started to show preliminary signs of self-recognition.

Who Is That Baby in the Mirror?   What about humans? At what age do human babies recognize that the image in the mirror is themselves? Self-recognition is one step along the way to self-concept development. But to appreciate the import of this developmental landmark, we need to start at the beginning of self-concept development. Table 5.1 summarizes the processes and major accomplishments of self-concept development (for more detail see Harter, 1998, 2003).

Table 5.1 How We Develop a Sense of Self: Important Milestones in the Development of Self-Concept, Self-Esteem, and Social Identity

Age	Developing Aspect of Self	Accomplishment
0–1 years	Physical self-awareness	Recognizing *Me* vs. *Not me*
1–2 years	Self-recognition	Mirror recognition
2–3 years	Self-esteem	Internalizing standards for behavior
3–4 years	Skills and abilities	Demonstrating new talents
5–12 years	Social comparison	Comparing abilities with others
	Private self-concept	Keeping secrets
Adolescence	Identity	Abstract thought
		Reflected appraisals
		Objective self-awareness
Adulthood	The self	Internalizing societal expectations

From birth to about 1 year of age infants are developing a sense of physical awareness. Rather than having an awareness of themselves in the world, they are still trying to discern what is part of them and what is part of the physical environment. If you have watched young infants in their cribs perhaps you've seen their momentary surprise and delight at a foot or an arm without the full recognition that it is their own limbs that are moving in such fascinating ways. Although there is some evidence that even newborns react differently to a recording of their own cry compared to the cry of another infant (Dondi, Simion, & Caltran, 1999)—indicating some basic self-recognition—an infant's self is really just a physical self (Meltzhoff, 1990).

Once children know that they are a physical being separate from other people and other objects, then they can begin to find out more about themselves (Harter, 1983). Have you ever tried the look-at-the-crying-baby-in-the-mirror trick to get an infant to calm down? Sadly, that "trick" works only until children recognize a familiar image in the mirror at around 4 or 5 months (Legerstee, Anderson, & Schaffer, 1998). But is this merely visual discrimination or do they really know that the image is them?

If you were thinking that we ought to do the mirror test to test for self-recognition, much like Gallup (1977) did with his chimpanzees, you would be right. When a spot of rouge is placed on an infant's nose by the mother, under the guise of wiping the infant's nose, infants are able to recognize themselves in a mirror at 18 months of age, on average. They touch their own faces and wonder at this new mark. Only about 25% of infants tested could recognize themselves as early as 9 to 12 months of age, yet by the age of 21 to 25 months about 75% of infant-participants could recognize themselves in the mirror (Lewis & Brooks-Gunn, 1979).

By ages 2 or 3, children are able to recognize themselves in the mirror and in pictures and have mastered language enough to use the words "I," "me," "my," "mine," and the phrase "I'm . . ." appropriately (Lewis & Ramsay, 2004). Perhaps a little too appropriately, as this baby sense of self is partially what makes the "terrible twos" so challenging. Children will often want to exercise their developing selves by doing things without parental help or by refusing to cooperate amid protests of "No!" Children at this age know certain facts about themselves such as their sex, age, ethnic group, and family, and their self-concepts reflect this information (Stipek, Gralinski, & Kopp, 1990).

Around this age we also see the very beginnings of self-esteem. Children start to understand parents' expectations for behavior and begin to internalize standards for good and bad behavior. They will often voluntarily offer that they are "a good girl" or respond positively to such praise ("good boy!") from an adult.

By ages 3 to 4 children's self-concepts reflect their developing skill and abilities in addition to physical attributes, preferences, and possessions (Harter, 1999). Children will often enthusiastically run up to visitors wishing to show off their latest accomplishments: "Look at me! I can jump!"

The Developing Self in School.   During ages 5 to 12 children are further developing their own abilities and at the same time becoming acutely aware of the abilities of other children as they enter school. Have you ever seen kids at a park run to the top of a hill and vie for the chance to declare "I'm king of the mountain!" Comparing themselves with peers becomes very important between ages 5 and 6 and becomes increasingly important (Ruble, 1983). Children gain a sense of their own talents by seeing how they measure up compared to others (Harter, 2005).

As early as ages 3 or 4 children recognize personality characteristics and can use them to describe other children. However, it is not until they are about 5 or 6 that children may further progress and come to describe kids in their class using personality attributes in addition to social comparison information. "He's the smart one." They may even be able to use traits to judge the past behavior of others as well as to make predictions about their future behavior. Imagine a child not wanting to invite another child to a birthday party because "she's a baby." Why is she a baby? "She cried in school yesterday." But it is not until ages 9 or 10 that children

> **THINK ABOUT IT**
>
> What is a 2-year old's favorite word?

The queen and kings of the mountain: At about ages 5 to 12, children's self-concept includes comparing their abilities with others.

SEE FOR YOURSELF

Did you have an imaginary friend as a child? How old were you at the time?

come to understand what a trait is and recognize traits as enduring qualities within a person that are stable across time and situations (Alvarez, Ruble, & Bolger, 2001).

Also between ages 5 to 12 children start to develop a private sense of self as they recognize that there are parts of themselves that others cannot see. They start to realize that they have thoughts, feelings, and desires that are uniquely their own and not automatically known by others. At younger ages this may appear as an imaginary friend. At a slightly older age the child may taunt another child with "I know something you don't know." Later, children realize that they can keep a secret as in "I know a secret." Of course, they won't realize until they are older that to truly keep a secret you cannot even tell that you know a secret!

Consider this response of a 5-year-old girl to the Twenty Statements Test:

> *My name is Lizzie. I look like my mommy. I play a lot in the summer time with my grandparents. I like to play at the beach. I have brown hair. My eyes are blue. My teeth are white. I like to eat. I'm a girl. I like my hair. I like my eyes. I like my teeth. I like everything I do. I am five years old. (Yavari, 2002).*

Or this 9-year-old boy, with his original spellings and emphasis:

> *My name is Bruce C. I have brown eyes. I have brown hair. I have brown eyebrows. I'm nine years old. I LOVE! Sports. I have seven people in my family. I have great! eye site. I have lots! of friends. I live on 1923 Pinecrest Dr. I'm going on 10 in September. I'm a boy. I have an uncle that is almost 7 feet tall. My school is Pinecrest. My teacher is Mrs. V. I play Hockey! I'am almost the smartest boy in the class. I LOVE! food. I love fresh air. I LOVE School. (Montemayor & Eisen, 1977, p. 317).*

Can you see how his self-description is very concrete? Compare Lizzie's and Bruce's responses with this one from an 11-year-old boy:

> *I'm a person who likes to look in space; I love astronomy. I love using rockets. I love playing outside and playing soccer. I love to swim. I'm smart. I'm a nice and sweet and loving person. I'm a great swimmer. (Yavari, 2002)*

Or this one from an 11.5-year-old girl:

> *My name is A. I'm a human being. I'm a girl. I'm a truthful person. I'm not pretty. I do so-so in my studies. I'm a very good cellist. I'm a very good pianist. I'm a little bit tall for my age. I like several boys. I like several girls. I'm old-fashioned. I play tennis. I am a very good swimmer. I try to be helpful I'm always ready to be friends with anybody. Mostly I'm good, but I lose my temper. I'm*

not well-liked by some girls and boys. I don't know if I'm liked by boys or not.
(Montemayor & Eisen, 1977, p. 317–318)

Adolescence and the Looking Glass Self. By the time we are adolescents, our self-concepts have become more abstract, incorporating motivations, beliefs, and personality characteristics in contrast to the more concrete descriptions of children's self-concepts (Harter, 1999). You can see this difference in the response by this 16-year-old male to the Twenty Statements Test:

> *I guess I would say I'm God's creation made for a purpose. I have a natural curiosity given to me by God. I have a strong will and desire to fulfill my purpose in life and I also believe that as a man I have my weaknesses and strengths. I sin and make mistakes, but I learn from them with God's help. As a Christian, I think that I am better prepared for the world's temptations and societies' manipulations. I am trying to strive for goals, which are to be successful, intelligent, spiritual, and happy. I think that my relationship with God helps me to accomplish my goals and fulfill my purpose in life. Who I am as a person is defined by my spiritual nature.* (Yavari, 2002)

And in this 17-year-old female:

> *I am a human being. I am a girl. I am an individual. I don't know who I am. I am a Pisces. I am a moody person. I am a very curious person. I am not an individual. I am a loner. I am an American (God help me). I am a Democrat. I am a liberal person. I am a radical. I am a conservative. I am a pseudoliberal. I am an atheist. I am not a classifiable person (i.e., I don't want to be).* (Montemayor & Eisen, 1977, p. 318)

Adolescents, especially ages 15 to 16, are particularly sensitive to how they are perceived and judged by others. This becomes a period of extreme self-consciousness, as anybody who's ever had a pimple can attest to! Adolescents experience **objective self-awareness** (Duval & Wicklund, 1972), as they start to see themselves as the object of others' attentions. They use the views of significant others as a social mirror to form the basis of their own self-views. Through these **reflected appraisals** adolescents internalize others' evaluations of them, especially people who are very important to them, such as family and peers. The American sociologist Charles Cooley (1902) calls this the **looking glass self** and this forms the basis of the adolescent's self-esteem. In the words of Ralph Waldo Emerson: "Each to each a looking-glass/Reflects the other that doth pass."

By the time the teenage years have ended, we not only respond to ourselves from the point of view of a particular person, but we also are able to respond to the views of a number of others. We combine these views and come to internalize the view of "the generalized other" (i.e. society; Mead, 1925).

We start to wonder during our teens about our place in society. We start to question our identities. An **identity** is socially defined. It includes definitions and standards that are imposed on us by others, including interpersonal aspects (e.g., roles, relationships), potentialities (e.g., who we might become), and values (e.g., morals, priorities) (Baumeister, 1986). People have identities from birth (Baumeister, 1997), but they may not be aware of their import until the teen years. That is, we may start to wonder if our ascribed identity matches what we've developed and recognize as our own unique self-concept.

Consider the following poem by a 13-year-old girl (Santana, 2005) struggling with the various identities she imagines people placing on her:

SEE FOR YOURSELF

What identity or identities are imposed on you and which have you willingly embraced?

The Girl

> *I am the girl who sits on her roof, who wishes she could fly*
> *free, fly free from the*
> *prison cell she lives in*

> *I am the girl that most fear, whose reputation was forged on*
> *terror.*

*I am the girl who tries her best, but people think she doesn't
try her best, who tries to be
but fails miserably.*

*I am the girl who you wouldn't know with a pen, whose
weapon of choice isn't the
one that draws blood, but the weapon that can leave a bigger
mark: WORDS*

*I am the girl who wears a disguise, who fools you on who she
really is.*
*What if I wasn't the girl who sits on her roof, who wishes she
could fly free?*
*What if I wasn't the girl whose reputation was forged on
terror, the one who most feared?*
*What if I wasn't the girl who tries her best, whom no one
thinks tries?*
*What if I wasn't the girl you would need a pen to know, who
didn't make her first
weapon of choice be words?*
What if I wasn't the girl who always wears a disguise?

*But I'm not that girl. If I was then I wouldn't be me, I'd just
be another face in the crowd.
So let's go back to the beginning,
When all you knew was that,
I am a girl.*

Source: "The Girl" by Santana, © 2005 in A. C. of Princeton (Ed.), Under age (Vol. 17, p. 16–17). Princeton, NJ: Arts Council of Princeton.

Many people believe, much as the psychologist Erik Erikson did, that an **identity crisis** in adolescence is inevitable, universal, and perfectly normal (Erikson, 1968). However, this popular view is not supported by current research evidence (see Baumeister, 1997, for a complete discussion). For example, only teens who openly question the beliefs, values, and goals of their parents may experience an identity crisis as they experience a great deal of confusion and anxiety over who they are and who they wish to be. For such teens, the choice is to either embrace these expectations or to form their own identity that is true to their self-concepts and yet satisfies the expectations of their social worlds. Other teens embrace their identity and do not experience a crisis.

Our Grown-Up Selves. As adults, we have for the most part a good sense of who we are (our self-concepts) and how we feel about ourselves (our self-esteem), and we can choose who we want to be or what aspects of ourselves we wish to present to others (social identity). Terms such as "wife," "bread-winner," "father," and "future doctor" are all social identities that may also be part of one's self-concept. The difference is that self-concept comes from within and identity comes from others (Baumeister, 1997). For example, some people may not fully embrace their new identity as a college student and may struggle to balance their studies

Starting at age 12, adolescents start to develop objective self-awareness and become concerned about how they appear to others.

and the expectations of parents and professors with their own desires or the expectations of friends. Similarly, people may impose identities on us—"Black man," "old woman," "disabled kid"—based on certain attributes without knowing who we really are on the inside.

Consider this poem from a 30-something woman (Missuz J, n.d.). Can you see what social identities she is alluding to?

> *I Am From ...*
> *I am from pink spongy curlers in my hair every Saturday night, for princess*
> *   hair on Sunday.*
> *I am from days in the car—writing letters on crackers in squeeze cheese,*
> *   playing and fighting and sitting.*
> *I am from job lists and sharing a room and "borrowing" my sisters clothes.*
> *I am from salt smells and waves and fog; and naked red rock and juniper*
> *   and sage.*
> *I am from The Mists of Avalon, The Red Tent, The Blue Sword, and*
> *   Dragonsinger.*
> *I am from a religion that spread guilt like cheap margarine.*
> *I am from the thrill and the burn, the laughter and hunger and sometimes*
> *   the truth.*
> *I am from long sticky nights on the couch, filled with kisses, Cheers and Taxi.*
> *I am from stony silence, and fighting it out, and talking it out, and loving*
> *   it out.*
> *I am from stretch marks and breast pumps and diapers and a baby bouncing*
> *   on my hip.*
> *I am from Funshine Bear and big girl panties and Twinkle Twinkle Little Star.*
> *I am from South Beach and Atkins and Phentemine and bulimia.*
> *I am from crying with Mandy, playing with Katy, singing with Kodie, dancing*
> *   with Jennifer, and regretting with Kelli.*
> *I am from apostrophes, settings, topic sentences, and make-up work.*
> *I am from driving with Janzen, reading to Sophie, and Erik holding my hand.*

Source: Reprinted courtesy of Rebecca Jorgensen.

"Missuz J" is a blogger who writes about being a mom, wife, teacher, sister, and woman, as well as an individual. She readily embraces all of these identities and integrates them into her self. This post was from November 2005 and was inspired by a writing assignment she gave her high school students.

Depending on the culture that we live in—and on our own characteristics—we may have an easier or a harder time embracing our identity (Aronson & Rogers, 2008; Cass, 1979; Cross & Cross, 2008; Helms, 1990; Swanson, Cunningham, Youngblood, & Spencer, 2009; Swartz, 2008). We may hold certain ethnic, racial, gender, sexual, or class identities that may be at odds with the dominant culture. For example, people who are made aware of their membership in a stereotyped group may be unable to perform up to their potential as a result of **stereotype threat**. This is when a person experiences distress when faced with a stereotype that threatens his or her self-esteem or social identity. This apprehension then causes the person's performance to suffer, which ends up confirming the very stereotype he or she felt threatened by (Aronson, Lustina, Good, Keough, & Steele, 1999; Aronson, Quinn, & Spencer, 1998; Aronson & Rogers, 2008; Steele & Aronson, 1995; Steele, Spencer, & Aronson, 2002; Walton & Spencer, 2009). One need not believe the stereotype—or an ascribed social identity—to feel upset by it (Aronson & Rogers, 2008). However, new research suggests that writing about things that are important such as creativity, family relationships, career, or having a sense of humor may counteract this effect by reinforcing a person's values and individuality (Miyake et al., 2010).

Impact of Culture on Self-Concepts

As should be clear to you by now, we develop our selves—our self-concepts, self-esteem, and social identities—by using three sources of knowledge: social comparison with others, the

SEE FOR YOURSELF

Do you currently struggle with aspects of your identity?

"The fact that everyone can use the term 'self' with such ease and familiarity suggests that the concept of selfhood is rooted in some simple, universal human experience."
Baumeister (1999, pp. 1–2)

Table 5.2 Coding Scheme for the Twenty Statements Test

Category	Description	Examples
Physical	Physical qualities without implying social roles or group membership such as the information you might find on a driver's license	"I am a male" "I am 18 years old" "I am short"
Social	Social roles, institutional memberships, socially defined status	"I am a student" "I am a mother" "I am Jewish"
Attributive	Psychological and physiological states or traits	"I am a warm person" "I am a high energy person" "I am introverted"
Global	Descriptions so comprehensive or so vague that they do not distinguish that person from any other	"I am a human being" "I am light" "I am me"

Source: Cousins (1989, p. 126).

reflected appraisals of others, and our own self-appraisals. The self is very much the product of social interaction, in addition to cognitive developments (Harter, 2003). Given this, do you wonder how you might be different if you were born at a different time? What if you were born in a different place? As strange as it may seem at first, who we are depends a lot on the culture we are born into.

Recall the Twenty Statements Test (TST) discussed in the study that opened this chapter (Kuhn & McPartland, 1954). One way of scoring the test is to classify participants' responses into one of four categories (Cousins, 1989; see Table 5.2). With this standardized scoring scheme we can compare the responses of people from various cultures to see if there are differences in self-concepts across cultures.

In one study, Japanese and American college students answered the TST and their answers were sorted into one of the four categories by three trained judges (Cousins, 1989). About 58% of the responses of the American students fell into the **Attributive self-description** category, referring to their own psychological attributes or traits, whereas for Japanese students Attributive descriptions made up significantly less, about 19% of their total responses (see Figure 5.1). When Japanese students did refer to themselves, it was generally to their preferences, interests, wishes, aspirations, activities, and habits more so than to their personal traits.

Figure 5.1 Mean proportion of psychological attributes endorsed by American and Japanese students in the two self-description tasks of Cousins (1989). *Source:* (Markus & Kitayama, 1991, Figure 3, p. 233. Markus, H. R., & Kitayama, S. (1991). Culture and the self: Implications for cognition, emotion and motivation. *Psychological Review,* 98(2), 224–253. Copyright American Psychological Association. Reprinted with permission.

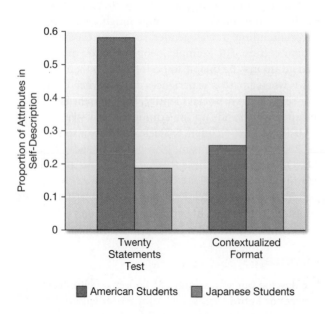

If they weren't describing themselves using Attributive or trait descriptions, how did the Japanese students define themselves? They described themselves in terms of the social groups to which they belonged. About 27% of the Japanese students' responses fell into the **Social self-descriptions** category compared to only 9% of the American students' responses. Japanese students were also more likely to refer to **Physical self-descriptions** (5%) than American students (2%). Interestingly, similar results were found when comparing Chinese and American college students (Trafimow, Triandis, & Goto, 1991), in that the Chinese students were more likely to describe themselves in social ways and the American students in attributive ways.

Individualism and Collectivism.   What is it about Japan and China that lead to similar self-descriptions by their natives that are very different from the self-descriptions of Americans? In a word: culture. According to psychologist Harry Triandis (1990), cultures may be described along two dimensions: individualism and collectivism. The extent to which cultures emphasize individualism and collectivism actually affects how people define their very selves!

Individualism focuses on the uniqueness of the individual and distinguishes the person as separate from the group. Under individualism, people develop their own selves including attitudes and values as distinct from the group's. Individualistic cultures place a value on bravery, creativity, and self-reliance (Triandis, 1990).

Collectivism places greater emphasis on the views, needs, and goals of the group rather than of the individual. Under collectivism, people emphasize being part of a social group and sharing beliefs and customs. In the extreme, one's beliefs, goals, attitudes, and values reflect those of the group. Collectivistic cultures value obligation, duty, security, tradition, dependence, harmony, obedience to authority, equilibrium, and proper action (Triandis, 1990).

Keep in mind that every culture has both individualistic and collectivistic components. Think of collectivism and individualism like water and ice. Instead of being opposites, they are two different states of the same substance (Triandis, 1990). Like water, we are connected to others, especially when we are young and dependent on family. However, as we grow we may separate ourselves and become individuals or nuclear families or social groups, much like ice crystals forming out of the water. Just as water may be turned into ice and ice can melt into water, we can form and dissolve social bonds with others. Cultures differ in the extent to which one state is emphasized over the other.

Cultures that emphasize individualism are considered **individualistic cultures;** cultures that emphasize collectivism are considered **collectivistic cultures.** About 80% of the world's population live in collectivistic cultures (e.g., Africa, Asia, South America; Dwairy, 2002). In Japan, for example, people value *wa,* the harmonious ebb and flow of interpersonal relations. Similarly, the Chinese have *jen,* the ability to interact with others in a sincere, polite, and decent fashion. Latinos talk of being *simpático* with each other, which means to both respect and share another's feelings (Markus & Kitayama, 1991).

Cultures may have developed to be more collectivistic or more individualistic due to cultural complexity, ecology, mobility (both social and geographic), and affluence (Triandis, 1990). As cultures become more complex, individuals must choose how to act from among conflicting norms and diverse worldviews. Without a clear culturally defined norm for behavior, people are forced to choose based on their own internal values and desires. Similarly, cultural complexity increases as the range of possible jobs within a society increases, forcing people to specialize rather than just do what everybody else does. Complexity also increases as people move from rural to urban settings. Together, these trends push a culture toward individualism.

Individualism also increases when a country's geography forces a separation among its people (e.g., mountains, islands) or when individuals have migrated to distant lands (e.g., Great Britain). This distance among members of a culture forces them to make individual choices, fostering individualism in the culture. Triandis (1990) suggested that democracy was born in ancient Greece because its geography of mountains and islands dispersed the population, forcing cities—and individuals living in the cities—to develop their own governments and ways of doing things. Finally, with affluence, individuals are less dependent on the group for survival and are free to cultivate their own interests.

How do these differing themes of individualism and collectivism play out in a culture? For example, in the United States, a place where individualism reigns, we tend to say "The squeaky wheel gets the grease" encouraging people to stand up for their rights. What do they say in Japan? "The nail that stands out gets pounded down," to encourage getting along with others and placing the harmony of the group above individual rights. Or, when you were growing up, what did your parents say to cajole you into eating your vegetables? Often, it was some variation of "Think of starving kids in Ethiopia, and appreciate how lucky you are." What do Japanese kids hear from their parents? "Think of the farmer who worked so hard to produce this rice for you; if you don't eat it he will feel bad, for his efforts will have been in vain" (Markus & Kitayama, 1991, p. 224). These cultural values are also reflected in literature and cartoons.

Or, consider having a friend over for lunch. In the United States we would either ask our guest what he would like to have or we would have a range of available foods and flavors so that he could make a choice that reflects his personal preferences. What might happen in Japan? For one, a good host wouldn't come out and ask her guest what she would want. That would be considered rude! Instead, she would anticipate—even read the mind of—her guest and prepare just the right food (Markus & Kitayama, 1991). Speaking up, not speaking up, eating what's put in front of you, no wonder we experience discomfort while trying to figure out what the polite thing to do or say is while interacting with someone from a different cultural background!

Independent and Interdependent Selves.   As a result of the contrasting emphasis placed on the individual person compared to the group under individualism and collectivism, people come to think of themselves differently. In individualistic cultures people develop an independent view of the self, whereas people living in collectivistic cultures develop an interdependent view of the self (Markus & Kitayama, 1991).

An independent self exists apart from other people and is autonomous and self-contained. Individuals are encouraged to embark on a process of self-actualization and self-discovery to develop their potential. People are their truest selves when alone, apart from the influence of others. In contrast, the interdependent self includes others. People cannot be understood when separated from their social group (e.g., family, friends, clan, coworkers, etc.); they are not truly themselves without others (Markus & Kitayama, 1991). However, this does not mean that a person with an interdependent self merges, or loses himself or herself with others or that the person is passive when interacting with others. These two views of the self are illustrated in Figure 5.2.

These two views of the self lead to differences in the demands that society places on people in their respective cultures. There are also differences in what role others take in our lives. Even the basis of healthy self-esteem depends on our view of the self and the culture to which we belong. Keep in mind that well-being and self-esteem come from attaining culturally valued outcomes, so that neither individualism nor collectivism is better than the other (Oyserman, Coon, & Kemmelmeier, 2002). You can see these differences for yourself in Table 5.3, and reflected in items from a scale measuring individualism and collectivism in Table 5.4.

An independent self is likely to be found in more individualistic cultures like American and western European (Markus & Kitayama, 1991) and also Canadian (Oyserman, Coon, & Kemmelmeier, 2002). An interdependent self is likely to be found in more collectivistic cultures like Asian, African, Latin American, and southern European (Markus & Kitayama, 1991). Of course, we need to be careful not to overgeneralize or to assume we know a person's self view based on his or her culture, as there are many cultures and countries that have not been directly tested (Oyserman, Coon, & Kemmelmeier, 2002) and people can define themselves as independent or interdependent—regardless of their culture—depending on the task (Oyserman & Lee, 2008; Trafimow et al., 1991).

In countries with very strong ethnic or religious identification, people may develop an interdependent self despite living in an individualistic culture. For example, in the United States, Hawaiians, Quakers, African Americans, Latinos, and women—not to mention Italians and others of southern European ancestry or people living in small towns and rural areas—may have a more

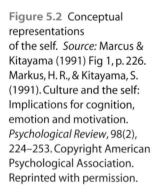

SEE FOR YOURSELF

Answer the questions in Table 5.4. Are you more individualistic or collectivistic? How do these values impact your self-concept and self-esteem? You may wish to reflect on Table 5.3 for features to think about.

Figure 5.2 Conceptual representations of the self. *Source:* Marcus & Kitayama (1991) Fig 1, p. 226. Markus, H. R., & Kitayama, S. (1991). Culture and the self: Implications for cognition, emotion and motivation. *Psychological Review,* 98(2), 224–253. Copyright American Psychological Association. Reprinted with permission.

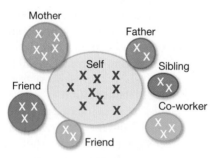

A. Independent View of Self

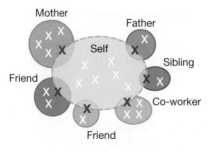

B. Interdependent View of Self

Table 5.3 Summary of Key Differences Between an Independent and an Interdependent Self

Feature Compared	Independent Self	Interdependent Self
Definition	Separate from social context	Connected with social context
Structure	Bounded, unitary, stable	Flexible, variable
Important features	Internal, private (abilities, thoughts, feelings)	External, public (statuses, roles, relationships)
Tasks	Be unique Express self Realize internal attributes Promote own goals Be direct: "say what's on your mind"	Belong, fit in Occupy one's proper place Engage in appropriate action Promote others' goals Be indirect: "read other's mind"
Role of others	*Self-evaluation:* others important for social comparison, reflected appraisal	*Self-definition:* relationships with others in specific contexts define the self
Basis of self-esteem	Ability to express self, validate internal attributes	Ability to adjust, restrain self, maintain harmony with social context

Note: Esteeming the self may be primarily a Western phenomenon, and the concept of self-esteem should perhaps be replaced by self-satisfaction, or by a term that reflects the realization that one is fulfilling the culturally mandated task. *Source:* (Marcus & Kitayama, 1991, Table 1, p. 230. Marcus, H. R., & Kitayama, S. (1991). Culture and the self: Implications for cognition, emotion and motivation. Psychological Review, 98(2), 224–253. Copyright American Psychological Association. Adapted with permission.

interdependent sense of self (Markus & Kitayama, 1991) as do many people living in the southern United States (Vandello & Cohen, 1999). As you can see, it would be a mistake to overgeneralize and assume that *all* Americans have an independent self!

In fact, some have claimed that earlier generations of Americans, say in the 1950s to 1960s, were more likely to describe themselves using social roles, much like the Japanese and Chinese college students of more recent times (Zurcher, 1977). This shifting of American self-concept from collectivistic to individualistic parallels the social upheavals of the 1960s to 1970s including the assassination of President John F. Kennedy, the civil rights movement, the Vietnam War, the women's rights movement, and the Watergate scandal of President Richard Nixon. What have sociologists named the generation that came of age during this time of individual rights and distrust of social institutions like government? The Me generation!

> **THINK ABOUT IT**
>
> Are today's college students more likely to describe themselves using trait terms or social terms? Why?
> Do you think this is likely to change in the near future?

Table 5.4 Selected Items Measuring Individualism and Collectivism

Individualism

In the end, achievements define the man/woman.

A mature person knows his/her abilities and acts to obtain maximum utility from them.

A man/woman of character attempts to act on his/her values and attain his/her goals without depending on others.

A man/woman of weak character forms his opinions in consultation with his/her friends.

I feel uncomfortable if I find I am very similar to the others in my group.

Collectivism

A mature person understands that he/she must act in accordance with the honor of the group.

A man/woman of character helps his/her group before all else.

A mature person understands the needs of the group and acts to fulfill them.

What is good for my group is good for me.

Without group loyalty there is no self-actualization.

Note: Questions were answered on a 5-point scale from 1 = *strongly disagree* to 5 = *strongly agree*.

Source: Adapted from Oyserman (1993, Table 1. p. 9). See Brewer and Chen (2007) for a review of various measures of individualism and collectivism. Reprinted with permission from Oyserman, D., Terry, K., & Bybee, D. (2002), "A possible selves intervention to enhance school involvement," *Journal of Adolescence*, 25, 313–326. Permission conveyed through the Copyright Clearance Center.

Possible Selves

According to modern-day psychologists, an important aspect of our self-concepts encompasses our hopes—and fears—of what we might become. For example, **hoped-for selves** might include the successful self, the creative self, the rich self, the thin self, or the loved and admired self. **Feared selves** might be the alone self, the depressed self, the incompetent self, the alcoholic self, the unemployed self, or the bag lady self. These images of our **possible selves** help us choose our aspirations, maintain motivation, and provide continuity in our self-concepts over time (Markus & Nurius, 1986).

A quote from William James stated (1890):

> *Not that I would not, if I could, be both handsome and fat and well dressed, and a great athlete, and make a million a year, be a wit, a* bon-vivant, *and a lady-killer, as well as a philosopher; a philanthropist, statesman, warrior, and African explorer, as well as a "tone-poet" and saint. . . . Such different characters may conceivably at the outset of life be alike possible to a man. But to make any one of them actual, the rest must more or less be suppressed. So the seeker of his truest, strongest, deepest self must review the list carefully, and pick out the one on which to stake his salvation. All other selves thereupon become unreal, but the fortunes of this self are real. . . . [We] . . . choose . . . one of many possible selves or characters [to become].* (pp. 309–310)

Possible selves also help us make sense out of our current experiences, as they give us a context to evaluate and interpret events. For example, a student with a possible self of physician will interpret a grade of A in organic chemistry differently from, say, a student with a possible self of lawyer. Or a person with a feared possible self of being alone or abandoned might react more negatively to a broken lunch date than someone without this negative possible self (Markus & Nurius, 1986).

Positive Possible Selves. Ideas for possible selves derive from our past experiences set against the backdrop of our time, place, and culture. Our immediate social context has a bigger influence on our possible selves than demographics such as age, gender, or socioeconomic status, and here again we see the influence of our social experiences in making us who we are (Lee & Oyserman, 2009). Role models, either in the media or as real people in our worlds, provide powerful images of what we might become, or what we might fear becoming. For example, about 33% of college students and 25% of adolescents mention physical appearance as part of their desired self (Bybee & Wells, 2006). Using her media impact, Oprah Winfrey started a "Live Your Best Life" campaign to help readers of her magazine and viewers of her talk show imagine, strive for, and achieve a positive possible self. This campaign provides very vivid and powerful images of women living well despite their circumstances or past failures and no doubt serves as a motivating possible self for people, especially women, to change their lives for the better.

Psychologists have investigated the possible selves of many different kinds of people including pregnant teens and teen moms (Nurius, Casey, Lindhorst, & Macy, 2006), young fathers in prison (Meek, 2007), low-income mothers (Lee & Oyserman, 2009), juvenile delinquent teens (Oyserman & Markus, 1990), young women in counseling (Dunkel, Kelts, & Coon, 2006), gay men and lesbian women (King & Smith, 2004), and young, middle, and elderly adults (Cross & Markus, 1991). Let's consider some of these findings in depth.

Have you ever imagined what your life would be like if you married? Do you picture yourself as a good provider? A good homemaker? Both of these roles are examples of possible selves (Eagly, 2009). Can our possible selves change what we think is attractive in a potential mate? Apparently they can.

College students were randomly assigned to imagine themselves as married with children in one of three future self conditions: a homemaker role, a provider role, or a control condition in which they imagined themselves in whatever role came to mind. Then, while holding this image of their future self, they rated how important various characteristics were in their future mate. Although women rated provider characteristics as more important than men,

The easier it is to imagine a possible self, like being a mom or a dad, the more likely this possible self will guide our aspirations and increase our well-being.

both women and men who imagined themselves as a future homemaker rated provider characteristics (e.g., status, ambition, career focus, salary) as more important than participants in the provider condition. Both men and women who imagined themselves as a future provider, however, rated homemaker characteristics (e.g., good cook, good with children, good housekeeper) as more important in a future mate. This study suggests that our possible selves can even change what we think is attractive in a future mate!

Sometimes people discover that they are growing up to be a person they didn't quite imagine. Such may be the case for gay men and lesbian women, especially those who are raised in conservative families or in a culture that assumes that heterosexuality is the norm. For example, in the United States of the late 20th century, many gays and lesbians grew up imagining themselves living the proverbial American dream of marrying someone of the other sex and having children. The realization that one is gay or lesbian requires that one abandon this straight possible self in favor of a gay possible self. How might an individual's ability to imagine one self or the other relate to well-being?

This question was investigated in a study in which gay men and lesbians were asked to imagine their best possible straight and gay/lesbian future selves (King & Smith, 2004). Participants 18 to 66 years old rated how easily and vividly they imagined these possible selves. They also rated the extent to which they were out to their family, friends, and coworkers. Finally, they also answered questionnaires that measured their psychological distress, degree of regret or second thoughts about their current gay/lesbian life, and feelings of well-being and life satisfaction.

The more salient a straight possible self was, the less life satisfaction and the more regrets a participant reported. In addition, the less likely they were to be out to others. In contrast, the more salient a gay/lesbian self was, the greater life satisfaction, the fewer regrets, and the more open about his or her life a participant was. Further, at a follow-up study conducted 2 years later, salience of straight possible selves was related to increased psychological distress whereas salience of gay/lesbian selves was related to lowered distress *2 years later*. The more people were invested in their best possible gay/lesbian self—that is, easily and vividly imagining a gay/lesbian life, being out to more people—the less distress participants felt over time.

Negative Possible Selves.   The studies reviewed so far focused on positive possible selves. What about negative or feared possible selves? Imagine that you are an adolescent, 13 to 16 years old, say, living in inner-city Detroit. Perhaps you've committed some minor crimes, perhaps you've gotten into more serious crime, perhaps you are trying to stay out of trouble. What kinds of possible selves are particularly salient to you?

This is the question investigated by Oyserman and Markus (1990). They identified four groups of youths differing in their rates of delinquency. One group attended a regular public school and had no history of crime. A second showed mild delinquency and were attending either an alternative school or a delinquency intervention program as part of regular public school. A third group showed moderate delinquency and attended a special school or lived in a group home. The fourth group had a record of severe delinquency and were attending a state training school as a last resort after other treatments had failed. The participants included Black and White males and females.

Each teen was interviewed one-on-one by a trained researcher and asked to imagine possible selves over the next year. Specifically, they were asked to list three of each of their expected selves ("What is most likely to be true for you in the next year"), hoped-for selves ("Possible selves that you most hope to describe you in the next year"), and feared selves ("What do you most fear or worry about being in the next year").

There were stark differences between the nondelinquent group and the severe delinquency group. Consider this reply from a young man in the public school group:

> I expect to be doing better in school, to be almost independent—ready to move out and to have a part-time job. I hope to study more, have a good paying part-time job, and be independent of my parents. I'm afraid I might not stay in school, I won't get a summer job, and I'll be homeless. (16-year-old male, public school; Oyserman & Markus, 1990, p. 117)

Now, compare this reply with the reply from a teen in the severe delinquency group:

> Next year I expect to be in trouble more, but trying to stay out of trouble, and trying to stay in school. I hope to graduate high school, not be in trouble with the police, and start a good job so I won't steal for cash. I'm afraid I might be a thief, in prison, dead—killed breaking into houses. (16-year-old male, maximum security training school for delinquent boys; Oyserman & Markus, 1990, p. 117)

Overall, the possible selves of this sample were more likely to include *criminal* than *having a job* or *getting along well in school.* Note that having a negative feared self—as part of a self-concept—doesn't necessarily set you up for failure, nor is holding a positive hoped-for or expected self enough to lead to success. In a follow-up of the public school and community placement teens 2 or 3 months later, those youths who had a balance of positive and negative selves committed fewer and less serious crimes than youths with more negative selves or more positive selves. For possible selves to have the greatest impact on motivation and long-term behavior change, we need both hoped-for and feared selves. That is, having a clear positive hoped-for self helps us imagine what we can do to avoid the negative feared self, and a negative feared self can help us be aware of what could happen if we don't achieve our positive hoped-for self.

Might it be possible to use these findings on possible selves to help teens develop alternative possible selves and to succeed in school? Researchers developed an after-school program specifically for African American middle school students from inner-city Detroit (Oyserman, Terry, & Bybee, 2002). The 9-week intervention included group

The right balance of hoped-for and feared possible selves can be particularly motivating.

activities and discussions to help the youths articulate academically oriented possible selves, identify specific strategies to help achieve these selves, connect their possible selves to the selves of successful adult role models, and improve their social skills.

An important aspect of this intervention was that it took account of their social context. For example, the workshops took place after-hours in their regular schools and involved other kids in their school and adults in the community. The workshops also addressed issues these kids face on a regular basis including racism and how to deal with it, positive aspects of racial identity, and academic achievement as part of racial identity. Compared to boys and girls who did not experience the intervention, participants showed a greater sense of bonding to school, a greater concern for doing well in school, more balanced possible selves, knowledge of more plausible strategies to achieve their possible selves, greater school attendance, and, for boys, a decrease in getting into trouble at school (Oyserman, Terry, & Bybee, 2002).

These results are pretty remarkable when you realize that without this intervention, these middle school kids would be at risk for delinquency, much like the teens of the Oyserman and Markus (1990) study discussed in the preceding pages. Other researchers have created similar programs for at-risk youth, university-level student athletes, and middle school children (Hock, Deshler, & Schumaker, 2006).

Then and Now: The Self

As I am writing this chapter a certain phone company is launching the debut of a new mobile phone that is, in the words of the company, "the first phone that becomes 100% you." The ad goes on to explain that you can "make your phone as unique as you are" with customizable accessories, applications, covers, and skins. As someone who can remember when phones were not mobile, came in basic black, and were rented to customers by the one and only phone company in existence at the time, the idea of customizing a phone would be like customizing a microwave oven! Clothes and living spaces sure, but when did choosing *utilities* become an important way of expressing ourselves?

According to Roy Baumeister (1987), the self has become a "problem." For psychologists the self is a fascinating puzzle and exciting research area and has been for the last 120 years or so! For the rest of us, the self is something we need to find, become, express, or even have a crisis over. Growing up in modern Western societies we view ourselves—and others—as unique and special. But this was not always the case.

Drawing on the historical record and themes in literature of the time, psychologist Roy Baumeister described how the self—including self-knowledge, potential and fulfillment, relation between individual and society, and self-definitions—has changed in the course of history (Baumeister, 1986, 1987; see also Gergen, 1991, and Leary, 2004).

The history of self-knowledge can be traced at least as far back as the ancient Greeks. The words "Know thyself" were inscribed over the entrance to the Temple of Apollo at Delphi. Of course, in ancient times this probably meant that one should appraise his talents to be able to carry out his duties effectively, with good judgment and common sense. Even up to medieval times, around the 11th to 15th centuries, a person's identity simply came from his or her duty or place in society, and depended on his or her social rank, family ties, and occupation (Baumeister, 1987).

Notions about the self at this time paralleled early Christian beliefs that salvation would come to humanity as a whole. However, this changed around the 12th century or so when the Christian concept of the Last Judgment emphasized individual salvation, suggesting that one's eternal fate depended on the sum of one's moral and spiritual life (Baumeister, 1987).

During the 16th to 18th centuries people became fascinated with the distinction between inner and outer life. Before that, people essentially equated the self with concrete outer appearance: People looked like their station in life and that is who they essentially were. However, this new fascination with misleading appearances led to recognition of a private, inner, real self that was hidden (Baumeister, 1987). Just think of the themes in Shakespeare that reflect the contrast

"[The self] has justly been regarded as the most puzzling puzzle with which psychology has to deal."
William James (1890, p. 330)

Under the repressiveness of the Victorian era people became self-conscious and developed a fascination with the hidden aspects of the self.

between appearances and realities: *Romeo and Juliet* ("O Romeo, Romeo, wherefore art thou Romeo? . . . 'Tis but thy name that is my enemy: Thou art thyself"), *The Merchant of Venice* ("Hath not a Jew eyes . . . if you prick us, do we not bleed?"), or *Twelfth Night* and other plays in which people switch places or pretend to be others.

Puritanism during the 16th and 17th centuries increased self-consciousness as individuals worried about their fate in the afterlife. Self-consciousness and self-awareness became important values and people became concerned with their own self-deception. The self was deemed difficult or impossible to know (Baumeister, 1987).

As people sought to understand this hidden side to the self, personality became more important, as reflected in the increased popularity of biography and autobiography in the literature of the 18th and 19th centuries. People recognized that personality, rather than social status, defined the individual. It is interesting to note the psychologist and philosopher William James and his brother, the writer Henry James, both tackled the problem of self from different perspectives during this time. Politically, economically, and socially, this period saw revolutions in America and in France, for example, and a rise in individual rights and social equality (Baumeister, 1997). As a result, the Romantic era of the late 18th to early 19th centuries emphasized the unique, individual, cosmic destiny that an individual was expected to discover and fulfill (Baumeister, 1987, 1997).

Victorian repressiveness of the middle and late 19th century only served to further emphasize the unique, but hidden self. High moral standards forced Victorians to become self-conscious and to hide their true selves, lest they appear to fall short of impossibly high standards of behavior (Baumeister, 1987). Victorians believed that the inner self could be revealed inadvertently, a feat exemplified by Sherlock Holmes with his keen powers of perception (Baumeister, 1987). Sigmund Freud may have captured this feeling best when he observed, "Betrayal oozes from every pore" (Baumeister, 1987; Freud, 1905/1959, p. 94). Perhaps Freud's ability to decode this hidden self explains his popularity then and continued popularity today.

As a result of increasing modernization and mass production during the early part of the 20th century, people felt an increasing alienation and discontent with work life. This set the stage for self-exploration and belief in personal uniqueness that marked the self of the latter part of the 20th century (Baumeister, 1987). By the time Erik Erikson coined the phrase *identity crisis* (Erikson, 1968) the fervor with which people embraced the idea suggests that he merely named, rather than discovered, an important human experience (Baumeister, 1999).

By the end of the 20th century and into our own time, we struggle for a balance between our individual uniqueness and our group membership (Brewer, 1991) as we embrace our diverse social identities. What about the self of the 21st century? We have yet to see the full impact of technology—such as the Internet with instant messaging (IM), social networking, and yes, customizable phones—that simultaneously brings us closer to friends, family, and strangers even as it invites deception or at least strategic self-presentation and experimentation with various identities.

Self-Esteem

Self-esteem, the "greatest love" according to a classic song, is just that: the amount of value people place on themselves (Baumeister, Campbell, Kreuger, & Vohs, 2003). People with high self-esteem have a favorable view of themselves, whereas people low in self-esteem have an unfavorable view of themselves. Keep in mind that self-esteem is more of a perception or an opinion and does not imply anything about whether the person *actually is* a good or a bad person. This might be confusing, as people who are high in self-esteem may have an accurate and justified appreciation of their own achievements and successes or they may have an inflated, arrogant, and conceited view of their talents. Similarly, low self-esteem may reflect an accurate view of one's shortcomings, or it may be a distorted and problematic view of one's perceived inferiority (Baumeister et al., 2003).

Self-esteem often refers to a general evaluation of one's self-concept (e.g., Rosenberg, 1965), but we can also have domain-specific self-esteem for work (e.g., Brockner, 1988), academics (e.g., Marsh, 1993), athletics (e.g., Fox & Corbin, 1989), appearance (e.g., Franzoi & Shields, 1984), and even toward one's social identity (Luhtanen & Crocker, 1992). Global self-esteem is moderately correlated with domain-specific self-esteem.

Self-Esteem Level

People vary in the amount of self-esteem they feel, so that even though we talk about people high or low in self-esteem, self-esteem is really a matter of degree. In fact, people rarely admit—at least not on questionnaires to psychologists—that they feel bad about themselves. Low self-esteem is really more like lacking positive views about the self (Baumeister et al., 2003). In many experiments people are classified as low in self-esteem if they fall in the bottom half or bottom third of a sample of people. You can get some idea of your own self-esteem by taking the Rosenberg Self-Esteem Scale (Rosenberg, 1965) in Table 5.5.

People with high self-esteem tend to agree with items such as "I feel that I'm a person of worth, at least on an equal plane with others" or "I take a positive attitude toward myself" and to disagree with items like "At times, I think I am no good at all" or "I feel I do not have much to be proud of" (Rosenberg, 1965, pp. 17–18). People low in self-esteem, rather than feeling bad about themselves and agreeing with the negative items and disagreeing with the positive items, tend to be more neutral toward all items, sometimes agreeing or disagreeing, but not very strongly. In the words of one researcher, "High scores are high, but low scores are medium" (Tice, 1993, p. 40).

Table 5.5 The Rosenberg Self-Esteem Scale

How do you feel about yourself? For each of the items below, strongly agree *SA*, agree *A*, disagree *D*, or strongly disagree *SD* by circling the appropriate response.				
1. On the whole, I am satisfied with myself.	SA	A	D	SD
*2. At times, I think I am no good at all.	SA	A	D	SD
3. I feel that I have a number of good qualities.	SA	A	D	SD
4. I am able to do things as well as most other people.	SA	A	D	SD
*5. I feel I do not have much to be proud of.	SA	A	D	SD
*6. I certainly feel useless at times.	SA	A	D	SD
7. I feel that I'm a person of worth, at least on an equal plane with others.	SA	A	D	SD
*8. I wish I could have more respect for myself.	SA	A	D	SD
*9. All in all, I am inclined to feel that I am a failure.	SA	A	D	SD
10. I take a positive attitude toward myself.	SA	A	D	SD

Scoring: SA = 3, A = 2, D = 1, SD = 0. Items with an asterisk are reverse scored, that is, SA = 0, A = 1, D = 2, SD = 3. Sum the scores for the 10 items. The higher the score, the higher the self-esteem. Scores below 15 suggest low self-esteem.

Source: Rosenberg, M. (1965). Society and the adolescent self-image. Princeton, NJ: Princeton University Press.

People with high self-esteem are better than people with lower self-esteem in coping with failure. They persist longer and bounce back quicker from setbacks (Shrauger & Rosenberg, 1970; Shrauger & Sorman, 1977). People with lower self-esteem are more vulnerable to the slings and arrows of everyday life, showing more reactivity to events and greater mood swings (Campbell, Chew, & Scratchley, 1991). Also, people with lower self-esteem are more easily persuaded by the social influence of others (Brockner, 1984). People with lower self-esteem experience a conflict between wanting success and approval and being afraid of falling short (Brown, 1993). People with higher self-esteem are even physically healthier than people with low self-esteem (Brown & McGill, 1989).

Self-Esteem Stability

In addition to level of self-esteem (i.e., whether one's self-esteem is high or low), researchers study how changeable one's self-esteem is. **Self-esteem stability** refers to how stable or variable people's general feelings of self-worth are over time (Kernis & Goldman, 2003). Although most self-esteem scales ask about how people typically feel about themselves or how they feel about themselves in general, self-esteem stability is measured by asking people how they feel about themselves at the moment that they are answering the question. Then, researchers ask people this question once or twice a day over a 4- to 7-day period.

People with stable self-esteem are consistent in how they feel about themselves. People with unstable or variable self-esteem feel good or bad about themselves depending on what's going on around them. They seem to be very responsive—almost too responsive—to events that are potentially relevant to their self-worth. These events may be actual events (e.g., a compliment or an insult) or their own thoughts and reflections (e.g., thinking about one's appearance). People with unstable self-esteem often feel fragile or vulnerable as if their self-esteem is continually in jeopardy (Kernis & Goldman, 2003).

There is some evidence that level of self-esteem interacts with stability of self-esteem. Low self-esteem may not be so bad if one is variable, compared to stable, in this negative self-view (Paradise & Kernis, 2002). However, people with unstable high self-esteem may have more difficulty coping in their everyday life compared to people with stable high self-esteem. People with unstable, high self-esteem tend to be more defensive (Kernis, Grannemann, & Barclay, 1992), self-aggrandizing (Kernis, Greenier, Herlocker, Whisenhunt, & Abend, 1997), prone to anger (Kernis et al., 1989), and to have less satisfying relationships (Kernis & Goldman, 2003) than people with stable high self-esteem.

Self-Concept Clarity

People with high and low self-esteem don't differ only in how they feel about themselves; they also differ in how they *think* about themselves. People with higher self-esteem know themselves better. **Self-concept clarity** refers to how well people know—or think they know—themselves. Although it is similar to self-esteem stability (Campbell et al., 1996), self-concept clarity refers to consistency of our self-concepts whereas self-esteem stability refers to consistency of our self-esteem, our feelings about our self-concepts.

In a very simple demonstration, college students described themselves using 15 pairs of adjectives and then rated how confident they were (Campbell, 1990). For example, they were asked how silly versus serious or how extravagant versus thrifty they were on a 7-point scale. A person who is clearer in his or her self-concept would give more extreme answers—that is, away from the midpoint—than a person who is more wishy-washy about himself or herself.

This is precisely what the researchers found. People with high self-esteem gave more extreme responses than people with low self-esteem. They were also more confident in their responses than people lower in self-esteem. In subsequent studies, participants high in self-esteem were also faster at making self-ratings and more consistent in their ratings, than participants lower in self-esteem (Campbell, 1990).

Similar results have been found by other researchers using different ways of defining and measuring self-concept clarity (Stinson, Wood, & Doxey, 2008) and related concepts including self-concept confusion (Campbell & Lavallee, 1993), self-certainty (Baumgardner, 1990; Wright, 2001), self-ambivalence (Riketta & Ziegler, 2006), self-concept integration versus compartmentalization

---

"I know who I am. No one else knows who I am. If I was a giraffe, and someone said I was a snake, I'd think, no, actually I'm a giraffe."

Richard Gere, to British newspaper The Guardian, *when asked if what the press says about his private life bothers him*

THINK ABOUT IT

Does knowing yourself cause high self-esteem or does having high self-esteem help you know yourself?

People with low self-esteem often self-handicap as a way of protecting their self-esteem.

The Personality of Everyday Life

Shooting yourself in the foot to protect your self-esteem

As strange as it may seem, **self-handicapping** is when we purposely set ourselves up for possible failure. If we fail, we have a ready-made excuse and some measure of self-protection. And if we succeed despite the sabotage? Why, we look even better and increase our worth in the eyes of others and ourselves! In this way self-handicapping can serve either self-enhancement or self-protection motives, depending on the task and the likelihood of success or failure.

In one experiment, participants who were high or low in self-esteem would have a chance to practice and then perform a task (Tice, 1991). Participants were randomly assigned to one of four conditions that differed in how important they thought the task was and whether success or failure was meaningful on the task. For example, in one condition participants believed success indicated that they had high ability but that failure indicated nothing about their ability. In another condition, participants believed that failure meant they lacked ability but that success indicated nothing about their ability. The differing instructions suggested to participants that self-handicapping, in the form of not practicing before their big evaluation, could either protect or enhance their self-esteem.

Sure enough, before their performance participants who were low in self-esteem practiced less and self-handicapped more than people high in self-esteem when they thought it would protect their self-esteem (when failure reflected badly on their ability, but that success was no big deal) whereas participants high in self-esteem practiced less and handicapped more than people low in self-esteem when they thought it would enhance their self-esteem (when success reflected well on their ability but that failure was no big deal). In a second study, these findings were replicated with participants choosing distracting music as a self-handicap (Tice, 1991).

There are many ways that people, especially college students, can self-handicap. Perhaps you've seen some of these strategies in yourself or others: making excuses, not getting enough sleep, not trying your best, eating badly, arriving late, being distracted, not practicing, not studying, trying to do too much, using alcohol and other drugs, and—everyone's favorite—procrastinating. Although self-handicapping strategies may provide a short-term benefit by taking the pressure off, they are often detrimental in the long run because they prevent us from performing our best. Even procrastination, despite most procrastinators thinking that they "work best under pressure," is detrimental (Tice & Baumeister, 1997). So the next time you are tempted to self-handicap—or procrastinate—think again!

(Showers, 1992; Showers & Zeigler-Hill, 2007; Story, 2004; Zeigler-Hill & Showers, 2007), contingent self-esteem (Crocker & Knight, 2005; Deci & Ryan, 1995), and fragile self-esteem (Kernis, Lakey, & Heppner, 2008). However, one puzzle still remains: Does self-concept clarity cause self-esteem or does self-esteem cause self-concept clarity? Perhaps they affect each other (Brandt & Vonk, 2006; Hoyle, 2006; Showers & Zeigler-Hill, 2006). Only with more research will we be able to know for sure.

THINK ABOUT IT

Is self-esteem important? Why?

Life Outcomes of High and Low Self-Esteem: Myths and Realities

Psychologists and the general public alike agree that self-esteem is important for individual well-being. In fact, in the 1980s the California legislature went so far as to fund a task force to increase the self-esteem of its residents. It believed—in the absence of scientific evidence—that an investment in the self-esteem of the citizenry would pay dividends in a reduction of welfare dependency, unwanted pregnancy, school failure, crime, drug addiction, and other social problems. Is it true that increasing self-esteem can do all this? Take a look at Table 5.6 and test your own knowledge about the supposed outcomes of self-esteem.

Myths? Truths? How can we know for sure? In 2003 the American Psychological Society (now the Association for Psychological Science) charged a task force, including four researchers in the area of self-esteem, to review and summarize available research to evaluate such claims (Baumeister et al., 2003). The statements in Table 5.6 come directly out of the task force's work. Let's take a closer look at some of what it found.

MYTH 1: Too many people suffer from low self-esteem.

FACT: There is no epidemic of low self-esteem in America or elsewhere in the world, for that matter. Quite the opposite: The average person sees himself or herself as better than average, in both the United States (Baumeister et al., 2003) and in 52 other cultures including European, South American, Australian, Asian, and African, and in both individualistic

Table 5.6 Myths (and Realities) of Self Esteem—Which Is which?

Can you separate the myths of self-esteem from the true research findings? Take this quiz to find out. Circle true or false to each of the statements below. The answers are given below and in the text.		
1. Too many people suffer from low self-esteem.	True	False
2. People with high self-esteem are smarter, more likable, and more physically attractive than people with low self-esteem.	True	False
3. People with high self-esteem do better in school and achieve more on the job, and have greater life satisfaction and happiness than people with low self-esteem.	True	False
4. Interventions that aim to increase achievement by increasing the self-esteem of school students are successful.	True	False
5. Relationships are more likely to break up if a partner has low self-esteem than if a partner has high self-esteem.	True	False
6. Bullies suffer from low self-esteem so they need to lash out and hurt others.	True	False
7. People with low self-esteem are more likely to abuse alcohol and other drugs than people with high self-esteem.	True	False
8. People with low self-esteem are more likely to engage in premature sexual activity and to have an unwanted pregnancy than people with high self-esteem.	True	False

Answers: All of the above statements are false.
Source: See the text and Baumeister et al. (2003) for details.

Although self-esteem is important, scientific evidence suggests that interventions to increase self-esteem may be misguided.

and collectivistic cultures (Schmitt & Allik, 2005). In many experiments, the "low self-esteem group," defined as scoring in the bottom portion of a sample of participants, often ends up scoring at least one standard deviation above the midpoint of the scale. In fact, the average score on self-esteem tests is actually *above* the midpoint of the scale (Baumeister, Tice, & Hutton, 1989). Although this lets us make comparisons between people higher and lower in self-esteem, it does not suggest that low self-esteem is a problem. We might well wonder if some of this self-reported high self-esteem is due to deliberate impression management, defensive self-enhancement, narcissism, or a tendency to see everything more positively (Baumeister et al., 2003). This *heterogeneity of high self-esteem,* where there may be different kinds of high self-esteem, makes it difficult to detect significant effects of self-esteem.

MYTH 2: People with high self-esteem are smarter, more likable, and more physically attractive than people with low self-esteem.

FACT: There is a strong correlation between self-esteem and being smart, likable, popular, and physically attractive, but this is true only for self-ratings. There is no correlation between self-esteem and others' ratings of how likable, popular, and physically attractive a person is, or with objective measures of intelligence. What's going on? People with high self-esteem *believe* all these things about themselves, but they are not true by objective standards. In fact, people high and low in self-esteem are equally likable and equal in physical attractiveness and intelligence.

For example, in one study male and female college students rated themselves on self-esteem, attractiveness, and intelligence, and took a standard intelligence test (Gabriel, Critelli, & Ee, 1994). Then, experimenters took their photographs and rated each one on attractiveness compared to the average college student. For both men and women, there was a significant correlation of $r = .35$ between self-esteem and self-rated intelligence but *no correlation* between self-esteem and scores on the intelligence test ($r = -.07$). The results for attractiveness were similar, but fell just short of statistical significance. There was a positive correlation between self-esteem and self-rated attractiveness ($r = .23$) but not between self-esteem and experimenter-rated attractiveness ($r = .01$). Both men and women were guilty of this self-inflation. However, men inflated their own attractiveness ratings more than women did.

MYTH 3: People with high self-esteem do better in school, achieve more in their job, and have greater life satisfaction and happiness than people with low self-esteem.

FACT: There is a correlation between self-esteem and success but self-esteem is the result—not the cause—of success in school, work, and life. We have to remind ourselves that correlation is not causation. In this case research has demonstrated that achieving commendable accomplishments, working hard for outcomes, developing our skills through effort and practice, and coping with negative events all make us feel good about ourselves whether in school, on the job, or in our lives.

All of the studies on workplace success and self-esteem are correlational in nature (Judge & Bono, 2001), but school success is one of the most studied outcomes of self-esteem (Baumeister et al., 2003). Numerous studies employing various methods, including longitudinal designs which can test for causality, find little (Valentine, DuBois, & Cooper, 2004) or no (Baumeister et al., 2003) effect of self-esteem on school achievement. Where there are significant correlations between self-esteem and achievement, they are small and most often due to achievement causing increased self-esteem rather than the other way around. There is also some evidence that third variables, like family background, can cause both increased self-esteem and increased school achievement.

MYTH 4: Interventions that aim to increase achievement by increasing the self-esteem of school students are successful.

FACT: Alas, not only are such programs less successful than other, more traditional, methods of increasing achievement (e.g., getting parents more involved), but such methods may actually backfire. For example, one study specifically targeted college students who got a C, D, or an F on the midterm of their introductory psychology class and randomly assigned them to one of three feedback conditions (Forsyth, Lawrence, Burnette, & Baumeister, 2007). For all students, this feedback was administered via a weekly e-mail message that included a review question on that week's material. The control condition received this review question only. In a second condition, students received feedback aimed at increasing their self-esteem. In a third condition, students received feedback aimed at increasing their sense of control and taking responsibility for their grades and study habits.

What happened when it came to the final exam? Take a look at Figure 5.3. The pattern of results was *opposite* to predictions! Bolstering self-esteem actually led to poorer performance especially among the weakest students. That is, students in the self-esteem bolstering feedback condition

Figure 5.3 Mean final exam scores for C and D/F students in the self-esteem bolstering condition (SE), the internal and controllable (I/C) condition, and the control condition. *Source:* From Forsyth et al. (2007, Figure 1, p. 453). Reprinted with permission from Forsyth, D. R., Lawrence, N. K., Burnette, J. L., & Baumeister, R. F. (2007), "Attempting to improve the academic performance of struggling college students by bolstering their self-esteem: An intervention that backfired," *Journal of Social and Clinical Psychology,* 26(4), 447–459. Permission conveyed through the Copyright Clearance Center.

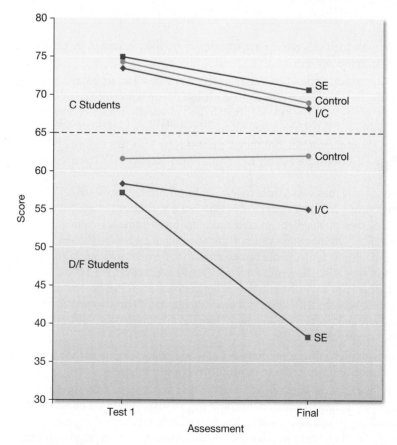

actually performed worse than the other two groups, and none of the groups improved their grades from the midterm to the final exam. The authors pointed out that not only did the self-esteem group of D/F students perform significantly worse than the other two D/F groups, but they also performed worse on a practical level: Their average final grade was below passing!

What went so wrong with this intervention? The authors agreed with the reasoning of Baumeister et al. (2003) who cautioned that boosting self-esteem regardless of performance encourages people to devalue their performance. After all, one very effective way of maintaining self-esteem in the face of failure is to withdraw your effort from the task and convince yourself that your self-esteem is not contingent on your performance (i.e., that failure doesn't matter). What happens to students who do not study, go to class, keep up with readings, or essentially withdraw their efforts from their studies? They do poorly in their classes but—and here is the amazing part—they don't feel bad about it! Perhaps feeling bad when we know we're not performing our best is not such a bad thing. After all, our self-esteem might suffer a bit in the short term, but our positive outcomes might increase in the long run.

MYTH 5: Relationships are more likely to break up if a partner has low self-esteem than if a partner has high self-esteem.

FACT: Both high and low self-esteem cause problems in relationships, so self-esteem has little to do with who stays together or who breaks up (Baumeister et al., 2003). However, low self-esteem does cause some problems in relationships, such as often distrusting a partner's expressions of love and support.

MYTH 6: Bullies suffer from low self-esteem so they need to lash out and hurt others.

FACT: There is no correlation between self-esteem and self-report bullying or peer-reported likelihood of bullying. People with *high* self-esteem, especially with unstable self-esteem, with unrealistically positive self-views as in narcissism, or with defensive high self-esteem, are more likely to react to perceived threats with violence than people with low self-esteem. These people are especially sensitive to evaluation and react badly if they don't measure up in their own minds to what they think they deserve (Baumeister et al., 2003).

MYTH 7: People with low self-esteem are likely to abuse alcohol and other drugs than people with high self-esteem.

FACT: There is no correlation between drug use and self-esteem (Baumeister et al., 2003).

MYTH 8: People with low self-esteem are likely to engage in premature sexual activity and to have an unwanted pregnancy than people with high self-esteem.

FACT: Experiencing sexual activity before one is ready or having an unwanted pregnancy are both events that make people feel bad about themselves and cause low self-esteem. Again, just because there is a correlation, we can't assume causation. If anything, people with high self-esteem are often less inhibited and more willing to take risks than people with low self-esteem (Baumeister et al., 2003). The problem appears to be with high self-esteem or the overconfidence of unwarranted high self-esteem. One of the biggest puzzles of self-esteem for researchers is to separate out true high self-esteem from overly high self-esteem or defensive self-esteem (e.g., Jordan, Spencer, & Zanna, 2005; Lambird & Mann, 2006).

These myths and facts involve but a few of the many variables that have been assumed by people to be related to self-esteem. In their review Baumeister et al. (2003) also discussed research on self-esteem and group behavior, leadership, delinquency, antisocial behavior, smoking, sexual orientation, and eating disorders, and came to similar conclusions. For most of these outcomes there are no significant correlations with self-esteem, and even when there are significant correlations, most of them are small, and evidence of a clear *causal* connection between self-esteem and these outcomes is lacking. Their report started a wave of controversy and renewed interest in understanding the correlates and outcomes of self-esteem (e.g., Swann, Chang-Schneider, & McClarty, 2007). For example, newer evidence suggests that when we look at aggression, antisocial behavior, and delinquency (including fighting, drug use, alcohol use, and illegal activities) outside the laboratory and over time, there are small to moderate correlations with low self-esteem (Donnellan, Trzesniewski, Robins, Moffitt, & Caspi, 2005). Clearly, this is an exciting time to be a researcher in the area of self-esteem!

THINK ABOUT IT

Which of these myths did you find the most surprising? Why?

"Think about yourself in the future, please tell me about the possible selves that you think are most likely to be true of you in the next year. These are possible selves you expect to be true of you. . . . Now think about ways you would not like to be next year. Ways you would like to avoid being or fear being."

Unemori, Omoregie, and Markus (2004, p. 326)

Research Methods Illustrated: Qualitative Data and Content Analysis

Suppose you were one of the researchers who posed these questions (see left margin) to their participants. You've collected responses from 150 college students at 5 different universities in the United States, Chile, and Japan (Unemori et al., 2004). Now what do you do?

This is an example of a study using **qualitative methods**, techniques that analyze broad themes or characteristics—qualities—reflected in participants' responses. In contrast to **quantitative methods**, where the data collected involve measures, questionnaires, test scores, or other numerical data—quantities, amounts—qualitative data are often verbal. Qualitative data collection is used more in sociology, anthropology, and sometimes in education. Psychology, and personality in particular, draws on both kinds of research, often in the same study (see Table 5.7 for a comparison of quantitative and qualitative research methods).

In personality psychology, sometimes the best way to study people's thoughts, feelings, and reactions is through open-ended questions (Woike, 2007). Examples of open-ended questions are sentence-completion tests, essays, stories, and diaries (Woike, 2007). The challenge for researchers is to figure out a way of judging, categorizing, and analyzing the content of these responses in a meaningful fashion (e.g., Bartholomew, Henderson, & Marcia, 2000). This is called **content analysis.**

Open-ended questions have several advantages over questionnaire measures (Woike, 2007). First, they allow participants the freedom to express themselves without the constraints of a questionnaire. Participants may express their innermost thoughts and emotional reactions, and reveal their frames of reference and cultural assumptions in open-ended responses. Even when questionnaires allow participants to choose between options, we have no way of knowing if the options are relevant for participants or if they are merely choosing "the lesser of two evils."

Second, what if we have left out some aspect of the topic that is important to participants? We would never know this from a questionnaire. Because open-ended responses are self-generated, we know that what participants say is personally relevant and important. Third, asking open-ended questions can minimize the researcher's unknown or hidden biases that may contaminate more traditional measures.

Finally, asking open-ended questions may be the only way to understand how participants think, feel, and react to a topic that has never been studied before.

So, how do researchers conduct a content analysis? Let's take a closer look at the steps involved (Smith, 2000; Woike, 2007) and see how they might apply to the study of the possible selves of young adults from four cultural backgrounds (Unemori et al., 2004).

Step 1: Identify the research question. What are we trying to identify, describe, or measure? Unemori et al. (2004) had two research questions in mind: What are the similarities and differences

Table 5.7 A Comparison of Quantitative and Qualitative Research Methods

Quantitative Research
Tests a hypothesis that the researcher begins with.
Concepts are in the form of distinct variables.
Data are in the form of numbers.
Theory is largely causal and is deductive (reasoning from general principles to particular facts).
Analysis proceeds by using statistics, tables, or charts.

Qualitative Research
Captures and discovers meaning from the data.
Concepts are in the form of themes, motifs, generalizations, taxonomies, and so on.
Data are in the form of words from documents, observations, transcripts, open-ended questions, and so forth.
Theory can be causal or noncausal and is often inductive (reasoning from particular facts to general principles).
Analysis proceeds by extracting themes or generalizations from evidence and organizing data to present a coherent, consistent picture.

Source: Adapted from Neuman (1997, p. 329, Table 13.1). Neuman, W. L. (1997). Social research methods: Qualitative and quantitative approaches. Boston, MA: Allyn & Bacon.

in possible selves (actual and feared) among young people of European American (EA), Japanese American (JA), Chilean (CH), and Japanese (JN) cultural backgrounds? Do people have a similar number of expected and feared possible selves, that is, a balance between the number of expected and feared possible selves? Or, does one kind or the other predominate?

Step 2: Decide if content analysis will answer the research question either alone or combined with other methods. Sometimes researchers will give a personality questionnaire like the NEO-PI-R to measure the five-factor model of traits (Costa & McCrae, 1985), a self-esteem scale (Rosenberg, 1965), or a measure of individualism–collectivism (Oyserman, 1993) along with open-ended questions. The Unemori et al. (2004) study used content analysis combined with background questions (gender, age, highest level of education attained by their parents, highest level of education they expected to achieve) to explore their two research questions.

Step 3: Decide what type of material will answer the research question and how best to obtain it. The key here is to make the instructions neither too broad and general ("Tell me the story of your life") nor too structured like a self-report questionnaire ("Are you more like a placid lake or a babbling brook?"). The questions Unemori et al. (2004) used ("Tell me about the possible selves that you think are most likely to be true of you in the next year" and "Ways you would like to avoid being or fear being") have the right amount of structure. Additional instructions to "rank the three that are most meaningful to you" made sure that the researchers captured what was most important to the participants. Mentioning the number three ensured that participants would give the right amount of information, neither too much (making coding difficult) nor too little (rendering analysis impossible).

Step 4: Determine the unit of analysis to be coded. This might be a phrase, a sentence, a paragraph, or even an essay. Once the unit is identified, we can create a scoring system to capture and quantify the concept we are after. In the Unemori et al. (2004) study the unit of analysis was the possible self described. For most participants, this was a short phrase or sentence.

Step 5: Select or develop a content coding system. In the Unemori et al. (2004) study, since the researchers were building on past research, they used a coding scheme that had been validated in previous research instead of devising their own scheme. Each of the expected selves and feared selves was classified into one of the following categories: Intrapersonal (e.g., anxious, happy, rich), Interpersonal (e.g., keep in touch with friends, strengthen relationships), Career/Education (e.g., worried about future job, applying to medical school), Extracurricular (e.g., involved in clubs, swim more), Attainment of material goods (e.g., have a regular income, have a car), and Health-related (e.g., in shape, less tired).

Step 6: Test and refine the coding system with pilot data. In the Unemori et al. (2004) study, this was not necessary because they used a coding system that had already been validated with college students. This step is crucial, however, when conducting research in a new area, with new measures, or with a population that has not been tested before. Often, further refinement of a coding system is necessary before researchers are ready to collect data.

Step 7: Train coders and obtain adequate intercoder agreement. While training coders in what to look for and how to make their judgments, researchers must ensure that the coders are not aware of the experimental hypothesis. This way the coders can be as free from bias in their ratings as possible.

Step 8: Collect responses. Here, researchers should be careful that data are collected under the same conditions for all participants. Ideally, data should not be collected by the coders, so that they do not inadvertently bias the responses.

Open-ended questions, an example of qualitative data, are often used to study people's thoughts, feelings, and reactions.

Step 9: Code the data. The first step here is to transcribe the responses and remove names and other identifying information to protect the identity of the participants. Researchers will often use code numbers or names to keep track of the data. Coders then make their judgments or ratings and the researcher should verify that coders are using the coding system correctly and show adequate agreement.

In the Unemori et al. (2004) study two groups of bilingual coders (English and Spanish; English and Japanese) who were unaware of the purpose of the study each read through a subset of responses. Once the coders achieved 92 to 96% agreement, one of each pair went on to read the remaining responses of the European American, Japanese American, Chilean, or Japanese samples.

Step 10: Analyze the data. Here, researchers might look for patterns, tally the percentage of responses that fall in various categories, calculate frequency data, conduct appropriate statistical analyses, and draw tables and figures. For example, in the Unemori et al. (2004) study, researchers tallied the number of possible selves that fell into each of the six categories for both expected and feared selves. See Figures 5.4 and 5.5 for their results.

So, what did Unemori et al. (2004) find? Basically, there were cultural differences in both expected and feared selves. The EA students reported more interpersonal selves whereas the JN, CH, and JA students reported more career/education selves. The EA and CH samples showed more balance in their expected and feared selves, whereas JA and JN samples showed more similarities between their expected and feared selves.

Step 11: Interpret the results. The more open-ended the questions are, the more challenging this part will be. Similarly, the more quantitative the coding system is, the easier this part will be. Regardless of method, the first part of interpreting the results is to see what the data have to say about the original research question. Then, researchers should think about how the results fit into what has been done before. Finally, researchers should think about what kinds of questions remain for future research. Often, the best studies raise more questions for future research than they actually answer!

In this study, Unemori et al. (2004) interpreted their results to mean that young adults who are attending elite universities share similar expectations and fears about their futures involving friendships, personal relationships, and careers, regardless of culture. However, the relative importance of these areas varies by culture, with students in individualistic cultures able to focus

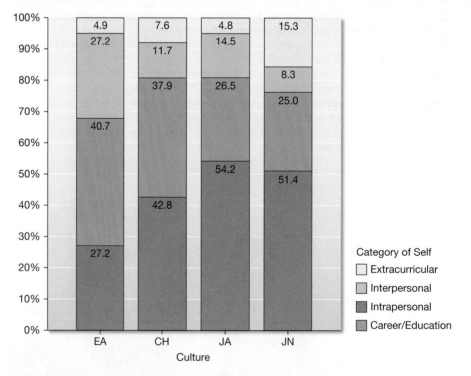

Figure 5.4 Percentage of expected selves across four categories of self in European American (EA), Chilean (CH), Japanese American (JP), and native Japanese (JN) participants. *Source:* Reprinted with permission from Unemori, P., Omoregie, H., & Markus, H. R. (2004), "Self-portraits: Possible selves in European-American, Chilean, Japanese and Japanese-American cultural contexts," *Self and Identity*, 3, 321–338. Permission conveyed through the Copyright Clearance Center.

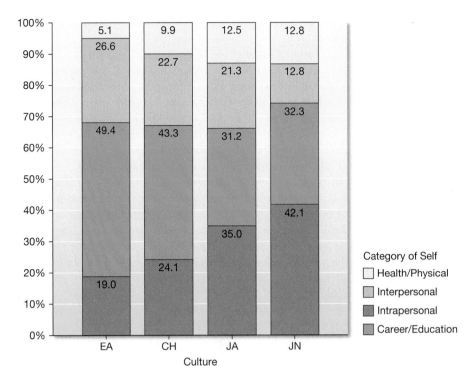

Figure 5.5 Percentage of feared selves across four categories of self in European American (EA), Chilean (CH), Japanese American (JP), and native Japanese (JN) participants. *Source:* From Unemori et al. (2004, Figure 2, p. 331). Reprinted with permission from Unemori, P., Omoregie, H., & Markus, H. R. (2004), "Self-portraits: Possible selves in European-American, Chilean, Japanese and Japanese-American cultural contexts," *Self and Identity, 3*, 321–338. Permission conveyed through the Copyright Clearance Center.

more on their internal attributes and relationships and students in more collectivistic cultures living up to parental and societal expectations about school success, further education, and future careers. Finally, more research is necessary to understand how similarities between expected and feared selves can be motivating for Japanese students the way that a balance between these selves is motivating to American students.

As you can see, the general process of conducting qualitative research is very similar to quantitative research. The biggest difference is in the development and validation of the coding system, the part we call content analysis.

Social Identity

An important part of who we are is who we are when we are with others. Do we purposely present ourselves in a certain light to gain the esteem of others? Do we act a certain way to fit into a situation? Perhaps William James's statement is even more true today as the Internet provides yet another way for us to define, refine, and present ourselves to others. In this section we will discuss the common self-presentation strategies and explore a personality variable that captures the extent to which people change who they are to blend into the social situation.

Self-Presentation

Imagine yourself getting ready for a big date. You have been attracted to this person for a long time, and now you will have the chance to go out one-on-one with the object of your affection. You hope to make a good impression, so that this first date turns into a series of dates culminating in a lifetime of happiness. To make the best impression possible, what do you do? How would you dress? What would you talk about (and avoid talking about) to make this person like you?

Or, think about going on a job interview for a job you really, really want. What image do you want to convey to the interviewer? What will you wear? Might you, modestly of course, talk about your talents and accomplishments? Would you try to steer the interviewer away from

"A man has as many social selves as there are individuals to recognize him."
William James (1890, pp. 189–190)

> "The image of myself which I try to create in my own mind in order that I may love myself is very different from the image which I try to create in the minds of others in order that they may love me."
>
> *W. H. Auden,* Hic et Ille *(1956)*

> "All the world's a stage, And all the men and women merely players."
>
> *William Shakespeare,* As You Like It *(Act II, scene vii, lines 139–166)*

THINK ABOUT IT

Sure, everybody wants to make a good impression on the first date, but what about the second date? Are you better off going with an authentic self-presentation or a strategic self-presentation? Why?

asking about your weakness? Would you find a way to put a positive spin on your faults (e.g., "My friends say I work too hard")?

For most of us, first dates (Rowatt, Cunningham, & Druen, 1998) and job interviews (Rosse, Stecher, Miller, & Levin, 1998) are two places where we are likely to engage in **self-presentation**: acting, speaking, or dressing in a certain way to convey a specific image of ourselves to others (Paulhus & Trapnell, 2008). According to this view, "All the world's a stage," to quote Shakespeare and elaborated by sociologist Erving Goffman. Actors (i.e., people) strategically present themselves in certain ways to establish, maintain, or refine a specific image in the mind of an "audience"—for example, another person, other people (Goffman, 1959). The regulation of public self-presentations is called **impression management** (Paulhus & Trapnell, 2008; Schlenker & Pontari, 2000).

People can present themselves as they truly are with an **authentic self-presentation** or they may attempt to create a specific image for some ulterior motive using a **strategic self-presentation** (Jones & Pittman, 1982). For example, people tend to do a fair amount of self-presentation in their online dating profiles to make themselves seem more attractive to a potential date (Toma, Hancock, & Eillison, 2008). Women lie more about their weight and men lie more about their height. Also, people further away from the mean, on either weight or height, are more apt to stretch the truth. People also report being the most accurate about their relationship information, but the least authentic in their photographs.

Although there are many different kinds of self-presentational tactics—up to 12 by one count (Lee, Quigley, Nesler, Corbet, & Tedeschi, 1999)!—the most common and the most influential ones are the classic quintet identified by Jones and Pittman (1982): **ingratiation**, **intimidation**, **self-promotion**, **exemplification**, and **supplication** (Paulhus & Trapnell, 2008). For each of these self-presentational tactics, the actor projects a specific image through verbal and nonverbal cues (DePaulo, 1992) and uses various psychological ploys to create a specific impression. There is always a danger that self-presentation may backfire: Once the audience sees it for what it is—a presentational strategy rather than an authentic self-presentation—the technique often stops working. Table 5.8 summarizes the most common tactics.

Who is more likely to use self-presentational strategies? First, we tend to use self-presentational strategies more with strangers than with friends (Tice, 1995). Second, people who are apt to tell little lies in their everyday life are more concerned with self-presentation than more truthful people (Kashy & DePaulo, 1996). Third, extroverts may be more apt to use self-presentational strategies than introverts. For example, when it comes to choice of picture on a social networking site, there is a lot of room for self-presentation as you might imagine. Turns out that extroverts are more likely than introverts to present themselves in a less conservative manner by the choice of a unique profile photograph (Krämer & Winter, 2008). Can you guess who the extroverts might be in the photo on page 135 Finally, some people—high self-monitors (Turnley & Bolino, 2001) and the politically astute (Harris, Kacmar, Zivnuska, & Shaw, 2007), for example—are more effective at using self-presentational techniques than others.

Table 5.8 The Five Most Common Self-Presentation Tactics

Strategy	Image Projected	Emotion Aroused	How Achieved	Avoid	Illustration
Ingratiation	Likable	Affection	Flattery Agreement Similarity Solidarity Interest	Being found out Seen as a sycophant	"Flattery will get you everywhere"
Intimidation	Dangerous	Fear	Respect	Being too threatening	"I'll huff and I'll puff"
Self-promotion	Competent	Respect	Claims of Performance	Conceit	"When you've got it flaunt it"
Exemplification	Good example	Guilt	Self-denial	Hypocrisy	"Do as I do"
Supplication	Helpless	Nurturance	Arouse empathy Invoke responsibility	Loss of self-esteem Victim blame	"You're my only hope"

Source: Reprinted with permission from Jones, E.E., & Pittman, T.S. (1982), "Toward a theory of strategic self-presentation," as appeared in J. Suls (Ed.), Psychological perspectives on the Self, p. 231–262. (Hillsdale, NJ: Erlbaum). Permission conveyed through the Copyright Clearance Center.

Self-presentation 2.0. Extroverts are more likely than introverts to present themselves as less conservative through the use of an unusual or stylized photograph rather than a realistic color picture. Pictures from the German social network site *StudiVZ* illustrate the normal style of photo (top left) and different types of photos. Top (from left to right): serious photo, partial face, different style (e.g., black and white). Bottom (from left to right): making a face, posing, location. *Source:* From Krämer and Winter (2008, Figure 1, p. 109).

Self-presentation is related to a whole host of social behaviors including the giving and receiving of help, conformity, reactance, attitude expression, attitude change, response to evaluation, aggression, and emotions (Baumeister, 1982). For example, putting our "best face forward" by trying to make a good impression on others actually improves our own mood (Dunn, Biesanz, Human, & Finn, 2007).

Yet, self-presentations can be hazardous to our health. One review suggested that reluctance to use sunscreen, use of certain cosmetics, engagement in unsafe sex, use of steroids, eating disorders, smoking, injuries and accidental death, failure to exercise, and alcohol and other drug use may all be related to the desire to present ourselves in a certain light when we are with others (Leary, Tchividjian, & Kraxberger, 1994).

Self-Monitoring

Is it possible for a person to use self-presentation *all* the time? Whereas most of us would monitor our behavior and emotional expressions at certain times, some people seem to be especially aware of the images they portray. **Self-monitoring** is a personality trait that describes the extent to which people are aware of and manage their self-presentations, expressive behaviors, and nonverbal displays of emotion to control the images and impressions others form of them (Snyder, 1979). Like other traits, self-monitoring describes behavior on a continuum from low to high.

High self-monitors are particularly sensitive to the behavior of others in social situations, and use other people as a guideline for their own behavior. In contrast, low self-monitors have less concern for social appropriateness and so pay less attention to what others in a situation are doing.

Table 5.9   Sample Items From the Self-Monitoring Scale

High self-monitors would agree with these statements:

1. I guess I put on a show to impress or entertain people.
2. In different situations and with different people, I often act like very different persons.
3. I'm not always the person I appear to be.
4. I may deceive people by being friendly when I really dislike them.

Low self-monitors would agree with these statements:

1. I find it hard to imitate the behavior of other people.
2. My behavior is usually an expression of my true inner feelings, attitudes, and beliefs.
3. At parties and social gatherings, I do not attempt to do or say things that others will like.
4. I can only argue for ideas which I already believe.

Source: From M. Snyder (1974, Table 1, p. 531). Snyder, M. (1974). Self-monitoring of expressive behavior. *Journal of Personality and Social Psychology, 30*, 526–537. Copyright American Psychological Association. Adapted with permission.

Low self-monitors audit and control their self-presentations far less than high self-monitors do. Ratings from the peers of high and low self-monitors confirm these differences (Snyder, 1974). When in a new situation, high self-monitors seem to ask themselves, Who does this situation want me to be and how can I be that person? (Snyder, 1979, p. 102). Low self-monitors are more apt to think, Who am I and how can I be me in this situation? (Snyder, 1979, p. 103). Table 5.9 presents sample items from the Self-Monitoring Scale (Snyder, 1974; Snyder & Gangestad, 1986).

Professional stage actors, as we might imagine, are higher than college students in self-monitoring whereas psychiatric inpatients are lower (Snyder, 1974). Self-monitoring may well be a skill good politicians have mastered to their advantage. For example, the popular Depression-era mayor of New York City, Fiorello LaGuardia, was reputed to have been so skilled at reading a crowd and adopting their mannerisms, that one could tell which ethnic group he was addressing by watching silent films of his appearances (Snyder, 1974).

Low self-monitors are more consistent in their expressive behavior across situations and show greater correspondence between their attitudes and behaviors than high self-monitors (Snyder, 1979). They also differ in their social interactions (Ickes, Holloway, Stinson, & Hoodenpyle, 2006). High self-monitors tend to take the lead in initiating conversations and managing smooth social interactions with a stranger, especially in an unusual situation (Snyder, 1979).

Although we might view high self-monitors as social chameleons, they see themselves as flexible and adaptable (Snyder, 1979). On the other hand, low self-monitors would agree with Polonius's advice to the college-bound Laertes in Shakespeare's *Hamlet:* "To thine own self be true" (Snyder, 1987).

In addition to differences in self-presentation, awareness of their own attitudes and emotions, and sensitivity to situational demands, high and low self-monitors also show differences in friendship choice, close relationships, consumer behavior, and even workplace behavior (Leone, 2006). High and low self-monitors seem to want different things in their friendships, romantic relationships, and long-term relationships (Leone & Hawkins, 2006). For example, imagine that you've won free passes to one of the hottest bands in town. Who would you rather take, your very best friend, or an ordinary friend who is really into this band?

When it comes to choosing friends for activities, high self-monitors choose friends for activities whereas low self-monitors choose activities for friends (Snyder, Gangestad, & Simpson, 1983). That is, high self-monitors think in terms of what the activity requires and then pick a friend to invite along accordingly (e.g., "Even though John's a better friend, he's just not the right person to go to a concert with"). Low self-monitors think in terms of a friend they want to spend time with, and then they pick something to do (e.g., "Jan's my best friend. Besides, she's the most fun to be around, whatever the activity"; Snyder et al., 1983, p. 1069). As a result, high self-monitors tend to have many separate groups of friends (e.g., "My soccer friends," "My work friends," "My school friends"). Low self-monitors tend to have overlapping groups of friends (Snyder et al., 1983).

High and low self-monitors seem to want different things in their romantic relationships, too (Jones, 1993). Low self-monitors report more pleasure in their relationships from simply being with their partners, and to value kindness and consideration, faithfulness and loyalty, and honesty in a potential dating partner more so than high self-monitors. High self-monitors report more external rewards from their relationships (e.g., social connections, opportunities) than low self-monitors, and to value the qualities of physical attractiveness, sex appeal, social status, and financial resources in their potential dating partners more so than low self-monitors.

High and low self-monitors also differ in the kinds of ads that appeal to them (DeBono, 1987, 2006; Snyder & DeBono, 1985). High self-monitors are attracted by glitzy ads that emphasize the image use of a product projects, whereas low self-monitors are more swayed by ads emphasizing the quality of the product. High and low self-monitors also evaluate consumer products differently (DeBono, 2006). For high self-monitors a quality product is one that can enhance their image. For low self-monitors, quality comes from product performance.

Even in the workplace high and low self-monitors act differently (Day & Schleicher, 2006). High self-monitors are better than low self-monitors at getting along with others and in job performance. They also tend to become leaders of their work groups. Self-monitoring is not related to rates of job turnover per se, but it is related to reasons for switching jobs (Jenkins, 1993). Low self-monitors are more likely to leave a job once their commitment flags. High self-monitors don't care as much about commitment to an organization, but are more likely to leave when the job becomes unsatisfying.

THINK ABOUT IT

Do you more often choose friends for activities or activities for friends?

"A man's Self is the sum total of all that he CAN call his, not only his body and his psychic powers, but his clothes and his house, his wife and children, his ancestors and friends, his reputation and works, his lands and horses, and yacht and bank-account. All these things give him the same emotions. If they wax and prosper, he feels triumphant; if they dwindle and die away, he feels cast down,—not necessarily in the same degree for each thing, but in much the same way for all."

William James (1890, p. 188)

Is there an advantage to being high or low in self-monitoring? Is one style any healthier than the other? People high and low in self-monitoring do not differ in neuroticism, intelligence, academic achievement, social anxiety, achievement anxiety, or vocational interests (Snyder, 1979). Also, high and low self-monitors do not differ in their rates of depression, but they do differ in what triggers depression. High self-monitors are more upset when their self-presentation is threatened, like when they fail to make a team, secure a part in a play, or land a job offer. Low self-monitors are more upset when they are unable to be their true selves, like working with people they do not like, being told they are hypocrites, or discovering that a close friend no longer shares important values or attitudes (Snyder, 1987). Basically, these are just two different ways of approaching and engaging the social world.

Chapter Summary

Who am I? By now you should have a better idea of how personality psychology answers this question. Our selves are made up of self-concepts (ideas about what we are like), self-esteem (how we feel about our selves), and our social identity (the parts of ourselves we show to others).

Our self-concepts develop from our experiences with the social world along with maturation and cognitive development. Self-recognition, as demonstrated by the mirror test, is a very sophisticated skill, one shared by great apes, dolphins, elephants, and humans. From our interactions with others, we come to develop and refine our self-concepts, develop our self-esteem, and understand our identity (i.e., how we are viewed by society). In short, we develop our selves through three sources of knowledge, two of which are based on our interactions with other people: social comparison, reflected appraisals, and our own self-appraisals.

Culture has a huge impact on how we think about ourselves. People who live in more individualistic cultures develop an independent self-concept, whereas people in more collectivistic cultures develop an interdependent self-concept. These self-concepts differ in definition, structure, features, tasks, the role of others, and the basis of self-esteem. The Twenty Statements Test has been used to compare self-concepts of people across cultures.

Also contained in our self-concepts are our possible selves, including how we expect to be, what we hope to be, and what we fear becoming in the future. These different selves can help us set goals and stay motivated to achieve those goals.

The idea of self, identity, and identity crisis is a modern one. What the self is has changed through the ages and has become more complicated since William James, the father of psychology, defined the self in 1890.

Self-esteem, the evaluative component of the self, can be described as high or low, and stable or unstable, and can be global or specific to a domain. People with high self-esteem have greater self-concept clarity than people low in self-esteem.

No doubt feeling good about ourselves is a good thing, but is low self-esteem the root of all social ills? Although people think that those with high self-esteem are smarter, more likable, and more physically attractive, do better in school, achieve more on the job, have greater life satisfaction and happiness than those with low self-esteem, this is not supported by research. Similarly, it is not true that low self-esteem is problematic, causing relationship problems, aggressiveness, alcohol and other drug abuse, premature sexual activity, unwanted pregnancies, and other social ills.

Many of these myths derive from misinterpreting research, the different kinds of high self-esteem masking the true effects of self-esteem, the inherent bias existing in self-ratings, not realizing that low self-esteem is really only moderate self-esteem, and mistaking correlation for causation. For example, self-esteem is often the result—not the cause—of achievement in school, work, and life. Also, the role of third variables (e.g., family background) has not been sufficiently investigated. Interventions that attempt to boost self-esteem through noncontingent rewards such as praise are misguided and may even backfire if they teach that one's efforts are unimportant.

Personality psychologists use quantitative and qualitative methods in their research. Quantitative methods involve measures or scores whereas qualitative methods involve the content analysis of verbal material. Many steps are involved in conducting a study using content analysis, the most important being to ask the right open-ended question and to take care in coding and categorizing participants' responses.

✓● **Study** and **Review** on **mysearchlab.com**

Go online for more resources to help you review.

Finally, our social identity is that part of ourselves that we share with others. We may show our true selves in an authentic self-presentation or we may use a strategic self-presentation to project a specific image or impression for others. Images may be agentic or communal. The regulation of public self-presentations is called impression management. The most common self-presentational strategies are ingratiation, intimidation, self-promotion, exemplification, and supplication.

Some people—that is, high self-monitors—seem to constantly monitor a situation and change their behavior accordingly. High self-monitors strive to be what a situation calls for; low self-monitors strive to be themselves in all situations. High and low self-monitors differ in behavioral consistency, self-presentation, awareness of their own attitudes and emotions, sensitivity to situational demands, friendship choice, close relationships, consumer behavior, and workplace behavior.

These are but a few of the many aspects of the self studied by personality psychologists. One thing we can say for certain: Studying our selves is among the most fascinating topics in personality psychology.

Review Questions

1. What are the three parts of the self studied by psychologists?
2. What is a self-concept? Do animals have a self-concept? How do we know? How does a self-concept develop? What are some major milestones in the development of self-concept, self-esteem, and social identity?
3. Describe the Twenty Statements Test. What are the four categories of responses in the TST? How does culture impact self-concepts? What are the important differences between an independent and an interdependent self?
4. What are possible selves? What are the different kinds of possible selves identified by psychologists? What impact do positive and negative possible selves have on adjustment? Can possible selves be changed? How?
5. How has the self changed through time? How do personality psychologists define the self now?
6. What is self-esteem? What are people high in self-esteem like? What are people low in self-esteem like? What is self-handicapping? Is this an effective strategy? Explain your reasoning.
7. What are some popular beliefs about self-esteem? What does research evidence have to say about these beliefs?
8. What is qualitative data? What is quantitative data? What is content analysis? What are some of the steps involved in doing content analysis?
9. What is a social identity? What is an authentic self-presentation? What is a strategic self-presentation? What are some ways of strategically presenting ourselves?
10. What is self-monitoring? What are some key differences between people high and low in self-monitoring? Is it better to be one or the other?

Key Terms

Twenty Statements Test (TST)	Individualism	Quantitative methods
Self-concept	Collectivism	Content analysis
Mirror test	Individualistic cultures	Social identity
Objective self-awareness	Collectivistic cultures	Self-presentation
Reflected appraisals	Independent view of the self	Impression management
Looking glass self	Hoped-for selves	Authentic self-presentation
Identity	Feared selves	Strategic self-presentation
Identity crisis	Possible selves	Ingratiation
Stereotype threat	Self-esteem	Intimidation
Attributive self-descriptions	Self-esteem stability	Self-promotion
Social self-descriptions	Self-concept clarity	Exemplification
Global self-descriptions	Self-handicapping	Supplication
Physical self-descriptions	Qualitative methods	Self-monitoring

6 GENETICS

Read the Chapter on
mysearchlab.com

"What a piece of work is man! How noble in reason! How infinite in faculty! In form and moving how express and admirable! In action how like an angel! In apprehension how like a god! The beauty of the world! The paragon of animals!"

William Shakespeare, Hamlet, *Act II, scene ii*

D o these words sound familiar to you? Of course they do, but do you recall the few lines preceding these classic words?

I have of late—but wherefore I know not—lost all my mirth.

And earlier in Act I, scene ii:

O, that this too, too solid flesh would melt,
Thaw, and resolve itself into a dew!
Or, that the Everlasting had not fix'd
His canon 'gainst self-slaughter! O God! God!
How weary, stale, flat and unprofitable,
Seem to me all the uses of this world!

Hamlet is depressed. Of course, he has good reason to be, with his father recently dead, his uncle trying to take over the kingdom, and his mother remarrying too soon. What makes a person depressed? Is depression caused by a genetic predisposition, such that some people are doomed to be depressed? Or is depression caused by experiences that are so devastating that *anybody* would be depressed by them?

For years, psychologists wondered what caused clinical depression: a debilitating combination of profound sadness, loss of interest in formerly pleasurable activities, lack of energy, hopelessness, feelings of worthlessness, and even thoughts of suicide. Although life events such as death of a parent, job loss, or stress no doubt cause people to be sad, what causes this devastating condition?

Because some psychologists had noticed that depression ran in families—or at least in some families—researchers tried to find a genetic mechanism of depression. Consider a study by Haeffel et al. (2008). They identified a sample of adolescent boys who were ordered by the courts to attend a residential juvenile delinquent detention facility in the Arkhangelsk region of northern Russia. The sample was not very diverse—about 98% of the sample was of Russian ancestry—but perfect for investigating possible genetic causes of depression.

The researchers looked for genetic and environmental differences between the youths who were depressed and those who were not. The amazing thing is that they found—nothing! That is, they found no impact of either genes or environment on rates of depression.

But, when they looked closer and divided up the sample depending on which of three specific gene combinations—called **genotypes**—a participant had, the results were startling, as Figure 6.1 shows. If a youth had both a stressful environment (as measured by maternal rejection in this study) and Genotype 3, there was a good chance that he was depressed.

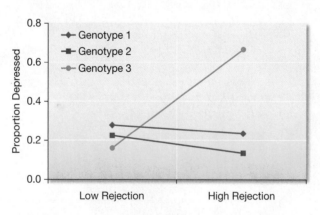

Figure 6.1 Incidence of clinical depression as a function of genotype and maternal rejection. *Source:* From Haeffel et al. (2008, Figure 1, p. 66), Haeffel, G. J., Getchell, M., Koposov, R. A., Yrigollen, C. M., DeYoung, C. G., af Klinteberg, B., et al. (2008), "Association between polymorphisms in the dopaminetransporter gene and depression," *Psychological Science,* 19(1), 62–69. Reprinted by permission of Blackwell Publishing.

However, if a youth had any of the three genotypes without maternal rejection or maternal rejection with either Genotype 1 or Genotype 2 he was not as likely to develop clinical depression. Further, this combination of environment (maternal rejection) and genotype predicted related outcomes such as suicide ideation and depressive symptoms but not *un*related psychological problems such as an anxiety disorder. This suggests that there is something magical (perhaps alarming is a better word) about this particular interaction of *these* genes with *this* environment.

Like Haeffel et al. (2008), other researchers have found it notoriously difficult to find main effects of genes on personality traits (Krueger & Johnson, 2008). This highlights an important theme of this chapter: The interesting question is not whether genes *or* environment affect our personalities, for surely both do. The real question is *how* do genes and environment *work together* to make us the kind of people we are? To answer this question we need to explore some basics of **behavioral genetics**, which is the study of the genetic and environmental contributions to individual differences in personality and behavior (DiLalla, 2004). (To get you thinking about these issues, you may want to try the self-assessment exercise in Table 6.1).

The goal of this chapter is not to present a catalog of personality characteristics that have a genetic component, for the list would be too long! Neither will we explore the molecular mechanism of specific genes important for personality development, for the research evidence is piling up too quickly for a textbook to keep up with. Instead, we will focus on understanding how genetic principles work in explaining differences in personality. Armed with this broad understanding as your groundwork, you will be able to understand the genetics behind any personality characteristic you encounter in this book and to understand the newest breakthroughs in genetics research that you may hear about in the news.

Table 6.1 How Much Do Genes and Environment Contribute to Personality?

Instructions: Identify four family members or friends who differ in their blood-relation to you and in whether you grew up in the same environment by using the following descriptions for Person 1, Person 2, and so on and filling in their names at the top of each of the four columns in the chart.

Person 1 = Genetic parent (of same sex as you, if possible).

Person 2 = Genetic sibling (of same sex as you, if possible). If you are an only child, use a cousin or other relative.

Person 3 = Unrelated person (or less related to you than Person 2) living in your household while you were growing up.

Person 4 = Unrelated person, not living in your household while you were growing up (e.g., best friend, peer, roommate).

If you are unable to identify any of Persons 1 to 3, then use people who lived in your household, even if you were not related to them, and compare them with unrelated people who did not live in your household while growing up.

Next, rate how similar you are to each of these people using the following scale:

1	2	3	4	5	6
Completely different	Different	More different than Similar	More similar than Different	Similar	Very similar, almost the same

	Person 1	Person 2	Person 3	Person 4
Name of person:				
Characteristic:				
1. Height				
2. Sense of humor				
3. Weight				
4. Political views				
5. Adventurousness				
6. Taste in music				
7. Extraversion				
8. Anxiousness				
9. Individualistic				
10. Tech-savy				

Based on your responses, can you venture a guess as to which has a greater influence on the development of each characteristic, genes or environment? Finally, do you think that each characteristic is caused more by genes and environment working separately, working together, or by influencing each other?

Nature and Nurture as Allies

Imagine that you are taking a standardized test and the following item appears in your test book:

Lemonade is

a. lemon juice.

b. water.

c. sugar.

How would you answer this question? Would you start to panic and wonder if this was a trick question? After all, *everybody* knows that lemonade is made up of all of these! In fact, we might say that lemonade is a compound solution entirely different from its constituent parts. So, this question, obviously, makes no sense. But consider this equally nonsensical question:

Extraversion is

a. genetic.

b. cultural.

c. familial.

d. due to all your idiosyncratic learning experiences.

When it comes to understanding human behavior, this question makes no sense either. That is, human behavior—and personality in particular—is an inextricable combination of both genetics and environment. In fact, taking sides in the nature–nurture debate is a massive "scientific mistake" (Krueger & Johnson, 2008, p. 287). So, if you are wondering *whether* genes determine your personality, stop right there: Personality is lemonade! (This fantastic example comes from Carey, 2003, pp. 2–3.)

The best characterization of the nature–nurture issue is that nature and nurture *transact.* That is, genes and environment can work separately, together, or they may influence one another (Canli, 2008, p. 299). When we talk about heritability and environmentality separately, we are assuming that genes and environment each have a unique contribution to the whole personality. That is, genes and environment may operate separately but in parallel (i.e., at the same time) to influence our personalities. You can think of genes and environment as co-actors (Cardno & McGuffin, 2002). This is the simplest case, as we shall soon see, and may not, in fact, be the way most aspects of personality develop.

A more interesting case is that genes and environment may interact with each other, such that they change aspects of human personality by acting together on a person. You know that saying *the whole is greater than the sum of its parts?* Well, it is possible that certain

Genes and environment as co-actors: Physically and psychologically, we are the result of an inextricable combination of both genetics and environment.

environments have different effects on people depending on their specific genetic makeup. We call this combination of nature and nurture a *genotype–environment interaction.* With more sophisticated ways of exploring the human genome, especially at the molecular level, this is the most exciting, and potentially groundbreaking kind of research that personality researchers are conducting. This is partially what we meant by lemonade in the discussion that opened this chapter: sugar, lemon, and water, when mixed in the right proportions, combine to make something fundamentally different (and better!) than each separate ingredient.

Yet another possibility is that it may be impossible to separate the effect of genes from the effect of the environment. What if people change environments and environments change people, so that we really can't separate the impact of genes on environment? This is called a *genotype–environment correlation.* This is yet another sense in which personality is lemonade: There is no way to separate out the ingredients, as they are inextricably combined.

In fact, some researchers advocate an even more complicated equation for understanding the manifestation of complex human traits—a concept known as **phenotype** (Cardno & McGuffin, 2002, p. 40):

$$\text{Phenotype} = \text{Genotype} + \text{Environment} + \text{Gene–environment correlation}$$

$$+ \text{Gene–environment interaction.}$$

We will consider each part of this equation in turn.

Genes and Environment as Co-actors

When we say that a characteristic is due to both genetics and environment, how do we know? Scientists are able to estimate how much of the differences among people on a given characteristic are because of their genes. For example, consider the students in your personality class. No doubt there are wide variations of height, with some taller people and some shorter people and lots of people of average height. The question is, how much of this observed height difference among people in your class is due to their differing genetic makeup? In this section we examine the concepts of *heritability* and *environmentality.*

Heritability

Heritability (h^2) is the amount of observed individual differences in some characteristic that can be accounted for by genetic differences (Carey, 2003). Heritability refers to differences across a group or population of people—not to a specific person. It is impossible to say how much of *your* height is due to *your* genes. But, considering a sample of people, like your personality class, we can estimate that about 80% of the observed differences in height is due to differing genetic makeup of your classmates and 20% is due to differing environments your classmates were raised in, plus some percentage of measurement error (because nothing, especially not our measurement instruments, is perfect).

To illustrate, imagine that you and your friends like to bake (and eat!) chocolate chip cookies, and each time you make them, they come out slightly different. Why might this be? Different brands of chocolate chips? Different types of flour? Is it possible that different bakers produce different cookies? You can readily see that the differences among batches could be due to differences in any of these factors. But suppose I asked you, which is more important to the flavor of *this particular cookie:* the flour or the eggs? Well, obviously we need both in order to have a good cookie! The question makes no sense. The same principle applies to understanding heritability: We cannot know what contributes more to the personality of a particular person, but we can know how much genetics and environment each account for differences in a particular personality characteristic of this particular sample of people.

Heritability, therefore, refers to the inheritance of *a particular trait in a particular population at a particular time,* so sometimes heritability estimates differ depending on the exact

"Everything is heritable."
Turkheimer (2004, p. 161)

THINK ABOUT IT

What environmental factors could account for differences in height among a group of people?

Heritability: Just as the variation among batches of cookies is due to variations in ingredients, the variation of a particular trait in a particular population at a particular time is due to differences in their genetic makeup.

sample and methods used by researchers (Plomin, DeFries, McClearn, & McGuffin, 2008, p. 86). To understand this, let's continue discussing height, a characteristic with a fairly large genetic component. The heritability of height is 80% or higher in the United States but it is only 65% in China and western Africa. And in Australia, one study estimated height heritability as 87% for men and 71% for women (Silvetoinen et al., 2003)! This is because of genetic variations among ethnic groups and because of the distinct environments they face. For example, Americans, Chinese, and Africans vary in native climates, lifestyle, and dietary habits, as do men and women in many cultures (Lai, 2006). This is why heritability is considered an estimate that refers to a specific population: Estimates vary between samples.

Environmentality

It's unlikely that genetics account for 100% of the variance in *any* personality variable, so what accounts for the rest of the variation? The environment, of course! We use the term **environmentality** (e^2) for that. Environmentality estimates the extent to which observed individual differences can be traced in any way to individual differences in environments (Carey, 2003). Together, heritability, environmentality, and measurement error account for all the differences we see among people on a given characteristic.

By now, it must be getting clearer to you that environment and genetics work together to impact human behavior so that it doesn't make sense to pit nature *against* nurture. As a general rule, the greater the heritability of a characteristic the less the environmentality. And the greater the environmentality, the less the heritability. Whereas height does have a large genetic component, the environmentality of height is fairly strong too, somewhere in the neighborhood of 20 to 40%. What kinds of environmental factors influence height? The biggest influence is childhood nutrition, especially protein, but also calcium, vitamin A, and vitamin D. In particular, childhood *mal*nutrition is particularly detrimental to adult height. Childhood diseases can also limit adult height, and by the same token human growth hormones can counteract some of these detrimental effects (Lai, 2006). This is how genetically similar populations may show differing heritability estimates: environmentality.

We see higher heritability estimates in equalizing environments (i.e., environments that are the same for everybody, and lower estimates in more variable environments; Plomin et al., 2008). This is because when everybody has access to resources in rich environments there is little variance in the effect the environment can have. For example, there's a limit to how much meat will increase height. Once all or nearly all of the people in a society have access to good health care, high levels of protein, and enriched foods, then we will see a very strong effect of genetics. Essentially, the only thing left to vary at this point *is* genetics. This is why heritability estimates for height are the greatest in developed countries such as the United States, and lower in less developed countries. In fact, average height in the United States has plateaued, meaning that as a nation we've gotten about as tall as we're going to get due to environmental effects (Lai, 2006).

SEE FOR YOURSELF

Consider your extended family of great-grandparents, grandparents, aunts, uncles, and cousins. Can you identify particular environmental factors that may account for height differences, especially between generations in your family?

Shared and Nonshared Environments

Traditionally, environment referred only to any part of the phenotype not accounted for by genes. However, these days researchers are trying to zero in on, and specifically identify, the exact aspects of an environment that account for differences in personality among a group of people. One way of thinking about environmental influences on characteristics such as height or personality is to identify aspects of the environment that are shared and unshared among relatives living together in a household.

Shared environment includes aspects of the family environment that are generally the same for all the children in the household (Krueger & Johnson, 2008) including physical, psychological, and social aspects (Carey, 2003). Physical aspects of a household may be the type of dwelling (e.g., apartment vs. house) and its layout, the number of computers or books in the home, or the presence of a video gaming system. Psychological aspects might include home atmosphere, parenting practices, the quality of sibling interactions, or psychopathology (e.g., alcoholism, drug use, depression) in the home. Social variables include socioeconomic status, family structure, educational attainment of the parents, an urban or a rural setting, and religion. In the broadest sense, *anything* not accounted for by genetics that makes relatives similar has been considered part of the shared environment (Carey, 2003).

In contrast, the **nonshared environment** includes experiences that relatives have which make them different from one another (Carey, 2003; Krueger & Johnson, 2008; Plomin, Asbury, & Dunn, 2001). These may include unique experiences within the family (e.g., being the eldest, being the only boy, spacing of siblings, differential parental treatment), or outside the family (e.g., peers, teachers, sports, hobbies). When it comes to personality, most of the environmental influence ends up being of the nonshared variety (Krueger & Johnson, 2008; Plomin & Caspi, 1999; Turkheimer & Waldron, 2000). The big surprise to researchers has been that when family members resemble one another it is more often due to heredity than to shared environment (Krueger & Johnson, 2008; Plomin & Caspi, 1999). That is, children growing up in the same family are not any more similar to one another than children growing up in different families. Even when children experience the same event, like a divorce, it may be experienced differently by each of the children depending on their individual personalities or ages (e.g., a relief, the end of the world; Hetherington & Clingempeel, 1992). Certainly environment is important; however, the important aspects of the environment for personality development do not appear to be shared by family members.

It may be that family environment makes children *different* from one another (e.g., "Jerry is the adventurous one; Tony is the thoughtful one") or it may be that researchers are looking too broadly and have not identified specific aspects of the environment that are shared (e.g., sense of humor, openness to ideas, cultural and aesthetic values). Also, parents may handle children differently depending on their personality, creating a unique environment for each child. For all of these reasons, researchers have had a difficult time identifying the precise shared and nonshared aspects of the child's environment that, along with genetics, account for differences in personality.

For example, although we know that teachers and peers have a big impact on children's development (e.g., Shaffer, 2009), is this part of the shared or the nonshared environment? In most behavioral genetic research the effect of schools, neighborhoods, and communities gets labeled as shared family experiences when they might not even be shared by siblings and they don't involve family! To untangle familial experiences from nonfamilial experiences one study employed an unusual control group.

Richard Rose and colleagues (Rose & Dick, 2004/2005; Rose et al., 2003) studied a sample of identical twins and nonidentical twins along with kids who were from the same neighborhood, school, and even classroom as each of the twins. The study took place in Finland, which at the time required parents to send their children to the closest neighborhood school. In this way, the researchers could estimate the separate effects of genetics (by comparing identical twins with nonidentical twins), familial environments (comparing twins with their matched control classmates), nonfamilial environments (comparing control kids from the same classes to one another), and personal environments (comparing kids from different neighborhoods to one another).

The twins were part of a longitudinal study known as the Finn Twin studies (Rose & Dick, 2004/2005). Only same-sex twins were used, and each member of the twin pair was matched to a child of the same sex from the same school, and in about 90% of the cases, they were from the same classroom. In all, there were 333 identical twins, 298 nonidentical twins, and 1,262 matched classmates for a total of 2,524 11- and 12-year-olds (Rose et al., 2003).

The participants were asked a series of yes-or-no questions about their smoking, drinking, and church activities (Rose & Dick, 2004/2005; Rose et al., 2003). From their responses, the researchers were able to estimate the amount of variance in the kids' self-reported behaviors that was due to genetics, familial environment, school environment, or personal environment.

Which source of variance was the most important? That depended on the behavior. In no case did genetics explain *all* of the variance in participants' self-reports. For some variables, notably smoking cigarettes, saying prayers, and seeing adults drunk, there was a greater effect of shared environment (i.e., the household) than shared genes. This makes sense because these are the kind of behaviors that parents model in front of their children. For alcohol use, both shared environment and shared genes had an impact.

When it came to drinking with peers without parents around, the neighborhood was more important than the household, as you might expect. After all, kids typically engage in these sorts of behaviors with their friends and do so far away from parental surveillance.

Finally, unique, unshared environment—what we might think of as a kid's personal environment—was more important for participation in church activities. You can see that even though the parents might encourage certain behaviors in the family such as saying prayers, it appears that kids themselves are choosing to get involved or not in church activities beyond Sunday services. And, indeed, the influence of family was the largest and genetics the smallest for having prayers in the home while growing up.

This study illustrates how the relative importance of genetics and environments varies depending on the question. Research designed to take account of various sources of social influence can shed light on shared and nonshared environments in accounting for personality and behavior.

SEE FOR YOURSELF

In what ways are you more similar to your friends than to your siblings? Why might this be?

Estimating Heritability

By now you must be wondering how researchers are able to measure heritability. We estimate the heritability of a characteristic by seeing if people who have similar genes show similar characteristics. If a characteristic has a strong genetic component, then we would expect identical twins, who share 100% of their genes, to be more similar than strangers in that characteristic. We can see this more clearly in physical characteristics, but it is harder to see the effects of genes and environment in personality, which is why so far in this chapter we've been looking at tangible things such as height.

Consider twins. As you know, there are two kinds of twins: identical and fraternal. Identical twins, called **monozygotic (MZ) twins,** are exact genetic duplicates of each other. This happens when a fertilized egg, the zygote, splits into two (or sometimes more) identical parts that each go on

One method of studying genetic influence is to compare personality traits in identical twins and in nontwin siblings.

Identical twins, called monozygotic (MZ) twins, are exact genetic duplicates of each other.

to develop into a fetus. Identical twins are quite rare in the population, occurring just over 32 times in 1,000 births in the United States.

In contrast, fraternal twins occur when two zygotes develop in utero at the same time. We call these kinds of twins **dizygotic (DZ) twins.** DZ twins result from the fertilization of two different eggs by two different sperm cells, hence they are genetically distinct. Essentially fraternal twins are no more alike than ordinary siblings, sharing about 50% of their genes (Carey, 2003). Although twins may look alike, the only way to be sure if they are identical (MZ) or fraternal (DZ) is to conduct a genetic test (of course, if the twins are of different sexes, then we know that they must be fraternal twins). Because of increased use of fertility drugs and in vitro fertilization the incidence of fraternal twins has been steadily increasing since the early 1980s (Plomin et al., 2008).

One measure of heritability, then, is to calculate the correlation (r) between twins on a given trait and compare the correlation between MZ twins and DZ twins (Plomin et al., 2008). The exact formula is to double the difference between these correlations or

$$h^2 = 2(r_{mz} - r_{dz})$$

A second way of estimating heritability is to compare identical twins who have been raised in separate environments (Plomin et al., 2008). We call these kinds of twins **MZA twins** (monozygotic twins raised apart). If such twins score similarly in a trait such as Extraversion, then we know that Extraversion has a strong genetic component. Studies of MZA twins are particularly powerful in disentangling the effects of genes and environment because they have identical genes but different environments. Here is a second formula for estimating heritability:

$$h^2 = r_{MZA}$$

We'll consider the logic behind adoption studies and twin studies in the Research Methods Illustrated section, in a moment. For now, note that both of these

Nonidentical twins, called dizygotic (DZ) twins, are no more alike than siblings, having about 50% of their genetic makeup in common.

estimates of heritability have limitations, and researchers may use more sophisticated formulas to account for these potential problems. The double-the-difference method assumes that twins were reared under equal environments (Cardno & McGuffin, 2002; Carey, 2003; DiLalla, 2004; Plomin et al., 2008). That is, it assumes that people have not treated MZ twins more alike than DZ twins. Whereas certainly *twins* are often treated differently than nontwins, the question is, are identical twins treated more similarly than are fraternal twins? If MZ twins are treated more alike, then they may score more similarly on a particular trait, artificially inflating the heritability estimate (you can see this for yourself by looking at our first formula). Essentially, what is really an environmental effect (similar treatment) gets mislabeled as a genetic effect (similar personality).

This **equal environments assumption** applies only to similar treatment that is related to the specific characteristic under study. For example, people often dress their twins alike in identical sailor suits or matching dresses. This probably happens more often to MZ twins than to DZ twins. If we were studying something like fashion sense, then this would violate our equal environments assumption. But unless wearing matching outfits affects a specific personality characteristic like shyness, then this assumption still holds (Carey, 2003).

You'll see that researchers often test this assumption by asking research participants (or their parents) to describe how they were treated while growing up. Indeed, such studies have concluded that for the most part, parents of MZ twins don't treat their twins any more alike than parents of DZ twins so that this equal environments assumption is a fair assumption (Cardno & McGuffin, 2002; Carey, 2003; Plomin et al., 2008).

The double-the-difference formula also assumes that twins are typical of the population. We call this the **assumption of representativeness** (Plomin et al., 2008). For example, twins are often premature and have a lower birthrate than single births. Twins, therefore, may not be representative of the general population on variables that are affected by prematurity or low birth weight. Again, this is something researchers may test for, and for the most part this assumption holds as well (Carey, 2003; Plomin et al., 2008).

The r_{MZA} method of estimating heritability also has its limitations. Here, researchers assume that the adopted families of each twin are different from each other. If the identical twins are placed in similar environments this may increase the similarity between the twins, artificially inflating our heritability estimate. That is, twins may be more alike on a certain characteristic due to **selective placement** during the adoption process and not to their genetics. Selective placement makes it impossible to see the effect of genetics apart from the effect of environment because it confounds the two (Plomin, DeFries, & Loehlin, 1977; Plomin et al., 2008).

Adoption studies of MZA twins also assume that families who adopt are the same as families who do not adopt. Again, if there is something special about adoptive families, then this environmental effect will get improperly labeled as a genetic effect. For example, prospective adoptive families often go through an interview to rule out extreme poverty, criminal behavior, drug abuse, and other factors that affect the ability of the family to provide a safe and secure environment for a child. We might wonder how representative adoptive families are. Although the mean income of adoptive families and the general population are not much different, there are fewer families in extreme poverty among adoptive families (Carey, 2003). This suggests a potential problem of range restriction among adoptive families, making it harder to detect a significant effect of environment. Again, whereas this might be a problem for some variables (e.g., antisocial behavior) it may not be a problem when it comes to personality traits (Carey, 2003). Both of these assumptions, selective placement and representativeness of adoptive families, have been tested by researchers and are not a problem for most studies (Plomin et al., 1977, 2008).

Research Methods Illustrated: Correlational Designs I: The Logic of Adoption and Twin Studies

What do we mean when we say that a certain trait "runs in families"? For example, families often share inside jokes and find the same sorts of things amusing. Does sense of humor run in families? If so, why might this be? When we say that a trait runs in families, is this because of shared genetics among family members? Or, is it because family members all live in the

THINK ABOUT IT

Do people treat identical twins differently from non-identical twins?

THINK ABOUT IT

Does being a twin affect one's personality more so than having a sibling close to your own age would?

same environment, where they might watch the same TV programs, tell amusing stories around the dinner table, and laugh at one another's jokes, for example? The trouble is, under ordinary conditions we can't tell the two apart.

Sure, we could design a kind of science-fiction experiment: Imagine a set of MZ twins who are identical in their genetic makeup. For about 9 months, let's say they share identical conditions inside their mother's womb (although in reality MZ twins grow in their own subenvironment of the womb). Then we would take these twins, separate them at birth, and randomly place them in contrasting environments. When they grow to adulthood we see what kinds of cartoons they think are funny and then see if this is more similar to their birth family's sense of humor or to their adopted family's sense of humor. This would be the way to design a true experimental test, but obviously such an experiment is completely unethical and impossible to do.

However, such natural experiments do happen in the world. Babies—both twins and nontwins—are adopted and raised in families that provide a nurturing environment but no genetic material. Similarly, twins—both genetically identical and not—are raised in the same environment. Thus adoption studies and twin studies go a long way to helping researchers understand both the genetic and environmental impact on human behavior, including personality.

Recall that a true experiment allows a researcher to infer causality between the presence or absence of a variable and some outcome measure. This is because the researcher is able to manipulate the independent variable and to randomly assign participants to various levels of that independent variable. Therefore, any difference in the outcome between the groups must be due to differences in what the experimenter manipulated. Of course, this assumes everything else was exactly the same for each and every participant. These two requirements—experimental control and random assignment to conditions—are the defining qualities of a true experiment.

However, there are times when one or both of these requirements are impossible. Like in our little sci-fi experiment, you can't randomly assign children to parents! That violates the random assignment to condition requirement. Similarly, you can't control whether children get raised in families with a dry sense of humor or into families with a corny sense of humor, violating the control of the independent variable requirement. So, sometimes it's unethical to conduct a true experiment and sometimes it's just impossible. Often, it's just impractical or inconvenient, due to limited time or resources.

As an alternative to a true experiment, researchers turn to correlational designs. In a correlational design the experimenter doesn't attempt to manipulate the presence or absence of the independent variable, but instead measures it along with some outcome measure. Because the independent variable is not under the experimenter's control, if we see a difference between participants in the outcome of the dependent variable, we can't assume that the independent variable is what *caused* the difference. In this case, the best we can say is that the two variables—our independent variable and our dependent variable—are related.

Although it is very rare to find identical twins who were separated at birth, studying such twins is a good way to understand the effects of genetics and environment on personality. For example, Bob and Bob first met as adults and discovered they had many similarities, including their name and occupation.

Recall that when two variables are related, there are always at least three possible explanations for the findings. First, it's possible that one variable causes the other, like being around the same people all the time causes people to develop a similar sense of humor. Second, it's also possible that the second variable causes the first one, like people who have a similar sense of humor spend more time hanging around each other. Finally, it's also possible that some third variable—like genetics—causes people to hang around each other (i.e., family) and to find the same jokes funny.

The beauty of twin and adoption studies is that they are able to rule out some of these explanations. For example, if adopted children are more similar to their birth parents than to their adoptive parents (or adopted siblings, even), then we can assume that the trait in question has a stronger genetic component. However, if adopted children are more similar to their adoptive parents than to their birth parents, then the trait in question must have a stronger environmental component.

An especially strong case for the relative contribution of genetics and environment may be made if we can study twins who were separated at birth. In these cases, we have two people with identical genetic makeup who have been exposed to different environments. If they respond similarly then we can conclude that genetics must have caused the similarity; if they respond differently then we can conclude that the environment must have caused the difference.

Take a look at Table 6.2 which shows the correlations between various family members in Extraversion and Neuroticism. Recall that positive correlations between two variables mean that the two variables are similar: as one variable increases (or decreases), the other variable increases (or decreases) too. Where are the correlations the highest? The lowest? As you can see, the more genetically similar two people are—for example, identical twins—the more similar they are in both of these characteristics. Being raised apart lessens the similarity, but being raised together without a genetic predisposition does little to make people similar on these traits. You can readily see how twin and adoption studies help us sort out the relative effects of genes and environment.

With all of this background on adoption studies, twin studies, and how to interpret correlations, we can now address our question: Does sense of humor run in families? And if so, why might this be? Using a sample of MZ and DZ female twin pairs, researchers had each twin rate how funny they found a series of five *Far Side* cartoons by Gary Larson (Johnson, Vernon, & Feiler, 2008). The researchers were careful to have the women rate the cartoons in separate rooms so they couldn't hear or see their twin's reaction.

How similar were the twins in their ratings of the cartoons? Overall, the ratings of each twin were pretty similar for each of the five cartoons. For one of the cartoons, for example, the correlation between ratings of one MZ with her twin was .50 and for DZ twins it was .41. This suggests that there is a medium, positive relationship between humor ratings of this cartoon in twins.

Take a closer look at these two correlations. Do you think that these correlations are different enough to suggest a genetic component to sense of humor? The researchers tested this idea using

Table 6.2   Twin, Family, and Adoption Correlations for Neuroticism and Extraversion

Type of Relative	Neuroticism	Extraversion
Identical twins reared together	.43	.52
Fraternal twins reared together	.19	.18
Identical twins reared apart	.31	.42
Fraternal twins reared apart	.23	.08
Nonadoptive parents and offspring	.14	.18
Adoptive parents and offspring	.05	.06
Nonadoptive siblings	.18	.19
Adoptive siblings	.12	−.05

Note: Based on a meta-analysis of 145 studies.

Source: From Johnson et al. (2008).

advanced statistical techniques and found that there was no significant impact of genetics on the ratings of these cartoons. However, they estimated that about 49% of the differences between twin pairs was due to differences in shared environment whereas 51% was due to nonshared environment. This suggests that sense of humor, at least for these kind of cerebral off-the-wall cartoons, is something that is partly learned at home and partly picked up from friends, and other aspects of a individual's unique environment.

Note that in this study the researchers did not randomly assign participants to be MZ twins or DZ twins, nor did they manipulate people to share 50 or 100% of the genes. And yet, we are able to estimate the relative contribution of genes, shared environment, and unique environment on people's sense of humor. Such is the value of correlational designs, adoption studies, and twin studies.

Heritability of Common Personality Characteristics

A solid finding in the research—one that has been well replicated across many samples and for both self-report and other report—is that virtually all individual differences in human behavior including cognitive abilities, personality, social attitudes, psychological interests, and psychopathology are moderately heritable (Bouchard & McGue, 2003). In the words of one researcher, "some degree of heritability is practically inevitable" (Turkheimer, 2004, p. 162).

The heritability of personality traits ranges from .40 to .60, and is the same for both men and women (Carey, 2003; Johnson et al., 2008; Krueger & Johnson, 2008; Plomin & Caspi, 1999; Plomin & Daniels, 1987; Plomin et al., 2008). In fact, one researcher went so far as to say that this is true for all known human differences (Turkheimer, 2000). In addition, shared environment typically accounts for very little variation (Johnson et al., 2008; Krueger & Johnson, 2008; Turkheimer, 2000), whereas nonshared environment accounts for a great deal (Johnson et al., 2008; Krueger & Johnson, 2008; Turkheimer, 2000). The variance in personality traits typically breaks down like this (Krueger & Johnson, 2008):

$$\text{Observed differences in personality traits} = 40\% \text{ Genetics} + 0\% \text{ Shared environment}$$
$$+ 40\% \text{ Nonshared environment} + 20\% \text{ Error.}$$

So even after we account for the 40 to 60% of variation in most personality traits that comes from genetics (Plomin et al., 2002), there is still plenty of variance left to be explained (Turkheimer, 2004)!

To illustrate this model, let's take a closer look at the heritability of the five-factor model (FFM) of traits. According to this model, human personality can be described using five broad categories of traits: Neuroticism, Extraversion, Openness, Agreeableness, and Conscientiousness (McCrae & Costa, 2008) (we learned about these factors in earlier chapters). Table 6.3 presents a summary of results based on 85,640 pairs of MZ twins, 106,644 pairs of DZ twins, and 46,215 nontwin kinships from 145 studies published from 1955 to 2006 (Johnson et al., 2008). As you can see, identical twins are very similar in the five-factor traits, even if they are raised apart, indicating a moderately strong genetic component to these traits. Indeed, the heritability of all five factors is in the .41 to .50 range, indicating that about 41 to 50% of the variation in these traits is due to genetic factors.

But look closely: Identical twins who were raised together have the highest correlations and indeed, even fraternal twins who are raised together look a bit like each other even though fraternal twins share only about 50% of their genes on average. This suggests that there is a moderate effect of the environment too. Indeed, the environment—both shared and nonshared—accounts for about 47 to 53% of the variance in these traits. Finally, the shared environment accounts for only about 8 to 17% of the variation in these traits. Other researchers have found similar results when looking at the individual facet traits that make up each of the five factors (Jang, McCrae, Angleitner, Riemann, & Livesley, 1998).

"Quantitative genetics is hardly needed any longer merely to ask whether and how much genetic factors influence behavioral traits because the answers are 'yes' and 'a lot,' respectively, for nearly all traits that have been studied, including personality and cognitive abilities"
(Plomin, Happé, & Caspi, 2002, p. 88).

SEE FOR YOURSELF

How similar are you and your siblings or parents in how emotional you are (Neuroticism)? In aesthetic sense such as appreciation for art and classical music (Openness)?

Table 6.3 Kinship Correlations, Heritability Estimates, and Environmentality Estimates for Traits of the Five-Factor Model

Type of Relative	N	E	O	A	C
Identical twins reared together	.43	.52	.48	.42	.47
Fraternal twins reared together	.19	.18	.24	.23	.22
Identical twins reared apart	.31	.42	.34	.19	.33
Fraternal twins reared apart	.23	.08	.14	.03	.09
Heritability	.41	.50	.46	.43	.49
Environmentality	.53	.47	.47	.49	.48
Shared environment	.08	.08	.12	.17	.11

Note: Based on a meta-analysis of 145 studies. N = Neuroticism, E = Extraversion, O = Openness, A = Agreeableness, and C = Conscientiousness.

A similar picture emerges from a study of 660 MZ and 200 DZ twins from Germany and Poland (Riemann, Angleitner, & Strelau, 1997). Each twin and two friends of that twin filled out questionnaires to measure the twin's personality on the five personality factors. The peer's ratings correlated .61 with one another and .55 with the twin's own rating indicating considerable agreement among the three raters in what the twin was like.

As you can see in Figure 6.2, although each of the five factors has moderate heritability—genetics accounted for about 35 to 60% of the variance in self-reported traits—there was a greater effect of nonshared environment on these traits (Plomin & Caspi, 1999). In fact, shared environment accounted for the smallest amount of variance in both self-reports and peer reports.

Here is a puzzle for you to think about. Notice that there is a strong genetic component to the peer ratings. Does this mean that we "inherit" the opinions of our friends? If not, then what might cause this correlation? It's easy to see how our genetic makeup would account for our own ratings, but why would our genetic makeup correlate with our friends' ratings? Stay tuned to find out!

Figure 6.2 Genetic and environmental influences for self-reports of Big Five personality traits. *Source:* From Plomin and Caspi (1999, Figure 9.1, p. 252). From L. A. Pervin & O. P. John, eds., *Handbook of Personality: Theory and Research* (2nd ed., p. 251–276). New York, NY: Guilford Press. Copyright © 1999 Guilford Press. Reprinted with permission.

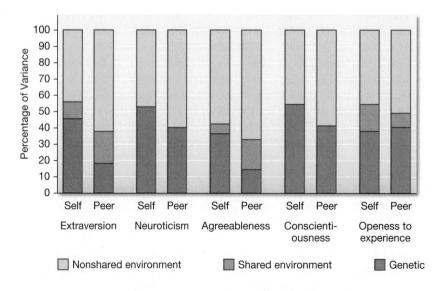

Then and Now: The Science of Genetics

To think the whole field of genetics started with a simple Augustinian friar named Gregor Johann Mendel (1822–1884), who was born and lived in what is now the Czech Republic, is mind-boggling. The son of a tenant farmer, he worked on the farm and learned about the grafting of fruit trees from his father. Mendel and his family recognized that he was too smart to simply follow in his father's footsteps working land that he could never own, so he joined the monastery and attended the University of Vienna to earn the credentials he needed to teach high school science. It was there that this farmboy "began to turn himself into one of the greatest experimental biologists of all time" (Mawer, 2006, p. 38). The friars of the Abbey of St. Thomas in Brno were unusual in their desire to practice public ministry, getting involved in political causes of the day (Mendel may have taken part in protests against the Austrian Empire as a student) and fostering intellectual pursuits. Although some brothers were philosophers and others were accomplished composers, the stout, amiable, shy, introverted, sensitive, and nearsighted Mendel spent his free time conducting experiments in the monastery gardens:

> Throughout each spring and summer the man spent hours and hours tending his plants, pollinating, scoring, labeling, harvesting, drying, putting seeds away for the next year, peering at the world through his gold-rimmed spectacles, puzzling and pondering, counting, and tallying, explaining to anyone who would listen what was going on. Visitors were in the presence of a man inspired—a Beethoven or a Goethe—and all they saw was a dumpy little friar with a sense of irony introducing them to his "children." (Mawer, 2006, p. 63).

His children were, of course, pea plants—over 28,000 of them! He studied the variation in plants and noticed that sometimes characteristics of plants seemed to skip a generation. He meticulously planted and recorded details of his pea plants and counted their offspring instead of merely generalizing the results as earlier researchers had done (Plomin et al., 2008). In particular, the nearly obsessive Mendel followed seven "characters" of plants over successive generations by crossing one kind of plant with another. These characteristics included smooth or wrinkled peas, yellow or green seeds, white seed coat with white flowers or gray seed coat with purple flowers, smooth or constricted peapods, green or yellow peapods, flowers at the top of the plant or all along the stem, and tall or dwarf plants (Mawer, 2006).

At the time, people believed that inherited characteristics—of people and plants—were blended. That is, the offspring of a pea plant with wrinkled peas and a plant with smooth peas would have moderately wrinkled peas. But that is not what Mendel found. Instead, he found that the next generation was all smooth. What happened to the genetic information for wrinkly peas? Mendel reasoned that the trait must still be present in the genotype even though it was not expressed in the phenotype. If this was true, then the genotype ought to be passed on to the next generation. Indeed, about 75% of the plants in the *next* generation were smooth and 25% were wrinkled. How can it be that each generation can seem so different? From such observations, Mendel developed two hypotheses, part of what we now consider his first law of inheritance (Plomin et al., 2008).

First, each parent plant passes on one form of the gene (Mendel used the word *element*) for a given characteristic to its offspring, who get two forms of the gene, one from each parent (note that different forms of the same gene are called **alleles**). These two alleles can either be the same or different. When the alleles are different, one characteristic will be dominant over the other. However, both alleles will be passed on to the next generation.

For example, say a pea plant with wrinkled peas breeds with a plant that has smooth peas. The next generation will each get some combination of alleles for smooth and wrinkly peas. If smoothness is the dominant characteristic, then the peas will look smooth, but the plants will still carry and pass on the recessive wrinkly pea trait to the next generation (see Figure 6.3). When a trait is recessive, the trait will appear only when a plant receives *two* alleles for the recessive trait—in this case wrinkly peas.

This concept of dominance explains the pattern of seeds Mendel observed in successive generations. In fact, such inheritance patterns where one trait dominates over another is called **Mendelian inheritance** and Mendel is now known as the founder of modern genetics (Mawer, 2006).

"When all the human genes are truly known, scientists will have produced a Periodic Table of Life."

Peltonen and McKusick (2001, p. 1224)

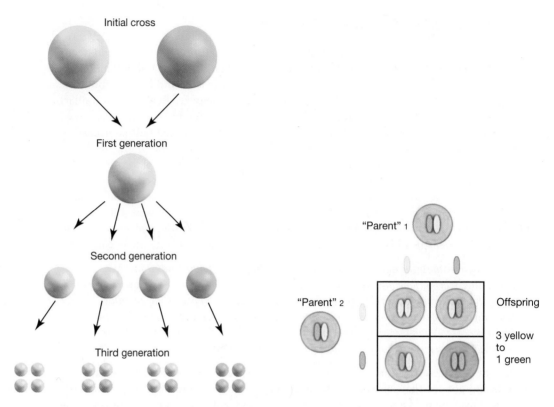

Figure 6.3 Summary of Mendel's experiments with peas. *Source:* From Mawer (2006, p. 54). Gregor Mendel: Planting the seeds of genetics. New York, NY: Abrams.

Fast-forward almost 150 years to the present day. Instead of inheritance of smooth or wrinkled peas, scientists are trying to understand what causes any number of human characteristics: physical diseases, psychological disorders, and even personality traits. Since the start of the century, a collaborative of international scientists have identified the 20,000 to 25,000 genes that make up the human genome (Mawer, 2006; Venter et al., 2001). Whereas about 99.9% of the human DNA sequence is the same for each and every one of us, it's that .1% that does differ that makes us unique individuals (Plomin, DeFries, Craig, & McGuffin, 2003).

Have researchers discovered a genetic, yet noninheritable means by which the environment fundamentally changes human functioning? Apparently so. This exciting new area of genetics research is called **epigenetics**. We know that a **gene** is a sequence of DNA that codes for a specific trait. Genes are composed of coding regions called **exons** and noncoding regions called **introns**. Of the 3.3 billion base pairs of DNA in the human genome, only about 2 to 3% are functioning genes. The remainder of the DNA—nearly 2 meters of it—was once thought to do nothing because it occurs outside genes (Mawer, 2006). This so-called junk DNA is actually turning out to be more interesting than the coding genes themselves. Some of this "junk" appears to orchestrate—alter its regulation to underexpress or overexpress—a nearby gene (Plomin et al., 2003). In fact, some of these noncoding sequences end up changing how the genes function in *direct response to the environment.*

What might this look like? Cole et al. (2007) identified a sample of older American adults, with a median age of 55 years, who scored in the top 15% of the UCLA Loneliness Scale. They were matched to adults of the same sex, age, ethnicity, and socioeconomic status who scored in the bottom 15% of the scale.

Previous research had established that people who are socially isolated are vulnerable to a host of cardiovascular and infectious diseases due to increased levels of the stress hormone cortisol. In the Cole et al. (2007) study both the lonely group and the socially connected group

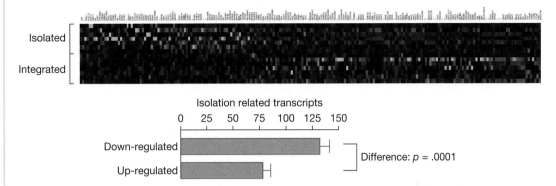

Figure 6.4 Gene expression as a function of loneliness status. The top strip indicates how the genes are functioning in isolated individuals, the bottom strip in connected individuals. Horizontal location indicates function of gene: Those on the left increase disease, those on the right prevent disease. Color indicates activity of genes: Green indicates overexpression (up-regulated) and red indicates underexpression (down-regulated). Here, the genes that code for disease are overexpressed in lonely people (green cells on the left) and underexpressed in socially connected people (red cells on the left). However, the genes that code for disease prevention are underactivated in lonely people (red cells on the right) and overexpressed in socially connected people (green cells on the right). Lonely individuals have significantly more underexpressed genes (red) than socially connected people. *Source:* From Cole et al. (2007, Figure 1, p. R189. 4). Cole, S. W., Hawkley, L. C., Arevalo, J. M., Sung, C. Y., Rose, R. M., & Cacioppo, J. T. (2007). Social regulation of gene expression in human leukocytes. *Genome Biology,* 8, R189 (doi:10.1186/gb-2007-8-9-r189)

gave samples of blood for genetic analysis to identify problems in the coding of glucocorticoid response genes that regulate how the body responds to stress hormones.

Figure 6.4 vividly shows the differences between these two groups in gene expression as a function of their feelings of isolation or connection. Significantly more genes that regulate immune functioning were turned down (not expressed at the same levels) in the lonely group than in the socially supported group. Specifically, those cells that protect against disease were turned down (red), whereas genes that increased disease were turned up (green). These results suggest that loneliness directly impacts immune functioning by regulating the specific genes that control immune functioning.

This is how epigenetics works for just one human behavior. As we learn more about genes involved in disorders and about the noncoding sequences of DNA that may turn out to regulate the genes, researchers may develop amazing new ways of treating diseases, both physical and psychological, perhaps in your lifetime. Scientists are searching for similar environmental effects behind diseases including (Carey, 2003) breast cancer, diabetes, high cholesterol, atherosclerosis, Alzheimer's disease, and also schizophrenia (Gottesman, 1991) and bipolar disorder (McGuffin, 2004).

For example, if a disease was inherited, once we have identified the exact gene involved in a disorder we can diagnose or screen who has the gene. Researchers then will be able to use this information to replace faulty genetic code with new and improved code that has been cloned to match as precisely as possible the recipient's genetics (McGuffin, 2004). This is called **positional cloning.**

In the words of one researcher:

It is now possible for behavior genetics to move beyond statistical analyses of differences between identical and nonidentical twins and identify individual genes that are related to behavioral outcomes. (Turkheimer, 2000, p. 163).

This is where the cutting-edge research is happening in behavioral genetics and the results are very exciting. We are finding that often the environment affects people differently depending on a specific genotype. We'll talk about some of these genotype–environmental interactions and the specific genes involved in the next section.

Genes and Environment: A Dialectical Synthesis

So far in this chapter we've been looking at the separate effects of genes and environment. But when it comes to personality, often genes and environment influence each other. We've briefly mentioned two ways this may happen—through genotype–environment interactions and genotype–environment correlations. Now it's time for us to take a closer look at these two processes.

According to the philosopher Hegel, a **dialectic** is a way of thinking in which contradictions are seen to be part of a higher truth. Take the nature–nurture debate. This phrase suggests that nature and nurture work in opposition. What happens if we think of "nature" and "nurture" not as opposing forces, but as forces that can be combined or synthesized in some fashion? What if genes and environment worked together as allies instead of working against each other as foes?

Recall our formula from the beginning of the chapter in which the amount of variance in an observed characteristic can be due to genetics, environment, and some combination of the two (Cardno & McGuffin, 2002, p. 40):

$$\text{Phenotype} = \text{Genotype} + \text{Environment} + \text{Gene–environment correlation} + \text{Gene–environment interaction}.$$

Until the 1980s, researchers had been considering genes and environment only as separate factors influencing phenotype. Plomin et al. (1977) suggested that researchers can increase the accuracy of their results—and detect new effects—by specifically testing for two ways in which genes and environment influence each other: a **genotype–environment interaction** and a **genotype–environment correlation**. A genotype–environment interaction occurs when a genotype *responds* differently to an environment; a genotype–environment correlation occurs when a genotype is *exposed* differently to an environment (Loehlin, 1992). These two effects are really examples of how nature and nurture work together and lead us to a higher truth. In this way, nature–nurture is more of a dialectic than a debate.

Two caveats are in order here. First, whereas we may be unable to see the joint effects of genes and environment in a single individual (remember lemonade?) we can explore only genotype–environment interactions and genotype–environment correlations within a population (Plomin et al., 1977). Although we will illustrate these concepts using individual examples, in practice we can really only gauge the genotype–environment effects in a group of people in which we are able to estimate key aspects of their genetic makeup and of their environment.

Second, Plomin et al. (1977) noted that in practice it is sometimes difficult to distinguish genotype–environment interactions from genotype–environment correlations. Researchers must be careful to define and measure aspects of both personality and the environment to truly see which kind of effect is occurring, ideally through a study that looks at these variables over time (Carey, 2003; Plomin et al., 1977). That is, it often comes down to sophisticated statistical tests to determine which effect—an interaction or a correlation—accounts for the data. Next we will define genotype–environment interactions and genotype–environment correlations in more detail and take a closer look at some interesting research findings that illustrate both kinds of effects.

Genotype–Environment Interactions

One way that genetics and environment work on each other is through a genotype–environment interaction. This is when people respond differently to the same environment because of their differing genetic makeup. That is, the environment has a different impact *depending* on a person's genotype (Plomin et al., 1977).

To illustrate how this works, let's go back to the study that opened the chapter. Recall that in a sample of juvenile delinquents in Russia even though many of the boys experienced maternal rejection in their lives (e.g., physical punishment, lack of respect for their point of view, public criticism), only those with a certain genotype experienced clinical depression (Haeffel et al., 2008).

As you can see now, this is an example of genotype–environment interaction. The same environment—maternal rejection—led to clinical depression only in boys with one specific

THINK ABOUT IT

Can you think of another example of a dialectic?

genotype (look back to Figure 6.1). In case you were wondering, maternal rejection was not correlated with clinical depression, so these really are separate effects.

To identify the specific genotype related to depression, researchers took blood samples from the participants. They then analyzed the samples to find out if the young men carried one of the three variations of a gene suspected to be related to depression. This gene (DAT1 or SLC6A3) is an important regulator of the neurotransmitter dopamine. Evidence suggests that prolonged exposure to dopamine may lead to depression.

Despite knowing which genes are related to dopamine functioning, scientists have been unable to prove that these genes cause depression. That is, no genetic difference has been found between depressed and nondepressed people. Recall that in this study researchers initially found no effect of genes alone or environment alone on clinical depression. But when they looked at the combination of a specific genotype with an environment of maternal rejection, that's when they found a significant genotype–environment interaction. In this case, genes and environment interacted with each other to cause a psychological outcome. We might well wonder what other genotype–environment interactions researchers may have missed out on by looking separately at genes and environment!

In fact, remember our earlier discussion of how shared environment effects on the development of personality traits have been difficult to find? Well, Lahey (2009) pointed out that shared environments may impact the personality trait of Neuroticism through genotype–environment interactions. By not considering interactive effects of environment on genes, researchers may have accidentally overestimated genetic effects and underestimated the impact of shared environments.

A second potential genetic risk factor for depression, anxiety, and other mood disorders involves a certain region of the serotonin transporter gene. The thinking here is that depression may be caused by a lack of the neurotransmitter serotonin in the spaces between the neurons. In fact, many popular antidepressant drugs, called selective serotonin reuptake inhibitors (SSRIs), work by blocking the cells that process serotonin so that it stays in the system a bit longer. People actually get two versions of the gene that regulates serotonin one from each parent. This leads to three different variations of the gene depending on which allele a person gets from his or her parents: *ss, sl,* and *ll.* These letters stand for the "short" (*s*) and "long" (*l*) versions of the gene. People with the short version (*ss* or *sl*), especially two short alleles (*ss*), are less efficient at regulating serotonin so they are at risk for depression, whereas people with two long alleles (*ll*) may have a measure of protection from depression.

Early research on the link between the short version of the gene and depression was, in the words of one group of researchers, "inconclusive" (Caspi, Sugden, et al., 2003, p. 387). These researchers wondered if there might be an interaction between life stressors and genotype. Using a longitudinal sample of 1,037 men and women in New Zealand who were studied extensively from ages 3 to 26, they were able to divide the sample into three groups depending on their genotype of the serotonin transporter promoter gene: *ss, sl,* and *ll.* In addition, participants noted if any of 14 major life events occurred to them between the ages of 21 and 26. These events included things such as a major change in employment, housing, finances, health, and relationships. Finally, participants were asked if they experienced any symptoms of depression, thoughts of suicide, suicide attempts, or a depressive episode in the past year. Interestingly, there were no differences in number of life stressors among the three genotype groups suggesting that genes did not cause people to experience more life stressors.

As you can see in Figure 6.5, for all of the outcomes studied, participants with the *ss* genotype were the most at risk whereas participants with the *ll* genotype were the least at risk for depression or symptoms of depression (Caspi, Sugden, et al., 2003). Participants with the *sl* genotype fell somewhere in between. In all cases, the environment—that is, having more life stressors—put a person at greater risk for symptoms of depression or a full-blown depressive episode, but there was little impact of genotype on symptoms or incidence of depression. However, when a person with a specific genotype—*ss*—encountered stressful life events, the person was particularly likely to develop depression or depressive symptoms. Thus the interaction between genes and environment was statistically significant in every instance (Caspi, Sugden, et al., 2003). No wonder early research was inconsistent; apparently it takes both the environment and a special genotype for a person to experience depression in his or her lifetime (see Monroe & Reid, 2008, for a review and Munafò & Flint, 2009, for a criticism of this work).

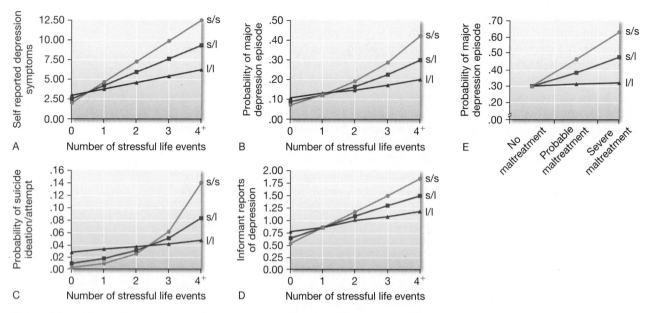

Figure 6.5 Incidence of clinical depression symptoms as a function of genotype and life stressors. *Source:* From Caspi, Sugden, et al. (2003, Figures 1 and 2, p. 388). From Caspi, A., Sugden, K., Moffitt, T. E., Taylor, A., Craig, I. W., Harrington, H., et al. (2003). Influence of life stress on depression: Moderation by a polymorphism in the 5-HTT gene. Science, 301(5631), 386–389. Reprinted by permission of the American Association for the Advancement of Science.

THINK ABOUT IT

What does it mean to say that there is a genotype–environment interaction between negative life events and Neuroticism? What kinds of people are more vulnerable to negative events?

These are just two examples of an increasing trend in personality where researchers look for genotype–environment interactions. One group of researchers suggested that such interactions probably occur more often than we realize, especially for psychopathology (Krueger, Markon, & Bouchard, 2003). Interactions between genes and environment have been found to account for religious upbringing lessening the impulsiveness of high sensation seekers (Boomsma, de Geus, van Baal, & Koopmans, 1999), parental bonding and family functioning decreasing emotional instability (Jang, Dick, Wolf, Livesley, & Paris, 2005), a monoamine oxidase A (MAOA) promoter gene and parental harshness increasing adolescent antisocial behavior (Krueger et al., 2003), the DRD2 gene and stress increasing alcoholism (Madrid, MacMurray, Lee, Anderson, & Comings, 2001), and negative life events increasing Neuroticism (Lahey, 2009).

Genotype–Environment Correlations

> "We propose that development is indeed the result of nature *and* nurture but that genes drive experience. Genes are components in a system that organizes the organism to experience its world."
>
> *Scarr and McCartney (1983, p. 425)*

It seems easy enough to think about the effects of genes and environment. However, researchers soon discovered a curious finding: Measures of environments showed evidence of genetic influence (Plomin et al., 2002). In other words, measures of environmental effects, such as parenting styles on, or peer ratings of, a child, for example, were not strictly environmental. That is, people's personalities affected the environments they found themselves in and also how they described those environments on questionnaires. This puzzle soon led to a breakthrough in personality research which led to many interesting findings (Plomin et al., 2002). Perhaps you can see now how this accounts for the genetic component of peer ratings in the twin study of the five-factor model of personality study discussed earlier (Riemann et al., 1997). Did you figure it out?

The answer to this puzzle is that people construct their environments. That is, we select, modify, create, and re-create in our memory (and on questionnaires administered by researchers!) our experiences (Plomin et al., 2002). When people's experiences are related to—that is, are correlated with—their genetic inclinations we call this a genotype–environment correlation. A genotype–environment correlation occurs when people with a gene for a specific characteristic find themselves in an environment that fosters—or discourages—the expression of that characteristic (Carey, 2003). Or, to think of it another way, people with different genotypes are exposed to different environments *depending on that genotype* (Plomin et al., 1977). Because both the genes and the environment occur together, we can't be sure which is causing the manifestation of that characteristic.

Table 6.4 Three Types of Genotype–Environment Correlations

Type	Description	Pertinent Environment
Passive	Children are given genotypes linked to their environment	Natural parents and siblings
Reactive	Children are reacted to on the basis of their genotype	Anybody
Active	Children seek an environment conductive to their genotype	Anytime

Source: From Plomin et al. (1977, Table 1, p. 311). Plomin, R., DeFries, J. C., & Loehlin, J. C. (1977). Genotype-environment interaction and correlation in the analysis of human behavior. *Psychological Bulletin*, 84(2), 309–322.

Another way to think about genotype–environment correlations goes back to our definition of what a correlation is. In this case, a genotype–environment correlation occurs when people with high "genetic values" (i.e., a strong genetic predisposition for a specific characteristic) find themselves in environments with high values (i.e., environments that push for that characteristic; Carey, 2003). Similarly, a genotype–environment correlation also occurs when people with low genetic values (i.e., no particular inclination for a characteristic) find themselves in environments with low values (i.e., environments with no particular demand for that characteristic). The interesting question is *why* people with certain genotypes find themselves in certain environments. There are three possible explanations, which lead to three types of correlations: passive, reactive, and active (Plomin et al., 1977; see Table 6.4).

Types of Genotype–Environment Correlations. When parents provide both the genes and an environment that is favorable (or unfavorable) to the development of those genes, we observe a **passive genotype–environment correlation** (Plomin et al., 1977). For example, imagine parents who have very high verbal skills—gifted even—who not only pass on these fabulous genes to their children but also provide a home filled with books and games and other activities that are likely to help their children develop good verbal skills (Plomin et al., 1977). Because the children did nothing to cause the environment to provide these resources—and in fact, such resources may have been in place long before children were even on the scene—the genotype–environment correlation is passive.

But consider the same highly verbal parents who see that their baby is babbling constantly and often seems as if she is trying to communicate to them. These parents may purposely try to engage the baby in conversation (e.g., "Who's Mama's precious little baby?") or encourage the baby to talk ("Say Dada!"). Because the parents are responding to something in the child, we call this kind of relationship a **reactive genotype–environment correlation** (Plomin et al., 1977). Just as with the passive genotype–environment correlation, we can't be sure if the child's genetics or environment caused him or her to be so verbal because the two co-occur.

Genotype–environment correlations occur when people are exposed to different environments depending on their genotype. Genotype–environment correlations can be passive, reactive, or active. This young boy is already an accomplished ballet dancer. Do you think this is an example of a passive or active genotype–environment correlation?

Now imagine that this child of highly verbal parents is spending the weekend with grandparents (with whom the child shares about 25% of her genes, on average). Suppose the baby babbles to both grandparents, but because Grandma is in the middle of cooking dinner, Grandpa investigates the noises coming from the crib. "Are you trying to talk, little baby?" he says while laughing. "Go on, tell me all about it." For the rest of the weekend, the baby crawls to Grandpa whereever he is and continues to babble at him. This would be an example of an **active genotype–environment correlation**. Here, the parents (or grandparents, in this case) have provided both the genes and the environment. The baby can either interact with Grandma or Grandpa, but she chooses to "talk" with, and indeed seeks out, the more responsive one, Grandpa. Here, her high verbal ability comes from both her genetics and the environment, but she is the one who specifically seeks out the environment.

Genotype–environment correlations can be either positive or negative. The previous examples illustrated **positive genotype–environment correlations**, where conditions were favorable for developing a certain characteristic. In this case, verbal behavior was encouraged in the child either by an environment that just happens to encourage verbal ability (passive), responded to the child (reactive), or which the child sought out (active). But we could easily imagine scenarios where verbal behavior was discouraged or where the child found herself in an environment that was unfavorable for developing verbal ability because the TV was on all the time (passive), where there was an older sibling who talked at the baby and interrupted her babbling (reactive), or where the baby preferred the company of a quiet relative to a talkative relative (active). These would be examples of **negative genotype–environment correlations**.

In the case of a negative genotype–environment correlation, people with high genetic values for a characteristic find themselves in environments with low values for that characteristic. Often, the result is that the environment discourages the expression of that characteristic. The inverse is also possible, where people with low genetic values for a characteristic find themselves in environments with high values for that characteristic. They may end up developing some of their less pronounced characteristics.

Keep in mind that whether a genotype–environment correlation is positive or negative does *not* depend on the ultimate outcome—the development or lack of development of a characteristic—but on the relative levels of the genotype and the environment (see Table 6.5). Often positive genotype–environment correlations encourage a specific characteristic whereas negative genotype–environment correlations discourage a specific characteristic, but this is not necessarily the case. For example, Scarr and McCartney (1983) described a negative passive genotype–environment correlation where parents might be highly skilled readers and have a child who is not reading so well. They may decide to enhance the environment for this child—because they are good at reading and not because of anything about the child—more than they might for a child who is already reading well or more than parents who are not highly skilled readers would do if they had such a child.

For personality characteristics, Raymond Cattell suggested that negative genotype–environment correlations were probably more common than positive correlations (Plomin et al., 1977). For example, a person who is too domineering will probably be put in her place by her peers, indicating a negative reactive genotype–environment correlation (Plomin et al., 1977). Although it may seem odd that people would seek out environments that work

Table 6.5 Positive and Negative Genotype–Environment Correlations

Type of Correlation	Genotype	Environment
Positive	High	High
Positive	Low	Low
Negative	High	Low
Negative	Low	High

Note: High or low indicates the amount of the characteristic present in the genes or in the environment.

against their natural inclinations, as is the case with negative active genotype–environment correlations, you could imagine a person who is anxious and easily upset seeking out stable and reassuring friends to calm him down (Plomin et al., 1977). What would a negative passive genotype–environment correlation look like? Imagine parents who are emotionally reactive and get angry easily and yet have a child who is similar to them in this regard. They are very likely to squelch any unseemly reaction in their child (Plomin et al., 1977).

According to Scarr and McCartney (1983):

> *People seek out environments they find compatible and stimulating. We all select from the surrounding environment some aspects to which to respond, learn about, or ignore. Our selections are correlated with motivational, personality, and intellectual aspects of our genotypes. The active genotype → environment effect, we argue, is the most powerful connection between people and environments and the most direct expression of the genotype in experience. (p. 427)*

Note that these three types of correlations differ in terms of what constitutes the environment. For passive, the environment is the child's immediate environment: parents, siblings, and other members of the household that he or she is born into. For reactive, the environment is any person who interacts with or responds to the child. For example, peers may reciprocate the affection of a sociable child or teachers may provide an enriched environment for a student who shows special aptitude. Finally, for active, the environment can be other people or indeed, the physical environment itself. For example, a musical child can rush to play the piano at Grandma's house, gravitate to the music store at the mall, or even bang on pots and pans in the kitchen to make music. Further, the relative importance of these environments—and hence the type of genotype–environment correlation that is operating—shifts over the life span. For example, passive genotype–environment influences may decrease from infancy to adolescence whereas active genotype–environment influences increase as the child experiences more of the world away from home.

What's the Evidence? Researching Genotype–Environment Correlations.

What evidence is there for this idea that social experiences are evoked by one's genotype? One way to find a reactive genotype–environment correlation is to look at twin studies over time, where we might be able to see changes in a child's behavior and if these changes correlate with changes in the environment. For example, comparing MZ twins and DZ twins, Narusyte, Andershed, Neiderhiser, and Lichtenstein (2007) found that childhood aggression was related to parental criticism that was related, in turn, to self-reported antisocial behavior in adolescence. The researchers suggested that this is an example of a reactive genotype–environment correlation: Children at risk for antisocial behavior are indeed more aggressive than children not at risk, and they are also more likely to elicit negative reactions in their parents.

A similar reactive genotype–environment correlation was found in an adoption study, where teens' antisocial behavior was correlated with both their biological parent's substance abuse or antisocial personality (genotype) and with the harsh or inconsistent disciplinary practices of their adoptive mothers and fathers (environment; Ge et al., 1996).

Another way to investigate a reactive genotype–environment correlation is to create one in the laboratory, something researchers have only begun to explore. Burt conducted an experiment in which undergraduate men were put in a controlled situation to see how they interacted with others (Burt, 2008, 2009). Would they elicit certain reactions from their peers as a function of their genotype? If they did, then this would demonstrate a reactive genotype–environment correlation in an experimental situation.

In this unusual experiment, Burt identified men who had either a G-allele or an A-allele for a certain serotonin receptor gene (5-HTR2A) and had them interact in small groups on two tasks. In previous research, the G-allele was associated with an increased response to selective serotonin reuptake inhibitors (SSRIs). When normal volunteers are given SSRIs they act friendlier (indeed, recall that the administration of SSRIs has been shown to reduce clinical depression). Burt hypothesized that participants with the G-allele would be more likely than

Can one person's gene code for other people's responses? A reactive genotype–environmental correlation occurs when our genes, as expressed in our personalities, influence the environment around us.

those with the A-allele to be friendly, smile, and socialize with others, eventually becoming one of the most popular members of the group.

The groups were charged with two sets of tasks: answering brainteasers and planning two parties, one with a strict budget and the other with unlimited funds and the instructions to "be creative and have fun." Afterward the participants rated how much they liked each person in their group. The researchers created a composite of group ratings for each participant indicating how likable each participant was perceived to be by the others in the group. In addition, observers took note of how often a participant joked, supported, or suggested, that the group break rules either during the planning of their party or as part of the entertainment at the party. For example, some participants suggested that they somehow steal money to supplement their limited budget, or, in the case of the creative second party, provide alcohol (even though all participants were under the legal drinking age), marijuana, other drugs, or even prostitutes. An overall composite measure of rule-breaking was created from these observer ratings along with self-reports. Burt reasoned that among young people, particularly men, rule-breaking is a way of establishing status and popularity.

As predicted, men with the G-allele were more likely to suggest or encourage rule-breaking and were, in fact, rated as more popular by their group-mates compared to men with the A-allele (Burt, 2008, 2009). As Burt explained, the funny thing is that it is biologically impossible for a person's gene to code for *another* person's response. It seems that this particular gene codes for behaviors like rule-breaking that then lead people to be perceived as more likable. Burt's results suggested that genes code for a particular behavior (e.g., rule-breaking) and for the social consequences of that behavior (e.g., popularity). This is an example of a positive reactive genotype–environment correlation, where genes cause behavior to which the environment, in this case other people, then responds.

Burt (2009) recognized that rule-breaking is just one aspect of popularity. He suggested that researchers explore other aspects of personality that are known to affect liking such as social dominance, extraversion, physical attractiveness, and perceived athletic ability, or specific gestures that affect first impressions such as eye contact and smiling, to see if these might help explain the correlation between genotype and popularity.

There are many examples of gene–environment correlations, especially in developmental psychology. Correlations between genes and environment have been found for adolescents' perceptions of parental warmth or conflict (Johnson & Krueger, 2006), physical punishment and misbehavior (Jaffee et al., 2004), parental harshness and antisocial behavior (Krueger et al., 2003), memories of childhood environment (Krueger et al., 2003), and family bonding and neuroticism (Jang et al., 2005).

The movie *Gattaca* portrays a futuristic world where parents select the exact genetic makeup of their offspring. As individuals and society we need to decide what to do with the results of genetic research.

The Personality of Everyday Life

What can genetics research do for us?

If the concept of cloning or prenatal genetic testing makes you nervous, you are not alone. Keep in mind that genetics is a tool, not a goal, so that understanding the human genome is really only the beginning (Carey, 2003). As a tool, genetics is value-neutral. The real moral question is, what do we do with the findings from genetic research? To make these kinds of decisions it is imperative that informed citizens understand what genetics can and can't do so that we can be involved in the issues and not leave the debate solely to the scientists or lawmakers.

One way that findings from genetics have been misused in the past includes the eugenics movement, which claimed the moral superiority of one group over another (witness the so-called Final Solution of the Nazis) and even went so far as to control who gets to reproduce or not (for example, the United States for a time instituted forced sterilization of people with supposedly lower IQs as part of a eugenics program; Mawer, 2006). Another questionable use of genetics is cloning, although some say human cloning may be nearly impossible (Smith, 2005).

Although gene therapy involving the cloning of the common cold virus has successfully cured some diseases, such as severe combined immune deficiency syndrome (SCIDS; Smith, 2005), sometimes the risk of this type of therapy is too great (Collins & Vedantam, 1999). The biggest fear may be that genetic testing will be used to modify or even select for traits that are not disease related such as gender, intelligence, eye color, physical strength, or sociability—a brave new world indeed!

And yet, the knowledge gleaned from genetics can be used for a world of good. Some possible goals currently under investigation by geneticists include identification of genetic risk indicators (Plomin et al., 2008), medical treatments individually tailored to our DNA (Plomin et al., 2008), the conservation of endangered animal and plant species (Mawer, 2006), a better understanding of evolution (Carey, 2003), identification of our common ancestors (Mawer, 2006), increased use of forensic evidence (Reilly, 2006), cures for cancers and other diseases (Reilly, 2006; Smith, 2005), improvement of crop production (Reilly, 2006), prevention of famine (Reilly, 2006), solutions to historical puzzles (Reilly, 2006), and a better use of the limited resources of our planet (Reilly, 2006).

We must not forget our discussion from the beginning of this chapter: Personality is lemonade. For personality psychologists, knowing that even when a personality trait

"[I]f you really want to engineer your child's IQ, stick to the old ways. Send them to Eton. And if governments want to improve the nations' intelligence, the best value for money would be to double teachers' salaries."
Geneticist Steve Jones as cited in Smith (2005, p. 188)

is genetic the environment still has a big impact suggests that mental health may be a public health issue (e.g., Lahey, 2009). Problems such as depression and antisocial behavior (Carey, 2003) may be preventable whereas increasing intelligence, cooperation, and a host of other prosocial traits may be possible. With genes as an early warning system (Plomin et al., 2003), behavioral and environmental engineering will work with genetic engineering (Plomin et al., 2008). It all starts with an understanding of the genetic—and environmental—influences on human behavior and personality (e.g., Moffitt, Caspi, & Rutter, 2006).

Chapter Summary

How does genetics make us who we are? Basically, we develop the personalities we do, as a result of the following:

1. Inheritance of specific genes (e.g., Gregor Mendel and his pea plants).
2. Genes and environment working together as co-actors (e.g., heritability, environmentality).
3. Genes and environment working together as a dialectic (e.g., genotype–environment interactions, genotype–environment correlations).
4. Environmental toxins, stressors, social situations (both nurturing and neglecting) that affect the regulation of specific genes (e.g., turning them up or turning them down). Environmental effects can not only trigger negative outcomes in a genetically vulnerable person, but can also offset genetic vulnerabilities for maladaptive outcomes.

Researchers often study twins (both MZ twins and DZ twins) to estimate the heritability of personality traits. Because it would be impossible to conduct a true experiment, researchers have relied on correlational designs (e.g., family studies, twin studies, adoption studies) to study genetics and personality.

We discovered that there are two ways of estimating heritability (double the difference in correlations between MZ twins and DZ twins; the correlation between MZ twins raised apart), and that heritability refers to a particular trait in a particular population at a particular time. Further, a phenotype (the observed manifestation of a gene) is a function of a person's genotype, environment (including shared and nonshared aspects), the interaction of both, the correlation of both, and measurement error.

When it comes to personality, just about every individual difference characteristic you can think of (e.g., Neuroticism, Extraversion, Openness, Agreeableness, Conscientiousness) has a substantial genetic component (about 40% of the variance in a trait is due to genetics) and a substantial environmental component. Further, the important part of the environment appears to be the part that is unique to us and not shared with siblings raised in the same environment (also about 40%).

Where once psychologists who studied the genetics of personality concerned themselves with the heritability of personality characteristics, they now think in terms of epigenetics, or how genes are regulated by events or experiences in the environment. In fact, researchers believe that most aspects of personality including mental and physical illness are controlled by complex genetics (e.g., involving many genes, interacting with the environment, and even regulated by environmental conditions). One day we may be able to treat disorders with drugs or behavioral interventions that operate at the level of gene regulation. With the foundation of this chapter you will be able to understand both the ethical issues and the implications of research breakthroughs that will no doubt emerge in your lifetime in this most exciting area of personality research. In sum: "This ain't your parents' genetics!"

Review Questions

1. If the real question is not whether genes or environment affect personality, what is the right question to ask? What does it mean to say that nature and nurture transact?

2. What is heritability? What is environmentality? What is shared environment? What is nonshared environment?

3. What are the two common ways of estimating heritability? What assumptions does each of these formulas depend on?

4. What is the logic behind adoption and twin studies? What makes a correlational design different from a true experiment? Based on research with twins, does sense of humor run in families? Why might this be?

5. What can we say about the heritability of the traits of Neuroticism, Extraversion, Openness, Agreeableness, and Conscientiousness? Which is more important for developing these traits, shared or nonshared environment?

6. How do noncoding sequences of DNA change how genes function in direct response to the environment? Explain using the example of loneliness and immune functioning.

7. What does it mean to say that genes and environment are a dialectic? What is a dialectic? What is a genotype–environment interaction? Describe how genotype and life stressors interact to cause clinical depression according to research by Caspi, Sugden, et al. (2003).

8. What is a genotype–environment correlation? What is a positive genotype–environment correlation? What is a negative genotype–environment correlation? What are passive, reactive, and active genotype–environment correlations?

9. What are some uses genetic research may be put to in the near future?

> "Genetic diversity is the essence of life."
>
> *Plomin et al. (2008, p. 91)*

Key Terms

Genotype
Behavioral genetics
Phenotype
Heritability
Environmentality
Shared environment
Nonshared environment
Monozygotic (MZ) twins
Dizygotic (DZ) twins
MZA twins
Equal environments assumption

Assumption of representativeness
Selective placement
Alleles
Mendelian inheritance
Epigenetics
Genes
Exon
Intron
Positional cloning
Dialectic
Genotype–environment interaction

Genotype–environment correlation
Passive genotype–environment correlation
Reactive genotype–environment correlation
Active genotype–environment correlation
Positive genotype–environment correlation
Negative genotype–environment correlation

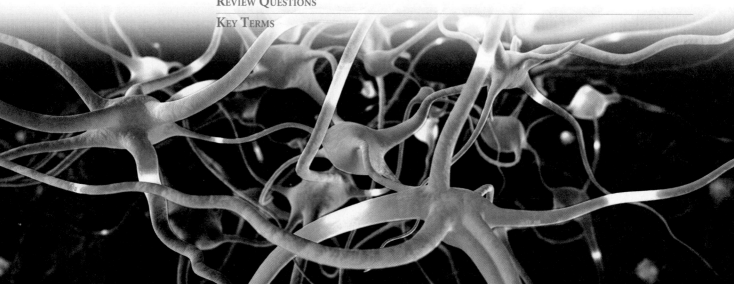

CHAPTER 7 THE NEUROSCIENCE OF PERSONALITY

Read the **Chapter** on
mysearchlab.com

> "As physicists had to learn that they were dealing with a space-time continuum, psychologists will have to learn that they have to deal with a mind-body continuum—not with Cartesian entities entirely separate from each other."
>
> *Eysenck (1997, p. 1224)*

SEE FOR YOURSELF

Take a few minutes to close your eyes, sit still, clear your mind, and focus on your breathing. Were you able to do this? Did you start to feel more relaxed?

THINK ABOUT IT

Does physiology determine personality or does personality determine physiology? Can it be both?

What if I told you there was a way that you could be healthier and happier? It's not a drug, it doesn't involve massive psychotherapy, it's not painful, and it's totally free. What is this miracle cure? Believe it or not, it's meditation!

Although some religious and cultural traditions embrace meditation as a powerful spiritual practice, modern medical research has traditionally scoffed at alternative treatments. However, Dr. Jon Kabat-Zinn, professor of medicine emeritus at the University of Massachusetts Medical School, has changed all this with his brand of Westernized stress reduction using Eastern principles of meditation. And he and his colleagues have been doing controlled experiments to test the effectiveness of these techniques.

In one study, participants who wanted to learn about meditation as a form of stress reduction were randomly assigned to either a meditation group or a control group (Davidson et al., 2003). The meditation group went through an extensive 8-week training in mindfulness-based stress reduction meditation, whereas people in the control group were put on a wait list for the 8 weeks to receive the training at a later time. In this way, both groups were essentially equivalent except for participation in the meditation training.

During the training, participants practiced being in the moment instead of planning, worrying, thinking, or fantasizing about the future, the way most of us do when given a few moments to sit still. The meditation group members tuned in to their breathing and practiced regulating their attention to *not* think about these things—to think about nothing, in fact (Kabat-Zinn, 1990).

At the end of the training session the two groups were compared on a number of measures. The researchers found that the group that had learned meditation showed less anxiety. This would be exciting enough—that people who meditate have less anxiety—but the real news is that they also showed differences in how their brains responded to emotional stimuli (Davidson et al., 2003). People who meditated showed greater brain activation on the left prefrontal cortex of their brains both at rest and in response to positive and negative emotional events. As a special bonus, participants in the meditation group also showed better immune functioning than participants in the control group.

Overall, the data suggest that regular meditation fundamentally changes how our brains work and that this activation is related both to the emotions we feel and to how we respond to stressful events. The researchers surmised that meditation makes people more open to experiencing positive emotions and less reactive to negative emotions with the overall effect of decreasing their anxiety and improving immune functioning (Davidson et al., 2003)—all of this without drugs!

When it comes to understanding our biological functioning and personality, it's like the question of which came first, the chicken or the egg: Does our physiology determine our personality, or does our personality determine our physiology? We may be born with a certain

Evidence suggests that the regular practice of mindfulness meditation makes people more receptive to positive emotions, decreases anxiety, and bolsters the immune system.

physiology that may cause us to develop certain traits, but the environment can modify aspects of our personality. Perhaps the best way to think of our physiology is as a package of potentialities for personality traits that may be developed, discouraged, or even modified by our experiences. However, at the same time research such as the meditation study suggests that our behavior also affects our physiology. How much so and for which specific aspects of our personality are still open questions.

In this chapter we briefly review the major physiological systems and discuss two personality theories that hypothesize that neurological differences cause differences in personality traits. Then we consider the physiology and neurology behind some common personality characteristics.

What Is Neuroscience and How Do We Study It?

Researchers who explore the neuroscience behind personality focus on the brain and the nervous system. A brief overview of the parts of the nervous system will help us better understand some of the recent findings in this area.

The nervous system is made up of the **central nervous system** and the **peripheral nervous system**. The central nervous system includes the brain and the spinal cord whereas the peripheral nervous system includes the **somatic nervous system**, which controls movements of the muscles, and the **autonomic nervous system**, which regulates smooth muscle (e.g., inner organs), cardiac muscle, and glands. The autonomic nervous system is further divided into the **sympathetic division** and the **parasympathetic division**. The sympathetic division mobilizes energy (e.g., for fight or flight), whereas the parasympathetic division supports systems that replenish the body's energy stores (e.g., salivation, digestion, etc.; Carlson, 2010).

The brain is protected by a bath of *cerebrospinal fluid (CSF)* that cushions the delicate brain and also flows through spaces in the brain called *ventricles.* CSF is similar to blood plasma, and is continually produced, circulated, and reabsorbed through the brain and the ventricles (Carlson, 2010).

The brain contains a number of structures and systems that control everything from thinking, reasoning, learning, and memory, to breathing, sleeping, and eating, to movement and the processing of sensory information, to the experience of emotions. Because all of these parts are crucial for basic functioning, we should not expect to see large differences among people. However, individuals can vary in all kinds of ways, from how they may respond to stress (e.g., heart palpitations, sweating) to what they think is happy or sad, to how they respond to hormones and drugs. Researchers hypothesize that differences in *bodily responses, brain structure, brain activity, and biochemical activity* are all related to individual differences in personality (Zuckerman, 2005). All of the research that has been done on exploring physiological and neurological differences in personality fits into one of these four categories. These categories and the common physiological measures of each are summarized in Table 7.1.

Bodily Responses

When our body responds to arousing events in the environment it is the autonomic nervous system that responds. When aroused, the sympathetic division responds by increasing heart rate, blood pressure, blood flow to the extremities, respiration, sweating, and muscle activity. Essentially the body curtails some of its regular maintenance functions to mobilize an immediate response.

Sweating is measured by **galvanic skin response (GSR)** which is a measure of skin conductance or how quickly a slight electrical current passes through two points on the skin. The faster the conductance of the current, the more moisture is present that indicates greater arousal.

Muscle activity is measured by **electromyography (EMG)** or myoelectric activity, which estimates the electrical impulses of the muscles during contraction and relaxation. EMG is often used in biofeedback to train people to perceive muscle contractions so that they can learn to relax their muscles.

> "It is unlikely that you would define your personality in terms of molecular and cellular brain processes. . . . Yet personality is the product of the brain."
> *Corr (2006, p. 519)*

Table 7.1 Common Markers of Neurological and Physiological Differences in Personality

Bodily Responses	Brain Structure	Brain Activity	Biochemical Activity
Cardiovascular	Dissection	Cortical stimulation	Neurotransmitters:
Heart rate	Cytology	EEG	Dopamine,
Blood pressure	CT scan	Evoked potential	Serotonin,
Blood flow	MRI	PET scan	GABA
Respiratory function		fMRI	Enzymes:
Galvanic skin response		Transcranial magnetic stimulation	MAO
Electromyography			Hormones:
			Epinephrine,
			Norepinephrine,
			Cortisol
			Drug responses

Note: See the chapter text for descriptions and explanations of abbreviations.

SEE FOR YOURSELF

Have you ever had a CT scan, CAT scan, or an MRI? What information was your doctor hoping to find that couldn't be found through other methods?

THINK ABOUT IT

Which of these four markers of neurological and physiological activity do you think are most promising for understanding personality: bodily responses, brain structure, brain activity, or biochemical activity? Why?

Brain Structure

Another place that researchers have looked for differences among people is in the relative size and weight of specific parts of the brain, or even in the kinds and number of cells found in various parts of the nervous system. In the past, the only way of studying differences in brain structure and cells was through dissecting the brain after death. During an autopsy the brain may be removed and sections of tissues preserved for cytological (cell) study.

Today, through the advent of more sophisticated techniques we can study the structure of a living human brain through noninvasive procedures. For example, **computerized tomography (CT)**, called a CT scan, takes a high-resolution x-ray picture of the brain. By looking at thin cross sections of the brain—often less than a millimeter!—we can detect abnormalities or differences in brain tissue. (This same technique was once called **computer axial tomography [CAT]**, or CAT scan.)

A similar technique involves **magnetic resonance imaging (MRI)**. Here radio frequency waves are used instead of x-rays. First, a strong magnetic field causes the nuclei of some atoms to resonate. Then radio frequency waves are used to detect the activity of these atoms. Because

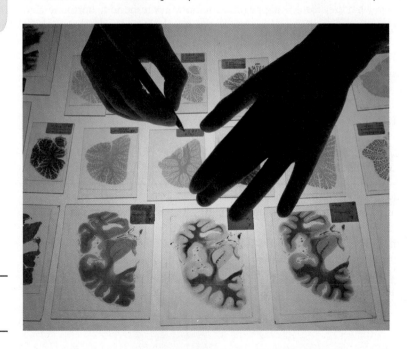

Paper-thin slices of human brain mounted on slides for study.

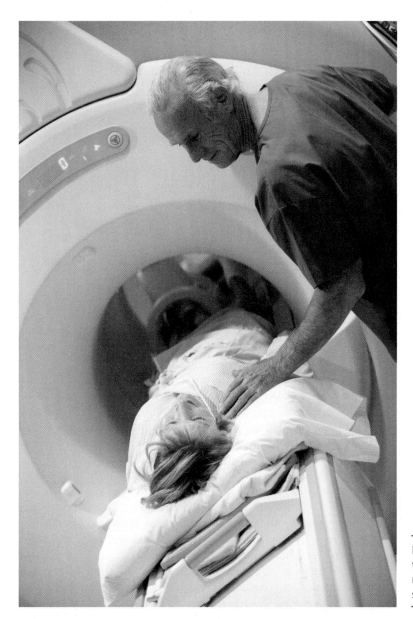

Non-invasive procedures, like the CT scan shown here, allow researchers to study brain structures.

hydrogen atoms are present in all tissues but in varying concentrations, the pattern of resonance formed by the hydrogen atoms forms a multidimensional picture of the brain.

Brain Activity

Both CT scans and MRIs can detect only static pictures of the brain—that is, pictures of brain structure at one moment in time. Measures of brain activity are ways of looking for differences in brain structures while the brain is stimulated. Often, participants are given a mental task to work on or other stimuli to react to while measures of brain activity are taken.

One early technique of studying brain activity is cortical stimulation. Using either electrodes implanted in the brain or direct electrical stimulation of parts of the brain, the patient is awake and can report on sensations as various parts of the brain are being stimulated. Today, we are able to use less invasive procedures. For instance, in an **electroencephalogram (EEG)** electrodes are placed on the scalp to monitor electrical activity of the brain. When electrical activity of the brain or other part of the nervous system is measured in response to a specific stimulus, this is called an **evoked potential (EP)**. Both EEGs and EPs indicate amount of brain activity in response to a stimulus. However, newer techniques identify the exact location of brain activity.

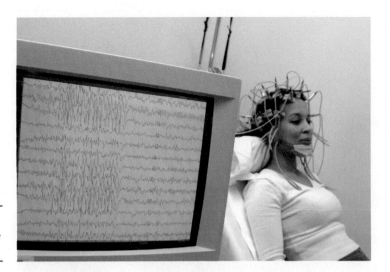

Electrodes are attached to this woman's head to measure brain activity.

In **positron emission tomography** (**PET**), called a PET scan, a slightly radioactive glucose-like substance with a very short half-life (rate of breakdown) is injected into the brain and the person is placed in a scanner similar to a CT scanner. Active regions of the brain use up more glucose than inactive regions and, with the aid of computer enhancement, scans of these regions appear in different colors related to their activity level.

The most detailed view of brain activity at a cellular level comes from **functional magnetic resonance imaging** (**fMRI**). This works the same as the traditional MRI except that brain activity levels are monitored over time by tracing blood oxygen levels in the brain. The more active areas use up more oxygen and this activity is translated into different color scans of the brain. Often images are taken while the participant is engaged in some cognitive activity or viewing stimuli, so that the researcher takes a series of these functional images over time.

Though the use of fMRI for personality research is on the rise, there are some notable problems with fMRI research. One problem is timing of response. When viewing a stimulus, our thoughts react within milliseconds whereas blood flow takes about 2 seconds. This makes it difficult to pinpoint the precise area that fired at the exact moment of a thought or reaction. Another problem is that the procedure is time-intensive and the equipment expensive so that often experiments use only a small number of participants. Small sample sizes make it difficult to find a reliable and significant effect (Yarkoni, 2009). A third problem, called the **nonindependence error**, is that researchers may unintentionally bias their results by not independently selecting which brain areas to correlate with, say, personality characteristics or other variables (Vul, Harris, Winkielman, & Pashler, 2009a). We'll talk more about this error and the controversy surrounding fMRI studies in the Research Methods Illustrated section.

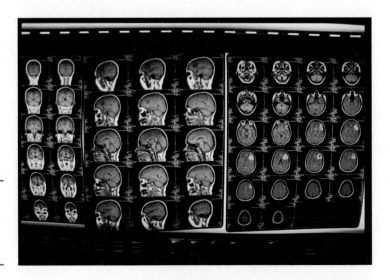

These fMRI images of a woman's brain show areas of her brain that are active while she is engaged in a cognitive task.

Finally, confounds such as time of day and nervousness of participants can also affect the results of neuroimaging studies (Dumit, 2004; Uttal, 2001).

One of the newest techniques for studying brain activity is **transcranial magnetic stimulation (TMS)**. With TMS a brief electrical current passes through a coil placed on the head. The magnetic field disrupts the regular activity of the neurons, sometimes impairing and sometimes enhancing function (Schutter, 2009). By carefully mapping parts of the brain that are stimulated and noting what kind of functioning is disrupted, researchers are able to pinpoint with greater accuracy than cortical stimulation or EP the exact area affected. Essentially TMS mimics a brain lesion, which allows researchers to draw inferences about cause and effect. This is a huge improvement over earlier techniques that only suggested a correlational relationship between brain activity and behavior (Walsh & Cowey, 2000). Although this technique has been used to treat various disorders including depression and anxiety (George & Bellmaker, 2000) and the pain of fibromyalgia (Sampson, 2006), we do not know yet how useful TMS will be for the study of personality.

This imaging research is very exciting, but there is one major problem with interpreting the results of brain scan research: What exactly does it mean when an area reacts in response to certain stimuli? According to critics of brain localization techniques, it could mean a number of things (Dumit, 2004; Uttal, 2001; Wade, 2006). First, it could mean that the area in question is indeed the center for that characteristic or response. But there could also be other areas that are less active but of equal or even greater importance that may have disinhibited the more active area. Also, when an area responds to stimulation we know that the area is necessary, but we don't know if it is a sufficient cause of the characteristic or response that we have observed. Maybe it's sufficient only if other parts of the brain are also involved. Finally, when a PET scan finds an area of increased glucose use, it may indicate activity or it may also indicate a neuron that is working less efficiently needing more glucose. However, by using fMRI, PET scans, and other neuroimaging techniques in the context of a controlled experiment we can figure out what brain activity really means.

Biochemical Activity

Finally, physiological differences may appear as differences in how the brain and body process various chemicals including neurotransmitters, hormones, and drugs. Depending on how and where these chemicals function, we might analyze cerebrospinal fluid, saliva, blood, or urine to monitor levels of these chemical substances.

Neurotransmitters are chemicals released by neurons to inhibit or excite the next neuron into action. In this way, neurotransmitters do just that: help transmit signals through the nervous system. Some important neurotransmitters are *norepinephrine, epinephrine, dopamine,* and *serotonin.* These all have a similar molecular structure, so that drugs that affect one tend to affect all of them. Norepinephrine (noradrenaline) and epinephrine (adrenaline) are also considered stress hormones. They help the body deal with threat by increasing blood flow to the muscles which increases heart rate and blood pressure. Dopamine is related to feelings of pleasure, and helps regulate movement, learning, attention, and rewards. Serotonin is involved with mood regulation, arousal, the control of sleeping and eating, and pain regulation. Depression, anxiety, and other mood disorders are related to how the body processes serotonin. The enzyme *monoamine oxidase (MAO)* regulates, to some degree, the availability of dopamine, norepinephrine, and epinephrine in the system.

Norepinephrine and serotonin may also be related to symptoms of depression (Thorn & Lokken, 2006). Some antidepressants, for example, work by blocking the reuptake of norepinephrine, serotonin or both, so that they stay in the spaces between the neurons a bit longer (Thorn & Lokken, 2006). Antianxiety drugs work by mimicking another neurotransmitter, *gamma-aminobutyric acid (GABA),* an inhibitory neurotransmitter (Thorn & Lokken, 2006).

Researchers may study neurotransmitters and the systems that process them by having participants engage in a task or activity and monitor the fluctuations in these chemicals. When it is impossible to directly measure the level of neurotransmitters—as with norepinephrine, for example—researchers indirectly monitor how the neurotransmitter is being used by measuring known byproducts of neurotransmitter metabolism. Another way is through a **challenge test** in which researchers administer a drug that is known to either increase or decrease a neurotransmitter's functioning and monitor the impact of this new substance on reactions presumed to be related to the neurotransmitter.

Research Methods Illustrated: Correlational Designs II: Scatterplots, Correlations, and the Alleged "Voodoo Science" of fMRI Studies

Are fMRI studies "voodoo science"? Are pretty scatterplots misleading? Oh, say it isn't so! In March 2009 the journal *Perspectives on Psychological Science* published a series of invited papers and made overt a debate that had been brewing on the Internet for some time (Diener, 2009). It seems that a small group of researchers noted that some fMRI studies of emotion, social cognition, and personality reported, in the words of one overzealous researcher, "insanely strong" correlations (Vul, Harris, Winkielman, & Pashler, 2009b, p. 320). The group suspected that these correlations were too good to be true. What they found set off a whole controversy (Vul et al., 2009a; see also Diener, 2010).

To understand all the fuss, we need to start with the concept of correlation. Recall that correlation is a measure of the relationship between two variables. If two variables increase or decrease at the same time—such as age and height—they are positively correlated. If one variable decreases (or increases) while the second variable increases (or decreases)—such as practice and typing errors—then the variables are negatively correlated. You can vividly see the relationship between two variables by graphing them against each other on the same graph.

Consider the graphs in Figure 7.1. The graph on the left shows Neuroticism scores on the *x*-axis plotted against thickness of a section of the orbital frontal cortex (OFC) on the *y*-axis. The graph on the right shows a similar graph for Extraversion scores. These are called **scatterplots or scattergrams** because they show the scatter, or spread, of the data. Many brain-imaging studies will use scatterplots to illustrate their results. Each point represents a participant in the study. In this graph, the blue circles represent females and the red squares represent males (ignore for a moment the diagonal lines drawn through the dots).

Notice how the cloud of data points on the left graph seems to slope downward. That tells us that as Neuroticism scores increase, thickness of this region of the OFC decreases. That suggests a negative correlation. Now look at the width of the cloud. Is it thinner or thicker? The thinner a cloud, the more closely related the two variables are and the stronger the correlation will be. The scatterplot on the left shows us that there is a moderately negative correlation between Neuroticism and thickness of the OFC. Indeed, the correlation of these data is −.65 (Wright et al., 2006). The line through the cloud of points is called a *linear regression line* and it estimates our best guess of how we can predict *y*-values from *x*-values.

What do you think about the correlation between Extraversion and thickness of the OFC as illustrated in the graph on the right? Here, the dots seem to be more scattered, making more of a circle than an oval. This tells us that there is not much of a correlation between the two variables, .18 in fact (Wright et al., 2006).

As you can see, a scatterplot is a very useful graphic. It can tell us at least three things about a set of data. First, it can alert us to outliers, or participants who score extremely high or low in one or

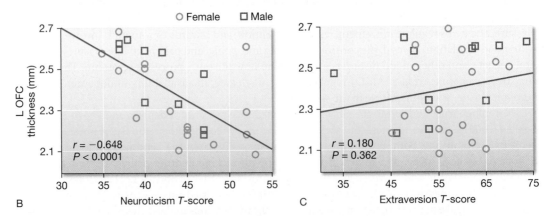

Figure 7.1 Scatterplots showing the relationship between cortical thickness and Neuroticism (left) and Extraversion (right) in the orbitofrontal cortex. *Source:* Adapted from Wright et al. (2006, Figure 3, p. 1814). From Wright, C. I., Williams, D., Feczko, E., Barrett, L. F., Dickerson, B. C., Schwartz, C. E., et al. (2006), "Neuroanatomical correlates of extraversion and neuroticism," *Cerebral Cortex*, 16(12), 1809–1819. Reprinted by permission of Oxford University Press.

both of our variables. There doesn't seem to be any outliers in the Wright et al. (2006) data, except for maybe the male who is very low in Extraversion in the graph on the right. Second, a scatterplot can tell us the direction of the correlation: whether it's positive (the cloud of dots points upward) or negative (the cloud points downward). Third, the thickness of the cloud or scatter of the dots tells us the strength of the correlation. The more the scatterplot looks like a circle, the less the two variables are related. The more the scatterplot looks like an oval, the more strongly the two variables are related. A perfect correlation will look like a straight line, whereas a zero correlation will look like random dots spread out around the graph. Check out the graphs in Figure 7.2 and try to guess whether the correlations are positive or negative, and high, medium, or close to zero.

Wright et al. (2006) also correlated cortical thickness in key areas with participants' scores on Extraversion, Neuroticism, Openness, Conscientiousness, and Agreeableness. Can you think of why they did this? They wanted to show specifically that Neuroticism was related to the thickness in some areas of the brain whereas Extraversion (and the other personality traits) was not. Because Neuroticism and Extraversion correlate with thickness in some areas and not in others, and only these two traits and not all five factors correlate with these areas of the brain, we have more confidence that the researchers have found a true result and not a significant result by chance alone.

Notice that Wright et al. (2006) cross-checked an area of the cortex that they thought was related to positive and negative emotions (Extraversion and Neuroticism, respectively) but was not related to other traits (Openness, Agreeableness, Conscientiousness). Other researchers are not so careful to cross-validate their findings. Instead, they selected which areas to study based on how well signals from that area correlated with their dependent variable (e.g., personality) and then calculated correlations based on this narrower range of values. That is, the same sample was used to decide what ought to be correlated and for the calculation of the actual correlation itself.

Figure 7.2 Scatterplots illustrating various correlations in hypothetical data. The correlations are (left to right): 0, −.3, .5, −.7, .90, −.99.

Technically, these two decisions should be made based on separate samples. It would be like deciding to have a state championship by choosing the best athletes in a specific sport—the sport you know your school excels in—instead of choosing a sport at random. Because the criterion and the outcome were determined within the same sample and not independent samples, the researchers made the nonindependence error (Vul et al., 2009a). This error caused artificially large correlations that made it seem like all kinds of social behaviors could be located in the brain. These "puzzlingly" large correlations led to accusations of fraudulence and claims that the researchers were conducting "voodoo science" and inflating their correlations on purpose (Vul et al., 2009b). Many of the researchers so accused defended the logic of their studies and claimed that Vul et al. (2009a) were exaggerating and that, in fact, the methods used by the authors to judge the studies in question were themselves flawed (Lazar, 2009; Lieberman, Berkman, & Wager, 2009; Lindquist & Gelman, 2009; Nichols & Poline, 2009).

The good news is that both sides agree that the methodology of fMRI studies correlating blood oxygen level dependent (BOLD) effect to personality are not perfect and can be improved. The problems that Vul et al. (2009a) identified, though not unique to fMRI studies, can be readily fixed, sometimes without collecting new data (Barrett, 2009; Vul et al., 2009a, 2009b; Yarkoni, 2009). The whole scientific community is now committed to understanding the debate—ceasing with the name-calling—and coming to a thoughtful resolution that will no doubt improve both our methods and our findings in behavioral neuroscience.

This brings us to a familiar caution: Our results are only as good as our measures. Think of it this way: Imagine beachcombing. You walk along a beach looking for interesting things that people may have lost. Part of your success comes from knowing where to look, like going to popular beaches or searching under the boardwalk where people may have dropped change from the food stands above. But part of your success comes from having the right equipment: your eyes versus a rake versus a metal detector. With a metal detector—especially a very powerful one—you are more likely to find coins, jewelry, watches, and other valuables buried inches under the sand. However, you may also find things such as old bottle caps, broken toys, and rusty nails. As researchers, we want to find good, significant effects, but we also want to minimize the "junk" we find along the way.

Neurological Theories of Personality

"Biological differences are innate and form the foundation upon which mature personality develops."
Clark and Watson (2008, p. 266)

In the 1998 revision to his 1947 classic book *Dimensions of Personality*, Hans Eysenck noted that even as we recognize that a substantial portion of our personality is inherited "there must be biological intermediaries between DNA and personality, and these intermediaries should be specified by theory and investigated" (Eysenck, 1998, p. xii). These biological intermediaries, what Eysenck's technology was not sufficiently advanced in 1947 to detect, are physiological differences.

Although Eysenck and others would like to be able to identify specific aspects of our physiology—be it bodily responses, brain structures, brain activity, or biochemical activity—that can account for differences in personality, this "holy grail" of personality research eludes us. Despite bigger and better and less invasive techniques and even with the ability to decode the smallest gene, protein, and neurotransmitter, scientists are not able to find consistent physiological differences that relate in a clear way to differences in personality characteristics (e.g., Eysenck, 1990). It may be that our techniques are not up to the task or it may be that aspects of the human nervous system interact in complicated ways that we have yet to untangle. Even when we are able to identify such differences, we still have a long way to go to prove that these differences actually cause us to develop the personalities that we have considering that our personalities have developed over a lifetime of interactions with other people.

THINK ABOUT IT

Are infants a blank slate at birth or are they born with a personality?

We can't be sure that differences in physiology cause us to develop different full-blown personalities, but perhaps we are expecting too much. Maybe biology has the biggest impact at a broader, more general level of personality, called **temperament**. What is temperament? Temperament is a set of personality characteristics that are (Zuckerman, 2005)

1. Relatively stable across the life span
2. Expressed through general energy level
3. Present from early childhood
4. Similar in other species of animals

Eysenck believed that temperament, determined by genes and passed on from parents to children, is the intermediary between DNA and personality.

5. Present at birth, at least in a general way
6. Determined by genetic factors
7. Changeable with maturation and experience

In their search for the biological basis of personality nearly all major personality typologies converge on three primary temperaments (Zuckerman, 2005), or clusters of related personality traits:

■ *Extraversion:* Positive emotion, reward sensitivity, social rewards, sociability, approach.
■ *Neuroticism:* Negative emotion, anxiety, punishment sensitivity, withdrawal.
■ *Impulsivity:* Psychoticism, lack of constraint, sensation seeking, novelty seeking, lack of conscientiousness, lack of agreeableness.

Indeed, there has been striking similarity in the various models that researchers have proposed. For example, Eysenck's Psychoticism, Extraversion, and Neuroticism model (PEN model; Eysenck, 1990), the five-factor model (FFM; Costa & McCrae, 1992; John, 1990; John et al., 2008), the Big Five (Goldberg, 1990; Norman, 1963), Gray's RST (Corr, 2008b), and Cloninger (1998) all posit at least two of these three dimensions as part of their theories. However, both the FFM and the Big Five split Eysenck's Psychoticism factor into Agreeableness and Conscientiousness (Digman, 1996). Other researchers write about an approach temperament (i.e., Extraversion) and an avoidance temperament (Neuroticism; Elliot & Thrash, 2008) or positive emotionality (Extraversion) and negative emotionality (Neuroticism; Depue, Luciano, Arbisi, Collins, & Leon, 1994).

Table 7.2 summarizes some of these relationships. Despite various names for the factors—and great debate about the "right" number of factors, something we investigated more closely in Chapter 2 on traits—when it comes to identifying basic *physiological* temperaments, the evidence from many theoretical backgrounds and different kinds of research methods converges on these three.

Table 7.2 Correspondences Among Three Personality Clusters and Major Trait Theories

	Cluster		
Theory	Extraversion	Neuroticism	Impulsivity
Eysenck	Extraversion	Neuroticism	Psychoticism
Gray	Behavioral Approach System	Behavioral Inhibition System	
Five Factors	Extraversion	Neuroticism	Low Conscientiousness
Cloninger	Reward Dependence	Harm Avoidance	Novelty Seeking

Note: The Openness factor of the five-factor model, the Intellect factor of the Big Five, and Gray's fight-flight-freeze system do not appear to correspond to any of the three primary traits identified by Zuckerman (2005).

To understand both the logic and the evidence supporting this assertion, let's take a close look at two important biological theories of personality: Hans Eysenck's PEN model and Jeffrey Gray's reinforcement sensitivity theory. Afterward, we'll look at the biological basis of the three temperaments of positive emotion, negative emotion, and impulsivity.

Eysenck's PEN Model

When Eysenck first started working in the 1940s, he was unusual in his desire to build a personality theory based on experimental findings (Eysenck, 1998). Further, he believed that a comprehensive theory should explain *how* people developed their personalities as well as predict consequences and outcomes of various personalities. While studying normal and psychiatric patients he developed his theory and identified two factors of personality, Extraversion and Neuroticism (Eysenck, 1998), and later he added Psychoticism, the third dimension. Together these three dimensions—Psychoticism, Extraversion, and Neuroticism—form the PEN model (Eysenck, 1952). This model is used to describe personality. People can be high or low on each of the three factors.

Overview of Eysenck's Three Dimensions.   The first of Eysenck's factors is **Extraversion**. People who are high in this factor, extroverts, tend to be sociable, popular, optimistic, and somewhat unreliable. Those low in Extraversion—introverts—tend to be quiet, introspective, reserved, and reliable, and to have a few close friends. Essentially, Extraversion refers to how outgoing people are, to both the social and the physical environments.

Eysenck's second factor is **Neuroticism**, which we might contrast with emotional stability. People high in this factor tend to be distressed, insecure, and upset in many areas of life. They are chronically worried, nervous, and moody, hold a low opinion of themselves, and find it difficult to get back on an even keel after an upsetting experience. In contrast, emotionally stable people are even-tempered, calm, relaxed, carefree, unworried, and somewhat unemotional, and return to their natural state quickly after an emotional experience (Eysenck & Eysenck, 1975).

Eysenck called the third factor **Psychoticism**. We might think of Psychoticism as being antisocial and contrast it with ego control. People high in Psychoticism tend to be loners, egocentric, troublesome, manipulative, impulsive, uncooperative, hostile, and withdrawn, and do not fit in anywhere (Eysenck, 1990; Eysenck & Eysenck, 1985).

In contrast, people low in Psychoticism tend to be altruistic, socialized, empathetic, and conventional. They care about others and are able to control their impulses to a greater extent than those high in Psychoticism.

Eysenck and Eysenck suggested that the pathological labels of Psychoticism and Neuroticism be dropped in favor of tough-mindedness and emotionality to emphasize that this is a theory of normal, nonpathological behavior and to eliminate the negative connotations of these labels (Eysenck & Eysenck, 1975, p. 3).

Eysenck drew on at least three pieces of evidence to support his view that these differences in personality are genetic and biological. First, cross-cultural universality in traits implies a strong biological component (Eysenck, 1990). After all, we would expect that large differences in culture and environment would produce different kinds of personality factors. However, this is not the case, as one study of personality in 25 diverse countries including Uganda, Nigeria, Japan, Mainland China, the United States, the Soviet Union, Hungary, Bulgaria, and the former Yugoslavia suggested (Barrett & Eysenck, 1984). The fact that three factors of Psychoticism, Extraversion, and Neuroticism occur in such diverse cultures suggests a biological, rather than cultural, explanation.

Second, people show tremendous consistency in these three traits over time, despite changing environments. Responses and habits might change over time and situations, but traits do not. This consistency suggests a strong biological component to these traits (Eysenck, 1990).

The third piece of evidence is the robust finding that Extraversion, Neuroticism, and Psychoticism each have moderate heritability (Eaves, Eysenck, & Martin, 1989). As Eysenck (1990) stated, "Genetic factors cannot directly influence behavior or cognitions, of course,

SEE FOR YOURSELF

Can you think of people you know or characters from movies, books, or TV who exemplify Eysenck's three factors?

and the intervening variables must inevitably be physiological, neurological, biochemical, or hormonal in nature" (p. 247).

Although Eysenck suspected that arousal and attention were involved with all three of his factors, he admitted that the research evidence did not suggest a clear hypothesis for a biological explanation of psychoticism (Eysenck, 1990; Eysenck & Eysenck, 1976). We now turn to a discussion of the physiological explanations Eysenck proposed for Extraversion and Neuroticism.

Neurology of Extraversion. Eysenck thought that the main difference between introverts and extraverts had to do with arousal, and on that score he was right (Eysenck, 1990). He considered two possibilities: that introverts and extraverts differed in arousal level or in arousability (Eysenck, 1967).

Eysenck thought that introverts had greater cortical arousal than extraverts, particularly in the **ascending reticular activating system (ARAS)**, a pathway transmitting signals from the limbic system and hypothalamus to the cortex (Eysenck, 1967; Eysenck & Eysenck, 1985). The ARAS processes the more cerebral aspects of arousal or emotion (e.g., thinking about a difficult calculus problem). Activation in the ARAS can make a person alert and mentally sharp or sluggish and mentally dull.

Because of their hypothesized overaroused baseline condition, introverts act more restrained and inhibited. That is, they avoid conditions that would aggravate their already overstimulated condition, preferring to stay to themselves and engaging in more quiet activities. In contrast, the system of extraverts, Eysenck reasoned, lets in too little stimulation so that their underaroused condition leads them toward more stimulating and unrestrained behaviors. Basically, extraverts are more outgoing and engaged with the world to raise their naturally low level of arousal. In this way, both extraverts and introverts attempt to regulate their own arousal striving to find their comfort zone: an optimal level of arousal (e.g., Hebb, 1955).

This sounds like a nice hypothesis, but is this true? Consider this: If there is a natural difference in arousal level between introverts and extraverts then we ought to see a difference between them even if they are sleeping or resting. Turns out we can readily test this hypothesis because arousal produced by the ARAS can be seen using EEG, whereas the arousal in the limbic system can be seen in the GSR and EMG (Eysenck, 1967).

Alas, using these traditional measures of arousal and even the newer methods (e.g., PET scans, cortical EPs) this is not the case. Indeed, over 1,000 studies have been conducted testing Eysenck's theory of arousal with no success (Geen, 1997). There is only a tiny, if any, difference in arousal level between extraverts and intraverts at rest. However, there is a significant difference in how extraverts and introverts respond to moderate stimulation, suggesting that the key difference between them is in their **arousability** or sensory reactivity (De Pascalis, 2004; Stelmack & Rammsayer, 2008; Zuckerman, 2005).

Is choice of study area related to personality? Which kind of study area do you think introverts and extraverts would prefer?

Given these differences in arousability, we would expect introverts and extraverts to differ in their choice of situations: noisy versus quiet. One study found that people studying in the quiet study spaces of their college library—spaces with individual carrels, small tables—tended to be introverted. Where did the extraverts prefer to study? In the noisy but highly sociable areas of the library: big rooms with open spaces and large tables (Campbell & Hawley, 1982).

But here's a question: Who performed better on their exams? Does noise level really matter when it comes to learning and performance? It sure does! Introverts and extraverts volunteered for a study in which they had to perform a moderately difficult cognitive reasoning task (Geen, 1984). Participants were given two words, one that fit a rule and the other that didn't. By observing a number of such pairs, participants had to figure out the rule. For example, the rule might be animal words or words that start with vowels.

While participants were viewing the words and trying to figure out the rule, they were bombarded with random bursts of white noise. Participants were randomly assigned to one of three conditions. In the choice condition, they were told that although they couldn't turn off the noise, they could select the volume that was "Just right for you." In the second and third conditions, participants were unable to control the volume. Instead, they were assigned the level of volume that matched what a participant in the first condition chose. In the assigned-same condition their volume was matched to the volume chosen by a personality just like them, either introverted or extraverted. However, in the assigned-different condition they were subjected to the volume chosen by a person different from them: an introvert, if they themselves were extraverted, or an extravert if they were introverted.

Who do you think chose the lower volume? Introverts in the choice condition chose a lower volume than extraverts in the choice condition. The difference was about that between a private office and a noisy group office. Second, who do you think experienced greater arousal as measured by heart rate and skin conductance? Well, it depended on which level of noise they were faced with. Both extraverts and introverts with noise levels at their optimum level of arousal—in either the choice condition or the assigned same condition—had similar levels of arousal as measured by heart rate and skin conductance. However, when faced with a level of noise not to their liking, introverts showed greater arousal and extraverts showed lower arousal. Essentially, introverts were overaroused by the loud "extraverted" level of noise whereas extraverts were underaroused by the soft, boring "introverted" level of noise.

Finally, how well did participants perform? By now you get the drill: It depended on if they were working at their optimum level of noise. Introverts assigned to the extravert's noise level performed the worst, needing more trials to learn the rule. Next came extraverts assigned to the introvert's noise level. The choice and assigned-same conditions performed best, learning the rule in the fewest number of trials. As you can see in Figure 7.3, what's just right for introverts—leading to their optimum performance—is too little for extraverts

Figure 7.3 Performance as function of noise intensity condition and personality. Higher numbers indicate more trials were needed to learn the rule. Note: Red line = Introverts, Blue line = Extraverts, Green dots = Assigned same condition. *Source:* From Geen (1984).

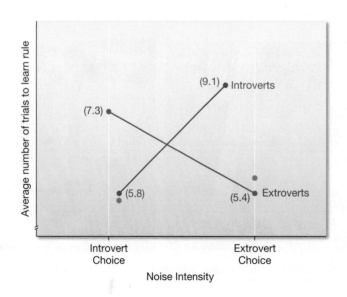

and what's just right for extraverts is too much for introverts. People's noise preferences and performance outcomes depend on their optimal level of arousal as determined by their personality (Geen, 1984). Keep this study in mind the next time you are trying to decide where to study!

Neurology of Neuroticism.   Eysenck hypothesized that physiological arousal could also account for individual differences in Neuroticism. In contrast to Extraversion, which was related to activation of the ARAS, he thought that Neuroticism had to do with stability or instability of the sympathetic nervous system (i.e., those parts of the brain that are involved in emotional regulation such as the hippocampus, amygdala, cingulum, septum and hypothalamus; Eysenck, 1967, 1990). Basically, the vulnerability of people high in Neuroticism to negative emotions such as fear and anxiety was due to an extrasensitive emotional or drive system (Eysenck, 1967, 1990). Whereas postulating separate physiological processes to account for Extraversion and Neuroticism, Eysenck acknowledged that the cortical and sympathetic systems were interconnected (Eysenck, 1967, 1990).

A vivid metaphor for how this might work is to think of Neuroticism as a smoke detector (Nettle, 2007). A good smoke detector alerts a building's occupants to a fire, but it doesn't go off for harmless events like someone burning the toast one morning. For the person high in Neuroticism, it's as if they are living in a house with an overly sensitive smoke detector that sends out a warning under the kinds of conditions that people low in Neuroticism would readily dismiss as safe. (If you're still thinking about how safe toast-burning is, then you are probably high in Neuroticism!) Extraversion and Neuroticism are similar in that both involve arousal; however, the big difference is in the valence or quality of that arousal. Extraversion is marked by positive arousal such as excitement and energy, whereas Neuroticism is marked by negative arousal such as fear and anxiety (Knutson & Bhanji, 2006; Zuckerman, 2005).

How did Eysenck's theory about Neuroticism fare in the face of research evidence? Well, it appears that Eysenck was on the right track. Simple measures of sympathetic nervous system activation (e.g., heart rate, skin conductance), both at rest and during stressful situations do not show any relationship with Neuroticism, but people who are high in Neuroticism do show an increase in heart rate in response to an intense stimulus (Zuckerman, 2005). So do introverts! However, people high in Neuroticism, but not introverts, show greater startle response to fearful pictures (Zuckerman, 2005). Together, these findings suggest that people high in Neuroticism may be more sensitive to negative emotions in particular, and not to arousing situations in general, the way that introverts are.

If it is true that the defining feature of Neuroticism is sensitivity to negative emotions, then it would be particularly difficult for researchers to identify specific physiological differences between people high and low in Neuroticism. This is because people vary greatly in their sympathetic responses (e.g., heart rate, skin conductance, breathing, blood flow, etc.; Eysenck, 1990). All in all, there is no support for Eysenck's hypothesis that Neuroticism is related to activation in the sympathetic nervous system (Strelau, 1998).

> **THINK ABOUT IT**
>
> If extraverts are more sensitive to positive emotions are they more vulnerable to happiness?

> **THINK ABOUT IT**
>
> If people high in Neuroticism are more sensitive to negative emotions, are they more vulnerable to depression?

Reinforcement Sensitivity Theory (RST)

An alternative theory was proposed by Jeffrey Gray. For Gray, personality *is* the variation in the functioning of brain systems. Indeed, the very essence of what makes people unique is differences in their responses to stimuli in the world (Corr, 2008b). Gray's idea was to (1) identify brain-behavior systems that accounted for important differences among individuals and (2) link these systems to standard measures of personality (Corr, 2008b). At first, he hypothesized two behavioral systems and linked these behavioral systems to Extraversion and Neuroticism in Eysenck's PEN theory (Gray, 1970, 1976, 1982). But now, after some 40 years of research and refinement, evidence suggests that there are three important behavioral systems that do not exactly map onto any existing measure of personality (Corr, 2004, 2008b; Gray & McNaughton, 2000; McNaughton & Corr, 2004, 2008; Pickering & Corr, 2008).

Overview of Three Neurological Systems. According to **reinforcement sensitivity theory (RST)** there are three hypothetical brain-behavior systems. These systems are presumed to exist based on evidence from neurology, physiology, behavior, and personality. Together they form a framework through which we can infer neural activity. Rather than identify isolated parts of the brain working separately, we can look for interconnected areas that function similarly and work together in accord with one of these hypothesized systems. Gray's great contribution was in recognizing that *everything* in the brain is interconnected. The conception of these three systems is his way of studying these interconnections. We may think of these systems as a kind of shorthand for a whole set of neural networks.

The first is called the **fight-flight-freeze system (FFFS)**. This system is associated with the emotion of fear and is responsible for orchestrating our reactions to aversive stimuli. We may opt to confront or fight the stimulus, avoid or escape it, or to remain frozen in place hoping the danger passes (Corr, 2004). The personality factor that matches this biological system is fearfulness and avoidance, which, if extreme, may lead to phobias and panic disorders (Corr, 2008b).

The second system, the **behavioral approach system (BAS)** organizes reactions to "appetitive stimuli," that is, stimuli that are enticing, pleasurable, and rewarding (Corr, 2004, p. 324). BAS makes a person more sensitive to reward. The related personality factor is optimism, impulsiveness, and the emotion of "anticipatory pleasure" (Corr, 2008b, p. 10). In the extreme, this system may lead to addictive behaviors, high-risk impulsive behaviors, and mania.

The third system, the **behavioral inhibition system (BIS)**, once thought to control the inhibition of behavior, is now hypothesized to resolve conflicts (Corr, 2004). These may be conflicts between two really good things, like deciding which movie to watch with friends, or between two distasteful things, like deciding which to open first, the electricity bill or the phone bill. Or between two options that have both upsides and downsides to them, such as whether or not to go to a party where you will see people you like as well as a few people whom you'd rather not hang out with. BIS also is activated when there is a conflict within one of the other systems (e.g., FFFS–FFFS or BAS–BAS conflicts; Corr, 2008b). Until the conflict is resolved, we

The fight-flight-freeze system (FFFS) regulates our reactions to aversive stimuli including fears, phobias, and panic disorders.

may experience anxiety, worry, rumination, risk assessment, vigilance for bad things, or a sense of possible danger or loss. Clinically, this system may lead to obsessive-compulsive disorder or generalized anxiety disorder (Corr, 2008b).

People may feel anxiety from BIS to a greater or a lesser degree depending on the specific rewards or punishments that are potentially in conflict. When BIS is activated, people become more sensitive to punishment (Corr, 2004) and often more cautious (Corr, 2008b). Further, there is an optimal level of BIS arousal. Too little leads to risk proneness, similar to Eysenck's notion of Psychoticism. Too much leads to risk aversion and generalized anxiety disorder (Corr, 2008b). RST suggests that choice—even between two rewarding options—has a negative component. Corr (2008b) wondered if having too many good things to choose from (e.g., Caribbean? Europe? Sports car? SUV?) may be a cause of discontent and depression in our affluent society.

BAS is very similar to Extraversion and BIS is very similar to Neuroticism. Current evidence suggests that they are quite similar but not identical (Smits & Boeck, 2006). The dimensions of FFFS/BIS and BAS are about 30 degrees off from Eysenck's dimensions of Neuroticism and Extraversion. Think of BAS as "2 parts Extraversion to 1 part Neuroticism" and BIS as "2 parts Neuroticism to 1 part Extraversion" (Smillie, Pickering, & Jackson, 2006, p. 323). Specifically, punishment sensitivity is manifested as neurotic-introversion and reward sensitivity is manifested as neurotic-extraversion. Sensitivity to punishment and sensitivity to rewards are the biological systems that together are hypothesized to develop into the traits of Extraversion and Neuroticism (Corr, 2004). Table 7.3 lists sample items from an early measure of BIS and BAS based on the original version of RST (Carver & White, 1994).

Think of it like this: Extraversion reflects the trade-off of rewards and punishments, whereas Neuroticism reflects the combination of rewards and punishments. For example, punishment makes a person less willing to take action—unless of course that action is to flee the situation—whereas the possibility of a reward increases the action. If the situation is clearly punishing or rewarding, then *everybody* will go for the reward or avoid the punishment.

However, the situations that define and challenge us are ones that are not clearly rewarding or punishing. That is, the real question of character is: What will you choose when rewards and punishments are both present? Because these situations involve some degree of conflict, BIS will

SEE FOR YOURSELF

Are you more willing to risk a punishment to gain a reward or to forego a reward to avoid a punishment?

Table 7.3 Sample Items From the BIS/BAS Scale

BAS Drive

1. When I want something I usually go all-out to get it.
2. If I see a chance to get something I want I move on it right away.

BAS Fun Seeking

1. I'm always willing to try something new if I think it will be fun.
2. I crave excitement and new sensations.

BAS Reward Responsiveness

1. When I'm doing well at something I love to keep at it.
2. When I get something I want, I feel excited and energized.

BIS

1. Criticism or scolding hurts me quite a bit.
2. If I think something unpleasant is going to happen I usually get pretty "worked up."

Note: Responses are indicated on a 4-point scale labeled *Very true for me, Somewhat true for me, Somewhat false for me,* and *Very false for me.*

Source: Adapted from C. S. Carver and White (1994, Table 1, p. 323). Carver, C. S., & White, T. L. (1994). Behavioral inhibition, behavioral activation, and affective responses to impending reward and punishment: The BIS/BAS scales. *Journal of Personality and Social Psychology,* 67(2), 319–333. Copyright American Psychological Association. Adapted with permission.

be activated and this will become manifested as Neuroticism. If rewards are more salient than punishments, then we will get a person who is willing to venture out into the world: a neurotic extravert. But if the punishment is more salient than the reward, or if the conflict is more salient than either the reward or the punishment, then we will get a person who would rather stay to himself or herself: a neurotic introvert. Who gets to decide if the rewards and punishments are in conflict? That's where Neuroticism comes in. Somebody who is low in Neuroticism would not experience conflict over the same situation that might cause consternation in somebody who was high in Neuroticism.

You can see that Gray suggested two things: our inherent behavioral systems—FFFS, BAS, and BIS—predispose us to respond to punishments, rewards, and conflicts in a certain way. Then, a lifetime of experiences refine our personalities (neurotic, emotionally stable, extraverted, introverted). In addition, RST suggests that the difference between healthy personality and psychopathology is one of degree: The underlying biological systems are essentially the same, differing only in their strength (See Table 7.4 for a summary of these three systems).

Neurology of FFFS, BAS, and BIS.   What evidence is there for these three systems? The short answer: Quite a lot! Although much of the research has been done on animals, RST appears to be a good general theory of emotion, motivation, and learning in humans too (Pickering & Corr, 2008; Smillie, 2008; Smillie et al., 2006). However, the long answer is that researchers are struggling with how to operationalize and test some of the propositions of RST (see Corr, 2001; Pickering et al., 1997; Smillie, 2008; Smillie et al., 2006; Torrubia, Ávila, Moltó, & Caseras, 2001 for reviews), especially the implications of RST for trait theory (Smillie et al., 2006). The biggest issue is that we cannot tell if there is a problem with Gray's theory or a problem with the scales designed to measure the personality traits exhibited by these brain systems. As a sign of just how lively the debate is, recently *The European Journal of Personality*

> If we could look through the skull into the brain of a consciously thinking person, and if the place of optimal excitability were luminous, then we should see playing over the cerebral surface, a bright spot with fantastic, waving borders constantly fluctuating in size and form, surrounded by a darkness more or less deep, covering the rest of the hemisphere.
>
> *Ivan Petrovich Pavlov*
> *(1928, p. 222)*

Table 7.4 Summary of Reinforcement Sensitivity Theory Systems

	FFFS	BAS	BIS
Input:	Punishment	Reward	Conflict Punishment (?)*
Response:	Avoidance Freezing Defensive attack	Approach Exploration Active avoidance	Passive avoidance Risk assessment Information processing Arousal
Emotion:	Panic Phobia Rage Fearfulness	Anticipatory pleasure Hope	Rumination
Trait:	Psychoticism Neurotic-introversion	Extraversion Neurotic-extraversion	Neuroticism Anxiety
Pathology:	Phobias Panic disorders	Addictive behaviors Mania	Obsessive-compulsive disorder Generalized anxiety disorder
Motto:	"Escape!"	"Go for it!"	"Be careful!"

*There is disagreement among researchers about whether some kinds of punishments (e.g., conditioned) are still under BIS control in the revised RST (cf. Corr, 2002).

Note: See the chapter text for descriptions and explanations of abbreviations.

Sources: Adapted from Corr and McNaughton (2008, Table 5.2, p. 182) and Smillie (2008, p. 362). Corr, P. J., & McNaughton, N. (2008). Reinforcement sensitivity theory and personality. In P. J. Corr (Ed.), The reinforcement sensitivity theory of personality (p. 155–187). Cambridge, UK: Cambridge.

The behavioral approach system (BAS) regulates our reaction to things that are enticing, pleasurable, and rewarding.

dedicated an entire special issue to personality and RST (Ávila & Torrubia, 2008; Carver, 2008; Chavanon, Stemmler, & Wacker, 2008; Cloninger, 2008; Corr, 2008a; Johnson & Deary, 2008; Matthews, 2008; McNaughton, 2008; Reuter & Montag, 2008; Revelle & Wilt, 2008; Smillie, 2008).

The theory does, however, suggest a number of important and intriguing hypotheses for understanding human personality. To give you a sense of the evidence that led to the formulation of RST and the biology behind it, let's review research on two key predictions of RST: individual differences in reward sensitivity and learning.

Consider one very important class of rewards for most people: Food. Given that BAS is related to how sensitive people are to rewards, we might wonder if people high and low in strength of BAS would have different reactions to images of food. But we're not talking about *taste* for food. RST suggests that the *brains* of people high and low in BAS will respond differently to food.

There are at least five parts of the brain that are related to responding to visual food cues: the ventral (underside) part of the striatum, the amygdala, the orbitofrontal cortex, the ventral (underside) part of the pallidum and the midbrain regions that are associated with increased dopamine activity (Beaver et al., 2006). Participants looked at color photos of appetizing food (e.g., chocolate cake, an ice cream sundae), disgusting food (rotten meat, moldy bread), bland food (e.g., uncooked rice, potatoes), and nonfood items (e.g., an iron, a videocassette). While viewing these photos, their brains were scanned using fMRI.

Researchers found that BAS drive significantly accounted for differences in signals to appetizing food and disgusting food compared to bland foods in all five of these regions related to reward. Further, these responses were not related to a BAS measure of fun seeking so that they were unique to BAS drive. Participants with a strong appetitive drive as measured by BAS scores showed stronger reactions to photos of appetizing and disgusting foods in these parts of the brain that are known to be related to food regulation (Beaver et al., 2006). This is an example of how neural differences may be related to BAS, BIS, and FFFS functioning.

An important individual difference, according to RST, is how quickly people learn from rewards and punishments. This reinforcement sensitivity is the whole premise on which the theory rests. People with a strong BAS are more sensitive to reward, meaning that they will condition—or learn responses—more quickly by responding than by withholding a response. However, people with a strong BIS are more sensitive to punishment, meaning that they will condition more quickly by withholding a response than by responding (Gray, 1970, 1976). Think about it: Would you learn better by concentrating on not doing things wrong and avoiding a punishment, or by doing things right and gaining a reward?

SEE FOR YOURSELF

Which statement do you agree with more: "Nothing ventured, nothing gained" or "Better safe than sorry"?

The behavioral inhibition system (BIS) regulates our reactions to conflicts between the fight-flight-freeze system and the behavioral approach system such as worry, rumination, vigilance, and obsessive-compulsiveness.

This question was explored in an experiment in which participants had to learn the right response to a computer task—either press the "3" key or do nothing—when presented with random two-digit numbers (Zinbarg & Mohlman, 1998). The participants had to learn which numbers required a response and which numbers required that they withhold a response. Every trial was different, so that participants had to figure out all over again which numbers to respond to (e.g., hit the "3" key) or to withhold a response from (e.g., do nothing).

To let participants know whether they were correct or not, they received rewards and punishments depending on their responses. But instead of being rewarded *every time* they were correct ("You won 25 cents") or punished *every time* they were wrong ("You lost 25 cents"), there was a twist. On some trials taking action was associated with gaining a reward. On other trials, *not* taking action would avoid a punishment (see Figure 7.4). This pattern of feedback gave participants enough information to master the task. However, there is a big difference between learning by doing and learning by not doing. The question is, do some people learn better by taking actions or by withholding actions?

As it turned out, just as RST predicts, people with a reactive BAS learned the correct responses faster from reacting than from withholding their responses. However, people with high scores on a mixed FFFS/BIS scale learned faster from withholding than from reacting. In addition, people who scored high on an anxiety scale also learned faster from withholding than from reacting (Zinbarg & Mohlman, 1998). This experiment shows differences in learning from rewards and punishments in humans as a function of BAS and BIS/FFFS (See The Personality of Everyday Life for an application of RST theory to test-taking). This study is the human equivalent of the many studies of rats and other animals that led to the original statement of RST.

Figure 7.4 Schematic of participant feedback in the Zinbarg and Mohlman (1998) study.

	Correct Answer			
	Respond		Do Nothing	
Participant's Response:	Respond	Do nothing	Respond	Do nothing
Answer:	Right	Wrong	Wrong	Right
Outcome:	Win 25 cents	(nothing)	Lose 25 cents	(nothing)
	Reward Trials		Punishment Trials	

The Personality of Everyday Life

Personality and the guessing penalty

Have you ever taken a test where you were faced with the dilemma of guessing or leaving a question blank? Some standardized tests such as the SAT or the ACT have what is commonly called a *guessing penalty*. Test takers get one point for a correct answer, but lose one-fourth point for a wrong answer. This scoring is meant to discourage a person from randomly guessing on a multiple-choice test with four choices. Is there an effective way to deal with these exams?

That depends on the relative strength of your BAS and BIS (Ávila & Torrubia, 2004). The participants in this study regularly faced exams in which they not only needed to know the material, but they had to decide whether they should respond to a question they were unsure of or to leave the question blank because there was a guessing penalty built into the exam.

How did participants deal with this conflict? Participants who scored high in sensitivity to reward made more incorrect responses and left fewer questions blank than participants who scored low in sensitivity to reward (see Table 7.5). Essentially, people who are sensitive to reward are more likely to go for it, but then they are also more likely to pay for it, compared to people who are less sensitive to reward (see Figure 7.5).

However, participants who scored high in sensitivity to punishment left more questions blank but gave more correct answers than participants who scored low in sensitivity to punishment. Participants who were sensitive to punishment seemed to go by the rule "when in doubt, leave it out."

Alas, Ávila and Torrubia (2004) did not report if there was a difference in grades as a function of high and low sensitivity to reward or punishment. However, an earlier study did (Torrubia, Ávila, Moltó, & Grande, 1995). Despite these differences in incorrect responses and omissions, there was no difference in overall exam scores between participants who were high in sensitivity to punishment or sensitivity to reward. This suggests that the contrasting strategies work equally well.

People who are more sensitive to reward—such as extraverts—seem to go though life with the philosophy "Nothing ventured, nothing gained." In contrast, people who are more sensitive to punishment—such as people high in anxiety and/or fear—would rather be safe than sorry. The good news is, both strategies can be effective.

Table 7.5 Sample Items From the Sensitivity to Punishment and Sensitivity to Reward Questionnaire (SPSRQ)

Sensitivity to Punishment Questions

1. Are you often afraid of new or unexpected situations?
2. Is it difficult for you to telephone someone you do not know?
3. As a child, were you troubled by punishments at home or in school?

Sensitivity to Reward Questions

1. Do you often do things to be praised?
2. Do you like being the center of attention at a party or a social meeting?
3. Do you spend a lot of your time on obtaining a good image?

Source: Adapted from Torrubia et al. (2001, Table 2, p. 846). Reprinted with permission from Torrubia, R., Ávila, C., Moltó, J., & Caseras, X. (2001), "The sensitivity to punishment and sensitivity to reward questionnaire (SPSRQ) as a measure of Gray's anxiety and impulsivity dimensions," Personality and Individual Differences, 29, 837–862. Permission conveyed through the Copyright Clearance Center.

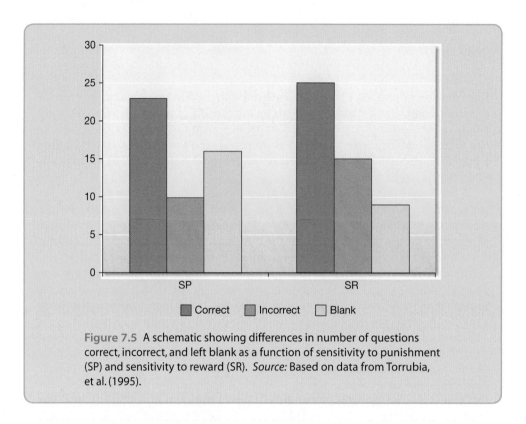

Figure 7.5 A schematic showing differences in number of questions correct, incorrect, and left blank as a function of sensitivity to punishment (SP) and sensitivity to reward (SR). *Source:* Based on data from Torrubia, et al. (1995).

"There is not the slightest resemblance between the phrenologist's localization of function that we find in physiological psychology."
Review of Charles H. Olin's 1910 book Phrenology *as cited in Seashore (1912, p. 227)*

Then and Now: Phrenology, the New Phrenology, and the Future of Neuroimaging for Personality and Beyond

Ever since ancient times, we humans have wondered, what makes us who we are? The ancient Greek philosopher Aristotle debated whether the heart or the brain was the seat of the soul or psyche, what we think of today as personality (Cowey, 2001). Since that time, others have wondered about the relationship between specific parts of the brain and personality. But it was the physician and anatomist Franz Joseph Gall in the 1790s who turned it into a science: **phrenology**. Gall reasoned—well ahead of his time—that certain functions of the brain were localized in parts of the cerebral cortex. That much, he had right. However, he also believed that the size of the cortex, as indicated by the size, shape, and in particular the location and size of bumps on the scalp, was related to particular mental or personality characteristics.

We know today that this system is completely without merit, "absolutely absurd," and "preposterous nonsense" according to the reviewer of a 1910 book on phrenology (Seashore, 1912, p. 227). However, Gall inspired a later phrenologist, George Combe, who made two interesting observations in 1836. Combe discovered that by pressing his thumb on parts of the exposed cortex of patients who had serious head injuries, he was able to change their behavior. He also noticed that some areas of brain tissue became filled with blood when the patient was thinking, dreaming, or talking (Cowey, 2001). The detection of blood-flow fluctuation eventually led to the development of fMRI, which one researcher viewed as the greatest single influence in neurological research in over 2,000 years (Cowey, 2001).

Then in 1884 William Wundt, a doctor, psychologist, and physiologist, viewed by many as the founder of experimental psychology, gave a lecture with the provocative title "Old and New Phrenology" (1894). In it he was critical of both phrenology and brain localization. Ironically, brain localization turned out to be the beginning of an important branch of psychology, as Combe's observations attested to, but at the same time Wundt was eerily on target when he cautioned that the "hypothesis of [localization] gives no account of the manifold forms of ideational and sensational connexion." (Wundt, 1894, p. 447). Indeed, his critique of brain localization was echoed 90 years later by a neuropsychologist who called neuropsychology "the currently fashionable name for phrenology" (Marshall, 1984, p. 210). The problem is that theories of localization fail to account for the connectivity of ideas in the mind, according to Wundt (1894), and the complex interaction of brain systems, according to Marshall (1984).

In the last decade or so, researchers came to realize that the various parts and systems of the brain, especially in humans, work in concert to impact behavior (Knight, 2007). Especially when it comes to understanding something as complicated as personality, we need to look at how systems within the brain work together (Uttal, 2001). Today, diffusion tensor imaging (DTI), a special type of fMRI that traces the diffusion of water in cells, is giving even more detailed pictures of the brain. But more importantly, DTI can highlight connections between cortical and subcortical regions (Cowey, 2001). DTI moves beyond localization and has the potential to enable researchers to study systems and functions as a whole rather than piecemeal.

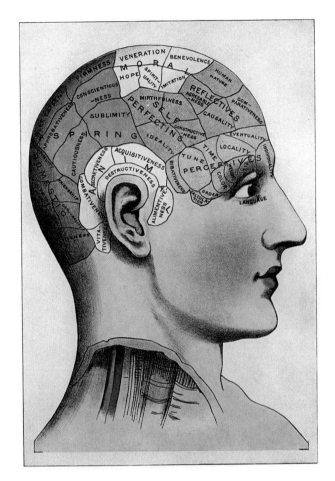

Are theories linking parts of the brain with differences in personality as simplistic and outdated as phrenology?

What might this new technology reveal? For one, we may be able to locate and study Gray's hypothetical BAS, BIS, and FFFS. For example, Whittle, Allen, Lubman, and Yücel (2006) suggested that the prefrontal cortex and limbic structures (including the amygdala) are associated with the three temperaments we have been discussing in this chapter: Extraversion, Neuroticism, and Impulsivity. Their model (see Figure 7.6) is based on neural circuitry that past research has suggested may be related to personality and psychopathology. Direct evidence for their model comes from imaging studies using fMRI, DTI, and even newer and more powerful technology still being

Visualization of a DTI measurement of a human brain. Coloured 3-dimensional magnetic resonance imaging (MRI) scan of the white matter pathways of the brain, side view. White matter is composed of myelin-coated nerve cell fibres that carry information between nerve cells in the cerebrum of the brain (top half of image) and the brain stem (bottom centre). This image was created by an MRI scanner sensitised to the movement of water around the brain. Blue represents neural pathways from the top to the bottom of the brain, green represents pathways from the front (left) to the back (right), and red shows pathways between the right and left hemispheres of the brain.

Figure 7.6 Structures proposed to comprise the neural circuits underlying the three temperaments: (a) Neuroticism (negative affect) (b) Extraversion (positive affect) and (3) low Impulsivity (high constraint). *Note:* NAcc = nucleus accumbens; OFC= orbitofrontal cortex; ACC = anterior cingulate cortex; DLPFC = dorsolateral prefrontal cortex. Solid colors indicate structures, shaded colors indicate resting state activity, red indicates positive correlation (more activity), blue indicates negative correlation (less activity). *Source:* From Whittle et al. (2006, Figure 1, p. 520). Whittle, S., Allen, N. B., Lubman, D. I., & Yücel, M. (2006), "The neurobiological basis of temperament: Towards a better understanding of psychopathology," Neuroscience and the Biobehavioral Reviews, 30, 511–525. Permission conveyed through the Copyright Clearance Center.

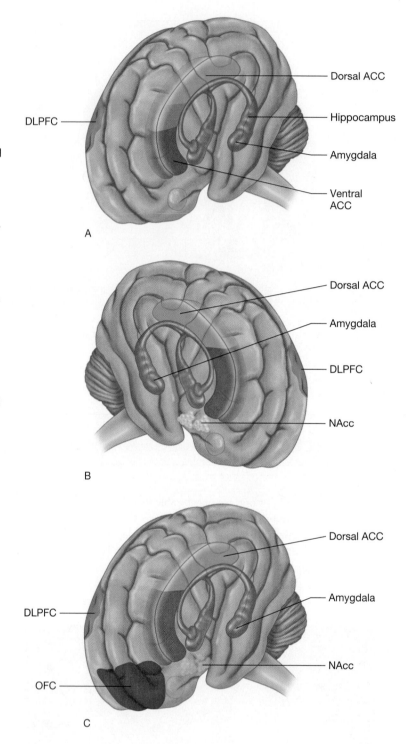

developed. Whittle et al. (2006) proposed to use these techniques to study the neural networks of young people who may be at risk for depression, anxiety disorders, or delinquency based on their temperament. By studying preteens whose brains are still growing and forming connections even as they are developing their own unique personalities, Whittle et al. (2006) hoped to relate changes in neural networks with behavior and psychopathology over time (Whittle et al., 2008).

Researchers in the Digital Media program at Drexel University have used Combe's observation of the change in cerebral blood flow caused by mental activity to design video games in which the gamer controls the character's actions *just by thinking!* There is no remote, joy stick, mouse, or other control in this game. Instead, infrared sensors, placed on a specially designed headband worn by the player, measure changes in blood oxygen levels in the frontal cortex.

Blood flow, as Combe discovered, increases with concentration. The computer monitors these fluctuations and allows the gamer to interact in a virtual world (CBS3 News, 2008). In a joint endeavor between video game designers and medical scientists, the research team has designed a game that is fun, engaging, and that studies brain function at the same time (*Drexel University Replay Lab*, 2009). Researchers hope that the game and associated technology can one day be used to help people with ADHD focus better or to enable people with severe disabilities to communicate through their computer (CBS3 News, 2008).

Neurological Correlates of Personality

If RST and Eysenck's PEN theory are beginning to blur in your mind, take heart: there's a good reason for that. Both theories make predictions for the three personality clusters, or temperaments, we identified earlier: Extraversion, Neuroticism, and Impulsivity.

A consistent finding is that a key difference between Extraversion and Neuroticism is in how emotions are experienced. Both extraverts and people high in Neuroticism have more positive emotions and negative emotions, respectively, and they also react more strongly to their positive or negative emotions than do introverts or emotionally stable people (Gross, Sutton, & Ketelaar, 1998; Larsen & Ketelaar, 1989, 1991). That is, extraverts experience more positive emotions and react to them more strongly than introverts, whereas people high in Neuroticism experience more negative emotions and react to them more strongly compared to people low in Neuroticism. In addition, extraverts experience more positive emotions but less negative emotions than people high in Neuroticism. Indeed, much of the day-to-day anxiety and moodiness experienced by people high in Neuroticism is due to their reactivity compared to people low in Neuroticism (Bolger & Schilling, 1991).

Keep in mind that positive emotions (a marker of Extraversion) and negative emotions (a marker of Neuroticism) are not opposites but rather two separate dimensions (Diener & Emmons, 1984). That is, people can have a lot of both kinds of emotions or a little of both. Being high in one does not imply being low in the other. Indeed, the lack of positive emotion is not negative emotion, but a state called **anhedonia**, which is the loss of or inability to experience pleasure that may or may not be accompanied by the presence of negative emotions. In fact, extraverts report experiencing more happiness, positive emotions, and life satisfaction than introverts, whereas people who are high in Neuroticism experience more negative emotions, unhappiness, and dissatisfaction with life compared to more emotionally stable individuals (Costa & McCrae, 1980).

Impulsivity, the third temperament, involves a lack of constraint or a state of being undercontrolled (Clark & Watson, 2008). Although this sounds very similar to Eysenck's third factor of Psychoticism, they are not the same. Eysenck maintained that his concept of psychoticism was a "more general higher-order concept" involving antisocial aspects of behavior than just impulsivity (Eysenck, 1990, p. 269). Impulsivity is related to a broader cluster of characteristics including sensation seeking, novelty seeking, or venturesomeness (Pickering & Gray, 1999).

The early work on RST proposed that Impulsivity was controlled by BAS. With the revised RST, there is consensus among researchers that BAS sensitivity is related to Extraversion (i.e., surgency: seeking incentives in the world) where impulsivity is

"When we deal with brain science, we are dealing with the organ that makes us unique individuals, that gives us our personality, memories, emotions, dreams, creative abilities, and at times our sinister selves."

Ruth Fischbach and Gerald Fischbach as cited in Ackerman (2006)

THINK ABOUT IT

How would impulsive behavior such as gambling relate to BAS and BIS functioning?

People high in extraversion show increased activity in parts of the brain to positive photos like these compared to when they viewed negative pictures.

caused by the failure of BIS to inhibit behavior, especially around novel or exciting stimuli (Smillie et al., 2006). As a result, there may be two very different motivations behind a seemingly impulsive behavior such as excessive alcohol use. People may drink frequently or excessively as a means of gaining a reward (strong BAS) or because they are incapable of inhibiting a response (weak BIS; Pardo, Aguilar, Molinuevo, & Torrubia, 2007).

At some level, all of these terms are related and define a temperament of a person who seeks novelty and excitement and who sometimes acts without thinking about the consequences. There are similar physiological processes involved in Extraversion and Neuroticism, but Impulsivity seems to have a very different underlying physiology. Let us take a closer look at the neurological correlates behind Extraversion, Neuroticism, and Impulsivity.

Extraversion and Neuroticism

Because people who are high in Extraversion or high in Neuroticism differ in their experience of emotions, it should come as no surprise that they also differ in the neurological structures and systems that are involved in the experience and regulation of emotion. We experience emotions as a result of complex systems that coordinate form and function across brain structures, brain activity, and biochemical processes. These differences in sensitivity to positive or negative emotion, although not reflected in heightened bodily responses, are reflected in differences in brain structures that control emotion, brain activity in response to emotional stimuli, and biochemical activity that regulates emotions. We'll review some of this evidence, focusing on this general picture of personality differences more so than the neuroscience of emotional regulation.

Brain Structure Differences in the Cortex and the Amygdala.   Two main areas of the brain show differences in size depending on personality differences in Extraversion and Neuroticism: the cortex and the amygdala.

The Cortex.   One area that is important for the experience of emotion is the prefrontal cortex; and introverts and extraverts show differences in the size of their cortexes. In one study, the brains of normal, healthy volunteers were scanned using MRI while at rest (Wright et al., 2006). Introversion was correlated with thickness of three sections of the right, but not the left, cortex. That is, introverts appeared to have more gray matter in these right hemisphere areas than extraverts (see Figures 7.7 and 7.8; Wright et al., 2006).

Wright et al. (2006) suggested that the relative thinning of these areas may be a neurological symptom of the lessened social inhibition found in extraverts. However, they also cautioned that smaller size doesn't necessarily indicate diminished function. We know that one way the nervous system works is to start out with a lot of neurons and connections that gradually get abandoned or cut back as connections become more refined. It's possible that neurons in these areas may have been pruned back during development, leading to greater efficiency in the system rather than reduced function.

In contrast, Neuroticism scores were negatively correlated with parts of the left, but not the right, cortex (Wright et al., 2006). That is, people high in Neuroticism had less gray matter in these left hemisphere areas compared to people low in Neuroticism (see Figure 7.9). This effect

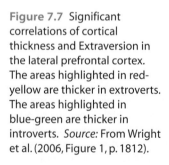

Figure 7.7 Significant correlations of cortical thickness and Extraversion in the lateral prefrontal cortex. The areas highlighted in red-yellow are thicker in extroverts. The areas highlighted in blue-green are thicker in introverts. *Source:* From Wright et al. (2006, Figure 1, p. 1812).

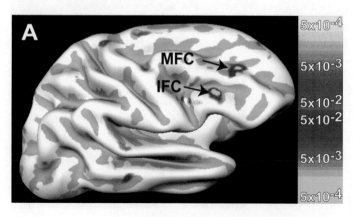

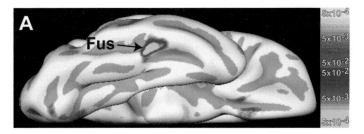

Figure 7.8 Significant correlations of cortical thickness and Extraversion in the right fusiform cortex. The areas highlighted in red-yellow are thicker in extroverts. The areas highlighted in blue-green are thicker in introverts. *Source:* From Wright et al. (2006, Figure 2, p. 1813).

was stronger in males than in females. These results confirm an earlier study that found that people high in Neuroticism, especially in anxiety and self-consciousness, had lower brain volume and that brain volume was not related to Extraversion nor to other traits (Knutson, Momenan, Rawlings, Fong, & Hommer, 2001).

The Amygdala. Extraversion and Neuroticism are also related to structural differences in the amygdala. Extraverts had a higher concentration of gray matter in the left amygdala as measured by MRI than introverts, and people high in Neuroticism had a lower concentration of gray matter in the right amygdala than people scoring low in Neuroticism (Omura, Constable, & Canli, 2005). Other studies have found that depressed people also have less gray matter in the amygdala. Because of its association with Neuroticism, Omura et al. (2005) stated that this reduction in the mass of the amygdala is not a result of depression, but instead, occurs before the depression hits.

Brain Activity Differences in the Cortex, Left–Right Asymmetry, and the Amygdala. In addition to differences in brain structures, there are differences in how the brains of people high in Extraversion or high in Neuroticism function. These are reflected in brain activity differences in the cortex, including left–right asymmetry, and in the amygdala.

The Cortex. Extraversion and Neuroticism are each correlated with activity in the temporal and frontal parts of the cortex, areas that control consciousness (frontal) and emotions (both temporal and frontal), but in different ways: Extraversion is correlated with activity for positive emotions and Neuroticism is correlated with activity for negative emotions (Canli et al., 2001).

To illustrate, consider the following experiment. Women participants saw 20 positive and 20 negative pictures while their brains were being scanned using fMRI (Canli et al., 2001). The positive pictures included a happy couple, sunsets, and pictures of appetizing foods such as ice

> **THINK ABOUT IT**
>
> Why would individual differences in positive but not negative emotions evolve?

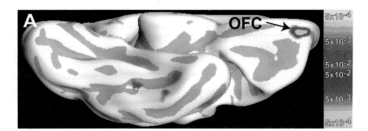

Figure 7.9 Significant correlations of cortical thickness and Neuroticism in the orbitofrontal cortex. The areas highlighted in red-yellow are thicker in people who are high in Neuroticism. The areas highlighted in blue-green are thicker in people low in Neuroticism. *Source:* From Wright et al. (2006, Figure 3, p. 1814).

People high in Neuroticism show increased activity in parts of the brain to negative photos like these compared to when they viewed positive pictures.

cream and brownies. The negative pictures included images of people crying, spiders, and a cemetery. While looking at the positive pictures, extraverts showed more activity in the temporal and frontal parts of the cortex compared to when they saw the negative pictures. However, people high in Neuroticism showed greater activity in the temporal and frontal parts of the cortex when looking at negative pictures than when looking at positive pictures. Further, one study identified an amazing 15 different cortical and subcortical regions of the brain where extraverts responded with greater brain activation to positive stimuli compared to negative stimuli (Canli et al., 2001).

Left–Right Asymmetry.   Although the two hemispheres of the brain are specialized for different processes (e.g., linguistic processes in the left hemisphere among right-handers), there are individual differences in how the cortex of the brain reacts to specific emotional stimuli as shown by EEG brain wave response or fMRI. Specifically, the right frontal and prefrontal cortexes are more active than the left during negative emotions, whereas the left portion of these regions are more active than the right portion during positive emotions (Davidson, 1992, 2004). But more importantly, people differ in how large these relative differences are in responding to positive and negative emotions. Further, these differences are present as early as the first year of life. We call these differences **left–right asymmetries**.

Some people show more left asymmetry: their left cortex responds to positive emotion more than their right cortex responds to negative emotion. Other people show more right asymmetry: their right cortex responds to negative emotions more than their left cortex responds to positive emotion. People with greater left asymmetry report more positive emotion to film clips than people with right asymmetry; people with greater right asymmetry report more negative emotion to film clips than people with left asymmetry (Davidson, 1992).

THINK ABOUT IT

If meditation changes left–right asymmetry and if left–right asymmetry shows consistent differences among people, does meditation change personality?

What kind of people are likely to show left or right asymmetry? Shy, inhibited children and depressed adults show greater right asymmetry, as do people who are high in Neuroticism, both at rest and in response to emotional stimuli (Davidson, 1992). People who experience positive emotion, like those high in extraversion, show greater left asymmetry both at rest and in response to positive emotion (Tomarken, Davidson, Wheeler, & Doss, 1992).

Do you recall the meditation study that opened this chapter? One of the results was that people in the meditation condition showed greater left brain asymmetry both at rest and in response to positive and negative emotional events (Davidson et al., 2003). Psychologist Richard Davidson actually conducted an fMRI of a Tibetan monk with over 10,000 hours of training in meditation (Savory, 2004). This monk turned out to have the most extreme left asymmetry that Davidson had ever seen! We can see now that meditation reduces reactions in the right brain to stress and increases reactions in the left brain to positive emotions. The net result is that little stressors don't bother people as much and they get more joy out of the small pleasures in life.

Of course we must be cautious, as these results may hold for only the kind of people who seek out and voluntarily invest the time and energy to learn and practice meditation. We can't be sure if there is something special about these people, compared to people who are uninterested in meditation, or if it is the meditation per se that causes these changes. It is possible that yoga, spirituality, or any form of relaxation can lead to similar results.

Richard J. Davidson meeting the Dalai Lama, the supreme leader of Tibetan Buddhism. The Dalai Lama visited Davidson's lab at the University of Wisconsin–Madison in May 2001 to discuss ways science could study meditation to promote human happiness.

The Amygdala. Extraversion is also related to activity in the amygdala, a brain region involved in the processing and memory of emotions (Canli, Sievers, Whitfield, Gotlib, & Gabrieli, 2002). While viewing happy faces, extraverts showed more activity in the amygdala than did introverts (see Figure 7.10). Other research confirms these results (see Gross, 2008, for a review).

However, there was no relationship between Extraversion and amygdala response to negative faces nor was there any relationship between amygdala activation and Neuroticism in response to any of the other emotional faces used (e.g., angry, fearful, happy, sad, or neutral). The researchers believed that response to threatening faces—at least at this gut emotional level—is an important survival mechanism and so is unrelated to individual differences in personality (Canli et al., 2002).

Biochemical Activity. Given that Extraversion and Neuroticism are associated with differences in brain structure and brain activity, it follows that there are biochemical differences as well. For Extraversion, these differences involve the dopamine system, whereas for people high in Neuroticism, serotonin seems to be key.

Dopamine and Extraversion. You know how introverts have greater sensitivity to sensory stimulation—that is, arousability—than extraverts? It turns out that introverts are also more sensitive to fluctuations in the neurotransmitter dopamine in the brain as a result of sensory

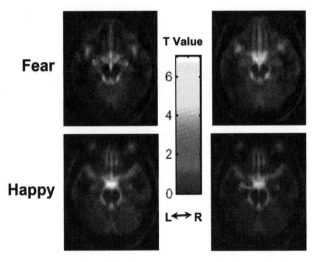

Figure 7.10 Response of the amygdala to emotional faces. The left fMRI images show significant activation to fearful (top) but not happy faces (bottom) across all participants. The right images show areas where greater activation to emotional images was significantly correlated with higher scores in Extraversion for happy (bottom) but not for fearful faces (top). Redder areas show greater activation. *Source:* From Canli et al. (2002, Figure 1, p. 2191).

input. This may explain their preference for quiet and solitude (Stelmack & Rammsayer, 2008). However, extraverts have greater dopamine activity than introverts in general. This may be due to either more extensive dopamine pathways in the brains of extraverts or a greater responsiveness to dopamine in general (Depue & Collins, 1999; Depue et al., 1994). This makes sense because the dopamine system connects with the amygdala, which is more responsive in extraverts, as we just saw (Gross, 2008; Knutson & Bhanji, 2006).

Serotonin and Neuroticism.   For people high in Neuroticism, the neurotransmitter serotonin and the serotonin receptors in the brain may be more important than dopamine and the dopamine system. Serotonin and parts of the brain sensitive to serotonin such as the cortex and amygdala but also the hippocampus, septum, and hypothalamus are involved with mood regulation, depression, and anxiety disorders (Canli, 2006). Therefore it's likely for these to be related to Neuroticism as well.

There is evidence that extreme levels of anxiety and depression, as found in clinical depression, posttraumatic stress disorder, chronic anxiety, and other kinds of pathology, may be related to low serotonin levels (Stelmack & Rammsayer, 2008; Zuckerman, 2005). Given that anxiety and depression are aspects of Neuroticism, this suggests that serotonin may also be related to individual differences in Neuroticism.

We know from the previous chapter on genetics that Neuroticism has a strong genetic component. People high in Neuroticism are more likely than emotionally stable people to have the short allele of a serotonin transporter that people low in Neuroticism lack (Lesch et al., 1996). People with this variation of the gene have less serotonin in their system and are therefore at increased risk for mood and anxiety disorders (Canli & Lesch, 2007; Lesch, 2007).

Recall that Neuroticism is associated with increased neural activity, as measured by fMRI, in the amygdala especially during negative emotions such as fear (Hooker, Verosky, Miyakawa, Knight, & D'Esposito, 2008). Additional research finds that people with a genetic variation in a serotonin transporter, which causes lower levels of serotonin in the system, showed greater amygdala reactivity to fearful faces, especially for people who were higher in BIS threat sensitivity (Cools et al., 2005). These studies suggest that people high in Neuroticism may have stronger and longer-lasting learned associations, especially to punishment (Hooker et al., 2008). This would account for the earlier findings from reinforcement sensitivity theory that extraverts are more sensitive to reward whereas people high in Neuroticism are more sensitive to punishment.

Impulsivity and Sensation Seeking

Sensation seeking is the "seeking of varied novel, complex, and intense sensations and experiences, and the willingness to take physical, social, legal, and financial risks for the sake of such experiences" (Zuckerman, 1994, p. 27). Sensation seekers are not so much into the danger of such behaviors—like risking all their money on a big bet; they are more into the fun part—like spending an entire evening at a casino.

Marvin Zuckerman first identified this personality trait while he was engaged in sensory-deprivation and social isolation research in the 1960s (e.g., Zuckerman, Persky, Link, & Basu, 1968). He and his colleagues found that many of their volunteers—people who were willing to go into physical isolation, alone in a dark, sound-proofed room, with heavy gloves covering their hands—were high in sensation seeking. Paradoxically, these high sensation seeking volunteers sought sensory deprivation in the hopes of having unusual sensory experiences like hallucinations as a result of the extreme deprivation in the experiments (Zuckerman, 2008). Low sensation seekers found such experiments particularly anxiety-provoking (Zuckerman et al., 1968). This led Zuckerman and his colleagues to realize that sensation seeking involved a desire for novel mental, internal sensations as well as exciting activities (Zuckerman, 2008). Sensation seekers were more likely to volunteer for studies involving unusual experiences such as hypnosis, ESP, meditation, encounter groups, or viewing pornography, but nor for more run-of-the-mill experiments in learning or social psychology (Zuckerman, 2008).

Sensation seeking is typically measured by the Sensation Seeking Scale which is divided into four subscales, each measuring a different aspect of sensation seeking (Zuckerman, 1971). **Experience seeking** measures the desire for moderate arousal through different kinds of experiences

"To me, one of the deepest motivations in the human spirit is to lead an interesting, exciting and thrilling life. It's not for everybody, but I think it's a powerful force."
Frank Farley as cited in Munsey
(2009, p. 40)

involving both the mind and the senses, perhaps through music, travel, or an unconventional lifestyle (Zuckerman, 1971, 2008). It is very similar to the concept of Openness from the five-factor model (McCrae & Costa, 1997a). **Boredom susceptibility** taps the need for change and variety and an aversion to routine and sameness (Zuckerman, 1971). **Thrill and adventure seeking** measures arousal seeking through physical sensations produced by speed, height, falling, danger, and unique experiences such as exploring an underwater world by scuba-diving (Zuckerman, 1971, 2008). Many extreme sports athletes are no doubt high in thrill and adventure seeking! **Disinhibition** is the extent to which people have lowered social inhibitions and enjoy letting loose in the company of others, without a thought about decorum, proper behavior, or social norms. Disinhibition often takes the form of alcohol use, partying, and sex (Zuckerman, 2008). Table 7.6 contains sample items of the Brief Sensation Seeking Scale (Hoyle, Stephenson, Palmgreen, Lorch, & Donohew, 2002) so you can see for yourself what these four dimensions look like.

Sensation seeking shows a consistent gender difference and an age difference, with men scoring higher than women and young people scoring higher than older people, on average (Zuckerman & Neeb, 1980). Sensation seeking peaks in the late teens and early 20s.

High sensation seekers differ from low sensation seekers in some interesting ways. High sensation seekers are more likely to be younger at the age of first intercourse, and to have more sexual partners, more varied sexual experiences, and risky sex, defined as sex with strangers or under the influence of alcohol or other drugs (Hoyle, Fejfar, & Miller, 2000; Zuckerman, 2007).

High sensation seekers are also more likely to smoke cigarettes than low sensation seekers, a finding that has remained consistent over some 30-plus years of research and across many countries including Switzerland, Norway, the Netherlands, Israel, and the United States (Zuckerman, 2008). Sensation seeking also correlates with drug and alcohol use including stimulants such as cocaine, amphetamine, marijuana and LSD, and depressants such as heroin (Zuckerman, 1979). Among people who use drugs, high sensation seeking is associated with the range of different kinds of drugs used, more so than with any one drug (Kaestner, Rosen, & Apel, 1977).

From the discussion so far, you might think that "sex, drugs, and rock 'n' roll" somehow go together. Well, at least when it comes to the tastes of the high sensation seeker, they do! These are new and, to some extent depending on the generation, unusual and antisocial experiences. High sensation seekers prefer rock, heavy metal, and punk music over movie soundtracks and religious music (Litle & Zuckerman, 1986). They also enjoy alternative, rap, and electronic dance music more so than people low in sensation seeking (McNamara & Ballard, 1999).

"Bones heal, chicks dig scars, pain is temporary, glory is forever."
Evel Knievel, American daredevil and entertainer

SEE FOR YOURSELF

How much of a sensation seeker are you? Why do you say this?

Table 7.6 The Brief Sensation Seeking Scale

Experience Seeking

1. I would like to explore strange places.
5. I would like to take off on a trip with no preplanned routes or timetables.

Boredom Susceptibility

2. I get restless when I spend too much time at home.
6. I prefer friends who are excitingly unpredictable.

Thrill and Adventure Seeking

3. I like to do frightening things.
7. I would like to try bungee jumping.

Disinhibition

4. I like wild parties.
8. I would love to have new and exciting experiences, even if they are illegal.

Note: To what extent do you agree or disagree? Answer using a 5-point scale from *Strongly disagree (1), Disagree (2), Neither disagree nor agree (3), Agree (4)*, and *Strongly agree (5)*. In a sample of 8th to 11th graders, females averaged 3.68 and males 3.54.

Source: Adapted from Hoyle et al. (2002, p. 405). Reprinted with permission from Hoyle, R. H., Stephenson, M. T., Palmgreen, P., Lorch, E. P., & Donohew, R. L. (2002), "Reliability and validity of a brief measure of sensation reliability and validity of a brief measure of sensation seeking," *Personality and Individual Differences*, 32, pg. 401–414. Permission conveyed through the Copyright Clearance Center.

Ice climbing is an example of an extreme sport that involves inherent danger.

High and low sensation seekers also differ in the kinds of careers they enjoy. Whereas sensation seekers are not drawn more to the military or to law enforcement than low sensation seekers, they are more likely to volunteer for riskier assignments in both careers (Zuckerman, 2008). Speeders and reckless drivers—and the officers who engage in high-speed criminal chases—are more likely to be high sensation seekers (Zuckerman, 2008). People who deal with risk on a daily basis such as air traffic controllers and rape counselors, or physicians, nurses, psychologists, and paraprofessionals who voluntarily work in an emergency room are all higher in sensation seeking than people working in more traditional settings (Zuckerman, 2008).

What might it be like to be in a close relationship with a high sensation seeker? It depends: People have greater marital satisfaction when their partners are similar to them on this trait (Schroth, 1991). However, couples are less likely to divorce if both partners are low in sensation seeking (Zuckerman & Neeb, 1980).

It isn't all fun and games for a high sensation seeker. Tragically, sometimes high sensation seekers behave a little too riskily or impulsively for their own good. Casual observations in the past had noted that spinal cord injuries often happen due to poor judgment and impulsivity (Mawson, Jacobs, Winchester, & Biundo, 1988). Might personality (i.e., sensation seeking) be related to type of injury? An interesting study was conducted in which 140 men with spinal cord injuries were matched with control subjects who were of the same age, gender, educational attainment, and lived in the same zip code (Mawson et al., 1988). Through phone interviews, both injured and control participants filled out the Sensation Seeking Scale (Zuckerman, 1971) and answered questions about their lives.

Sure enough, the spinal cord injured participants scored higher than the matched control participants on boredom susceptibility and disinhibition. Even more interesting, when the researchers selected the injured participants who scored in the top and bottom 10% of the Sensation Seeking Scale (i.e., the highest and lowest sensation seekers, respectively) the highest sensation seekers were significantly more likely than the lowest sensation seekers to have an arrest record, be younger at the time of their injury (26.1 vs. 41.5 years of age), and to have been using alcohol or taking drugs at the time of their injury (Mawson et al., 1988).

Recently, Zuckerman has refined the concept of sensation seeking to the more specific impulsive sensation seeking (Zuckerman, 1993a, 2002). Impulsive sensation seeking is very close to Eysenck's concept of Psychoticism. In contrast to high scorers, low scorers show restraint, responsibility, and inhibition (Zuckerman, 2008). Impulsive Sensation seeking is part of an alternative five-factor measure of personality that includes Impulsive Sensation Seeking, Neuroticism-Anxiety, Aggression-Hostility, Sociability, and Activity (Zuckerman, 1993a, 2005).

Bodily Responses.   Why are some people high in sensation seeking and impulsiveness and others not? Zuckerman once thought that high sensation seekers were merely trying to increase their arousal to some optimum level of arousal, much like Eysenck thought extraverts and introverts do (Zuckerman, 1969). However, experimental tests failed to support this idea (Geen, 1997). More recently, evidence suggests that the key difference may be in orienting—or how people react to a novel stimuli—which may involve the reactivity of the nervous system, which is regulated by neurotransmitters (Geen, 1997).

Physiological reactions to novel stimuli, as measured by GSR, heart rate, and cortical activity (e.g., EPs), suggest that what is viewed as a potential threat by the low sensation seeker may be of keen interest to the high sensation seeker. That is, high and low sensation seekers differ in how they react to a novel stimulus. High sensation seekers are more likely to react with a physiological pattern of responses that are more similar to an orienting reflex, indicative of interest and a desire to approach. In contrast, low sensation seekers are more likely to react with a defensive startle reflex, indicative of danger and a readiness for action (Geen, 1997; Zuckerman, 2005, 2008). For example, at the onset of a moderate noise, both high and low sensation seekers react with a spike in heart rate. As the noise continues, high sensation seekers will quickly habituate to the noise and their heart rate will rapidly decrease. In contrast, the heart rate of low sensation seekers will continue to increase, indicating a readiness to fight, flight, or freeze. Eventually, they too will habituate to the noise, but at a rate slower than high sensation seekers (Zuckerman, Simons, & Como, 1988).

Other evidence suggests that high sensation seekers have greater pain tolerance, higher Extraversion, less hypochondriasis, and higher sensory thresholds compared to low sensation seekers (Goldman, Kohn, & Hunt, 1983; Kohn, Hunt, & Hoffman, 1982). This suggests that high sensation seekers are not trying to maintain an optimal level of arousal, but that they are able to handle and even enjoy more intense sensory stimulation (Stelmack & Rammsayer, 2008).

Brain Activity.   There are remarkably few studies done looking at brain imaging and sensation seeking. One of these few compared fMRI scans of high and low sensation seekers while they viewed positive and negative emotional images (Joseph, Liu, Jiang, Lynam, & Kelly, 2009). Some of the images were highly arousing, depicting things such as violence, extreme sports, and erotica. Other images, such as pictures of objects, people, or food, were not as arousing. High sensation seekers, compared to low sensation seekers, had stronger reactions in parts of the brain related to arousal and reinforcement while viewing the highly arousing pictures, regardless of whether they were positive or negative (Joseph et al., 2009). In contrast, low sensation seekers showed faster and stronger activation in regions related to emotional regulation and decision making. Overall, high sensation seekers were more reactive to the arousal level of the pictures and were less sensitive to their positive or negative content compared to low sensation seekers.

Biochemical Activity.   Do you recall the important neurotransmitters dopamine, norepinephrine and epinephrine, and how they are all broken down by the enzyme MAO? All of these—dopamine, norepinephrine, epinephrine, MAO—show correlations with sensation seeking and impulsivity (Carver, 2005; Rawlings & Dawe, 2008; Ruchkin, Koposov, af Klinteberg, Oreland, & Grigorenko, 2005; Zuckerman, 1984, 1994, 1995, 2007, 2008). Zuckerman's (2008) latest model suggests that high sensation seeking comes from an interaction of these three systems: dopamine reactivity (which increases exploration of novel stimuli), low serotonin (which fails to inhibit behavior) and low norepinephrine/noradrenaline (which lessens the stress response to novel stimuli and the threat of punishment).

Much evidence suggests that high sensation seekers either have higher levels of dopamine or a more reactive dopamine system than low sensation seekers (Pickering & Gray, 1999; Stelmack & Rammsayer, 2008; Zuckerman, 1993b, 2008). And, indeed, high sensation seekers have lower levels of serotonin than low sensation seekers (Rawlings & Dawe, 2008; Zuckerman, 2007). Because MAO regulates dopamine and norepinephrine we would expect differences in MAO between high and low sensation seekers (Geen, 1997). Some have compared the action of MAO to the braking system of a car: less braking power (e.g., less MAO) means more forward motion (e.g., more dopamine, serotonin, or norepinephrine). Though researchers have hypothesized that high sensation seekers have lower levels of MAO (e.g., Zuckerman, 1995), until recently, the results have been inconsistent (Geen, 1997).

THINK ABOUT IT

Why were high sensation seekers more sensitive to the arousal than to the content in this study?

Conclusion: What Have We Learned From the Neuroscience of Personality?

> *Putting together a [physiological approach] to personality is like assembling the pieces of a jigsaw puzzle or fitting words into a crossword puzzle. In the crossword puzzle, horizontal words (relationships between traits and behaviors) require vertical words (between traits and behaviors and underlying biological traits) to confirm them. The puzzle . . . is beginning to form some semblance of a theoretical model, although many pieces are missing and many words are disconnected.* (Zuckerman, 2006, p. 51)

Although Zuckerman wrote these words referring to sensation seeking, this statement could apply to any personality characteristic. We know that about 40% of the variance in a personality trait is due to genetics (Krueger & Johnson, 2008; Turkheimer, 2000) and, as Eysenck suggested, genetics must work through physiology and neurology. There are a few theoretical models, notably Eysenck's PEN model and Gray's RST, that try to account for personality in terms of genetics and neurological differences. But even this equation leaves us with the question of where the other 60% of the variance in personality traits comes from. Generally we say the environment, but really the answer is more complicated, as we know that experiences, including thoughts and behaviors, can affect our physiology. Think about the experiment that opened this chapter showing that meditation caused changes in brain functioning (Davidson et al., 2003).

Ultimately, even if we were to find a "Neuroticism" area of the brain, does this mean that neurology *causes* us to develop a certain personality? Does it mean that a lifetime of acting anxious *causes* our brains to develop a certain way? Maybe having a rough life filled with many unfortunate events makes one neurotic *and* changes our brains. No matter how good our imaging techniques are, we are unable to determine the answer to this fundamental causal question without conducting a true experiment.

What might such an experiment look like? Right now, a standard treatment for patients with severe tremors in their hands or other limbs is to implant a tiny electrode. When switched on, a slight electrical current inhibits the tremor and the person is able to function without shaking. Could you imagine such a device implanted in an area of the brain that is related to Extraversion? Would turning on the electrode make a person want to be with other people? Would turning off the electrode make a person want to sit quietly and read a book?

Or, what if we randomly gave some people a drug that artificially lowers their levels of serotonin? Would they become more anxious? It is this *random assignment* to condition or a treatment that is the only way of determining causality. This serotonin study was actually conducted. What did they find? The result depended on the level of the participant's BIS. Participants with high BIS were more sensitive to negative stimuli as measured by BOLD levels in the amygdala (Cools et al., 2005). That is, serotonin level alone is not enough to *cause* a difference in brain functioning. This study highlights two important lessons from this chapter. First, we need to think of personality in terms of brain systems and not just localized areas of the brain. Second, we need to move beyond correlational methods if we hope to figure out how much of our personalities is due to our physiology and neurology.

> "As the Dalai Lama himself said in his book *The Art of Happiness*, we have the capacity to change ourselves because of the very nature, of the very structure and function of our brain."
> *Richard J. Davidson as cited in Savory (2004)*

Chapter Summary

· ·

✓● Study and Review
on mysearchlab.com

Go online for more resources to help you review.

How does our neurology and physiology make us who we are? The answer to this chicken-and-egg question is still a bit murky. Let's start with what we do know:

1. The field of neuropersonality studies the relationship between neurology and personality by studying bodily responses, brain structure, brain activity, and biochemical activity related to personality and personality functioning.

2. There appear to be broad, inborn, biological differences among individuals, called temperaments, that develop into personality characteristics over a lifetime of interacting with the social environment.

3. Three broad temperaments or clusters of personality traits are Extraversion, Neuroticism, and Impulsivity (e.g., sensation seeking).

4. These three traits are related to physiological and neurological differences in dopamine and dopaminergic systems, emotion systems, and serotonin and serotonergic systems.

5. Just as phrenology, the science of determining personality from bumps on the head, is outdated, looking for correlates of personality in specific areas of the brain is outdated as well. Neuroscientists now think in terms of brain systems.

We learned how Hans Eysenck's Psychoticism–Extraversion–Neuroticism model and Jeffrey Gray's reinforcement sensitivity theory are models of personality grounded in physiological and neurological differences and refined and revised in light of research evidence. These two theories are good examples of the questions—and answers—pursued by personality psychologists.

We discovered that high sensation seekers are driven toward excitement and novelty. Evidence suggests that they have different reflexes or gut-level reactions to unusual stimuli. Sensation seekers appear to thrive on levels of excitement that would make low sensation seekers' heads spin. This is a personality trait with a strong physiological correlate.

Now for what we don't know. When it comes to neurology and personality, researchers often rely on correlational designs using neuroimaging techniques such as fMRI. These techniques and designs, though imperfect, can tell us which part of the brain is active in which kinds of people on which kinds of tasks. Although it might be tempting to conclude that the brains of extraverts are this way whereas the brains of introverts are that way, we ultimately don't know *why* the brains and physiologies of people differ. The techniques used by neurologists cannot tell us the ultimate answer, of whether our physiology causes us to develop certain personalities or whether certain personalities develop certain neurology or whether certain experiences alter both our brains and our personalities. The answer will have to wait for more sophisticated methods and methodologies.

Review Questions

1. What are the four types of common markers of neurological and physiological differences in personality? What are some examples of each?

2. What is a correlational design? How does it compare to a true experiment? What are scatterplots? Why are some fMRI studies suspect?

3. What is Eysenck's PEN model? What is the main physiological difference between introverts and extraverts?

4. What are the three main systems of Gray's reinforcement sensitivity theory? What kind of people learn better from rewards? What kind of people learn better from punishments?

5. What is phrenology? What is brain localization? In contrast to these methods, what do researchers today focus on? What are some preliminary findings from these cutting-edge methods in personality neuroscience?

6. How do extraverts and people high in Neuroticism respond to emotion? What differences in brain structure, brain activity, and biochemical activity are related to Extraversion and Neuroticism?

7. What is sensation seeking? How do high and low sensation seekers differ from one another? What three systems appear to be related to sensation seeking?

Key Terms

Central nervous system
Peripheral nervous system
Somatic nervous system
Autonomic nervous system
Sympathetic division
Parasympathetic division
Galvanic Skin Response
(GSR)
Electromyography (EMG)
Computerized Tomography
(CT)
Computer Axial Tomography
(CAT)
Magnetic Resonance Imaging
(MRI)
Electroencephalogram (EEG)
Evoked Potential (EP)

Positron Emission Tomogra-
phy (PET)
Functional Magnetic Reso-
nance Imaging (fMRI)
Nonindependence error
Transcranial Magnetic Stim-
ulation (TMS)
Neurotransmitters
Challenge test
Scatterplots or scattergrams
Temperament
Extraversion
Neuroticism
Psychoticism
Ascending Reticular Activat-
ing System (ARAS)
Arousability

Reinforcement Sensitivity
Theory (RST)
Fight-Flight-Freeze System
(FFFS)
Behavioral Approach System
(BAS)
Behavioral Inhibition System
(BIS)
Phrenology
Anhedonia
Left–right asymmetries
Sensation seeking
Experience seeking
Boredom susceptibility
Thrill and adventure seeking
Disinhibition

8 INTRAPSYCHIC FOUNDATIONS OF PERSONALITY

Read the Chapter on
mysearchlab.com

"Probably the sexiest woman I know is my mother. She's an ethereal angel. Nobody looks like that woman. If I could meet my mother and marry her, I would. I would be with my mother now, if she weren't my mother, as sick as that sounds."

Actor Shia LaBeouf, in an interview June 2009

SEE FOR YOURSELF

Have you ever felt an inexplicable bond with a person you just met?

"We sometimes encounter people, even perfect strangers, who begin to interest us at first sight, somehow suddenly, all at once, before a word has been spoken."

Fydor Dostoevsky

"Freud, like Elvis, has been dead for a number of years but continues to be cited with some regularity."

Psychologist Drew Westen (1998a, p. 333)

D o you believe in love at first sight, the sense that there is something so powerful, so attractive in another person that your realize that he or she is THE ONE? Imagine that you are perusing the personal ads hoping to find the Love of Your Life—or at least an interesting person to date! You read two different descriptions and imagine what it would be like to date each of them. Though they both seem nice enough, you seem to feel an inexplicable bond with one of them and, despite some slight nervousness, you could definitely picture yourself dating this person.

This was the exact task faced by participants in an interesting study (Brumbaugh & Fraley, 2006). Undergraduate men and women read the personal ads of two potential dates. Unbeknownst to them, the two profiles were designed so that one resembled their most significant past romantic relationship whereas the other resembled the past love of another participant. Participants read both descriptions and rated whether each person seemed like someone they could date and to describe what it would be like to be in a relationship with each of them.

Participants imagined relationships with their potential dates in ways that were eerily similar to the kinds of relationships that they described having with their past love, especially when the potential date resembled their past love. Participants felt a greater degree of closeness and intimacy, were more interested in dating, and yet felt more susceptible to rejection with potential dates who resembled a former partner than potential dates who resembled another participant's former partner. In particular, people were especially likely to feel anxious when contemplating dating a person who resembled their very first love (Brumbaugh & Fraley, 2006).

Why does this happen? According to *attachment theory* (Ainsworth, Bell, & Stayton, 1974; Bowlby, 1969), we form emotional bonds with our caregivers, which become mental representations, called *internal working models,* of all future intimate relationships. Researchers in this area would say that our feelings from past significant relationships, including our early love relationships with parents and caregivers, become transferred onto future potential partners, especially if they resemble these significant people in terms of personality characteristics and typical behaviors (e.g., Geher, 2000).

Are we, like actor LaBeouf in the quote that opened this chapter, destined to fall in love with our parent of the other sex, or at least with somebody who resembles him or her? These ideas of relationship styles and of **transference** come from—you guessed it—the work of Sigmund Freud (1856–1939). Freud defined psychoanalysis as a theory of personality, a method for investigating unconscious processes, and a technique of treatment (Freud, 1923/1961). A key premise of psychoanalytic psychology, the branch of psychology based on Freud's theories and methods of psychoanalysis, is that we form mental representations of ourselves, others, and our relationships from early experiences (Westen, 1998a). However, the field of psychoanalysis today is undergoing a revolution, becoming more empirical and more open to findings from other areas of psychology (Westen, Gabbard, & Ortigo, 2008). Ironically, this change is occurring even as the theories, methods, and findings of the founder of psychoanalysis, Sigmund Freud, are being discounted.

In this chapter we consider intrapsychic aspects of personality through a brief review of the controversy surrounding Sigmund Freud and his theory of personality, empirical evidence for key aspects of his theory, and other psychoanalytic approaches, including the research-based attachment theory.

Sigmund Freud and Psychoanalysis

A huge controversy has been brewing in psychology, made public by a 1993 cover of *Time* magazine that asked, "Is Freud dead?" Critics lined up on either side of the debate claiming that if he wasn't dead, his outdated, discredited, and at times misogynistic theories ought to be laid to rest (see, for example, Azar, 1997; Crews, 1996, 1998; Macmillan, 1991; Webster, 1995).

At one extreme, a critic noted "there is literally nothing to be said, scientifically or therapeutically, to the advantage of the entire Freudian system or any of its component dogmas" (Crews, 1996, p. 63). Others pointed out that empirical data do not support this view (Westen, 1998a; see also Azar, 1997; Damasio, 1999; Fisher & Greenberg, 1996; Guterl, 2002; Muris, 2006; Weinberger & Westen, 2001; Westen, 1998b). Regardless of which side is correct, we have got to marvel at a theorist who manages to stir up such controversy—not to mention make the cover of a major magazine—some 53 years after his death, even as his major works are at least 100 years old!

Perhaps Drew Westen had it right when he compared Sigmund Freud to Elvis Presley (Westen, 1998a). Just as it would be impossible to imagine rock 'n' roll music without its founder, it would be difficult to imagine psychoanalysis today without its founder. Similarly, just as you wouldn't hear Presley's music on today's pop or top 40 radio stations—his music is relegated to oldies stations nowadays—you wouldn't see Freud's theories appear in the top research journals of the field today exactly as he posited them. Yet the impact of Freudian thought on current research in personality, clinical, and developmental psychology—and even areas outside psychology including sociology, political science, cultural studies, literary studies, and especially religion—is indelible, just as Presley's impact is on rock music today.

Rather than ask "Is Freud Dead?", maybe we should ask, "Why is Freudian theory still alive?" (Horgan, 1996, p. 106). One reason may be that it provides a "compelling framework within which to ponder our mysterious selves" (Horgan, 1996, p. 106; Malcolm, 1994; Vaillant, 1995b). As mentioned in Chapter 5, Freud's claim that the unique but hidden self is revealed in our unconscious behavior subverted the Victorian repressiveness of the day. Another reason that Freud's ideas captured the fancy of both American scholars and the popular culture may be because they suggested that personality can change, which resonated with the sense of opportunity and possibility in America at the turn of the 20th century and still does even today (Horgan, 1996). Finally, no other paradigm has emerged to conquer Freudian thought.

So, why study Freud? For better or for worse, Freud's ideas and terminology are an important part of the history of psychology as well as the greater culture (Dunn & Dougherty, 2005). Further, his theories greatly influenced personality psychology and clinical psychology (Dunn & Dougherty, 2005). No doubt, a review of a major icon of Western thought will be fun, challenging, and perhaps even surprising (Anderegg, 2004). But don't take my word for it: In this chapter, you will learn about Freud's theories and decide for yourself if they contribute to a science of personality.

Background

Instincts: The Connection Between Mind and Body. Freud was very much influenced by scientists and philosophers of his day, including Charles Darwin (Gay, 1988). He believed that he had an answer to the mind–body problem: instincts. Just as the body used energy to carry out its bodily functions of breathing, blood circulation, muscular and glandular activity, he reasoned that there had to be a similar source of energy for the mind. He called this energy *psychic energy* and believed that psychic energy fueled the functions of the mind including thinking, imagining, and remembering. According to the law of conservation in physics, Freud reasoned that energy within the mind–body system must also be conserved, that is, neither created nor destroyed. He hypothesized that body energy and psychic energy could be turned into each other through an instinct, a "mental representation of a physical or bodily need" (Freud, 1915/1957, p. 122).

THINK ABOUT IT

Which Freudian theory should we debate, Freud's original formulations or the current reformulations of others?

Sigmund Freud, the famous Viennese neurologist and founder of psychoanalysis, lived from 1856 to 1939.

THINK ABOUT IT

Can you see a relationship between these ways of handling impulses and certain personality traits?

Freud's original German word for what we call **instincts** was *trieb,* but the English word *impulse* really comes closer to capturing the concept Freud was trying to describe. We can think of an instinct or impulse like a tension, or an excitation originating from within the body. There are as many impulses as there are bodily needs. We first feel an impulse in the body that, like an itch, must somehow be satisfied. Impulses are always present in the body, therefore we always feel a certain amount of tension. There are many ways a particular impulse may be satisfied in the body or in the mind. The habitual ways we choose to deal with our impulses by gratifying them, inhibiting them, turning them into something more acceptable, or denying their very existence, form our personality.

According to Freud, there are two broad categories of instincts: life instincts, which he called **Eros**, and the death instincts, which he called **Thanatos** (Freud, 1914/1957). The life instincts are concerned with survival of the individual and the species, and include the needs for food, water, air, and sex. The psychic energy of the life instincts is called **libido**. The most important of the life instincts, according to Freud, is sex. Today, most contemporary psychodynamic psychologists would deemphasize sex and instead emphasize the needs for relationships and self-esteem as important life instincts (Westen, 1998a).

Freud noted that all living things decay and die, and reasoned that death and destruction must be inborn instincts as well (Freud, 1920/1955). His discussion of Thanatos was not as fully developed as his discussion of Eros, and he discussed only one death instinct: aggression. Today, the death instinct is one aspect of Freudian theory that is rejected by most psychologists as false, being evolutionarily unsound (Westen, 1998a).

Taken together—the death instinct, and aggression in particular, and the life instincts, with an emphasis on sex—you can see why many people believe that all of Freudian theory reduces to sex and aggression. Though tempting to conclude, this would be an oversimplification of Freudian theory.

Here is a puzzle: If these two instincts provide the energy and direction for personality, then we should be able to see these sexual and aggressive instincts bubble to the surface demanding that we immediately gratify them. Why do we not spend more of our time engaged in sexual or aggressive acts? Freud reasoned that we have been socialized to consciously hide our sexual and aggressive impulses and to express them only in socially acceptable ways (Freud, 1929/1989). What happens to these ungratified instincts? Going back to the law of conservation of energy, libido cannot be destroyed. Instead, instincts become expressed in *un*conscious ways.

Uncovering the Unconscious. How does Freud propose we get at this unconscious material? Unacceptable urges are likely to leak into our everyday behavior when our normally vigilant consciousness is relaxed. This may happen in any number of ways, including hypnosis, free association, dreams, Freudian slips, humor, and symbolic behavior.

THINK ABOUT IT

Can unconscious thoughts affect our everyday behavior? In what ways?

Free Association. Freud's famous talk therapy, *psychoanalysis,* started when a colleague of his realized that people revealed their private thoughts and desires while under hypnosis. Freud started using hypnosis with his patients, and soon discovered that they needn't be in an altered state, but just very relaxed (Freud, 1955). This is why, even today, psychoanalysis is often conducted with the patient lying down on a couch, with the therapist sitting slightly behind and out of sight of the patient. In this way the patient relaxes and says whatever comes to mind without consciously trying to control, monitor, or censor what he or she says. This **free association** of one thought to the next may lead the patient to reveal unconscious thoughts.

To illustrate how free association might work, let's consider an incident from Freud's own life. One day, when he left his office in a hurry to catch a train on his way to meet a new patient, he grabbed the wrong implement from his desk (Freud, 1901/1960). In trying to figure out why he took the tuning fork instead of the reflex hammer, he followed his associations to both tools. Of course, he might just have been in a hurry, but might there have been a deeper meaning to this mistake?

First, he recalled that the last person who touched the tuning fork was a slow-witted child who played with the tuning fork while Freud conducted his examination. Freud then wondered if he, himself, was an idiot for taking the wrong tool. He confirmed this passing thought in the very next moment by his realization that the Hebrew word for "hammer" was *Chamer* or "ass."

But why was Freud moved to censure himself with such harsh language? He immediately remembered that the train station he was running to was the location of an earlier and particularly embarrassing misdiagnosis he had made. Freud suddenly realized that he had better be careful at his upcoming consultation to not repeat this mistake. By not taking the hammer, he was avoiding being an ass! Thus the ultimate meaning of picking up the wrong implement was a self-reproach:

> *You idiot! You ass! Pull yourself together this time, and see that you don't diag-*
> *nose hysteria again where there's an incurable illness, as you did years ago.*
> (Freud, 1901/1960, pp. 165–166)

Tuning fork, child, hammer, *Chammer,* ass, idiot, train station, hysterical woman, and a misdiagnosis—as disconnected as these may seem to us—make sense in Freud's unconscious as revealed through his thoughts of free association.

Dream Analysis.   Free association was particularly useful for patients describing their dreams. Freud believed that "the interpretation of dreams is the royal road to a knowledge of the unconscious activities of the mind" (Freud, 1900/1953, p. 608). He used **dream analysis**, the detailed examination of the content and symbolism of dreams in order to decipher their hidden, unconscious meaning. When we are asleep, it is the perfect time for our unconscious thoughts, dreams, and wishes to make themselves known. Freud believed that dreaming acted as a safety value allowing a controlled release of unconscious tension built up by our instincts.

Because it would still be unsafe to directly express the dark urges of our instincts, our instinctual urges reveal themselves through the symbolism of dreams. Dreams allow wish fulfillment and gratification of our instincts in a safe, symbolic form. On waking, many people are able to describe in great detail what they saw in their dreams, called the **manifest content**. For Freud, both the dream symbolism and our reactions to the dream, expressed through free association under the guidance of a therapist, are important for understanding the **latent content** or true meaning of the dream.

There is some evidence that Freud was partially correct that suppressed thoughts are likely to reveal themselves in dreams. This was tested in an experiment in which undergraduate students were instructed to suppress thoughts of a specific person, right before falling asleep (Wegner, Wenzlaff, & Kozak, 2004). Would this suppression force the unexpressed thoughts to appear in participants' dreams?

First, participants either thought about a crush ("a person you have never been in a romantic relationship with—but whom you have thought about in a romantic way") or a noncrush ("a person you feel fondly about, but to whom you are not attracted").

This painting, *The Dream* by Henri Rousseau, was inspired by a poem about a young woman who dreams of hearing enchanted music in a lush green jungle under a moonlit sky that mesmerizes all who hear it, human and animal.

Then participants were randomly assigned to one of three presleep thought conditions. In the suppression condition, participants were instructed to not think about their target person. In the expression condition, participants specifically thought about and focused on their target person. In the final, mention condition participants were not to specifically think about or avoid thinking about their target person, but to note if thoughts of the target person nonetheless came to mind. Participants spent 5 minutes before going to bed writing a stream of consciousness of whatever thoughts came into their heads. On waking, participants noted if they dreamed during the night and what they dreamed about.

As you can see in Figure 8.1, participants in the suppression condition, who were instructed to not think about their target person, actually ended up dreaming more about that person than participants in either the mention condition or the expression condition. However, it made little difference if the person participants were trying not to think about was a crush or a noncrush: Both kinds of targets appeared later in their dreams as measured by self-rated dreaming and the number of times the target person appeared in their dream reports.

This suggests that whereas Freud had the process correct—that suppressed thoughts will appear later in our dreams—he was incorrect that this had anything to do with our hidden desires or wishes. Instead, researchers believe that this is an example of cognitive ironic processes of mental control, rather than unconscious motivation from our instincts (Wegner, 1994).

Parapraxes: Mistakes in Speaking and Acting.   Another way that our unconscious urges can reveal themselves is through mistakes in thought or deed. For Freud, nothing is ever done by accident. He believed that slips-of-the-tongue, bungled actions (such as the incident described

Figure 8.1 Dreaming about the target and nontarget persons as a function of presleep thought instruction: mean self-ratings (on a scale from 1 to 5) of whether the person appeared in the previous night's dreams (a) and mean number of coded mentions of the target person in dream reports (b). Error bars show standard error. *Source:* From Wegner et al. (2004, Figure 1, p. 234). Wegner, D. M., Wenzlaff, R. M., & Kozak, M. (2004), "Dream rebound: The return of suppressed thoughts in dreams," *Psychological Science,* 15(4), 232–236. Copyright © 2004 by Sage Publications. Reprinted with permission of Sage Publications.

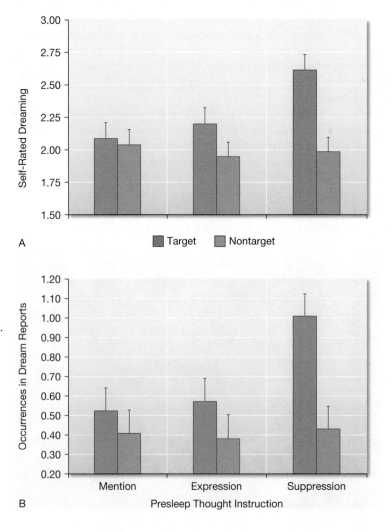

previously where Freud picked up the tuning fork instead of the hammer), mistakes and errors, forgotten names and words, lost and mislaid objects, misreadings, slips of the pen and misprints, and other chance actions all reveal our hidden desires. Freud called mistakes caused by unconscious desires **parapraxes** (plural; *parapraxis,* singular). Freud collected examples of parapraxes and wrote about the many ways we reveal our hidden, and often unacceptable, urges in his classic book *The Psychopathology of Everyday Life* (Freud, 1901/1960).

One type of parapraxis is a **Freudian slip**, or a mistake in speech. One of Freud's examples came from the president of the Lower House of the Austrian Parliament at the time, who opened a session by saying (in German, of course), "Gentlemen: I take notice that a full quorum of members is present and herewith declare the sitting closed!" (Freud, 1901/1960, p. 59). Could he have been expressing his deepest wish that the session were already over?

Despite many vivid examples, research suggests that not all slips are Freudian. People are likely to make verbal errors as a result of priming from whatever is on their mind, not necessarily from forbidden id impulses (Motley & Baars, 1979). In particular, such slips may be caused by cognitive indecision over word choice (Motley, 1985).

Another type of parapraxis is an accident or a mistaken action. Consider a woman I knew, who had a terrific case of prewedding jitters. In the week leading up to the momentous event, her fiancé slammed the car door on her fresh-from-the-boutique gown and bridal veil, causing a slight tear in the delicate material of the veil. When she and her sister tried to repair it, they made it worse, and had to cut a few inches off the veil to hide their mistake. Then, while cleaning her apartment in preparation for the wedding night, a small bookcase collapsed as she was trying to move it, breaking her food processor and nearly breaking her own foot! The final "accident" came while she was washing a drinking glass that broke into pieces in her hands cutting her thumb. Would it surprise you to find out the couple divorced a few short—and very sad—years later?

Humor.   Even jokes, especially spur of the moment quips and comebacks and spontaneous reactions, can be analyzed, much like dreams, to uncover the unacceptable desires they satisfy (Freud, 1905/1960). Jokes give us a socially acceptable means of expressing aggression and sexual desires through laughter. Many people who would not ordinarily express these impulses find sexual jokes, bathroom humor, and jokes playing on unflattering stereotypes about gender, height, hair color, religion, ethnicity, or profession quite funny. Somehow these normally taboo thoughts are socially acceptable in jokes. Though consciously we might be thinking "I was only kidding" the impulses expressed are quite real to our unconscious.

Symbolic Behavior.   Another way in which we may express our hidden instincts is through actions that seem innocent enough on the surface, but that actually represent deeper motives. These **symbolic behaviors** allow us to safely express our id impulses under the guise of a benign behavior. For example, no doubt you've heard of people with an oral fixation, a personality type we will discuss shortly, who gratify their urges through smoking, eating, or even biting sarcasm. These oral behaviors symbolize or stand in as more acceptable ways of getting sexual (smoking, eating), or aggressive (sarcasm) gratification.

Then and Now: The Word Association Test and the Implicit Attitudes Test

Over 100 years ago, an important historical event took place: Sigmund Freud and his disciple at the time, Carl Jung, came to America to speak at Clark University in Worcester, Massachusetts. Freud spoke about psychoanalysis, infantile sexuality, and dream interpretation. Jung also gave three lectures, two introducing his audience to the **word association method** (Benjamin, 2009).

The word association method was used by many psychologists of the day to identify the connections people made between words. Jung, however, took it to a new level by using the test to identify unconscious **complexes**, or important concerns for a person that he or she may not even be aware of. Complexes, what we call a **schema** today, are patterns of thoughts, memories, and perceptions organized about a theme (Jung, 1934/1960).

THINK ABOUT IT

Are all slips of the tongue or accidents expressions of our unconscious desires?

SEE FOR YOURSELF

Have you ever had an accident that may have been the result of an unconscious wish?

THINK ABOUT IT

Have you ever heard of an Oedipus complex? What does the word *complex* suggest in this phrase?

Carl Jung and Sigmund Freud at Clark University in September 1909. The organizer of the conference, G. Stanley Hall is in the center of the front row with Freud on his left, both holding hats; Jung is standing next to Freud in the front row, third from right.

In the word association test, Jung would slowly read 100 words out loud to subjects who were instructed to "Answer as quickly as possible the first word that comes to mind" after hearing each word. Jung would record not just the response, but also the reaction time and physiological responses. He maintained that the test assessed not just verbal fluency, but also whether there were some emotional connotations to the words that interfered with responding and caused the person to respond slower or with an unusual response (Jung, 1910).

For example, sometimes there might be too many ways of answering so that a subject might give more than one word. Sometimes a subject might be moved to give an explanation for his or her idiosyncratic answers. Other times, a subject might repeat the stimulus word, repeat the same answer to multiple stimulus words, stammer, exhibit a slip of the tongue, or just give up responding at all (Jung, 1910). All of these behaviors indicated that the stimulus word was provoking an emotional reaction in the person.

Jung would also calculate average reaction times and see which words elicited a faster or a slower response. These, too, could indicate a complex or a hidden problem. Consider the chart in Figure 8.2. These are the results of a 30-year-old woman, married for 3 years, who claimed to be happily married. From the pattern of slower reaction times and unusual responses, Jung deduced that she was not as happy in the marriage as she first claimed: She disliked that her husband was Protestant whereas she was Catholic; she often thought about being untrue to her husband and leaving the marriage; and she was afraid, either of her husband or of the future. When Jung revealed all this to her, she denied it at first, but then admitted her true feelings and told him even more about her unhappy life.

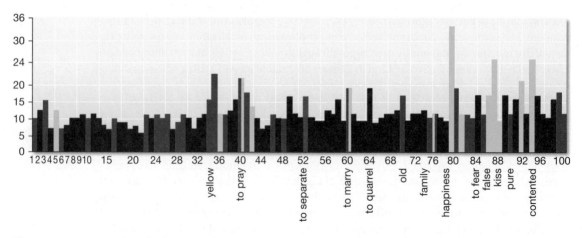

Figure 8.2 Reaction times for the word association test of a young woman who reported being happily married. Height of the bars indicates reaction time (unit = 0.2 second). Selected stimulus words appear under the bars. Blue bars = no answer; green bars = repetition of stimulus word; yellow bars = mistakes or multiple word responses; black bars = average responses. Based on these results, do you think she is as happy as she claims? *Source:* Jung (1910, color plate following p. 238).

Even today, researchers and clinicians use variations of the word association test to assess verbal fluency and semantic memory (Ross et al., 2007), personality (Stacy, Leigh, & Weingardt, 1997), brain injury (Silverberg, Hanks, Buchanan, Fichtenberg, & Mills, 2008), and more.

The idea that our reaction times can reveal our hidden thoughts and feelings is also behind a more modern assessment technique: the **Implicit Association Test**, or **IAT** (Greenwald, McGhee, & Schwartz, 1998). When it comes to self-reports, people may be reluctant to give their true responses, especially on sensitive subjects. They might also try to fake their responses, or present themselves in a positive light. Might our unconscious responses, like our reaction times, reveal our true attitudes?

The IAT uses reaction times to measure the strength of associations between concepts (Greenwald, Nosek, & Banaji, 2003; Greenwald, Poehlman, Uhlmann, & Banaji, 2009; Nosek, Greenwald, & Banaji, 2005). The more related two concepts are, the easier it will be to sort them on a computer task if they require the same response than if they require different responses. Because people will react faster to related concepts than to unrelated concepts, we can present participants with various pairings of concepts and infer their attitude based on when they respond the fastest. For example, people respond faster when liked items and positive words require the same response (e.g., hit the space bar) than when unliked items and positive words require the same response. We can pair photos, say, with positive or negative words and judge if people feel positive or negative to the objects or people in the photos based on their relative reaction times.

To illustrate how the IAT works, let's take a look at an experiment using German undergraduate students to compare self-reported anxiety with IAT-measured anxiety (Egloff & Schmukle, 2002). For the IAT measure of anxiety, participants had to categorize words reflecting the self (*I, self, my, me, own*) and other (*they, them, your, you, others*) along with anxiety-related words (*nervous, afraid, fearful, anxious, uncertain*) and calmness related words (*relaxed, balanced, at ease, calm, restful*).

Participants who scored higher on a questionnaire measure of anxiety found it easier to classify the self words with the anxiety words than with the calmness words. This suggests more of an association in their minds between self and anxiety than between self and calmness. Further, participants' scores on the IAT predicted poor performance after failure and an increase in nervous behaviors such as mouth movements, speech errors, and hand movements under stress better than their self-reported anxiety did.

Although it is more difficult to lie or fake your way through an IAT (Greenwald et al., 2009), does this mean that the IAT is a better measure of our true attitudes and beliefs? Not necessarily. IAT and self-report measures are actually different evaluations of the same object and each predict slightly different outcomes (Greenwald et al., 2009). The key difference between self-report and IAT measures of attitudes appears to be depth of processing or how conscious we are of our beliefs. Perhaps our true attitudes and beliefs, like our true motivations, lurk deep in our unconscious just as Freud and Jung hypothesized.

Freud's View of Personality: The Structural and Topographic Models

Freud described personality using a structural model, which outlined the parts of personality, and a topographic model, which described the regions in our mind where the parts of personality resided. He even drew a graphic to illustrate the relationship between both models (see Figure 8.3).

The Structural Model of Personality: Id, Ego, and Superego.   The **structural model of personality**, which is indeed what we think of when we think of the self today, is made up of three parts: the id, the ego, and the superego (Freud, 1923/1961). In German, Freud referred to the *id* as *das es* or "the it" to emphasize that the id contains pure instinctual energy and is a bundle of reflexes and urges. The id operates through **primary process thinking** meaning that it makes decisions without logical rules and conscious thought (Freud, 1923/1961). The

THINK ABOUT IT

Why might the IAT reveal hidden or unconscious thoughts better than a questionnaire?

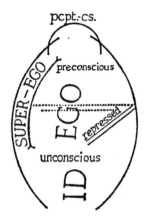

Figure 8.3 This is how Freud imagined the relationship between the topographical model of the mind and the structural model of personality. Note that *pcpt-cs* stood for the *perceptual consciousness*, Freud's early term for the conscious. He placed it to illustrate how thoughts bubble up from the preconscious. Note how the unconscious, preconscious, and conscious blend into one another, illustrating Freud's view of the continuity of mental life. *Source:* From Freud (1933/1990, p. 98). Freud, S. (1933/1990). The anatomy of the mental personality (Lecture 31). In New introductory lectures on psychoanalysis. New York, NY: Norton. (Original work published 1933).

id is completely out of our control, being housed completely in the unconscious. This is why we are apt to see the workings of the id in unconscious behaviors like dreams and parapraxes. The id operates according to the **pleasure principle** (Freud, 1923/1961), wanting what it wants when it wants it, and demanding immediate gratification as in the phrase "It [id] just came over me" (Westen et al., 2008).

There are two ways of satisfying an id instinct: reflex action and wish fulfillment. In keeping with Freud's attempt at reconciling the mind–body problem, one way involves the body and the other involves the mind. A **reflex action** is when the id seeks gratification through immediate physical action. If it is not possible or not practical to carry out a reflex action, then the id may try **wish fulfillment**. Here the id seeks gratification by imagining what it wants (Freud, 1911/1958). For the id, fantasy can be just as satisfying as reality, at least temporarily. In this way, for example, dreams can serve as wish fulfillment for the impulses of the id (Freud, 1923/1961).

What part of personality decides whether the id will be satisfied or not? That's up to the *ego* or *das ich* in German. The "I" or ego must try to match the wishes of the id with objects and events in the real world through a process called **identification** (Freud, 1923/1961). To identify with an object means that the object fulfills a wish of the id. The ego, therefore, must operate according to the **reality principle** where it tries to satisfy the id within the constraints of social and physical reality (Freud, 1923/1961). That is, the ego must figure out how to get the most amount of pleasure for the id with the least amount of negative consequences from both reality and from the superego. The ego operates using **secondary process thinking**, what we might think of as logical thinking, weighing the costs and rewards of possible courses of action (Freud, 1923/1961).

What is this *superego* that can reward or punish the ego for making a wrong decision in satisfying id impulses? *Das über ich,* the "over I" or the "above me," contains moral standards for thinking and acting, standing like a harsh judge looking down over everything we do ready to inflict punishment on the ego for allowing id impulses to escape. The superego strives for perfection, and is just as unrealistic as the id. The superego contains society's standards of behavior that we have learned from our parents while growing up.

The superego has two parts: the conscience and the ego ideal. The **conscience** (not to be confused with the *conscious* mind) contains knowledge of what we should not do. This is where we have internalized, or accepted as our own, actions from our past for which we have been punished. The conscience punishes us when we do something wrong with feelings of guilt, shame and embarrassment (Freud, 1923/1961).

The **ego ideal** contains knowledge of what we should do. This is where we have internalized experiences for which we have been rewarded. The ego ideal rewards us with feelings of pride when we have done the right thing (Freud, 1923/1961).

Do you remember how we said earlier that fantasizing about expressing id impulses—wish fulfillment—was a good way of satisfying the id within the constraints of reality? Well, you can see how this may also satisfy the superego, since the person is not actually doing anything wrong. A 5-year-old patient of Freud's summed it up succinctly when describing his desire to masturbate: "wanting's not doing, and doing's not wanting" (Freud, 1909a/1955, p. 31; see the Research Methods Illustrated feature for more about Little Hans). However, a person with a very strong superego, indicating very high moral standards, would not buy this argument and instead would believe that thinking is just as bad as doing ("I lusted in my heart").

In sum, the human personality is made up of id impulses that demand instant gratification. However, the superego, as the arbiter of moral standards, won't let the id directly express itself. Instead, the ego must think of a way to gratify the id within the bounds of decency demanded by the superego, all the while taking into account the constraints of reality. As Freud tells it:

> *The ego's relation to the id might be compared with that of a rider to his horse. The horse supplies the locomotive energy, while the rider has the privilege of deciding on the goal and of guiding the powerful animal's movement. But only too often there arises between the ego and the id the not precisely ideal situation of the rider being obliged to guide the horse along the path by which it itself wants to go. (Freud, 1933/1990, p. 96)*

SEE FOR YOURSELF

Suppose you are in a class right before lunch and become very hungry. What do you do to deal with these feelings?

THINK ABOUT IT

Where do the conscience and ego ideal get their moral standards from?

THINK ABOUT IT

Though Freud talks of the id, ego, and superego as structures, are they truly parts of our brain or more like hypothetical concepts or metaphors?

How well does the structural model hold up to empirical support? Alas, critics, even psychoanalytic psychologists, suggest that we abandon Freud's structural model of personality (Brenner, 2003; Westen et al., 2008). There is no evidence that our personalities or our minds are divided into parts that are more or less logical than other parts (Brenner, 2003). However, the idea of conflict inherent in this model, and the idea that behavior represents a compromise among forces of desire, conscience, reality, and social acceptability, remain important and do influence our thoughts, behaviors, and personality (Westen et al., 2008).

The Topographic Model of Personality: Conscious, Preconscious, Unconscious. The **topographic model of personality** consists of the conscious mind, the preconscious mind, and unconscious mind. The *conscious* mind contains the thoughts and sensations that we are currently aware of. The *preconscious* mind contains thoughts that are just outside of our awareness, thoughts that are easily accessible and that we could readily summon into our consciousness (Freud, 1923/1961).

The *unconscious* mind contains urges, thoughts, wishes, desires, and memories that we are unable to know about "in itself and without more ado" (Freud, 1923/1961, p. 15). That is, we are unable to retrieve thoughts from the unconscious by our own efforts except under the special circumstances discussed earlier (e.g., through dreams, free association, symbolic behavior, parapraxes, etc.) (Freud, 1923/1961).

Although we may be able to move from topic to topic in our consciousness, pull out observations at will from our preconscious, or push thoughts into our unconscious, we cannot consciously retrieve thoughts directly from our unconscious. The unconscious can produce particular thoughts, feelings, behaviors, and defenses in us related to our impulses and for this reason is often called the **motivated unconscious** (Westen et al., 2008).

Keep in mind that the terminology of conscious, preconscious, and unconscious suggests three separate parts of the mind, when really Freud believed in the continuity of mental life. That is, thoughts or memories became conscious—or unconscious for that matter—not as if they were passing through a curtain to a separate room, but more like how a camera lens makes a picture come in and out of focus.

How does Freud's model of mind and memory compare to what we know about the mind today? Freud was eerily close to what modern cognitive psychology is just now finding out about how the mind works, albeit with some notable exceptions.

First, Freud was correct in realizing that there is really more of a continuum between conscious and unconscious rather than a clear cut line between the two states (Erdelyi, 2006b). You can see this in Freud's original drawing as a dotted line between the conscious and the unconscious in Figure 8.3. Also, we can have multiple levels of awareness even for thoughts in our unconscious (Glaser & Kihlstrom, 2005; Hilgard, 1977). Perhaps we should not talk about the unconscious as a location; instead we should talk about unconscious *processes* (Westen, 1998b). The important question becomes—especially for therapy (Westen, 1998b)—to what extent are people aware of their defenses and motives, not what part of the mind is involved.

Second, Freud was also correct in suggesting that the unconscious influences our conscious experiences, including our thoughts and actions (Westen, 1998a, 1998b). However, Freud believed the unconscious operated in service of our drives; we know today that this view is too simplistic.

Third, current research suggests that the **cognitive unconscious** is motivated and goal-driven, as Freud hypothesized, but not quite in the way that he thought. The unconscious is not preoccupied with the satisfaction of id impulses, nor is it concerned with infiltrating our consciousness with its darker motives, or in betraying our true motives. Instead, the unconscious mind, much like the conscious mind, can help regulate our thoughts, emotions, motivations, goals, and even intentions, without all the "conflict and drama" of the psychoanalytic unconsciousness (Uleman, 2005, p. 6). The unconscious is more like a helpful and efficient Jeeves-like butler and less like a conniving and controlling dark force.

Anxiety and the Defense Mechanisms

Recall that in Freud's model of personality the ego must satisfy the id impulses in a socially acceptable way so as not to upset the superego, but must also take into account reality.

THINK ABOUT IT

How does Freud's notion of the unconscious compare to automatic thinking from cognitive psychology?

Anna and Sigmund Freud on holiday in the Dolomites, Italy, 1913.

Sometimes this balancing of id, superego, and reality is too much for the ego and causes anxiety. This anxiety may come out in—and here's that mind–body dualism again—a physical symptom (what Freud called a **conversion reaction**) or a psychological symptom (e.g., anxiety, a neurosis, a phobia). However, the ego can take measures to defend itself from the anxiety. One way the ego can prevent or lessen anxiety and achieve a balance among desire (id), morality (superego), and reality is to use a **defense mechanism**. Defense mechanisms are the ego's way of handling a threatening thought or an unacceptable impulse to protect itself and minimize anxiety and distress.

Today, psychoanalysts have abandoned the idea that sexual and aggressive impulses are the most threatening for people (Westen, 1998a). Instead, we are more concerned with threats to our self-esteem rather than to our egos (Baumeister, Dale, & Sommer, 1998). Perhaps in Freud's day, acknowledging that one had sexual and aggressive impulses was particularly threatening to a person's self-esteem (Baumeister et al., 1998).

In truth, most of the so-called Freudian defense mechanisms were interpreted and described in detail by Anna Freud, Sigmund Freud's daughter and psychoanalyst in her own right. Anna identified 10 defense mechanisms in her father's work (A. Freud, 1937/1966). Others have identified additional defenses (e.g., Vaillant, 1995b) including some 50 or more since that time (Clark, 1998)!

We will focus on the basic defense mechanisms, first identified by Freud, that are not indicative of serious pathology, and which have inspired later work in personality (Baumeister et al., 1998). Do not be surprised if you recognize seeing these in yourself or in people around you! Defense mechanisms can be useful, short-term ways of handling stress and anxiety.

Reaction Formation. In a **reaction formation**, instead of expressing a threatening id impulse, people express the *opposite* id impulse. A good clue to a reaction formation is that the reaction is out of proportion to the actual event, either more extreme or more intense than usual. For example, have you ever noticed that when a dating couple suddenly breaks up they immediately hate each other? How can love so quickly turn to hate? Sometimes, the circumstances may warrant the extreme reaction, but I wonder if anxiety over the thought of a love lost doesn't make it easier for some people to express the opposite emotion—hate—as a way of coping.

An example of a reaction formation comes from an elderly friend of mine who had just gotten cable television. Instead of being entertained by the range of choices now available to her, she expressed her shock and outrage at an R-rated movie shown on one of the movie channels. She took a good 10 minutes explaining to me, in minute and embarrassing detail, the various love scenes and how angry watching each scene made her. When I asked her why she didn't just change the channel, she exclaimed, "Well, I had to see how it all ended!" Obviously, it was too threatening for a usually prim and proper little old lady to admit that she was enjoying, or being aroused by, the love scenes so she expressed the opposite emotion, disgust.

Reaction formation may be one of the most often used defenses, especially when we fear others may be judging us badly. One review of the research found that we respond with extreme and opposite feelings when we are in danger of showing undesirable sexual feelings, prejudiced

"The lady doth protest too much, methinks."
Hamlet, Act 3, scene ii, 222–230

attitudes, or incompetence, for example (Baumeister et al., 1998). It's as if we are trying to prove these accusations wrong, by publicly demonstrating the opposite feeling. The evidence for reaction formation is strong; however, it remains to be determined just how conscious or unconscious some of our reactions may be.

Isolation.   **Isolation** occurs when we mentally isolate a threatening thought by keeping it separate from other thoughts and feelings. One way of doing this, as Freud observed in his patients, is to create a pause or gap between one train of thought and another.

One form of isolation is **intellectualization**, when we isolate the emotion so that we can experience thoughts or memories without the disturbing feelings. For example, people may use intellectualization to logically understand a traumatic event. Also, intellectualization may allow people to relate horrible stories without being overwhelmed by their emotions.

Isolation is easily understood within a cognitive model. Our thoughts are associated in our minds and memories so that a negative thought can trigger other negative thoughts. By mentally isolating negative thoughts—perhaps by consciously thinking of a neutral or positive thought—we can indeed make ourselves feel better. In fact, many articles that support isolation are from cognitive psychology and don't even cite Freud (Baumeister et al., 1998)!

Baumeister et al. (1998) suggested ways that people may use isolation to protect themselves, such as keeping failure feedback separate from performance standards, trivializing a misdeed, and isolating past experiences by thinking of the present self like a different person. This may be why declaring oneself a "born-again Christian" or a "born-again virgin" are such meaningful designations for some.

Denial.   **Denial** is when we refuse to believe or even acknowledge a threatening or traumatic event, or the emotions associated with the event. For example, we may exclaim "Oh, no!" immediately on hearing bad news, an effective use of denial that buys us a moment to process the shock. Or, we might daydream or have fantasies about how things might have been. Denial may be a helpful coping strategy in the short run, but less effective than other strategies in the long run (Suls & Fletcher, 1985).

For example, Freud believed that when little boys see that girls' genitals are different from theirs, they "disavow the fact and believe that they do see a penis, all the same" (Freud, 1923b/1961, pp. 143–144). Freud theorized that boys use this denial to allay their supposed castration anxiety, a point we will come back to later.

There is plenty of evidence that people deny feedback that is threatening to their self-esteem. For example, people may think a test is unfair (Pyszczynski, Greenberg, & Holt, 1985)

Oh, no! Students who lived in potentially unsafe residence halls were more likely to deny that they could be at risk in case of an earthquake (Lehman & Taylor, 1987).

or that research evidence is flawed (Liberman & Chaiken, 1992) if it helps them think well of themselves despite a poor performance or unhealthy behaviors. People may even convince themselves, with unrealistic optimism, that their futures are likely to be rosier than that of their peers (Weinstein, 1980). People may also experience denial in the aftermath of a trauma as a way of coming to grips with the event slowly (Janoff-Bullman, 1992). Denial has also been seen in people who deny the seriousness of a breast cancer diagnosis (Carver et al., 1993), the likelihood of being in harm's way due to an earthquake (Lehman & Taylor, 1987), and even their chances of experiencing an unwanted pregnancy (Burger & Burns, 1988).

Undoing.   In **undoing**, a person who has either thought about performing or who has already performed an unacceptable behavior attempts to nullify that action with a later action. Of course, we rationally know that the behavior or thought has occurred, but through: " . . . a procedure that may be called magical, of "undoing" [Ungeschehenmachen or un-make-happen] what has been done" we can take it back or cancel it out (Freud, 1915/1957, p. 164). Freud described it as: "negative magic . . . by means of . . . symbolism to "blow away" not merely the consequences of some event (or the experiences or impression) but the event itself" (Freud, 1925/1959, p. 119).

Freud believed undoing occurred as a part of obsessional disorders, popular customs, and also religious ceremonies (Freud, 1925/1959). For example, perhaps you've heard of the superstition whereby people must undo the bad luck of having spilled the salt by throwing a pinch of it over their left shoulder.

More serious examples of undoing might be a woman with an eating disorder who tries to undo eating by purging. Or an abusive man who might bring his wife flowers to atone for having harmed her the night before. Both of these involve some pathology where a person is truly convinced that she or he can undo the undesirable behavior. This extreme form of undoing, whereby people attempt to alter the past, has not been documented in healthy individuals (Baumeister et al., 1998).

However, a more common and less serious type of undoing that many people unconsciously do is to ruminate over past events, imagining how they might have gone differently and mentally undoing the damage (Baumeister et al., 1998; Roese, Sanna, & Galinsky, 2005). This *counterfactual thinking* was studied in a sample of athletes at the 1992 summer Olympic games (Medvec, Madey, & Gilovich, 1995). Bronze medal winners were happier than silver medalists both at the time of their performance and on the medal stand.

Why would the people who performed worse be happier? In a subsequent study, researchers were able to interview athletes competing in New York State's 1994 Empire State Games directly after their performance. The researchers discovered that the silver medalists were more occupied than the bronze medalists with thoughts of "I almost did better" than with thoughts

THINK ABOUT IT

Can you think of other examples of undoing in superstition or children's games?

Due to undoing, bronze medalists may be happier than silver medalists.

of "at least I did this well." Silver medalists were preoccupied with thoughts of how they could have undone their failed performances. Unfortunately, this counterfactual rumination only made them feel worse.

In sum, the evidence for undoing is mixed, depending on how strict an interpretation one takes of Freud's original idea. In either case, magically or mentally undoing the past does not seem to protect a person, or their self-esteem, from negative events. It might help a person develop alternative strategies to help a future performance, but it doesn't change the reality of a negative event. For this reason Baumeister et al. (1998) suggested that undoing is best viewed as a coping mechanism to deal with negative events, rather than a defense mechanism.

Projection.   In **projection**, we attribute our own disturbing or unacceptable impulses to another person. For example, say we fight with a friend. Afterward in recalling the incident we might remark "She was very hostile" instead of admitting our own feelings of aggression. Oftentimes, what we find annoying in other people is actually more revealing of our own insecurities: It is safer to project them onto others than to admit the failings in ourselves.

In a compelling demonstration of projection, participants attributed their undesirable traits to another person using an elaborate cover story and three-part procedure (Newman, Duff, & Baumeister, 1997). First, the researchers gave participants false feedback about their personalities. They were told that they possessed four positive traits and two undesirable traits (e.g., inflexible, indecisive, dishonest, disturbed) on a fake personality test.

Then, for the next 5 minutes participants were instructed to think about the results of the personality test and to free associate, verbalizing their thoughts out loud as they occurred. However, participants were instructed to not think about one of their negative trait ratings, which was determined ostensibly at random.

Finally, participants watched a video, without sound, of a college student talking about herself. From watching her nonverbal behavior they had to rate her personality on the same six trait dimensions that they had received feedback on in the first part of the experiment.

Would their own false feedback affect their ratings of the target student? It would if they were using the defense mechanism of projection to deal with the blow to their self-esteem from the unflattering feedback on the personality test. Participants rated the target more negatively but on only one of their negative trait dimensions: the one they had been asked *not* to think about! In other words, they were more likely to project an unflattering trait that they were trying not to think about than either a positive or negative trait that they were able to think about.

Based on the results of this and other related experiments, the researchers concluded that not thinking about an undesirable trait actually increases the tendency to see that trait in other people. So Freud was right about projection!

However, the evidence also suggests that projection occurs as a result of trying to suppress thinking about one's own faults; it is another example of ironic processing as in the dream study discussed earlier. That is, thought *suppression*—not projection—is the defense mechanism; projection is a result of thought suppression and not a way to avoid thinking about one's own faults. Paradoxically, thought suppression makes people more aware of the very traits they are trying not to think about, both negative and positive (Newman, Duff, Hedberg, & Blitstein, 1996). This increased accessibility makes it more likely that people will use these very traits to interpret the ambiguous behavior of others.

The bottom line is that Freud identified an important phenomenon: defensive projection. But it took current research in social and cognitive psychology to fully explain the process. Our view of ourselves influences our view of others, for both positive and negative traits. But we commit this projection as a result of thought suppression, not as a way of rejecting these traits in ourselves.

Displacement.   In **displacement** the true id impulse is expressed but the target of that impulse is changed into a more acceptable one. Perhaps you've seen a child who is angry at her mother. It would be too threatening to express that anger directly at her mother, so instead she might express that anger by slamming the door to her room.

> **THINK ABOUT IT**
>
> How are the defense mechanism of projection and the ideas behind projective tests similar?

Freud's famous case of Little Hans concerned a 5-year-old boy who was afraid of his father, but displaced this fear onto horses. Why horses? The horse had "black round their mouths" and blinders that resembled his father's mustache and glasses (Freud, 1909a/1955, p. 42). For more about Hans and why he feared his father, see the Research Methods Illustrated feature in this chapter.

Despite the popular appeal of this defense, there is very little evidence for displacement (Baumeister et al., 1998). Often alternative explanations account for the results better than the notion of displacement. For example, we know that frustration, direct retaliation, or being in bad mood all increase aggression, but none of these involve displacement (Baumeister et al., 1998). In fact, the one study that was specifically designed to test for displacement found no significant effects (Bushman & Baumeister, 1998). Participants in this study were most aggressive toward the person who angered them and did not take out their aggression on an innocent person.

The idea of displacement hinges on Freud's notion of catharsis (from the Greek word for *cleanse* or *purge*). The idea was that tension from unsatisfied id impulses builds up, like steam in a closed system, and must somehow be released or else cause damage to the system in the form of psychological symptoms. This release of the id energy is called **catharsis** (Breur & Freud, 1893/1955). Acting aggressively (body) or viewing aggression (mind) should satisfy the impulse and lead to less aggression. But does it?

To test this, participants in an experiment wrote an essay and then were later insulted by a confederate who called their essay the worst they had ever seen (Bushman, Baumeister, & Stack, 1999). Half the participants immediately got a chance to work out their aggression by hitting a punching bag for 2 minutes, whereas the other half didn't. Then all participants played an aggressive video game against the very same confederate who had insulted them. Would participants who worked out their aggressiveness against the punching bag be less aggressive toward their tormentor?

According to the catharsis hypothesis, they ought to, having already released and satisfied the aggressive impulses triggered by the insulting confederate. However, that's not what the researchers found! Participants who played with the punching bag were actually *more* aggressive—almost three times as much—toward their insulter than participants who were told to sit there. Not only is the concept of catharsis completely without merit, but acting aggressively or even viewing aggression actually increases later aggressive behavior (Bushman et al., 1999).

THINK ABOUT IT

What other popular notions about catharsis are also invalid? For example, would watching a violent sport on TV increase or decrease later aggressiveness?

Despite its intuitive appeal, there is no empirical support for the notion that people sublimate their sexual drives into creative ones.

Sublimation. Another way of dealing with an unacceptable id impulse is to change the impulse into something more acceptable, a process called **sublimation**. For example, aggressive urges might be morphed into the less psychologically threatening energy for sports, dangerous hobbies, or healthy competition. Similarly, Freud believed that sexual urges could be safely expressed through hard work, the fine arts, and other creative activities. Freud noted that society, in socializing us, demands that we sublimate our sexual and aggressive urges to be productive members.

Again, despite the intuitive appeal of sublimation, Baumeister et al. (1998) adamantly claimed that there is no support whatsoever for sublimation. They were unable to find even a single article in a top research journal that showed convincing evidence for sublimation. So instead they tried, unsuccessfully, to find at least correlational evidence of possible sublimation effects.

For example, Baumeister et al. (1998) looked at historical periods of great creativity and found no corresponding increase in sexual abstinence; in fact, they found quite the opposite. Periods of intellectual creativity—think of the Italian Renaissance, Elizabethan England, or ancient Greece, for example—were generally periods of sexual freedom as well. Similarly, the lives of the most famous writers, musicians, and painters of the 20th century are marked by "sexual excess and misadventure" rather than sublimation of sexual impulses (Baumeister et al., 1998, p. 1106).

Until research evidence suggests otherwise, the defense mechanism of sublimation should be abandoned.

Repression.   According to Freud, "the essence of repression lies simply in the function of rejecting and keeping something out of consciousness" (Freud, 1915b/1957, p. 147). Keeping an undesirable thought out of consciousness protects a person from anxiety.

Freud originally believed that repression could be conscious or unconscious, going along with his belief in the continuity of mental life (Erdelyi, 2006b). His daughter Anna made the distinction between **suppression** and **repression** in her interpretation of his defense mechanisms (A. Freud, 1937/1966). In suppression the ego consciously keeps unacceptable thoughts or urges outside of our awareness whereas in repression the process is unconscious. For example, if we are faced with an event or a thought that makes us anxious we can consciously put it out of mind or suppress thinking about it. However, if this forgetting happens unconsciously, without our awareness, or out of our control, it would be an example of repression.

Freud believed that some traumatic events could be so anxiety-provoking that the ego would bury the event deep in the unconscious. You can see this in Freud's original graphic in Figure 8.3. He depicts repression as a one-way slide channeling thoughts directly from the conscious into the very heart of the unconscious.

Defense mechanisms can work on both an explicit level and an implicit level (Vaillant, 1998) and indeed, evidence suggests that one way people cope with trauma is to avoid thinking about it, either consciously or unconsciously (Brewin, 2003; McNally, 2003a, 2003b). But does this mean that people have completely forgotten about the traumatic event?

Probably not. First, we know from cognitive psychology that putting a thought out of our mind consciously, through suppression, or unconsciously, through repression, only makes the thought occur *more* frequently (Najmi & Wegner, 2006; Wegner, 1989, 1994; Wegner & Erber, 1992; Wegner, Schneider, Carter, & White, 1987).

Second, generally people do not forget the traumatic event, rather, they cope with the trauma by managing their emotional responses to the event (Boden, 2006; Foa, Riggs, Massie, & Yarczower, 1995).

Third, there is no evidence that memories can be repressed and kept out of consciousness for significant periods of time (Boden, 2006; Crews, 2006; Hayne, Garry, & Loftus, 2006; Holmes, 1995; McNally, 2003a, 2003b; Pope, Oliva, & Hudson, 1999). However, many victims would

Don't think about this bear: Paradoxically, trying to not think of something, as in repression, makes the thought occur more frequently.

THINK ABOUT IT

Why would there be no need for the other defense mechanisms if repression were completely effective?

SEE FOR YOURSELF

Have you ever used a rationalization to hide your true motivation for an unacceptable behavior?

rather not remember the event so they may consciously choose not to share their memories with friends, family, therapists, or researchers. What may seem on the surface to be repression may really be due to fear, guilt, or embarrassment (Boden, 2006; Freyd, 2006).

Though the controversy is not entirely over, in light of the evidence available today, repression probably ought to be removed from a list of effective defense mechanisms (Rofé, 2008). Instead, more research on related topics in cognitive psychology such as cognitive avoidance, retrieval inhibition, or memory bias is needed (Erdelyi, 2000).

Rationalization. **Rationalization** is when people reinterpret their behavior to hide their true motivations for their actions. Essentially, the behavior is acknowledged, but it is reinterpreted to seem more acceptable. In this way, the id can be gratified without the superego disapproving.

Freud noted that a person suffering from an obsessive neurosis might justify his compulsive behavior by explaining why he did what he did in a rational way. He described a patient of his, who having tripped on a branch in a park, threw the branch into some nearby bushes. On the way home, the man was suddenly struck with the thought that the branch might be more dangerous to passers-by in this new place than in the original place along the path. Freud believed that the man's anxiety caused him to go back and replace the branch on the path, but instead of acknowledging this compulsion, the man rationalized it by convincing himself the branch was safer in its original place, even though, objectively, it wasn't (Freud, 1909b/1955).

The idea that we rationalize our decisions, beliefs, feelings, and attitudes forms the basis of cognitive dissonance theory from social psychology (Gray, 2001; Kay, Jimenez, & Jost, 2002). According to this theory, when we are faced with an inconsistency between our attitude and our behavior or between two beliefs, it causes us to feel dissonance; that is, to feel like hypocrites (Festinger, 1957). To feel better—and to convince ourselves that we are indeed logical people—we find ways of rationalizing or justifying our behavior and beliefs. What cognitive dissonance calls justification is a specific example of the Freudian defense mechanism of rationalization.

Cognitive dissonance theory was later revised to suggest that we feel the need to rationalize our beliefs and behaviors only when our actions make us feel bad about ourselves (Aronson, 1968). In this way cognitive dissonance acts as a defense mechanism to preserve our self-esteem. The empirical support for cognitive dissonance theory is overwhelming. For example, by motivating people to explain themselves using the defense mechanism of rationalization, cognitive dissonance theory has been used to help people overcome eating disorders (Wade, George, & Atkinson, 2009), engage in safer sex (Stone, Aronson, Crain, Winslow, & Fried, 1994), and conserve water (Dickerson, Thibodeau, Aronson, & Miller, 1992), to name just a few applications of the theory.

You can see how the defenses all involve some kind of transformation of either the impulse, the target, or the person feeling the impulse (Freud used the colorful word *vicissitudes* to describe the changing nature of the instincts). Keeping these three processes separate will help you distinguish among the various defense mechanisms.

As you can see, there is quite a lot of evidence for the defense mechanisms. Psychologists continue to explore these and other defense mechanisms in their practice and in their research in personality, social psychology, developmental psychology, and cognition (Cramer, 2000, 2006).

Psychosexual Stages

"[Psychosexual hypotheses] are better understood metaphorically or discarded altogether. Knowing which ones to discard, however, is not always an easy task."
Westen et al. (2008, p. 65)

One of the foundations of Freudian psychoanalysis is that adult personality is formed as a result of childhood experiences. Freud set out to describe the process of development based on the recollections of his patients in a series of stages called the **Psychosexual stages** of development. However, much of what Freud hypothesized about development is controversial. To be able to evaluate Freud's theory, we need to understand just what his claims are. As you read about his theories below, see if they make sense to you from what you know about child development from other classes you've taken, or from your own experience with children.

Because the sexual instinct was of utmost importance to Freud, he interpreted the psychological phenomena he observed within a sexual framework. Each psycho*sexual* stage of development starts with a libidinal urge that is experienced in a specific, biologically determined, part of the body (Freud, 1955). The infant or child feels tension in an **erogenous zone** and must find a way of gratifying the id impulse in a socially acceptable way.

Once the id instinct is gratified, the tension subsides and the child is psychologically able to move into the next stage. However, if the child has received too much or too little gratification—and Freud did not differentiate between the two—then some libidinal energy gets left behind (Fenichel, 1945/1995). The child then has fewer psychological resources left to deal with the challenges of the next stage. The result is a **fixation**, where psychic energy is still devoted to resolving the earlier issue instead of moving fully into the next stage.

A person who is fixated at one of the stages will show certain adult personality characteristics and engage in behaviors directly related to the fixation. In addition, the person will show symbolic activities related to the fixation. In keeping with Freud's emphasis on the interconnectedness of body and mind, we see evidence of the fixation in both the body (erogenous zone-related activity) and in the mind (symbolic activity).

Freud hypothesized that we are born with an id, the source of these libidinal urges, so that id impulses are present from birth (Freud, 1915/2000). By age 2, the ego is formed as we learn to control our bowel functions, and by age 5 the superego is formed as a result of resolving the Oedipal complex. By the time a child is around 5 years old, the three parts of the personality—id, ego, and superego—are formed and work together. This is why Freud believed that the first 5 years were the most important for development and believed that personality was set by the age of 5. Table 8.1 summarizes the key elements of Freud's psychosexual states of development.

> **THINK ABOUT IT**
>
> Do you agree that personality is set by age 5? Why or why not?

Table 8.1   Summary of Freud's Psychosexual Stages of Development

Name of Stage	Erogenous Zone	Ages	Task	Adult Fixation		
				Personality Characteristics	**Activities**	**Symbolic Activity**
Oral stage	Mouth	0–18 months	Early: feeding	Oral, incorporative personality: dependent	Eating, drinking, smoking, kissing	Collecting things, good listener, gullible
			Late: weaning	Oral sadistic personality: aggressive	Gum chewing, nail-biting, overeating	Sarcasm, cynicism, ridicule
Anal stage	Anus/ buttocks	1–3 years	Early: feces expulsion	Anal expulsive personality: self-confident, uninhibited, resistant to authority	Lack of sphincter or bowel control, bed-wetting	Overly generous, gives things away, creative
			Late: feces retention	Anal retentive personality: rigid, compulsive, live up to expectations of others	Constipation	Stinginess, orderliness, stubbornness, perfectionistic
Phallic stage	Genitals	2–5 years	Boys: Oedipus complex, castration, anxiety	Phallic character: hyper-masculinity	Concern with virility, machismo	Power tools, cars, trucks, large machinery
			Girls: Oedipus complex, penis envy	Hysterical character: Hyper-femininity	Flirtatiousness, seductiveness	Promiscuity, castration of men: male-bashing
Latency stage	(None)	5–puberty	Sublimation	(A period of psychological rest—no fixation at this stage)		
Genital stage	(None)	Adulthood	To marry, procreate, be a productive member of society: *"Lieben und arbeiten"* which means "To love and to work"			

Source: Bornstein 2005, Table 1, p. 327. Bonstein, R. F. (2005). Reconnecting psychoanalysis to main stream psychology. Psychoanalytic Psychology, 22(3), 323–340. Copyright American Psychological Association. Adapted with permission.

THINK ABOUT IT

Did you know that Freud loved to collect Greek, Roman, and Byzantine antiques? He was seldom without his trademark cigar and, as a therapist, was a good listener.

Oral Stage.   At birth and until about 18 months of age, an infant's life revolves around feeding (Freud, 1915/2000). The erogenous zone of the oral stage is the mouth. The child gains pleasure through the mouth, as she takes in nourishment. Early in the oral stage infants are concerned with feeding, sucking, and swallowing. Later in the oral stage, the child develops teeth. Now the oral pleasures change from taking in to biting and devouring. If a child gets too much or too little pleasure from these activities—taking in while very young or biting when a little older—then the infant may develop an oral fixation as an adult.

If the lack of appropriate gratification occurred early in the stage, the results might be the **oral incorporative personality**. As an adult, this person would replay this early infantlike state by showing excessive dependency and by trying to gain oral satisfaction by eating, drinking, smoking, or kissing. She might also try to get satisfaction through symbolic oral incorporative activities like collecting things, being a good listener, and being gullible (taking in what people tell her).

However, if the lack of gratification occurred later in the stage, then a person might develop the **oral sadistic personality** showing aggressive behavior, oral activities like gum chewing, nail-biting, or overeating, and the symbolic biting behaviors of sarcasm, cynicism, and ridicule.

Anal Stage.   Once an infant has been weaned, the next biological milestone is learning bowel and sphincter control, as this is the age that most children must face toilet training. Between the ages of 1 and 3 years, the child must learn where and when it is appropriate to relieve himself. This is the first time that a child must adhere to societal expectations, as enforced by the parents, instead of being totally indulged. How the child reacts to the monitoring and control of the parents can determine adult personality.

A child might react by feces expulsion, obtaining gratification by letting loose whenever and wherever. As an adult, this **anal expulsive personality** will show the personality traits of being self-confident, uninhibited, nonconventional, and resisting of authority. He may show the physical behaviors of lack of sphincter or bowel control, and bed-wetting. He may also show the symbolic behaviors of being overly generous and giving things away, and also by being highly creative.

Alternatively, a child might react to parental control of her feces by refusing to go, holding on to her bowel movements. This adult **anal retentive personality** is rigid, compulsive, and lives up to the expectations of others. She might have physical anal problems (e.g., constipation), and also show the symbolic anal retentive activities of being stingy, highly organized, stubborn, and perfectionistic (Freud, 1908/1959).

Today we know that in adults, bowel and bladder problems are real physical disorders and are not related to an anal fixation.

Phallic Stage.   The phallic stage is the most complicated and the most controversial of Freud's stages of development. So far, the developmental stages have tracked the id impulses from the mouth to the anus. Now, in the course of toilet-training the child discovers his penis (Freud couched everything in terms of masculine development, so let's put aside for a moment what happens if you don't happen to have a penis). In the phallic stage, the child feels id impulses in the penis and seeks gratification here by masturbation.

The young boy feels sexual feelings toward the mother and wants to marry his mother. However, there's one problem: the father. The boy starts to harbor hatred for his father, as the father is his rival for the love and attention of the mother. The boy must now find some way of resolving this **Oedipus complex** (Freud, 1925/1961), named for the mythical Greek king of Thebes who unwittingly killed his father and married his mother.

At the same time, the boy discovers that girls are missing a penis. He reasons that girls must have had one, and therefore must have had it cut off and reacts with "horror at the mutilated creature" (Freud, 1925/1961, p. 252). Because his penis is the source of both pleasurable feelings and sexual feelings toward his mother the boy develops **castration anxiety** and lives in fear that the father will cut his off as well. Freud noted that this fear may have originated with actual castration threats, not uncommon at the time in children who had been admonished to not touch themselves.

As a result, the boy then realizes that he must repress his desire for his mother and his hostility for the father or else he may face retribution from the father. So he represses these feelings and instead identifies with the father. By identifying with the father, imagining that he is the father, he gets to possess his mother, at least in mind, through wish fulfillment of the id. Through identification, he also internalizes the father's superego, taking on his father's morality.

If a boy does not resolve his Oedipus complex and identify with the father he may become fixated at this stage. Such a man develops a **phallic character** marked by an overly exaggerated sense of masculinity or machismo. This phallic character continually strives to prove his virility by engaging in hobbies that are symbolic of the phallus: power tools, cars, trucks, and a desire for large machinery.

In girls, the process works slightly differently, with a much less satisfactory ending. Like the boy, the girl starts out strongly attracted to the mother, after all she is the source of comfort and food. The girl makes a "momentous discovery" that boys have a penis "strikingly visible and of large proportions, [and] at once recognize it as the superior counterpart of their own small and inconspicuous organ, and from that time forward fall a victim to envy for the penis" experiencing **penis envy** (Freud, 1925/1961, p. 252).

The girl reasons that she must have had one, but that it was somehow cut off. And because the only person close enough to have done so is her mother, she thinks that her mother must have cut off her penis. At the same time, she is sexually attracted to the father, but she is also angry and jealous because he has a penis and she doesn't.

The sad conclusion Freud comes to is that there is no satisfactory way for a girl to resolve her Oedipus complex: "it may be slowly abandoned or dealt with by repression or its effects may persist far into women's normal mental life" (Freud, 1925/1961, p. 257). A girl's penis envy essentially keeps her fixated at this stage until she can achieve symbolic possession of a penis through having a baby (ideally, a male baby) with a man who resembles her father. "She gives up the wish for a penis and puts in place of it a wish for a child: and with that purpose in view she takes her father as a love-object" (Freud, 1925/1961, p. 256).

Because girls do not come to identify with their fathers, they have no way of developing a superego. Therefore women are lacking in moral character and are naturally inferior to men: "I cannot evade the notion (though I hesitate to give it expression) that for women the level of what is ethically normal is different from what it is in men" (Freud, 1925/1961, p. 258). This is why Freud believed that anatomy is destiny.

Many people oversimplify Freud by thinking that the lack of a penis is what makes women inferior to men. But it's the lack of a superego that is more damaging for the status of women, according to Freud.

A woman who is fixated at this stage develops a **hysterical character**, marked by an exaggerated femininity and activities such as flirting, seducing men, and promiscuity (think of Scarlett O'Hara the Southern belle from *Gone With the Wind*). She may find ways of symbolically remedying her penis envy by trying either to gain the penis she lacks through promiscuity, or to begrudge men the penis they have by symbolically castrating men through insulting and belittling them.

What did Freud have to say to women at the time who objected to his theory? "We must not allow ourselves to be deflected from such conclusions by the denials of the feminists, who are anxious to force us to regard the two sexes as completely equal in position and worth" (Freud, 1925/1961, p. 258).

Latency Stage. The latency stage, from age 5 until puberty, is a time of no significant developments, at least in terms of id impulses and activity in erogenous zones. Freud hypothesized that id impulses are sublimated into other activities like schoolwork, athletics, and friendships with same-sex peers (Freud, 1915/2000). Because of the child's reproductive immaturity, these impulses cannot be satisfied and so must be defended against with sublimation. However, today we know that this is an important time for physical, cognitive, social, and emotional development in children.

THINK ABOUT IT

Which is more important for Freudian theory, the lack of a penis or the lack of a superego?

THINK ABOUT IT

What kinds of developmental changes do children go through from ages 5 until puberty?

Freud failed to recognize that the latency period, ages 5 to 13, is an important time of physical, cognitive, social, and emotional development in children.

THINK ABOUT IT

When does a person become an adult in today's society? Why?

"Freud was one of the most creative thinkers in psychology, but that doesn't mean he was right about everything."

Psychologist Roy Baumeister as cited in Azar (1997, p. 28)

"The process of moral internalization may have already begun long before young children would have even experienced much of an Oedipal or Electra complex, much less have resolved it. . . . [P]erhaps it's time to lay his theory of Oedipal morality to rest."

Shaffer (2009, p. 343)

Genital Stage.   Once young people reach puberty they are, or least they were in Freud's day, considered adults. If people passed successfully through the oral, anal, phallic, and latency stages, getting proper gratification, then they would be able to face the responsibilities of adulthood. To be an adult—and Freud was very clear on this, reflecting his conventional, conservative, and narrow Victorian sensibility—meant that you would be heterosexual, marry, have children, and be a self-sufficient, productive member of society. This philosophy is summed up in his phrase "*Lieben und arbeiten*" which means "To love and to work" (Erikson, 1950).

If, however, a person was unsuccessful in resolving the tasks or challenges of each of the psychosexual developmental stages, he or she would have problems in adulthood caused by a fixation in one of the stages. And how did Freud suggest that we resolve a fixation? Why, by psychotherapy of course, where these unconsciously repressed urges and ungratified id impulses could be explored and the fixation resolved.

Problems With Freud's Psychosexual Stages of Development.   A thorough critique of Freud's claims, even if we just limit it to a discussion of the Oedipus complex, would take an entire volume by itself! However, because much of what he said is very controversial, it is worth discussing some of the major critiques. Indeed, some of these apply to other aspects of his work as well.

First, he worked out his theory of psychosexual development by analyzing the recollections of his patients and himself. Further, we know that his patients were generally suffering from some sort of emotional problem. Essentially, he started with adults who had problems, and asked them to remember their childhoods, instead of studying children at each of the stages or by studying a handful of children as they progressed through the stages, or by comparing the childhoods of adults with and without problems. As a result, his theory is based on biased methods and biased sampling.

Second, think about what Freud's theory of the Oedipal complex starts with: knowledge of genital differences between males and females. Do children between the ages of 2 and 5 really know about genital differences? Apparently, they do not know enough to either feel inferior or to fear castration as Freud claims (Bem, 1989; Brillesliijper-Kater & Baartman, 2000; Katcher, 1955).

Third, boys and girls do not differ in morality, despite the theorized lack of superego formation in girls. One author, after finding no differences in morality of boys and girls and finding that children are able to behave morally much sooner than Freud imagined by toddlerhood even, urged psychologists to abandon this invalid Oedipal morality theory (Shaffer, 2009).

Finally, his whole theory of psychosexual development hinges on the notion of sexual fantasy. However, what if his adults were remembering not just thoughts, wishes, or fantasies of sexual acts, but memories of *actual* sexual assaults?

Originally, Freud believed that his patients, both men and women, were victims of sexual assault as children. He presented a paper in 1896 called "Etiology of Hysteria" (Masson, 1984a, 1984b). Of the 18 patients with hysteria undergoing therapy with Freud at the time, all of them had a history of sexual assault, with independent corroborating evidence in some cases.

Jeffrey Masson—a leading Freud scholar and project director of the Sigmund Freud Archives until he went public with Freud's original ideas over the objections of the officers of the archives, including Anna Freud herself—described the assault theory based on Freud's correspondences of the time. Freud believed that the assaults were real and not a result of false memories or leading questions on the part of the therapist because

> Freud's patients recalled their traumas "with all the feelings that belonged to the original experience"; that is, they took the permission to remember as a permission to feel, and the feelings apparently absent from the original assault were at last experiences: the anger, the disgust, the sense of helplessness and betrayal, all these powerful emotions surfaced. Freud was like an explorer who has chanced on a long-submerged world. (*Masson*, 1984b, p. 35)

Even one of Freud's colleagues at the time, Sándor Ferenczi, reportedly found similar evidence in his patients, but found the reports hard to believe because they suggested that the sexual abuse of children was widespread at the time. However, in 1905 Freud recanted the 1896 paper and instead concluded that the incidents were fantasy, emanating from the sexual feelings of the child. Masson believed—based on original unpublished documents and correspondence at the time, much of which had been censored by Freud and his followers to eliminate any mention of his unfortunately named seduction theory—that Freud capitulated to pressures at the time and was forever haunted by this decision. Instead of exposing a powerful and respected colleague at the time as a fraud, implying that other respected colleagues at the time could be child molesters and exposing child abuse for the widespread problem it was, Freud claimed he was mistaken and withdrew the theory.

By blaming the victim of a botched operation for her own physical problems saying that she nearly bled to death "deriving from repressed wishes not an unskilled surgeon" and Freud's own negligence in the case, he saved his own reputation and the reputation of the colleague (Masson, 1984b, p. 41). However, by hypothesizing that children have sexual feelings for adults, Freud was able to excuse the suspect behavior of a few of his colleagues, including perhaps his own father, and essentially blamed the victim for his or her own abuse.

Let's consider for a moment if Freud's theory of psychosexual development was indeed a theory, not of normal development, but of the development of a child who had been abused. Does childhood sexuality originate within the child, or with the child's experience with an adult? Could early sexual abuse account for how children would know about genital differences at so young an age? Also, why must a girl hate her mother instead of merely identifying with her like boys do with their fathers? Might the girl be angry at her mother, not for cutting off her penis, but for failing to protect her from an abusive father? And why must a girl also be angry at her father? Could he have been the perpetrator of the abuse? No wonder that being able to marry and have sexual relations in marriage became the benchmarks of healthy development. We might well ask ourselves which theory accounts for the data better, Freud's original assault theory or his later theory of childhood sexuality?

Masson (1984b) claimed that some of Freud's case histories make more sense if reread with sexual abuse in mind. Consider Freud's description of a session with a young woman:

> I told her that I was quite convinced that her cousin's death had had nothing at all to do with her state, but that something else had happened which she had not mentioned. At this, she gave way to the extent of letting fall a single significant phrase; but she had hardly said a word before she stopped, and her old father, who was sitting behind her, began to sob bitterly. Naturally I pressed my investigation no further, but I never saw the patient again. (p. 45)

THINK ABOUT IT

Do you agree with Masson that some of Freud's case studies make more sense if reread with sexual abuse in mind?

However, critics refute Masson's claims and argue that Freud either lied about his patient's reports, incorrectly inferred abuse from their symptoms, or created false memories in his patients, and that the medical community of the time rejected Freud's claims for these reasons and not because they found his allegations of abuse repugnant (Gleaves & Hernandez, 1999).

The seduction theory, combined with Freud's notion of repression, fueled the false memory controversy of the 1980s (Erdelyi, 2006a). At the time, there were a number of cases in the news of people who claimed to have remembered traumatic events that had happened to them years before. Later, these traumatic events were shown to be false. The popular press perpetuated the invalid belief that memories could be repressed for years and then suddenly come to the surface. Past incidences of abuse were believed to be responsible for a whole list of psychological and physical complaints, even if the person involved couldn't recall any such abuse.

What causes false memories? First, memory does not work like an electronic recording; it is constructive and vulnerable to inconsistencies including the implantation—and recovery—of false memories (Loftus, Garry, & Feldman, 1994; Schacter, 1987; Sedikides & Green, 2006). Second, false memories may also occur due to leading questions or suggestions by inept or unscrupulous therapists (Loftus & Bernstein, 2005; Kihlstrom, 2006), a charge leveled by some critics at Freud himself (Esterson, 1993, 1998, 2001, 2002a, 2002b). However, some recovered memories may be real.

Although scholars continue to debate the status of Freud's seduction theory (see Gleaves & Hernandez, 1999, for a good summary), alas, the failure to take childhood sexual abuse seriously from the start has done damage to the field and to countless individuals. We must keep in mind that "false alarms do not imply the absence of true hits" (Erdelyi, 2006a, p. 40). The true tragedy is that these concepts have entered the culture so that most people, especially those who have *not* taken a psychology class, somehow continue to believe that childhood sexuality and the Oedipus complex are real, psychologically meaningful concepts, instead of misguided and invalid theories.

As long as we expect to see Oedipal behaviors—or oral or anal for that matter—we are apt to recognize them in the world around us as a result of our own self-fulfilling prophesies and confirmation biases, and not due to Freud's alleged genius in shedding light on important aspects of human experience. Certainly, Freud was on the right track in identifying the importance of early family experiences on later development, but he was wrong in hypothesizing that it revolves around sexual feelings. The empirical evidence does not support Freud's psychosexual stages of development.

THINK ABOUT IT

Why do people continue to believe in the Oedipus complex, despite no supporting evidence for its existence?

Research Methods Illustrated: Case Study and Psychobiography

Case study, an in-depth study of a single person, has traditionally been an important technique in medicine and clinical psychology to illustrate disorders. *Psychobiography* is the use of psychological theory, usually personality theory, to organize a person's life into a coherent story (McAdams, 1988). Notable case studies in personality include Jenny (Allport, 1965), Henry Kissinger (Swede & Tetlock, 1986), a man who sailed solo around the world (Nasby & Read, 1997), and various U.S. presidents (Simonton, 1999).

A case study can help us reach a greater understanding of the personality of a specific person (Elms, 2007), showing us how a person is unique, especially after we've discovered commonalities among people or between this person and other people (Schultz, 2005). Like any research method, there are strengths and weaknesses to the case study method. Of course, the major weakness is that we can draw conclusions only about this particular person; we can't generalize to other people and we can't demonstrate causality in the way a true experiment can.

However, rather than supporting or disconfirming a theory, like experiments, a case study can be used to generate theory. Whereas the logic of an experiment is deductive (generalizing from a general principle to a specific instance), the logic of a case study is inductive (generalizing from a specific instance to a general principle). In this way, the life of an individual person can inspire a new theory (Carlson, 1988). Case studies can help us understand a theory better by seeing how the theory may work in a real person with all of his or her idiosyncrasies (Elms, 2007). Case studies provide useful evidence, explanation, and interpretation of how a theory may work when applied to a single person (Elms, 2007).

The strength of a case study depends on the choice of subject and on the thoroughness of the researcher. Researchers, whenever they conduct research but especially when doing a case study, need to be aware of their own personal biases that may unduly influence their work. Also, researchers need to remain open to the possibility that they could be wrong about a person and should take pains to verify, ideally though multiple sources of data, their conclusions about the subject of their case study.

Freud was known for a number of famous case studies, including Leonardo Da Vinci (Freud, 1910/1964) and Woodrow Wilson (Freud, 1967). Let's take a look at his case of Little Hans, the 5-year-old boy who developed a fear of horses (Freud, 1909a/1955). Hans was the son of one of Freud's associates who carried out the analysis of the boy himself and reported the events as they unfolded to Freud. Of course, Hans's case was met with great excitement, as this was a chance to see how the theorized sexual instincts of the phallic stage would play out in an actual child.

Hans's father reported that between ages 3 and 4 Hans was very curious about "wiwimakers" (unfortunately translated as *widdlers* in English). He quickly understood that horses and dogs had one but that tables and chairs didn't. When his father drew a picture of a giraffe after an outing to the zoo, Hans insisted that they add the giraffe's wiwimaker as well (see Figure 8.4). He noticed that his 3-month-old baby sister Hannah had a "tiny, little one." He saw his father's, but when he asked if his mother had one, she replied that of course she did. At the same time, Hans would often touch himself, a habit his parents wished to break him of. They even threatened to cut off his penis if he didn't stop.

At about age 5, Hans developed a phobia about going out, for fear that a horse would bite him. When he was taken outside, he would immediately wish to return home and be comforted in the arms of his mother. Later, they discovered that he was particularly afraid of horses with blinders on and black harnesses around their mouths (see Figure 8.5).

Hans's fears seemed to increase after an extended summer vacation in the country. While his father worked in the city, Hans could spend time alone with his mother. He especially liked to cuddle with her in the morning. He even had a dream during this time that his mother left him and he had nobody to cuddle with. Hans's father blamed his mother for spoiling the boy by spending so much time with him as well as, in his mind, excessive displays of affection. His father noted that Hans still had not stopped touching himself, but grew increasingly anxious about this habit (recall Hans's "wanting's not doing" quote during our discussion of wish fulfillment and the superego).

One night Hans had a telling dream: "In the night there was a big giraffe in the room and a crumpled one; and the big one called out because I took the crumpled one away from it. Then it stopped calling out; and then I sat down on top of the crumpled one" (Freud, 1909a/1955, p. 37). A few days later Hans expressed his fear that one or both of his parents might leave him, and this came out later at breakfast. Hans's father got up to leave and Hans remarked: "Daddy, don't trot away from me!"

For Freud and Hans's father, this unusual choice of words suggested the unconscious reason for his fear: His father was the horse! Of course, they interpreted the fear to be that Hans was afraid that the horse (his father) would hurt him because he wanted his mother all to himself.

In the case study method, psychologists study a single person in great depth. Pictured here is Bertha Pappenheim, whom Freud wrote about as "Anna O" in a famous case study.

Widdler

Figure 8.4 The picture of a giraffe drawn by Hans's father. The *wiwimaker* was added by Hans himself. *Source:* S. Freud, 1955/1909a, p. 13. Freud, S. (1955/1909a). Analysis of a phobia in a five-year old boy. In Standard edition: Volume 10. (p. 5–149). London, UK.: Hogarth Press. (Original work published 1909).

Figure 8.5 The picture Hans's father drew of a horse with black around his mouth and blinders on. *Source:* S. Freud, 1955/1909a, p. 49. Freud, S. (1955/1909a). Analysis of a phobia in a five-year old boy. In Standard edition: Volume 10. (p. 5–149). London, UK.: Hogarth Press. (Original work published 1909).

Freud and Hans's father believed that this was all part of Hans's Oedipal complex. First, Hans was obviously in love with his mother. Second, though he claimed to be fearful when his father was away, he really wanted his father out of the picture so he could have his mother all to himself. Freud reasoned that Hans wanted to do away with his father (the big giraffe) to have his mother (the crumpled giraffe). Then, Hans developed a castration anxiety and feared that his father would cut off his penis as revenge for wanting his mother. So instead of fearing his father, Hans displaced that fear onto horses and came to fear horses. This was later confirmed by his fear, actually a disguised wish, that his father would fall down and die like in an actual horse-and-cart accident he unfortunately witnessed while out with his mother.

But, can you think of an alternative explanation for his fear? How might a small child react to an accident involving carts and horses? How might a typical 3-year-old react to a new baby in the house? How might a 4-year-old react to his father being away from home for an extended period of time? Finally, not long after these events Hans's parents separated and eventually divorced. Does this suggest to you a different interpretation of events?

This classic case demonstrates both the advantages and the problems of the case study method. Though this case allegedly illustrates Freud's theory of childhood sexuality including id impulses, the Oedipus complex, and castration anxiety, Freud himself realized the biases contained in the case. He cautioned, "psychoanalysis is not an impartial scientific investigation, but a therapeutic measure" (Freud, 1909a/1955, p. 104).

Psychodynamic Theory Since Freud

"The assumption that there are unconscious mental processes, the recognition of the theory of resistance and repression, the appreciation of the importance of sexuality and of the Oedipus complex—these constitute the principal subject matter of psycho-analysis and the foundations of its theory. No one who cannot accept them all should count himself a psycho-analyst."

Sigmund Freud (1955, p. 247)

There have been a number of movements within psychoanalysis since Freud's time. In the early days, some of Freud's colleagues broke with him and started their own systems. These *neo-Freudians* included Alfred Adler, Carl Jung, Karen Horney, Eric Fromm, and Harry Stack Sullivan. Like Freud, they developed their own theories of personality and techniques of therapy (Westen et al., 2008).

In particular, some objected to Freud's "id psychology" and developed their own *ego psychology,* which focused on the development and functions of the ego rather than the impulses of the id. These early pioneers included Heinz Hartmann and Freud's own daughter Anna Freud (Westen et al., 2008).

Karen Horney (1885–1952) took issue with many of Freud's concepts and established feminine psychology.

Systems such as object relations theory, self-psychology, and relational psychology soon followed (Wolitzky, 2006). All were rooted in psychoanalysis, but placed a greater emphasis on mental representations of the self and others and less of an emphasis on sex and aggression. Object relations theory, for example, focuses on the cognitive and emotional processes involved in intimate relationships: how we form close relationships, bond, and cognitively represent important others. Object relations theory is concerned with the impact of actual experiences instead of fantasy (Westen et al., 2008). Major theorists in object relations theory include Heinz Kohut (1966, 1971, 1977, 1984), Otto Kernberg (1975, 1984), Charles Brenner (1982), and Stephen Mitchell (1988, 1993, 1997; Greenberg & Mitchell, 1993).

What does psychoanalysis look like today? There are five postulates that define contemporary psychoanalytic theory. These are aspects of Freudian theory that are supported by experimental data and which are endorsed by most psychoanalytic psychologists today (Westen, 1998a, 2000):

1. Much of our thoughts, feelings, motives, defenses, fears, and wishes are unconscious. Unconscious processes remain central to contemporary psychoanalysis.

2. Part of being human is recognizing that we have conflicting thoughts, feelings, and motivations. Behavior is often an imperfect compromise among these forces. Our unconscious is more rational than Freud thought; feelings influence our cognitions more than modern cognitive psychology originally thought.

3. Personality begins to form in childhood and shows continuity into adulthood. Childhood experiences are important in making us who we are as adults, especially when it comes to our relationships with others.

4. Mental representations of self, others, and relationships are important. These representations guide the way we form later relationships and the kind of psychological problems we may experience.

5. Personality development and growth involves moving from an immature, dependent state to a mature interdependent state. Development involves more than managing our sexual and aggressive urges; it includes managing feelings of dependency, independency, and interdependency in socially appropriate ways.

To see what these five postulates look like in a contemporary theory, let us consider a current theory, developed through and supported by empirical research. Attachment theory has been described as the resurrection of the psychodynamic theory of personality (Shaver & Mikulincer, 2005). Though originally grounded in psychoanalytic thinking, attachment theory has moved beyond these roots to become an influential theory of personality, close relationships, and developmental psychology and has already changed psychoanalytic theories of child development (Westen et al., 2008; see also Fonagy, Gergely, & Target, 2008; Shaver & Mikulincer, 2007).

Attachment Theory

Brief History

Imagine a typical children's hospital in the United States or Europe during the early part of the 20th century. Infants and toddlers were kept in individual cubicles and were tended by masked and hooded nurses and doctors who walked carefully to avoid stirring up germs. Parents were not permitted to touch, hug, cuddle, comfort, or even see their children for the duration of their hospital stay, sometimes up to 1 year. The attending medical staff would handle the children only minimally, propping bottles on pillows to feed them efficiently and antiseptically (Karen, 1994).

As chilling as this sounds to us, that was pretty much the standard way hospitals and orphanages worked in those days. People were more concerned about sterility, orderliness, and the physical needs of children than about their emotional needs. How did infants and children raised in these conditions fare? Not very well. Despite better nutrition and a cleaner environment, the children healed slower, seemed listless and depressed, and when they returned home (or were eventually adopted) they had behavioral problems ranging from anger to delinquency to detachment. Parents complained that the child they brought home was a very different child from the one they checked in a short time ago (Karen, 1994).

John Bowlby, a child psychiatrist originally trained as a psychoanalyst, was one of the young interns caring for children in a clinic very much like this. He was disturbed by what he saw in hospitals and clinics of the day and set out to document that children's emotional needs were just as—if not more—important than their physical needs. Bowlby believed that emotional ties with mother, the primary caregiver for most children at the time, had an impact on emotional regulation, interpersonal relations, and mental health across the life span (Shaver & Mikulincer,

"There are very few analysts who follow all of Freud's formulations."
Morris Eagle, president of the psychoanalysis division of the American Psychological Association as cited in Horgan (1996, p. 106)

THINK ABOUT IT

Why is the distinction between fantasy and reality important to object relations theory? Why was fantasy more important to Freudians?

"[The child] may be ill-fed and ill-sheltered, he may be very dirty and suffering from disease, he may be ill-treated, but, unless his parents have wholly rejected him, he is secure in the knowledge that there is someone to whom he is of value and who will strive, even though inadequately, to provide for him."
John Bowlby as cited in Karen (1994, p. 64)

THINK ABOUT IT

What is it like for hospitalized children today?

The Personality of Everyday Life

Taking the trauma out of a hospital stay

While observing children in the hospital, Bowlby noticed a distinct pattern of emotional responses to separation from the primary caregiver, be it the mother, the father, or a nurse. First is protest, where the infant cries, clings to, and tries to actively seek out the mother to either prevent her from leaving or to reestablish contact with her. Second is despair, where the infant shows sadness, passivity, and an increased hopelessness that the mother will return and appears to be mourning her loss. Finally, there is detachment, where the infant responds to the returning mother with loss of interest, turning away, apathy, and a lack of attachment behaviors seen before the separation (Bowlby, 1969). After reunion with the primary caregiver some children returned to normal after a number of days, but some children remained affected for a very long time.

This same pattern was also found in primate infants. Infant monkeys, separated from their mothers, preferred a warm, cuddly, terrycloth monkey over the cold, hard wire mesh surrogate mother even though only the wire mesh mother had food. Though psychologists at the time predicted that the monkey would prefer the mother who provided it with nourishment, Harlow discovered that contact comfort was a more powerful force, and the observations of Bowlby bear this out in human infants (Harlow, 1958).

Even Anna Freud noticed that during the Second World War, some children preferred to sleep next to their mothers in a dark and scary air raid shelter under the streets of London than alone in the sterile but safe clinic for children she ran just outside the city. Alas, she failed to appreciate the full import of her observations (Karen, 1994).

Today, hospitals make arrangements for a parent or guardian to stay in the room with the child for the entire length of the child's hospital stay. Some hospitals, such as the world-renowned St. Jude's Children's Research hospital in Memphis, Tennessee, avoid hospitalizing children entirely! They recognize that a child's parents and family are a great source of emotional and social support, especially during an illness. By encouraging families to stay together and to stay in a homelike setting rather than in the hospital, these hospitals aim to fulfill the attachment needs of children for a secure base and a safe haven.

2007). Although he agreed with Freud's view that much of adult behavior has its roots in childhood social experiences, he wanted to observe these events directly and over time rather than rely on adults' reminiscences (Shaver & Clark, 1994).

Bowlby theorized that the attachment system evolved to keep infants close to their mothers and safe from harm. According to Bowlby: (1) An infant who trusts that the mother will be accessible and responsive will be less fearful than an infant who does not have confidence that the mother will be available. (2) This confidence is built up slowly from birth through adolescence and will remain relatively unchanged through adulthood. (3) These expectations are fairly accurate reflections of the experiences individuals have actually had. Bowlby referred to these expectations as **internal working models** (Bowlby, 1973).

As a result of our early attachment relationships we form two sets of internal working models: working models of others and working models of our self. The working model of others comes from our expectations of our primary caregiver's responsiveness. The working model of our self comes from our feelings of worthiness, lovability, and competence, as individuals deserving of help (Bowlby, 1969). These internal working models of others and of ourselves remain with us throughout our lives and form the basis of subsequent close relationships: They organize our memories and guide future interactions with people we would like to be close with.

But more than that, according to Bowlby, having secure attachments allows us to function better out in the world. With a secure base, we show increased exploration of our world, and develop self-regulation and the ability to rely on others when necessary. Insecure people are not

THINK ABOUT IT

Can internal working models account for supposed love at first sight?

Securely attached children will use their parents as a safe base from which to explore the world.

able to explore the world or make healthy connections with others. A person with an anxious attachment may be overly dependent on others, whereas an avoidant person may be overly self-reliant (Shaver & Mikulincer, 2007).

Bowlby's work would be merely theoretical musings if not for the research of Mary Ainsworth. Ainsworth and her colleagues regularly visited infants and mothers in the Baltimore area multiple times during the baby's first year and watched how they interacted while the mother attended to the baby's needs during a 4-hour visit (Ainsworth, Blehar, Waters, & Wall, 1978). Researchers rated the mother's sensitivity to the infant's signals; acceptance, as opposed to rejection, of the infant and his or her needs; cooperation with the infant's desires and rhythms, rather than being interfering, demanding, or intrusive; and availability to the infant, rather than ignoring the infant's signals. For example, Ainsworth and her assistants recorded every time the mother or baby touched, cuddled, smiled, vocalized, made eye contact, or had face-to-face interactions. She noticed that some mothers were particularly sensitive and responsive to the infant's signals. Then—inspired by Bowlby's work—she wanted to see how the infants reacted when separated from their mothers. She developed a laboratory technique called the **Strange Situation**.

In the Strange Situation a mother and her infant are brought to a laboratory room filled with toys. Over the next 30 minutes, the mother and the baby go through a series of separations and reunions, lasting about 3 minutes each. The infant's reactions are carefully monitored during three key periods: free play with the mother in the room, separation where the mother departs, and reunion when the mother returns.

Not only did Ainsworth and her colleagues see remarkable differences in infants' behavior in the Strange Situation, but they also were able to relate the infants' attachment behaviors to the mothers' sensitivity and responsiveness in the home (Ainsworth et al., 1978). They identified three patterns of attachment.

At home, children of sensitive and responsive mothers cried less, communicated better, obeyed more, and enjoyed close bodily contact more than children of less responsive mothers. Though they enjoyed physical contact, they were not clingy and actually sought physical contact less than infants in the other two groups. According to Ainsworth these infants showed **secure attachment**. In the Strange Situation of the laboratory they used the mother as a **secure base** from which to explore the toys in the lab and as a **safe haven** to return to for safety and comfort when danger is near, such as the approach of the laboratory assistant (Ainsworth et al., 1978).

In contrast, other mothers were less affectionate during the child's first 3 months and frequently disliked and avoided close bodily contact with the child during the first year. These infants showed **avoidant attachment** to their mothers in the Strange Situation. Even though they actively explored the toys in the lab, they seemed oblivious to their mother's departure and return and did not seek her out as a safe haven. Whereas these children appeared to be

SEE FOR YOURSELF

The next time you are around a child, watch carefully to see if you can see the child using his or her caregiver as a secure base from which to explore the world or as a safe haven to return to when things get scary.

independent and unemotional during separation, their heart rates were as high as the secure infants', suggesting that despite outward appearances they were greatly distressed by the separation (Spangler & Grossmann, 1993).

Finally, a third group of mothers frequently ignored their babies' signals but did not reject close bodily contact. These mothers were inconsistent in responding to their infants or seemed to respond in an interfering, nonsensitive way. At home, their infants cried more than usual even in the mothers' presence, and explored their environments less, a pattern repeated in the Strange Situation. Though the infants showed distress upon separation from their mothers in the Strange Situation and ran to them when the mothers returned, the infants did not seem to accept the comfort the mothers attempted to offer, arching away as mothers attempted to hug them. Overall, these infants seemed generally anxious. These infants have an **anxious-ambivalent attachment** to their mothers (Ainsworth et al., 1978).

Later, a fourth **disorganized/disoriented** group was identified in the Strange Situation (Main & Solomon, 1990). Parents of these infants are often full of fear, themselves, or inadvertently behave in ways that are frightening to an infant (e.g., showing anxious facial expressions or awkward postures). Because it is difficult for the infant to approach such a parent, the child has no idea of how to respond. Sadly, many of these parents have experienced their own attachment-related traumas, such as the loss of a parent or caregiver through death or separation. Parents who maltreat their infants tend to have infants with a disorganized/disoriented attachment but not all disorganized/disoriented children have a history of abuse.

As you might expect if the attachment system is important for survival, using the mother as a secure base is universal—at least across the United States, Japan, Israel, Columbia, Germany and Norway—but what makes for an ideal infant or a secure infant varies somewhat by culture (Posada et al., 1995; Rutter, 2008). Across many cultures, the essential ingredients of attachment are a caregiver who notices the baby's signals, interprets them accurately by taking the baby's perspective, responds promptly and appropriately, and can be depended on to do so (Ainsworth et al., 1974; Bretherton, 1990). The mother's sensitivity to her infant appears to play a greater role in the infant's attachment than the child's temperament at this early age (Fraley & Shaver, 2008).

Attachment Patterns for Life?

Bowlby described the patterns of attachment from cradle to grave as being like a railway system (Bowlby, 1973). Though the system may start with a single main route, it often forks into a number of individual lines depending on life experiences (see the photo below). A recent

> "What is more natural than that we should persist in looking for happiness along the path on which we first encountered it? . . . We are never so defenseless against suffering as when we love, never so helplessly unhappy as when we have lost our loved object or its love."
> *Sigmund Freud (1929/1989, p. 33)*

Bowlby used the metaphor of a railway to describe attachment trajectories across the life span.

meta-analysis of 27 different samples across various ages between 1 to 16 years suggests that these lines indeed remain very close to their original routes despite life experiences that cause them to diverge (Fraley, 2002). The correlation between early attachment and attachment at any later point in time is approximately $r = .39$.

Even more impressive is that recent studies find a 70 to 75% agreement between an infant's secure or insecure attachment in the Strange Situation and his or her attachment in late adolescence and young adulthood. Where participants changed their attachment style, it was due to life stresses, including death of a parent, parental divorce, or a life-threatening illness of the participant or a parent that often changed a secure environment into an insecure one (Crowell, Fraley, & Shaver, 2008). This suggests that internal working models are more like updated representations modified by life experiences and events, as Bowlby suggested, as opposed to the very psychodynamic suggestion that they are residues from childhood (Shaver & Mikulincer, 2005).

There is also some evidence that attachment patterns are socialized into the next generation, which is not a surprise if attachment comes from a caregiver's responsiveness. To assess an adult's attachment pattern, researchers developed the **Adult Attachment Interview**, or **AAI** (Main, Kaplan, & Cassidy, 1985; see Hesse, 2008, for a review). Adults are asked to recall their childhoods and the kind of interactions they had with a parent. The manner in which participants revealed their memories was very telling. Participants fell into one of three categories of attachment styles, very similar to the three styles of infant attachment (Main, 1996).

In numerous studies using the AAI, parents' recollections of their own childhood experiences predicted the attachment of their children in the Strange Situation 76 to 85% of the time (Karen, 1994). In fact, one study was able to trace attachment patterns across three generations! Mothers were given the AAI when they were pregnant and again when their child was 11 months old. The AAI was also given to their mothers. Then, when their child was 23 months of age, the mothers and infants were placed in the Strange Situation.

Attachment Styles in Adulthood

By the time we are adults, we have formed internal working models of ourselves and others in close relationships. Researchers hypothesized that people will have different expectations for romantic love depending on their adult attachment style, that is, their internal working models. Their adult romantic relationships will look very much like their childhood attachment behavior patterns (Fraley & Shaver, 2008; Mikulincer & Shaver, 2007; Mohr, 2008).

To test this, researchers ran a "Love Quiz" in the *Rocky Mountain News,* a major newspaper in their area (Hazan & Shaver, 1987). Part of the quiz asked respondents to answer a questionnaire about their experiences and to choose which one of three paragraphs best described their feelings (see Table 8.2). The description of the three adult attachment styles was based on the original description of infants in the Ainsworth et al. (1978) study rewritten to apply to adult romantic behaviors.

Over 1,200 people aged 14 to 82, with an average of 36 years old, responded to their ad. People could readily identify with one of the three paragraphs in proportions comparable to the

> **THINK ABOUT IT**
>
> What kind of experiences could make attachment patterns become less secure? More secure?

> **THINK ABOUT IT**
>
> Is attachment still important in adulthood?

> **SEE FOR YOURSELF**
>
> Which paragraph in Table 8.2 best applies to you?

Table 8.2 Adult Attachment Styles

%	Attachment	Description
56	Secure	"I find it relatively easy to get close to others and am comfortable depending on them and having them depend on me. I don't often worry about being abandoned or about someone getting too close to me."
25	Avoidant	"I am somewhat uncomfortable being close to others; I find it difficult to trust them completely, difficult to allow myself to depend on them. I am nervous when anyone gets too close, and often love partners want me to be more intimate than I feel comfortable being."
19	Anxious-Ambivalent	"I find that others are reluctant to get as close as I would like. I often worry that my partner doesnt really love me or won't stay with me. I want to merge completely with another person, and this desire sometimes scares people away."

Source: From Hazan and Shaver (1987, Table 2, p. 515). Hazan, C., & Shaver, P. R. (1987). Romantic lover conceptualized as an attachment process. *Journal of Personality and Social Psychology, 52*(3), 511–524. Copyright American Psychological Association.

original findings with children (Ainsworth et al., 1978). There were no differences in childhood experiences with separation from parents between the three groups, but people with different adult attachment styles seemed to experience love differently.

People who described themselves as secure described their most important love experience as happy, friendly, and trusting. They believed that romantic feelings of love come and go over the course of a relationship, and that such feelings could return to the high intensity of the early days of a romance. Secure adults reported warmer relationships with both of their parents and also that their parents had a warmer relationship with each other than the other two groups.

Avoidant lovers demonstrated a fear of intimacy, and relationships marked by emotional highs and lows and jealousy. They believed that the romantic head-over-heels-love depicted in movies does not exist. They also believed that true romantic love seldom lasts and that it is rare to find a person whom they could really fall in love with. Avoidant adults described their mothers as cold and rejecting.

Anxious-ambivalent lovers experienced obsession, a desire for reciprocation and union, emotional extremes, strong sexual attraction, and jealousy with their partners. They fell in love easily, but seldom found true love. They also believed that romantic feelings come and go over the course of a relationship. In a second study, anxious-ambivalent lovers reported the most loneliness and secure lovers the least (Hazan & Shaver, 1987).

If we develop our attachment style from our early experiences, how might divorce affect attachment? This question was explored in a study of undergraduate men and women who reported on their parents' marriages and identified their adult attachment style (Brennan & Shaver, 1993). They found evidence that the quality of the parents' relationship, not the status itself, had a greater impact on a child's attachment style.

Brennan and Shaver (1993) found that there was no relationship between adult attachment style and parents' marital status. However, among parents who were still married, there was an effect on adult attachment. Parents who were described as being happily married had children with all three kinds of adult attachment styles. But parents who were unhappily married tended to have fewer securely attached adult children and more insecurely attached adult children, especially with the avoidant style.

On a hopeful note, these styles could be modified if the parent, especially the custodial parent, remarried happily. In this case, more adult children turned out secure. If both parents remained unmarried, then the adult child was likely to describe themselves as one of the insecurely attached styles.

Attachment and Adult Personality Functioning

Let's consider for a moment how adults react to separation from their attachment figures. Although we wouldn't be able to place an adult in the Strange Situation for children, some researchers discovered an adult equivalent of the Strange Situation. In a clever operationalization of the concept of separation, researchers observed 109 couples at the airport, aged 16 to 68 years, about half of whom were married (Fraley & Shaver, 1998). A bit more than half of the couples were separating; the rest were traveling together. The experiment took place at a time when people could walk right up to the gate to say goodbye to a traveling friend and even wave at them from the window while watching the plane take off!

In this study, one researcher asked couples to fill out a survey about their attachment style, the nature of their relationship, and, if separating, their distress at leaving their partner. Meanwhile, a second experimenter who knew nothing about the couple rated their separation and attachment behaviors by observing their behavior from a short distance away in the departure lounge while the participants were saying goodbye to their partners or entering the airplane with their partners.

Couples separating at the airport reacted very much like children separated from their mothers in the Strange Situation; their reactions were a reflection of their attachment style. First, there were more attachment behaviors in separating couples than in couples traveling together. Couples who were separating were particularly likely to sit close to their partner; kiss, hug, stroke their partner's head or face in a comforting manner; and perhaps even well up with tears or cry.

Do adults separating at an airport show attachment behaviors like those shown by children in the Strange Situation?

Second, the longer a couple had been together, the less distress they reported at separation. Longer-term couples also showed less attachment behaviors than shorter-term couples at separation. Finally, there was an interaction between gender and attachment style in separation behavior.

Women with attachment anxiety reported more distress when facing separation than women in couples who were traveling together, even though they didn't seem to show different separation behaviors. However, women with attachment avoidance showed more withdrawal and avoidance of their partners and less contact, contact-seeking, care-seeking, and caregiving than women in couples traveling together.

Men with attachment anxiety showed less contact with their partners than men who were traveling with their partners. Men with attachment avoidance who were separating showed no particular pattern of responses or behaviors. This study illustrates that, just as Bowlby suggested, attachment behaviors operate to maintain contact with caregivers when separation is imminent.

What about breaking up? Loss or threat of the loss of an important relationship should also elicit attachment-like behaviors. In one study, over 5,000 internet users voluntarily filled out a questionnaire asking about their anxiety and avoidance in close relationships and to describe a recent breakup of a serious relationship (Davis, Shaver, & Vernon, 2003). Participants who were secure in their attachments, scoring low in both anxiety and avoidance, reported using more social coping strategies like using friends and family as a safe haven to deal with the breakup of a relationship.

However, participants who showed attachment anxiety or attachment avoidance reported more distress and a harder time in dealing with their breakups. As you might expect, participants high in avoidance were more likely to use self-reliant coping strategies, preferring to go it alone rather than seek solace with friends and family. They also blamed themselves for the loss rather than their partners.

Participants with attachment anxiety reported the hardest time of all three attachment styles. They reported greater physical and emotional distress, a preoccupation with their lost love, and interference with exploration. Paradoxically, they would show angry and vengeful behaviors and yet went to great lengths in their attempts to reestablish the relationship. Rather than rely on friends or go it alone, they turned to more dysfunctional ways of coping including alcohol and other drugs.

If adult love relationships parallel children's attachment patterns, what about exploratory behavior? Might secure adult attachments provide support for exploration in the adult world of work? This hypothesis was tested in a study of attachment styles, job satisfaction, leisure activities, and well-being (Hazan & Shaver, 1990).

Participants for this study were readers of the *Denver Post* newspaper who responded to a questionnaire that appeared in the Sunday magazine section. This questionnaire assessed their adult attachment style using the paragraph measure (Hazan & Shaver, 1987; see Table 8.2). As a follow-up they were sent a two-page questionnaire specifically asking about work-related attitudes and behaviors. As expected, there was a significant relationship between attachment and attitudes toward work.

Secure respondents reported a positive approach to work, and showed the least likelihood of the three groups to procrastinate, fear failure, and have difficulty completing work tasks. They were also least likely to fear rejection from coworkers. They had a healthy balance between their personal life and their work life, taking time off to enjoy vacations, putting relationships before work, and not letting work jeopardize their health. They reported the highest ratings of work satisfaction and success of all three groups. Essentially, feeling secure, they have the confidence to explore safely in the world of work and focus on their careers out of their own interests and desires.

In contrast, anxious-ambivalent respondents preferred to work with others on projects, yet felt misunderstood and underappreciated at work and resented the perceived intrusiveness of others. They seemed to be motivated by the approval of others, worried that others would not appreciate their efforts, and were likely to fear rejection for poor performance. They reported that their personal lives interfered with their work life. For these people, exploration—in the form of performance, achievement, and respect and admiration from others—had become a way of satisfying unmet attachment needs rather than a way of pursuing their own interests or developing their own talents. This group had the lowest average income of the three attachment groups even after controlling for differences in education.

Finally, avoidant respondents seemed to use work as a way of avoiding close relationships with others. They reported an almost compulsive approach to work, feeling nervous when not working and deriving little pleasure from vacations. They also preferred to work alone and found that work left little time for relationships. Avoidant adults used work as an excuse for avoiding interacting with others and to distract themselves from the anxiety associated with unmet attachment needs. Other studies find similar results for the relationship of adult attachment styles and achievement motivation (Elliot & Reis, 2003).

Overall, studies find that attachment patterns are related to a whole range of positive outcomes in adults. For example, secure adults show less defensive behaviors including self-enhancement biases and intergroup biases (Fraley & Shaver, 2008). Insecure adults show less tolerance of out-group members, less humanistic values, and are less compassionate and altruistic (Fraley & Shaver, 2008). Facing the world without a secure base and safe haven leads to a consistent struggle for stable self-worth as an adult (Foster, Kernis, & Goldman, 2007; Fraley & Shaver, 2008).

Secure adults are more likely than insecure adults to show the defining features of what the humanistic psychologist Carl Rogers (1968) called the **fully functioning** person: openness to new experiences, trust in oneself and the world, lack of fear of disapproval or rejection,

THINK ABOUT IT

What attachment experiences might help people achieve a better balance of work and relationships?

Adults with an avoidant attachment style may use work to avoid intimate relationships with other people.

experiencing thoughts and emotions deeply, sensitivity and responsiveness to others' needs, and volunteering in their communities (Fraley & Shaver, 2008).

Evidence suggests that, indeed, attachment styles are powerfully related to many different outcomes in adulthood related to both love and work. Maybe Freud wasn't too far off when he suggested that "to love and to work" was the goal of healthy development!

Chapter Summary

So, what do you think? Is Freud dead? Does Freudian theory contribute anything to the science of personality? Or, have researchers and clinicians taken the useful parts of Freudian theory, expanded, revised, and built on it so much so that what remains of the original theory is indeed useless? Does Freudian theory belong "along with other Mesozoic curiosities, in a museum of natural history," a view challenged by psychologist Drew Westen (1998a, p. 356)?

Freud hypothesized that humans were driven by the unconscious life and death instincts. Though these impulses, especially for sex and aggression, stay hidden in the unconscious, they occasionally infiltrate our consciousness through hypnosis, free association (e.g., the word association test championed by Carl Jung), dreams, parapraxes, jokes, symbolic behaviors, and projective tests. Freud's structural model of personality (id, ego, and superego) remains a useful metaphor for describing personality functioning; his topographical model (conscious, preconscious, unconscious) is best viewed as a continuum. The ego must find ways of satisfying these id impulses within the bounds of morality (internalized in the superego as the conscience and the ego ideal) and reality. Defense mechanisms are ways the ego can deal with unacceptable impulses. Current research clearly supports some of the defenses Freud suggested (reaction formation, isolation, denial, rationalization), provides mixed support for two (undoing, projection), and provides no support for others (repression, displacement, sublimation).

Freud interpreted psychological changes associated with growth and development in children with biological changes across a series of psychosexual stages: oral, anal, phallic, latency, and genital. Freud was correct in recognizing the importance of early relationships on later development but was misguided in interpreting them as sexual in nature and as fantasies. Especially controversial is the phallic stage where boys go through castration anxiety and must resolve their Oedipus complex and girls suffer from penis envy. Freud used the case study method to draw and support many of his conclusions.

Experimental evidence supports certain aspects of Freud's theory including the impact of the unconscious, role of conflict and compromise of motives, the importance of childhood experiences in shaping adult personality, mental representations of the self and other, and that healthy personality development requires learning to regulate sexual and aggressive feelings.

Psychoanalytic approaches today build on some of the basic principles of Freudian theory: the importance of unconscious processes, conflict, continuity of personality across the life span, mental representations of the self and others, and the importance of childhood experiences on adult personality. These ideas are championed by current approaches including ego psychology, self-psychology, and object relations theory.

Attachment theory, developed by John Bowlby and Mary Ainsworth, confirms that we form internal working models of key attachments from our early childhood that affect our adult relationships. Secure attachment develops out of a relationship with a caregiver who is sensitive, responsive, and dependable. Attachment is assessed in infants by observing them interact with their primary caregiver in the laboratory Strange Situation. For adults, there is the Adult Attachment Interview, a paragraph measure, and questionnaire measures. People's attachment patterns tend to be somewhat consistent over their lives, and across generations. Attachment in adulthood is related to beliefs about love, reactions to separation from a partner, and even to achievement and satisfaction at work, that is, "To love and to work," just as Freud predicted.

One demonstration of the impact of internal working models on later love relationships is the experiment that opened this chapter: People felt that a relationship with a potential dating partner who resembled a past love was likely to be particularly intimate compared to a

"Freud should be placed in the same category as Darwin, who lived before the discovery of genes."

Neuroscientist Jaak Panksepp as cited in Guterl (2002, p. 51)

✓●─ **Study** and **Review** on **mysearchlab.com**

Go online for more resources to help you review.

description of a person who did not resemble a past love. People were particularly vulnerable to a potential date who resembled their first love.

The debate on Freud will not be over anytime soon. Certainly, there are parts of Freudian theory we can lay to rest. Perhaps we should keep Freudian theory in its place as an interesting theory from a historical point of view and instead focus on modern empirical incarnations such as attachment theory.

Review Questions

1. What were the results of the Brumbaugh and Fraley (2006) study where participants rated personal ads that resembled a past romantic relationship? How would Freud explain these results? How would attachment theory explain these results?

2. Why does Drew Westen compare Freud to Elvis Presley? Is Freud dead?

3. What are instincts? What two categories of instincts did Freud posit? What is libido?

4. What techniques are used to uncover the unconscious? What are parapraxes? What are symbolic behaviors?

5. How did Carl Jung use the word association test to study unconscious processes? What did he find? What technique is a modern-day equivalent of the word association test?

6. What three parts make up the personality? At what three levels do these parts function?

7. What is primary process thinking? What is the pleasure principle? In what two ways does the id seek gratification?

8. What is identification? What is the reality principle? What is secondary process thinking?

9. What are the two parts of the superego?

10. What are the three kinds of anxiety? How does the ego cope with anxiety? Which defense mechanisms have the strongest research support? Which ones have mixed support? Which ones have no support?

11. What are the psychosexual stages of development? What is a fixation? In what two ways is a fixation expressed? How does a fixation affect adult personality?

12. What is the Oedipus complex? How do boys and girls resolve this complex? What do the male and female adult fixations at this stage look like? What is the seduction theory? What is the evidence for Freud's psychosexual stages of development?

13. What is the case study method? What are some pros and cons of the case study method? How does Freud's case of Little Hans illustrate these pros and cons?

14. What five postulates define contemporary psychoanalytic theory?

15. What is attachment? What is an internal working model? What two sets of internal working models do we develop as a result of our early attachment experiences?

16. What is the Strange Situation? What are the four attachment patterns seen in the Strange Situation?

17. Do early attachment patterns stay with us for life? Are attachment patterns similar across generations?

18. What is the relationship between attachment style and adult expectations of romantic relationships? What impact does divorce have on attachment? How do adults respond to a separation from their loved one? Do adult attachment styles predict work behavior?

Key Terms

Transference
Instincts
Eros
Thanatos
Libido
Free association
Dream analysis
Manifest content
Latent content
Parapraxes
Freudian slip
Symbolic behaviors
Word association method
Complex
Schema
Implicit Association Test
 (IAT)
Structural model of
 personality
Primary process thinking
Pleasure principle
Reflex action
Wish fulfillment
Identification

Reality principle
Secondary process thinking
Conscience
Ego ideal
Topographic model of
 personality
Motivated unconscious
Cognitive unconscious
Conversion reaction
Defense mechanism
Reaction formation
Isolation
Intellectualization
Denial
Undoing
Projection
Displacement
Catharsis
Sublimation
Suppression
Repression
Rationalization
Psychosexual stages
Erogenous zone

Fixation
Oral incorporative
 personality
Oral sadistic personality
Anal expulsive personality
Anal retentive personality
Oedipus complex
Castration anxiety
Phallic character
Penis envy
Hysterical character
Case study method
Internal working models
Strange Situation
Secure attachment
Secure base
Safe haven
Avoidant attachment
Anxious-ambivalent
 attachment
Disorganized/disoriented
Adult attachment interview
 (AAI)
Fully functioning

9 REGULATION AND MOTIVATION: SELF-DETERMINATION THEORY

Read the **Chapter** on
mysearchlab.com

> "When we are motivated by goals that have deep meaning, by dreams that need completion, by pure love that needs expressing, then we truly live life."
>
> *Greg Anderson, American athlete and trainer*

When I was in my first year of college, students in the Psychology 101 class (some 500 of them) were required to do a special project: pick a behavior of their own to modify. Although my friends chose to quit smoking or apply their acne medications more regularly, I decided to increase my violin-playing, something that I had, regrettably, let lapse since starting college.

My university had a number of practice rooms in the basement of the student center. Students could sign out a room and pick up and return the key at the front desk, which also happened to be where they sold candy by the pound. For every half hour of practicing I did, I would buy a small bag of M&Ms as my reward. Given that the reward followed directly after the desired behavior (practicing), and was something I really liked (chocolate), I thought my plan was foolproof.

Sure enough, I started practicing regularly and was able to revisit pieces I had mastered in high school. I was enjoying rediscovering the violin so much that one day, after about a week or so of this training, I was halfway back to my residence hall before I realized—with horror thinking that I would fail the assignment—that I forgot to give myself the reward. *And that I had forgotten to reward myself for the past few days!* And yet, the behavior persisted in the absence of the reward. I was certain that I would fail the assignment because of this anomaly. However, when I received my grade, I was pleased to find that I had actually discovered the right answer: There's more to motivation than rewards and punishments. And in some cases the intrinsic reward of mastery can be more effective that the extrinsic reward of candy—even chocolate!

According to the **self-determination theory** of Edward Deci and Richard Ryan, there is a big difference between engaging in an activity because of extrinsic reasons and engaging in the same activity for intrinsic reasons (Deci & Ryan, 1985b; Ryan & Deci, 2000). When we are **extrinsically motivated**, acting because of some external pressures like rewards (M&Ms) or punishments (failing an assignment), we may not enjoy the activity as much, perform our best, or continue the behavior on our own. However, when we are **intrinsically motivated** acting out of our own desires and by our own choice doing things that are fun or satisfying to us (making music), we enjoy what we are doing and increase our well-being in the process. According to self-determination theory, the reasons *why* we do something are often more important than what we do.

Consider the following experiment (Vansteenkiste, Simons, Soenens, & Lens, 2004). Students in a high school physical education class participated in a unit on Tae Bo, which combines the martial arts movements of Tae Kwon Do with the speed and rhythm of boxing. The students, in Grades 10 to 12, were randomly assigned to conditions that varied in whether the instructor emphasized an intrinsic or extrinsic goal for the activity and whether he communicated these goals in a supportive or a controlling manner.

SEE FOR YOURSELF

Is there some behavior you wish you engaged in more regularly like studying, exercising, or practicing an instrument or a hobby?

SEE FOR YOURSELF

What kinds of activities do you engage in just for the fun of it?

Doing a little Tae Bo for intrinsic reasons with a supportive instructor leads to greater motivation than doing it for extrinsic reasons or with a controlling instructor.

For example, the instructor who introduced students to the Tae Bo unit emphasized intrinsic goals by telling the students that "Doing a little Tae Bo helps you to remain physically fit and prevents you from becoming sick at a later age." In other classes, he emphasized extrinsic goals by saying "Doing a little Tae Bo helps you to remain physically appealing to others and prevents you from gaining weight at a later age."

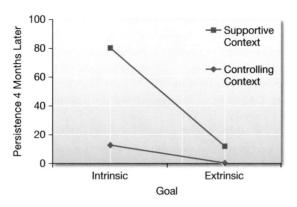

Figure 9.1 Students who learned Tae Bo in a supportive context and with an intrinsic goal were more willing to demonstrate their skills 4 months later. *Source:* Based on means reported by Vansteenkiste et al. (2004).

At the same time, in the supportive conditions, the instructor demonstrated various exercises to students while emphasizing that students had the option of trying the Tae Bo exercises by using phrases such as "we ask you to," "you can," or "you might" during the class. In the controlling conditions the instructor used phrases such as "you are obligated," "you should," or "you have to" to emphasize that the students had little choice about whether they would participate in the exercises.

After this introduction, a certified Tae Bo instructor entered the room and, unaware of which conditions the students were in or that they were even part of an experiment, proceeded to teach exercises and practice with the students for the next two classes.

What impact did goal and context have on students' motivation and performance? Quite a big one! Students with an intrinsic goal for learning Tae Bo put in greater effort during classes than students with an extrinsic goal. They also performed the exercises better when tested a few days after learning the exercises. Also, students in the supportive context put in greater effort and performed better than students in the controlling context.

The impact of goal and context was even greater on persistence (see Figure 9.1). To test the students' willingness to engage in Tae Bo even after the unit had ended they were asked if they would be willing to demonstrate some Tae Bo exercises in another class. The request came 1 week later, 1 month later, and 4 months after the Tae Bo unit ended. Although students in the supportive context and students with an intrinsic goal persisted longer than students in the controlling context or students with an extrinsic goal, students who had *both* a supportive context and an intrinsic goal for learning Tae Bo showed the greatest persistence of all 4 months later. They were even more likely to join the school's official Tae Bo club!

These results illustrate two important predictions of self-determination theory. First, the reasons *why* we do something—intrinsic or extrinsic reasons, for example—are important for effort, performance, and task persistence. Second, the *way* another person communicates his or her expectations and instructions to us also has a big impact on our effort, performance, and task persistence. Given that we are surrounded by people who wish to impart their expectations on us—such as health care professionals, parents, bosses, and teachers—and the fact that we are likely to be in these very same positions imparting our expectations on others, self-determination theory has a lot to say about motivation and performance.

In this chapter we will learn about self-determination theory and how people vary in how self-determined they feel. We will also consider aspects of the situation that can help people feel motivated and happily engaged in their activities at work and play rather than unmotivated, disengaged, and depressed. Then we will apply this theory to understand health behaviors (like following the doctor's orders, staying healthy), sports behaviors, work behaviors, and the pursuit of happiness.

SEE FOR YOURSELF

How might parents, teachers, or bosses communicate their expectations to you in a way that would be more supportive and less controlling?

Three Fundamental Psychological Needs

Self-determination theory is grounded in the **humanistic tradition** which emphasizes responsibility, growth, and the actualizing tendency (Deci, 1980; Deci & Ryan, 1985b). It views the

THINK ABOUT IT

How does the humanistic tradition compare to the behavioristic tradition with its emphasis on the reinforcement of behavior?

SEE FOR YOURSELF

What was the worst class you've ever been in? Why?

SEE FOR YOURSELF

What was the best class you've ever been in? Why?

individual as an active organism seeking the best way, not merely to survive, but also to grow and develop. Carl Rogers (1951) called this the **actualizing tendency:** the motive to actualize or bring about growth and positive change. Think of a wild flower that is so destined to grow that it blossoms even in a sidewalk crack. Of course, not all environments support the growth of an individual—flower or human—but according to the humanistic tradition, when people are not being pushed around by the environment they have the ability to find what they need for growth.

In addition to the physiological needs of food, water, and air, people have inborn psychological needs that must be met to survive and thrive. According to self-determination theory, there are three basic and universal psychological needs: **autonomy, competence,** and **relatedness** (Deci & Ryan, 1985b; Ryan & Deci, 2000). In fact, of all the psychological needs that have been studied by psychologists such as Henry Murray (1938) and Abraham Maslow (1954)—including self-actualization (Maslow, 1954), security, money, influence, popularity, health, self-esteem, self-respect, and pleasure—the three needs of autonomy, competence, and relatedness appear to be the most important (Sheldon, Elliot, Kim, & Kasser, 2001). Further, these needs are important for *all* people in a wide range of cultures studied, regardless of whether they were born and raised in a collectivistic or individualistic culture with traditional or egalitarian values (Deci & Ryan, 2008b; Sheldon et al., 2001).

First, individuals must feel that they can freely choose what to pursue, instead of being pushed around, forced to do things, or burdened with a lot of *have to*s, *shoulds,* or *musts* from the people or situations around them or even from themselves. This is the need for autonomy. Autonomy is feeling free and able to make choices about one's actions, being self-regulating and able to determine one's own actions and plans, as opposed to feeling like a pawn at the mercy of others or fate (Deci & Ryan, 1985b).

Second, individuals also need to feel competent at their pursuits, achieving mastery at tasks that are neither too easy nor too hard for them. This is the need for competence. Competence is feeling effective in one's actions and having the opportunities and experiences to exercise, expand, and express one's abilities (Deci & Ryan, 1985b).

Finally, individuals also need to feel they have meaningful relationships with people around them, like peers or supervisors. This is the need for relatedness. Relatedness is feeling connected to others, having people to care for, and to receive care from (Ryan & Deci, 2000). Relatedness can also come from feeling a sense of belonging within a community like a school, a work organization, a club, or a town (Reis & Patrick, 1996).

When these three needs of autonomy, competence, and relatedness are met, people will feel motivated and will happily participate in some activity—that is, they will feel intrinsically motivated, perform well, and, as a result, build skills and increase their well-being (Ryan & Deci, 2000). These three basic psychological needs are universal and essential for healthy development. Everybody requires these psychological nutriments whether they are explicitly aware of them or not (Ryan & Deci, 2008a).

To illustrate these three needs, think back to one of the worst classes you've ever encountered either in high school or in college. When I ask my students

Humans, like all living things, seek out conditions in which they can survive and grow to their full capabilities. Self-determination theory describes the conditions that foster motivation and well-being.

this question, they often describe experiences where they felt that one of their needs was not being adequately met, although they didn't think of it in these terms at the time. For example, students often have a bad experience in a class that is too difficult for them or in which they are totally bored. A sense of competence is missing in both of these situations. Students often dislike classes where there are a lot of required readings or heavily structured assignments where they have little choice about what to do and how to do it. These are examples of classes where autonomy is sorely lacking. Finally, students sometimes say that they didn't get along with a teacher who might have been uncaring, cold, or disrespectful. Other students will explain that they just didn't enjoy being in a class where they didn't have an opportunity to get to know the other students very well. These are examples of where relatedness is lacking.

By the same token, imagine a class that you really enjoyed. Was it because you worked hard but saw that hard work pay off as you mastered the material? Was it because the teacher gave a lot of freedom to students and encouraged creativity in the completion of assignments? Or was it because you had a strong group of friends suffering with you or a teacher who went out of his or her way to reach you? In these cases, classes that met your needs for competence, autonomy, and relatedness may have increased your motivation, learning, and well-being. In fact, I bet you can imagine a class or a work situation in which you felt incompetent, pushed around, and yet you got through it due to a bunch of dedicated friends sharing the experience with you!

How Do We Satisfy These Needs?

Just like flowers need soil and water provided by the environment to grow and thrive, people need to get their needs met by the context or situation in which they find themselves. People must balance their internal needs for autonomy, competence, and relatedness with the nutriments provided by external environments (Ryan & Deci, 2008a). Certain aspects of the environment can foster the fulfillment of the three needs (see Table 9.1).

"He cultivates rare orchids. And people."

The chair of a small psychology department talking about a clinical psychologist on staff.

Table 9.1 How to Foster the Three Psychological Needs

Need	Provided By	In These Ways
Autonomy	Autonomy support	Recognize individual's unique perspective Give choices where possible Use minimal pressure Encourage initiative Link to the individual's goals, values Support individual's choice Help the individual live with the consequences of the choices at a level he or she can cope with
Competence	Structure	Clear expectations Clear contingencies Feedback provided Break task into smaller, manageable pieces
	Optimal challenge	Task not too hard Task not too easy
Relatedness	Involvement	Time Interest Energy

Source: Connell and Wellborn (1990).

"It is our choices, Harry, that show us what we truly are, far more than our abilities."
Professor Dumbledore as cited in Rowling (1999, p. 333)

Fostering Autonomy: Autonomy Support

For persons to satisfy their need for autonomy they must feel they can act out of their own volition (i.e., from their own wishes, preferences, and desires). For example, parents, teachers, coaches, therapists, work supervisors, and even our close friends can help us make our own choices and develop our own way of doing things, or they can attempt to control and pressure us into doing or thinking as they want us to. Strategies that help individuals develop and express their own self are autonomy supportive; the opposite of autonomy support is control. Ideally, parents, teachers, coaches, therapists, work supervisors, friends, and partners will have our own best interests at heart and wish to help us develop our own autonomy. However, this may not always be the case, like at certain jobs for example, or when parents must set limits to help teach or protect a child from harm. Even under these conditions, there are ways of being autonomy supportive without being pressuring, authoritarian, and directive or resorting to controlling and punitive methods.

One way to support autonomy is by providing choice (Connell, 1990). For example, a parent will have better luck getting a toddler to eat vegetables by asking: "Would you like peas or carrots?" than by saying "Eat your vegetables." Recall that this is how the instructor in the Vansteenkiste et al. (2004) experiment introduced Tae Bo in the supportive condition. Similarly, a parent or a teacher can support the autonomy of a child by using the minimal amount of pressure necessary to gain the child's compliance instead of immediately using threats to get the child to obey. When a friend of mine visited the doctor for swollen feet the doctor didn't come right out and tell him to lose weight; instead he was sort of blasé and said something like "I find that my patients have the most difficulty in losing weight," implying that it would be nice if my friend lost weight but that the doctor wasn't going to pressure him into it or make him feel bad for not doing it.

Another way that a person can support another's autonomy is by encouraging initiative—that is, to give people a chance to decide for themselves what they would like to do or how they would like to do it without fearing repercussions for choosing poorly (Connell, 1990). Autonomy cannot be developed if a person is hesitant or fearful to make any choice whatsoever. Children learn to regulate and control their own behavior by making choices on trivial matters, like choosing what to wear as a toddler, and then gradually learning how to make bigger decisions, like choosing their own friends and activities as teenagers.

To do this, parents, teachers, supervisors, therapists, or doctors need to support their child's, worker's, or patient's, choice, even if they disagree with it (Connell, 1990). For example, students are often required to write a paper, but most of the time professors allow students to choose their own topics—even if it is a topic the professor has already read a hundred papers on! Good professors may limit topics or preapprove topics to make sure that all students work on a fruitful topic; bad professors may limit topics to only the ones they do research on. Making the choice of what topic to write on helps build a sense of autonomy in students.

At the same time, parents and teachers should then stand by to help their children or students live with the consequences of these decisions—after all, that's how we learn—but at a level the child or student can cope with (Connell, 1990). A psychology professor I knew would take his children with him to run errands on Saturdays. When they were finished, they would visit the local candy shop where the children could choose any kind of candy they wanted as a treat. The only catch was that the children couldn't cry or make a fuss if they didn't like what they picked (the store had a strict no-return policy on the beautiful handmade candies

Giving children choices over some behaviors, even if parents may not agree with those choices, helps children build a sense of autonomy. This girl is well on her way to developing autonomy, if not her fashion sense.

displayed in cases throughout the shop). Most of the time their choices worked out, but occasionally they ended up with something they didn't like. Their father, an expert in motivation, would say something like "Oh, those are your mom's favorites! Go see if she has something she'd be willing to swap with you for those." By this seemingly small treat, his two children learned to make decisions, try new things, take responsibility, and to live with their decisions. In short, he helped them develop autonomy in an age-appropriate way by applying these principles of autonomy support.

Even when it is not possible to give others choice and control, there are things that people can say to help the individual retain some sense of autonomy. For example, recognizing and respecting the individual's point of view and feelings about the matter or helping individuals see how their actions relate to their personal goals, beliefs, or values, goes a long way toward helping people regulate their own behavior and stave off helplessness (Connell, 1990). For example an advisor might say: "I know you're not happy about having to study for the LSATs while everybody else is out enjoying the nice weather. But it's only for a few more weeks, and besides, you want to get into a good law school so you can become a lawyer. It will all be worth it in the end."

Using these principles, researchers were even able to get kids to paint neatly. First and second graders were asked to draw a picture of a house they would like to live in using watercolors and paper neatly laid out in front of them in the experimental room (Koestner, Ryan, Bernieri, & Holt, 1984). Children were randomly assigned to one of three conditions in which an adult explained the rules to them. Children in the controlling limits condition were told "Before you begin, I want to tell you some things that you will have to do. There are rules that we have about painting. You have to keep the paints clean . . . . I want you to be a good boy (girl) and don't make a mess with the paints." Children in the autonomy supportive limits condition were told "I know that sometimes it's really fun to just slop the paint around, but here the materials and room need to be kept nice for the other children who will use them." There was also a control group that were given no limits on how they were to paint.

After this painting activity, the children were given the opportunity to continue to paint or to switch to another activity while the experimenter was out of the room for a few minutes. During this time, an assistant, unaware of which condition the child was in, surreptitiously monitored the child's activity. The experimenters wanted to know how the differing instructions would affect the child's intrinsic motivation, as measured by their choice to continue to paint or not. They also wanted to know if setting limits affected the children's creativity and enjoyment of painting.

The children in all three groups did as they were told and did not make a mess with the paints. However, that was not the big news: Children in the autonomy supportive limits condition actually had greater enjoyment of painting and more artistic and creative paintings than children in the controlling limits condition (see Figure 9.2). Specifically, their paintings were higher in creativity, technical merit, overall quality, the number of colors used, and the level of detail. Further, the autonomy supportive limits condition and the no limits condition were not significantly different from each other on these variables. Even more amazing is that these differences between groups carried over into the free choice period where children in the no limits and autonomy supportive limits conditions painted longer than children in the controlling limits condition (see Figure 9.3). These results suggest that limits can be communicated to children without undermining their autonomy, in a way that increases their motivation and the quality of their performance.

THINK ABOUT IT

Which is better: to tell a child "It's your bedtime now" or "Your bedtime is in 5 minutes"? Why?

Limits and rules need not undermine intrinsic motivation if they are communicated in an autonomy-supportive way.

Figure 9.2 Overall quality of children's paintings as a function of condition. *ns* = not a significant difference between these groups; other comparisons are significant *Source:* Koestner et al. (1984).

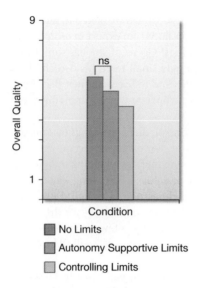

Fostering Competence: Structure and Optimal Challenge

To build competence, people need tasks that are aimed at the right level—not too easy, not too hard—with steps that are clear and doable. Specifically, people need to know exactly how to carry out a task and what the results of their actions will be. For example, if you are learning how to edit a document on the computer for the first time, it might be helpful to know that if you right-click on the mouse a menu will appear. People also need to know what is expected of them (e.g., "You need to choose *copy* from the menu") and they need to get immediate feedback from the task ("Uh oh, *cut* is highlighted, where's *copy?*") or from another person so that they can learn the correct way to do a task ("*cut* is just above *copy*"). Large or difficult tasks need to be broken down into smaller steps, the way a basketball coach might institute drills to work on skills like passing, shooting, and dribbling, with the ultimate goal of winning a game. By attempting a task that is at the right level, where the steps necessary to carry out the task are clear and doable, and where there is immediate feedback, people learn very quickly how to master a task, building their sense of competence (Connell, 1990).

You can see this in action by coaches in how they train their players, by parents who set up household chores for their children (little kids set the table; bigger kids load the dishwasher), by work supervisors ("10 sales calls is a great goal for today"), and even in many computer games. Amazingly enough, this kind of structure is built into the Wii Fit game system. First, as part of the initial setup, the system calibrates an appropriate fitness level based on a player's age and weight. This ensures that people are working toward a fitness goal that is neither too easy nor too hard for them. Then, as players start a game, the screen gives visual feedback to let players know exactly how they are doing.

For example, in one activity that trains players to control their balance on a board, the screen shows two columns visually indicating how much weight they have placed on each leg. Users must match their weight distribution to some standard set by the computer, leaning left or right to get the two columns to line up a certain way. In the early trials, players don't have to be too exact to hit the standard. But as the game progresses, the computer demands that players get more and more precise in their movements. That is, the game trains players by successive approximation to become better at controlling their movements and balance. Of course, during the entire process players get both the visual feedback on the screen and a host of happy sounds when they achieve the goal ("Yay!") or sad sounds when they don't ("Awww!"). These features help players master physical activities like balance, agility, and coordination, and presumably increase their fitness level in the process.

An important part of satisfying the need for competence is working on tasks that are **optimally challenging** (Connell, 1990; Csikszentmihalyi, 1975; Deci, 1975). Tasks that are too difficult, where the demand outpaces the person's skills, may cause the person to feel frustrated and then worried and anxious. Tasks that are too easy may cause relaxation and then boredom. Engagement in tasks that have a clear set of goals, that require appropriate responses, give immediate feedback, and in which people are operating at their maximum capacity can lead to a positive state called **flow** (Csikszentmihalyi, 1975, 1997; see Figure 9.4).

Figure 9.3 Time spent painting during the free choice period as a function of condition. *ns* = not a significant difference between these groups; other comparisons are significant *Source:* Koestner et al. (1984).

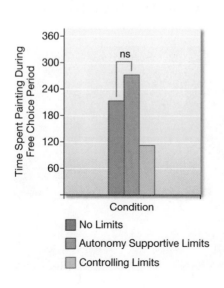

People can develop competence at an activity when expectations are made clear, contingencies between behavior and outcomes are explained, tasks are broken down into manageable pieces, and feedback is given, even if all of this is provided by a computer game.

Flow is an experience marked by complete absorption, deep enjoyment, intense concentration, and almost an altered state, as people block out all irrelevant stimuli and focus entirely on the task at hand (Csikszentmihalyi, 1975, 1997). Athletes call this being in the zone; religious mystics call it ecstasy (Csikszentmihalyi, 1997). Think of an artist who persists single-mindedly on a painting, ignoring hunger and fatigue (Getzels & Csikszentmihalyi, 1976). When in a state of flow, people have no sense of time, reporting that minutes seem to pass in mere moments.

Flow experiences are especially likely to happen when people are engaged in creative activities, music, sports, games, and religious rituals. A composer explained how it felt when his music writing was going well:

> *You are in an ecstatic state to such a point that you feel as though you almost don't exist. I have experienced this time and time again. My hand seems devoid*

SEE FOR YOURSELF

Have you ever experienced flow? When?

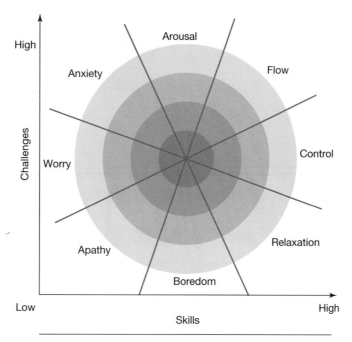

Figure 9.4 Tasks that are optimally challenging lead to a state called flow. Intensity of experience increases with distance from a person's average levels of challenge and skill, as shown by the concentric rings. *Source:* From Nakamura and Csikszentmihalyi (2009, Figure 18.2, p. 201). Nakamura, J., & Csikszentmihalyi, M. (2009). Flow theory and research. In S. J. Lopez & C. R. Snyder (Eds.), Oxford handbook of positive psychology research (p. 195–206). Oxford, UK: Oxford University Press.

of myself, and I have nothing to do with what is happening. I just sit there watching in a state of awe and wonderment. And the music just flows out by itself. (Csikszentmihalyi, 1975, p. 4)

Even just immersing oneself in everyday activities that are highly meaningful and which demand the right balance of challenge and skill can produce flow. Flow states are by no means the only way that a person can have their need for competence met, but they certainly are a powerful means of feeling competence, which together with autonomy, fosters motivation and engagement (Shernoff, Csikszentmihalyi, Schneider, & Shernoff, 2003). Tasks that are just a bit beyond a person's skill level, personally meaningful, highly enjoyable, engrossing, or worth doing for their own sake, lead to the greatest amount of intrinsic motivation and positive emotion.

Fostering Relatedness: Involvement

Autonomy support and task structure both occur within a relationship, whether it be patient–doctor, teacher–student, parent–child, boss–worker, therapist–client, partner-to-partner, or friend-to-friend. The quality of these relationships can increase the likelihood that autonomy and competence needs will be met. People feel related or connected to others through involvement: the interest shown in them and their concerns, the time a person spends with them, and the energy that others invest in them (Connell, 1990; Grolnick & Ryan, 1987, 1989). For example, you may recall a teacher or coach who spent extra time with you or who took a special interest in your progress. Or perhaps a parent or grandparent helped you with a school project or shared their expertise with you, like teaching you to cook or fish. These efforts made you feel connected and made it easier for you to feel motivated.

One experiment's failed attempt at a control condition inadvertently demonstrated the importance of relatedness. In this experiment, 4- to 5-year-old children played with colorful markers under various reward conditions (Anderson, Manoogian, & Reznick, 1976). In the control condition, where the child merely drew in the presence of a neutral experimenter, both the child and the experimenter found it awkward and unsettling to *not* interact with each other. Even as the experimenter didn't make eye contact with the child, attend to his or her drawings, and ignored the child's overtures, children persisted at getting the attention of the experimenter. Compared to the reward conditions, children in this control condition showed the lowest intrinsic interest of all conditions, when their motivation to draw with the markers was assessed a week later.

Part of what makes teachers autonomy-supportive is that they establish a warm, supportive relationship with their students (Reeve & Jang, 2006). Autonomy-supportive teachers spend time listening to students, give students time to talk, and take the students' perspective. These behaviors establish a sense of warmth, affection, and acceptance of students, fostering relatedness. In contrast, controlling teachers seem to ignore the teacher–student relationship altogether and focus on correct answers and desired classroom behaviors instead (Reeve & Jang, 2006). Autonomy-supportive teachers show a sensitivity and attunement to

Relatedness, along with competence and autonomy, is important for the motivation and engagement of college students.

> **THINK ABOUT IT**
>
> Is there something unique about parental attachments or can attachments to any adult meet a child's need for relatedness?

The Personality of Everyday Life

Relatedness in college students

Early research on students' motivation for attending college focused on feelings of competence and autonomy, ignoring relatedness (Vallerand & Bissonnette, 1992). But for college students of color, relatedness to family, peers, and professors is especially important for their motivation and engagement. Students of color who perceive their campuses as hostile and unfriendly—indicating a lack of relatedness—are at risk for performing poorly in college and eventually dropping out (Smedley, Myers, & Harrell, 1993).

To study the relatedness of college students, researchers developed the Need for Relatedness at College Questionnaire (NRC-Q) to measure connectedness with friends and family back home, and faculty, staff, and peers at college (Guiffrida, Gouveia, Wall, & Seward, 2008; see Table 9.2).

Using this questionnaire, researchers discovered that relatedness was an important source of motivation for *all* college students regardless of their cultural background. Students were engaged in college for the relationships they hoped to develop (e.g., with friends), the teaching they looked forward to receiving (e.g., with professors), and the love and support of their family and friends back home. Researchers also found that friends and family back home could provide both intrinsic reasons (e.g., to give back to people who have supported and helped you) and extrinsic reasons (e.g., to keep up with others around you) for attending college. Intrinsic reasons, along with relatedness to peers and relatedness to faculty and staff, lessened a student's intention to drop out of school. Extrinsic reasons were not related to a student's intention to drop out of college.

These results highlight the predictions of self-determination theory that relatedness is an important but often overlooked variable in predicting motivation and engagement. Whether we are talking about students attending college or children in a classroom, involvement of parents, teachers, and peers can help fulfill a person's need for relatedness.

Table 9.2 The Need for Relatedness at College Questionnaire (NRC-Q)

I go to college …

How well does each statement reflect your reasons for attending college? Rate each statement on a 1 (*Does not correspond at all*) to 7 (*Corresponds exactly*) scale.

Relatedness with peers at college (*M* = 11.03):

12. To make new friends
2. To meet friends who can relate to me and around whom I am comfortable
9. To become a member of an interesting and fun student organization

Relatedness with family and friends from home (helping them, making them proud, giving back to them) (*M* = 13.12):

1. To give back to my family
11. To be able to help my family
4. Because I want to make my family and friends from home proud of me

Relatedness with faculty and staff (*M* = 10.96):

5. Because I am interested in connecting with faculty who have expertise in my areas of interest
7. To get to know faculty and staff whom I can learn from and feel comfortable around
3. To connect with a mentor who will support me and look out for me

Relatedness with family and friends from home (to keep up with them) (*M* = 7.51):

10. To keep up with family members or friends from home
6. To relate to my friends from home who have gone to college
8. To help me talk to my friends or family members

Note: Responses are summed for each subscale. Average score for a group of college students on each of the subscales is given in parentheses. Numbers refer to the order of the items as presented on the original questionnaire.

Source: Adapted from Guiffrida et al. (2008, Appendix, p. 261). Guiffrida, D., Gouveia, A., Wall, A., & Seward, D. (2008). Development and validation of the need for relatedness at college questionnaire (NRC-Q). *Journal of Diversity in Higher Education*, 1(4), 251–261. Copyright American Psychological Association. Adapted with permission.

students by sensing the cognitive and emotional states of their students and adjusting their instruction accordingly.

Then and Now: Undermining Intrinsic Interest

Is rewarding kids for getting good grades a good thing? In the Philadelphia area at the end of the 2009–2010 school year kids could cash in on their As to get pizza, ice cream, fast food, and even trading cards at some national chains, including Pizza Hut (Buckman, 2010). And that doesn't even count the summer reading programs at local libraries that also promise kids rewards for reading on their own!

We can all agree that diligent work and reading skills are important for kids, but what if these extrinsic rewards inadvertently prevented kids from developing a lifelong love of reading for its own sake? Just what is the effect of extrinsic factors like rewards, and also external controls like deadlines, imposed goals, competition, surveillance, and evaluations, on intrinsic motivation (Ryan & Deci, 2008a)?

This question of the impact of extrinsic rewards on intrinsic behavior has a long history in social psychology, and in fact was the inspiration behind self-determination theory (Deci, 1971; Ryan & Deci, 2008a). One of the earliest experiments was a landmark study rewarding nursery school children for drawing with markers (Lepper, Greene, & Nisbett, 1973).

Researchers selected children who had shown an interest in drawing with markers to take part in an experiment on children's drawing. Children came to the laboratory, one at a time, and were randomly assigned to one of three conditions. In the *expected reward* condition, children were told that they would earn "A Good Player Award" for drawing. In the *unexpected reward* condition, children received the same "Good Player Award" but only *after* they drew with the markers. This condition tested whether merely getting a reward lowers intrinsic interest or if explicitly contracting for the reward lowers interest. In a third *no reward* (control) condition, children drew with the markers but did not hear about nor receive an award.

All the children drew with the markers, received their awards (if they were in the expected or unexpected conditions), and returned to their regular classrooms. Then, after about a week or so, markers appeared in the children's regular classrooms and the children were observed from behind a one-way mirror. The experimenters recorded how much of their free play time the children spent drawing with the markers.

Despite what a behaviorist might predict—that rewards will increase the desired behavior—rewards actually had the *opposite* effect! Not only were the drawings made by the children in the expected reward condition during the experiment rated by judges as inferior, but the children also played with the markers *less* when back in their regular classrooms and the experiment was over than children in the unexpected reward and no reward conditions (see Figure 9.5).

This effect is called the undermining of intrinsic interest or the **overjustification effect**. When intrinsic interest in an activity is already high, like drawing was for these children, if extrinsic factors are made more salient, by giving a reward, for example, then people will discount their own intrinsic reasons for doing the behavior. It's as if they say to themselves, "This must be one of those times when people have to make me to do something that's not very fun to begin with." As a result, people come to see the activity as the means to some end and cease to view the activity as desirable in itself. Both cognitive dissonance theory (Festinger, 1957) and self-perception theory (Bem, 1967, 1972) support this logic.

In the almost 40 years since this work was done, over 128 well-controlled experiments have tested the effect of extrinsic rewards on intrinsic interest. According to a meta-analysis the results are clear and consistent: tangible rewards—including anything from money to marshmallows—undermine the intrinsic interest of participants, both children and college students (Deci, Koestner, & Ryan, 1999). In particular, rewards that are given explicitly for reaching a level of performance or for finishing a task are more likely to have an adverse effect than rewards that do not require engaging in a specific task or which are not contingent on completion, quality of output, or reaching

> **THINK ABOUT IT**
>
> What kinds of activities do people get paid for doing? Are they generally fun to begin with?

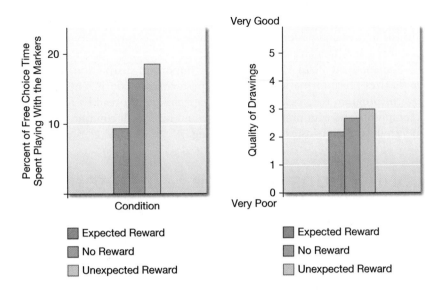

Figure 9.5 Judges' ratings of drawing quality during the experiment and percentage of free play time spent drawing with the markers after the experiment as a function of reward condition. *Source:* Lepper et al. (1973). Quality was rated on a 1 to 5 scale.

some standard of excellence (Deci et al., 1999, but see also Eisenberger, Pierce, & Cameron, 1999, for a dissenting view).

The key to predicting when rewards or threats of punishments will have negative effects on motivation and performance is to realize that external motivators can convey two meanings: control and information (Ryan & Deci, 2008a). The controlling aspect of an extrinsic factor suggests that the behavior is under external control ("You are doing the activity because I am giving you this reward"), essentially thwarting people's satisfaction of the need for autonomy. The informational aspect provides feedback about people's performance on the task ("One more and you'll have 10!") so that they can adjust their behavior and thereby satisfy their need for competence. A reward that is experienced as controlling ("Excellent! You should keep up the good work.") will rob a person of auton-omy and undermine intrinsic interest. But a reward that is experienced as informational ("Excellent! You're doing great.") will increase feelings of competence and not undermine intrinsic interest.

So it is not the reward per se that is good or bad, but how the reward is communicated and interpreted that determines whether the control or the information aspect will be more salient with the ultimate impact on motivation and performance. External motivators such

> **THINK ABOUT IT**
>
> What meanings does the phrase "I am proud of you" convey?

> **THINK ABOUT IT**
>
> What meanings does the phrase "See, I knew you could do it" convey?

> What is the impact of rewarding people for getting good grades?

THINK ABOUT IT

What could you say to somebody to praise him or her without undermining the person's intrinsic motivation?

as deadlines, imposed goals, competition, surveillance, and evaluations may also undermine intrinsic interest and performance if they are used to control (robbing autonomy) instead of for information (to increase competence).

Somebody at Pizza Hut grasped this important distinction, for now their website emphasizes the informational and non-performance-contingent nature of the reading rewards program by proclaiming, "Motivate children to read by rewarding their reading accomplishments with praise, recognition, and fun!"—all conditions that are less likely to undermine their intrinsic interest in reading.

Connections Between Self-Determination Theory and Other Theories in Personality

If some aspects of self-determination theory sound familiar to you that's because the theory builds on and unites previous research in psychology. In particular, other theorists and researchers have recognized the importance of autonomy, competence, and relatedness. In this section, we highlight and clarify some of these connections.

Autonomy and Locus of Causality

People can differ in their beliefs about control (Rotter, 1966). Those with an internal locus of control believe they can influence what happens to them through their own efforts, behavior, or characteristics. Those with an external locus of control believe that what happens to them is due to chance, luck, fate, or other people. They believe that they have little control over what happens to them. **Locus of control** describes the connection between behavior and outcomes. The opposite of having control is feeling helpless (we discuss the importance of control beliefs in more depth in Chapter 10).

THINK ABOUT IT

What causes a person to feel guilty? Is that internal or external?

Autonomy describes the connection between choice and behavior; the extent to which people feel free to choose their own behaviors or follow their own interests. Personality psychologists refer to the connection between choice and behavior as **locus of causality** (DeCharms, 1981). As you can see, locus of causality (autonomy) is slightly different from locus of control. People may understand the contingency between their behavior and some outcome and are able to control their behaviors (locus of control), but they may not *want* to or feel free to engage in those behaviors (locus of causality).

The opposite of autonomy is compliance (including conformity to norms and obedience to a direct order) or defiance, both of which occur in direct response to the controlling actions of another (Patrick, Skinner, & Connell, 1993). Anytime a person gives in to external (e.g., rewards, punishments) or internal (e.g., guilt) pressures to behave in a certain way, he or she is behaving without autonomy.

Sadly, school, especially in the lower grades, is often structured to reward compliance instead of autonomy (Patrick et al., 1993). For example, have you ever been faced with the choice of writing what the teacher wanted rather than what you believed on an essay or a paper? In both cases—either writing what the teacher wants or writing what you believe—the behavior of writing is completely under your control. However, the feeling of pressure to just do what you are told and the lack of being able to act in a way that is truly and authentically yourself illustrates an external locus of causality as well as a lack of autonomy.

Competence and Self-Efficacy Theory

Feelings of competence are very similar to a sense of self-efficacy. **Self-efficacy** is the belief that one can be competent and effective at some activity (Bandura, 1977a, 1982, 2000b, 2001). There are two parts to self-efficacy beliefs (see Figure 9.6). First is the **outcome expectation**, the belief that behaving in a certain way will produce a certain outcome. Then there is the **efficacy expectation**, the belief that one is capable of acting in a certain way; that is, the expectation about whether a person will succeed or fail at performing the required action.

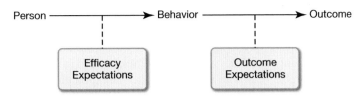

Figure 9.6 The two parts of self-efficacy: efficacy expectations and outcome expectations. *Source:* Lepper et al. (1973). Quality was rated on a 1 to 5 scale. Bandura, 1977, Figure 1, p. 193. Bandura, A. (1977a). Self-efficacy: Toward a unifying theory of behavioral change. *Psychological Review,* 84(2), 191–215. Copyright American Psychological Association. Reprinted with permission.

For example, imagine a person recovering from a back injury who is told that one way of preventing such injury is by strengthening her abdominal muscles. Her physical therapist tells her that if she does certain exercises every day she will get stronger. This describes how her behavior (exercising) will lead to an outcome (increased strength). Is this enough for her to be motivated to do her exercises? She may indeed hold this outcome expectation, but she also needs to hold an efficacy expectation and believe that she is capable of physically getting down on the ground to do the sit ups or whatever the exercise demands. According to self-efficacy theory, the efficacy expectation is more important than the outcome expectation. There are many situations where people know what they ought to do—or not to do—but feel incapable of actually doing it. Self-determination theory would call this a lack of perceived competence.

Knowing people's self-efficacy predicts how motivated they will be before and during an activity (Bandura, 1977). Self-efficacy determines which activities people are likely to engage in or avoid; how much effort they will put into that activity; whether they are likely to persist or give up, especially when the going gets tough; how well they perform; and what their emotional reactions might be before, during, and after the activity. Although self-efficacy theory predicts amount of motivation, it does not differentiate among types of motivation the way that self-determination theory does.

We develop our self-efficacy beliefs from four sources of information (Bandura, 1977, 1982). The most direct way is through personal experience. Successes build efficacy whereas failures decrease efficacy. Having a bad experience while skiing is likely to keep a person off the slopes for a long time and maybe even forever!

The second way is through the vicarious experience of watching another person enact the behavior and succeed or fail and then trying it ourselves. From observing others we can see what the task is all about so that we can anticipate what might happen when it is our turn. We also learn strategies to improve our own chances of succeeding. Have you ever witnessed a spectacular move of an athlete or dancer and thought that maybe you could do that? Or maybe, you've had the opposite experience of realizing that you could *never* do that! Then you've experienced how self-efficacy beliefs can be increased or decreased through observational learning and social modeling. Especially empowering are personal stories of people who have overcome difficulties in their lives through determination and effort (Bandura, 1977a).

Whee! Self-efficacy beliefs come from direct experience, watching others, persuasion, and our physical and emotional reactions while engaging in an activity.

THINK ABOUT IT

Can systematic desensiti-
zation or guided imagery
techniques decrease fear
and increase self-efficacy?
Why?

Self-efficacy beliefs can also develop or change through social persuasion. That is, friends, coaches, teachers, or therapists, for example, might be able to convince another person that he or she is capable of taking a desired action (e.g., Miserandino, 1998). Their persuasion often involves changing efficacy expectations ("Yes, you can call him up. Just take a deep breath and dial his number"), but can also involve outcome expectations ("Here's his number, what's stopping you?" "Keep your eye on the ball, not the other player!").

Finally, self-efficacy beliefs can come from physical and emotional states. According to self-efficacy theory, we read our own physical and emotional reactions and adjust our self-efficacy beliefs accordingly. Do you have a gut reaction to the thought of giving a speech in front of the class or to the memory of a scary amusement park ride? Activities or the thought of activities that make us sweat, tire us out, or cause aches and pains lower our self-efficacy and may prevent us from attempting an activity ("I'm getting dizzy just looking at that ride") or may cause us to stop the activity ("OK, three times on that roller coaster is enough"). Activities that energize us or occur in the absence of negative visceral reactions increase our self-efficacy and make us want to attempt the activity ("OK, I'll give it a shot.") or continue at it ("Hey, this isn't so bad. Let's go on it again!"). Tension, anxiety, and depression on many tasks, as well as feelings of fatigue and pain on tasks that require stamina and strength may be interpreted as signs of low self-efficacy (Bandura, 2000b).

Psychologists have used principles of self-efficacy theory to decrease people's fears of traveling by automobile, using elevators and escalators, climbing stairs to high levels, dining in restaurants, shopping in supermarkets, and entering public places (Bandura, Adams, Hardy, & Howells, 1980). In addition to treating phobias, self-efficacy theory has been used to help people recover from cardiac arrest (Bandura, 1982), to explain the effectiveness of groups (Bandura, 2000a), and the academic achievement and career choices of students (Bandura, Barbaranelli, Caprara, & Pastorelli, 2001).

Relatedness and Attachment Theory

Relatedness is very much like attachment, and in fact, self-determination theory builds on work in attachment theory. Recall from Chapter 8 that an attachment figure can be a secure base from which to explore the world and a safe haven to retreat to in times of stress (Bowlby, 1973; Shaver & Mikulincer, 2007). In the same spirit, self-determination theory recognizes the fundamental importance of this need to be connected or attached to, not just caregivers or partners, but to friends, coworkers, teammates, peers, and other people in our world. Feeling connected to others, along with autonomy and competence, gives us the motivation to engage with the world, persistence when the going gets tough, and increased well-being.

Research Methods Illustrated: Path Analysis

Research in self-determination theory often uses a statistical technique called **path analysis** to test how variables affect each other. Though the mathematics behind this technique are pretty complicated, the logic is fairly straightforward and builds on the logic of regression.

Generally, researchers have some idea of how they think variables are related and path analysis is a way of testing their hunches. In a path analysis, researchers use statistics to test their hypotheses about how variables relate to one another. Researchers then draw a **path diagram** visually showing the significant effects of the variables on each other. Variables can have a direct effect on another variable, an indirect effect on another variable, or no effect on another variable. Direct effects are generally identified by a solid line; indirect effects by a dotted line, and no effect by the absence of a line. The head of the arrow tells us the direction of the effect. Lines with double arrows indicate that two variables affect each other.

Each of the lines connecting variables represents the regression coefficient, which is how much the x variable is weighted when it is used to predict the next variable in the model. The higher the weight the greater the impact one variable has on the other. A weight can be positive, indicating that it causes an increase in the next variable, or negative, indicating that it causes a decrease in the next variable.

For each model researchers propose, they test (1) if the overall model accounts for a significant amount of variability in the data; (2) if the weights are significantly different from 0; and (3) if the effects are direct or indirect. Once these questions have been answered, researchers draw a path diagram of the results, with variables, lines, arrows, and significant weights identified.

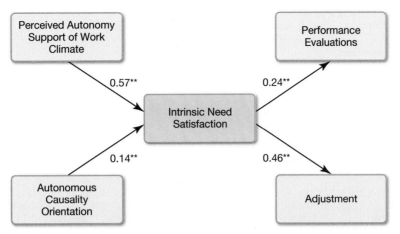

Figure 9.7 Path analysis of work performance and adjustment. *Source:* From Baard et al. (2004, Figure 1, p. 2061). Reprinted with permission from Baard, P. P., Deci, E. L., & Ryan, R. M. (2004), "Intrinsic need satisfaction: A motivational basis of performance and well-being in two work settings," *Journal of Applied Social Psychology*, 34, pp. 2045–2068. Permission conveyed through the Copyright Clearance Center.

Consider the path diagram shown in Figure 9.7. This comes from a study of 528 employees from a major U.S. investment banking firm (Baard, Deci, & Ryan, 2004). The researchers wanted to test predictions of self-determination theory in the workplace. This overall model was better than other models the researchers tested in explaining their results. For example, gender was not a significant predictor in the model, so it was not included in this path diagram. As you can see, all of the pathways are direct (the lines are solid), one way (arrow heads on one end only), and highly significant (starred weights).

This analysis suggests that workers' perceived supportiveness of their work environment had a direct impact on the satisfaction of their needs for autonomy, competence, and relatedness (measured in this study as one big variable called intrinsic need satisfaction). Also, approaching the world in an autonomous, intrinsically motivated way as opposed to being extrinsically motivated or feeling like the world pushes you around, also had a direct effect on workers' need satisfaction.

Further, having their needs met had a direct effect on workers' performance evaluations and adjustment. Because these two weights are positive, it means that having their needs met increased the quality of workers' performance and increased their psychological adjustment in the work environment (Baard et al., 2004). Workers whose needs were met by an autonomy supportive climate showed greater emotional stability and better health than workers whose needs were not being met. Notice that the arrow between need satisfaction and performance evaluations is one way, so we know that having good performance evaluations does not satisfy workers' needs for autonomy, competence, and relatedness. That is, need satisfaction is a cause, not a result, of high performance.

Now that you understand the basics of what path analysis is and how to interpret a path diagram, you can understand some of the fascinating research which has been done applying self-determination theory in various domains.

> **THINK ABOUT IT**
>
> Is it possible for good performance evaluations to increase personal adjustment at work? The researchers tested this hypothesis. What did they find?

What It Means to Be Self-Regulated

When faced with a task that is not particularly intrinsically interesting, say an assignment for school or work, what do you say to yourself to get yourself to do it? Do you give up and avoid thinking about it? Do you think of the dire consequences that could happen if you don't do it? Do you promise yourself a treat if you do it? Do you remind yourself of how this activity is related to important goals you hold, a strategy of providing autonomy support, as we saw earlier in the chapter? Or, does doing it come naturally to you, as an extension of who you are, so that doing it is really no big deal? Although the behavior may look identical to an outsider when done for *any* of these reasons the outcomes are radically different.

Motivation is best characterized on a continuum, ranging from extrinsic to intrinsic, varying in how much volition or autonomy a person feels they have (Ryan & Deci, 2000). There is even a kind of motivation called **amotivation** that is a state of having no motivation, where people are neither extrinsically nor intrinsically motivated, perhaps feeling apathetic or alienated. Being self-regulated means adjusting our own behaviors and attitudes somewhere along this continuum of motivation depending on the situation and the activity at hand (see Figure 9.8). Self-regulation embodies the

> **SEE FOR YOURSELF**
>
> Think of something you have to do this week. What do you tell yourself to get motivated for it?

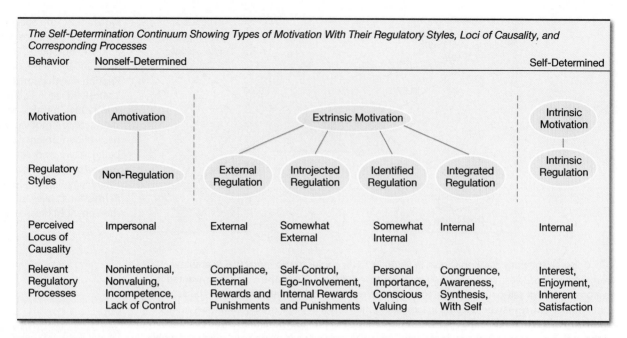

The Self-Determination Continuum Showing Types of Motivation With Their Regulatory Styles, Loci of Causality, and Corresponding Processes

Behavior	Nonself-Determined					Self-Determined
Motivation	Amotivation	Extrinsic Motivation				Intrinsic Motivation
Regulatory Styles	Non-Regulation	External Regulation	Introjected Regulation	Identified Regulation	Integrated Regulation	Intrinsic Regulation
Perceived Locus of Causality	Impersonal	External	Somewhat External	Somewhat Internal	Internal	Internal
Relevant Regulatory Processes	Nonintentional, Nonvaluing, Incompetence, Lack of Control	Compliance, External Rewards and Punishments	Self-Control, Ego-Involvement, Internal Rewards and Punishments	Personal Importance, Conscious Valuing	Congruence, Awareness, Synthesis, With Self	Interest, Enjoyment, Inherent Satisfaction

Figure 9.8 The types of motivation and regulation within self-determination theory, along with their placement along the continuum of relative self-determination. *Source:* Ryan and Deci (2000, Figure 1, p. 72). Deci and Ryan (2008a, Figure 1, p. 17) Deci, E. L., & Ryan, R. M. (2008a). Facilitating optimal motivation and psychological well-being across life's domains. *Canadian Psychology,* 49(1), 14–23. Copyright American Psychological Association. Reprinted with permission.

humanistic values of freedom, responsibility, and authenticity, all part of being fully functioning according to Carl Rogers (1968), which is at the very heart of self-determination theory.

Types of Motivation

Intrinsic motivation and **intrinsic regulation** occur when people engage in an activity due to reasons inherent in the activity itself, like satisfaction or pleasure. Actually, very few activities we undertake in the course of a typical day are intrinsically motivating. Yet, most of our activities—such as walking to class, grocery shopping, returning phone calls, going to the library, brushing our teeth—are undertaken with some measure of volition; that is, we are generally not forced or coerced into grocery shopping or brushing our teeth, yet there is nothing inherently pleasurable about pushing a bristled implement around in your mouth with some special soaplike substance! We engage in many activities in our day, especially chores and other activities that are not particularly intrinsically interesting, by being self-regulating.

In contrast to intrinsic motivation, **extrinsic motivation** occurs when an activity is undertaken for reasons that are external or separable from the activity itself, like gaining a reward or avoiding a punishment (Ryan & Deci, 2000). There are four types of extrinsic motivations, which vary in how much autonomy or volition is involved (Deci & Ryan, 2008b). At one extreme is **external regulation** , which is completely extrinsic and controlled by something or someone outside ourselves. Perhaps as a child you brushed your teeth to gain a reward like watching your favorite TV show or the praise of being called "good boy" or "good girl."

Next comes **introjected regulation** in which the behavior is controlled by something within ourselves. Introjected regulation is experienced as just as controlling as external regulation, except that we act as our own controlling agents, using guilt, anxiety, conditional self-esteem, obligation, approval, or other thoughts to control ourselves. For example, I doubt that there is a parent who is going to tell you to brush your teeth before bed tonight and say "good boy" or "good girl" when you do (external regulation). However, you might make yourself brush your own teeth and perhaps feel good about yourself when you do (introjected regulation).

Both external and introjected regulation are considered controlled and therefore part of extrinsic motivation because the person feels pressured or controlled by demands and

"[B]eing controlled by oneself can be fully as uncomfortable and detrimental to intrinsic motivation . . . as being controlled by another."
Deci and Ryan (1985b, p. 106)

Experiences with extrinsic regulation as a child are often internalized as introjected regulation as an adult.

contingencies (Deci & Ryan, 2008b). Despite all appearances of being actively engaged in an activity, when people are acting under external or introjected regulation they may also experience apathy, lower creativity, drug and alcohol abuse, and poor psychological health (Deci et al., 2001).

Two other kinds of extrinsic motivations are autonomously regulated but are still considered kinds of extrinsic motivation because they are not inherent in the activity (Deci & Ryan, 2008b). **Identified regulation** is when we accept the activity as personally meaningful, perhaps for some greater goal which is more important than hassles involved in the task at hand. Under **integrated regulation**, people have internalized the goals and values of the enterprise (e.g., work environment, maintaining a healthy lifestyle, getting an education) even though the particular activity (e.g., preparing reports, quitting smoking, taking an exam) is not inherently interesting.

For example, people who believe that they should take care of their bodies would probably show identified regulation for brushing their teeth and might not mind the momentary discomfort of hard bristles and medicine flavored toothpaste. However, if the *only* reason a person brushes her teeth is to avoid having a nasty case of gingivitis, that would be an example of external regulation.

Consider a person who maintains a healthy lifestyle: He regularly exercises, doesn't smoke, eats five servings of vegetables, avoids sugary drinks, uses organic products, and enjoys outdoor activities on the weekend. Suppose taking care of his teeth is just one of the many ways he expresses this aspect of his personality, it's part of who he is, and he probably doesn't even have to think about it. In this case, brushing his teeth is an example of integrated regulation where the identification with the activity is integrated into other aspects of the self (Ryan & Deci, 2000). Activities that are integrated are generally expressions of our true, authentic selves.

Getting back to the questions that opened this section, how *do* you motivate yourself for an activity that is not particularly interesting? The possible strategies suggested there represent the different kinds of regulation just discussed—nonregulation, external regulation, introjected regulation, identified regulation, and integrated regulation.

This discussion of the different kinds of motivation and how people can regulate their own behavior suggests that people can willingly undertake even uninteresting tasks if the meaning and greater value behind the activities is understood. People who are more autonomous or self-regulated in their motivation can take up activities with identified, integrated, or intrinsic regulations and engage in these activities with more interest, enthusiasm, confidence, and show greater performance, persistence, and creativity (Deci & Ryan, 1991; Sheldon, Ryan, Rawsthorne, & Ilardi, 1997) in these endeavors than people who are more controlled in their activities (Ryan & Deci, 2000). They also show increased vitality (Nix, Ryan, Manly, & Deci, 1999), self-esteem (Deci & Ryan, 1995), general well-being (Ryan, Deci, & Grolnick, 1995), and longer-lasting changes in health behaviors (Deci & Ryan, 2008b).

THINK ABOUT IT

Recall the activity you identified at the beginning of this chapter. Why do you want to do it? What does it suggest about your motivation for the task?

Perhaps you can also see now why the various ways of providing autonomy support summarized in Table 9.1 work: They help people find ways of regulating their behavior along this continuum. By supporting autonomy, agents such as parents, teachers, coaches, therapists, work supervisors, and friends foster internal motivation and self-determination. By being controlling, these agents foster external motivation and non-self-determination (Deci & Ryan, 1985b; Grolnick & Ryan, 1989). When we choose activities that are intrinsically interesting where possible, and regulate our behavior when choice is not possible, we maintain our own self-determination.

Causality Orientations

By the time we reach adulthood, we have a lifetime of experiences that can build our autonomy, lead us to develop competencies, and connect us with family, friends, and others. For people who have their needs for autonomy, competence, and relatedness met, the world is a very different place than for people who have had a lifetime of being pushed around, not developing a sense of their own competencies, or feeling unsupported by people around them. People differ in their **causality orientations** or their typical ways of self-regulating (Deci & Ryan, 2008b). These are important individual differences in what people expect from the world and how they approach specific situations.

Though people may express each of these orientations to some extent, generally one orientation is stronger than the others. People show consistent, general ways of approaching tasks across many behaviors (brushing your teeth, practicing foul shots), situations (at work, at home), and even domains (academics, sports).

There are three causality orientations: autonomous, controlled, and impersonal. The **autonomous orientation** describes the degree to which people interpret a situation as autonomy supportive, providing information for their own self-regulation (Ryan & Deci, 2008a). People develop an autonomous orientation when all three basic needs are regularly met. People with an autonomous orientation are attracted to situations that have the potential to stimulate their intrinsic motivation and which they find optimally challenging. The autonomous orientation is associated with autonomous self-regulation, greater initiative, good performance, and psychological well-being (Deci & Ryan, 2008b). You may recall the study, discussed earlier, of work performance at an investment banking firm (see Figure 9.7) in which workers with a more autonomous orientation were more likely to have all three of their needs met and to have more positive performance evaluations and better psychological adjustment (Baard et al., 2004).

> **THINK ABOUT IT**
>
> Can causality orientations be changed?

A **controlled orientation** describes the degree to which people look for controls in the environment and let the environment or their own introjects determine and regulate their own behavior (Ryan & Deci, 2008a). People develop a controlled orientation when some degree of their needs for competence and relatedness are satisfied, but the need for autonomy is not. People with a controlled orientation approach situations ready to respond to situational demands and contingencies. People with the controlled orientation self-regulate through introjects and external contingencies, are dependent on rewards and other controls, and show diminished well-being (Deci & Ryan, 2008b).

An **impersonal orientation** describes the degree to which people feel they lack control over important outcomes (Ryan & Deci, 2008a). An impersonal orientation develops from consistently having all three needs thwarted. People with an impersonal orientation approach situations through amotivation with detachment and apathy, believing that there is little they can do to attain desired outcomes. People with an impersonal orientation show poor functioning and poor well-being (Deci & Ryan, 2008b).

Causality orientations are measured through the General Causality Orientations Scale (GCOS; Deci & Ryan, 1985a). The GCOS presents respondents with 12 hypothetical situations and 3 ways they might respond (see Table 9.3). Respondents rate each possible reaction on a 1 to 7 scale of how likely they would be to react in each of these ways. Each of the possible responses represents one of the causality orientations. Responses are totaled separately for each orientation, and respondents receive a score indicating the strength of each of the orientations.

Table 9.3 Sample Item and Orientations From the General Causality Orientations Scale

How likely is each outcome?

You have been offered a new position in a company where you have worked for some time. The first question that is likely to come to mind is:	
I wonder if the new work will be interesting?	Autonomous Orientation
Will I make more at this position?	Controlled Orientation
What if I can't live up to the new responsibility?	Impersonal Orientation

Source: Deci and Ryan (1985a, p. 118). Reprinted from Deci, E. L., & Ryan, R. M. (1985), "The general causality orientations scale: Self-determination in personality," *Journal of Research in Personality,* 19, 109–134. Copyright © 1985, with permission from Elsevier.

Self-Determination Theory Applied

We can understand the three psychological needs and the conditions that foster these needs in one model of motivation and engagement (Connell & Wellborn, 1990; see Figure 9.9). According to this model, the context provides the nutriments for meeting the three needs, that is, structure for competence, autonomy support for autonomy, and involvement for relatedness. When these needs are met, we feel motivated for action and will experience positive emotions and feel like being engaged in the task at hand, be it school (Miserandino, 1996; Skinner, Furrer, Marchand, & Kindermann, 2008), work (Gagné & Deci, 2005), health maintenance (Ryan, Patrick, Deci, & Williams, 2008; Williams et al., 2006, 2009; Williams, Grow, Freedman, Ryan, & Deci, 1996; Wilson, Mack, & Grattan, 2008), close relationships (La Guardia & Patrick, 2008), therapy (Ryan & Deci, 2008b), or parenting (Joussemet, Landry, & Koestner, 2008). Across all of these contexts, as a result of our actions we will increase our skills, abilities, and general well-being.

However, if our needs are not met in a context that fails to provide either involvement, structure, or autonomy support, we will not feel motivated. Instead of engaging in the activities of the enterprise (e.g., studying, working, exercising, etc.) we may feel disaffection. For example, people who are engaged in a context show productive behaviors such as attention, effort and persistence, whereas people who are disaffected show behaviors such as lack of effort and withdrawal (Skinner et al., 2008). Instead of positive emotions like curiosity or enjoyment, they may express negative emotions like depression, frustration, or boredom (Skinner et al.,

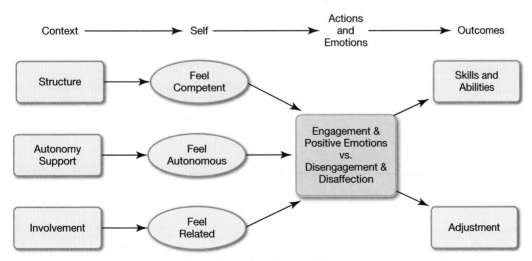

Figure 9.9 A motivational model of the effects of psychological needs on engagement. *Source:* From Connell and Wellborn (1990, Figure 2.2, p. 51). Reprinted from Connell, J. P., & Wellborn, J. G. (1990), "Competence, autonomy, and relatedness: A motivational analysis of self-system processes," as appeared in M. Gunnar & L. A. Sroufe (Eds.), The Minnesota Symposia on Child Psychology Vol. 22, p. 43–77 (Minneapolis, MN: University of Minnesota Press). Permission conveyed through the Copyright Clearance Center.

2008). As a result of disaffection, as shown in these behaviors and emotions, we will miss out on the chance to increase our skills and abilities, and may even end up experiencing the distress of poor psychological adjustment.

If all of this sounds a bit abstract to you, that's what a theoretical model is. But if we apply this model to a specific context the model may make more sense. Part of the power of this model is that it can apply to many different situations. Let's take a closer look at some of these.

Health Behaviors

Researchers and practitioners have applied the principles of self-determination theory to help patients take better care of themselves (Ryan et al., 2008). The more autonomy, competence, and relatedness patients feel, the more willing and able they are to quit smoking (Williams et al., 2006), successfully manage blood sugar levels (Williams et al., 2009), lose weight (Williams et al., 1996), and exercise regularly (Wilson et al., 2008). The self-determination model of motivation and engagement has even been used by dentists and hygienists to get people to take better care of their teeth (Halvari & Halvari, 2006; see Figure 9.10).

In the beginning of this study, patients in a dental clinic had their motivation for taking care of their teeth measured and their teeth examined for plaque and evidence of the gum disease gingivitis (Halvari & Halvari, 2006). About 1 month later, all participants had their teeth cleaned. Then, about 2 months later, patients were randomly assigned to receive either a special intervention or standard care. Patients in the intervention group returned to the clinic for a one-on-one session with a dental hygienist. Patients in the standard care condition did not return to the clinic and did not have this extra session about home oral health care. The lack of specific instruction was standard treatment at the time.

During the intervention, the hygienist asked patients in this condition about any dental problems they might have been experiencing. They listened to and acknowledged the patient's feelings and perspectives, and then gave feedback and suggestions. If a patient was having a problem, the hygienist presented patients with a combination of x-rays, pictures, examples, and information about how to remedy and prevent common gum problems. Patients were given options about treatments they could do at home to prevent problems along with a meaningful rationale for each option. The hygienist demonstrated the correct techniques of flossing and brushing and gave patients a chance to practice these techniques.

> **THINK ABOUT IT**
>
> What prevents people from taking steps to protect themselves from preventable diseases?

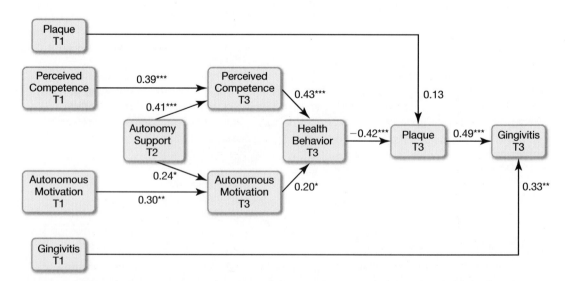

Figure 9.10 Self-determination theory model of oral health care: Self-determination theory predicted the amount of plaque patients had at the end of the experiment better than amount of plaque at the start of the experiment did. Significant pathways are marked by asterisks: *$p < .05$, **$p < .01$, ***$p < .001$. T1 = Beginning of experiment, T2 = Two months later, T3 = End of experiment. *Source:* Halvari and Halvari (2006, Figure 1, p. 300) Halvari, A. E. M., & Halvari, H. (2006). Motivational predictors of change in oral health: An experimental test of self-determination theory. Motivation and Emotion, 30, 295–306.

All the while, she encouraged and conveyed confidence in their ability to do these tasks. During the entire intervention controlling or pressuring language was kept to a minimum. At the end of the session, patients were given toothbrushes, floss, and brochures reinforcing good dental care at home.

Then, 7 months later, all participants returned to the clinic where their motivation, perceived competence for dental care, attitudes toward dental care, and dental health behaviors were assessed. Finally, all participants had an oral examination in which plaque and gingivitis were again measured.

The researchers hypothesized that the intervention would increase patients' perceived competence for dental care and their sense of autonomy in practicing good dental hygiene. Patients with greater competence would floss and brush better, and as a result, show less plaque and gingivitis at the end of the experiment. Figure 9.10 shows the results of the path analysis testing this model.

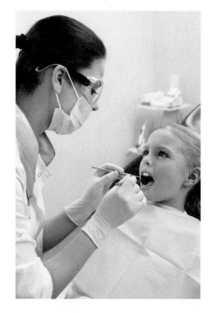

Open up and say ahh . . . tonomy! Patients who are competent at brushing and flossing and who take responsibility for doing so have less plaque than patients who lack competence and autonomy.

The results supported these predictions. The intervention (the box labeled *autonomy support T2*) was successful in giving patients an increased sense of competence and autonomy (the boxes labeled *perceived competence T3* and *autonomous motivation T3*, respectively). Patients whose competence and autonomy needs were being met either through the intervention or because they had a strong sense of autonomy to begin with were more likely to take better care of their teeth and to have less plaque than patients who believed they lacked competence and autonomy. This self-determination theory pathway was a better predictor of plaque at the end of the experiment than was the amount of plaque patients had at the beginning of the study! In addition, gingivitis at the end of the study was indirectly influenced by feelings of competence and autonomy through the amount of plaque patients had at the end of the study and directly through the amount of gingivitis patients had at the beginning of the study.

This study illustrates that feelings of autonomy and competence, nourished by autonomy support and task structure, motivated people to take better care of their teeth. Increased motivation led to increased health behaviors which led to a healthier mouth.

SEE FOR YOURSELF

What kinds of things does your dentist or hygienist say to you? Do you feel competent and motivated or incompetent and pressured after a visit?

Sports Behaviors

Which phrase do you agree with more: "Winning isn't everything; it's the only thing" or "It's not whether you win or lose but how you play the game"? As we saw earlier in this chapter, feedback can communicate two meanings: control and information (Ryan & Deci, 2008a). The mere outcome of a game played against another opponent—winning or losing—conveys information about a person's skill. So there is nothing inherently motivating or demotivating about competition by itself. However, the context in which the competition occurs can undermine intrinsic motivation if athletes experience the situation as controlling (Reeve & Deci, 1996).

College students who solved a block puzzle faster than their opponents, regardless of whether they were specifically instructed to beat their opponent or to just do their best, reported greater perceived competence than participants who lost the competition. However, participants who were pressured into winning (e.g., winning is the only thing that matters; focus your attention on being the winner) felt less intrinsic motivation and lowered perceived autonomy than participants without the pressure (Reeve & Deci, 1996). This suggests that coaches can have a huge impact on how their players interpret and experience practices and competitions to the benefit or detriment of their motivation.

In a study of soccer players aged 12 to 16 in Valencia, Spain, researchers found that coaches influence both the ability of their players to self-regulate their motivation and the emotional experiences of their players while playing and practicing (Álvarez, Castillo, & Duda, 2008).

Coaches have a direct effect on players' motivation and well-being.

Using path analysis, they discovered that the extent to which players' needs for autonomy, competence, and relatedness were met, directly and indirectly increased their enjoyment and decreased their boredom of the game (see Figure 9.11). The more players perceived that coaches provided autonomy support, structure and involvement, the more the players were self-regulated and engaged in practice using intrinsic or identified regulation instead of external or introjected regulation or amotivation (see Table 9.4). Self-regulated motivation, in turn, also increased players' enjoyment of the game.

As promising as these results are, keep in mind that these athletes were studied at one moment in time, so we are unable to know for sure if coaches behaviors *caused* the athletes to feel that their needs were being met. Recall our caveat that correlation is not causation. To answer definitively what impact coaching has on athletes' motivation and well-being, we need to study coaches' behaviors and athletes' experiences over time. This is precisely what was done in a study of gymnasts (Gagné, Ryan, & Bargmann, 2003).

Using a diary study, researchers followed the day-to-day motivation to attend practice, satisfaction of the three needs, emotions, energy level, and self-esteem of a team of 45 female gymnasts, 7 to 18 years of age (Gagné et al., 2003). Gymnasts were part of a competition team that practiced an average of 7 hours a week. They filled out questionnaires before and after every practice for 15 practices over the course of a month. The researchers wanted to know how fluctuations in an athlete's feelings of motivation, energy, and self-esteem related to perceptions of their coach's and parents' autonomy support, structure, and involvement, and feeling that their needs were being met during practice (see Table 9.5).

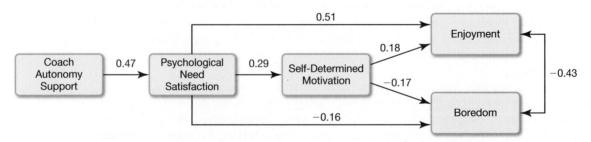

Figure 9.11 Self-determination theory path analysis of soccer players' context, need satisfaction, motivation, and emotions. All marked pathways are significant. Numbers marked are standardized beta weights. Negative numbers indicate that one variable decreases the next variable in the path. *Source:* Adapted from Álvarez et al. (2008, Figure 3, p. 145). Reprinted with permission from Álvarez, M. S., Balaguer, I., Castillo, I., & Duda, J. L. (2008), "Coach autonomy support and quality of sport engagement in young soccer players," *The Spanish Journal of Psychology*, 12(1), 138–148.

Table 9.4 Why Do You Practice Your Sport? Sample Items From the Sport Motivation Scale

Item	Type of Regulation
For the excitement I feel when I am really involved in the activity	Intrinsic Motivation
Because it is one of the best ways I have chosen to develop other aspects of myself	Identified Regulation
Because I must do sports to feel good about myself	Introjected Regulation
For the prestige of being an athlete	External Regulation
I don't know anymore; I have the impression that I am incapable of succeeding in this sport	Amotivation

Note: Self-determined motivation was assessed with a Spanish version (Balaguer, Castillo, & Duda, 2007) of the Sport Motivation Scale (SMS; Pelletier et al., 1995). Responses are rated on a 7-point Likert scale ranging from 1 (*Does Not Correspond at All*) to 7 (*Corresponds Exactly*).

Source: Adapted from Álvarez et al. (2008, p. 142).

As you might expect, these gymnasts were highly self-determined in their motivation, scoring the highest in identification and intrinsic regulation. Younger gymnasts showed more introjected regulation than older gymnasts. Gymnasts who were high in identification attended practices more regularly.

The more autonomy-supportive parents and coaches were perceived by the gymnasts to be, the more self-regulating the gymnasts were, showing more identified and intrinsic motivation. Gymnasts who were more self-regulated experienced more positive emotions during practices, like feeling excited, alert, enthusiastic, and inspired. They also showed more energy and vitality during practice (e.g., feeling alive, energized, spirited) and more stable self-esteem, and attended more practices. Gymnasts who were less self-regulating, feeling more controlled by their parents or the coach, reported more introjection and external motivation, experienced more negative emotions during practice, such as feeling distressed, nervous, sad, and irritable. They also showed less energy and vitality, and more unstable self-esteem.

During a practice session, gymnasts who reported that the practice fulfilled their needs for autonomy, competence, and relatedness experienced a boost in positive affect, energy, and stability of self-esteem by the end of that practice compared to how they felt at the beginning of practice. In particular, gymnasts who perceived the coach was highly involved in their training on a given day had more stable self-esteem during a practice session than gymnasts who perceived their coach as being uninvolved.

This study illustrates two parallel effects. First, there is the self-regulation style that gymnasts bring to practice. This style is developed over the course of a lifetime of experiences with parents as well as through past interactions with their coach. We might think of this as the backdrop for what goes on in a particular practice. The self-regulatory style of individual gymnasts is part of their personality, and was fairly stable over the month that these gymnasts were studied. In general, gymnasts who were more self-regulated showed greater engagement and well-being than gymnasts who were less self-regulating.

THINK ABOUT IT

Why did younger gymnasts show less self-determined motivation than older gymnasts?

Table 9.5 Selected Items From the Need Satisfaction Scale

Need	Item
Autonomy	My coaches helped me choose my own direction during practice
Competence	I was good at gymnastics
Relatedness	I felt like I was part of the team

Note: This scale assessed the extent to which gymnasts felt that their needs were met during a practice session. Responses were rated on a 5-point Likert scale ranging from 1 (*Completely Disagree*) to 5 (*Completely Agree*).

Source: Adapted from Gagné et al. (2003, p. 378).

Second, what did vary over the course of the study, was the impact of each practice session on the engagement and well-being of the gymnasts. Each practice session affected the extent to which gymnasts felt their needs were met. A good practice session—one in which their needs for autonomy, competence, and relatedness were met—left them feeling better than when they came in: more excited, alert, inspired, energetic, enthusiastic, and so on. However, a bad practice—one in which their needs for autonomy, competence, and relatedness were not met—made them feel worse than when then came in: more distressed, nervous, sad, irritable, lonely, dispirited, discouraged, and not so sure of themselves.

Comparing the results of this study with the Álvarez et al. (2008) study of Spanish soccer players (see Figure 9.11), we can confidently say that the extent to which a coach fosters the three needs within their players during a given practice session *causes* an increase in the self-regulation, engagement, and well-being of their players.

Work Behaviors

SEE FOR YOURSELF

How important to you are prestige, money, and freedom in a job?

According to Stone, Deci, and Ryan (2009), today's workplace has changed in recent years and so managers need to change their ways of thinking as well. Where management once applied a carrot-and-stick approach to motivating their workers by offering rewards or punishments to control them, we now know that such controlling methods are problematic. At the very least, these methods require continual monitoring and surveillance, and at the very worst, they often undermine intrinsic interest. Further, the nature of work today in our information economy requires more thought and creativity than routine factory jobs of earlier times. One simply cannot foster creativity and talent with controlling methods, as we saw with children's artwork in the Then and Now feature. Finally, because of the cost and effort required to hire and train skilled workers, organizations are shifting their focus and caring more about the retention and satisfaction of employees than they once did, seeking to boost well-being of workers in addition to organizational productivity. Self-determination theory provides the tools to increase motivation, creativity, satisfaction, and job performance of workers (Deci, Connell, & Ryan, 1989; Stone et al., 2009).

There are a number of steps that managers can take to foster the motivation of their workers, leading to a sustainable motivation—that is, a self-directed, rather than externally controlled, motivation that persists in the absence of direct surveillance (see Table 9.6). These steps are all ways of providing autonomy support, structure, and involvement to help satisfy workers' needs for autonomy, competence and relatedness. As we saw, when people feel that their needs are being met they will be more engaged in the work at hand.

These principles were put into action to help employee morale in the Xerox Corporation during a period of downsizing in the late 1980s (Deci et al., 1989). The participants in this study were nearly 1,000 technicians and their field managers. Technicians spent practically all of their time on the road dealing with clients, whereas field managers were responsible for about 18 technicians who formed their work team. Individual technicians had little contact with the other technicians except for monthly team meetings and saw their field manager only once a week or so to hand in time cards.

Table 9.6 How to Create Autonomous Motivation in a Work Setting

1. Ask open questions and invite participation in problem solving.
2. Actively listen and acknowledge employee perspectives.
3. Offer choices within structure including the clarification of responsibilities.
4. Provide sincere, positive feedback that acknowledges initiative and factual, nonjudgmental feedback about problems.
5. Minimize coercive controls such as rewards and comparisons with others.
6. Develop talent and share knowledge to enhance competence and autonomy.

Source: From Stone et al. (2009, Table 1, p. 80). Beyond talk: Creating autonomous motivation through self-determination theory. *Journal of General Management, 34*, 75–91.

During this period of uncertainty, wages were frozen and layoffs were widespread. Both technicians and managers were understandably upset by the pay freeze, and felt tremendous pressure to perform fearing that they could easily be the next person laid off and lose their jobs. Technicians reported that instead of feeling supported by their managers—who were no doubt feeling pressure of their own from above—they felt pressured and controlled. Managers reported feeling isolated and avoided talking to other managers for fear of revealing weakness in themselves or in their team. As you can see, the needs of autonomy and relatedness were both lacking under these conditions, although corporate management didn't think of the problems in these terms.

To help remedy this situation, corporate management wanted to change the organizational climate to include more participative management (which would increase autonomy) and employee involvement (which would increase relatedness). It instituted special training, established problem-solving groups, restructured work teams, and brought in external consultants to help implement these changes. Some of these consultants were trained in principles of self-determination theory. During the intervention, these consultants modeled autonomy-supportive behaviors and involvement in their interactions with the managers so that managers would experience for themselves the power of the self-determination theory model of motivation and engagement.

As part of the intervention, field managers met together and were given a chance to express their negative feelings about the work climate and to have their perspective acknowledged. Then, managers shared strategies that had worked for them with their own teams. During the process, the consultants modeled how to listen empathetically, taking the perspective of the managers, and acknowledging their feelings. Field managers were then trained in how to support their workers' self-determination using aspects of autonomy support including giving them choice whenever possible, providing them with noncontrolling feedback, and showing acceptance and acknowledgment of their perspective.

In the process of mastering these skills, managers learned to support and encourage each other. Then, when they returned to their regular work teams, they were able to use these skills with their own technicians. As a result, technicians felt less pressure and control, and more support and freedom in the workplace. For example, instead of passing the pressure they were feeling onto the technicians, managers sought support from the other managers. Managers also supported initiative in their workers, and helped them be more self-regulating.

Over the 18 months of the study, technicians' satisfaction with their work increased as a direct result of the field managers' support of their self-determination. At the beginning, the researchers were likely to hear things like "This is the kind of company that doesn't give a damn about its people" (Deci et al., 1989, p. 586). But by the end of the study workers with managers who supported their self-determination started to feel better and more positive about most aspects of their work situation. Workers with controlling managers continued to feel bad and to express negativity about most aspects of their work.

> **THINK ABOUT IT**
>
> Many people today face an uncertain work environment. Could similar interventions improve employee morale and motivation?

Autonomy, competence, and relatedness can increase workers' motivation and job satisfaction.

The more managers supported the self-determination of their technicians, the more trusting of the corporation technicians were and the less pressure they felt at work. Technicians also reported greater satisfaction with feedback from their managers, opportunity for input, and job security over the course of the study.

The Pursuit of Happiness

What leads to happiness? Does pursuing the ideals of achieving fame, fortune, and good looks lead to well-being? Though these goals are pursued by many people, both in the U.S. and in other countries, some researchers wonder if the pursuit of these extrinsic goals disconnect people from their family, friends, and community, making it difficult to achieve a sense of well-being and mental health.

For many people, pursuing the "American Dream" of financial success does indeed have a dark side (Kasser & Ryan, 1993, 1996). That is, young people who aspire to financial goals (e.g., being able to buy things they want, being their own boss, having a prestigious job) are more depressed, more anxious, and less self-actualized than people who strive for self-acceptance (having a meaningful life, knowing and accepting themselves) or affiliation (having friends, spouse, children).

This is true even in a formerly communist country like Russia, where young people today are able to pursue the values of a free-market economy even though they were not raised in such a climate (Ryan et al., 1999). U.S. and Russian college students who value intrinsic goals more than extrinsic goals have higher subjective well-being, life satisfaction, self-esteem, and self-actualization.

However, that's not the whole story: Well-being also depends on people's reasons for pursuing financial success (Carver & Baird, 1998). For example, students who agreed that it would be fun to have a job that paid well or that it was important to them to have the freedom to do what they choose or who felt that it would be satisfying to have a job that paid well, had higher self-actualization. In contrast, students who believed that achieving financial success is something you're supposed to do, or that it would make their family proud, or that people will respect them if they are financially successful were less self-actualized.

> "The U.S. Constitution doesn't guarantee happiness, only the pursuit of it. You have to catch up with it yourself."
>
> *Ben Franklin*

The trouble is, too often the pursuit of fame, fortune, or good looks involves relying on external standards rather than on a person's internal standards (Kasser & Ryan, 1996). That is, it involves extrinsic motivation rather than intrinsic motivation. So, it is both *what* you choose to pursue and *why* you pursue it that is important for well-being and happiness (Sheldon, Ryan, Deci, & Kasser, 2004). Fame, fortune, or good looks, in and of themselves, do not lead to well-being and happiness but rather freely choosing what to pursue, feeling competent in one's endeavors, and being meaningfully related to others along the way does lead to happiness (Kasser & Ryan, 1996).

The Tae Bo Study Revisited

Do you recall the study that opened this chapter on teens learning about Tae Bo in their gym class? The experimenters manipulated the autonomy supportiveness of the instructor (Vansteenkiste et al., 2004). In one condition he emphasized the students' own choice in whether to participate or not in the exercises, whereas in the other, he pressured students into participating. At the same time, the experimenters also manipulated whether students would engage in Tae Bo for intrinsic or extrinsic reasons. Both autonomy support and an intrinsic goal led to greater effort by the students, better performance, and higher persistence up to 4 months later. And the combination of both autonomy support and an intrinsic goal had the best outcomes of all!

You can see now how these manipulations helped foster a sense of autonomy in the students. Having their need for autonomy satisfied increased the students' motivation for learning and practicing Tae Bo. Further, being fully engaged in their Tae Bo class, they no doubt developed competence at this new skill.

Imagine a lifetime of such experiences in which people build autonomy and competence while having warm, supportive relationships with peers and adults. By the time we reach adulthood, we have some generalized notions about what to expect from the world. People differ in the extent to which they feel pushed around or supported by the world. These causality orientations account for differences between people in how they approach new situations and interpret feedback which impacts their psychological functioning and well-being (Ryan & Deci, 2008a, 2008b). So, a little Tae Bo may be good, but autonomy, competence, and relatedness are even better!

Chapter Summary

Self-determination theory suggests that people's intrinsic or extrinsic reasons for undertaking an activity are related to important outcomes. When people act because they feel pressured to, they lose motivation, their performance suffers, and they experience a loss of well-being. However, when people act out of their own volition, they are able to sustain motivation, perform well, and increase their well-being. This illustrates the need for autonomy, one of three primary psychological needs.

According to self-determination theory, all people, regardless of cultural background, have three inborn psychological needs that are necessary to survive and thrive: autonomy (choice, volition), competence (mastery, skillfulness), and relatedness (connection with others). These needs have been studied extensively by psychologists from many different traditions. Self-determination theory builds on the work of related theories including locus of causality (autonomy), self-efficacy theory (competence), and attachment theory (relatedness). People get these needs met from the social situation. Autonomy support helps people feel autonomous, structure and optimal challenge helps people feel competent, and involvement helps people feel relatedness.

One prediction of self-determination theory is that rewards and punishments may backfire, causing people to lose interest in an activity and to not perform their best, especially at activities that require creativity. This overjustification effect has been demonstrated in children and adults, with all sorts of rewards (e.g., monetary, praise, candy, etc.). External motivators such as deadlines, imposed goals, competition, surveillance, evaluations, and rewards that communicate information about competence at a task do not necessarily undermine motivation and performance. However, rewards that signal lack of autonomy and the presence of control will be detrimental to motivation and performance.

Part of being autonomous is having the ability to self-regulate one's behaviors especially when it comes to engaging in activities that are not intrinsically interesting. Motivations can vary in how self-determined they are, from amotivation (or nonregulation), external regulation, introjected regulation, identified regulation, integrated regulation, and intrinsic regulation. The least self-determined regulation is amotivation, when people feel apathetic and disengaged. The most self-determined motivation is intrinsic regulation, when people act because of inherent interest in the task.

After a lifetime of having one's needs for autonomy, competence, and relatedness met—or not—people develop expectations about the world called causality orientations. People may have an autonomous, controlled, or impersonal orientation and differ in their motivation, engagement, psychological adjustment, and overall well-being.

Path analysis is a statistical technique researchers use to test that a hypothesized model accounts for a significant amount of variance in the data better than do other models. Path analysis identifies direct and indirect effects of variables on each other. The results are generally summarized in a diagram with significant paths drawn between variables. Path analysis can tell us which causal paths are more likely among a set of variables, but cannot prove causality unless the variables are measured at different times or were manipulated as part of a true experiment. Researchers have used path analysis to test predictions from the self-determination theory model of engagement.

✓•⌐**Study** and **Review**
on **mysearchlab.com**
Go online for more resources to help you review.

According to the self-determination theory model of engagement, the three needs can be fostered or thwarted by the social context. When these needs are met, people feel motivated, engaged, perform at a high level, build skills, and increase their well-being. When these needs are not met, people will feel disengaged and disaffected, show low motivation, experience negative emotions, not increase their skills, and overall have poor well-being. This model has been applied to numerous domains including school, work, health, close relationships, therapy, and parenting.

For example, when health professionals help their patients meet these needs, people take more responsibility over their health and experience greater health as a result. Coaches who help their players meet these needs have players who are more motivated and enjoy practices more. At work, employees who feel more autonomous, competent, and related to their coworkers and supervisors show greater work satisfaction and work more independently. Finally, freely choosing what goals to pursue, feeling competent at one's pursuits, and feeling meaningfully related to others while doing so leads to lasting happiness. Accepting external goals such as pursuing fame, fortune, or good looks because of societal pressures is a recipe for unhappiness.

Review Questions

1. What is self-determination theory? What two predictions of self-determination theory are illustrated by the Tae Bo study?

2. What are the three fundamental psychological needs? How do we satisfy these needs? What are some specific examples of how these needs may be met in a particular situation?

3. What two meanings might rewards and punishments for performance convey? What kind of feedback is likely to undermine intrinsic interest?

4. How are autonomy and locus of causality similar? How are competence and self-efficacy similar? How does relatedness build on attachment theory?

5. What is path analysis? When understanding a path diagram, what do solid lines, arrow heads, and weights indicate?

6. What does it mean to be self-regulated? What are the different kinds of regulation? What are the different types of motivation?

7. What are the three causality orientations? How do people with each of these orientations approach new situations?

8. What is the motivational model of engagement that describes how aspects of the context, self, and actions can lead to positive or negative outcomes?

9. How has self-determination theory been applied to dental care, athlete's motivation, work motivation, and the pursuit of happiness?

Key Terms

Self-determination theory
Extrinsically motivated
Intrinsically motivated
Humanistic tradition
Actualizing tendency
Autonomy
Competence
Relatedness
Optimal challenge
Flow

Overjustification effect
Locus of control
Locus of causality
Self-efficacy
Outcome expectation
Efficacy expectation
Path analysis
Path diagram
Amotivation
Intrinsic motivation

Intrinsic regulation
Extrinsic motivation
External regulation
Introjected regulation
Identified regulation
Integrated regulation
Causality orientations
Autonomous orientation
Controlled orientation
Impersonal orientation

10 COGNITIVE FOUNDATIONS OF PERSONALITY

Read the Chapter on
mysearchlab.com

After graduating from college with a degree in psychology, I wanted to save the world. I spent about a month doing volunteer work in a remote village in Mexico. My fellow workers and I organized various programs to help these people by administering a government-sponsored literacy program, staffing a health clinic, participating in teen outreach programs, visiting the sick, and running a day camp of sorts for the youngest villagers. On one of my first days, I was astounded to discover a small girl about 4 years old just staring blankly at the crayons in front of her. While the children around her giggled and grabbed crayons from the center of the table, merrily scribbling on their papers, Elena sat mute.

When I asked her why she wasn't drawing, she merely shrugged and sank into herself. I was amazed that a 4-year-old might not know how to color, so I gently placed my hand around hers and together we clutched a crayon and started to scribble. But lack of practice coloring was not her problem; despite my instruction and encouragement Elena never did get the hang of drawing with crayons. As the other children filled their papers with elaborately colored designs, her paper remained strangely blank except for the few tiny scribbles we had done together.

The image of a helpless child staring at a table full of crayons stayed with me. What would make a child so helpless that she couldn't or wouldn't draw like the other children? I thought back to my psychology classes and wondered if this was what learned helplessness looked like. Today, I might be inclined to say that Elena was depressed, or at least depressed at the thought of drawing with crayons. Can mere thoughts depress us? If so, can changing our thoughts change our depressive feelings? And if we change how we think, are we also changing something fundamental about our personality?

The possibility of changing people's thoughts was tested in an experiment conducted by Seligman and his colleagues (Seligman, Steen, Park, & Peterson, 2005). They randomly assigned volunteers to one of five treatments. Every day for a week they were instructed to think about certain things such as expressing gratitude; reflecting on good things in their lives; and either identifying, reflecting on, or developing character strengths such as curiosity, zest, leadership, forgiveness, hope, kindness, and love. In a sixth, control condition, participants wrote about their early memories. Finally, participants' levels of depression and happiness were measured immediately, 1 week, 1 month, and 6 months after this treatment.

Despite being somewhat depressed at the start of the study, participants who thought about the good things that happened to them and about why they happened, and participants who developed one of their character strengths by using it in a new way, showed decreases in

Exercising one's character strengths such as curiosity, zest, leadership, forgiveness, hope, love, and kindness can prevent depression and increase happiness.

symptoms of depression and increases in felt happiness over the course of the experiment. People who wrote and delivered a letter of gratitude felt better, but the positive effects lasted only a month. However, recalling early memories or identifying and reflecting on a character strength did nothing for depression or happiness (see Figure 10.1).

What is particularly amazing about this experiment is that the interventions were delivered, not by a human therapist, but by a *computer!* Participants never talked or interacted with another person and never even stepped into a laboratory. The recruitment, measurement, and intervention took place on the Internet via a website. Many therapeutic interventions depend on the expertise or empathy of the therapist, but here is an example of an intervention working in the absence of human interaction. Seligman et al (2005) believed that these interventions may be even more effective when combined with the support of a caring and effective counselor or life coach, based on preliminary data. This study demonstrates—literally and figuratively—the power of positive thinking!

Many psychologists have identified consistent and specific differences between people in the way they perceive and think about the world. For example, some people are more dependent on visual cues and are more sensitive to the context. Those who are **field-dependent** tend to see the big picture rather than details. In contrast, people who are **field-independent** rely on their own physical sensations and have selective attention to a particular object without being distracted by the surrounding details (Witkin, Moore, Goodenough, & Cox, 1977). Whereas field-independent people are good at learning languages in a traditional classroom setting, field-dependent people learn best by being totally immersed in everyday situations where they are surrounded by a new language (Brown, 1994).

In addition to these differences in perceptions, people can differ in the constructs or schemas they use to interpret the world (Kelly, 1955), whether intelligence is fixed or if it can be increased through effort and experiences (Dweck, 1999), and in their expectations, beliefs, and goals (Mischel & Shoda, 1995). In this chapter we focus on individual differences in expectations

"Cogito ergo sum," I think therefore I am.

Philosopher René Descartes

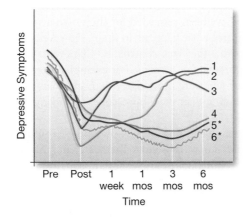

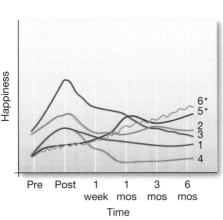

Key

1 = Identifying strengths
2 = Gratitude visit
3 = Control
4 = You at your best
5 = Using strengths
6 = 3 Good things

Figure 10.1 Depressive symptoms and levels of happiness over time as a function of condition. Although some of the interventions have an immediate impact, using only strengths (5) and explaining three good things (6) led to lasting changes. *Source:* Based on Seligman et al. (2005, Figures 1 and 2, pp. 417–418).

and beliefs and take an in-depth look at an area of current focus in personality: how people think about the causes and impacts of events in their lives and how these differences in locus of control, learned helplessness, optimistic and pessimistic explanatory styles, and dispositional optimism make us who we are.

Locus of Control

> To be, or not to be—that is the question:
> Whether 'tis nobler in the mind to suffer
> The slings and arrows of outrageous fortune
> Or to take arms against a sea of troubles
> And by opposing end them?
> From *Hamlet*, by William Shakespeare (Act 3, scene i)

Which side of Hamlet's dilemma do you agree with more: that we must put up with what life throws at us or that we can control what happens to us?

Although Shakespeare identified these two ways of viewing the world, personality psychologist Julian Rotter was the first to define **locus of control** as people's beliefs about the control of reinforcements and outcomes in their lives. People vary in the extent to which they believe that an outcome depends on their own behavior or personal characteristics, falling on a continuum of control beliefs. People who believe that they have some control over what happens to them have an *internal locus of control* and are often called *internals*. In contrast, *externals,* or people with an *external locus of control,* believe that they have little control over what happens to them and instead believe that reinforcements or outcomes are due to chance, luck, fate, powerful others, or are unpredictable (Rotter, 1966). Though people may have a mix of internal and external beliefs, generally one way of thinking will occur more often.

People develop these expectations from their experiences in the world (Rotter, Chance, & Phares, 1972). If people have been rewarded for their own actions, they will come to believe that they can indeed control what happens to them. However, if their actions have not been rewarded they will think that they lack control and that events happen due to external causes or for unknown and unpredictable reasons. For example, externals who believed that events happen due to chance or fate were more likely than internals to believe in astrology, and to act on their beliefs by reading their daily horoscopes or buying books about astrology (Sosis, Strickland, & Haley, 1980).

Internals and externals also differ in how they process information. Internals pay more attention to information that may be useful to them later and they also retain more information than externals (Wallston, 2001). For example, both hospitalized tuberculosis patients (Seeman & Evans, 1962) and prisoners facing parole (Seeman, 1963) who were internal retained more information related to their conditions than externals. People with an internal locus of control act as if knowing more about one's condition or situation is an important step toward changing one's circumstances.

Measures of Locus of Control

Locus of control is often measured with the Internal-External Locus of Control Scale (Rotter, 1966; see Table 10.1). Respondents are presented with 29 pairs of statements in a forced-choice format. Each pair includes one internal locus of control statement and one external locus of control statement. Participants must decide which statement they agree with more. Six of the pairs are filler statements and are not scored. Scores can range from 0 to 23 with higher scores indicating a greater external locus of control, and lower scores a more internal locus of control.

More recently, researchers have developed scales to measure locus of control in specific goals areas (Lefcourt, 1979, 1981, 1991) including health (Wallston, Wallston, & DeVellis, 1978), weight management (Saltzer, 1982), personal finance management (Furnham, 1986), wealth

THINK ABOUT IT

Who do you think is more likely to buy a lottery ticket? Why?

Table 10.1   Items From the Rotter Internal–External Locus of Control Scale

People who are internal tend to agree with these statements:

1. People's misfortunes result from the mistakes they make.
2. In the long run people get the respect they deserve in this world.
3. Trusting to fate has never turned out as well for me as making a decision to take a definite course of action.
4. In the case of the well-prepared student there is rarely if ever such a thing as an unfair test.
5. Becoming a success is a matter of hard work, luck has little or nothing to do with it.

People who are external tend to agree with these statements:

1. Many of the unhappy things in people's lives are partly due to bad luck.
2. Unfortunately, an individual's worth often passes unrecognized no matter how hard he tries.
3. I have often found that what is going to happen will happen.
4. Many times exam questions tend to be so unrelated to course work that studying is really useless.
5. Getting a good job depends mainly on being in the right place at the right time.

Note: Based on a scale of 0 = *no chance* to 100 = *certainty.*

Source: Generalized expectancies for internal versus external control of reinforcement. Psychological Monographs: General and Applied, 80(1), (Whole number 609), 1–28. Copyright American Psychological Association. Reprinted with permission.

accumulation (Steed & Symes, 2009), interpersonal relationships (Lewis, Cheney, & Dawes, 1977), marital outcomes (Miller, Lefcourt, & Ware, 1983), headache pain (Martin, Holroyd, & Penzien, 1990), work (Spector, 1988), sleep (Vincent, Sande, Read, & Giannuzzi, 2004), alcohol use (Donovan & O'Leary, 1978), and intellectual, physical, and social domains (Bradley, Stuck, Coop, & White, 1977).

Numerous studies have been done on locus of control which suggests that more positive outcomes in achievement, work, health, and relationships are associated with having an internal locus of control. However, Rotter himself warned that it would be too simple to declare an internal locus of control the better or healthier way to think and external locus of control as a bad way of thinking (Rotter, 1975). People with an external locus of control are not particularly distressed by their beliefs. Many—but not all—important life outcomes are related to an internal locus of control. Let's consider some of the major findings in these areas.

Locus of Control and Achievement

Internals take more action than externals (Rahim, 1997), including taking political action (Gore & Rotter, 1963; Strickland, 1965), and achieving greater academic success by studying more, performing better on tests, and getting better grades (Nord, Connelly, & Daignault, 1974; Prociuk & Breen, 1974) than externals. In fact, internal locus of control scores at age 10 predicted greater educational attainment in adulthood (Flouri, 2006). Internals even daydream more about achievement and less about failure than do externals (Brannigan, Hauk, & Guay, 1991).

Internals are better at planning and working at long-term goals (Lefcourt, 1982) and at establishing more realistic goals (Gilmor & Reid, 1978). For example, internals finished their college degrees faster than students with an external locus of control (Hall, Smith, & Chia, 2008). Children in Grades 3 to 5 with an internal locus of control were better able to delay gratification than those with an external locus of control (Strickland, 1973). They were more willing to forgo a single lollipop to obtain three lollipops 2 weeks later.

Internals assume more responsibility for themselves and hold others to high standards of responsibility as well (Phares & Wilson, 1972). For example, they are more likely to support the death penalty (Butler & Moran, 2007). Internals also have higher credit ratings, even after controlling for income, education, and negative life events such as medical expenses, unemployment, or a reduction in income. Internals also have higher income and more financial knowledge than externals and are more highly educated (Perry, 2008).

THINK ABOUT IT

Why would somebody with an internal locus of control show more intrinsic motivation than somebody with an external locus of control?

Locus of Control and Work Behavior

Having an internal locus of control quite literally pays off when it comes to career and work behavior. Based on a meta-analysis of 222 studies, workers with an internal locus of control showed greater satisfaction with their pay, promotions, coworkers, and supervisors than did workers with an external locus of control (Ng, Sorensen, & Eby, 2006). Internals showed greater job commitment, intrinsic motivation, productivity, career success, and job challenge and worked more hours than externals. In contrast, externals experienced greater job overload, work problems, stress, burnout, absenteeism, and conflicts between family and work responsibilities.

College students with an internal locus of control show better career decision-making skills (Millar & Shevlin, 2007). An internal locus of control was associated with greater work involvement in both skilled and unskilled workers across six countries (Reitz & Jewell, 1979). Internals are particularly sensitive to pay incentives and work particularly well under incentive systems such as sales or piecework. People with an internal locus of control tend to be more satisfied with their jobs (Spector, 1982) whereas people with an external locus of control were among the most stressed and burned out in a sample of distressed nurses in Germany (Schmitz, Neumann, & Oppermann, 2000).

Entrepreneurs, people who start their own business, though more internal than nonentrepreneurs, are not necessarily more successful than people who work for others (Venkatapathy, 1984). Entrepreneurs with an internal locus of control did more business-related activities such as working longer hours, expanding the business, and setting goals for the business than externals did (Durand & Shea, 1974). The authors suggested that people with an internal locus of control are better able to turn their thoughts and dreams into actions.

Business owners who were more internal coped better with a devastating hurricane and flood that hit central Pennsylvania in June of 1972, damaging some 430 businesses in the area (Anderson, 1977). By 8 months after the devastation, internals had engaged in more problem-solving behaviors as a way of coping rather than emotion-focused coping and did things such as managing their anxiety, anger, or other emotional reactions. Externals found the whole situation more stressful than internals did.

Even 3 ½ years later, the businesses of internals were still doing better than the businesses of externals as indicated by a higher credit rating. The researchers found that business owners with an internal locus of control took more productive actions during this period which, in turn, led the owners to become even more internal and to bring their businesses back to their pre-flood levels of performance. External business owners whose businesses improved became even more external in the years after the flood (Anderson, 1977). This study illustrates Rotter's original contention that locus of control affects performance and that performance also affects future locus of control beliefs.

THINK ABOUT IT

Why do externals fail to take steps to protect themselves?

Locus of Control and Physical and Psychological Health

The belief that they can control what happens to them combined with a greater willingness to take action contributes to the overall better physical and mental health of people with an internal locus of control (Lefcourt, 1982; Selander, Marnetoft, Åkerström, & Asplund, 2005). For example, internals have a decreased risk of heart attacks, presumably due to taking preventative measures like exercising more and eating a healthy diet (Stürmer, Hasselbach, & Amelang, 2006).

Internals are also more likely than externals to wear seatbelts (Hoyt, 1973), exercise (Norman, Bennett, Smith, & Murphy, 1997), quit smoking (Segall & Wynd, 1990), use birth control (MacDonald, 1970), keep track of their medications (Hong, Oddone, Dudley, & Bosworth, 2006), and take steps to reduce their risk of breast cancer (Rowe, Montgomery, Duberstein, & Bovbjerg, 2005). British children with an internal locus of control at age 10 were less likely to be overweight as adults and to have a lowered risk of obesity, better self-rated health, and less psychological distress at age 30 (Gale, Batty, & Deary, 2008). Individuals with chronic illness who had an external locus of control, believing that good health is in the hands of their doctors, reported more emotional distress (Shelley & Pakenham, 2004).

People with an internal locus of control are more likely to take better care of themselves, such as regularly using seatbelts and eating a healthier diet.

Externals are more vulnerable to anxiety and depression (Benassi, Sweeney, & Dufour, 1988), and are less able to cope with stressful life experiences (Lefcourt, 1983). Adolescent externals have a greater risk of suicide than internals (Evans, Owens, & Marsh, 2005). People with an internal locus of control tend to be happier (Lefcourt, 1982; Ye, She, & Wu, 2007).

For example, imagine living in Israel during the Persian Gulf War, when civilians faced nightly SCUD missile attacks for 5 weeks. Adolescents with an internal locus of control reported fewer physical symptoms (e.g., headaches, fatigue, insomnia, loss of appetite, etc.), less fear, and better cognitive functioning under stress (e.g., concentration, memory, decision making) than those with an external locus of control (Zeidner, 1993).

There is also evidence that individuals handle stressful situations differently depending on their control beliefs. Across many studies, a consistent finding is that people with an internal locus of control use more problem-focused coping, looking for possible solutions and taking concrete steps to make things better. In contrast, externals use more emotion-focused coping, relieving their feelings of anger, anxiety, or sadness by talking with others, for example (Ng et al., 2006). In the previous section we saw how this difference in business owners led to better economic recovery years after a devastating flood (Anderson, 1977).

Locus of Control and Social Behavior

Locus of control even leads to differences in how individuals interact with others. People who believe that their social relationships are established and maintained as a result of their own efforts are more socially skillful and show greater social sensitivity than people without these beliefs (Lefcourt, Martin, Fick, & Saleh, 1985). People with an internal locus of control are also more likely to show independence and resistance to social influence than externals (Crowne & Liverant, 1963). Externals are more vulnerable to persuasion, social influence, and conformity pressures (Avtgis, 1998).

Internals participate in more campus activities (Brown & Strickland, 1972) and hold more campus leadership positions than externals do (Brown & Strickland, 1972; Hiers & Heckel, 1977). Internals are also more likely than externals to opt for a position of power—for example sitting at the head of the table—when choosing where to sit with others (Hiers & Heckel, 1977).

In accord with where they perceive the rewards to be, internals and externals differ in which aspects of a situation they pay more attention to. Externals are more sensitive to the social demands of a situation whereas internals are more sensitive to the task demands of the situation. In one experiment, externals paid more attention when feedback for their performance came from the experimenter instead of directly from the task. Internals, of course, preferred to receive feedback directly from their performance (Pines & Julian, 1972).

However, when interacting with a stranger, externals talked more and looked at their partners more than internals did (Rajecki, Ickes, & Tanford, 1981). Again, we can see that this is due to where externals and internals expect to receive their rewards, either from their own behavior or from the behavior of others.

Cultural Differences in Locus of Control

Believing one has control or not seems to be a human universal in that the basic differences between internals and externals hold across a variety of cultures. However, differences exist between cultures in the amount of control people believe they have (Cross & Markus, 1999). Individualistic cultures, such as in the United States and western European countries, tend to have a more internal locus of control. In fact, individualistic cultures tend to be so internal that they are actually vulnerable to an **illusion of control** where people believe they have control even in situations where, objectively, they do not (Taylor & Brown, 1988).

In contrast, collectivistic cultures, such as in countries in East Asia, tend to be more external. They believe that supernatural forces, fate, or even destiny determine outcomes. For example, Japanese students feel less control over both positive and negative events than American college students do (Heine & Lehman, 1995).

However, John Weisz and his colleagues suggested that there are two ways of taking control (Weisz, Rothbaum, & Blackburn, 1984). First, people can exercise **primary control** and attempt to make themselves feel better or less distressed by changing circumstances. To do this, of course, one must have an internal locus of control.

Alternatively, people can choose to exercise **secondary control** and attempt to fit into, accommodate, or accept a situation or an event in ways that make themselves feel better, or at least less distressed. This also requires an internal locus of control. They cited an example of the Japanese cultural value of *akirame* which means being "at peace with what fate has given" (Weisz, Eastman, & McCarty, 1996, p. 67). Similarly, Hinduism places a value on giving up control and detaching oneself from a situation, which leads to better psychological health (Berry, Poortinga, Segall, & Dasen, 1992). Evidence suggests that as Americans move from young adulthood into middle age they show primary control, but then show secondary control as they move into old age (Schultz, Heckhausen, & Locher, 1991). That is, in the face of being able to do less, people turn to more cognitive ways of maintaining control rather than admit that they have no control over a situation.

The crucial difference between an internal and an external locus of control may be that externals have almost a "victim mentality" in which they feel helpless, act passively and believe that there is nothing they can do to change their outcomes or reinforcements. These feelings of helplessness and hopelessness are risk factors for depression, as we shall see later in this chapter. The notion of primary and secondary control suggests that just because collectivistic cultures

THINK ABOUT IT

Just how much do standards of psychological health and pathology vary by culture?

People in collectivistic cultures, such as in countries in East Asia, tend to be more external than people in individualistic cultures, such as in the United States.

appear to have an external locus of control, they are not necessarily adapting less well or feeling more victimized by their circumstances. Rather, they are asserting their control differently than what Americans do (Sosis et al., 1980). This also suggests that standards of psychological health and what is considered normal are determined by culture.

Then and Now: Locus of Control

Here is a puzzle for you: Since the time that Julian Rotter first identified the concept of locus of control young Americans have shown an interesting trend. Do you think college students have become more internal or external since 1960?

On the one hand, American culture has become more individualistic during this time (recall our earlier discussion of this finding from Chapter 5). We might expect that along with an emphasis on the individual, more people would believe in the power of the individual person as well. Or, as Twenge, Zhang, and Im (2004) put it, "Modern people are, in theory, strong, independent individuals in control of their own destinies and free of the confines of social forces" (p. 309). Objectively, people today do have more control over their environments than we did over half a century ago. Think about changes like birth control, increased opportunity for travel, a more diverse and tolerant society, and technological advancements that facilitate shopping, communication, and entertainment. Does this translate into an increased sense of personal control?

Maybe not. During this same time Americans have also become more cynical, mistrusting, alienated, and litigious (Twenge et al., 2004). In addition, there has been an increase in the divorce rate, violent crime, and the suicide rate. Perhaps blaming outside forces for our own troubles might be a way of protecting ourselves from a more dangerous world.

So which hypothesis is correct, the independence model that suggests that Americans have become more internal, or the alienation model that suggests that Americans have become more external? The beauty of locus of control is that because it is one of the most studied personality variables in the history of personality research, Twenge et al. (2004) were able to graph changes in mean level of locus of control scores over time. They found a correlation of $r = .70$ between scores on the Rotter I-E scale and the year the sample was collected for college student samples and among children in Grades 4 or 5. Or, to put it another way, the average college student in 2002 scored more externally than 80% of college students in the early 1960s (Twenge et al., 2004).

Twenge et al. (2004) wondered if being moderately external is not as bad as it once was, if *everyone* has similar beliefs. That is, which is more important, absolute level of locus of control (e.g., internal or external) or level relative to one's peers and the society at large? Perhaps, like in collectivistic cultures, Americans are turning to secondary control more and more as a way of maintaining control. This shift toward secondary control is reflected in a more external locus of control.

> **THINK ABOUT IT**
>
> Which is more important, absolute level of locus of control (e.g., internal or external) or level relative to one's peers and the society at large?

College students from the 1960s (left). College students today (right) have a more external locus of control than college students in earlier times.

Learned Helplessness

Locus of control is not the only consistent difference between people in how they think about the world. The opposite of having an internal locus of control is not having an external locus of control; it is feeling helpless in the present and hopeless about the future. It is to this topic of learned helplessness—of which locus of control is but one part—that we now turn.

At around the same time that Julian Rotter realized the importance of locus of control, Martin Seligman and his colleagues were trying to figure out why dogs, after being exposed to inescapable shock, were unable to escape from a later escapable shock (Overmier & Seligman, 1967). The explanation seems obvious to us now—that the dogs had somehow learned that their responses were useless and gave up trying—but the notion that the dogs had expectations about future payoffs in a totally new situation flew in the face of years of research evidence on instrumental conditioning. Yet this is precisely what the dogs had learned!

Overmier and Seligman (1967) reasoned that when dogs or humans find themselves in a situation where they are exposed to aversive stimuli that they cannot reduce, eliminate, or control in any way, they may experience **learned helplessness** and come to believe that their actions will be useless in future situations as well. The authors hypothesized that lack of control causes this state of learned helplessness, whereas having control over aversive stimuli prevents later helplessness. Helplessness leads to loss of motivation, problems in thinking and learning, and negative emotions such as sadness, depression, and anger (Maier & Seligman, 1976).

To test the learned helplessness explanation, dogs were randomly assigned to one of three conditions (Seligman & Maier, 1967). In the Escapable Shock condition, the dogs first went through a training phase where they received a shock, but could make the shock stop by touching a panel with their heads. In the Inescapable Shock condition, dogs received shocks for the same amount of time as dogs in the Escape condition did; the only difference was that there was nothing the dogs could do to stop the shocks. Researchers call this **yoking** when a treatment that participants in one condition receive depends on how participants in another condition behave. In the third, Experimental Control condition, dogs did not have this training with shocks like the dogs in the Escape and Inescapable conditions did. The **triadic design** of this experiment using these three conditions tests that the *controllability* of the shock, not the shock itself, causes the helplessness.

After this initial training, 24 hours later the dogs in all three conditions took part in the testing phase of the experiment. Here they were placed in a shuttle box that had two compartments separated by a wall at the dogs' shoulder height. For each trial, dogs were placed in one side of the box and then the lights in the box would dim signaling that they were about to receive a shock. Sure enough, 10 seconds later the dogs would receive a shock through the floor of the compartment. However, if the dogs jumped over the wall into the adjacent compartment, the shock would terminate. Would dogs be able to figure this out for themselves?

As you can see in Table 10.2, all of the dogs that went through the Escapable Shock training figured out rather quickly that they could escape or even avoid the shock altogether by jumping over the barrier as soon as the lights dimmed. But most of the dogs in the Inescapable Shock condition did not. Having learned in the training phase that there was nothing they could do to avoid the shocks, they did nothing in the testing phase.

Can dogs learn to be helpless?

They just gave up and passively endured the shocks. However, if the experimenters forcibly dragged the dogs over the barrier, they eventually learned that they could escape the shock on their own (Maier & Seligman, 1976).

Keep in mind that the shocks were painful enough to make the dogs want to avoid them, but not so painful as to harm the dogs. Generally, researchers do not like using such methods except where they are unavoidable and have great potential to make a contribution to alleviate human suffering. Of course, many people object to using animals in research at all.

The results of this experiment were so surprising that critics suggested many alternative explanations to learned helplessness. Some suggested that the dogs, rather than learning that they had no control, instead learned that *not* responding paid off. Essentially the dogs learned to be passive, rather than helpless. To test this alternative explanation, experimenters used the same triadic design and exposed dogs to the same training and testing phases as in the Seligman and Maier (1967; Maier, 1970) experiments. But this time during the training phase, dogs in the Escapable Shock condition needed to remain perfectly still to make the shocks stop. In this way escaping the shocks was still under the dog's control, but they were controllable only by being passive. In the testing phase, where dogs were placed in the shuttle box and given escapable shocks that they could escape by jumping over the barrier, the experimenters wondered if the dogs would indeed be passive, because this is what worked in the first part, or if they would manage to escape the shock.

As predicted by learned helplessness theory, the dogs escaped the shock, albeit a bit slower than dogs in the original experiment, after realizing that keeping perfectly still did not terminate the shock. The key to avoiding helplessness is not learning that a *particular* response is effective, but learning that *any* response is effective. Dogs who are not helpless will keep moving around, trying new behaviors, and eventually hitting on the right response in a given situation.

The flip side of helplessness, especially for humans, is personal control. Imagine participants in an experiment who are seated at a table in front of a red button (Hiroto, 1974). They are told, "From time to time a loud tone will appear. When that tone comes on, there is something you can do to stop it." Suddenly, they hear an obnoxious, high-pitched tone about as loud as a chainsaw. How do you think a participant might react?

Most participants immediately hit the button. However, this worked only to terminate the noise if they were in the Escapable Noise condition. Despite these instructions, in the Inescapable Noise condition there was nothing participants could do to terminate the noise. In fact, they had to endure it for a full 5 seconds. There was also a Control Group that did not go through this training phase.

Then, participants in all three conditions were seated at a different table with a different apparatus in front of them: a wooden box that looked like an extraordinarily long shoebox, with a knob protruding out of the top locked in some sort of a track that ran from one end of the box to the other. A red light located at the top of the box would go on for 5 seconds and when the light went off, the same obnoxious noise from the first part of the experiment would come on.

As you probably recognized, this box was the human equivalent of the shuttle box used with dogs in the early helplessness studies. Participants could stop the noise if they pushed the knob from one side to the other. Sure enough, just like in the animal studies, human participants who were trained with the Inescapable Noise were significantly slower at figuring out how to escape the noise during the testing phase. Participants in the Control Group and the Escapable Noise conditions were faster at figuring out how to make the noise stop and even managed to prevent the noise from starting in the first place. Participants in the Inescapable Noise condition never quite realized that they could prevent the onset of the noise.

Participants in this experiment were also given a measure of locus of control. Based on Rotter's research on locus of control, the experimenters wondered who would be faster at figuring out how to make the noise stop during the testing phase of the experiment. True to the belief that they can control their own outcomes, internals were faster than externals to escape noise in this human shuttle box.

Table 10.2 Percentage of Dogs That Were Unable to Escape Shocks in the Testing Phase as a Function of Training Condition

Escapable Shock	0%
Inescapable Shock	75
Experimental Control Group	12.5

Source: Seligman and Maier (1967).

THINK ABOUT IT

Was Elena, the child who was unable to color, more like participants in the escapable noise or inescapable noise conditions?

In yet another twist to this experiment, some participants were led to believe that terminating the noise involved skill: "What you do is really up to you to figure out. You are potentially in control of the situation." Other participants were told that the task involved chance: "The way to stop the tone is up to [the experimenter]. This is a guessing game. If you guess wrong the tone stays on." Participants who thought that preventing or stopping the noise was due to their own skill were faster at the task than were participants who believed the task was due to chance.

This experiment demonstrated that learned helplessness comes from people's beliefs about control, their expectations about a specific task, and their past experiences with uncontrollable outcomes (Hiroto, 1974). Each one alone is enough to cause helplessness in humans.

Learned helplessness in humans, just like in animals, causes problems in motivation, cognition, and emotion (Maier & Seligman, 1976). Exposure to inescapable shocks, uncontrollable loud noises, or unsolvable anagrams causes a state of helplessness that makes people give up responding (Hiroto & Seligman, 1975). Even if one of their responses should be effective, helplessness will make it difficult if not impossible for people to recognize that their response worked (Maier & Seligman, 1976). Helplessness first causes anxiety; then, after continued exposure, it causes depression (Seligman, 1975).

In both humans and animals, learned helplessness is marked by the same three parts (Peterson, Maier, & Seligman, 1993). First, there must be a noncontingency or disconnect between people's actions and their outcomes, such that people truly have no control over their outcomes in a given situation. But exposure to uncontrollable outcomes is not enough to cause helplessness; people must also come to expect that their actions will also be ineffective in the future. Finally, people give up and act passively when they recognize that their actions are fruitless.

However, when they discover that they are helpless, humans, unlike animals, ask themselves, "Why am I helpless?" (Abramson, Seligman, & Teasdale, 1978). The way people understand the cause of their helplessness is very important for determining how devastating the feelings of helplessness will be. This led to a reformulated theory of learned helplessness in humans (Abramson et al., 1978) which eventually led to the current **hopelessness model of depression**. Here, the belief that one lacks control—is helpless in the face of a negative event in the present—combines with the belief that the helplessness will continue in the future. This causes a person to lose hope, stop trying, and feel sadness (Abramson, Metalsky, & Alloy, 1989).

Hopelessness depression, like other kinds of depression, causes changes in motivation (e.g., passivity and giving up), cognition (e.g., failure to perceive an opportunity to control outcomes), emotions (e.g., sadness, guilt), and lowered self-esteem (e.g., feeling useless and incompetent; Abramson et al., 1989).

People can feel helpless without feeling hopeless if they anticipate that circumstances might be different in the future (Abramson et al., 1989). For example, believing that somebody else might

THINK ABOUT IT

What costs are involved in believing that something is wrongly due to chance? In believing that something is wrongly due to skill?

Can humans learn to be helpless?

step in to help or that the external circumstances could change for the better (e.g., the task becomes easier) are hopeful beliefs. The combination of helplessness in the present and the hopelessness that negative consequences will continue into the future makes people vulnerable to depression when a bad event occurs or when an important good event fails to occur.

Explanatory Style

An interesting side note to the original learned helplessness experiments with dogs is that Seligman and his colleagues used more than 150 dogs in their experiments (Maier & Seligman, 1976). Of these, about 33% could not be made to feel helpless, even though they were exposed to inescapable shocks. Also, about 5% of the dogs never learned that they could escape the shock, even without experience with the inescapable shock. The experimenters wondered, was there something in the past history of these dogs that taught them to be helpless or immunized them against helplessness before they even came to the lab?

If you think about it, just like the dogs that were helpless or not helpless before the experiment began, people have a lifetime of experiencing good and bad events. Essentially, the laboratory is not the first time or place that a person—or a dog—may have felt that his or her efforts are useless. After many such experiences, people develop habitual ways of explaining both the bad and the good things that happen to them in life. This is called **explanatory style**. How people differ in explanatory style is an important aspect of personality.

People who view negative events as their own fault (internal) likely to happen again (stable), and undermining other aspects of their lives (global) are at risk for depression (Peterson & Seligman, 1984; Sweeney, Anderson, & Bailey, 1986). This is called a **pessimistic explanatory style**. In contrast, people with an **optimistic explanatory style** view negative events as not their own fault (external), unlikely to happen again (unstable), and limited to just one aspect of their lives (specific). With an optimistic explanatory style people are faster at bouncing back from a negative event and are less likely to experience symptoms of depression.

There are also pessimistic and optimistic ways of explaining good events. People with an optimistic explanatory style believe that they caused the good thing to happen, that they are able to make it happen again, and that their good fortune makes everything in their life better. In contrast, people with a pessimistic explanatory style believe that they had little to do with their good fortune, that good things may or may not happen again, and that the good event affects just one aspect of their lives.

Explanations for events can vary in three ways. As we saw with learned helplessness, when trying to understand a situation in which they feel helpless, people may think that there is nothing they can do to remedy the situation (i.e., that they lack control). So one way that explanations can vary is in how **internal versus external** the cause might be.

"No sense being pessimistic. It wouldn't work anyway."
Phillip Mueller

Tis nothing good or bad but thinking makes it so. Shakespeare.
From Hamlet, by William Shakespeare (Act 2, scene ii)

How might a person with an optimistic explanatory style respond to this event?

For example, imagine that Olivia does poorly on her psychology test. Why might this be? She could think that the test was difficult (external) or unfair (external), or she might think that she didn't study enough (internal), or that she is not smart enough (internal). However, not all explanations are created equal! Some explanations may lead her to feel helpless in the future, whereas others will actually help her prevent a bad grade from happening again. If she truly believed that she didn't study hard enough due to lack of effort—a temporary condition—she could study harder next time. However, if she believed that she doesn't have the brain power to do any better than a D (lack of ability), then why should she bother studying at all next time? The difference between lack of effort and lack of ability has to do with how permanent or stable the cause is. So, the second way that explanations can vary is in how **stable versus unstable** the cause might be.

Consider another situation. Imagine that Tamika just told Jamal that she didn't want to see him again after their first date. Jamal could think that this was because Tamika is extra busy this semester (external) or that she finds him boring (internal). But even if Tamika finds Jamal boring, this doesn't mean that other potential dates will find him boring as well. Being boring, although an internal explanation, is also an unstable cause of Jamal's failure to get a second date with Tamika. However, suppose Jamal is so devastated by the news that he starts to believe that his friends barely tolerate him, he is convinced that he will make a poor impression on a future employer, and that he will be a failure in life! Here the cause of the breakup is not only internal and stable, but it affects other aspects of his life as well, not just his chances of dating again. Jamal's beliefs about the breakup have broad repercussions in his young life. The third way that explanations can vary is in how **global versus specific** the cause might be.

To summarize, when *any* good or a bad event occurs, people come up with possible explanations to understand what caused the event (see Table 10.3). These explanations differ in three dimensions, as illustrated by our examples of Olivia and Jamal. Explanations can vary in locus of control (internal or external), stability (how stable, permanent, or recurrent a cause is vs. how unstable, temporary, or intermittent it is), and generality (how global, affecting many aspects of a person's life, or limited to a specific domain a cause is).

In fact, undergraduates who had either an increase in good events or an increase in optimistic explanatory style for positive events (attributing good events to stable and global factors) recovered from depression faster, showing fewer depressive symptoms than students with a more pessimistic style (Needles & Abramson, 1990). In addition, students with an optimistic style (making stable and global attributions) benefited the most from good events whereas students who made pessimistic attributions for good events (unstable, specific) didn't seem to derive much cheer from the good events in their lives. In addition, an increase in participants' hopefulness for future success in their career or personal lives was a significant predictor of recovery from depression.

Optimistic and pessimistic explanatory styles, like locus of control, have been associated with outcomes in achievement, career and work behavior, physical and psychological health, and social

> **SEE FOR YOURSELF**
>
> Think about a recent negative event. What caused this event? Is your explanation more internal or external? Stable or unstable? Global or specific?

Table 10.3 Optimistic and Pessimistic Explanatory Styles

	Optimistic Style	Pessimistic Style
	External: "It's not me"	Internal: "It's me"
Bad events	Unstable: "It's just a temporary setback"	Stable: "It's going to last"
	Specific: "It's just this one situation"	Global: "It's going to undermine everything I do"
	Internal: "I did it"	External: "It happened to me"
Good events	Stable: "I can do it again"	Unstable: "It's a one-time thing"
	Global: "Life is good"	Specific: "It's just this one situation"

Note: Causal explanations for both good and bad events vary in three dimensions: internal–external, stable–unstable, and global–specific.

Source: Abramson et al. (1978).

behavior (Wise & Rosqvist, 2006). An optimistic explanatory style is associated with increased motivation, achievement, physical health, lower depression, and overall well-being (Buchanan & Seligman, 1995; Peterson & Steen, 2002; Wise & Rosqvist, 2006). In contrast, a pessimistic explanatory style is associated with negative affect, depressive symptoms, lower academic achievement, poorer physical health, poorer athletic performance, lower marital satisfaction, and even political losses (Gillham, Shatté, Reivich, & Seligman, 2001). A pessimistic explanatory style is a risk factor for depression (Gladstone & Kaslow, 1995; Joiner & Wagner, 1995; Sweeney et al., 1986).

Measures of Explanatory Style

How is explanatory style measured? There are basically two different ways: questionnaires and content analysis (a research method discussed in Chapter 5). The most extensively used questionnaire is the **Attributional Style Questionnaire** (**ASQ**) (Peterson et al., 1982). The ASQ contains 12 hypothetical good and bad situations. Respondents imagine the situation happening to them and write down what they think would be one major cause of that situation. Then they rate each cause on a 1 to 7 scale of internal–external, stable–unstable, and global–specific. The situations include things such as becoming very rich, getting a raise, getting complimented by a friend, having a date go badly, giving a bad presentation, and not getting all your work done on time. Generally, researchers average a participant's responses on all three dimensions yielding a score for bad events, for good events, and a composite of the two. Higher numbers indicate a more pessimistic explanatory style (internal, stable, global for negative events and external, unstable, specific for good events) and lower numbers indicate a more optimistic explanatory style. Researchers can also measure a participant's hopelessness by scoring the two dimensions of stable–unstable and global–specific for bad events only (Needles & Abramson, 1990).

The ASQ has been revised and expanded (Peterson & Villanova, 1988). There is also an ASQ for use with elderly populations (Houston, McKee, & Wilson, 2000), the Occupational Attributional Style Questionnaire for work situations (OASQ; Furnham, Sadka, & Brewin, 1992), and the Cognitive Style Questionnaire to measure vulnerability to hopelessness depression (CSQ; Alloy et al., 2000; Haeffel et al., 2008).

The second method of measuring explanatory style is the content analysis of verbatim explanations called the **CAVE technique** (Peterson, Luborsky, & Seligman, 1983). The technique works very much like the ASQ. First, one must find a direct quote of a person explaining why a good or a bad event happened to him or her. The researcher then quotes the event and the explanation and presents both to trained judges who rate the explanation on the three dimensions of internal–external, stable–unstable, and global–specific using the same 1 to 7 scale as on the ASQ (Zullow, Oettingen, Peterson, & Seligman, 1988). Ratings are averaged for each dimension and for good and bad events. Higher scores indicate a more pessimistic explanatory style, lower scores a more optimistic one.

THINK ABOUT IT

If you could discover the explanatory style of any person, who would it be and why? Could you use the CAVE technique with him or her?

Using the CAVE technique, researchers found that teams with optimistic players performed better after a loss than teams with pessimistic players.

Table 10.4 The CAVE Technique: Sample Events, Explanations, and Ratings

Event	Explanation	Ratings
Player is in a slump (bad event)	"I've been putting too much pressure on myself. Now I'm relaxed"	I/E = 7 S/U = 3 G/S = 6
"I'm not frustrated" (good event)	"Because I have confidence that I have what it takes"	I/E = 7 S/U = 7 G/S = 7
Player missed an easy shot (bad event)	"My timing was off for a second"	I/E = 7 S/U = 1 G/S = 1
Player hadn't scored for two quarters (bad event)	"They were playing great defense for a change"	I/E = 1 S/U = 1 G/S = 1

Note: Causal explanations for both good and bad events vary in three dimensions: internal–external (I/E; higher numbers more internal, lower numbers more external), stable–unstable (S/U; higher numbers more stable, lower numbers more unstable), and global–specific (G/S; higher numbers more global, lower numbers more specific).

Source: From Rettew and Reivich (1995, Table 10.1 p.175). Reprinted with permission from Rettew, D., & Reivich, K. (1995), "Sports and explanatory style," as appeared in G. M. Buchanan & M. E. P. Seligman (Eds.), Explanatory style, pp. 173–185 (Hillsdale, NJ: Erlbaum). Permission conveyed through the Copyright Clearance Center.

The power of the CAVE technique is that a researcher can measure the explanatory style of historical figures, famous people, politicians, athletes—pretty much anybody who has left behind a sample of his or her words in letters, speeches, interviews, diaries, journals, school essays, newspaper stories, and other archival material (Zullow et al., 1988).

Table 10.4 illustrates how the CAVE technique might work. Quotations from members of the 1982–1984 Celtics, Knicks, Bullets, Sixers, and Nets basketball teams were taken from the weekly journal *The Sporting News* and from the hometown newspapers of the players. Judges then rated each explanation on the three dimensions of internal–external, stable–unstable, global–specific and calculated each player's explanatory style. Across both seasons, teams with more optimistic players performed better following a loss than teams with more pessimistic players (Rettew & Reivich, 1995).

In another study, researchers were able to predict the ups and downs of a patient's mood from the kind of explanations he made during a therapy session using the CAVE technique (Peterson et al., 1983). Mr. Q, as the patient was called, demonstrated very unusual mood swings during therapy sessions which often took him and his therapist by surprise. But as you can see in Figure 10.2, his mood shifts were actually preceded by certain types of explanations he made. When he made more pessimistic explanations his mood became more depressed and his explanations more pessimistic. But when he made less pessimistic explanations his depression seemed to improve and his explanations became more optimistic as the session continued.

An optimistic explanatory style as assessed by the CAVE technique has also been linked to political victory (Zullow, 1995), military assertiveness (Satterfield & Seligman, 1994), and quality of life while living in a politically free country (Zullow et al., 1988). For example,

Figure 10.2 Means of attributions for negative events before and after Mr. Q's mood shifts. Higher numbers indicate a more pessimistic explanatory style (numbers in parentheses refer to the number of therapy sessions on which means are based). *Source:* From Peterson et al. (1983, Figure 1, p. 100). Peterson, C., Luborsky, L., & Seligman, M. E. P. (1983). Attributions and depressive mood shifts: A case study using the symptom-context method. *Journal of Abnormal Psychology*, 92, 96–103. Copyright American Psychological Association. Reprinted with permission.

in 9 out of the 10 U.S. presidential elections held between 1948 and 1984, the more pessimistic candidate in his nomination acceptance speech lost the election, especially if he was prone to ruminate or dwell on depressive thoughts (Zullow & Seligman, 1990). What about the 10th election? That candidate started out optimistic enough during his acceptance speech, but then became much more pessimistic and ruminative as the campaign wore on. What about our current president? Optimism won again! (See the photo on the right.)

"A joint analysis of candidate optimism has determined that, once again, the more hopeful candidate, Barack Obama, has won an election. We believe that hopefulness has played a major role in this election. When it comes to celebrating what is good about America and to acknowledging our ability to make lasting positive change in the world, Obama wins out over McCain. That message appeals more to Americans at this time apparently," according to Stephen Schueller of the Positive Psychology Center at the University of Pennsylvania. Here, then senator Barack Obama poses in front of the Superman statue in downtown Metropolis, IL, after his 50th town hall meeting in Massac County.

Explanatory Style and Achievement

Across many different contexts, people with an optimistic explanatory style outperform expectations—and often their pessimistic peers and rival teams—in school and on the playing field (Gillham et al., 2001; Rettew & Reivich, 1995; Schulman, 1995). In college, optimistic students achieve at a level beyond what would be expected based on their high school grades, class rank, SAT scores, or achievement test scores (Schulman, 1995). Optimistic teams and individual athletes bounce back faster from a loss or a bad performance than pessimistic teams or athletes (Gillham et al., 2001).

School. Optimistic college students do better in their classes than students with a pessimistic explanatory style, even after controlling for ability (Metalsky, Abramson, Seligman, Semmel, & Peterson, 1982; Metalsky, Halberstadt, & Abramson, 1987; Peterson & Barett, 1987). What leads optimists to outperform expectations? Students with an optimistic explanatory style show greater motivation and persist longer in the face of adversity, strategies which are related to higher achievement (Wise & Rosqvist, 2006).

In one study, first-year college students filled out a series of questionnaires measuring explanatory style, how they coped with academic failures and frustrations, SAT scores, and grades. Students with a pessimistic explanatory style performed worse in their first year in college, averaging about a C, compared to students with an optimistic explanatory style who averaged almost a B-, even when SAT scores were used to control for natural ability (Peterson & Barett, 1987). Students with an optimistic style remained motivated in the face of setbacks and, as a result, obtained a higher GPA, whereas students with a pessimistic explanatory style tended to give up after academic frustrations. Their GPA reflects a lack of motivation rather than a lack of ability.

Similar results have been demonstrated with elementary school children. Kids with a pessimistic explanatory style showed poor achievement on standardized tests and grades in both the United States (Nolen-Hoeksema, Girgus, & Seligman, 1986) and in China (Yu & Seligman, 2002). In addition, teachers in China reported that students with a pessimistic explanatory style showed behavioral problems as well, something not measured in the U.S. sample.

However, there are times when a more pessimistic explanatory style—focusing on failure and discounting success—may work to improve achievement such as when faced with highly demanding academic programs like law (Satterfield, Monahan, & Seligman, 1997) and marketing (LaForge & Cantrell, 2003). In one study, students with a pessimistic explanatory style (internal, stable, global for negative events and the opposite pattern for positive events) the summer before starting law school achieved a higher GPA and greater success working on their school's law journal than those with an optimistic explanatory style. Some aspects of the pessimistic explanatory style, such as taking responsibility for one's failures to remedy them, may be more adaptive and conducive to future achievement than explaining them away as external, unstable, or specific. Law school programs are intense, and maybe performance in law school *is* everything to a faltering law student. Perhaps viewing failures as internal may be a way of keeping oneself on track or motivated for success. Of course, the authors cautioned, we don't know if these pessimists were at greater risk for depression or if these negative attributions merely served as defenses keeping their expectations low to keep themselves performing their best (Satterfield et al., 1997).

Pessimistic explanations tend to be self-fulfilling: Students with a pessimistic explanatory style were less likely to have specific academic goals and less likely to seek academic advising, symptoms of passive rather than active strategies to school achievement (Peterson & Barett, 1987). In the academic life of a typical student—as many readers of this book can attest—there are many frustrations, from failed quizzes, difficult problem sets, a lost textbook, a surprise quiz, an incomplete reading assignment, difficulty starting an upcoming paper, or an unintelligible lecture, for example, that students must face on a daily basis. Successful students are not necessarily the smartest, but those who are able to cope with these inevitable setbacks and continue to strive rather than give up.

Athletics.   Even in the sports arena, individuals and teams with an optimistic explanatory style perform better than those with a pessimistic style (Gillham et al., 2001; Rettew & Reivich, 1995; Seligman, Nolen-Hoeksema, Thornton, & Thornton, 1990), especially after defeat (Seligman et al., 1990). We saw this earlier with professional basketball teams using the CAVE technique (Rettew & Reivich, 1995).

In a different study using similar methods with baseball players, teams with more optimistic players won more games the following season than teams with pessimistic players (Rettew & Reivich, 1995). Explanatory style was just as good a predictor of the next season's performance as was the team's performance in the current season (see Figure 10.3). Optimistic soccer players also play better after a loss than do players with a pessimistic explanatory style (Gordon, 2008).

Why does explanatory style have such a strong effect on athletic performance? Researchers think that the key to a winning athletic performance is the ability to persist despite setbacks. This was studied more closely in elite male and female swimmers.

For this experiment, the participants were members of the University of California at Berkeley's men's and women's swim teams, both nationally ranked, in which several members

Figure 10.3 Explanatory style and baseball wins: Average explanatory style of players for negative events during the 1985 season by percentage of games won during the 1986 season. Higher numbers indicate a more pessimistic explanatory style. *Source:* From Rettew and Reivich (1995, Figure 10.1, p. 180). Rettew, D., & Reivich, K. (1995). Sports and explanatory style. In G. M. Buchanan & M. E. P. Seligman (Eds.), Explanatory style (p. 173–185). Hillsdale, NJ: Erlbaum.

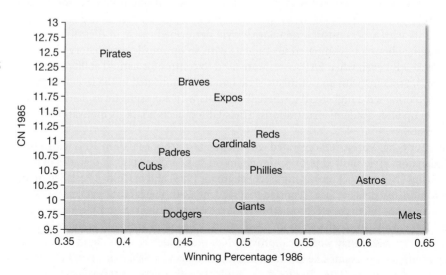

at the time held national and world records and were preparing for the 1988 Olympic trials. At the beginning of the season, the swimmers indicated their explanatory style and their coaches rated how likely the swimmer was to bounce back after a bad performance. Then, after every swim meet during the regular season, coaches rated whether the swimmer performed better than expected or worse than expected. Swimmers with a pessimistic explanatory style and swimmers who were rated by the coach as unlikely to bounce back after a defeat performed worse than expected over the course of the season (Seligman et al., 1990).

The researchers hypothesized that one reason why optimists outperform pessimists is because they are better able to bounce back after a defeat. Having a pessimistic explanatory style, where they believe that bad events are likely to recur, causes pessimists to become helpless after a failure and give up trying. However, as you no doubt recognized, this study

Optimistic swimmers bounce back better than pessimistic swimmers after a failed performance.

merely showed that the two are correlated. We do not know if a bad performance *caused* the pessimists, but not the optimists, to give up and try less hard the next time around (Seligman et al., 1990).

In a second experiment using the same participants, the researchers specifically imposed defeat on each swimmer and watched what happened to his or her performance. To do this, after competing in their best event, swimmers were told that they swam at a time significantly slower than their actual time. Although the times were large enough so that each swimmer would feel that he or she performed poorly, the times were small enough to be undetected by the swimmers themselves. After a 30-minute rest swimmers swam the same event again. How would optimists and pessimists perform after this manipulated failure?

The optimistic swimmers did at least as well on their second swim as they had on the first swim, but the pessimistic swimmers swam slower. Despite no time difference between the optimists and the pessimists on the first swim, the difference between the optimists and the pessimists on the second swim was enough to lose the event if it had been an actual swim meet (see Figure 10.4; Seligman et al., 1990).

Another study found a similar effect in professional basketball teams: Teams with an optimistic explanatory style were more likely than teams with a pessimistic style to bounce back from a loss by winning the next game (Rettew & Reivich, 1995). When it comes to athletic performance, it's like the old saying: When the going gets tough, the tough—the optimists in this case—get going! By the way, when the going gets tough the *pessimists* go shopping. Or something like that, as pessimists tend to use avoidance as a way of coping with negative events (Scheier, Carver, & Bridges, 2001).

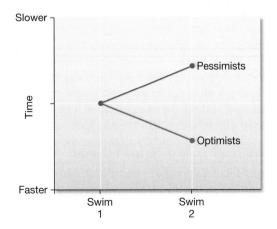

Figure 10.4 Swim times of optimists and pessimists after false failure feedback. Optimistic swimmers perform better than pessimistic swimmers after failure. *Source:* Seligman et al. (1990).

Explanatory Style and Work Behavior

In the United States, as well as in other countries including Greece (Xenikou, 2005) and Australia (Henry, 2005), with managers, nonmanagers, or laborers and across many types of work including hospitals, schools, sales, banking, or information technology, workers with an optimistic explanatory style are more motivated, persist longer in the face of adversity, perform better, and experience less burnout and turnover than workers with a pessimistic explanatory style.

When it comes to sales, in particular, an optimistic explanatory style really pays off. Whether it is insurance, telecommunications, real estate, office products, auto sales, or banking, whenever persistence is necessary to overcome difficulties, salespeople with an optimistic explanatory style outsell salespeople with a pessimistic explanatory style by about 20 to 40 percent (Schulman, 1999). Why is this the case? Salespersons often must make "cold calls" where they contact a potential buyer who is not expecting the call or whom they do not yet know. Understandably, the likelihood of landing a sale under these conditions is quite slim, so the successful salesperson must be able to take a rejection and forge ahead with his or her calls.

Imagine two recently hired insurance salespeople, Carlos and Manny, who have just finished making 20 cold calls and were rejected on every single one. Carlos says to himself: "I made 20 calls without a hint of a sale. What's wrong with me? I'm just not cut out for this (internal). I guess I'm not good with people or not very persuasive" (stable and global; Schulman, 1999, p. 32). With this attitude, how likely will Carlos be to ever pick up the phone again?

Now consider Manny who says: "That was a tough stretch, but that can happen to the best of them (external). Maybe they don't need what I'm selling or were too busy (external). Also, I'm new at this and it takes time and practice to learn the ropes and sharpen my sales pitch (unstable and specific). As my boss said, this is a numbers game—you have to make lots of calls to find those few customers who are interested enough to buy" (Schulman, 1999, pp. 32–33). With this attitude, Manny is able to face the next call and even the next rejection.

Obviously, Carlos has a pessimistic explanatory style whereas Manny has an optimistic one. These two imaginary salespeople are fairly representative of participants in a study of explanatory style of 104 insurance agents working for the Met Life Insurance Company (Seligman & Schulman, 1986). Agents with an optimistic explanatory style sold more life insurance than agents with a pessimistic explanatory style. They were also less likely to quit or be fired in the first 2 years of employment. In fact, optimists sold about 35% more insurance than the pessimists. Pessimists may be more easily overwhelmed by cold calling, and come to avoid it. They start to lose their confidence in a self-fulfilling prophesy of helplessness, hopelessness, and pessimism, which may eventually lead to their quitting, if they are not fired first (Schulman, 1999). In contrast, optimists are more likely to see adversity as a challenge or as a puzzle that they can solve with the right strategy or enough effort. They may spend long hours refining their interpersonal skills and striving to maintain their confidence after a rejection so that they can rebound quickly after setbacks, and persist in the face of challenge.

But how can we be so sure that explanatory style *caused* workers to persist longer leading to other good outcomes? After all, because none of these studies randomly assigned workers to explanatory style, it is possible that job success led workers to become more optimistic in their explanatory style. However, we can randomly assign some workers to a treatment designed to make them more optimistic and compare them to workers who did not go through the treatment. Will changing a worker's explanatory style to a more optimistic one also lead to better outcomes at work?

The answer is a resounding yes! Employees of a major British insurance company that had just undergone a massive reorganization took part in an intervention designed to help them develop a more optimistic explanatory style (Proudfoot, Corr, Guest, & Dunn, 2009). Before the intervention, the reorganization hit employees hard; some 37% of employees experienced levels of psychological distress high enough to warrant professional help.

For this experiment, half the participants were randomly assigned to participate in a special training group immediately; the others were placed on a wait-list control and would have the same exact training but 5 months later. In this way the researchers made sure that both the treatment group and the control group were comparable except for the training. The experimental group attended weekly 3-hour sessions for 7 weeks. Using a combination of Socratic questioning, group discussions, self-observation, reflection, and assignments, these sessions used principles of cognitive behavior therapy to change employees' work-related explanatory style.

THINK ABOUT IT

In what other jobs do workers face similar conditions? Might people with an optimistic explanatory style excel there as well?

The intervention did more than make employees in the intervention group more optimistic compared to employees who had not yet experienced the intervention: It also led to positive psychological and work-related outcomes. Both immediately after the intervention and 3 months later, employees in the experimental group reported greater self-esteem, job satisfaction, and productivity compared to before they started the program. They also reported lowered psychological distress, intention to quit, and job turnover. Employees in the control group also showed these improvements, but only after they had gone through the training (Proudfoot et al., 2009; see Figure 10.5).

As you can see, an optimistic explanatory style not only leads to better outcomes at work but it can also help workers successfully weather the changes and stresses of a corporate reorganization.

Explanatory Style and Physical and Psychological Health

Physical Health. We've already seen how a pessimistic explanatory style can be detrimental to good psychological health (Peterson & Seligman, 1984; Sweeney et al., 1986), but a pessimistic explanatory style can be bad for one's physical health as well (Peterson & Bossio, 2001).

An optimistic explanatory style is linked to better immune functioning (Brennan & Charnetski, 2000; Kamen-Siegel, Rodin, Seligman, & Dwyer, 1991). People with an optimistic explanatory style take better care of themselves, seeking and following medical advice more so than people with a pessimistic explanatory style. They are also more likely to engage in healthier behaviors that can prevent illness. Optimists have greater social support—that is, number and quality of friendships—and more quality personal relationships, both of which have been shown to bolster immune functioning (Seligman, 1990). College students with an optimistic explanatory style had fewer illnesses, made fewer visits to the doctor, and were more confident that they could prevent health problems than their more pessimistic peers (Peterson, 1988; Peterson & De Avila, 1995).

The effects of explanatory style in young adulthood set the stage for good psychological and physical health later in life. Students with an optimistic explanatory style in college also had better physical health in middle age (Peterson, Seligman, & Vaillant, 1988). Among men who

> **THINK ABOUT IT**
>
> Why might optimists and pessimists show differences in number and quality of friendships? Could a vicious cycle or self-fulfilling prophesy be operating here?

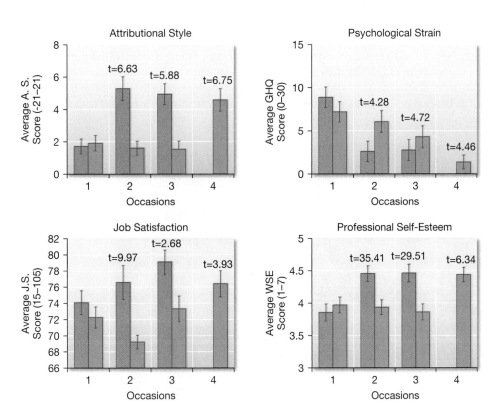

Figure 10.5 Comparison of experimental group with wait-list control group: 1 = before intervention for experimental group; 2 = after intervention; 3 = 3-month follow-up of experimental group and baseline for control group; and 4 = after control group intervention. *Source:* From Proudfoot et al. (2009, Figure 2, p. 150). Reprinted from Proudfoot, J. G., Corr, P. J., Guest, D. E., & Dunn, G. (2009), "Cognitive-behavioural training to change attributional style improves employee well-being, job satisfaction, productivity, and turnover," Personality and Individual Differences, 46, 147–153. Copyright © 2009, with permission from Elsevier.

had a previous heart attack, those with an optimistic explanatory style had a greater survival rate (Buchanan, 1995).

Psychological Health: Depression.   One of the most robust findings is that a pessimistic explanatory style is a risk factor for depression in both children (Gladstone & Kaslow, 1995; Joiner & Wagner, 1995) and adults (Gillham et al., 2001; Robins & Hayes, 1995). That is, although everybody might feel sad when a bad thing happens or a good thing fails to happen to them, people with a pessimistic style feel sadder longer and more deeply than people with an optimistic explanatory style (Peterson & Seligman, 1984). This finding has been demonstrated in cross-sectional correlational studies, longitudinal studies, field experiments, laboratory experiments, and case studies (Peterson & Seligman, 1984). In addition to depression, pessimists experience more negative emotions such as anxiety, guilt, anger, sadness, despair and hopelessness in the face of negative events than optimists (Isaacowitz & Seligman, 2003).

The tricky part of proving that a pessimistic explanatory style actually causes depression is that we can't randomly assign people to one style or the other. Also, it would be unethical to purposely cause bad things to happen to people and see who becomes depressed. As a result, much of the evidence for the effect of explanatory style on depression is correlational. However, the logic behind many of these studies does lead to the conclusion that pessimistic explanatory style is a risk factor for depression.

For example, much research finds a correlation between explanatory style and depression at the same point in time. As you recall, this could be because a pessimistic explanatory style causes depression, depression causes a person to develop a pessimistic explanatory style, or because some third variable, like Neuroticism, causes both depression and a pessimistic explanatory style.

One way around this problem is to start with a sample of optimistic and pessimistic people who do not differ in depressive symptoms and then attempt to predict who actually becomes depressed when a naturally occurring negative event—like failing a test, not getting into the college of your dreams, being rejected from a highly desirable fraternity or sorority, or having a heart attack—hits. Many studies have used such naturally occurring negative events to track explanatory style and depression and do indeed find that a pessimistic explanatory style often leads to depression after a negative event (e.g., Abela & Seligman, 2000).

College students, for example, regularly face naturally occurring negative events: exams. Undergraduate students in an intro psychology class took the ASQ and indicated what grade on the upcoming midterm exam would make them happy or unhappy. Then their mood was measured right before and right after the dreaded midterm exam. Among students who performed badly on the midterm exam—by their own definition—students with a pessimistic explanatory style were more likely to be depressed when they found out their grade than students with an optimistic explanatory style (Metalsky et al., 1982). Explanatory style was not correlated with exam grades.

> **THINK ABOUT IT**
>
> If a pessimistic explanatory style causes depression, can attribution therapy prevent or alleviate depression?

Students regularly face naturally occurring negative events. However, students with an optimistic explanatory style bounce back better and are less likely to become depressed after doing badly on an exam than students with a pessimistic explanatory style.

Similarly, undergraduate students in an abnormal psychology class who learned that they did badly on a midterm exam were understandably upset. However, students with an optimistic explanatory style seemed to bounce back within a day or two, whereas students with a pessimistic explanatory style still showed symptoms of depression. Pessimistic students with low self-esteem who failed the exam—a triple whammy of risk factors—continued to show symptoms of depression up to 5 days after receiving their grades, long after students with high self-esteem recovered from their failing grades (Metalsky, Joiner, Hardin, & Abramson, 1993).

Even children are vulnerable to depression when bad events happen to them, if they have a pessimistic explanatory style (Nolen-Hoeksema et al., 1986). Third, fourth, and fifth graders who had a pessimistic explanatory style were more likely to show symptoms of depression both in the present and a few months later, especially if they experienced negative life events than children with a more optimistic explanatory style. The children also reported engaging in more helpless behaviors, an observation verified by their teachers, and showed lower scores on state achievement test scores. Overall, helpless behaviors and depression were associated with poor achievement on standardized tests. There was also evidence in this study that depression can cause a pessimistic explanatory style.

A second strategy researchers may use to effectively demonstrate that a pessimistic explanatory style causes depression is to track both explanatory style and depressive symptoms over time and see how they relate to each other. Studies that have taken this tack do indeed find that a pessimistic explanatory style predicts increases in depressive symptoms over time (Gillham et al., 2001). One study found that the greater the number of daily hassles people experienced over 6 weeks, the more likely they were to experience depressive symptoms, especially if they had a more pessimistic way of explaining events (Gibb, Beevers, Andover, & Holleran, 2006).

Yet a third strategy is to design a treatment that changes explanatory style and see if this leads to changes in depression. Of course, it would be unethical to attempt to change an optimistic style to a more pessimistic one, so researchers opt to change a pessimistic style to a more optimistic one. An even more powerful demonstration would be to compare the intervention group to a control group of participants who are similar to them in explanatory style and depression, but who do not receive the intervention. If we see improvements in the experimental group but not in the control group, it suggests that it was the manipulation of explanatory style that caused the lessening of depressive symptoms.

Both of these studies have been done (Gillham et al., 2001). Martin Seligman and his colleagues at the University of Pennsylvania have devised the Penn Resiliency Program (PRP). This program was designed to change a pessimistic explanatory style to a more optimistic one. Indeed, not only do these programs change explanatory style, but they also prevent depression in both adults (Seligman, Schulman, DeRubeis, & Hollon, 1999) and children (Gillham et al., 2001). These programs have met with great success in the United States (Gillham, Reivich, Jaycox, & Seligman, 1995; Jaycox, Reivich, Gillham, & Seligman, 1994) and in China (Yu & Seligman, 2002). We'll take a closer look at how these programs work to increase optimism and lessen depression in The Personality of Everyday Life box later in this chapter.

Another kind of treatment is therapy. As adults successfully progress through cognitive therapy for depression, their explanatory style changes from a pessimistic one to a more optimistic one (Peterson & Seligman, 1984; Seligman et al., 1988). Conversely, a pessimistic explanatory style predicts a relapse in depression after termination of therapy (DeRubeis & Hollon, 1995; Ilardi, Craighead, & Evans, 1997). For example, one study monitored the thought processes of four patients who were in cognitive therapy for depression after a loss of a loved one. According to the transcripts of their therapy sessions from the beginning, middle, and end of therapy, these people showed the most internal stable and global explanations for negative events at the beginning of their therapy and the least internal, stable, and global explanations during their last session (Peterson & Seligman, 1984).

However, not all research supports the finding that pessimistic explanatory style is a risk factor for depression (Gillham et al., 2001; Norem, 2003). A few inconsistent studies find that explanatory style does not predict changes in symptoms of depression up to one year later (Bennett & Bates, 1995; Hammen, Adrian, & Hiroto, 1988; Tiggemann, Winefield, Winefield, & Goldney, 1991). All three of these studies looked at the impact of everyday hassles on depression.

Figure 10.6 Depressive symptoms at 6 months in optimists and pessimists on the Beck Depression Inventory (BDI) as a function of negative live events. *Source:* From Isaacowitz and Seligman (2001, Figure 1, p. 264). Reprinted from Isaacowitz, D. M., & Seligman, M. E. P. (2001), "Is pessimism a risk factor for depressive mood among community-dwelling older adults?" Behaviour Research and Therapy, 39, 255–272. Copyright © 2001, with permission from Elsevier.

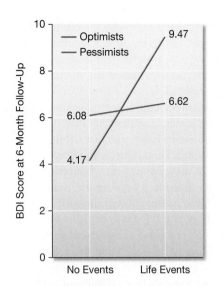

Perhaps everyday stress is not enough to cause depressive symptoms in people with a pessimistic explanatory style.

Other studies find that a pessimistic explanatory style may be more adaptive in certain situations. Recall our earlier discussion of how pessimistic college students in high-pressure courses of study achieved higher grades than students with an optimistic explanatory style (LaForge & Cantrell, 2003; Satterfield et al., 1997). Because neither of these studies looked at depressive symptoms, we do not know if the higher grades of pessimists came at a psychological cost. However, there is some evidence that a pessimistic explanatory style is better for the mental health of elderly people (Isaacowitz & Seligman, 2001).

In one sample of elders living in the greater Philadelphia region, those with a optimistic explanatory style showed the least symptoms of depression 6 months later *unless* they were faced with a negative event such as the death of a loved one or deterioration in physical health. In this case, optimists showed the *most* amount of depression. Pessimists, regardless of negative events, scored in between these two extremes on depressive symptoms (see Figure 10.6; Isaacowitz & Seligman, 2001).

Isaacowitz and Seligman (2001) surmised that the optimists' lifetime habit of viewing negative events as temporary and changeable is suddenly thrown into doubt when negative events occur for elders. Whereas for young people failing an exam is temporary, events such as changes in health status, death of friends, or other lifestyle changes associated with aging are permanent for elders and in most cases really do impact many domains of their lives. For elders, attributing bad events to unstable causes may actually increase depression if the causes turn out to be a permanent part of the elders' lives.

Similarly, aging may be harder for optimists who apply their typical active problem-focused coping to unsolvable problems. Pessimists may be more able to accept that some things happen outside their control. So, even though a pessimistic explanatory style is generally a risk factor for depression in young people, an optimistic explanatory style may be a risk factor for elders given the reality of their lives. Realism—however depressing one's prospects may be—may be a better coping strategy for elders, just as it may be for law students and marketing majors.

SEE FOR YOURSELF

The next time you are feeling lonely, consider it a temporary situation and think about what you could do, at least in the short term, to feel better.

Explanatory Style and Social Behavior

People with optimistic and pessimistic explanatory styles also differ in social behaviors like loneliness and marital satisfaction. Just as how people can stave off depression and achieve good things by blaming negative events on external, unstable, and specific causes—the optimistic explanatory style—people who make such attributions for their spouses' behavior feel better about their marriages (Gillham et al., 2001). After all, who would you rather be married to: a cranky, selfish mate or a distracted sweetie who is just going through a rough patch at work? The kind of attributions we make for our friends and life partners, giving them the attributional benefit-of-the-doubt, leads to better outcomes, like marital satisfaction 1 year later, the same way it does for our own behaviors (Fincham & Bradbury, 1993).

People who are lonely, compared to nonlonely people, and those who are depressed, compared to nondepressed people, make more internal, stable, and global explanations for their loneliness or depression (Anderson & Arnoult, 1985; Anderson, Horowitz, & French, 1983). Lonely people and depressed people blame their problems in interacting with others on their own lack of ability or personal defects, attributing interpersonal failures to stable causes in themselves. In contrast, nonlonely or nondepressed people blame their interpersonal failings on lack of effort or poor strategies. This suggests that lonely people experience helplessness

Cultural differences in explanatory style: Chinese students tend to be more pessimistic than American students.

when it comes to interacting with other people, which if true, also suggests how to cure loneliness: realize that you can take concrete steps, such as reaching out to others, doing volunteer work, or contacting a friend, to ease your feelings of loneliness (Cacioppo & Patrick, 2008). As mentioned in the section on physical health, social isolation has been linked to health problems (Cobb, 1976) and, as we saw in Chapter 6, to negative genetic changes in immune functioning (Cole et al., 2007).

Cultural Differences in Explanatory Style

As you might expect, given that there are cultural differences in locus of control, there are also cultural differences in explanatory style (Peterson & Chang, 2003). Recall that people in collectivistic cultures, such as in countries in East Asia, tend to be more external whereas people in individualistic cultures, such as in the United States, tend to be more internal (Heine & Lehman, 1995). The same pattern is found for explanatory style: Chinese people tend to have a more pessimistic and less optimistic explanatory style than Americans (Lee & Seligman, 1997).

Undergraduate students in China and the United States took the ASQ in their native language. As you can see in Figure 10.7, Chinese students were the most pessimistic, American students the most optimistic, with the Chinese American students falling somewhere in between. In particular, European Americans were more likely to show a self-serving bias, attributing good events to themselves and negative events to external factors, than were the Chinese Americans or the mainland Chinese. Both groups of Chinese students attributed their good events to circumstances outside themselves, as would be expected in Chinese culture which values modesty. Across all three samples, pessimism related to lower grades, worse health, and less confidence.

Clearly, there is something about cultural values that fosters an optimistic or a pessimistic explanatory style. What specific aspect of Chinese or American culture might do this? In a study of explanatory styles of Asian American and European American students, those who grew up in families emphasizing submissiveness—a value important in Chinese culture—were more global in their explanations for negative events *regardless of their cultural background* providing direct evidence that cultural values, as reinforced by parents as well as by the dominant culture, affect explanatory style (Kao, Nagata, & Peterson, 1997).

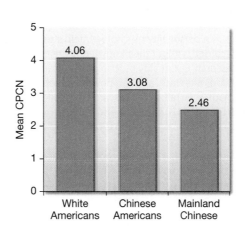

Figure 10.7 Mean composite scores of optimism between White Americans, Chinese Americans, and mainland Chinese. Higher numbers indicate a more optimistic explanatory style. *Source:* From Lee and Seligman (1997, Figure 1, p. 36). Lee, Y., & Seligman, M. E. P. (1997), "Are Americans more optimistic than the Chinese?," *Personality and Social Psychology Bulletin,* 23(1), 32–40. Copyright © 1997 by Sage Publications. Reprinted with permission of Sage Publications.

Research Methods Illustrated: Field Studies and Natural Manipulations

I knew a particularly amazing professor back in graduate school. Ron Mack was a caring person and a bit of a character around the psychology department. But as a clinical psychologist, he often felt uncomfortable by the kinds of research done by social and personality psychologists that involved making people feel bad or sad, distressed them, or made them fail at seemingly important tasks. His philosophy was simple: There is enough pain in the world; we don't need to add to it by putting participants through stressful manipulations in the laboratory.

Ron Mack was right: There are many naturally occurring tragic events in the world that challenge people's beliefs and expectations and even send some into a tailspin of depression. Because it would be unethical to *purposely* induce a depression in people or psychologically distress them, researchers often design experiments or correlational studies around such natural manipulations using **field studies** (McGuire, 1967).

A field study is a study that takes place outside the laboratory. Field studies can be experimental or nonexperimental (Aronson, Ellsworth, Carlsmith, & Gonzales, 1990). When researchers are unable to control the independent variable or when randomly assigning participants to conditions that may be harmful or disturbing is impossible or inadvisable (Aronson et al., 1990), researchers may use nonexperimental methods rather than a true experiment. Designs that are nonexperimental are often called **quasi-experimental** or correlational designs. Quasi-experimental designs strongly suggest a causal link, but, like a correlation, must be interpreted with caution because they can't *prove* one (Aronson et al., 1990).

Because research questions can be investigated in a number of ways researchers must pick the best method for investigating their hypothesis. Often, this results in a compromise (Aronson et al., 1990). For example, when studying people who are coping with a catastrophic event—say a hurricane and a flood—experimenters must sacrifice experimental control and random assignment to gain insight into a real-world tragedy. Researchers might also apply different methods so that the shortcomings of one study can be compensated by the strengths of another (Aronson et al., 1990). This is why many researchers identify causal effects in the laboratory where they can conduct a true experiment and then attempt to extend their findings to a field study where they can't (Aronson et al., 1990). One of the best examples of this is how researchers investigating learned helplessness first identified the causes of helplessness by doing laboratory experiments with dogs (Seligman & Maier, 1967) and then they applied the findings to understand human behavior in naturally occurring situations through quasi-experimental field studies.

Another advantage of field research, in addition to the ethical advantage, is that participants may give a more natural response, lessening experimental demand characteristics, because they are often unaware that they are even in an experiment. At the same time, because participants are unaware that they are in an experiment there may be invasion of privacy issues (Aronson et al., 1990).

Both laboratory and field research involves a trade-off between experimental control and generalizability (Dunn, 1999). Laboratory experiments generally have a lot of experimental control—so much so that we can identify the causes of an effect—but they have limited generalizability or applicability to situations that may differ from the strict, controlled conditions of the laboratory. Conversely, field research has very high generalizability, but lower levels of experimental control.

In personality psychology, field studies where people are observed and their behavior is recorded without their knowledge are less common than in social psychology or sociological research. Personality psychologists often use a blend of laboratory and field methods to study things like stress and coping with adversity that naturally occur in the world. For example, in this chapter we talk about research that followed people as they coped with tuberculosis (Seeman & Evans, 1962), parole (Seeman, 1963), hurricane and flooding (Anderson, 1977), lost swim meets (Seligman et al., 1990), possible unemployment (Proudfoot et al., 2009), failed exams (Metalsky et al., 1982; Metalsky et al., 1993), death of a loved one (Peterson & Seligman, 1984), heart bypass surgery (Scheier et al., 1989), and cancer (Scheier et al., 2001). In *none* of these studies did experimenters manipulate or cause these bad things to happen. Instead, researchers looked at how people handled these distressing situations differently depending on their locus of control, explanatory style, or dispositional optimism.

Consider the following field experiment, in which the participants were residents of a nursing home who didn't even know they were being studied (Langer & Rodin, 1976). The experimenters wondered if part of the decrements associated with old age is due to the loss of personal responsibility and feelings of helplessness rather than failing health or the natural process of aging.

To test this hypothesis, elderly residents of two floors of a nursing home in Connecticut were randomly assigned to one of two conditions: a responsibility-induced group and a control group. Note that the residents were not individually assigned to condition; instead residents on entire floor were assigned to the same condition. Even though not fulfilling the requirement of random assignment, this lessened the possibility that residents could talk with each other and contaminate the treatment effects. Because the residents on the two floors were similar in physical condition, psychological health, and prior socioeconomic status, and were assigned to rooms based on availability, the researchers accepted this compromise in experimental control to gain the realism and generalizability of their results.

Elders who are given responsibility and retain control over aspects of their daily lives show better health than elders who experience loss of control in their lives.

One day, the administrator of the nursing home called a meeting in the lounge of each floor. To the residents on the responsibility-induced floor, he emphasized that they were responsible for decorating their rooms, caring for themselves, and deciding how they wanted to spend their time. Residents of the control floor were reminded of how much the home had provided for their care and comfort, such as nice rooms, taking care of them, and allowing them a range of activities. Then, residents in the responsibility-induced group had the option of choosing a plant, if they wanted, which was theirs "to keep and take care of as you'd like." Residents in the control group were told "The plants are yours to keep. The nurses will water and care for them for you." Finally, residents in the responsibility-induced group were reminded that they could choose which of two nights they wanted to see a movie the following week; residents in the control group were informed that they would be told which night they were scheduled to see the movie.

Though residents of both the experimental and control floors scored similarly on the dependent variables before the experiment started, there were significant differences between the two groups 3 weeks after this treatment. Residents of the responsibility-induced group reported greater increases in happiness and activity than the control group. They were also rated by an interviewer as being more alert, and by the nurses as engaging in more activities, such as visiting other residents, talking to the staff, and attending movie nights. Overall, 93% of the responsibility-induced group showed improvements in eating, sleeping, and mood since the study started, whereas only 21% of the control group showed these positive changes. In fact, 71% of the control group actually became more debilitated despite receiving the same high-quality care provided by the institution. (Neither the interviewer nor the nurses were aware of which condition a resident was in.)

These differences were still seen 18 months later (Rodin & Langer, 1977). Although the overall death rate for the facility during the 18 months prior to the original experiment was 25%, the rate for the two floors in the 18 months after the treatment was strikingly different: 30% in the control group had died compared to 15% of the residents on the responsibility-induced floor.

The results of this experiment are quite striking, especially in light of what we know today about learned helplessness and the power of control on people's physical and psychological health. Of course, we should still interpret these results with caution because this was not a true experiment.

That is why researchers always end their papers with the caveat "More research is necessary"!

THINK ABOUT IT

Imagine that your grandmother wants to help with food preparations for a big family dinner on Sunday. Your mom is concerned that it may be too much for her. Based on this research, what do you think?

Twin 1: Hey, let's get out of here. This old barn smells terrible!

Twin 2: No, wait, with all this manure there's got to be a pony around here somewhere!

"When God closes one door He opens another."

Dispositional Optimism

In addition to an optimistic explanatory style, another way personality psychologists define optimism is closer to what most people believe optimism is: an expectation that things will get better (Isaacowitz & Seligman, 2003). **Dispositional optimism** is a general expectation that good things will happen in the future (Scheier & Carver, 1985, 1993). People with dispositional optimism approach life with positive expectations—even in the face of adversity—and believe that good things will happen, events and circumstances will work out for the best, and that good will overcome bad (Carver & Scheier, 2001; Wise & Rosqvist, 2006). People low in dispositional optimism, whom we might call pessimists, hold negative expectations and believe that things will not work out and that bad things will happen and continue to happen in the future. As a result of their belief that things will work out, optimists tend to be confident and persistent. In contrast, pessimists are doubtful and hesitant (Carver & Scheier, 1998, 2002). These beliefs help optimists weather challenging experiences as well as everyday stressors better than pessimists.

Charles Carver and Michael Scheier developed their ideas of dispositional optimism and pessimism from their early work on self-regulation theory (Carver & Scheier, 2001; Scheier & Carver, 1988). While striving toward desired goals, people experience positive emotions (e.g., pride, gratitude, relief) when making progress toward those goals or negative emotions (e.g., shame, anger, and resentment) when their progress is impeded (Carver & Scheier, 1990; Scheier & Carver, 1992). But what happens when a person encounters an obstacle that he or she believes is too great to overcome?

First, if people are forced to abandon their efforts toward a goal they still want very badly, they may feel helplessness and distress (Carver & Scheier, 2003b). But if they give up on the goal or give up on their current efforts toward the goal, they could choose an alternative path to the same goal or even choose a different goal and avoid feelings of helplessness. This new goal may be more modest, the same, or even bigger than the original goal. Under these conditions, giving up doesn't cause helplessness and may actually be adaptive. However, if no adjustment is made and people give up their commitment toward a goal without choosing an alternative goal, they might end up feeling aimless and empty (Carver & Scheier, 2003b). Healthy self-regulation requires persistence in the face of adversity as well as giving up and changing to other, presumably more likely, goals in the same or in alternative domains (Carver & Scheier, 2001).

People regulate their current behaviors based on their future goals and their beliefs about their chances of achieving those goals. In this way, confidence (optimism) or doubt (pessimism) leads to different behaviors in the present and huge differences in achievement, psychological and physical health, and work behaviors and social behaviors in the future (Carver & Scheier, 2001). These differing expectations of optimists and pessimists become self-fulfilling prophecies: Giving up makes failure a sure thing whereas persistence makes success more likely.

Unlike people with an internal locus of control or an optimistic explanatory style, people with dispositional optimism do not necessarily need to be in control of their destinies to feel this confidence. Good things could happen because they are talented, hardworking, blessed, lucky, have friends in the right places, or some combination of all of these causes (Carver & Scheier, 2003a).

Rather than sit back and wait for good things to happen, optimists agree with Thomas Jefferson's observation: "I'm a great believer in luck and I find the harder I work, the more I have of it." In the face of difficulties, optimists continue working to find alternative ways to achieve their goals and believe that they can achieve their goals; pessimists are not so sure. Dispositional optimism leads to continuing efforts and perseverance whereas pessimism leads to giving up (Carver & Scheier, 2003a). As a result, optimists and pessimists differ in how they approach, cope with, and how effectively they prevail over challenges and problems (Carver & Scheier, 2003a).

As we saw with learned helplessness, people's actions are regulated by their beliefs about the likely outcome of their actions (Scheier & Carver, 1987). When people see desired outcomes as attainable, they will persevere toward that goal even when the going gets tough. But when people believe that outcomes are unattainable, either due to their own inadequacies or due to circumstances, they will give up and choose another activity. People's general expectations of what good or bad outcomes will happen to them is reflected in their dispositional optimism and pessimism: how likely good things will happen for them regardless of the cause. As a result, everyday obstacles will be less disruptive to optimists.

Both explanatory style and dispositional optimism start with the belief that expectations impact people's actions and experiences (Carver & Scheier, 2003a). Though they come from different approaches, both lines of research converge on two important conclusions. First, holding negative expectations for the future leads to giving up, negative emotions, symptoms of depression, feelings of stress, slow recovery from stressors, social isolation, and a shorter life expectancy (Scheier & Carver, 1987). Second, holding positive expectations for the future leads to persistence, good morale, positive affect, active problem solving, problem-focused coping, a long life, social support, and greater well-being (Peterson, 2000). Even though optimists achieve better outcomes in life, dispositional optimism is not correlated with intelligence, wealth, or academic achievement (Aspinwall, Richter, & Hoffman, 2001).

Is this glass half empty or half full? People with dispositional optimism believe that good things will happen, events and circumstances will work out for the best, and that good will overcome bad.

For example, across different populations (e.g., college students, elderly people), and among people with varied medical conditions (e.g., cancer, pregnancy, bypass surgery, AIDS risk, joint replacement, rheumatoid arthritis), and their caregivers (e.g., nurses, family members, Alzheimer's caregivers), dispositional optimism was associated with fewer symptoms of depression and distress, better mood, and higher quality of life before, during, and after treatment (Affleck, Tennen, & Apter, 2001; Scheier et al., 2001).

The research evidence for optimism is overwhelming: People with dispositional optimism are better than pessimists at realistically revising their goals and coping with negative events in their lives (Scheier et al., 2001). However, unrealistic optimism (Weinstein, 1980), wishful thinking (Peterson, 2000), or overconfidence—which are all different from dispositional optimism—may cause problems if a person is so overly optimistic or optimistic in unproductive ways that he or she chooses to sit back and passively wait for good things to happen (Scheier & Carver, 1993). Dispositional optimism is similar to hopefulness (Needles & Abramson, 1990) or what Martin Seligman and his colleagues call a flexible optimism (Seligman, 1990).

Optimists differ in their expectations about the future, but what about their past and present? Undergraduate men and women answered a questionnaire measuring how satisfied they were with their present lives (e.g., "I am satisfied with my current life"), past lives ("I am satisfied with my life in the past"), and anticipated future lives ("I will be satisfied with my life in the future"). Both pessimists and optimists saw their lives as becoming more satisfying over time, a common finding in life satisfaction research. However, as you might expect, optimists reported more life satisfaction at all three time periods than pessimists (Busseri, Choma, & Sadava, 2009).

There was also an interaction between time perspective and optimism/pessimism, such that optimists saw their present and future lives as similarly rosy, whereas pessimists anticipated a better life in the future—just not as good as the future lives the optimists imagined. That is, pessimists see their present lives as more similar to their past lives than optimists do (see Figure 10.8). The researchers concluded that life satisfaction is relative depending on one's dispositional optimism: For optimists their present lives are "as good as it gets" whereas for pessimists "the best is yet to come."

THINK ABOUT IT

What is the difference between unrealistic optimism and dispositional optimism?

SEE FOR YOURSELF

Which do you agree with more: Is your life today as good as it gets or is the best yet to come?

Figure 10.8 Past, present, and anticipated future life satisfaction by optimism/pessimism group. Life satisfaction means, plus and minus one standard error, are shown on the y-axis. *Source:* From Busseri et al. (2009, Figure 1, p. 354). Reprinted from Busseri, M. A., Choma, B. L., & Sadava, S. W. (2009), "As good as it gets" or "The best is yet to come"? How optimists and pessimists view their past, present, and anticipated future life satisfaction," Personality and Individual Differences, 47, 352–356. Copyright © 2009, with permission from Elsevier.

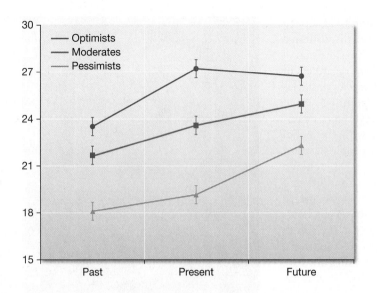

Measures of Dispositional Optimism

Individual differences in dispositional optimism and pessimism are measured by the Life Orientation Test (LOT; Scheier & Carver, 1985), now in a revised version (LOT-R; Scheier, Carver, & Bridges, 1994). The LOT-R has 10 items, 3 for optimism, 3 for pessimism, and 4 that are fillers to help disguise the purpose of the test. Respondents must agree or disagree with each of the items on a 5-point scale. Scores from the individual items are combined to form a single score of optimism, although more recent research suggests that separate optimism and pessimism scores predict to different outcomes (Isaacowitz & Seligman, 2003; Peterson, 2000). You can see how optimistic or pessimistic you are by taking the LOT-R for yourself in Table 10.5.

Table 10.5   The Life Orientation Test—Revised (LOT-R)

Read each statement and circle your response. Please be as honest and accurate as you can throughout. Try not to let your response to one statement influence your responses to other statements. There are no "correct" or "incorrect" answers. Answer according to your own feelings, rather than how you think "most people" would answer.

A = I agree a lot
B = I agree a little
C = I neither agree nor disagree
D = I disagree a little
E = I disagree a lot

1. In uncertain times, I usually expect the best.	A	B	C	D	E
2. It's easy for me to relax.	A	B	C	D	E
3. If something can go wrong for me, it will.	A	B	C	D	E
4. I'm always optimistic about my future.	A	B	C	D	E
5. I enjoy my friends a lot.	A	B	C	D	E
6. It's important for me to keep busy.	A	B	C	D	E
7. I hardly ever expect things to go my way.	A	B	C	D	E
8. I don't get upset too easily.	A	B	C	D	E
9. I rarely count on good things happening to me.	A	B	C	D	E
10. Overall, I expect more good things to happen to me than bad.	A	B	C	D	E

Note: Items 2, 5, 6, and 8 are fillers and are not scored. Responses to the optimistic items 1, 4, and 10 are scored: A = 5, B = 4, C = 3, D = 2, E = 1. Responses to the pessimistic items 3, 7, 9, are reversed scored: A = 1, B = 2, C = 3, D = 4, E = 5. Add up scores for individual items to get the total score for the scale. Higher numbers indicate more optimism.

Source: From Scheier et al. (1994, Table 6, p. 1073). Scheier, M. F., Carver, C. S., & Bridges, M. W. (1994). Distinguishing optimism from neuroticism (and trait anxiety, self-mastery, and self-esteem): A reevaluation of the Life Orientation Test. Journal of Personality and Social Psychology, 67, 1063–1078.

Dispositional Optimism and Coping

Echoing the findings for locus of control and explanatory style reviewed earlier in this chapter, dispositional optimism is associated with positive outcomes in school and work, physical and psychological health, and social behavior. However, researchers on dispositional optimism have taken optimism and pessimism in a slightly different direction and have focused on how people cope with major life events. When faced with a negative event, people high in dispositional optimism report fewer depressive symptoms, greater use of effective coping strategies, and fewer physical symptoms than pessimists (Scheier & Carver, 1992, 1993). Dispositional optimism is associated with greater well-being and better adjustment to life stressors over time (Scheier et al., 2001).

For example, among middle-aged women who experienced a negative event, those who were lower in dispositional optimism reported more depressive symptoms (Bromberger & Matthews, 1996). Similarly, a study following middle-aged women over a 1-year period found that caregivers were less optimistic and more pessimistic than noncaregivers. However, pessimism predicted changes in anxiety, perceived stress, and worsening self-rated health of both caregivers and noncaregivers (Robinson-Whelen, Kim, MacCallum, & Kiecolt-Glaser, 1997).

Dispositional optimism is also associated with better adjustment to the demands of college life in medical students, law students, and first-year undergraduates. Optimistic students showed greater achievement, less loneliness, less stress, fewer symptoms of depression, less chronic anger, and less anger suppression (Scheier et al., 2001).

Men with greater dispositional optimism prior to coronary bypass surgery showed more problem-focused coping and a faster recovery, returning to their regular activities faster than pessimists, and reporting a higher quality of life 6 months after the operation (Scheier et al., 1989).

Overall, optimists cope better, in both the short term and in the long run, than pessimists. Let's take a closer look at why this might be (see Table 10.6).

Optimistic Beliefs and Expectations. Optimists fare better than pessimists when confronted with stressful situations because their beliefs and expectations help them cope, whereas the beliefs and expectations of pessimists hurt them (Scheier et al., 2001). In the face of stress, optimism makes people resistant to depression (Carver, 2004), keeps them working toward their goals (Carver et al., 2005), and improves coping with life-threatening health issues (Carver et al., 1993; Stanton & Snider, 1993). Like this quote by Christine, optimists are likely to believe that much can be learned from trying experiences (Carver & Gaines, 1987). Just as civil engineers analyze bridge and building disasters and use this knowledge to build better structures, optimists embrace failure and are ready to analyze past negative experiences to make things turn out better next time (Wise & Rosqvist, 2006). "It's all a learning experience," you might hear an optimist declare.

For example, dispositional optimism predicted adjustment to diagnosis and treatment for cancer. In women with breast cancer, and in men with prostate cancer, optimism predicted less distress immediately after surgery and up to 1 year afterward. In patients undergoing radiation treatments, optimism was associated with better adjustment throughout the process (Scheier et al., 2001). Optimism has been shown to predict better emotional and psychological well-being and lower distress in breast cancer patients during and just after diagnosis (Carver et al., 1993, 1994; Epping-Jordan et al., 1999; Stanton & Snider, 1993) and also up to

"If every difficult experience makes you stronger . . . then I should be brilliant . . . amazing . . . and strong as hell after all this."
Christine "Spoon Lady" Miserandino, 32-year-old lupus survivor and founder of www.ButYouDontLookSick .com, November 25, 2009

Table 10.6 Why People High in Dispositional Optimism Fare Better

1. Optimistic beliefs and expectations are more advantageous than pessimistic ones.
2. Optimists use better strategies to cope in a crisis.
3. Optimists take action, make plans, and engage in healthy behaviors.
4. Optimists are good at judging whether a situation is controllable or not and change strategies accordingly.
5. Optimistic beliefs alter physiological functioning and protect the body from stress.

13 years after treatment (Carver et al., 2005). Optimists were also able to return faster than pessimists to the social and recreational activities of their daily lives. These activities, in turn, lowered their emotional distress and protected them from depression as a result of enduring cancer treatments (Carver, Lehman, & Antoni, 2003). Pessimistic women did not experience these benefits.

In men and women recovering from coronary bypass surgery, dispositional optimists showed lower levels of hostility and depression than pessimists, and reported more happiness, relief, satisfaction with their medical care, emotional support from friends and family, and higher quality of life immediately after the operation and up to 5 years later (Scheier et al., 2001).

In women of child-bearing age, dispositional optimism was associated with less anxiety during pregnancy, fewer depressive symptoms during pregnancy and after childbirth, and better adjustment to abortion, whereas dispositional pessimism was associated with distress of infertile couples (Scheier et al., 2001).

One need not be facing a major life illness to benefit from dispositional optimism. Among first-year college students, optimists held higher academic expectations than pessimists and were more energized by the challenges of college, seeing them as opportunities rather than threats. As a result, they were less stressed, happier, healthier, better adjusted, and achieved higher grades during their first year of college than pessimists (Chemers, Hu, & Garcia, 2001).

Remember how stressful high school was, especially when it came to thinking about your future? Among Australian suburban high school students in Grades 8 to 12, those with higher levels of optimism, compared to students low in optimism, showed more career exploration and planning, career decision-making certainty, and held more career-related goals. Students with higher levels of pessimism, compared to students low in pessimism, knew less about the world of work, used decision-making strategies less, knew less about potential careers, were more indecisive, and had lower levels of school achievement. Overall, higher optimism in these teens was also associated with greater psychological health as shown by higher levels of self-esteem and less reported psychological distress (Creed, Patton, & Bartrum, 2002).

Optimism and Coping Strategies.   Even though optimists and pessimists use different coping strategies, the strategies of optimists are more effective at managing stress (Scheier & Carver, 1985). Optimists approach problems head-on, doing whatever they can to improve their predicament, engaging in active problem-focused coping. **Problem-focused** coping is when people work to solve their problems or do something concrete to change the source of the stress. This may involve planning, calling on friends to help fix the situation, focusing on fixing the problem and ignoring other activities, or engaging in any activity that is aimed at lessening the stress itself (Carver, Scheier, & Weintraub, 1989). Optimists are especially likely to use problem-focused strategies when they perceive the stressful situation as controllable. When things are not controllable, optimists use more adaptive coping mechanisms such as positive reframing, seeing the best in a situation, learning from a bad situation, accepting what can't be changed, realistically revising goals, and using humor. Optimists keep trying whereas pessimists are more likely to get upset and give up (Brown & Marshall, 2001; Scheier & Carver, 1987).

Pessimists show more **emotion-focused coping**, where they attempt to reduce or manage the negative emotions and distress they feel as a result of the stress (Carver et al., 1989). This may involve being preoccupied with their emotional distress, accepting the stress, putting a positive spin on events, denying the stress, turning to religion, or seeking friends for comfort. Pessimists might also engage in **avoidant coping** such as giving up on goals, distancing, denying, escaping, abusing substances, and failing to take constructive steps to fix the situation.

Problem-focused coping works to reduce the threat whereas emotion-focused coping works to lessen the emotional distress caused by the threat (Scheier & Carver, 1987). People generally apply a combination of both problem-focused and emotion-focused coping depending on the circumstances. Often emotion-focused coping reduces the anguish and distress people feel, allowing them to carry out problem-focused coping.

To study these differences in coping styles, one study asked undergraduate students to imagine themselves in five hypothetical situations (Scheier, Weintraub, & Carver, 1986). The

---

THINK ABOUT IT

How can one be optimistic while going through cancer treatment?

THINK ABOUT IT

What are some other ways of engaging in problem-focused coping?

THINK ABOUT IT

What are some other ways of engaging in emotion-focused coping?

situations were moderately stressful and somewhat controllable, such as managing multiple final exams on the same day, and other situations highly relevant to college students. As predicted, optimists and pessimists differed in their coping strategies, with optimists using more problem-focused coping and pessimists using more emotion-focused coping.

There is an interesting cultural difference between Asians and Americans in the coping strategies of optimists and pessimists (Chang, 2001). Self-identified Asian American college students (an admittedly broad, heterogeneous category) showed similar amounts of dispositional optimism as White Americans, but greater pessimism. This greater pessimism was associated with more avoidance coping and psychological problems (e.g., anxiety, fear, panic attacks, alienation, feelings of inadequacy, thought disorders, and other symptoms) among Asian Americans as demonstrated in previous studies. But, this pessimism and avoidance coping was *not* associated with more depressive symptoms in Asian Americans as it generally is among White Americans. Instead, among those high in pessimism, Asian Americans use more problem-focused coping than White Americans. Perhaps this is how Asians can have higher pessimism and yet not be vulnerable to depression like American college students are. If these pessimistic thoughts are an important way for Asians to cope, Chang (2001) suggested that therapists of Asian Americans should try to increase optimistic thoughts in their clients rather than decrease pessimistic thoughts, as is standard practice with cognitive behavioral therapy (Beck, 1976).

Optimists Take Action.   In contrast to pessimists, the direct, active, problem-solving approach of optimists causes them to act in ways that promote health. Optimists are more likely than pessimists to seek out information, adhere to medical regimes, eat a healthy diet, get regular exercise, and regularly engage in behaviors to promote health and reduce risk (e.g., engaging in safer sex practices if HIV-positive, or using sunscreen regularly if at risk for skin cancer; Scheier et al., 2001). Compared with pessimists, optimists take vitamins on a regular basis, eat healthier lunches, lower their levels of body fat, reduce smoking, reduce alcohol consumption, exercise, and enroll in cardiac rehabilitation programs more than pessimists do (Scheier & Carver, 1992). Optimism is associated with fewer physical symptoms in both elderly people and in college students (Scheier & Carver, 1987).

Part of problem-focused coping involves formulating a plan of action for dealing with a crisis, and optimists are more likely than pessimists to do this (Scheier & Carver, 1987). In one study, optimistic coronary bypass patients were more likely to make plans for their recovery by setting goals for themselves and by getting as much information as possible about the recovery process. In contrast, pessimists blocked out thoughts of what their recovery might be like. As a result, optimists showed a faster rate of recovery and fewer signs of complications from their bypass surgeries.

Optimism and Judging Controllability.   As mentioned earlier, optimists are more likely to change strategies or goals when faced with an uncontrollable situation. The key here is that optimists appear to be better able than pessimists to judge when situations are controllable or uncontrollable so they can choose more appropriate strategies (Aspinwall et al., 2001).

For example, in one study students tackled anagrams (scrambled word puzzles) that they believed tested their verbal intelligence (Aspinwall & Richter, 1999). The students had 20 minutes to solve as many anagrams as they could. Unbeknownst to them, the first 7 anagrams were unsolvable. For participants in the No Alternatives condition, this was the only task they were given. But participants in the Alternatives condition were given two additional sets of anagrams that were solvable (of course, the participants didn't know this). At the same time, half of the participants in both conditions were allowed to return to an anagram they missed while the other half was not.

When participants had no alternative tasks to work on, all participants—both optimists and pessimists—worked on the puzzles until time was up. But when alternatives were available and participants couldn't return to their previously unsolved problems—forcing them to admit defeat on a test of verbal intelligence—participants high in optimism gave up on the unsolvable problems 4 minutes sooner than pessimistic participants. Further, they performed better on the new tasks than pessimistic participants (Aspinwall & Richter, 1999; see Figure 10.9).

> **THINK ABOUT IT**
>
> Might the emotion-focused strategy of seeking the comfort of others be especially useful in a collectivistic culture compared to an individualistic culture?

> "God grant me the serenity to accept the things I cannot change; courage to change the things I can; and wisdom to know the difference."
> *"The Serenity Prayer" by Reinhold Niebuhr*

Figure 10.9 Time spent on unsolvable anagrams as a function of dispositional optimism and whether returning to previous anagrams was prohibited or permitted. *Source:* From Aspinwall and Richter (1999).

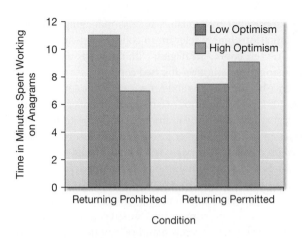

This may remind you of the Serenity Prayer. Optimists are better able to change the things they can change, accept the things they cannot change, and they do seem to have the wisdom to tell the difference—at least more wisdom than pessimists do (Aspinwall et al., 2001). Or, in the words of the legendary vaudevillian comedian W. C. Fields: "If at first you don't succeed, try, try again. Then give up. There's no use in being a damn fool about it."

Optimistic Beliefs and Physiological Functioning. Optimism seems to have a protective effect on the body's physiological reactions to stress, preventing stress from doing the kind of damage it might otherwise cause (Scheier & Carver, 1987). The relationship between optimism and physical and psychological health persists even after controlling for other personality variables that are known to be related to health, like neuroticism, anxiety, and depression. This suggests that there must be other ways that optimism impacts health. One such mechanism may be the immune system: Optimism seems to make the immune system function better and protect the body from the harmful effects of stress.

Previous studies have found significant correlations between optimism and immune functioning, but these studies were all correlational. For example, in a sample of HIV-positive men and women, greater optimism was associated with greater immune functioning over time, although this enhanced immune function did not affect disease progression. Greater pessimism was associated with greater disease progression over time but not due to enhanced immune function (Milam, Richardson, Marks, Kemper, & McCutchan, 2004). In another study, optimistic students showed greater T-cell and natural killer cell activity, two cell types that help fight infection, during times of academic stress than pessimists (Segerstrom, 2001, 2005; Segerstrom, Taylor, Kemeny, & Fahey, 1998). In a study of women undergoing breast cancer diagnosis and treatment, dispositional optimism counteracted the usual association between high perceived stress and lowered activity of natural killer cells (Von Ah, Kang, & Carpenter, 2007).

The best evidence that optimism causes changes in the functioning of the immune system comes from a recent experiment that used a placebo control group to compare the effects of dispositional optimism and stress on immune functioning (Brydon, Walker, Wawrzyniak, Chart, & Steptoe, 2009). The experimenters manipulated the psychological stress of healthy male undergraduates and exposure to illness by randomly assigning them to one of four conditions.

Vaccines work by physiologically stimulating the body into making antibodies to fight an infection. Using a **double-blind** technique, where neither the experimenters nor the participants know who received the

THINK ABOUT IT

Why does a placebo control group provide the best evidence that optimism causes changes in immune system functioning?

Evidence suggests that dispositional optimists have strong immune systems and are better able to fight colds than dispositional pessimists.

placebo and who received the vaccine, some participants received a typhoid vaccine whereas others received a harmless saline solution. Then half of the participants rested while the other half faced two psychologically stressful tasks. One task was the classic Stroop test, where participants were presented with names of colors displayed in various colored lettering on a computer screen. Participants had to indicate the color of the lettering, not what the word said (this task is harder than it looks, and is often used by experimenters to induce stress in participants). For the second task, participants had to imagine that they were falsely accused of a theft and had to give a speech defending themselves. They believed that the speeches would be videotaped and judged.

During these tasks, experimenters measured mood, stress responses, and immune functioning of participants. They were particularly interested in interleukin-6, an inflammatory cytokine, the level of which increases when the immune system is activated. A short-term increase in inflammatory response is necessary to help fight infection. But a prolonged inflammatory response, which occurs when a person is under chronic stress, can be damaging. A side effect of interleukin-6 is an increase in tension and anxiety. The experimenters wondered, would psychological stress (Stroop test and speech) increase interleukin-6, what impact would a participant's dispositional optimism have on this immune system response, and would this response compromise participants' ability to ward off infection later?

First, when experiencing an immediate stressor—getting a needle in the arm as part of an experiment—optimists showed a smaller increase in tension and anxiety, indicating a smaller spike in interleukin-6.

Second, when faced with the anxiety-provoking Stroop test and the possibility of giving a speech, optimism moderated people's stress responses. That is, the immune system of optimists showed a steady response to these stressors rather than the five-alarm-end-of-the-world-all-hands-on-deck immune response of pessimists. This limits long-term inflammation and preserves the body's ability to fight infection.

You can see this for yourself in Figure 10.10. At 2 hours after the stressful experience, the interleukin-6 levels of pessimists were still elevated, whereas those of optimists had dropped significantly. This provides direct evidence that when faced with a stressor, dispositional optimism *causes* better immune functioning.

Third, as a result of this more efficient response to stress, the immune system of optimists is better able to fight physical infection, as reflected in their response to the typhoid vaccine, three weeks later.

Think of it like this: imagine driving down the highway with your friends in the car and suddenly seeing a pothole. Some drivers might scream and swerve sharply to avoid the pothole, momentarily loosing control of the car and upsetting their passengers. Everyone may need a few moments to collect themselves before settling back into an otherwise pleasant road trip. However, other drivers might only gasp instead of scream, swerving a bit more gently to avoid the pothole. Their ability to retain control of the car isn't as disruptive, making for a safer and more pleasant trip for them and their passengers. In general, stress compromises the body's

Figure 10.10 Optimists' immune systems rebound faster than pessimists' after a stressful event. This graph shows the mean change in interleukin-6 at 2 hours poststress in relation to dispositional optimism scores, grouped from lowest (pessimistic) to highest (optimism) in five equal-sized groups. Whereas pessimists still show an inflammatory response to stress, the levels of interleukin-6 in optimists is greatly reduced. Optimism appears to protect the body from long-term inflammation by quickly reducing levels of interleukin-6 in the hours after a stressful event. *Source:* From Brydon et al. (2009, Figure 2, p. 813). Reprinted from Brydon, L., Walker, C., Wawrzyniak, A. J., Chart, H., & Steptoe, A. (2009), "Dispositional optimism and stress-induced changes in immunity and negative mood," Brain, Behavior, and Immunity, 23, 810–816. Copyright © 2009, with permission from Elsevier.

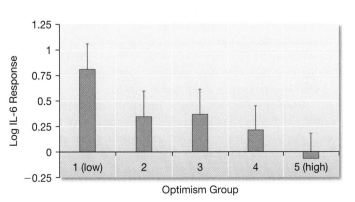

ability to fight off infections. However, optimists, perhaps by being not so physiologically reactive to stress, are less vulnerable than pessimists to physical infections.

The results of this experiment suggest that optimism protects against the long-term inflammatory effects of psychological stress (Brydon et al., 2009). Interleukin-6 is correlated with depressive symptoms in healthy people and is elevated in some patients with clinical depression (Irwin & Miller, 2007). Circulating levels of interleukin-6 are also elevated in some conditions such as cardiovascular disease, arthritis, pain, and certain cancers, all health conditions under which optimists have been shown to fare better than pessimists. This experiment suggests that the reason why appears to be due to optimists having optimal immune system responses. Smaller long-term interleukin-6 responses in optimists may protect them against stress-related depressive illness. Optimism acts like an antioxidant—think of chocolate, green tea, berries, spinach—to help protect the body from long-term inflammation after a stressful experience!

In sum, the expectations, beliefs, coping strategies, readiness to spring into action, and immune systems of optimists combined with an ability to size up their chances of achieving their goals and a willingness to change strategies serve them well, especially in times of stress, protecting them and fostering both psychological and physical health. So, what can you do if you are not so high in dispositional optimism? Read the The Personality of Everyday Life box for a description of how psychologists have been able to change people's thoughts for the better.

> "Perpetual optimism is a force multiplier."
> *Colin Powell*

> "Optimism is the foundation of courage."
> *Nicholas Murray Butler*

The Personality of Everyday Life

Making people more optimistic

Can we make people more optimistic—both in their explanatory style and in their dispositional optimism—by changing their thoughts? Two methods have proven successful in making people more optimistic: cognitive behavioral therapy (Carver & Scheier, 2002) and attributional retraining (Miserandino, 1998; Peterson, 2000; Proudfoot et al., 2009). Both of these principles were taught to children in a special program called the Penn Resiliency Program (PRP) through comics, stories, videos, role-playing, games, and discussions (Jaycox et al., 1994).

The program was based on the ABC model of Albert Ellis (Ellis, 1962) and the cognitive behavioral therapy of Aaron Beck (Beck, 1976). When *adversity* hits (A), it stirs up *beliefs* (B) which have *consequences* (C) for how we feel. The children learned that sometimes negative thoughts occur automatically (e.g., "I'm no good at anything") much like how a song gets stuck in our heads. By learning to *dispute* the automatic negative thoughts (step D, added to the ABC model by the facilitators; Seligman, 1975) and evaluating if the negative feelings go up or down (step E for *energization* of negative feelings) children can start to choose thoughts to make themselves feel better and dispute thoughts that make them feel bad.

The children followed the adventures of Hopeful Holly and Hopeful Howard. This optimistic pair would regularly challenge the negative thinking and pessimistic explanatory styles of Gloomy Greg and Pessimistic Penny and help them find ways to cope with their problems. Children were encouraged to act like Sherlock Holmes—and not his caustic counterpart Hemlock Jones—using steps ABCD and E to think about alternatives, rather than believing their automatic thoughts, which were often internal, stable, and global explanations for a negative event (Seligman, 1995).

Before the program, 24% of these fifth- and sixth-grade children in both the wait-list control and prevention groups had moderate to severe symptoms of depression. Immediately afterward, whereas children in the control group still showed symptoms, children in the prevention group had fewer symptoms. By 2 years after the program ended, children in the prevention group were half as likely to be depressed as children in the control group (Gillham et al., 1995; Seligman, 1995). Children in the prevention group were less likely to attribute negative events to stable causes, becoming slightly more optimistic in their explanatory style. They were also less likely to show behavioral problems at home and at school.

The PRP is successful in many settings including inner cities, suburban, and rural schools and with European American, African American, and Latino children and adolescents'. Comparable programs in Australia and China were similarly effective. The PRP significantly reduces depression, prevents anxiety, prevents behavioral problems, and leads to a more optimistic explanatory style, less helplessness, fewer automatic thoughts, increased self-esteem, and better coping with adversity and problem-solving skills (Brunwasser, Gillham, & Kim, 2009; Gillham, Brunwasser, & Freres, 2007).

Chapter Summary

In this chapter on cognitive approaches to psychology we witnessed the power of words: how our thoughts, beliefs, and expectations lead us to see and experience the world differently and become self-fulfilling prophesies in our lives.

One very important belief is in one's own power to bring about important outcomes. Some people, those with an internal locus of control, believe that they can control their own destinies. Others, those with an external locus of control, believe that what happens to them is due to luck, chance, powerful others, fate, or any number of causes outside their control. Generally an internal locus of control is related to responsibility for one's actions, higher achievement, greater success and satisfaction on the job, better physical and psychological health, and greater social sensitivity. People with an internal locus of control cope better with stressful events. People living in individualistic cultures tend to be more internal than people living in collectivistic cultures. American college students have become more external since 1960. Locus of control is measured by questionnaires.

A sense of control is so important that when people, dogs—or small children, as in the story of Elena with the crayons which opened this chapter—discover that they are unable to control important outcomes or prevent negative events from happening, they become helpless. Learned helplessness causes problems in motivation, cognition, and emotion, and may be a risk factor for hopelessness depression.

Over a lifetime of interacting with the world and being socialized by parents, teachers, coaches, and the media, people may develop habitual ways of explaining why things happen to them. These explanations can vary in three dimensions: internal or external, stable or unstable, and global or specific. People with an optimistic explanatory style see good events as internal, stable, and global; people with a pessimistic explanatory style see good events as external, unstable, and specific. People with an optimistic explanatory style see bad events as external, unstable, and specific. People with a pessimistic explanatory style see bad events as internal, stable, and global.

As a result of these beliefs, people with an optimistic explanatory style persist despite setbacks and achieve more at school, in athletic competitions, and on the job, compared to people with a more pessimistic explanatory style. An optimistic explanatory style is related to better physical and psychological health; a pessimistic explanatory style is a risk factor for depression and loneliness. Like locus of control, there appear to be cultural differences in explanatory style: people living in collectivistic cultures tend to be more pessimistic than people living in individualistic cultures. Explanatory style can be measured through questionnaires or through a content analysis of people's words.

Much of the research on locus of control, explanatory styles, and how people cope with adversity comes from field studies and natural manipulations. Researchers may study people outside the laboratory and often in real-world predicaments to see how they cope with heart disease, cancer, tuberculosis, hurricanes, unemployment, and other tragedies that cannot be

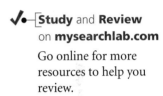

Study and **Review** on **mysearchlab.com**

Go online for more resources to help you review.

"Where there is room for doubt, people should fill the gap with hope."

Christopher Peterson (2000, p. 51)

purposely manipulated or controlled, and where participants cannot be randomly assigned to condition. Researchers will turn to quasi-experimental designs when a true experiment cannot be done for ethical or practical reasons. While a quasi-experimental design can suggest how a potential cause and an effect may be related, it cannot prove cause and effect the way a true experiment can.

Finally, people can differ in their general expectations that things will get better or worse for them in the future. Dispositional optimism, like locus of control and explanatory style, is related to achievement and better physical and psychological health. When the going gets tough, optimists have the coping skills and persistence to rise above their challenges and not give up. Dispositional optimism is measured through questionnaires.

Throughout this chapter, the research evidence is strong and clear that our thoughts and beliefs have a huge impact on how we experience life and cope with negative events: Optimists fare better. The real good news of this chapter is that explanatory style and dispositional optimism can be changed either through cognitive behavioral therapy or special workshops that challenge automatic pessimistic thoughts and foster a more optimistic explanatory style or even an online intervention conducted by a computer therapist, as we saw in the study that opened this chapter. These programs have successfully immunized children and adolescents from depression and anxiety. If, according to the cognitive approach, you are what you think, then this chapter ought to give you something to reflect on. For, to paraphrase the words of Thomas Paine, "The real *optimist* smiles in trouble, gathers strength from distress, and grows brave by reflection."

> "When I started, I was like Pessimistic Penny. I always felt really crummy and thought that I always messed things up . . . . The people from Penn came to our school and helped us be less gloomy all the time."
> *Seligman (1975, p. 129)*

Review Questions

1. Describe the Seligman et al. (2005) online study where participants went through 1 of 6 possible interventions for depression. Which two treatments were the most effective?

2. What is locus of control? How is it measured? What are some important differences between people who are more external or more internal in their locus of control when it comes to achievement, work behavior, physical and psychological health, and social behavior? Are there cultural differences in locus of control? Have American college students changed in locus of control over time?

3. What is learned helplessness? Describe the Seligman and Maier (1967) triadic design study where some dogs failed to learn how to escape shocks. What happens to humans who are placed in a similar situation? What is the hopelessness model of depression?

4. What is explanatory style? What three dimensions determine a person's explanatory style? What kind of attributions do people with an optimistic explanatory style make? What kind of attributions do people with a pessimistic explanatory style make? In what two ways is explanatory style measured? What are some important differences between people who are more optimistic or more pessimistic in their explanatory style when it comes to achievement in school and athletics, work behavior, physical and psychological health, and social behavior? Are there cultural differences in explanatory style?

5. What is a field study? What are some advantages and trade-offs of field research?

6. What is dispositional optimism? How is it measured? Why do people high in dispositional optimism cope better with major life events?

7. Is it possible to train people to think more optimistically?

Key Terms

Field-dependent	Illusion of control	Learned helplessness
Field-independent	Primary control	Yoking
Locus of control	Secondary control	Triadic design

Hopelessness model
  of depression
Explanatory style
Pessimistic explanatory style
Optimistic explanatory style
Internal versus external

Stable versus unstable
Global versus specific
Attributional Style
  Questionnaire (ASQ)
CAVE technique
Field studies

Quasi-experimental design
Dispositional optimism
Problem-focused coping
Emotion-focused coping
Avoidant coping
Double-blind technique

Read the **Chapter** on
mysearchlab.com

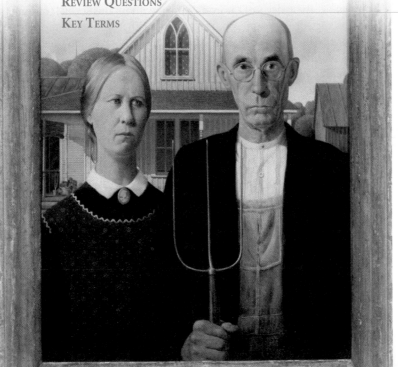

Imagine that you woke up tomorrow morning as a person of the other sex. What would be different in your life? Would you dress differently? Would you be friends with the same people? Would you have the same college major? Hairstyle? Would you still be the same person inside? Would you have the same personality?

This is the basic question of this chapter: How does gender—including genetics and physiology as well as cultural and societal expectations—make us who we are? Or, to put it differently, if we view personality as a consistent way of behaving, are men and women consistent in behaving differently? Certainly, there are biological and physical differences between men and women, but are there psychological differences as well? Are these gender differences real or in the eye of the beholder? If real, where do these differences come from? Are they a result of biological and evolutionary forces that are resistant to change or are they a result of social and cultural forces that can change?

To illustrate why gender differences and where they come from are important take, for example, a commonly held belief that men are better than women at mathematics. This turns out to be a myth, something we'll explore in more depth later in this chapter. However, it *is* true that men are better than women when it comes to one type of mathematical ability: spatial reasoning. In fact, the difference between men and women on mental rotation, one aspect of spatial reasoning where participants have to mentally rotate a figure (see Figure 11.1), is one of the largest gender differences in cognitive ability.

Where does this gender difference in mental rotation come from? Given that differences in mental rotation can be seen in infants as young as 3 to 5 months of age (Moore & Johnson, 2008; Quinn & Liben, 2008), psychologists assume that this difference was somehow hard-wired into the biology of men and women as a result of our evolution. After all, it takes more visual spatial ability to judge the distance of a quarry and to gauge how fast and how far to throw a weapon to take down a potential meal than is involved in the birthing and raising of children. Are differences in spatial rotation a legacy of how men and women have evolved?

Until recently, this is what many people thought. However, researchers gave undergraduate men and women 10 hours of training on either a 3-D puzzle video game or a 3-D action video game that required them to aim and shoot at targets (Feng, Spence, & Pratt, 2007). As a result of the training, not only did participants get better at their respective games, as you would imagine, but those who played the action game (but not the puzzle game) improved their performance on a mental rotation task. Surprisingly, women benefited more from the training than did men. Even more impressive, the difference in mental rotation abilities between men and women—something once thought to be an innate gender difference and impossible to change—was greatly reduced so that women who trained on the action game caught up to the spatial ability level of the average man without this special training (see Figure 11.2). These results suggest that some gender differences that were once thought to be fixed may actually be changeable as a result of life experiences, opportunities, preferences (girls generally do not enjoy playing action video games), or expectations, rather than set in stone and due to innate differences. The catch is that we can't always know which kind of gender difference—inborn or socialized—we are dealing with!

THINK ABOUT IT

Are gender differences in mathematics more innate or more learned?

Figure 11.1 A sample mental rotation task. Participants choose which two of the four pictures shown on the right portrayed an object identical to the one shown on the left, when rotated. *Source:* Feng et al. (2007, Figure 1b, p. 851). Reprinted from Feng, J., Spence, I., & Pratt, J. (2007), "Playing an action video game reduces gender differences in spatial cognition," *Psychological Science,* 18(10), 850–855. Used with permission.

Some gender differences, such as spatial rotation abilities, once thought to be evolutionarily programmed can be eliminated with certain opportunities and experiences.

In this chapter we consider the question: Are there personality differences between men and women? To answer this question, we attempt to sort out facts from fiction about actual gender differences, evaluate the size of gender differences, debate where these gender differences might come from, consider the impact of gender beliefs, and take a look at how the definition and assessment of gender has changed through the years.

"People do not have to be the same to be equal."

Psychologist Diane Halpern (2004), researcher on gender differences in cognitive abilities

Beliefs About Personality Similarities and Differences Between Men and Women

THINK ABOUT IT

Do you think that men and women have different personalities?

According to some psychologists, the American majority culture is so taken with gender differences that differences between men and women are seen as large, unchangeable, present from birth (if not sooner), and part of the very essence of what it means to be a man or a woman (Zurbriggen & Sherman, 2007).

We tend to believe that men and women differ in personality, social roles, physical attributes (in addition to the obvious reproductive ones), emotional experience and expression, and even the way we think (see Table 11.1). Beliefs about what men and women are like are remarkably stable and consistent across many cultures, both in the United States and abroad: Women are believed to be more concerned with nurturing whereas men are more concerned with actions and accomplishments (Kite, Deaux, & Haines, 2008; Williams & Best, 1990).

Men and women are also believed to pursue different careers

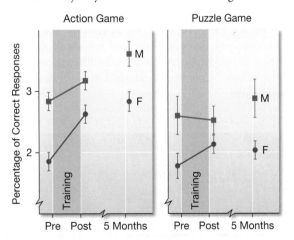

Figure 11.2 Performance on a mental rotation task after training with an action video game (left panel) or nonaction puzzle video game (right panel). Means are shown for males (M) and females (F) before training ("Pre"), after training ("Post"), and 5 months after training ended. *Source:* Adapted from Feng et al. (2007, Figure 3, p. 853) Feng, J., Spence, I., & Pratt, J. (2007), "Playing an action video game reduces gender differences in spatial cognition," *Psychological Science,* 18(10), 850–855. Copyright © 2007 by Sage Publications. Reprinted by permission of Sage Publications.

Table 11.1 Traditional Stereotypes of Males and Females

Category:	Men Are:	Women Are:
	Agentic and Instrumental	Expressive and Communal
Personality	active, competitive, independent, self-confident	emotional, gentle, understanding, devoted
Social Roles	leaders, financial providers, head of households	caregivers, provide emotional support, homemakers
Physical Attributes	athletic, brawny, broad-shouldered, physically strong	dainty, pretty, soft-voiced, graceful
Emotional Experience	anger, pride	more emotionally expressive, experience a wider range of all other emotions
Cognition	good at abstract thinking, problem solving	good at verbal reasoning, artistic

Source: From Kite et al. (2008).

as well as hobbies and favorite activities (Twenge, 1999). Traditional masculine occupations include auto mechanic, carpenter, jet pilot, and civil engineer. Traditional feminine occupations include nurse, art teacher, and social worker. Men are presumed to spend their free time working on computers or playing chess; women shopping.

Overall, these beliefs suggest that women are concerned with other people and the social group, being interdependent, and feeling connected with others and with the group. In contrast, men focus on the individual and feelings of self-protection and self-assertion. These contrasting ways of approaching the social world have been called **communion** and **agency** (Bakan, 1966) and reflect traditional feminine and masculine socialization (Eisenberg & Lennon, 1983).

No doubt you recognize these as **stereotypes** of what men and women are like. A stereotype is a generalization about a group of people, in this case men or women, in which attributes are assumed to be true of all members of the group regardless of the actual variation among group members (Aronson, Wilson, & Akert, 2001). Gender stereotypes describe traits and behaviors that people believe occur more frequently in one gender or the other (Best & Williams, 2001). They describe what men and women are like as well as what they should be like (Kite et al., 2008). Often, these stereotypes reinforce traditional sex roles (Best & Williams, 2001).

Is there any truth to these beliefs? We know what "people" and the media say, but what does the psychological research say about differences in personality between men and women? Luckily, gender and gender differences are among one of the most studied topics in psychology. To compare findings across studies we will need to understand something called **effect size**.

A young Indian couple during their wedding ceremony. Gender stereotypes are amazingly similar around the world, but is there any truth to them?

Research Methods Illustrated: Effect Size and Meta-Analysis

Say that you are making salsa (Doherty, 2004). You will need tomatoes, peppers, onions, cilantro, lime juice, salt, and perhaps a few other ingredients. But suppose you are in the middle of preparations for a dinner party and discover that you are out of lime juice. With guests due in 15 minutes, would you quickly run to the store to get some or would you just go without? Many cooks would just do without; after all, lime juice adds very little to the final flavor of salsa. However, suppose you discovered that you forgot to buy tomatoes. Can you make salsa without tomatoes? No way! It just wouldn't be salsa without the tomatoes.

This analogy can help us understand the concept of effect size (Cohen, 1988). Just as how tomatoes and lime juice each have a different impact on the final flavor of salsa, effect size tells us the impact or importance of a variable to the overall observed effect. Whereas significance tests, such as a *t*-test or an ANOVA, tell us whether there is a significant difference in average scores between men and women, for example, effect size tells us the size of that difference.

We can calculate the effect size within an individual experiment, but the real power comes from conducting a **meta-analysis** (Hyde, 2005, 2007; Johnson & Boynton, 2008; Ozer, 2007; Roberts, Kuncel, & Viechtbauer, 2007). Here, researchers combine the individual results of different experiments to calculate an estimate of how large an effect is across many different participants, samples, experimenters, methods, and measures. Meta-analysis and effect size can help us understand just how large a gender difference is and to evaluate if the difference is real or if it is due only to a particular sample or measure.

Effect size is estimated using the statistic *d:*

$$d = \frac{M_m - M_f}{s}$$

where M_m is the average score for males and M_f is the average score for females and *s* is the average standard deviation of the male and female scores (Hyde, 2004, p. 93). You can see from this formula that when males score higher than females on average, then *d* will be positive. When females score higher than males on average, then *d* will be negative. When there is no significant difference between the genders on this variable, then *d* will be close to zero (see Table 11.2).

Figure 11.3 graphically illustrates various effect sizes. As you can see in the left part of Figure 11.3, when an effect size is small there is huge overlap in the distributions of the scores of men and women. Even though a small difference between men and women may be statistically significant, it does not necessarily have practical significance. A *d* of 0.2 is often too small to be noticeable in everyday life and would be only detectable in a controlled research study with lots of participants. By the same logic, a moderate difference of 0.5, the middle graph in Figure 11.3, will probably be noticeable in everyday life. When differences reach 0.8 or greater people are generally already aware of the difference between men and women on this variable (see the right graph in Figure 11.3; Lippa, 2005a).

That men and women differ on some characteristic is not nearly as important as understanding the size of that difference. After all, people vary across all sorts of variables. The formula for *d* expresses the difference between the averages of two groups in relation to the amount of variability in each distribution. This means that where there is a lot of variation in a characteristic among individuals (e.g., height) it will take a larger difference between men and women to make a significant gender difference. But where people don't vary so much (e.g., scores on a 1 to 7 scale) smaller differences in averages can be significant. When doing a meta-analysis we are trying to see if—on average—there is more variation between the genders than among individuals within a gender.

Consider Figure 11.4, which shows the distribution of spatial ability scores in men and women. Is the difference between the genders greater than the difference within a gender? As you can see, the average of the

Table 11.2 Meta-Analysis: How Large a Difference?

Range of *d*	Size of Effect
−0.1 to 0 and 0 to +0.1	Trivial
−0.11 to −0.35 and +0.11 to +0.35	Small
−0.36 to −0.65 and +0.36 to +0.65	Medium
−0.66 to −01.0 and +0.66 to +1.0	Large
Greater than 1.0	Very large

Note: Positive numbers mean males scored higher than females. Negative numbers mean females scored higher than males.

Source: Effect size interpretations from Hyde (2007), after Cohen (1988).

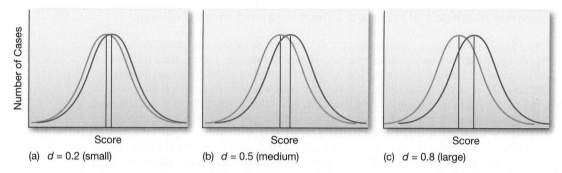

Number of Cases

Score

Score

Score

(a) $d = 0.2$ (small)   (b) $d = 0.5$ (medium)   (c) $d = 0.8$ (large)

Figure 11.3 A graphic illustration of small, moderate, and large effect sizes. For example, a small difference, $d = 0.2$, is the difference between men and women in self-esteem (left). A medium difference, $d = 0.5$, is the difference between boys and girls in activity level (middle). A large difference, $d = 0.8$, is a bit larger than the difference between men and women in knowledge of sports (right). Notice that in all cases there is substantial overlap between the curves. *Source:* Lippa (2005a, Figure 14, p. 8). Lippa, R. A. (2005). Gender, nature, and nurture. Mahwah, NJ: Lawrence Erlbaum and Associates.

men is greater than the average of the women, but there is substantial overlap between the two curves. The area that is shaded represents those women who scored higher than the average man, which is about 23% of the women. So even though there is a large gender difference, it does not mean that *every* man scored higher than *every* woman on this variable.

Like any type of review, a meta-analysis is only as good as the data that go into it. Ideally, researchers should identify and compile all of the studies ever conducted on a topic. As a general rule, the larger the number of studies that are combined into an effect size estimate—especially of different experimenters and various methods—the better our estimate of the true gender difference will be. However, if all of the studies that went into a meta-analysis used the same dependent variable then the resulting effect size estimate may have limited generalizability and not apply to other measures. Researchers will often include a table describing all of the studies they combined into their effect size estimate, including the methods, measures, sample size, age, gender, and so on of each one. This allows researchers to generate and test specific hypotheses about what might account for an observed gender difference.

Finally, keep in mind that one-item measures, such as willingness to help or conformity as measured in many experiments on social behavior, may underestimate the true effect size (Lippa, 2005a). To the extent possible, this chapter reviews the findings on gender similarities and differences based on meta-analyses and review articles and not on single studies.

Now that you are familiar with effect size, we can evaluate just how large—and how important—gender differences are compared to individual differences (see Table 11.2). Because of variability in individual differences there will always be some overlap in the distributions of men

Figure 11.4 The distribution of scores of males and females on a test of spatial ability. The difference between the two curves represents a large gender difference: $d = 0.73$.

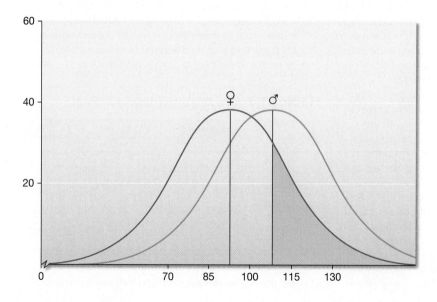

and women. That's why our estimate of effect size *d* is calculated as a ratio of difference between genders compared to individual variability within a gender. For *every single personality variable* that was been studied, there is overlap in the distributions of scores of men and women. Just how much overlap? Read on to find out!

Personality Differences Between Men and Women: Fact or Fiction?

Men and women are thought to be different in social behavior, physical attributes, emotional experiences, cognition, occupations, interests, moral reasoning, sexual behavior, and personality, but are we really? We can attempt to answer this question by considering the size of gender differences, the consistency of these differences, and possible interpretations of these differences.

In a very careful and strict summary of meta-analytic research on gender differences, including some very extensive national studies, Janet Hyde (2007) found that 78% of the effects reported were small (48%) or nonsignificant (30%). To give you a sense of what the research she reviewed looked like, consider Table 11.3.

> "[M]en and women are especially alike in their beliefs about their own differences. To the extent that males and females share expectations regarding intrapsychic and behavioral differences between the sexes, the expression of such differences constitutes a sex similarity."
>
> *Rhoda K. Unger (1979, p. 1086)*

Table 11.3 Summary of Meta-Analyses of Gender Differences

Variable	Type of Variable	% Non-overlap	d	Effect Size
Height (2.60)	Physical		2.6	
			2.5	
			2.4	
			2.3	
Throwing velocity (2.18)	Physical	81.1%	2.2	
			2.1	
Throwing distance (2.0)	Physical		2.0	
			1.9	Very Large
			1.8	
			1.7	
			1.6	
			1.5	
			1.4	
People–things dimension (1.35)	Occupations		1.3	
			1.2	
			1.1	
Desire realistic occupation (1.06)	Occupation	55.4	1.0	
Technology knowledge (1.04)	Interests			
Electronics knowledge (0.98)	Interests			
Throwing accuracy (0.96)	Physical	51.6	0.9	
Masturbation (0.96)	Sexuality			Large
Number of ideal partners in a lifetime (0.87)	Sexuality			
Aggression measured by projective tests (0.86)	Social behavior	47.4	0.8	
Aggression measured by fantasy (0.84)	Social behavior			
Attitude toward sex in a casual relationship (0.81)	Sexuality			
Sports knowledge (0.75)	Interests	43	0.7	
Mental rotation (0.73)	Cognitive			

(Continued)

Table 11.3 *(Continued)*

Variable	Type of Variable	% Non-overlap	d	Effect Size
Extraversion: assertiveness (0.67) Grip strength (0.66) Jealousy over sexual vs. emotional infidelity (0.64) Aggression measured by peer reports (0.63) Aggression, physical (0.60)	Personality Physical Social behavior Social behavior Temperament	38.2	0.6	Medium
Science knowledge (0.58) Desire physical attractiveness in mate (0.54) Knowledge of general information (0.51) Activity (0.5)	Interests Sexuality Interests Social behavior	33	0.5	
Attitude toward sex in a committed relationship (0.49) Spatial perception (0.44) Attitudes toward sex when engaged (0.43) Aggression measured by self-reports (0.40)	Sexuality Cognitive Sexuality Social behavior	27.4	0.4	
SAT math (earlier than 2004) (0.39) Arousal to erotic material (college students) (0.38) Surgency (0.38)	Cognitive Sexuality Temperament			
Helping behavior (0.34) Self-esteem at ages 15–18 (0.33) Activity (0.33) Homosexuality (0.33) SAT math (2004) (0.31) Arousal to erotic material (0.31) High-intensity fun (0.30)	Social behavior Personality Temperament Sexuality Cognitive Sexuality Temperament	21.3	0.3	Small
Number of sexual partners (0.25) Self-esteem at ages 11–14 (0.23) Self-esteem (overall) (0.21) Empathy (less than 0.20)	Sexuality Personality Personality Social behavior	14.7	0.2	
Justice reasoning (0.19) Self-esteem at ages 19–22 (0.18) Self-esteem at ages 7–10 (0.16) Mathematics (0.16) Spatial visualization (0.13)	Moral reasoning Personality Personality Cognitive Cognitive	7.7	0.1	
Self-esteem at ages 23–59 (0.10) SAT verbal (0.06) Desire for conventional occupations (0.06) Extraversion: activity (0.01) Openness: intellect/ideas (0.00) Pride frequency (ns) Pride intensity (ns) Guilt frequency (ns) Ideas-data dimension (ns) Literature knowledge (ns) Business knowledge (ns) Arts knowledge (ns) Leadership effectiveness (0.03) Self-esteem at age 60 + (−0.03) Balance (−0.09) GPA (−0.04) Arousal to erotic material (adults) (−0.04) Anger frequency (−0.05) Sexual satisfaction (−0.06) Extraversion: gregariousness (−0.06) Guilt intensity (−0.07)	Personality Cognitive Occupations Personality Personality Emotion Emotion Emotion Occupations Interests Interests Interests Social behavior Personality Physical Cognitive Sexuality Emotion Sexuality Personality Emotion	0	0.0	Trivial

Table 11.3 *(Continued)*

Variable	Type of Variable	% Non-overlap	d	Effect Size
Openness (−0.07)	Personality			
Reading comprehension (−0.09)	Cognitive			
Neuroticism: impulsiveness (−0.10)	Personality			
Verbal ability (in studies done after 1973) (−0.10)	Cognitive			
Verbal ability (−0.11)	Cognitive			
Fearfulness (−0.12)	Temperament	7.7		
Conscientiousness: order (−0.12)	Personality			
Contentment frequency (−0.13)	Emotion			
Negative emotions frequency (−0.14)	Emotion			
Anger intensity (−0.14)	Emotion			
Conscientiousness (−0.14)	Personality			
Extraversion (−0.15)	Personality		−0.1	Small
Joy frequency (−0.16)	Emotion			
Sadness frequency (−0.16)	Emotion			
Symptoms of depression (−0.16)	Emotion			
Fear frequency (−0.17)	Emotion			
Contentment intensity (−0.18)	Emotion			
Self-disclosure	Social behavior			
Positive emotions frequency (−0.20)	Emotion	14.7		
Democratic leadership (−0.22)	Social behavior			
Agreeableness: trust (−0.22)	Personality			
Positive emotions intensity (−0.23)	Emotion			
Verbal ability (in studies before 1973) (−0.23)	Cognitive			
Influenceability (−0.26)	Social behavior			
Joy intensity (−0.26)	Emotion		−0.2	
Fear intensity (−0.26)	Emotion			
Affection intensity (−0.25)	Emotion			
Negative emotions intensity (−0.25)	Emotion			
Neuroticism: anxiety (−0.25)	Personality			
Care reasoning (−0.28)	Moral reasoning			
Sadness intensity (−0.28)	Emotion			
Affection frequency (−0.30)	Emotion	21.3	−0.3	
Agreeableness (−0.32)	Personality			
Conformity in the Asch paradigm (−0.32)	Social behavior			
Medical knowledge (−0.32)	Interests			Medium
Perceptual sensitivity (−0.38)	Temperament	27.4	−0.4	
Smiling (−0.40)	Social behavior			
Food and cooking knowledge (0.48)	Interests			
Emotional stability (−0.49)	Personality			
		33	−0.5	
Desire for social occupation (−0.62)	Occupation	38.2	−0.6	
Desire for artistic occupation (−0.63)	Occupation			
Desire ambitiousness in mate (−0.67)	Sexuality			
Desire status in mate (−0.69)	Sexuality			
		43	−0.7	
		47.4	−0.8	
Agreeableness: tender-mindedness (−0.92)	Personality	51.6	−0.9	Large
		55.4	−1.0	

Key:

d = The average difference between males and females in standard deviation units.

+ Positive numbers mean that males score higher than females on this variable.

− Negative numbers mean that females score higher than males on this variable.

Source: Compiled from various sources.

THINK ABOUT IT

What personality characteristics do you think men and women differ the most in? The least in?

Table 11.3 summarizes the results of many meta-analyses (e.g., Feingold, 1992, 1994; Hyde, 2005, 2007; Lippa, 2005a, 2007) including some not reviewed by Hyde (2005, 2007). The first column lists the variable and gives the exact effect size *d* in parentheses. The second column classifies that variable into type of variable (e.g., social behavior, physical attributes, emotional experiences, cognition, occupations, interests, moral reasoning, sexual behavior, and personality). The third column lists the percentage of overlap between the distribution of males and females on that variable. The fourth column lists the effect size (*d*) of the difference between males and females. The last column groups effect sizes by size: trivial, small, medium, large, and very large according to the guidelines used by Hyde (2007; see Table 11.2).

There are a number of things to notice about Table 11.3. First, and most obvious, is that there are many characteristics that have been studied! This table represents the results of over 1,500 studies compiled into a single table by effect size. Can you think of any characteristic that is *missing* from this table? Second, how large are the vast majority of these effects? As you can see, almost half of the effects are trivial. In fact, if you were to eliminate the small and non-significant correlations from the table, that would eliminate the vast majority of effects. What kinds of variables are represented among these trivial effects?

Next, take a close look at the categories that are represented at the extreme of large and very large effects. Be sure to look at both ends where women score higher than men (the negative numbers) and where men score higher than women (the positive numbers). What kinds of variables account for the largest differences? Finally, even where there are significant differences, remember to consider the percentage overlap between men and women. For many of these variables, there is considerable overlap in the performances of men and women.

Table 11.3 doesn't claim to represent *every single* study that has ever been done, but it does summarize some of the major meta-analyses that have been conducted by psychologists. The results of the many effect size analyses summarized here suggest that men and women are the most different when it comes to physical attributes such as height and strength (Easton & Enns, 1986; Thomas & French, 1985); some aspects of sexuality (Oliver & Hyde, 1993; Petersen & Hyde, 2010), such as reported pornography use, frequency of masturbation, and attitudes toward casual sex; and qualities desired in a potential mate (Feingold, 1992; Sprecher, Sullivan, & Hatfield, 1994). The largest gender differences in personality and social behavior between men and women parallel the largest sex differences between males and females.

Men and women differ in ways you might expect and yet are similar in ways you might not. Table 11.4 highlights some of these interesting effects. As you can see here and in Table 11.3 there are effect size differences between men and women in occupational preferences. Men prefer realistic occupations more so than women. These occupations involve working with machines, equipment, and inanimate objects. Instead, women prefer people-oriented occupations that involve managing and interacting with other people. There are no gender differences in preference for occupations that require creative thought and intellectual effort; routine data-oriented occupations; or conventional occupations that involve following set procedures and routines such as office manager and secretarial positions (Lippa, 2005a).

THINK ABOUT IT

Do you find any of these results surprising? Why?

There is also no gender difference in general intelligence (Halpern, 2000; Halpern & LaMay, 2000), but there are some differences on specific types of mental abilities. Though traditionally people think that women show greater verbal ability than men, the difference is rather trivial ($d = -0.11$) and has been narrowing over time (Hyde & Linn, 1988). Similarly, there is no gender difference in mathematical ability ($d = -0.05$) (Hedges & Nowell, 1995; Hyde, Fennema, & Lamon, 1990). However, there is a slight ($d = 0.12$) difference in performance on word problems (Hyde & Linn, 2006). But as you can see in Figure 11.5, the far greater problem is that both American boys and girls lag far behind children in other countries in mathematics performance! Globally, girls and boys show comparable performance in mathematics in wealthier countries where women are better educated, and hold a proportional share of seats in parliament and in research positions (Else-Quest, Hyde, & Linn, 2010).

Table 11.4 Yes, No, Maybe So?: Gender Similarities and Differences in Personality and Social Behavior

There are no gender differences in these characteristics

Neuroticism: impulsiveness
Extraversion
Extraversion: gregariousness
Extraversion: activity
Openness
Openness: intellect
Conscientiousness
Conscientiousness: order
General Intelligence
Mathematics ability
Verbal ability
Leadership effectiveness
Self-confidence

There Are Gender Differences in These Characteristics

Agreeableness: sympathy
Extraversion: assertiveness
Sexuality
Nonverbal behavior
Aggressiveness
Risk taking
Occupational preferences
Mental disorders
Leadership style

There May Be Gender Differences in These Characteristics

Empathy
Emotions
Anxiety
Helping behavior
Influenceability
Self-esteem
Spatial ability

However, as we discussed earlier, there are slight differences in spatial ability (Linn & Petersen, 1985; Voyer, Voyer, & Bryden, 1995). When it comes to spatial visualization, like finding hidden figures in a picture, there is a small difference between men and women ($d = 0.13$; Linn & Petersen, 1985). But there are large gender differences in spatial perception of true vertical or horizontal ($d = 0.44$; Linn & Petersen, 1985) and mental rotation ($d = 0.73$ according to Linn & Petersen, 1985, but 0.56 according to Voyer et al., 1995).

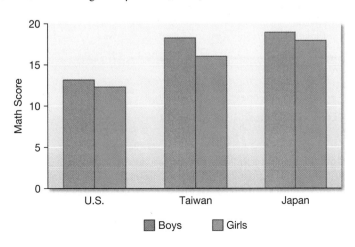

Figure 11.5 Cross-national and gender differences in math. Differences in fifth-graders' performance on word problems are larger between countries than between genders. Boys' scores are shown in orange; girls' scores are shown in yellow. *Source:* Hyde and Linn (2006, p. 600). Reprinted with permission from Hyde, J. S., & Linn, M. C. (2006), "Gender similarities in mathematics and science," *Science,* 314(5799), 599–600. Permission conveyed through the Copyright Clearance Center.

When it comes to mental disorders, there seem to be some differences in the number of males and females affected depending on the disorder (Hartung & Widiger, 1998). Substance-related disorders (e.g., alcohol, drugs), childhood disorders (e.g., mental retardation, reading disorders, autism), and sexual and gender identity disorders (e.g., sexual masochism, fetishism, pedophilia) are more frequent among men than women. However, mood disorders (e.g., panic disorders, bipolar disorder, anorexia and bulimia), and depression (Nolen-Hoeksema & Hilt, 2009) are more frequent among women. Some personality disorders (e.g., schizotypal personality disorder, antisocial personality disorder, narcissistic personality disorder, compulsive personality disorder) occur more among men whereas others (e.g., borderline personality disorder, histrionic personality disorder) occur more among women.

Although interesting, none of these characteristics are, strictly speaking, personality. Are there differences in the personality of men and women? Let us turn now to a discussion of some of the differences in personality and social behavior.

Gender Similarities and Differences in the Five-Factor Model

That men and women differ in sexuality and physical attributes is not surprising, given the differing reproductive roles of males and females. What is surprising to most people is the number of similarities between men and women in personality (Hyde, 2005, 2007). Take the traits of the five factors (see Table 11.5). This table includes data from an extensive study of observer ratings of personality in 50 cultures, including the United States, using the NEO Personality Inventory—Revised (NEO-PI-R; Costa & McCrae, 1992). Neuroticism shows the largest gender difference, with women averaging higher Neuroticism scores than men across all samples. Openness shows the smallest difference, where the genders are virtually identical. Across all cultures, women tend to be only slightly higher than men in Conscientiousness, Extraversion, and Agreeableness.

Table 11.5 Gender Similarities and Differences in The Five-Factor Model

Factor and Facets:	d	Trivial	Small	Medium	Large
Neuroticism	−0.49			✓	
Anxiety	−0.25		✓		
Impulsiveness	−0.10	✓			
Extraversion	−0.15		✓		
Gregariousness	−0.06	✓			
Assertiveness	0.67				✓
Activity	0.01	✓			
Openness	−0.07	✓			
Ideas	0.00	✓			
Agreeableness	−0.32		✓		
Trust	−0.22		✓		
Tender-Mindedness	−0.92				✓
Conscientiousness	−0.14		✓		
Order	−0.12		✓		

Note: Meta-analysis of the five-factor model from observer ratings of the NEO-PI-R in adults from 50 cultures ($N = 10,690$; Meta-analysis of the facets from self-ratings combined across 4–8 different personality tests in 8 samples of U.S. Adults ($N = 19,546$; Feingold, 1994). Positive numbers mean males scored higher than females. Negative numbers mean females scored higher than males. *Sources:* Feingold (1994); McCrae et al. (2005a).

Recall our caveat that when it comes to effect size estimates multiple measures give the most generalizable estimate. Whereas this study looking at the five-factor model in 50 cultures included thousands of participants, all participants were measured using the same dependent variable. What evidence do we have that these gender differences are not somehow due to something about the NEO-PI-R questionnaire?

An earlier meta-analysis looked at possible differences in the five-factor model by summing results from many personality questionnaires including the NEO-PI-R, the revised Eysenck Personality Inventory, and the Minnesota Multiphasic Personality Inventory (MMPI; Hathaway & McKinley, 1940), which were given to various samples of adults (see Table 11.5). Because each test measured different aspects of personality, the researchers were able to calculate effect sizes for only those variables of the five-factor model that were measured on more than one personality test. This limits the conclusions we can draw—data comparing men and women on *all* of the facets is frustratingly absent—but the effect estimates are more reliable and have greater generalizability.

As Table 11.5 shows, there are large differences in the facets of assertiveness (men score higher) and tender-mindedness (women score higher). Further, there are only small differences in anxiety, trust, and order, with women scoring higher in all three facets than men. The remaining facets that have been studied with multiple measures—impulsiveness, gregariousness, activity, and openness to ideas—show only trivial differences. The bottom line: When it comes to personality, men and women are more similar than different (Hyde, 2005).

Gender Differences in Other Aspects of Personality and Social Behavior

Aggression. One of the most consistent findings, both within the United States and in other countries, is that men are more aggressive than women (Archer, 2004; Bettencourt & Miller, 1996; Eagly & Steffen, 1986; Hyde, 1984, 1986; Knight, Fabes, & Higgins, 1996; Maccoby & Jacklin, 1974). However, recall that one of the benefits of meta-analysis is that if the sample and range of studies is large enough we can test specific hypotheses. It turns out that men are more *physically* aggressive than women ($d = 0.40$), but only slightly more *verbally* aggressive ($d = 0.18$; Eagly & Steffen, 1986)—unless women have been directly threatened. Then there is no difference in aggression between men and women (Bettencourt & Miller, 1996).

Bettencourt and Miller (1996) found that gender differences are most apparent under experimental conditions of unprovoked aggression ($d = 0.43$) but disappear when people have been directly threatened ($d = 0.06$; Bettencourt & Miller, 1996). Overall, men are more likely than women to resort to physical aggression whether provoked ($d = 0.21$), or not ($d = 0.48$). But when provoked, women are slightly more likely than men to respond with verbal aggression ($d = -0.11$). What kinds of situations do people find threatening enough to respond with physical or verbal aggression? Men and women respond equally aggressively to a physical attack, an insult, or a negative evaluation. Men are more likely than women to respond aggressively to frustration ($d = 0.17$) or an insult about their intelligence ($d = 0.59$).

Most of these studies focused on aggression in the laboratory, when experimental participants are no doubt on their best behavior. In fact, the gender difference in aggression is even larger than these early meta-analyses suggested according to a more recent meta-analysis of field studies conducted in the United States and nine other countries including India, Japan, Australia, and Canada (Archer, 2004). Men were indeed more aggressive than women in physical and verbal aggression, with *d*s for overall aggression ranging from 0.42 to 0.57 across peer, teacher, observer, and self-reports. Gender differences across all kinds of aggression were the greatest during young adulthood, ages 18 to 22 ($d = 0.66$) and then decreased with age. Men were particularly higher than women in physical aggression, ranging from a low of 0.39 for self-reports to a high of 0.84 for observer reports. However, during late childhood and adolescence, girls engaged in more indirect or relational aggression

THINK ABOUT IT

Where might gender differences in assertiveness and tender-mindedness come from?

THINK ABOUT IT

Why do men and women show no difference in aggression when provoked but a medium difference in unprovoked aggression?

than boys ($d = -0.74$). Observational studies found that girls were more likely than boys to purposely hurt others by rejecting or excluding them, turning others against them, or spreading gossip about them.

In sum, the evidence across multiple meta-analyses, ages, cultures, types of aggression, and conditions of aggression is that boys and men are more aggressive than girls and women. This gender difference plays out daily where men are more often the perpetrators of violent crime than women are, both in the United States and in other countries (Daly & Wilson, 1988). This is not to say that *all* men are aggressive or that all men are more aggressive than all women. As Lippa (2005a) noted, most people—regardless of their gender—do not assault or murder others (Bussey & Bandura, 1999).

Risk Taking.   Are there gender differences in risk taking? Men are higher in impulsive sensation-seeking, like bungee jumping while on vacation (Zuckerman & Kuhlman, 2000), but they are only slightly more likely than women ($d = 0.13$) to engage in risky behaviors that may have undesirable or dangerous outcomes in their daily lives, like speeding or running yellow lights (Byrnes, Miller, & Schafer, 1999). The size of the gender difference in risk taking depends on the context, the type of risk involved, and to some extent, age (Byrnes et al., 1999). As you can see in Table 11.6, the effect sizes, although small to medium, consistently show that men take more risks than women. Gender differences are the greatest in the amount and kind of risky behaviors people have actually engaged in and least when it comes to attitudes toward risky activities.

The largest gender differences occur for volunteering for experiments with a chance of physical or psychological harm; engaging in games of physical skill under high stakes, like shuffleboard or ring toss; and intellectual risk taking, where one's lack of skill might be uncovered. Differences are smaller for self-reported risk taking while driving (e.g., damage to one's vehicle, physical injury, traffic tickets), gambling (playing chance games with little or no skill involved), observed driving (e.g., making a left turn in front of oncoming traffic, gliding through a stop sign rather than coming to a complete stop), and engaging in physical activities that involve the potential for physical harm such as climbing a steep embankment, playing in the street, trying out gymnastics equipment (e.g., a balance beam), and taking a ride on an animal (e.g., a donkey). Gender differences are trivial for engagement in self-reported risky behaviors like smoking, drinking, drug use, and sexual activities.

Table 11.6 Gender Differences in Risk Taking

Task	Mean d Value	Trivial	Small	Medium	Large
Self-reported Behavior					
Smoking	−0.02	✓			
Drinking/Drug use	0.04*	✓			
Sexual Activities	0.07*	✓			
Driving	0.29*		✓		
Observed Behavior					
Physical activity	0.16*		✓		
Driving	0.17*		✓		
Gambling	0.21*		✓		
Risky experiment	0.41*			✓	
Intellectual risk taking	0.40*			✓	
Physical skills	0.43*			✓	

Note: Positive numbers mean males scored higher than females. Negative numbers mean females scored higher than males. Asterisks (*) indicate effects which are significantly different from zero. *Source:* Byrnes et al., (1999).

Men are more likely than women to engage in risky behaviors.

Even though there were significant gender differences across all age groups, from childhood to adulthood, what was considered risky tended to vary by age. For example, men showed a sharper increase in drinking and drug use from high school to college than women. Women were more likely to smoke in college than men. Yet after college, the drinking and drug use of women increased, surpassing that of men.

Another interesting gender difference is that boys and men tended to take more risks even when it was a bad idea to do so. Girls and women tended toward the opposite: avoiding risks even in situations where risk might have paid off, such as the intellectual risk taking that is involved on practice SATs, for example. Byrnes et al. (1999) surmised that males may encounter failure or other negative consequences more often than females, but the risk-averse strategy of females may inadvertently hold girls and women back from achieving success in many areas.

Finally, these gender differences in risky behaviors may be lessening over time. The mean effect size for studies conducted from 1964 to 1980 ($d = 0.20$) was larger than for those conducted from 1981 to 1997 ($d = 0.13$). Has this trend continued into the present day? That question will have to wait for the next round of meta-analyses.

> **THINK ABOUT IT**
>
> Why do you think these gender differences in risky behaviors are lessening over time?

Gender Differences? It Depends

Let's take a closer look at some of the gender differences in personality and social behavior. When we say "it depends," what does that mean?

Empathy. As we saw, one of the largest personality differences—in an area with many trivial and small differences—is that women show more empathy and sympathy than do men. Tender-mindedness, a facet of Agreeableness, shows the largest gender difference in all 50 cultures studied to date, including the United States ($d = -0.39$ for observer ratings; $d = -0.28$ for self-ratings; McCrae et al., 2005), and in a meta-analysis using various measures of tender-mindedness ($d = -0.92$; Feingold, 1994). This would suggest that women are indeed more empathic and sensitive to the plight of others than men are.

> **THINK ABOUT IT**
>
> What does it suggest when men and women differ in self-reports but not in actual behavior?

But this isn't the whole story. These findings were all based on self-report measures of feelings, rather than actual performance or accuracy in understanding another person's emotions (Feingold, 1994; McCrae et al., 2005).

In many studies of empathetic accuracy, participants view a videotaped interaction between two people and try to identify what one of the people in the scenario is feeling. In some experiments, participants estimate how accurate they think they were whereas in other experiments responses are scored as correct or incorrect. According to one meta-analysis, women reported greater accuracy at judging emotions than men did ($d = -0.56$). However, there was no difference between men and women in their actual performance ($d = -0.04$; Ickes, Gesn, & Graham, 2000). The researchers surmised that women present themselves as more empathic in self-reports than men do, perhaps in keeping with gender role stereotypes.

This finding echoes the results of an earlier meta-analysis looking at empathy across many types of tasks including emotional responsiveness after hearing about or viewing pictures of others, physiological measures, observation of facial expressions, tone of voice, and self-reported empathy (e.g., "Seeing people cry upsets me"; Eisenberg & Lennon, 1983). The researchers noted inconsistent results across the seven types of measures studied. However, one clear effect emerged: Females showed more empathy than males on self-reports or other measures obviously related to empathy, but there was no gender difference on unobtrusive measures of empathy like facial expressions or physiological distress. Again, the pattern suggests that there is a demand characteristic operating such that participants act differently—and in line with gender roles—when they know that their empathy is being monitored (Eisenberg & Lennon, 1983).

Women are also more likely to feel the emotions of people around them according to a self-report measure of emotional contagion (Doherty, 1997). The scale included items such as "If someone I'm talking with begins to cry, I get teary-eyed" or "I tense when overhearing an angry quarrel." Women reported that they felt the emotions of happiness, fear, anger, or sadness while being around people who were experiencing these emotions more often than men reported catching these emotions from others.

This greater responsiveness of women to what another person is feeling is reflected in women's greater nonverbal perceptiveness (Hall, 1978, 1984, 2006b). Women are better at reading other people's body language and facial expressions ($d = -0.43$) and recognizing faces ($d = -0.34$). Women are also better at expressing emotions nonverbally ($d = -0.52$), particularly in the face ($d = -1.01$), and they engage in more eye contact when interacting with others than men do ($d = -0.68$).

Emotions.   Are women more emotional than men? Are men less emotional than women? Gender differences in emotions depend more on cultural factors, situational influences, gender role pressures, and the measures used rather than differences in the actual experience of

Men and women both feel empathy for others; however, men may be more reluctant to show nonstereotypical masculine behavior when they know they are being monitored.

emotion (e.g., Brody, 2000; Ickes et al., 2000; LaFrance & Banaji, 1992; Shields, 1995; Wester, Vogel, Pressly, & Heesacker, 2002). The problem is compounded by the lack of a single measure of emotion (LaFrance & Banaji, 1992). For example, researchers might measure emotional intensity, frequency, duration, range, onset, accuracy, and congruence among different modes of expression (e.g., body, face, voice, words, etc.; LaFrance & Banaji, 1992). Or, researchers might use measures of experienced emotion, nonverbal expressions, or physiological reactions, which each tap different aspects of emotional experience and expression.

For example, there are no gender differences in women's and men's physiological experience of emotions. However, women report more emotion if asked directly, using self-reports, about an emotion that is readily observable and that involves other people. Women also report more emotion if asked about general emotion rather than about a specific emotion (LaFrance & Banaji, 1992).

Women report more intense feelings of sadness, depression, and being in a bad mood than do men (Brody & Hall, 2008). Men report more intense feelings of pride, confidence, guilt, and excitement than do women (Brody, 1993). Finally, gender differences in shame (Brody, 2000), anger, contempt, guilt, and loneliness (Brody & Hall, 2008) are inconsistent, depending on the situational context and the methods used.

These findings suggest that differences in men's and women's self-reported emotions parallel gender role expectations. In keeping with the expectation that admitting vulnerability, sadness, or self-consciousness is seen as unmanly, men report feeling negative emotions like disgust, sadness, fear, anxiety, hurt, shame, and embarrassment less than women do (Brody, 1999, 2000). Similarly, women find it less appropriate to express any emotion that might threaten a social relationship such as pride and lack of guilt or remorse. Instead, women feel social pressure to express emotions that protect and foster relationships like warmth, support, and cheerfulness (Brody, 2000). Is this truly a gender difference in the experience of emotion, or have men and women internalized appropriate gender roles?

Women and men in many countries feel similar pressures to adhere to gender expectations about emotional expression. In one study involving participants from 37 countries, women reported expressing emotions more publicly, feeling emotions more intensely, and experiencing emotions for a longer period of time, than men within their own culture did (Fischer & Manstead, 2000).

How large are these differences? There is no easy way to say, as the methods and measures vary greatly. In fact, no one has been able to conduct a meta-analysis combining individual effects from across these varied studies. However, a more recent study of undergraduates in 41 countries did try to estimate the size of the gender difference in emotion (Brebner, 2003). They asked participants how frequently and how intensely they felt four positive emotions (affection, contentment, joy, pride) and four negative emotions (anger, fear, guilt, sadness).

To help interpret their results, the researchers calculated the effect size of the difference between men and women in self-reported intensity and frequency of the eight emotions. Recall that effect size summarizes multiple effects in the case of meta-analysis, or single effects, as in the case of one study. We can compare the size of the effect in this study to other gender effects discussed in this chapter.

As you can see in Table 11.7, the effects are in the trivial to small range (Brebner, 2003). If anything, we would expect these effects based on self-reports to exaggerate the difference between the genders in the experience of emotion (LaFrance & Banaji, 1992). Until more research—and meta-analyses comparing effects across multiple methods and measures—is conducted, we can safely conclude that gender differences in emotional experience may have more to do with gender role expectations or experimental methods than a dispositional difference between men and women.

Anxiety.   Which gender is more anxious? According to meta-analyses, women are more anxious ($d = -0.30$). However, this is based on self-report (Maccoby & Jacklin, 1974). Are women really more anxious than men or are they just more willing to admit to being more anxious—because it's more socially acceptable for a woman to publicly admit vulnerability? When researchers actually observe the reactions of men and women to stressful events there

THINK ABOUT IT

Why might men and women differ in self-reported emotional experiences?

Table 11.7   Effect Sizes for Gender Differences in Emotions

Emotion	Frequency	Intensity
Positive Emotions	−0.20	−0.23
Affection	−0.30	−0.25
Joy	−0.16	−0.26
Contentment	−0.13	−0.18
Pride	*ns*	*ns*
Negative Emotions	−0.14	−0.25
Fear	−0.17	−0.26
Anger	−0.05	−0.14
Sadness	−0.16	−0.28
Guilt	*ns*	−0.07

Note: Positive numbers mean males scored higher than females; negative numbers mean females scored higher than males; *ns* indicates that the difference between males and females was not significant.

Source: Brebner (2003).

SEE FOR YOURSELF

What image comes to mind when you picture a "hero"?

are no gender differences in anxiety (Maccoby & Jacklin, 1974). Other studies have shown that men are actually more physiologically reactive than women, showing greater heart rate, skin conductance, and breathing when anxious (see Gottman, 1993, for a review).

Helping Behavior.   Meta-analyses show that, overall, men engage in more helping behavior than women ($d = 0.34$), especially if onlookers are present and the participant knows that he or she is being watched ($d = 0.74$; Eagly & Crowley, 1986). But if there are no witnesses, this gender difference disappears ($d = -0.02$)! Consider, too, that men and women may not differ in the amount of helping but in the kind of helping they provide. Women are more often the primary caregivers of children and elderly parents, but men are more often rescuers and heroes, especially where conditions rely on physical strength (Eagly, 2009a; Eagly & Crowley, 1986). Women's helping behavior is more communal, often taking place in close relationships, whereas men's is more agentic, taking place with strangers (e.g., bystander intervention), a type of helping most often studied in social psychological experiments (Eagly, 2009a; Wood & Eagly, 2010).

Leadership.   Similarly, there is no gender difference in leadership effectiveness ($d = 0.03$). However, women and men tend to have different styles of leadership (Eagly, Karau, & Makhijani, 1995). The effect size for democratic leadership ($d = -0.22$) suggests that women tend to share the power whereas men tend to be more autocratic (Eagly & Johnson, 1990). The difference is one of style rather than effectiveness (Eagly & Johannesen-Schmidt, 2001; Eagly, Johannesen-Schmidt, & van Engen, 2003; Eagly & Johnson, 1990). Other studies echo this finding, with men more likely to emerge as leaders in situations involving task leadership, where getting the task done and maintaining productivity is the most important ($d = 0.33$). Women are more likely to emerge as leaders in situations involving social leadership, and where working well together and maintaining the integrity of the group is important ($d = -0.21$; Eagly & Karau, 1991).

Influenceability.   Consider the social behavior of influenceability, or how likely people are to go along with others. Meta-analyses show that women are somewhat more influenceable than men ($d = -0.26$) (Eagly, 1978; Eagly & Carli, 1981). Women are more easily swayed by the conformity pressure of peers—think of the classic Asch line length experiment—especially if they must respond in front of others ($d = -0.32$). Women were also more easily persuaded

Men and women have different but equally effective styles of leadership. Here, then U.S. secretary of state Madeleine Albright meets Russian Orthodox patriarch Alexy II at the Danilov Monastery in Moscow, February 1997.

than men to change their attitude when interacting with another person who holds a different position on a topic ($d = -0.16$; Eagly & Carli, 1981).

As you might expect, women conform and change their attitudes more than men when the stimulus materials involve traditionally masculine topics such as sports, military, or technology. For example, the topic showing the greatest gender difference in influenceability is football ($d = 1.05$). At the same time, males are more easily swayed when it comes to traditionally female topics like social work, education, health habits, day care, domestic issues, abstract art, or judgment of artistic creativity. Men are particularly influenced when it comes to judging birth control ($d = -0.75$). There are no gender differences in conformity or attitude change if the subject matter is gender-neutral (Eagly & Carli, 1981).

Curiously, Eagly and Carli (1981) also found that women were more swayed than men in experiments conducted by males ($d = -0.28$). There was no gender difference in influenceability in experiments by female authors. At the time of this meta-analysis some 79% of the conformity and persuasion studies they summarized were conducted by men. The authors wondered if the impact of author gender might be due to a bias of male authors in choice of topic used in experiments or to not mentioning insignificant gender differences.

Overall, the difference between men and women in influenceability is small to medium. As we said earlier, a meta-analysis is only as good as the research that goes into it, and there are many unanswered questions on the topic of gender and influenceability. For example, we don't know the extent to which these effects carry over outside of psychology experiments to the real world and everyday situations of social influence (Becker, 1986). We don't know if these results apply to a non-college-aged population, or if they still apply today, considering many of these studies were done well over 30 years ago. Finally, we don't know how long lasting the attitude change of men and women might be (Becker, 1986).

Figure 11.6 Effect size of self-esteem over the life span. *Source:* Kling et al., 1999.

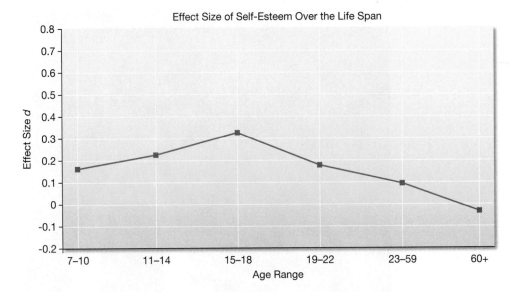

Self-Esteem and Self-Confidence. Perhaps the most interesting gender difference is the case of self-esteem. Based on the combination of 216 studies, men have slightly higher self-esteem ($d = 0.20$) than women, but this difference varies—getting higher or lower—depending on age (see Figure 11.6). The gender difference in self-esteem occurs in White participants ($d = 0.20$), but not in African American samples ($d = -0.04$).

Recall that self-esteem is a general evaluation about one's self. This is different from self-confidence, or belief that one will be successful at a task. Though early reviews found that women have less self-confidence than men (Maccoby & Jacklin, 1974) a more recent review concluded that under certain conditions women may merely appear less confident than men depending on the specific task involved, the availability of performance feedback, and the emphasis placed on social comparison with others (Lenney, 1977).

These findings were borne out in a later experiment. First-semester undergraduate women and men predicted what GPA they expected to achieve that semester either out loud to another student who was conducting the experiment or written privately and sealed in an envelope so the student-experimenter wouldn't be able to see it. Participants' estimates were later checked against their actual GPAs. Women predicted significantly lower estimates than men, showing an underconfidence, but only in the public condition. The estimates of women and men did not differ in the private condition (Heatherington et al., 1993).

In a second experiment, using similar methods, women gave lower estimates of their GPA in front of a weaker student. Interestingly, there was no gender difference in the participants' actual GPAs in either of these experiments. The researchers surmised that women underestimate their GPAs to appear modest or out of concern for another person's feelings. That is, what appears as a difference in self-confidence is really a difference in modesty or sensitivity to others.

Subsequent research has discovered that the difference is due as much to men *overestimating* their chances of success as women *underestimating* their chances of success. Men may be a bit overconfident, even as women may be a bit underconfident (Beyer, 1999; Mednick & Thomas, 1993). We should be sensitive to how our interpretation of the data unnecessarily projects female deficit or nonconsciously sets male behavior as the standard (Hyde, 2004).

What Causes Gender Differences?

Perhaps men and women are more similar than you thought; after all, many psychological gender differences are trivial. The reality is that medium and large differences do exist so we should be careful not to embrace a simplistic conclusion that men and women are the same or that men and women are different (Lippa, 2006). The real questions for researchers is why do these gender differences exist and where do they come from, so that we can start to untangle the biological and social forces that generate these similarities and differences (Lippa, 2006).

By now, from our discussion of gender similarities and differences, you probably have some idea of what causes men and women to develop the kind of personalities that we do. For the most part, psychologists have proposed variations of the nature and nurture question to explain gender differences. Let's briefly review some of these explanations (see Table 11.8).

First, at the nature extreme, are biological explanations. These explanations suggest that the differences between the genders are innate and due to biological causes like hormones, genetics, and evolution. One study of families, including identical and nonidentical twins, estimated that 25% of the variance in gendered behavior for teenage males and 38% for females was due to genetic influences (Cleveland, Udry, & Chantala, 2001). The remaining 75 and 62% was due to nonshared environmental influences, like differential treatment by parents, and measurement error. Also, psychologists are now discovering the extent to which prenatal hormones as well as daily fluctuations in testosterone (in males), monthly fluctuations in estrogen (for females), and even lifetime exposure to estrogen (in females) affect cognitive abilities (Halpern, 2004).

Or, consider the recent finding that when under stress, the sympathetic nervous system of females releases oxytocin in addition to epinephrine and norepinephrine. Oxytocin leads to a "tend-and-befriend" response in women under stress. In contrast to men, where testosterone interacts with norepinephrine to increase the "fight-or-flight" response, women seek out company and become more maternal, taking care of others (Taylor et al., 2000). In a double-blind study, men performed better at a test of nonverbal sensitivity when they had been given oxytocin compared to when they had a placebo (Domes, Heinrichs, Michel, Berger, & Herpertz, 2007). Oxytocin could well account for the sex difference in tender-mindedness and nonverbal sensitivity.

At the nurture extreme are social explanations. Social learning theory, for example, suggests that differences between the genders are not innate, but are socialized in us from our parents or learned from peers, teachers, or society via the media (Bandura, 1977; Mischel, 1966). For example, many supposed cognitive differences between males and females turned out to have been socialized. These have been reduced or eliminated altogether due to educational opportunities and changing social expectations (Halpern, 2004). For example the gender difference in mathematics is due to girls' choices (Ceci & Williams, 2010), such as opting out of mathematics courses in high school (Hyde, 1993), and not to an innate deficit in ability.

However, toy preference and color preference—characteristics thought to be a product of **gender socialization**—may actually be innate (Hurlburt & Ling, 2007). Infant girls 3 to 8 months old showed greater visual interest in a pink doll over a blue truck, whereas boys preferred the truck to the doll (Alexander, Wilcox, & Woods, 2009). Female and male monkeys

"When examining the multifaceted topic of gender, it may be useful to remember that human males and females are, after all, only slightly variant forms of the same animal species. By this we mean that anatomically and physiologically, males and females are much more similar than they are different, and as a result, they are for the most part interchangeable with regard to social behaviors and roles—childbearing being the major exception."

Deborah L. Best and John E. Williams (1993, p. 215)

THINK ABOUT IT

Do sex hormones account for all gender differences?

Table 11.8 Possible Explanations for Gender Differences

Explanation	Example
Biology	Aggressiveness, nonverbal sensitivity
Genetics	Physical characteristics
Evolution	Sexuality
Socialization	Spatial ability
Social context	Helping behavior
Social role theory	Extraversion: assertiveness
Feminist theory	Empathy
Social construction	Emotions
Biopsychosocial model	Personality

show similar toy preferences (Alexander & Hines, 2002; Hassett, Siebertand, & Wallen, 2008). That these sex differences occur in monkeys and that they occur in infants so young makes it hard to argue that socialization is responsible for gender differences in toys and colors.

Alexander (2003) believed that humans have evolved sex differences in color and form preferences that prepare them for their adult reproductive roles. Females, whether human or monkey, prefer pink objects which cue nurturing behavior. Males prefer objects which signal movement and location. Further, there is evidence that the hormone androgen, which stimulates and controls the development of masculine characteristics, also affects the structures of the visual system including the visual cortex. Androgens may be responsible for sex differences in color naming and spatial perception, in addition to color and function preferences.

Then there are theories that fall somewhere in between these two extremes. Some differences between men and women are due to the social situation or context in which the behavior occurs, as we saw in our discussion about emotional expression, anxiety, and self-confidence. What appears to be a gender difference may change or disappear under different circumstances. Other social explanations suggest that differences between men and women reflect the different roles they hold in society. **Feminist theories** question the status quo nature of these roles.

According to feminist views, too often gender differences become translated into value judgments of females as inferior to males (Halpern, 1997; Unger, 1979). Halpern (1997) noted that we all know that men's and women's genitals differ, so to ask if one set is superior to the other doesn't make sense. Yet, this is often what happens when it comes to psychological differences between the genders.

Feminist perspectives also point out how the power differential between men and women in our society colors the kind of questions researchers pursue. For example, instead of focusing on differences between men and women in reproduction—a deterministic view held by evolutionary psychologists—researchers should explore broader questions about women and sexuality beyond reproductive role (Hyde & Oliver, 2000).

Finally, psychologists are recognizing that the answer to the question of what causes gender differences may not be as simple as biology or social forces. Instead, some have proposed a biopsychosocial model, where biological and psychosocial forces influence each other (Halpern, 2004).

Others are realizing that the answer to the puzzle of what makes women and men the way they are may be a combination of all these explanations (Sternberg, 1993; see Halpern et al., 2007, for an extensive review of how all these theories can be applied to understanding the gender gap in science and mathematics). The trouble is, we may never know for sure which variables and in what precise combination explain a given gender difference. Table 11.9 presents psychology's best guess for documented gender difference in light of current research evidence.

Evolution

According to **evolutionary psychology**, humans have evolved certain characteristics to solve adaptive problems, that is, how to adapt to and survive under various biological and environmental conditions

THINK ABOUT IT

If men and women were to occupy different social roles, would some gender differences disappear?

There are many possible explanations for gender differences. Is this woman a doctor or a nurse? Why do you think that?

Table 11.9 Gender Differences in Personality and Social Characteristics Revisited: Possible Explanations

Characteristic	Current Best Explanation
Sexuality	Evolution
Aggressiveness	Evolution
Risk taking	Evolution
Toy preferences	Evolution
Pink–blue color preference	Evolution
Nonverbal behavior	Biological (oxytocin)
Agreeableness: tender-mindedness	Biological (oxytocin)
Mental rotation	Socialization
Occupational preferences	Socialization
Leadership style	Socialization
Extraversion: assertiveness	Social role theory
Mental disorders	Biopsychosocial

Note: These explanations are based on current research findings and represent psychology's best guess in light of the evidence. Some explanations are open to debate and may change as more evidence emerges.

(Buss, 2004, 2005). To the extent that all humans must face similar challenges, such as finding adequate food or shelter for survival, men and women will develop similar characteristics (for example, taste preferences for high-caloric sweet and fatty foods). However, when men and women face different adaptive problems—as they do for reproduction—then gender differences are likely to emerge. Those characteristics which lead to reproductive success are more likely to be passed on to successive generations (Buss, 1995a). How do we know that a characteristic has been selected? We look for similarities across time and cultures. Particularly valuable characteristics will appear as universal gender differences across many different environments and cultures (Kenrick & Trost, 1993). Differences between men and women in physical attributes (e.g., height), aggressiveness, sexuality, and in qualities desired in a mate are hypothesized to exist due to the different adaptive problem each sex must face to successfully reproduce (Buss, 1995b, 2003).

How do sex differences in reproduction lead to different dating and mating strategies in men and women? For females, reproduction involves a tremendous investment of time and energy. The opportunity for reproduction occurs only once a month, they must carry the embryo for 9 months, and then feed and care for a relatively helpless creature for an additional amount of time. Above all, females need to secure resources to carry them and their offspring through times when food might be scarce and their mobility might be limited due to pregnancy or birth. In contrast, reproduction for males is less costly. As a result, different mating strategies have evolved to solve these differing adaptive problems (Buss, 1995b).

Females have evolved to be more particular about whom they mate with, seeking a mate who has the resources to invest in them and their progeny to help their genes survive. This is why, according to evolutionary psychologists, women are much less in favor of casual sex and value status and ambitiousness in a potential mate (Buss, 1995b).

In contrast, males have evolved strategies to increase their chances of passing on their genes through aggression and risk taking to beat out the competition for a female; casual sex; desire for multiple partners in a lifetime; and the valuing of physical attractiveness (as a gauge of health and fertility) in a potential mate (Buss, 1995b).

In addition, whereas both males and females experience jealousy over a partner's emotional infidelity and sexual infidelity, there is a large effect size difference between the importance women and men place on each that follows from their differing reproductive strategies (Confer et al., 2010). Across all cultures studied, women's jealousy is triggered more by emotional

SEE FOR YOURSELF

Which would upset you more, discovering that your partner is having a sexual relationship or an emotional relationship with another?

infidelity whereas men's jealousy is triggered more by sexual infidelity ($d = 0.64$; Hofhansl, Voracek, & Vitouch, 2004, cited in Confer et al., 2010). This difference in jealousy has been documented using self-reports and physiological measures (Buss, Larsen, & Westen, 1992) and is not easily explained by other theories (Buss, Larsen, & Westen, 1996).

Similarly, according to evolutionary psychology, males develop better spatial skills because these skills were required by successful hunters who lived to reproduce, thus passing on these crucial genes to the next generation. However, one could argue that traditional female skills like weaving or fitting objects together such as required in sewing, quilting, or housekeeping require spatial skills more so than traversing large distances or throwing spears (Halpern, 2004; Pontius, 1997). Psychologists have proposed alternatives to evolutionary explanations of sex differences and the evolutionary perspective of human behavior is not without its critics (Confer et al., 2010).

THINK ABOUT IT

Why should gender differences depend on the social situation in which they are measured?

Social Context

Gender differences in the characteristics discussed earlier—helping behavior, leadership, anxiety, empathy, and influenceability—all depend on the context in which they occur or in how they are measured. For example, people may behave differently—often more in line with social expectations for gender—if other people are present or if assessed using self-report. Are men really more interested in sex than women, or do women feel uneasy admitting this on surveys? Are women really more sensitive to others or do they feel they need to appear so? That these differences in the behavior of men and women change depending on the situation suggests that these differences have more to do with the social context than with any important difference between men and women (Yoder & Kahn, 2003). We will never be able to answer the ultimate question and truly understand the essence of what a man is and what a woman is until social influences are minimized. This is why it is important to consider what causes gender differences. For example, the norms of a given situation may change how people behave, or, as we saw in Chapter 5, people may change their behavior to present themselves in a certain light.

For example, for years psychologists and others thought that the gender difference in spatial ability was "hard-wired" into the brains of males and females. However, the experiment that opened this chapter demonstrating that practice with certain video games can actually eliminate this gender difference in mental rotation suggests otherwise (Feng et al., 2007). Even something as simple as stimuli (human figures vs. abstract figures; see Figure 11.7; Alexander & Evardone, 2008) or task instructions can eliminate gender differences on a mental rotation task (Sharps, Price, & Williams, 1994; Sharps, Welton, & Price, 1993). When a mental rotation task was described as "an evaluation of some of your spatial abilities, of your abilities to reason

Figure 11.7 Examples of human figure stimuli. Both males and females perform better on a mental rotation task when human figures are used and the gender difference between men's and women's performance was reduced by half.

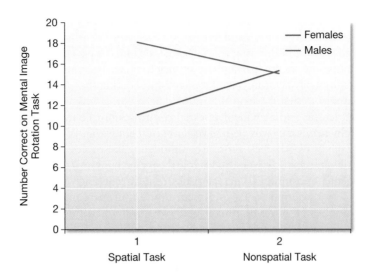

Figure 11.8 Performance in mental image rotation task as a function of participant gender and instructional set. Men and women perform equally well on a mental rotation task when it is not labeled as a test of spatial ability. *Source:* Sharps et al. (1993).

and solve problems regarding physical objects in space. Such abilities are involved in mechanical skills, and in navigation, map reading, and work with tools" we see the standard gender difference in spatial abilities, with men performing better than women. But when the same task was described as "an evaluation of some of your mental abilities, of your abilities to reason and solve problems" without any mention of the spatial nature of the task, men and women performed equally well (see Figure 11.8).

Social Role Theory

Social role theory suggests that men and women have developed differences due to the different roles they hold in society (Eagly, 1987; Eagly & Wood, 1999). What appears to be a gender difference may really be a power or status difference, due to the greater value placed on men and more power afforded to men in a patriarchal society. For example, perhaps the reason why women are more nurturing is because they do much of the caregiving in our society. If men did more caregiving, the reasoning goes, they would develop more empathy. Similarly, if women were better represented among the Fortune 500 CEOs and positions of political power, or earned salaries equal to what men in similar positions earned, they would develop more confidence, competitiveness, and business acumen, and stereotypes of what makes a good leader would start to change (Eagly & Sczesny, 2009).

Social role theory of gender differences suggests that men and women develop different aspects of their personality because of the different social roles they occupy in our society. By changing these roles, we may eliminate some gender differences.

Society's division of labor between the two sexes provides both opportunities and restrictions that cause males and females to develop differently. This leads to a concentration of men and women in differing roles. Historically, men have ended up in roles with greater power, status, and wealth, particularly as societies have become more complex, with sex differences traditionally favoring men. From accommodating these roles, men develop dominant behavior and women develop subordinate behavior. Dominant behavior is assertive, controlling, autocratic, and may involve sexual control. Subordinate behavior is more yielding to social influence, less overtly aggressive, more cooperative, and may involve a lack of sexual autonomy (Eagly & Wood, 1999). From accommodating these roles, men and women develop role-related skills and characteristics. Social role theory explains how men and women develop their typical agentic or communal characteristics, respectively (Eagly & Wood, 1999).

For example, one experiment found that men and women assigned to a supervisory role showed more dominant behaviors, but when these same participants were assigned to the underling role they acted more submissive. When the roles were reversed, the same participants showed completely different behaviors. That is, the former supervisors became more submissive and the former underlings became more dominant (Moskowitz, Suh, & Desaulniers, 1994).

Social role theory does explain some gender differences in nonverbal communication. For example, that men tend to interrupt others more may be a function of dominance or men's higher social status (Hall, 2006a). However, dominance or status doesn't explain all the gender differences in nonverbal communication.

Another way to see if gender role might be causing differences in personality between men and women is to eliminate the gender role and see if this eliminates the difference in behavior. To test this, researchers took advantage of a social phenomenon called **deindividuation** (Zimbardo, 1969). Deindividuation is when people feel unaccountable and not responsible for their actions. When people are anonymous and part of a group, they stop feeling like individuals and experience a loosening of ordinary social norms and social roles. When deindividuated, people act in nonnormative, often antisocial and aggressive ways. Because part of the social role of being a man is to act aggressively and for a woman to inhibit her aggressiveness, would loosening these social roles reduce gender differences in aggression?

Male and female participants played a video game in which they could attack their opponents by dropping bombs. In the individuated condition, the experimenter first introduced them to the other participants, gave them large name tags, and had them answer personal questions about their background and interests out loud. In the deindividuated condition, participants were part of a small group, no introductions were made, no names or name tags were used, and no personal questions were asked. How did these conditions affect later behavior in an aggressive video game?

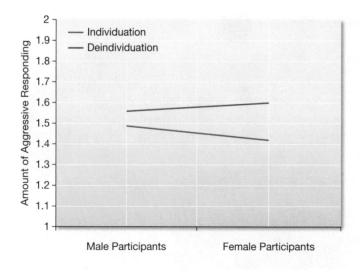

Figure 11.9 Aggressive responding as a function of deindividuation and participant sex. This graph shows a significant interaction between participant sex and deindividuation. Females were more aggressive when the social role prohibiting female aggressiveness was weakened. *Source:* Lightdale and Prentice (1994).

As you can see in Figure 11.9, females dropped fewer bombs than males in the individuated condition but not in the deindividuated condition. When the pressure to adhere to gender norms was eliminated through deindividuation women became *more* aggressive and the usual gender difference in aggression disappeared! Just in case you were thinking that maybe these participants were somehow going along with what they thought might be expected of them in an aggressive game or when deindividuated, a previous experiment verified that undergraduates are unaware of how deindividuation might affect their later aggressiveness.

Social role theory also proposes an alternative explanation for some of the differences in reproductive strategies like the qualities desired in a potential mate. Men and women must choose partners and potential mates who fit in with society's sexual division of labor in marital roles. Because women lack status, power, and wealth they must choose a mate who can provide these resources. Indeed, in a study of 37 cultures, women in cultures with greater gender equity were less likely to prefer an older man, or a potential mate with high earning capacity. Men in these cultures were less likely to prefer a younger woman, or to choose future mates based on domestic skills. Gender differences in these mating preferences decreased in cultures with greater gender equity. However, the gender difference for men preferring an attractive mate more than women still held regardless of the gender equity of the culture. Perhaps the emphasis on physical attractiveness is driven by evolution but other mating preferences are driven more by social roles (Eagly & Wood, 1999).

To test this alternative explanation for mate selection, male and female college students imagined themselves as married with children in either a homemaker role, a provider role, or a control condition where they imagined themselves in whatever role came to mind (Eagly, 2009b). Both women and men who imagined themselves as future homemakers rated status, ambition, career focus, and salary as important in a future mate. However, women and men who imagined themselves as a future provider rated good cook, good with children, and good housekeeper as important in a future mate. Notice that the qualities these participants desired in a future mate depended on the role they saw themselves in and not on their gender. This study suggests that some gender differences, like some aspects of mate preference, may be more a function of social role than of biological sex (Eagly, 2009b).

Social Construction

Imagine the following scenario:

> *Chris was really angry today! Enough was enough. Chris put on the gray suit, marched into work, and went into the main boss's office and yelled: "I've brought in more money for this company than anybody else and everyone gets promoted but me! You hand out promotions like candy!" The boss saw Chris's fist slam down on the desk. There was an angry look on Chris's face. They tried to talk but it was useless. Chris just stormed out of the office in anger.* (Beall, 1993, p. 127)

While reading this passage, did you imagine Chris as a man or woman? Perhaps the part about choosing the gray suit made you think of a woman, putting care into her appearance. Perhaps the part about the fist slamming down on the desk made you think Chris was a man, his aggressiveness coming to the fore. Go back now and reread the passage imagining Chris differently than you had before. If you look carefully, there is nothing in this paragraph to indicate gender—except your own expectations.

The idea that we define or construct our own reality is at the heart of **social construction-ism**. According to Gergen (1985), we construct our perceptions based on our cultural background. Some constructions, like stereotypes about gender, may persist because they support the current social order or rationalize differential treatment of groups (Beall, 1993). Social construction explanations claim that gender differences have more to do with people's beliefs about gender than any innate differences between men and women. This view suggests that gender is in the eye of the beholder.

SEE FOR YOURSELF

Imagine yourself as married with children. Do you see yourself more as a home-maker or as a provider? What qualities are important for your future mate?

THINK ABOUT IT

How do our beliefs about what men and women are like color our perceptions of people?

For example, in one study, male and female undergraduates watched a short video clip of a 9-month-old infant reacting to various toys, including a jack-in-the-box (Condry & Condry, 1976). The infant's response to the jack-in-the-box was ambiguous. At first the infant appeared startled when Jack popped up. Then the infant became more and more agitated and started to cry. Later, the infant screamed when Jack popped up, and then dissolved into tears. Participants watched the same video, but were randomly assigned to believe that they were watching a boy ("David") or a girl ("Dana"). They judged what emotion the baby was feeling and how intensely he or she was feeling it.

What emotion is this baby feeling and what does gender have to do with it?

Despite watching *the same infant,* participants judged the emotion of the infant very differently depending on whether they thought they were watching a girl or a boy (see Figure 11.10). Both male and female participants thought that "David" was equally angry or afraid of the jack-in-the-box but that "Dana" was more afraid and less angry at the toy.

Many studies have been done manipulating the ascribed (assigned) gender of infants, children, and even adults and the common finding is that the way people see emotions (Condry & Condry, 1976), choose toys (Seavey, Katz, & Zalk, 1975; Sidorowicz & Lunney, 1980), judge physical attributes (Vogel, Lake, Evans, & Karraker, 1991), rate aggression (Condry & Ross, 1985), and a host of other variables depends on the gender of the person participants believe they are watching and not on the target's actual sex.

Biopsychosocial Model

When it comes to understanding gender differences, the biological and the social influence each other (Halpern, 2004). As we saw in Chapter 6, nature and nurture work together to make us who we are. A **biopsychosocial model** suggests that gender differences are caused by a combination of social forces acting on biological processes and, in turn, biological processes

Figure 11.10 Gender is in the eye of the beholder. While watching the same videotape of an infant playing with a jack-in-the-box, participants who believed they were watching a girl viewed her as less angry and more afraid of it. The boy was judged as equally likely to be angry or afraid. *Source:* Condry and Condry (1976).

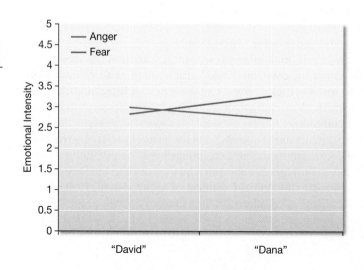

operating on psychological and social process (Halpern, 2004; Sternberg, 1993; Wood & Eagly, 2002).

For example, boys and girls may seek out different experiences based on their interests and abilities, thus further developing these abilities (Halpern, 2004). What appears to be a biologically determined sex difference in ability might really be a gender difference in interests, an active genotype–environment correlation, or a reactive genotype–environment correlation if people provide certain opportunities to children on the basis of their sex alone (you may want to review these concepts from Chapter 6). If kids naturally gravitate toward, or avoid pursuing, certain activities, that would be one thing. However, if some children are discouraged from pursuing activities they like or forced to engage in activities they don't like, then this would be an example of social forces changing a genetic predisposition. This example suggests how hard it is to separate out the effects of nature (genetics) from nurture (social forces) in trying to explain gender differences.

For example, take the gender differences in mental rotation. Though this difference occurs in very young infants (Moore & Johnson, 2008), we saw how the difference between college students can be eliminated by framing the task as gender appropriate (Sharps et al., 1993) or by providing women with special training (Feng et al., 2007). Even if this difference turns out to be innate and biological, the gender difference as it exists is not large enough to account for the finding that women earn only 10% of bachelor degrees in engineering in the United States (Hyde, 2004).

Why is this so? Women might not see themselves as fitting the stereotype of a scientist (Thomas, Henley, & Snell, 2006) or computer programmer (Cheryan, Plaut, Davies, & Steele, 2010) or they may find the demands of a science career unappealing (Cheryan et al., 2010). Overwhelmingly, both male and female college students picture "a scientist" as male (Thomas et al., 2006; see Figure 11.11). Among undergraduates, women found majoring in computer science or even learning a computer language far less interesting than men when sitting in a computer science classroom decorated with Star Trek posters, video game boxes, computer parts, technical books, and junk food. However, when the same classroom contained nature posters, water bottles, general interest books, and healthy snacks—objects not considered stereotypical of computer science majors—women's interest in computer science increased and was equivalent to the men's interest in this as a possible career (Cheryan et al., 2010; see Figure 11.12).

What was it about the environment that turned the women off to the field of computer science? Later studies confirmed that regardless of decisions the participants were asked to make (choose a major, join a work team, work for a generic company, or work for a web design company), or the gender representation of a work group (majority male, entirely female, or gender balanced), women avoided the stereotypical environment, which was viewed by both men and women as masculine. The masculine work environment discouraged women, even when gender proportion, salaries, work hours, and job descriptions were identical across the masculine and neutral environments (Cheryan et al., 2010).

These findings were echoed in a recent report by the American Association of University Women which found that the reason why there are so few women in science, technology, engineering, and mathematics has little to do with biology or innate sex differences in mathematics but everything to do with the social environment (Hill, Corbett, & St. Rose, 2010). Equality requires that we provide equal opportunities to all people; it makes no promises about equal outcomes from those opportunities.

Perhaps the most curious examples of how a biopsychosocial model can apply to gender differences are recent cross-cultural studies of personality (Costa, Terracciano, & McCrae, 2001; Guimond, 2008; Schmitt, Realo, Voracek, & Allik, 2008). Which kind of culture do you think has greater gender differences in personality: countries with a poorer standard of living and far less gender equity or more affluent cultures with equality, prosperity, and health? If you're thinking that social and economic equality would make the genders more similar— think again. Men and women in more affluent countries have more resources to pursue their own interests and talents and, strangely enough, this actually *increases* the personality differences between the genders (Schmitt et al., 2008).

SEE FOR YOURSELF

What image comes to mind when you picture a scientist?

THINK ABOUT IT

Which kind of culture do you think has greater gender differences in personality: countries with less gender equity or countries with more gender equity?

BEFORE

AFTER

Figure 11.11 After a field trip to the Fermilab proton collider in Batavia, Illinois, where students met with three physicists (a White male, a White female, and an African American male) who explained the tools, methods, and applications of Fermilab science, including cancer therapy, seventh graders changed their views of what a scientist was like. The image on the left is what Amy thought "a scientist" looked like before the tour. On the right is her view afterwards. *Source:* From http://ed.fnal.gov/projects/scientists/amy.html.

I think of a scientist as very dedicated to his work. He is kind of crazy, always talking quickly. He is constantly getting new ideas. He is always asking questions and can be annoying. He listens to other's ideas and questions them.

I know scientists are just normal people with a not so normal job.... Scientists lead a normal life outside of being a scientists. They are interested in dancing, pottery, jogging, and even racquetball. Being a scientist is just another job that can be much more exciting.

Amy

Figure 11.12 Reported interest in computer science by women ($N = 22$) and men ($N = 17$) when sitting in a room with objects stereotypically associated with computer science or not stereotypically associated with computer science. *Source:* Cheryan (2010, Figure 1, p. 1049). Cheryan, S., Plaut, V. C., Davies, P. G., & Steele, C. M. (2010). Ambient belonging: How stereotypical cues impact gender participation in computer science. *Journal of Personality and Social Psychology*, 97(6), 1045–1060. Copyright American Psychological Association. Reprinted with permission.

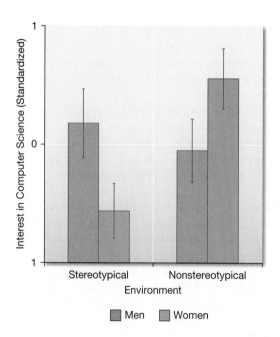

Cultures with a higher standard of living and greater gender equity show the largest differences in personality (McCrae et al., 2005a). In both self-reports and observer-reports, Asian and African cultures show the smallest gender differences in personality whereas European and American cultures show the largest (Costa et al., 2001; McCrae, 2002; Schmitt et al., 2008). For example, Figure 11.13 shows sex differences in the five factors across 50 cultures grouped by region (Schmitt et al., 2008). This graph shows that gender differences in personality decrease as one moves from Western to non-Western cultures.

When Schmitt et al. (2008) tried to figure out what accounted for this effect, they discovered that gender differences correlated with men's personality but not women's. This suggests

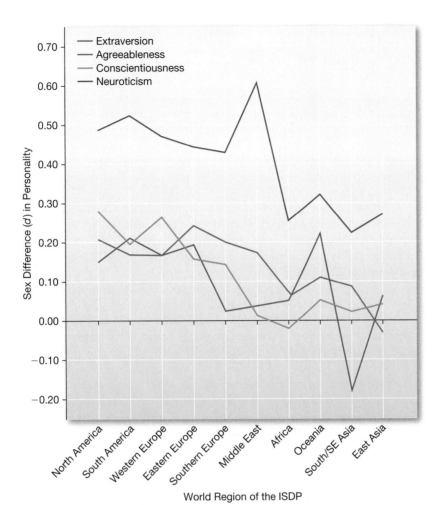

Figure 11.13 Magnitude of sex differences (*d*) in Extraversion, Agreeableness, Conscientiousness, and Neuroticism, across the 10 major world regions of the International Sexuality Description Project (ISDP). Gender differences in personality decrease as one moves from Western to non-Western cultures (from left to right). *Source:* Schmitt (2008, Figure 1, p. 175). Schmitt, D. P., Realo, A., Voracek, M., & Allik, J. (2008). Why can't a man be more like a woman? Sex differences in big five personality traits across 55 cultures. *Journal of Personality and Social Psychology, 94*(1), 168–182. Copyright American Psychological Association. Reprinted with permission.

that as countries become more affluent, men's personalities are changing more than women's. Specifically, men are becoming less similar to women, showing less Neuroticism, more Introversion, less Agreeableness, and less Conscientiousness. Affluence allows men and women to pursue their individual interests, which brings out and develops their innate temperament and—in the case of men—seems to make them more agentic and less communal in the process.

Schmitt et al. (2008) surmised that genetics and environment work on personality differences in a way similar to height, our example from Chapter 6. Once the environment is enriched for everybody, then differences between people are caused by the only variable that can still vary: genetics. Gender differences in personality start to appear once the environment is good enough so that people can choose their activities, careers, and mates and develop aspects of their personality in the process.

This finding that gender differences are greater in more affluent cultures suggests that the differences between men and women are exaggerated in Western or affluent cultures, the very same cultures in which psychologists have been looking for gender differences. Have we artificially exaggerated the differences between the genders by looking for gender differences within Western cultures (Guimond, 2008)? With affluence, men become less neurotic, more introverted, less agreeable, and less conscientious, all characteristics of the universal masculine stereotype (Williams & Best, 1990).

There's a saying, The answer you get depends on the question you ask. This is particularly true of the research on gender differences (Sternberg, 1993). Psychologists once framed questions about gender as questions about whether gender differences were due to biology or

The Personality of Everyday Life

Gendered beliefs about personality: What difference does it make?

Certainly there are differences between men and women, but these differences have become magnified and obscure the many similarities and commonalities that we share. Why is this important? There are many reasons. First, by seeing men and women as "opposites" or as enemies in a "battle of the sexes" we do ourselves and each other a disservice. This view makes it hard to see people as individuals instead of as representatives of their gender. It also sets us up for competition with each other instead of cooperation.

Second, stereotypes establish standards and norms for behavior and attitudes. Society does not take kindly to people who do not fit in, especially when it comes to norm violations for sex and gender. For example, women who do not fit the norm of being nurturant may face problems with evaluation in the workplace (Eagly, Makhijani, & Klonsky, 1992; Rudman & Glick, 1999).

Third, gender stereotypes may become **self-fulfilling prophecies**. When people hold beliefs about what another person is like based on their sex, whether true or false, it influences how they act toward that person. This causes the man or woman to act consistent with those gendered beliefs, making the original gendered expectations come true (Jussim, 1986; Rosenthal & Jacobson, 1968).

For example, parents, teachers, and even kids themselves hold expectations that boys are likely to do better academically than girls (Bhanot & Jovanovic, 2005; Jussim & Eccles, 1992; Yee & Eccles, 1988). Adults may prevent girls from ever having the opportunity to improve their skills, and as a result, the false belief of academic inferiority becomes a reality. Similarly, how will a man ever develop insight into his own emotions or sensitivity to the emotions of others if we don't expect a man to be in touch with his emotions?

Fourth, focusing on gender differences, especially those which are trivial or nonexistent, may take the attention away from more serious gender issues. For example, with an emphasis on the lower self-esteem of girls we may be disregarding boys who, contrary to the stereotype, are also at risk for self-esteem problems (Kling, Hyde, Showers, & Buswell, 1999). Similarly, talented girls may be overlooked if parents and teachers expect girls to be bad at mathematics (Hyde, 2005; Lummis & Stevenson, 1990).

Finally, *stereotype threat,* as you'll remember from Chapter 5, is when a person experiences distress when faced with a stereotype that threatens him or her, causing the person's performance to suffer thereby confirming the very stereotype he or she felt threatened by (Aronson et al., 1998; Aronson & Rogers, 2008; Spencer, Steele, & Quinn, 1999; Steele et al., 2002). For example, when faced with a challenging math problem, an otherwise capable woman might choke under the combined pressures of wanting to get the right answer and not wanting to be just another woman who is bad at math.

For each person to develop his or her own unique talents and to thrive in life we need to allow people to be their true selves without limitations set by stereotypes, society, expectations, or even our own self-inflicted limitations.

due to the environment. As you've realized by now, there is no simple answer to this question: Both biology and the environment influence each other, and the impact of each varies over time and place (Sternberg, 1993). As we pose the question of gender in more complex ways, our answers—and the psychological research on which they are based—get more advanced. By now, you've become more sophisticated as well during this process and have gained an appreciation of the biological and social mechanisms that affect similarities and differences between the genders.

"Consider a rainbow. Given the full spectrum of color, we perceive red and magenta as being similar. If, however, we eliminate all other hues, red and magenta are now perceived as being different. But the price of emphasizing this difference is the loss of the rest of the spectrum. Similarly, relationships relevant to both sexes have been obscured by the limitation of research to the difference between them." Rhoda K. Unger (1979, p. 1093)

Then and Now: Definition and Assessment of Gender

Are you: male or female? (circle one)

"Experimental results are based on group averages, and no one is average."
Psychologist Diane Halpern (2004)

   If you are male then you are masculine and if you are female then you are feminine, right? Maybe not. Traditionally, psychologists assumed that people developed a set of personality traits depending on their biological sex: males are masculine and females are feminine. Today, we have a richer and broader definition of gender that takes into account biological sex as well as personal feelings and social experiences.

   Let's start with the basics. *Sex* refers to a biological classification depending on a person's combination of chromosomes and hormones. *Gender* refers to a social classification (Unger, 1979). Psychologists generally use the terms *male* and *female* to refer to biological sex and *masculine* and *feminine* to refer to social gender (of course, it's not always easy to decide if a difference is due to biology or social role). In the early days of personality measurement, gender was measured as a *typology,* meaning that people would be one type or the other—masculine or feminine—as if being placed in a box. Further, it was assumed that a person's gender was the same as his or her sex: males are masculine and females are feminine. Any deviation from this norm was considered problematic.

THINK ABOUT IT

Do definitions of masculinity and femininity change over time? Why?

   Psychologists soon recognized the limitations of a gender typology and combined masculinity and femininity into a single **bipolar** (two-ended) dimension of masculinity–femininity: The more masculine a person is, the less feminine that person is. Like the earlier typology model, this **unidimensional model** was also limiting, as people could either be masculine or feminine but could not display aspects of both.

   A personality test that illustrates gender as a single dimension is the Minnesota Multiphasic Personality Inventory (MMPI; Hathaway & McKinley, 1940), of which a 1989 revision, the MMPI-2, is used today (Butcher et al., 1989). Both versions consist of 10 different scales, one of which is the masculinity–femininity scale. On the MMPI, if a man scores too high on the masculinity scale (indicating more femininity) or if a woman scores too low (indicating more masculinity) this is a sign of pathology.

THINK ABOUT IT

Is measuring gender like trying to hit a moving target?

   By the 1970s personality psychologists started to realize that a unidimensional scale did not fully capture the possible range of people's gendered behavior (Constantinople, 1973). Why couldn't a woman be gregarious *and* assertive? Why couldn't a man be self-sufficient *and* nurturing? Psychologists started thinking of masculinity and femininity as two separate unidimensional scales. A person could be high or low on one or both of the scales. That is, a person could be high in both stereotypically masculine traits such as leadership and analytical thinking, and in stereotypically feminine traits such as being affectionate and compassionate. Two scales, the Personal Attributes Questionnaire (PAQ; Spence, Helmreich, & Stapp, 1974, 1975) and the Bem Sex Role Inventory (BSRI; Bem, 1974) measure gender in just this way. Both the PAQ and the BSRI yield very similar results and correlate with each other (Spence, 1991). Further, there is no correlation between the masculinity and femininity scales of each test, suggesting that these are separate dimensions (Spence & Helmreich, 1979).

In the PAQ, respondents use a 5-point scale to rate which of a pair of statements best describes their personalities (see Table 11.10). The masculinity items measure goal-oriented and instrumental attributes. The femininity items measure interpersonally oriented and expressive attributes. Even though the masculine items tend to be stereotypically more characteristic of men and the feminine items stereotypically more characteristic of women, all attributes were rated as being equally desirable in men and women. Undergraduates imagined—back in 1975 at least—that the ideal man or woman would possess these attributes (Spence et al., 1975).

In the BSRI, respondents rate each of 60 adjectives on a 7-point scale from 1 (*never or almost never true*) to 7 (*almost always true*). Responses for the 20 feminine and the 20 masculine

Table 11.10 The Personal Attributes Questionnaire

1. Not at all aggressive	A	B	C	D	E	Very aggressive
2. Not at all independent	A	B	C	D	E	Very independent
3. Not at all emotional	A	B	C	D	E	Very emotional
4. Very submissive	A	B	C	D	E	Very dominant
5. Not at all excitable in a major crisis	A	B	C	D	E	Very excitable in a major crisis
6. Very passive	A	B	C	D	E	Very active
7. Not at all able to devote self completely to others	A	B	C	D	E	Able to devote self completely to others
8. Very rough	A	B	C	D	E	Very gentle
9. Not at all helpful to others	A	B	C	D	E	Very helpful to others
10. Not at all competitive	A	B	C	D	E	Very competitive
11. Very home oriented	A	B	C	D	E	Very worldly
12. Not at all kind	A	B	C	D	E	Very kind
13. Indifferent to others' approval	A	B	C	D	E	Highly needful of others' approval
14. Feelings not easily hurt	A	B	C	D	E	Feelings easily hurt
15. Not at all aware of feelings of others	A	B	C	D	E	Very aware of feelings of others
16. Can make decisions easily	A	B	C	D	E	Has difficulty making decisions
17. Gives up very easily	A	B	C	D	E	Never gives up easily
18. Never cries	A	B	C	D	E	Cries very easily
19. Not at all self-confident	A	B	C	D	E	Very self-confident
20. Feels very inferior	A	B	C	D	E	Feels superior
21. Not at all understanding of others	A	B	C	D	E	Very understanding of others
22. Very cold in relations with others	A	B	C	D	E	Very warm in relations with others
23. Very little time for security	A	B	C	D	E	Very strong need for security
24. Goes to pieces under pressure	A	B	C	D	E	Stands up well under pressure

Note: The items above inquire about what kind of person you think you are. Each item consists of a pair of characteristics, with the letters A–E in between. Each pair describes contradictory characteristics—that is, you cannot be both at the same time, such as very aggressive and not at all aggressive. The letters form a scale between the two extremes. You are to choose a letter that describes where you fall on the scale. For example, if you think you are not at all aggressive, you would choose A. If you think you are aggressive, you might choose D. If you are only somewhat aggressive, you might choose C, and so forth.

To score, assign numbers based on the letter you circled: A = 0, B = 1, C = 2, D = 3, E = 4. Based on the responses you circled, enter the appropriate numbers for the remaining items in the spaces to the left of the items. To compute your score on the femininity scale, add up the numbers next to items 3, 7, 8, 9, 12, 15, 21, and 22. To compute your scores on the masculinity scale, add up the numbers next to items 2, 6, 10, 16*, 17, 19, 20, and 24. Note that item 16 must be reverse scored so that a 4 is scored as a 0; 3 as a 1; 2 as a 2; 1 as a 3; and 0 as a 4.

Source: Spence and Helmreich (1978).

items are averaged. The remaining 20 are applicable to either gender and are not scored. Then using their masculinity and femininity scores, researchers classify respondents into one of four categories (see Table 11.11).

Women who score high in femininity and low in masculinity are classified as **feminine sex-typed**. Men who score high in masculinity and low in femininity are classified as **masculine sex-typed**. Women and men who score high in both masculinity and femininity—possessing attributes of both males and females—are called **androgynous** (from the Greek: *andro* = male and *gyn* = female). People who score low in both masculinity and femininity are **undifferentiated**. However, women who score high in masculinity (and low in femininity) and men who score high in femininity (and low in masculinity) are considered **cross sex-typed** (Bem, 1977).

Since the BSRI was designed and validated on a sample of college students from Stanford University in the 1970s, society has changed a lot. For one, undergraduates have become more androgynous over time (Twenge, 1997). That is, it has become more acceptable for men to be expressive and for women to be instrumental. A replication of Bem's original study with students at Franklin and Marshall college in 1999 discovered that both men and women found it more acceptable for a woman to demonstrate certain masculine traits like assertiveness and athleticism and to avoid feminine traits like being soft-spoken and not using harsh language (Auster & Ohm, 2000). Second, Sandra Bem, the originator of the scale, recognized that the test and the theory that it was built on suggested that androgyny was somehow better than being sex-typed or undifferentiated and that being cross sex-typed was particularly problematic, which was never her intention (Bem, 1981, 1993). Her utopian goal had been to create a climate in which gender matters only where it is biologically relevant (Bem, 1993). Recognizing that this may be impossible, she now advocates omitting gender categorization altogether and letting people be fluid in their biological sex, social gender, and sexual desires (Bem, 1995).

On both the BSRI and the PAQ women have become more masculine over time, showing an increase in the extent to which they say that stereotypical masculine traits apply to them and eliminating the difference between men and women on these scales. However, even though cultural changes from the 1970s to the 1990s have encouraged the development of instrumental traits in women, there has not been a similar increase in the acceptability of expressive and communal traits in men (Twenge, 1997). Perhaps the expectations for gender behavior, at least for women, are less strict today than they were when the BSRI and the PAQ were developed.

The idea of being sex-typed or androgynous comes from gender schema theory (Bem, 1981, 1984, 1993). Bem found that for those people who scored as sex-typed on the BSRI, gender was a highly salient and important organizing principle or schema for them, which they used to make judgments about themselves and the world. For example, sex-typed participants were more likely to organize words by gender when recalling them on a memory test (Bem, 1981). They were also faster at judging sex-congruent traits (e.g., female–sensitive; male–competitive) as descriptive of

Table 11.11 Gender as Two Dimensions: The Personal Attitudes Questionnaire and the Bem Sex Role Inventory

	Low Masculine	High Masculine
Low Feminine	Undifferentiated	Masculine sex-typed (if male)
		Cross sex-typed (if female)
High Feminine	Feminine sex-typed (if female)	Androgynous
	Cross sex-typed (if male)	

Note: Participants are classified as scoring high or low depending on whether they are above or below the median of their peers. People who are undifferentiated have a lower self-esteem than people in the other categories, which echoes our earlier discussion of self-esteem and self-concept clarity from Chapter 5.

Sources: Bem (1977); Spence et al. (1975).

themselves than sex-incongruent traits (e.g., female–forceful, male–loves children) (Bem, 1981). The BSRI may be a better measure of cognitive orientation or the strength of one's schema for gender than a measure of gender itself (but see Spence, 1993).

Today, there is a trend among researchers to define gender using not just one or two dimensions, but multiple dimensions (e.g., Twenge, 1999). For example, Janet Spence and her colleagues have suggested that masculinity and femininity (or instrumental and expressive traits) as measured by the PAQ or the BSRI is but one such dimension of gender identity. She suggested that our **gender identity**, a psychological sense of our own maleness and femaleness, like our self-concept, is established early in life (Spence, 1993; Spence & Sawin, 1985). Recall from our discussion in Chapter 5 that gender identity is one of many possible social identities (Wood & Eagly, 2009). Adult men and women reported that their gender identity included physical attributes, such as appearance, movements, and speech; social roles; interests and hobbies; social behavior; biological sex; and sexuality, in addition to instrumental and expressive personality traits (Spence & Sawin, 1985). People display only modest consistency in their gender-typical behavior across many aspects of their lives, from toy preference to careers, to preferred relationship partners to activity preferences (Egan & Perry, 2001). A multidimensional view of gender identity accounts for people's experiences of themselves as male or female better than either one- or two-dimensional models.

In two studies, the gender identity of middle school students was related to their psychological and social adjustment over the course of the school year (Carver, Yunger, & Perry, 2003; Egan & Perry, 2001). Researchers hypothesized that gender identity was made up of four dimensions:

1. **Membership Knowledge.** Knowledge of membership in a gender category: male, female.
2. **Gender Compatibility.** Felt compatibility with one's own gender compared to the other gender. Self-perceptions of how typical a person feels for his or her gender. Contentment with one's gender assignment, emerging sexuality, and sexual orientation.
3. **Gender Conformity Pressure.** The extent to which participants feel compelled to engage in gender-appropriate activities and to avoid gender-inappropriate activities and fearing punishment or ridicule from teachers, parents, peers, or themselves, instead of feeling free to explore a wide range of activities regardless of gender appropriateness.
4. **Intergroup Bias.** Attributing positive qualities to one's own sex and negative qualities to the other sex, such as showing favoritism for own sex and a bias against the other sex, or exaggerating the positive aspects of own sex and the negative aspects of the other sex.

Both studies found that these four dimensions were not strongly related to each other, supporting a multidimensional view of gender identity, and that all were related to psychological and social adjustment. Children showed better adjustment as measured by self-esteem, social competence, and acceptance from peers if they felt secure in themselves as typical for their gender and yet free to explore cross-sex behaviors when they wanted to. Poor adjustment was related to feeling greater pressure to conform to gender expectations and showing greater intergroup bias. Interestingly, boys had higher scores than girls on gender typicality, gender contentedness, and felt pressure, which goes along with other findings that suggest that boys are more sex-typed than girls and experience more pressures to act in accord with expectations for their gender. In addition, felt pressure to behave in accord with one's gender led to reduced agentic behaviors (e.g., assertion, daring, competitiveness) in girls and less communal behaviors (e.g., cooperation, maintaining of harmony, showing of fear or weakness) in boys (Carver et al., 2003).

As a final note, the results of both studies suggest that masculinity and femininity are indeed two ends of a single bipolar dimension: The more masculine one feels the less feminine one feels or the more expressive one is the less instrumental one is. So, when it comes to the measurement of gender, researchers have come back to thinking of masculinity and femininity as aspects of a single scale and not as two separate scales. But as these two studies show, there is more to our gender identity than the single dimension of masculinity–femininity.

Chapter Summary

Are there personality differences between men and women? People in Canada, the United States, and around the world hold amazingly consistent notions about what men and women are like. People believe that men and women differ in personality, social roles, physical attributes, emotional experience, emotional expression, cognitive skills, careers, hobbies, interests, and activities. Women are seen as communal, focusing on nurturing and feeling connected to others. Men are seen as more agentic, focused on individual actions and accomplishments.

Meta-analysis, a way of statistically combining results across methods and measures to estimate an average effect size (d), can help us evaluate if there are gender differences in these characteristics and estimate how large and how consistent gender differences are. Based on meta-analysis, there are many similarities and a few differences between males and females. Most of the differences tend to be physical or sexual; most of the similarities are in personality.

Men and women are the same when it comes to impulsiveness, Extraversion, gregariousness, activity, Openness, ideas, Conscientiousness, order, intelligence, mathematical ability, verbal ability, leadership effectiveness, self-confidence, and many more traits. Men and women are different when it comes to tender-mindedness, assertiveness, sexuality, nonverbal behavior, aggressiveness, risk taking, occupational preferences, and in the incidence of certain mental disorders. Other differences in personality and social behavior depend on the context in which they occur, how they are measured, and how they are defined. For example, men and women may not differ in empathy, emotions, helping behavior, leadership style, anxiety, and self-esteem. Differences in spatial ability can be eliminated by practice and how the task is presented to participants.

What causes gender differences? Psychologists have suggested that sex and gender differences may be due to biology, genetics, hormones, evolution, socialization, the social situation in which the behaviors occur, social construction, social roles, and biopsychosocial theory.

What difference do gendered beliefs make? When we judge people based on how we think they ought to behave for someone of their gender we fail to see them as individuals. Our stereotypical beliefs may become norms for behavior and we may negatively evaluate or even shun people who don't follow norms for sex or gender. Beliefs about gender can lead to a self-fulfilling prophesy in the behavior of others, take attention away from more serious gender differences, cause people to perform badly because of stereotype threat, and to wrongly think of men and women as opposites.

Finally, definitions of gender have become more sophisticated, moving from single-dimensional measures, to two-dimensional measures, to multidimensional measures. Gender identity is much richer than a single dimension of masculinity–femininity and includes biological sex, gender compatibility, gender conformity pressures, and intergroup bias.

Recall our thought experiment that opened the chapter. Would you answer differently now? Would you be the same person inside? Would you have the same personality? I suspect that most of us would have the same personality, but perhaps we would express it differently. Just as the facets of a diamond can look different depending on the light and the setting, perhaps men and women are not quite alien species to each other after all. Let's focus on our commonalities while celebrating—and not exclusively focusing on—our differences. Whatever male and female differences there are, we are not the *opposite* of each other (Lippa, 2005a). Ideally, gender and gender roles should fit comfortably like a favorite pair of jeans rather than uncomfortable hand-me-downs that pinch and restrict in places.

"I'm just a person trapped inside a woman's body."
Comedian Elayne Boosler

✔•─**Study** and **Review**
on **mysearchlab.com**
Go online for more resources to help you review.

Review Questions

1. Is spatial rotation skill learned or innate? What does this suggest about the cause of the gender difference between men and women in this skill?

2. What do people believe men and women are like? Are these stereotypes different depending on culture?

3. What is effect size? How is it measured? How can we interpret effect sizes? What questions about gender differences can a meta-analysis help answer?

4. What kinds of variables show the largest gender differences? What kinds of variables show the smallest gender differences? When it comes to the factors and facets of the five-factor model, are men and women more similar than different or more different than similar?

5. Are there gender differences in aggression and risk taking? Are there gender differences in empathy, basic emotions, helping behavior, leadership effectiveness, anxiety, influence-ability, self-esteem, or self-confidence? Explain your reasoning.

6. What are some possible explanations for gender differences put forth by psychologists? Explain how each of these explanations can account for gender differences.

7. What impact on ourselves and people around us does holding gendered beliefs about personality have?

8. How have definitions and assessments of gender changed over time?

Key Terms

Communion	Evolutionary psychology	Unidimensional model
Agency	Social role theory	Feminine sex-typed
Stereotypes	Deindividuation	Masculine sex-typed
Effect size	Social constructionism	Androgynous
Meta-analysis	Biopsychosocial model	Undifferentiated
Gender socialization	Self-fulfilling prophecies	Cross sex-typed
Feminist theory	Bipolar scale	Gender identity

12 SEXUAL ORIENTATION: AN INTEGRATIVE MINI-CHAPTER

Read the Chapter on
mysearchlab.com

"The important thing is not the object of love, but the emotion itself."

Gore Vidal

I n December 2010 Barbara Walters interviewed the legendary Oprah Winfrey about what she would do after ending her long-running daytime talk show. As part of the interview, Walters asked Oprah if she was gay. Rumors seemed to abound speculating about her relationship with her best friend Gayle King and questioning why she never married her love of many years, Stedman Graham.

The fact that this bold question made national news is pretty astounding. After all, what business is it of ours what celebrities do in their private lives? Indeed, many people also wonder about the sexual orientation of comedienne Wanda Sykes, *Sex and the City* actress Cynthia Nixon, Drew Barrymore, Angelina Jolie, Lady Gaga, Ellen DeGeneres, Anne Heche, and Portia De Rossi, in addition to that of Oprah. Why are people not similarly confused about the sexual orientation of male celebrities? Is sexual orientation different in men? Perhaps sexual orientation is just that important, either because it tells us something fundamental about a person's personality or else because American society *thinks* a person's sexual orientation is important. Either way, sexual orientation is an interesting question from a psychological standpoint and a politically charged topic from a societal standpoint.

"Labels? Okay, fine. I'm bisensual. Heteroflexible. And life-curious. That about covers it."

Morgan Torva

What makes a person straight, bisexual, gay, or lesbian? Is it something you choose or something you just *know?* Sexual orientation is an affinity, attraction, leaning, or longing toward one sex or the other or both. We can think of sexual orientation as partner orientation (Diamond, 2003b). Psychologists once thought that sexual orientation was pretty much set around puberty and stayed constant throughout one's life. However, now we are realizing that people can vary in just how set or **fluid** their sexual orientation is (Diamond, 2008b).

For example, the traditional labels of gay/lesbian, heterosexual, or bisexual may not accurately describe the sexual orientation of many people. As you will soon see, defining sexual orientation is not so easy. There is often a mismatch among a person's attractions, behaviors, and identity, suggesting that labels may be an oversimplification of how we experience our sexuality.

For women, in particular, the traditional labels of lesbian, heterosexual, or bisexual seem to be especially misleading. One study tracked the gender identity of 18- to 25-year-old lesbian and bisexual women over the course of 10 years. Every 2 to 3 years they were interviewed in person and asked, "How do you currently label your sexual identity to yourself, even if its different from what you might tell other people? If you don't apply a label to your sexual identity, please say so" (Diamond, 2008a, p. 8). About two thirds of the women in this study changed their identities at least once and 36% changed their identities more than once over the course of the study. Surprisingly, "unlabeled" was the most common identity adopted. These women may think of themselves as unlabeled as a way of indicating a questioning of their current sexual orientation, an openness to future changes in sexual orientation, or a not-quite-exclusive same-sex attraction that defies traditional lesbian or bisexual categories (Diamond, 2008a).

SEE FOR YOURSELF

How do you currently label your sexual identity to yourself, even if its different from what you might tell other people?

For a while, people thought that many women experienced a temporary state of same-sex attractions, but this is not so (Diamond, 2003a). In a study of nonheterosexual women who were interviewed over a period of 8 years, from late adolescence into their young adulthood, Lisa Diamond identified three distinct groups of women. Some women were consistent in how they labeled themselves, either as lesbian (stable lesbians) or not (stable nonlesbians). Note that these stable nonlesbians were behaving as bisexuals, experiencing attraction to women and men, but were not labeling themselves as such. However, a third group, which Diamond called fluid lesbians, alternated between the two identities, sometimes identifying themselves as lesbians and sometimes not using a label at all, despite having attractions to women and men. Table 12.1 shows the percentage of participants who changed their identity over time.

THINK ABOUT IT

Is sexual orientation best thought of as one dimension (sameness or otherness of partner) or two dimensions (sameness or otherness of partner and flexibility)?

To illustrate, one participant reported that at the start of the study she was lesbian and 100% attracted to women. However, after 2 years she reported being lesbian and only 90% attracted to women. By the fifth year, she was reluctant to label herself as anything and reported that her attraction to other women was about 70%. By the eighth year of the study, she was only 50% attracted to women and refused to label herself.

Table 12.1 Sexual Identity Transitions of Young Women

Category	Defections	Adoptions
Lesbian	25%	19%
Bisexual	33	23
Unlabeled	33	37
Heterosexual	10	21

Sources: From Savin-Williams (2007, Table 2.2, p. 41); data from Diamond (2003a). Savin-Williams, R. C. (2007). The new gay teenager. Cambridge, MA: Harvard University Press.

Stable nonlesbians and fluid lesbians—people who are behaving in a bisexual manner or having bisexual attractions but not labeling themselves as bisexual—were more likely to agree with the statement: "I'm the kind of person that is attracted to the person rather than their gender" (Diamond, 2003a, p. 126). In light of how women's attractions shifted over time and how the women themselves avoid labels, Diamond (2005) suggested that the sexual categories of lesbian and bisexual do not account for nonheterosexual women's experiences and should be abandoned. Instead, Diamond (2003a) recommended that we think of sexual orientation and flexibility, what she called fluidity, as two separate dimensions of individual difference.

This fluidity of sexual orientation explains the seemingly contradictory behavior of celebrities like Wanda Sykes, Cynthia Nixon, Drew Barrymore, Angelina Jolie, Lady Gaga, and others whose sexual orientation defies labels. Compare the stability of Ellen DeGeneres's lesbianism with that of her two recent partners, Anne Heche and Portia De Rossi, who were exclusively heterosexual at one point in their lives. Women with a fluid sexual orientation are capable of experiencing a wider range of erotic experiences and feelings than the label lesbian, bisexual, or heterosexual implies (Diamond, 2008b).

In this chapter, we discuss what sexual orientation is, difficulties with identifying how many people are gay, lesbian, straight or bisexual, and what determines sexual orientation. Though psychologists from all different areas—biology, genetics, neuroscience, social, developmental—have weighed in on this question, we are a long way from understanding one of the most intimate and interesting areas of our lives: our sexuality.

Myths and Misperceptions About Sexual Orientation

Before we get started, perhaps it's best if we establish what we know and—merely think we know—about sexual orientation. Consider the statements in Table 12.2. In fact, read them now before you go any further.

Though all of them may seem reasonable—no doubt you know people who believe some of these things—all of them are, in fact, false.

We saw in Chapter 11 that sex is biologically determined, that gender is socially defined, and that people have a psychological sense of their own maleness or femaleness called gender identity. We can add to this an additional dimension: sexual orientation. So, although a gay man may fall in love with other men, this in no way compromises his masculinity or sense of himself as a man or means that he would rather be a woman. By the same token, if a particular lesbian woman does not care about shopping, makeup, or wearing the latest clothes, this does not make her masculine or imply that she would rather be a man. Gay men and lesbian women vary in their masculinity and femininity—and indeed, in all characteristics—in the same way that heterosexual men and women do. Because who we feel sexual desire and emotional attachment for is a fundamental part of who we are, it cannot be changed, it cannot be faked, it cannot be taught, and we cannot convert others to our lifestyle.

"The trouble with people is not that they don't know but that they know so much that ain't so."
American humorist Josh Billings (1818–1885)

"There's this illusion that homosexuals have sex and heterosexuals fall in love. That's completely untrue. Everybody wants to be loved."
Boy George

Table 12.2 Myths and Misperceptions About Gays, Lesbians, and Bisexuals

1. Gay men really want to be women.
2. Sexual orientation can be corrected with the proper intervention.
3. Gay and lesbian teenagers are militant activists.
4. Gays and lesbians are at higher risk for suicide, alcoholism, and other problems than the general population.
5. Same-sex sexuality is a mental illness.
6. Gay men are likely to be child molesters.
7. Being gay or lesbian is just a phase.
8. Bisexuality is just a phase.
9. All gay men will die of HIV/AIDS.
10. Gay men are only interested in sex and do not care about long-term relationships.
11. Gay men are feminine.
12. Lesbians are masculine.
13. Bisexual people are confused.
14. Bisexuals are more promiscuous than straight people and cannot remain faithful or monogamous.
15. Very few people have feelings for a person of the same sex.
16. Homosexuality doesn't exist in nature.
17. Gay men and lesbians should not be allowed to teach in elementary or high schools because they will try to convert their students to a gay lifestyle.
18. Gay men are more similar to women than to other men.
19. Lesbians are more similar to men than to other women.
20. You can tell who is gay or lesbian by the way they dress and look.
21. People become gay, lesbian, or bisexual because of childhood sexual abuse.
22. Gay parents raise only gay children.
23. Gay and lesbian people are inherently areligious and immoral.
24. Bisexuality is just a transitional phase on the way to being gay or lesbian.
25. Gay men frequently rape straight men, or want to.
26. Lesbians really want to be men.
27. Gays, lesbians, and bisexuals should not be considered a protected minority because they could just act straight in public.

Note: Every one of these statements is false.

The Personality of Everyday Life

The heteronormativity of American life

It is not easy to be a nonheterosexual person in the world today. Most, if not all, cultures view heterosexuality as the natural, correct, and normal way to be (Berlant & Warner, 1998; Herek, 2010). This view is called normative heterosexuality or **heteronormativity**. Heterosexuality is taken for granted and provides people with distinct legal, political, and social advantages in American society (Herek, 2010).

For example, unmarried partners are not allowed in emergency rooms during a life-and-death emergency because they have no legal rights to be present at the bedside of a loved one, nor can they make important health decisions if their partner is incapacitated. Marriage gives husbands and wives a number of legal rights in many states, such as inheritance, social security, health insurance, next-of-kin rights, and access to private health status information of a partner. Some religions and moral convictions condemn same-sex sexuality, but is it fair to deny civil rights to people based on their sexual orientation?

Of course, partner rights and same-sex marriage laws are working to change all this, and there is evidence that the attitudes of Americans are becoming less antihomosexual, more tolerant, and increasingly accepting of same-sex relations. According to a poll by the National Opinion Research Center (NORC) at the University of Chicago, the percentage of Americans who believe that *sexual relations between adults of the same sex is always wrong* dropped from 74% in 1973 to 55% in 2002. Still, nonheterosexuals face social rejection, prejudice, and discrimination (Davis, Smith, & Marsden, 2010).

As a result, adolescents and adults who are not heterosexual face greater challenges and difficulties including higher levels of depression, anxiety, substance use, and suicidality than their heterosexual peers (Meyer, 2003). However, there is evidence that this is changing and that young people today are less concerned with labeling their sexuality and instead are living not as a "gay person" but as a person who happens to be gay or lesbian, facing the same challenges about dating, friends, classes, and parents as their peers (Savin-Williams, 2007).

What Is Sexual Orientation?

Until the sex researcher Alfred Kinsey came along in the 1940s, people thought that a person's sexual orientation could be classified into one of two or maybe three (at most!) boxes: heterosexual, homosexual, and bisexual. From interviewing 5,300 males (Kinsey, Pomeroy, & Martin, 1948) and 5,940 females (Kinsey, Pomeroy, Martin, & Gebhard, 1953) about their sexual history, Kinsey and his researchers realized that sexual behavior occurred more on a continuum, from exclusively heterosexual at one end to exclusively homosexual at the other (Kinsey et al., 1948, 1953; see Figure 12.1).

Before Kinsey conducted this research, people believed that a person's sexual orientation followed from his or her personality: People assumed that a feminine man was gay and that a masculine woman was lesbian. Though there is a slight correlation between sexual orientation and masculinity–femininity and gender-related interests (Lippa, 2005b), personality, or gender identity more specifically, is a separate dimension from sexual attraction and desire. That is, being a feminine man or a masculine woman doesn't make a person gay or lesbian; these are unfortunate stereotypes that persist today.

Although Kinsey conducted his sexual history interviews with great care and precision, using an elaborate coding system to protect the identities of his participants, he was guilty of biased sampling. He often recruited people with unusual sexual practices to become part of his study. Given the times—he collected data between 1938 and 1949—the kind

"You know what, I am gay, but my sexuality has never been my defining quality. . . . It's just a fact. My life is defined by my friends and by my interests, and I happen to be passionate about good design."

Thom Filicia, designer on the Bravo TV show Queer Eye for the Straight Guy *as quoted in Finn (2004, p. B2)*

THINK ABOUT IT

What's the difference between classifying sexual orientation as a box or as a continuum?

Same-sex marriage gives gay and lesbian couples the same legal rights as heterosexual couples including making health decisions, inheritance, social security, health insurance, and next-of-kin rights.

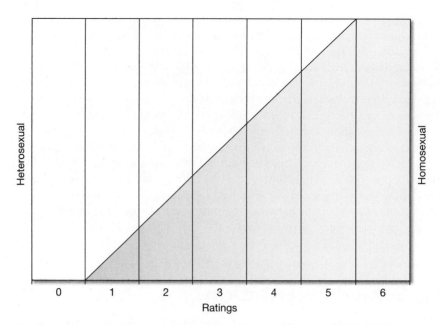

Figure 12.1 The Kinsey Heterosexual-Homosexual Scale. Alfred Kinsey and his researchers used this scale to rate participants on what proportion of his or her psychological reactions and/or overt behavior was heterosexual and homosexual:
1 = Largely heterosexual, but with incidental homosexual history
2 = Largely heterosexual, but with a distinct homosexual history
3 = Equally heterosexual and homosexual
4 = Largely homosexual but with a distinct heterosexual history
5 = Largely homosexual but with incidental heterosexual history
6 = Entirely homosexual
Source: Kinsey et al. (1948, Figure 161, p. 638). Reprinted with permission from Kinsey, A. C., Pomeroy, W. B., & Martin, C. E. (1948), *Sexual behavior in the human male,* Bloomington, IN: Indiana University Press. Permission conveyed through the Copyright Clearance Center.

of people who were willing to talk about their sexual histories were probably more open about sexuality than the average person. As a result, many researchers believe that Kinsey's estimates of how often same-sex sexuality occurs in the general population is probably an overestimate (Pomeroy, 1972).

Kinsey was correct in realizing that sexual orientation occurs on a continuum; however, it is much more fluid and far less fixed than his system suggested. As we saw in the opening study of this chapter, the sex drive of women is more flexible than men's (Baumeister, 2000), and women may shift their sexual orientation over the course of their lives (Diamond, 2007, 2008a).

Another criticism of the Kinsey scale is that sexual orientation includes more than behavior. After all, a person has a sexual orientation even if he or she has yet to have a sexual experience. Sexual orientation has many aspects, encompassing thoughts, feelings, behaviors, and identity. For example, Klein, Sepekoff, and Wolf (1985) measured sexual orientation through sexual attraction, sexual behaviors, sexual fantasies, emotional preferences, social preferences, self-identifications, and lifestyles across a person's past, present, and ideal life. Researchers today define **sexual orientation** as the prevalence of erotic arousals, feelings, fantasies, and behaviors one has for males, females, or both (Savin-Williams, 2006). Sexual orientation may be expressed in sexual attraction, sexual behavior, or sexual identity.

Sexual attraction includes thoughts, feelings, wants, or desires for sexual relations or to be in a loving sexual relationship with another person; it does not include behavior. Many people have feelings, thoughts, or fantasies of being intimate with another person without acting on those feelings. All of these are aspects of sexual attraction (Savin-Williams, 2006).

Sexual behavior refers to a person's actions, that is, those sexual activities they have actually engaged in. This may include any genital contact and sexual excitement, with or

THINK ABOUT IT

Can one have a sexual orientation without having a sexual experience?

without intercourse or orgasm, occurring with mutual consent of both partners (Savin-Williams, 2006).

Finally, **sexual identity** includes labels people associate with their sexuality, whether personally selected or socially ascribed. Recall from Chapter 5 that identity includes interpersonal aspects (e.g., roles, relationship), potentialities (e.g., who we might become), and values (e.g., morals, priorities) (Baumeister, 1986). All of these aspects of identity are inherent in the labels of *gay, lesbian, bi,* and *straight.* Identifying oneself with one of these labels is as much a political statement as a psychological one (Savin-Williams, 2007).

To illustrate these different facets of sexual orientation, imagine a young woman coming out to her parents. How might their reaction differ depending on what she says?

For many young people self-identifying as gay, lesbian, or bi means taking on a social identity as well as a sexual one.

> *Mom, Dad . . .*
> *I'm attracted to girls.*
> *I'm dating girls.*
> *I'm having sex with girls.*
> *I'm a lesbian.*

Each of these statements reveals a different aspect of her sexual orientation (Savin-Williams, 2007, p. 64).

Thinking of sexual orientation as encompassing these three aspects can help us understand sexual orientation in other cultures. In many cultures, people can engage in sexual behaviors and express a range of sexual desires without being labeled gay, lesbian, or bisexual (Peplau, 2001). In Sumatra, they call a woman who acts like a man a *tomboi,* from the English "tomboy." A tomboi sees herself as a man, acts like a man, and is attracted to a traditionally feminine woman. However, there is no special label for the lover of a tomboi; she is considered the same as other women in the culture (Blackwood, 2000). Similarly, among the Mojave Indians, as long as a woman adequately performed the traditional male social role, she could choose to live as a man and even marry a woman. Her wife, often a traditionally feminine woman in the tribe, is not considered homosexual or cross-gendered (Blackwood, 1984, discussed in Peplau, 2001).

Consider another example: 168 of the 250 Native American languages still spoken in the United States contain terms for people who are not considered male or female. Instead, these people contain two spirits: a male and a female one. They might dress and act as either male or female, and have relationships, including sexual ones, with a man or a woman, and they can even marry a person of either gender. These people take on a spiritual-sexual identity in the community and are considered blessed (Tafoya, 1997, discussed in Garnets, 2002).

Cultures can also vary in their acceptance of same-sex behavior. For example, African American communities in the United States are less tolerant of same-sex behavior, especially among men (Greene, 2000; Icard, 1996). Similarly, Latin American cultures are less tolerant of same-sex behavior than Anglo culture, particularly among women (Gonzales & Espin, 1996).

In still other cultures, there are different standards for what constitutes homosexuality. In Mexico, two men who are engaged in sexual relationship take on one of two exclusive roles in the relationship: either the receptive partner or the inserting partner. The receptive partner is considered feminine, unmanly and gay; the inserting partner is considered masculine and is not labeled as gay (Magaña & Carrier, 1991). A similar distinction occurs in many Arab cultures,

SEE FOR YOURSELF

When did you become aware of your sexual orientation? Was it a conscious choice, or something you just knew?

THINK ABOUT IT

Why should a culture's tolerance of same-sex behavior be different for a man than for a woman?

like Egypt, for example (Miller, 1992). Often the inserting partner in Mexican or Arab cultures later marries and raises a family and is considered heterosexual; he would never be called or even label himself bisexual despite his earlier behavior.

"I'm not bisexual or homosexual, I'm just sexual."

Female participant in the study by Diamond (2005, p. 126)

How Many People Are Gay, Lesbian, Straight, or Bisexual?

Given our discussion of what constitutes homosexuality in other cultures, you can see how this seemingly straightforward question, in practice, is not so easy to answer. The percentage of people who consider themselves gay, lesbian, straight, or bisexual varies depending on how the question is worded (see Table 12.3). Even then, many surveys fail to ask what percentage of respondents' attractions or behaviors are toward one sex or the other leading to possible inconsistencies and errors of classification between studies (Savin-Williams, 2006). Further, even within a single study, people's classifications can shift depending on whether the survey refers to attraction, behavior, or identity. In one study, only about 20% of gay and lesbian adults in the United States were consistently classified as gay or lesbian on all three dimensions, according to Savin-Williams (2006, reporting data collected by Laumann, Gagnon, Michael, & Michaels, 1994). Asking about same-sex attractions elicits the greatest prevalence whereas asking about identification elicits the least. However, only a very small percentage of people who report *any* same-sex attractions or engage in *any* same-sex behavior self-identify as gay or lesbian. People who call themselves gay or lesbian are actually a very small, and perhaps exceptional, fraction of the general population (Savin-Williams, 2006).

> **THINK ABOUT IT**
>
> Are these problems with defining sexual orientation due to methodological problems or to something fundamental about sexual orientation?

These differing definitions of what counts as gay, lesbian, bisexual, and heterosexual can explain the wide range of estimates of sexual orientation across studies. Alfred Kinsey and his associates reported the largest estimate. They found that 37% of men and 13% of women recounted at least one adult sexual experience with another member of the same sex that resulted in orgasm. However, far few people—4% of men and 3% of women—reported being lifelong homosexuals (Kinsey et al., 1948, 1953). The 37% figure made for sensational headlines back in the day, but as we saw, was probably an overestimate of what occurs in the general population.

More recently, the National Opinion Research Center (NORC) at the University of Chicago conducted a more extensive and better designed survey of sexual behavior in the United States (Laumann et al., 1994). They used sound scientific sampling methods and face-to-face interviews, followed up by anonymous questionnaires to find out about the sexual behavior of American adults aged 18 to 59, including a large representative sample of ethnic minorities. According to the National Health and Social Life Survey (NHSLS), about 0.9% and 0.4% of men and women report having had same-sex relations since age 18, yet 2% of men and 0.9% of women self-identify as gay or lesbian. Similarly, 4% of men and 3.7% of women report

Table 12.3 Prevalence of Homosexuality Among Females and Males in Four Countries According to Component of Sexual Orientation

Country and Population	Attraction		Behavior		Identity	
	Female	Male	Female	Male	Female	Male
United States: Young adults	13%	5%	4%	3%	4%	3%
United States: Adults	8	8	4	9	1	2
Australia: Adults	17	15	8	16	4	7
Turkey: Young adults	7	6	4	5	2	2
Norway: Adolescents	21	9	7	6	5	5

Note: Numbers indicate percentage of sample endorsing that response.

Source: Adapted from Savin-Willams (2006, Table 2, p. 41). Reprinted with permission from Savin-Williams, R. C. (2006), "Who's gay? Does it matter?," *Current Directions in Psychological Science,* 15(1), 40–44. Permission conveyed through the Copyright Clearance Center.

Table 12.4 Sexual Behavior, Attraction, and Identity Among Men and Women

	Men	Women
Sexual Behavior		
No partners, last year	10.5%	13.3%
Opposite-gender partners only, last year	86.8	85.4
Same-gender partners only, last year	2.0	1.0
Both male and female partners, last year	0.7	0.3
No partners since age 18	3.8	3.4
Opposite-gender partners only since age 18	91.3	92.5
Same-gender partners only since age 18	0.9	0.4
Both male and female partners since age 18	4.0	3.7
Sexual Attraction		
Only opposite gender	93.8%	95.6%
Mostly opposite gender	2.6	2.7
Both genders	0.6	0.8
Mostly same gender	0.7	0.6
Only same gender	2.4	0.3
Sexual Identity		
Heterosexual	96.9%	98.6%
Bisexual	0.8	0.5
Gay/lesbian	2.0	0.9
Other	0.3	0.1

Note: Numbers indicate percentage of sample endorsing that response.

Source: Adapted from Laumann et al. (1994, Table 8.3A and 8.3B, p. 311). From Laumann, E. O., Gagnon, J. H., Michael, R. T., & Michaels, S. (1994), "The social organization of sexuality: Sexual practices in the United States," Chicago, IL: University of Chicago Press. Copyright © 1994. Used with permission.

having sex with both men and women since age 18; yet only 0.8% of men and 0.5% of women self-identify as bisexual (Laumann et al., 1994; see Table 12.4). Still, it is possible that these figures underestimate the actual figures if people are reluctant to reveal same-sex attractions and behaviors due to the stigma associated with these activities in our culture.

In a 2002 update of this survey, 6% of men and 11.2% of women aged 15 to 44 reported having any same-sex sexual contact ever in their lives, but only 2.3% of men and 1.3% of women gave their sexual orientation as gay or lesbian. Only 1.8% of men and 2.8% of women said they were bisexual (Smith, 2006a).

What Determines Sexual Orientation?

"Love does not have an orientation of its own."
Researcher Lisa M. Diamond (2003b, p. 174)

Until very recently, the research on sexual orientation has been colored by three assumptions. First, many theories take a heteronormative view and assume that different-sex sexuality is the norm and same-sex sexuality is an exception or abnormality that must be explained. Refreshingly, current theories focus more on the orientation part, or what drives sexual arousal or attraction, and less on the sameness or otherness of the partner eventually chosen. Second, scientists have assumed that the same processes operate on men and women and have looked for theories that can explain the orientation of both gay men and lesbians. Again, newer theories suggest that given the large differences in sexuality of males and females—recall our discussion from Chapter 11—perhaps the causes of sexual orientation are different in males and females too (Chivers, 2005; Peplau, 2003). Finally, researchers are also starting to wonder if, at least in men, there is not just one type of same-sex sexuality, but many types, each determined by different factors (Bell, 1974). That is, social factors might explain why some men are gay but genetic factors might account for the orientation of others.

Do differences in sexual orientation reflect differences in social experiences, differences in biological factors unrelated to social experiences, or both? Let's take a closer look at biological, social, and interactionist theories.

Biological Explanations of Sexual Orientation

THINK ABOUT IT

Because there is a genetic component to same-sex sexuality, then what is the evolutionary advantage of same-sex sexuality?

Evolution.   Same-sex sexuality presents a Darwinian paradox: If gays and lesbians reproduce less than heterosexuals, how is this trait maintained in the population (Ciani, Corna, & Capiluppi, 2004)? There are at least three possible solutions to this problem: male alliance theory (Muscarella, 2006), the kin altruism hypothesis (Confer et al., 2010; Wilson, 1978), and increased female reproductive success (Ciani et al., 2004).

Some have reasoned that male–male sexual behavior evolved as a way of regulating dominance–submission and of forming alliances among a group of males living together, both of which increase survival and reproductive success of males (Muscarella, 2006). However, the alliance theory can't account for exclusive male same-sex behavior, nor does it apply to the same-sex behavior of women. To date, the evidence for this theory has been indirect; no studies have been conducted testing the theory.

From an evolutionary perspective, genes that code for behaviors that are important for an individual's or species' survival will be selected and genetically passed on. However, people who do not reproduce do not directly pass on their genes. So, how did same-sex sexuality survive natural selection? According to the kin altruism hypothesis of male same-sex sexuality, gay men adapt by shifting from investing in offspring to investing in next of kin, such as the children of their sisters and brothers (Confer et al., 2010; Wilson, 1978).

The evidence for this hypothesis is weak, at best. In one study, gay men and heterosexual men and women in Samoa were asked how willing they would be to engage in various activities for their nieces and nephews or for an unrelated child living nearby. Activities included babysitting, buying toys for the child, tutoring the child, helping expose the child to art and music, and contributing money toward the child's welfare. Gay men were more willing to engage in these behaviors toward nieces and nephews than were heterosexual women or men. However, all three groups showed the same low levels of willingness to help nonkin. Because only the gay men showed higher willingness to help kin than nonkin, it suggests that same-sex sexuality does pay off. Gay men become "helpers-in-the-nest" caring for their nieces and nephews and increasing their fitness indirectly (Vasey & VanderLaan, 2010).

However, another study in the United States comparing not just the willingness to help nieces and nephews, as in the Samoan study, but actual altruistic behaviors found no evidence for the kin altruism theory (Bobrow & Bailey, 2001). They found there was no difference between gay and straight men, of comparable income level, in their willingness to give financial or emotional resources to family members or in the willingness to channel resources toward nieces and nephews. More importantly, there was also no difference in altruistic behaviors, including giving monetary resources to family members over the past year. If anything, gay men tended to feel more distant and estranged from their families than heterosexual men (Bobrow & Bailey, 2001).

THINK ABOUT IT

Notice that these three theories attempt to explain male sexual orientation. How might an evolutionary explanation account for the same-sex orientation of females?

Based on the available evidence, there is no evidence for the kin selection theory of same-sex sexuality (Confer et al., 2010). However, another way that evolutionary forces could have selected for same-sex sexuality is if somehow the gene or genes that code for same-sex sexuality also code for the greater reproductive success of *relatives* (Ciani et al., 2004).

Two recent studies in Italy found evidence for an increase in the fertility of female relatives of gay men. Maternal relatives of gay men, that is, their aunts and mothers, had more children than the aunts and mothers of heterosexual men, even after controlling for differences in family size (Ciani et al., 2004; Iemmola & Ciani, 2009). Maternal relatives of gay men averaged 2.17 children whereas the maternal relatives of straight men averaged 1.83 children (Ciani et al., 2004). There was no difference in the number of children of fathers and uncles or grandparents of gay and straight men.

Table 12.5 Concordance Rate of Same-Sex Orientation

Sibling	Men	Women
Identical twin	52%	48%
Fraternal twin	22	16
Biological (nontwin) sibling	9.2	14
Adopted (nonbiological) sibling	11	6

Note: Numbers indicate percentage of sample with a gay or lesbian sibling as a function of relationship.
Sources: Bailey et al. (1993); Bailey & Pillard (1991).

In addition, there are more gay relatives among a gay man's mother's extended family than among his father's side of the family, a pattern that is not found in the families of heterosexual men (Ciani et al., 2004; Iemmola & Ciani, 2009). Gay men were also less likely to be firstborns than heterosexual men and to have more older brothers. These findings suggest that same-sex sexuality, in males, is genetic and transmitted at least partially through the X chromosome (Iemmola & Ciani, 2009). Scientists have not theorized an evolutionary explanation for female same-sex sexuality.

Genetics.   In addition to the findings just discussed, other studies suggest that part of the variation in same-sex orientation is accounted for by genetic variance (Bailey & Pillard, 1991; Bailey, Pillard, Neale, & Agyei, 1993; Kendler, Thorton, Gilman, & Kessler, 2000; Kirk, Bailey, Dunne, & Martin, 2000). In a study of gay men and their twin brothers (Bailey & Pillard, 1991) and lesbian women and their twin sisters (Bailey et al., 1993), there was a much greater chance that an identical twin than a fraternal twin or an adopted sibling would be gay or lesbian as well (see Table 12.5). The researchers estimated that the heritability, or proportion of variance in same-sex orientation that is accounted for by genetic variation, was 0.31 to 0.74 in gay men and 0.40 to 0.76 in lesbian women. More recent research gives a narrower estimate of heritability of same-sex sexual behavior in men as 0.34 to 0.39 and in women as 0.18 to 0.19, with unique, nonshared environmentality estimates of 0.61 to 0.66 in men and 0.64 to 0.66 in women (Långström, Rahman, Carlström, & Lichtenstein, 2010).

The concordance rate of sexual orientation suggests a strong genetic component in addition to an environmental component.

These findings suggest that there is a moderate genetic component to same-sex orientation and that the impact of genetics is stronger in men than in women. However, because the concordance rate in identical twins—those with identical genetic material—is not 100%, this suggests that there is a substantial impact of environmental factors on same-sex orientation as well. In particular, nonshared environments, including both social and biological ones, have a moderate to large effect on sexual orientation (Långström et al., 2010).

Building on these results, Michael Bailey and his colleagues found evidence that two aspects of same-sex sexuality also have a genetic component: childhood gender nonconformity and adult masculinity–femininity (Bailey, Dunne, & Martin, 2000).

As we saw in Chapter 6, research on human genetics is often misunderstood. Though research teams are trying to identify the exact gene responsible for sexual orientation, the results to date are inconsistent (Bailey et al., 1999; Bailey & Pillard, 1995; Hammer, Hu, Magnuson, Hu, & Pattatucci, 1993; Marshall, 1995; McKnight & Malcolm, 2000; Rice, Anderson, Risch, & Ebers, 1999). In their exuberance over a possible "gay gene" people tend to forget that the environment accounts for a large part of the variance in same-sex orientation as well. Any gene associated with sexual orientation will only confer a predisposition rather than definitively cause same-sex or different sex-orientation (Mustanski & Bailey, 2003).

Brain Structures.   Only a handful of studies have investigated whether parts of the brain differ between people with a same-sex orientation and those with a different-sex orientation (Allen & Gorski, 1992; Byne et al., 2001; LeVay, 1991; Swaab & Hofman, 1990). Sadly, these studies have a small number of participants, inconsistent findings, and a noticeable lack of women, lesbians in particular, making it difficult to draw conclusions. However, the most promising—and controversial—study found sex and sexual orientation differences in the hypothalamus (LeVay, 1991). Because the hypothalamus is the center for many kinds of sexual behavior, differences between people here may be related to differences in sexual arousal, reproduction, gender identity, gender identity disorders, and sexual orientation (Swaab, 2005).

LeVay (1991) studied the brain tissue of 18 men who were gay and died of AIDS, 16 men who were presumed to be heterosexual (6 died of AIDS), and 6 women who were presumed heterosexual (1 died of AIDS). He replicated a previous finding and verified that the third interstitial nucleus of the anterior hypothalamus (called INAH-3) was less than half as large in heterosexual women as in heterosexual men. However, his real discovery was that the INAH-3 of gay men was indistinguishable from that of heterosexual women and was also half the size of heterosexual men. Despite the difference in volume of the INAH-3 in gay and straight men there was no difference in the number of neurons found in this area. A later study replicated and extended these findings in gay men, straight men, and straight women (Byne et al., 2001).

This research came under intense scrutiny and was criticized on methodological grounds. The major critique was that AIDS, and not sexual orientation, could have caused the difference between the INAH-3 of the gay and straight men. However, LeVay (1991) still found a significant difference even when he compared only the brains of gay men with the straight men who had died from AIDS.

A second criticism concerned the heterosexual men. Because their orientation was not assessed directly and merely presumed, they could have been gay or bisexual. However, if this were the case, then LeVay (1991) would have actually ended up *underestimating* the true difference between the INAH-3 of gay and straight men. That is, mislabeling these men as straight would have only made it harder for him to find a difference.

Third, a major omission of the LeVay (1991) study and other studies in this area (e.g., Swaab & Hofman, 1990) is that they did not include lesbian women. To gain a complete picture of sexual orientation we need to study both men and women, of various orientations including bisexual.

Finally, there is no way to tell if these men were gay because they had smaller sections of the hypothalamus, or if being gay causes this part of the hypothalamus to develop smaller, or if some other neurohormonal process influences both sexual orientation and brain structure, as may be the case with other areas of the brain (Allen & Gorski, 1992). That is, we cannot infer causality from this kind of correlational study. We need larger, more extensive—and inclusive—studies, using the latest noninvasive techniques from neuroscience including PET scans and MRIs to understand these initial findings (Bailey, 2003).

THINK ABOUT IT

What is the controversy over finding a so-called gay gene?

THINK ABOUT IT

Why might there be difference in brain structures between gay and straight men?

Ultimately the question remains, why do differences in brain structures between gay and straight men occur? Newer research on prenatal hormone exposure and maternal immune response, which we shall cover shortly, suggests a possible mechanism by which these brain differences develop (Blanchard & Bogaert, 1996). Exposure to prenatal hormones during a critical period may affect the development of brain structures that influence sexual orientation (Bailey, 2003).

Prenatal Factors.   Hormonal Theories   One early view of sexual orientation was that circulating levels of hormones determined choice of sexual partner (Mustanski, Chivers, & Bailey, 2002). Research soon found that there is no difference in circulating levels of male hormones between gay and heterosexual men (Meyer-Bahlburg, 1984). Experimentally regulated levels of male hormones appear to affect the strength, not the direction, of the sex drive in men (Barahal, 1940). Studies of hormones and sexual orientation in women have been inconsistent or contain methodological problems (Mustanski et al., 2002). One thing we can say for sure is that there is no causal relationship between adult hormonal status and sexual orientation (Byne, 1995). However, there is evidence that prenatal hormones may indirectly affect later sexual orientation.

During prenatal development, all embryos start out developing exactly the same. At around the 7th week, the chromosomes direct the gonads (testes and ovaries) to begin sexual differentiation. Once the ovaries and testes have formed, they begin to produce different sex hormones that continue the development of the rest of the internal and external sex characteristics (Hyde & DeLamater, 2006). From 7 to 24 weeks of development and peaking at the 18th week, sex hormones also impact development of the brain. Exposure to prenatal hormones during this critical period affects the development of certain brain structures that appear to influence sexual orientation (Bailey, 2003). Prenatal sex hormones may affect later brain development and sexual development.

Based on animal experiments and human studies of endocrine disorders present at birth, it appears that masculine hormones (e.g., testosterone and similar substances, called **androgens**) regulate sexual behavior, potential attraction to females, and the brain structures that support these behaviors. High androgen exposure during a critical period of prenatal development is thought to be associated with heterosexuality in men and same-sex sexuality in women, whereas low androgen exposure may be associated with same-sex sexuality in men and heterosexuality in women (Bailey, 2003; Ellis & Ames, 1987). However, other studies found that women who had prenatal exposure to high levels of the female hormone estrogen were more likely to be classified as bisexual or lesbian than women without such exposure (Meyer-Bahlburg, 1997; Meyer-Bahlburg et al., 1995). The idea that androgens regulate the sexual differentiation of brain structures in humans is generally accepted; why it happens during development remains speculative (Bailey, 2003).

Currently, science lacks the technology to monitor these prenatal hormones so we cannot directly correlate later sexual orientation with events that occurred during development in the womb (Mustanski et al., 2002). However, as an alternative we can *indirectly* see the effect of prenatal hormones by studying traits thought to be affected by them, such as characteristics and behaviors typical of the other sex including cross-gender interests (Berenbaum & Snyder, 1995) and physical markers (Ellis & Ames, 1987). Physical markers indicative of one sex or the other have included dermatoglyphics (fingerprint ridge patterns), otoacoustic emissions (faint sounds generated by the inner ear), waist-to-hip ratio, spatial ability, finger length ratio, and handedness. Though all of these have some association with sexual orientation, only cross-gender behavior, finger length ratio, and handedness produce the most consistent and reliable results (Lippa, 2003; see Mustanski et al., 2002, for a review).

Gender Nonconformity.   Early research on sexuality hypothesized that gays and lesbians have a **gender inversion**. People believed that a biological defect occurred during development that turned a male into a female and a female into a male in both psychological characteristics and body type (Ellis, 1928; Krafft-Ebing, 1908/1986). Sigmund Freud even described psychological processes that could lead to gender inversion and same-sex attractions (Freud, 1915/2000).

> **THINK ABOUT IT**
>
> Should strength of sex drive be added to sameness or otherness of partner and flexibility as a third dimension of sexual orientation?

Obviously, this very simplistic view of sexual orientation and gender identity is wrong (Peplau, Spalding, Conley, & Veniegas, 1999). However, there is some truth to the notion that gay men are more similar to women than to other men, and lesbians are more similar to men than to other women but only when it comes to career interests and hobbies, not to personality.

One study investigated the difference between men and women, both gay or lesbian and straight, in career interests, hobbies, instrumentality, expressivity, masculinity and femininity, characteristics known to differ between the genders (Lippa, 2000). There were significant sex and sexual orientation differences in this college student population.

First, there was no evidence for the gender inversion hypothesis. The overall pattern did not indicate that the personalities of gay men were more like women or that the personalities of lesbian women were more like men. Despite significant differences in masculinity, femininity, instrumental traits, and expressive traits, the overall pattern suggests that gay men were more similar to straight men than to straight women, and lesbians were more similar to straight women than to straight men. That is, people tend to be similar in personality to others of their sex, regardless of their sexual orientation.

For example, although gay men scored the same as straight men on expressive traits, they scored lower on instrumentality. Lesbian women scored the same as straight women on instrumental traits, but they scored lower on expressive traits. Gay men and lesbians fell in between straight men and straight women on measures of occupational interest, hobbies, masculinity, and femininity. That is, gay men and lesbians are less masculine than straight men but not as low in masculinity as straight women. Gay men and lesbians are also more feminine than straight men, but not as feminine as straight women.

Other studies have found similar effects using the five factors. Although lesbian women scored higher on Openness and lower on Neuroticism than straight women, they were not more similar to straight men in their NEO-PI-R profile. However, gay men were more similar to women, scoring significantly higher than straight men on Neuroticism, Openness, Agreeableness, and Conscientiousness factors of the NEO-PI-R (Lippa, 2005b).

Second, regardless of sexual orientation, men scored higher than women on the more traditionally masculine measures of personality and women scored higher than men on the more traditionally feminine measures of personality. The difference between gay and straight men and between lesbian and straight women was the greatest in interests and hobbies, followed by self-ascribed masculinity and femininity. The differences were the lowest on instrumental and expressive traits (Lippa, 2000).

Finally, gay men and lesbians were more similar to the other gender in their interests and hobbies. Lesbians, compared to heterosexual women, and straight men, compared to gay men, were less likely to show interest in becoming a beauty consultant, interior decorator,

In men, but not in women, gender nonconformity as a child is related to adult sexual orientation.

fashion model, or grade school teacher, but were more interested in becoming a poet, carpenter, computer programmer, or jet pilot. There was no difference in preference for gender-neutral occupations such as lawyer, physician, newspaper reporter, or psychologist. Later studies confirmed these findings: Having gender nonconforming interests and hobbies as a child or teenager shows the highest correlation with sexual orientation as an adult, but having instrumental or expressive traits does not correlate with sexual orientation as an adult (Lippa, 2000, 2002, 2005b).

Although there is no evidence for the gender inversion hypothesis of personality traits, the research does suggest that gender nonconformity of behaviors and interests during childhood is related to sexual orientation as an adult. Indeed, a meta-analysis of 41 retrospective studies found that adults with same-sex attractions recalled substantially more cross-sex-typed behavior in childhood than heterosexual adults, and this was especially true for gay men (Bailey & Zucker, 1995). Even as children and adolescents, men who would grow up to be gay often felt that their interests and activities did not fit in with those of their male playmates (Green, 1987; Zucker, 1990). However, whereas gender nonconformity during childhood is one of the strongest predictors of a man's adult sexual orientation (Bailey & Zucker, 1995), no research has followed lesbians from girlhood into adulthood to see if this is predictive of women's adult sexual orientation as well (Bailey & Zucker, 1995; Peplau & Huppin, 2008).

Gender nonconformity in girls often takes the form of being a tomboy, the name given to girls who like traditional boy games and activities (Peplau et al., 1999). Lesbian women in the United States, the Philippines, Brazil, and Peru all reported more gender nonconformity in childhood than heterosexual women. Lesbians in these countries were more likely to play with boys' toys and to be labeled as a tomboy by others (Whitam & Mathy, 1991). However, being a tomboy was not predictive of adult sexual orientation: the overwhelming majority of tomboys grow up to be heterosexual women (Bailey & Zucker, 1995). This was even true for women who showed extreme gender nonconformity as children.

How is it that childhood gender nonconformity is a poor predictor of adult sexual orientation in women? First, women have more latitude to explore cross-gender behavior than men both in childhood and in adulthood, so that a girl faces less ostracism and rejection than a boy would for cross-gender behavior (Peplau, Garnets, Spalding, Conley, & Veniegas, 1998). Second, as mentioned, many heterosexual women recall being tomboys as children, so tomboyism may be less related to sexual orientation in women (Peplau et al., 1998). Finally—and we'll see hints of this throughout the chapter, as we have already—women's sexuality may be fundamentally different from men's (Baumeister, 2000). We'll take up the question of how well these theories apply to women's sexuality in the final section.

> **THINK ABOUT IT**
>
> While growing up, did you enjoy any toys or activities typically associated with the other gender?

> **THINK ABOUT IT**
>
> Might differences between traditional boys' and girls' toys and hobbies like moving parts, challenge, outdoors, activity level, and so on make boy's activities more fun and appealing to both boys and girls?

> **THINK ABOUT IT**
>
> Is gender nonconformity determined by social norms or by an individual's personality?

The majority of tomboys grow up to be heterosexual women.

Stressors During Development   Based on evidence from animal research, maternal stress during pregnancy may feminize and demasculinize male rat progeny because of a delay in the androgen surge necessary for proper sexual development. However, only a few studies have been done in humans testing this notion, with some finding a significant effect of maternal stress on males but not on females (Ellis, Ames, Peckham, & Burke, 1988), and others on females but not on males (Bailey, Willerman, & Parks, 1991).

For example, one study involved over 7,500 male and female heterosexual, gay, lesbian, and bisexual college students from 20 U.S. and Canadian universities and their mothers (Ellis & Cole-Harding, 2001). Mothers were asked if they had experienced any of 76 potentially stressful experiences just before, during, and just after their pregnancy, including physical stress, health- and pregnancy-related stress, emotional or intrapersonal stress, marital and sexual stress, nuclear family stress, extended family and friendship stress, and social or natural disaster stress. Mothers also rated their overall stress for each month of their pregnancy and indicated their drug, alcohol, and nicotine use.

The study found that mothers of gay men were more likely than mothers of straight men to report stress during the first trimester of their pregnancy. Mothers of lesbian women were no more likely to report stress during their pregnancy than mothers of straight women. There was no relationship between alcohol or drug use during pregnancy and children's sexual orientation, but mothers of lesbians had greater nicotine use during the first trimester of their pregnancy combined with higher stress in the second trimester than mothers of straight women (Ellis & Cole-Harding, 2001).

Even though the results of this study are promising, we need to interpret them with caution. The results were based on mothers' recollections, which could be flawed, or to demand characteristics, because some of the mothers knew that sexual orientation of their children was the focus of the study. Also, this is the first study to identify a link between nicotine use and sexual orientation in women and the results need to be replicated. The researchers noted that smoking mothers and their daughters had higher levels of testosterone than nonsmoking mothers and their daughters. However, more research is necessary to discover if nicotine, or the androgen testosterone, or some other variable that affects both testosterone levels and tendency to smoke affects sexual orientation in women (Ellis & Cole-Harding, 2001).

Fraternal Birth Order and Maternal Immune Response   Fraternal birth order refers to the birth order of brothers in a family. A robust finding in numerous studies is that gay men tend to have a larger number of older brothers than nongay men (Blanchard, 1997, 2001; Blanchard & Sheridan, 1992; Blanchard & Zucker, 1994; Blanchard, Zucker, Bradley, & Hume, 1995). However, there is no difference in birth order or number of older male or female siblings between lesbian and straight women (Blanchard, 1997, 2001). This **fraternal birth order effect** in males is not due to the number of older sisters, the time interval between births, or an artifact of the more advanced age of mothers and fathers by the time younger siblings come along (Blanchard, 2001).

According to one estimate, 14.5 to 15.2% of gay men can attribute their sexual orientation to this fraternal birth order effect (Cantor, Blanchard, Paterson, & Bogaert, 2002). Another estimate suggests that each additional older brother increases the odds of same-sex attraction by 33% (Blanchard & Bogaert, 1996). Because statistical significance is not the same as practical significance, we are a long way from predicting the sexual orientation of a male child based on his number of older brothers. The probability of a couple's having a gay son rises from only 2% for their first son to 6% for their sixth son, still an overall small probability (Blanchard, 2001).

In one test of this hypothesis, gay adolescents and children who later self-identified as gay were matched to nongay controls. All participants were currently under treatment at a psychiatric clinic. The children in the gay group were referred to the clinic because of cross-gender behavior or gender identity problems, whereas the adolescents were openly gay and were referred to the clinic for other problems. Each participant was matched to a nongay male of the same age and the same number of siblings in the family. These control participants came to the clinic for a range of childhood disorders, but mostly disruptive behavior disorders and developmental disorders (Blanchard, Zucker, & Hume, 1995).

The researchers found that gay and pregay participants had a total of 149 brothers and 106 sisters whereas participants in the control group had 130 brothers and 125 sisters. Statistical analyses confirmed that both being later-born and having older brothers was related to being gay or pregay. Merely being in a large family or having a large number of older sisters was not related to sexual orientation. These findings suggest that same-sex orientation may be caused by prenatal factors and not childhood social factors (Blanchard, Zucker, & Hume, 1995).

Why does this fraternal birth order effect occur? Many possible explanations have been investigated, but the one with the most support is that the male fetus provokes an immune response in the mother. The likely suspect in this process is one of the H-Y androgens (male hormones regulated by a gene on the Y chromosome), which are different enough from the mother's antigens so as to trigger an allergic response. According to the **maternal immune hypothesis**, H-Y antigens that, by definition, are present in male but not in female fetuses get into the mother's circulation triggering the immune system. The mother's antibodies react by attacking the H-Y antigen which prevents the fetal brain from developing male-typical brain structures and behaviors. Each male fetus increases the sensitivity of the mother's immune system to the antigen, triggering a stronger immune response with successive males increasing the chances that later-born male children will be gay (Blanchard, 2001; Blanchard & Bogaert, 1996).

Both direct and indirect evidence, from a combination of human and animal research, supports this hypothesis (see Blanchard & Klassen, 1997, for a review). Animal studies suggest that H-Y antigens, which are necessary for male brain development, are not necessary for male genital development. Anti-H-Y antibodies *in utero* have been shown to disrupt later sexual behavior in male mice. The mother's immune system, by attacking the H-Y antigens, disrupts brain development—but not physical development—by diverting it from the male-typical pathway. In humans, this may explain how a man can have a male-typical body but be attracted to other men, have feminine characteristics, or possibly feel that he is a female "trapped" in a man's body, as experienced by transsexual men.

Given that the animal models are quite promising, what about evidence in humans? We know that in humans H-Y antigens play a role in the sexual development of males and females and that the mother's immune system does respond to fetal H-Y antigens. Also, H-Y antigens can cross the blood-brain barrier and move from the mother's body into the fetus's brain. Finally, cytology research does show that the maternal immune response is greater to cells from male than female children.

An interesting finding is that newborn boys with older brothers tend to have a lower birth weight than boys with older sisters. In addition, gay men weighed even less at birth than straight men. This suggests that earlier male pregnancies influence the development of later male fetuses. The fetuses most strongly affected by this process as indicated by lower birth weights also happen to be those who grow up to be gay (Blanchard, 2001).

Researchers suspect that some prenatal process—like maternal immune response—impacts both birth weight and the sexual orientation of males. Lower birth weight may be a side effect of maternal immune response to the developing male fetus (Blanchard, 2001). Again, direct evidence for this comes from animal studies. The maternal immune response hypothesis suggests that a growth-inhibiting process rather than a feminization process is at work. Perhaps this is an evolutionary way of limiting the number of children later offspring can bear to ensure the greater reproductive success of relatives. If this is the case, then why don't mothers with many sons produce even more gay sons (Blanchard, 2001)?

The maternal immune hypothesis cannot account for men who are gay but who do not have older brothers. In one study, there was no difference in birth weight between firstborn gay men and firstborn straight men, nor between gay and straight men who had older sisters only. Because their birth weights do not show signs of maternal immune attack, there must be other explanations for sexual orientation in addition to prenatal factors (Blanchard, 2001).

As promising as the maternal immune response hypothesis is, and how parsimoniously it unites the findings on brain structure, there is a lack of direct evidence in humans. Obviously, more research is necessary, and this appears to be one of the most fruitful paths for understanding sexual behavior and sexual orientation.

THINK ABOUT IT

Where else in this book have you seen evidence of the immune system affecting psychological processes and vice versa?

THINK ABOUT IT

Can sexual desire be taught?

Environmental Theories

If a same-sex orientation is not due to nature, then it must be due to nurture, right? Although the notion that we learn how to be gay or straight has intuitive appeal, it has very little research support. Men and women are indeed socialized into gender roles, but these social pressures push people to be heterosexual (Hyde & Jaffee, 2000). People become gay, lesbian, or bisexual *despite,* not because of, socialization. Similarly, being raised by lesbian or transsexual parents does not make children grow up to be lesbian or transsexual (Golombok, Spencer, & Rutter, 1983; Green, 1978; Kirkpatrick, Smith, & Roy, 1981). In fact, most lesbian women and gay men were raised by heterosexual parents (Bailey & Dawood, 1998; Patterson, 1997). Not only does socialization by peers and family have little impact on a person's sexual orientation, but the person himself or herself doesn't exactly *choose* whom to be attracted to (Ellis, 1996).

Even studies investigating early childhood experiences of gay men and lesbians have failed to find any evidence *whatsoever* for the Freudian notion that certain experiences in childhood (e.g., domineering mother, weak father, failure to identify with same-sex parent, etc.) make people gay or lesbian (Bell, Weinberg, & Hammersmith, 1981a; Downey & Friedman, 1998; Magee & Miller, 1997).

Despite the fact that in our society heterosexuality is modeled and reinforced whereas same-sex attractions are invisible and often punished, people do grow up to be gay, lesbian, or bisexual (Bohan, 1996). No matter how hard researchers have looked, they found no childhood events or activities that are reliably related to later bisexual or lesbian attractions in adult women (Bohan, 1996).

Interactionist Theories

Psychologists believe that sexual orientation is not due to biology or learning alone, but is multiply determined, especially for women (Peplau & Garnets, 2000). These newer theories hypothesize that people are gay, lesbian, or bisexual due to an interaction of biological and social factors.

The Exotic Becomes Erotic.   One such interaction theory is Daryl Bem's notion that what we find unusual or exotic, piques our sexual interest, and becomes sexually attractive to us (Bem, 1996, 1998, 2000). According to the **exotic becomes erotic (EBE) theory**, cultures that emphasize the differences between men and women and organize social life, norms, and expectations for behavior of children and adults around this dichotomy (e.g., S. L. Bem, 1993) end up polarizing the genders (remember our discussion from Chapter 11 about Mars and Venus?). The result is that the other gender becomes foreign, mysterious, and a source of interest.

According to EBE theory, biological variables such as genes do not directly cause sexual orientation, but rather determine aspects of childhood temperament like aggression or activity level, both of which have a strong biological basis and are greater in boys than in girls (Easton & Enns, 1986; Else-Quest, Hyde, Goldsmith, & Van Hulle, 2006; Hyde, 1984). Children will choose activities and interests on the basis of their temperament. For example, some children, perhaps the more active or aggressive ones, will enjoy rough-and-tumble play or competitive sports, which are male-typical behaviors. Others will prefer to socialize quietly or play with dolls, female-typical behaviors. Children will seek out playmates who share their interests in these activities, so that children who prefer baseball or football will choose boys to play with, whereas children who prefer dolls or arts and crafts will choose girls.

THINK ABOUT IT

If a child grows up in a family with girls and boys, will the other sex still seem exotic to them?

Depending on the activities and playmates chosen, children may be conforming or nonconforming to the gender expectations of their culture. Children who prefer same-sex playmates and sex-typical activities are gender conforming, whereas children who prefer other-sex playmates and sex-atypical activities are gender nonconforming. Children who are gender conforming will feel different from their other-sex peers and see them as dissimilar, unfamiliar, and exotic. But children who are gender nonconforming will feel different from their same-sex peers and see them as dissimilar, unfamiliar, and exotic.

These feelings of differentness cause arousal, either in childhood, adolescence, or adulthood. Bem gives the example of how a girl may feel timid, shy, and apprehensive around boys or how boys might feel contempt in the presence of "yucky" girls. Bem also suggests that boys who face teasing for being a "sissy boy" might come to feel anger or fear in the presence of boys. Similarly, a girl who is teased for being a tomboy by her peers may feel anger and arousal in their presence. In both cases, this arousal is later transformed into a sexual arousal and an attraction for same-sex peers.

The strongest piece of evidence for the EBE theory is the robust finding that more gay men than heterosexual men were gender nonconforming as a child, a finding reviewed earlier. However, because this is not the case for women, as discussed, critics suggested that EBE theory cannot account for sexual orientation of women (Bem, 1998; Peplau et al., 1998, 1999). Bem answered these criticisms by analyzing data from studies of male and female, monozygotic and dizygotic twins. He found a significant effect of genetics on gender nonconformity and indeed, in both males and females, a direct effect of childhood gender nonconformity on adult sexual orientation (Bem, 2000, 2008). However, there was no direct effect of genetics on sexual orientation, suggesting that the genetic influence on sexual orientation works through gender nonconformity.

EBE theory has also been criticized for failing to account for other findings on sexual orientation (Peplau et al., 1998). For example, in a study cited by Bem (1998), most men and women—regardless of their sexual orientation—reported that most or all of their childhood friends, including their best friend, were of their own sex (Bell et al., 1981a; Bell, Weinberg, & Hammersmith, 1981b). This goes against EBE theory, which assumes that gay men and lesbian women must have spent more time among children of the other gender.

As it stands, EBE theory has identified gender nonconformity as an important childhood precursor of adult sexual orientation. However, empirical evidence will have to determine if the cause of this nonconformity is more social, due to conformity pressures and feeling different; biological, due to prenatal androgens or genetics; or some combination of the two such as gender polarization of society and children's inborn temperament.

The Biobehavioral Model of Love and Desire: Accounting for the Experiences of Women.

As we have seen in this chapter, much of the research reviewed does not explain same-sex sexuality in women. There are many ways in which sexuality and sexual orientation is experienced differently by women and men (Diamond, 2007). As you may recall from Chapter 11, men and women differ the most when it comes to sexuality. On average, women have lower sexual desire than men and more conservative attitudes toward premarital sex (Hyde & Oliver, 2000). When it comes to understanding sexual orientation, there are sex differences as well: "the male model of sexual orientation has been rejected in women" conclude some researchers (Mustanski et al., 2002, p. 127).

Why do we think that sexuality and sexual orientation is experienced differently by women? For one, adolescent and adult women are more likely to report bisexual attractions than to report exclusive same-sex attractions (Diamond, 2007). In contrast, men are more likely to report exclusive male or female attractions than to report bisexual attractions (see Figure 12.2). This same pattern also holds for other aspects of sexual orientation including physiological arousal and sexual desire.

"Men are lust; they lead with the gonads. Women are limerence; they lead with their hearts."
Daryl J. Bem (1998, p. 397), summarizing Peplau and colleagues' (1998) discussion of sex differences in sexuality

"It is therefore unwise to generalize from the male to the female situation."
Linda Garnets (2002, p. 118)

Female sexuality may be fundamentally different from male sexuality. For women, sexual desire involves a longing to be emotionally close to another person.

Figure 12.2 Fluidity of female sexuality illustrated: A scatter plot of attraction to men (*x*-axis) and attraction to women (*y*-axis) for men (top panel) and women (bottom panel). Men tend to be attracted to either men or women in accord with their sexual orientation. Women are often attracted to both men and women, regardless of their sexual orientation. *Source:* From Lippa (2006b, Figure 1, p. 51). Reprinted with permission from Lippa, R. A. (2006b), "Is high sex drive associated with increased sexual attraction to both sexes?," *Psychological Science,* 17(1), 46–52. Permission conveyed through the Copyright Clearance Center.

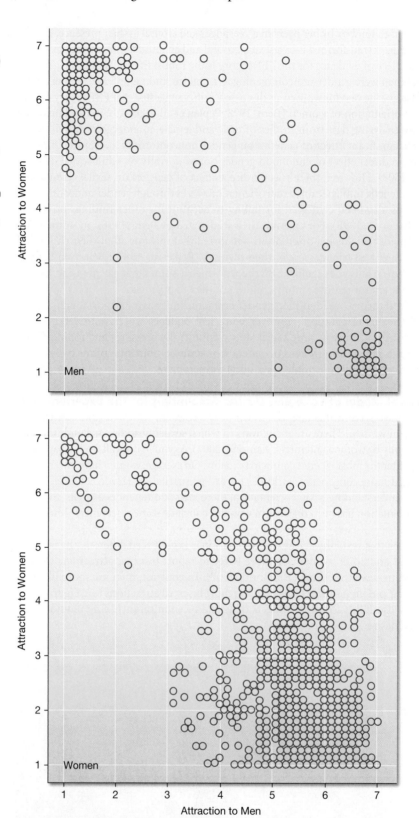

Second, men's attractions, whether they are toward the same or the other sex, tend to stay stable over their lifetime whereas women's attractions can change over time and across situations (Diamond, 2007). Daryl Bem characterizes this difference by noting that men who come out later in life might say "[I've] finally discovered [my] true sexual orientation," but lesbians in the same situation are more likely to say "That's who I was then, and this is who I am now" (Bem, 1998, p. 398).

Third, because female sexuality is more sensitive than male sexuality to situational, interpersonal, and contextual factors, psychologists describe it as more fluid than male sexuality (Baumeister, 2000; Diamond, 2007; but see Hyde & Durik, 2000, for an alternative view). As a result, women often report that their attractions can vary depending on the circumstances and the person involved, whereas men often report that their attractions originate from within themselves. Most women have a relational or partner-centered orientation to sexuality; most men have a physical or body-centered orientation (Peplau, 2001; Peplau & Garnets, 2000) developing an attraction "to the person not the gender" (Diamond, 2008a, p. 12), as we saw in the study that opened this chapter.

To illustrate, consider how one young heterosexual man defined sexual desire: "Sexual desire is wanting someone . . . in a physical manner. No strings attached. Just for uninhibited sexual intercourse." A young woman from the same study said: "Sexual desire is the longing to be emotionally intimate and to express love for another person" (Regan & Berscheid, 1996, p. 116).

Finally, men tend to experience their first sexual attractions before puberty, regardless of whether it is to females, in the case of straight men, or other males for gay and bisexual men. In contrast, many women report experiencing their first same-sex attraction in adulthood as a result of meeting a lesbian or bisexual woman, encountering the idea of a same-sex attraction, or having the opportunity for same-sex contact (Diamond, 2007).

Why should this be the case that sexuality is different in women? Psychologist Lisa Diamond (2006a) suggested that women's sexual desire evolved to be flexible so that females are able to reproduce not just during ovulation, when desire peaks, but at any time in their cycles.

Biologists distinguish between **proceptivity**, the motivation to initiate sexual activity, and receptivity in the case of animals, or **arousability** in the case of humans, that is, the capacity to become aroused to sexual stimuli. As higher primates evolved from having a limited and readily observable period of heightened fertility and receptivity called *estrus,* to being sexually active at any time in their cycles, proceptivity and arousability separated into two systems. Fluidity in women evolved at the same time that the processes of proceptivity and arousability evolved into independent systems (Diamond, 2006a).

Although women have heightened proceptivity linked to their reproductive cycles, peaking during ovulation, they have arousability at any time in their cycles. Men, however, experience continual proceptivity due to high testosterone levels. In contrast to men, women's day-to-day experience of sexual desire is more influenced by arousability than proceptivity. Arousability is more general and does not necessarily orient a woman toward a specific sex the way that proceptivity does. Because arousability is more dependent on the situation, some women show greater malleability in their desires across time and situations and can experience same-sex, other-sex, or both desires (Diamond, 2006a).

SEE FOR YOURSELF

Does your own pattern of sexual arousal match what the research shows?

Proceptivity, the motivation to initiate sexual activity, is when a woman is feeling sexual desire. Animals signal their readiness to engage in intercourse through physical or olfactory signals. Proceptivity in women peaks during ovulation when they are the most fertile. Proceptivity is more likely to orient a woman toward one sex or the other.

Arousability, the capacity to become aroused, occurs when a woman is not feeling strong sexual desire, but could be open to it if the circumstances and the partner are right. Human females have the capacity to become aroused at any point in their cycle. Arousability is more general and does not necessarily orient a woman toward a specific sex the way that proceptivity does.

More and more, researchers are suggesting that we need a new view of sexuality and sexual orientation to account for the diversity of men's and women's sexual experiences (Garnets, 2002; Peplau et al., 1999; Peplau & Garnets, 2000). Instead of viewing sexual orientation as dichotomous, defined by behavior, fixed at an early age, and established by a single pathway, research suggests that sexuality and sexual orientation, are flexible and multifaceted, and defined by attractions and attachments, in addition to behavior. Sexual orientation, especially for women, is fluid and changeable, with many possible pathways for developing an orientation or an identity. Recently, Lisa Diamond (2003b) proposed a biobehavioral model of sexual orientation based on her research with young women.

The biobehavioral model of sexual orientation combines both biological processes and social ones. Diamond (2003b) suggested that there are two components to sexual orientation: sexual desire and emotional attachment. She proposed that these two components of sexual orientation are controlled by two separate biological systems rooted in evolutionary processes. Because of the way these two systems interact with sex hormones, sexual orientation in men tends to be fixed as either gay or heterosexual, whereas for women it tends to be more fluid, defying set labels of either lesbian, heterosexual, or even bisexual.

One system, **sexual desire**, is regulated by the sexual mating system that promotes sexual union for the purpose of reproduction (Fisher, 1998). Sexual desire is a wish, need, or drive to be with or to engage in sexual activities with a person we find sexually attractive (Regan & Berscheid, 1995).

The second system, **emotional attachment**, maintains romantic relationships and causes us to fall in love (Hazan & Shaver, 1987). This system is regulated by pair-bonding which, evolutionarily, keeps couples together to protect and care for their young. Human and animal species with pair bonding are more likely to birth developmentally immature young at birth who need additional care. Often, fathers are involved in the care of offspring of pair bonds (Fraley, Brumbaugh, & Marks, 2005).

In contrast to the sexual desire system, which for evolutionary reasons must be oriented toward a member of the other sex, attachment orients emotional bonds without concern for gender. That is, attachment is gender-blind. We can form an attachment to members of the same sex or the other sex. This makes perfect sense, after all, if the attachment system is meant to keep a caregiver close to its young, or a young close to its caregiver (Diamond, 2003b). Although sexual desire is oriented toward one sex or the other or both, romantic attraction is person-, rather than sex-, oriented.

The distinction between these two systems is illustrated by the following. One gay man reported that he found sex with his former girlfriend "satisfying physically, but not emotionally." Another gay man said that he had been in love with his high school girlfriend, but that "physically, I didn't want her" (Savin-Williams, 1998, p. 110). For most people these two systems lead to the same sexual orientation, but for some people—often women more than men—this is not the case. Some lesbian and bisexual women report that they fall in love with the person, not the gender (Diamond, 2003b).

In humans, these two systems are separate so that we can mate without bonding and bond without mating (Diamond, 2003b). Yet, both systems play off each other so that sexual desire can lead to attachment and attachment can lead to sexual desire. The finding that women are more jealous over emotional infidelity and men over sexual infidelity supports the idea that these two systems are separate and have evolutionary roots (Buss et al., 1992). Because spending time together, feeling a sense of togetherness, and touch can foster feelings of romantic love (Hazan & Zeifman, 1994), we can, according to Diamond (2003b), experience romantic love without sexual desire even for people we may not be sexually oriented to. By the same token, it is also possible to develop sexual feelings for a same-sex friend.

Women are more likely than men to have sexual feelings for a same-sex friend, a finding that may be bolstered by biological as well as cultural and social factors (Diamond, 2003b). In humans, oxytocin facilitates both sexual behavior and pair bonding, particularly in women (Diamond, 2004; Taylor, Klein, et al., 2000). Also, it is more socially acceptable for women to develop strong emotional bonds with other women (Diamond, 2004). Because of their flexibility of responding to situational cues, women are more likely than men to fall in love with their female friends and, because of the release of oxytocin, override their general sexual orientation (Diamond, 2004).

Diamond's biobehavioral model of sexual orientation is too new to have been directly tested in humans. Right now, much of the evidence is indirect or comes from animal research (e.g., DeVries, Johnson, & Carter, 1997). However, the theory is very exciting because it presents a model of sexual orientation that applies to both men and women. This is an improvement over current theories with inconsistent or nonexisting findings for women. Still, there are aspects of sexual orientation the theory cannot account for.

When the theory says that a woman falls in love with the person and not the gender, what aspects of the person sparked that love? The biobehavioral model cannot predict who a person will fall in love with; then again, *no* theory can account for this most magical and mysterious of human experiences. Similarly, the theory is also not able to predict why some people have sexual feelings for one gender or the other. As discussed earlier, Diamond is continuing her research and has identified some people who are more flexible in their sexual orientation. The next step, of course, is to try to find out what makes these people more flexible. Is this where genetics or prenatal hormones have an impact?

In light of her research, Diamond recommended a new definition of sexual identity as something more individually constructed, rather than socially constructed (Diamond, 2006b): a chosen perspective from which to understand one's sexual feelings and behaviors (Weinberg, Williams, & Pryor, 1994). No doubt this newer research, in aiming to explain sexual orientation in women, will help us understand sexual orientation in both men and women.

> **THINK ABOUT IT**
>
> If Diamond is correct, do we need a different definition of sexual orientation than the one given earlier in this chapter?

Chapter Summary

• •

In this chapter we reviewed what sexual orientation is and saw how the number of people who are gay, lesbian, or bisexual changes depending on whether we define orientation as attraction, behavior, or identity. Back in the 1940s, Alfred Kinsey and his associates were the first to conduct a survey of the sexual behavior of the American public, and to conceptualize same-sex sexuality and other-sex sexuality on a continuum, using the famous 0 to 6 Kinsey scale. However, due to

✓• **Study** and **Review**
on **mysearchlab.com**

Go online for more resources to help you review.

sampling bias they overestimated the number of people who are gay, lesbian, or bisexual. Today the National Health and Social Life Survey provides a better estimate. More people report having same-sex attractions than identify themselves as gay or lesbian. The study by Diamond (2008a) that opened this chapter illustrated how sexual orientation can be fluid, especially for women, and that some women may change how they experience their sexual identity over their lifetime. We also identified a number of common myths and misperceptions about sexual orientation.

These problems with defining same-sex sexuality and the finding that sexual orientation may be fluid and changing within a single person over the life span make it difficult to interpret some of the studies that have been done on the causes of sexual orientation. Some psychologists have theorized that sexual orientation is innate, determined by biological factors, including evolution, genetics, brain structures, and prenatal factors (hormones, brain structures, the invalid gender inversion hypothesis, gender nonconformity, maternal stress, fraternal birth order, and maternal immune hypothesis). Other psychologists have suggested that sexual orientation is a pattern that is learned or develops out of childhood experiences. Still other psychologists believe that sexual orientation is determined by biological and social factors interacting together (such as Daryl Bem's exotic becomes erotic theory). Finally, newer research suggests that none of these theories explains the sexual orientation of women and has suggested a biobehavioral model of sexual desire and emotional attachment. This model has the advantage of accounting for the wide spectrum of sexual experiences of both women and men. As our models become more sophisticated and our operationalizations more precise, the research in this most intimate area of our personality will lead to new findings and increased understanding of human sexual orientation in the near future.

Review Questions

1. Why might the labels of lesbian, bisexual, and heterosexual be inaccurate and inadequate for describing human sexual orientation?

2. What are some common myths and misperceptions about sexual orientation?

3. How do psychologists define sexual orientation today? How did Kinsey define sexual orientation? What are some criticisms of Kinsey's studies? What is the difference between thinking about sexual orientation as separate categories or as a continuum? How is sexual orientation defined in other cultures?

4. About how many people in the population consider themselves gay, lesbian, bisexual, or straight?

5. What are some possible biological explanations of sexual orientation including evolution, genetics, brain structures, and prenatal factors?

6. Is there any evidence that sexual orientation is learned?

7. What is the exotic becomes erotic theory of sexual orientation?

8. What is the biobehavioral model of love and desire in women? What is proceptivity and arousability? How do these relate to sexual desire and emotional attachment?

Key Terms

Fluid sexuality
Heteronormativity
Sexual orientation
Sexual attraction
Sexual behavior
Sexual identity
Androgens

Gender inversion
Fraternal birth order
   effect
Maternal immune
   hypothesis
Exotic becomes erotic
   (EBE) theory

Proceptivity
Arousability
Sexual desire system
Emotional attachment
   system

13 RESILIENCE: AN INTEGRATIVE MINI-CHAPTER

Read the **Chapter** on
mysearchlab.com

*"He's a million rubber bands
in his resilience."*

Alan K. Simpson

When I think of resilience, I think of my older brother Jerry. He is a certified ski instructor in an adaptive ski program for people with disabilities. He spends his winters training and teaching across New England. He spends his summers kayaking, fishing, surfing, and engaging in other outdoor sports with a group of young men and women as part of the Wounded Warrior Project. What makes my brother truly amazing is that over 45 years ago, he was a wounded veteran himself, returning from Vietnam with two prosthetic arms.

Nearly 20% of military service members returning from Iraq and Afghanistan report symptoms of posttraumatic stress disorder (PTSD) or major depression (Ramchand, Karney, Osilla, Burns, & Caldarone, 2008). As tragic as this figure is, consider the flipside: Some 80% of returning soldiers—the vast majority—*don't!*

Why are some people able to snap back from adversity whereas others have considerable difficulty? Consider a study of Army National Guard and reservist medical units that had recently returned from serving in the first Gulf War (Bartone, 1999). The average age of the sample was 34 years and it included both men and women. The personnel were deployed in the Persian Gulf (Saudi Arabia or Kuwait), U.S. Army stations in Germany, or remained in the U.S.

First, as you might expect there was a significant effect of location on physical and psychological health. Personnel who worked closer to the Persian Gulf reported the most amount of stress, PTSD, and health problems followed by those deployed in Germany, with those serving stateside reporting the lowest of all.

But the question the researchers were most interested in was, is there a type of person who is less likely to experience distress after exposure to active combat? Take a look at Figure 13.1. Participants were divided into two groups depending on their personalities. The dotted line suggests that for one group of people, high exposure to combat stress was related to more psychological symptoms of distress such as anxiety and depression. However, this was not the case for participants in the second group (the solid line); they had low levels of distress no matter what their exposure to combat stress was.

The same effect was found for PTSD and for physical symptoms of stress: Participants in the second group showed fewer signs of physical and mental distress under conditions of high combat stress than people in the first group.

What was this special personality variable that protected some of the reservists from the negative effects of witnessing combat? It all came down to resilience. Some people have certain personality traits, cognitions, values, and beliefs that protect them in times of stress. In this study, people who were high in hardiness experienced less distress than people who were low in this characteristic.

In this integrative mini-chapter, we discuss how personality traits and cognitions together act on the body's physiology to protect some people from the physical and psychological harm normally associated with stress. This chapter builds on material covered in earlier chapters to give you a sense of how the separate aspects of personality that we have been discussing

Figure 13.1 The effect of combat stress and hardiness on psychological distress. *Source:* Bartone (1999, Figure 3, p. 79). Bartone, P. T. (1999). Hardiness protects against war-related stress in army reserve forces. *Consulting Psychology Journal: Practice and Research,* 51(2), 72–82.

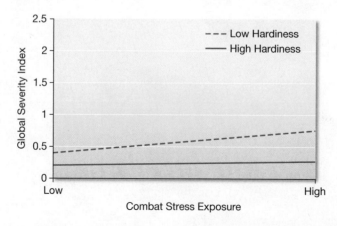

Jerry Miserandino surfing in the summer of 2010 with the Wounded Warriors. The Wounded Warrior Project provides programs and services to injured service members. According to its website, the organization's vision is "to foster the most successful, well-adjusted generation of wounded warriors in this nation's history."

throughout the book work together. Resilience builds on research in physiology, traits, cognition, attachment theory, and regulation and motivation.

What Is Resilience?

Resilience is the ability to recover from tragedy, adversity, hardship, or to adapt to ongoing life stressors (Newman, 2005; Tugade & Fredrickson, 2007). When hit with a traumatic event, everyone is momentarily thrown off balance. But just like how the body regulates temperature through homeostasis, humans also have an amazing, even *magical* (Masten, 2001) capacity to maintain psychological equilibrium and rebound to our former states of well-being (Carver, 1998). The great surprise of research in resilience is that the astounding ability of the human spirit to rebound and achieve good outcomes despite adversity is actually quite common (Masten, 2001, p. 228): We all have the capacity to be resilient (Bonanno, 2004; Masten, 2001; Tugade & Fredrickson, 2007).

When a traumatic event hits, such as the death of a loved one, diagnosis of a major illness, a terrorist attack like September 11, 2001, combat, or violent crime, there are at least four possible responses (Carver, 1998; see Figure 13.2). After the initial shock of the event passes, some people may not survive the event (succumbing) whereas others might be permanently traumatized or

"What does not kill me, makes me stronger."
Friedrich Nietzsche

THINK ABOUT IT

What's so magical about resilience?

Figure 13.2 "Potential responses to trauma. A downturn (physical or psychological) in response to a traumatic or stressful event can be followed by a downward slide and eventual succumbing, by survival in an impaired condition, by recovery to the prior level of functioning, or by the eventual attainment of a level of functioning superior to that displayed earlier—thriving." *Source:* From Carver 1998, Figure 1, p. 246). Reprinted with pernission from Carver, C. S. (1998), "Resilience and thriving: issues, models and linkages," *Journal of Social Issues,* 54(2), 245–266. Permission conveyed through the Copyright Clearance Center.

[Figure 13.2: Graph showing Level of Functioning (y-axis) versus Time (x-axis). An "Adverse Event" marked by a downward arrow divides the graph. Four response curves are shown: Thriving (rises above the baseline), Resilience (recovery) (returns to baseline), Survival with Impairment (partial recovery below baseline), and Succumbing (continues to decline).]

crippled by the event (survival with impairment). We are interested in the two groups of people who may recover (resilience) or even achieve a better level of functioning (thriving) than before the event, such as people who say that their illnesses or tragedies were the best things that ever happened to them because these events challenged them to live better.

Psychologists have proposed at least four kinds of models of how personality impacts health (Smith, 2006b). First, according to **health behavior models**, some people, like those higher in Conscientiousness or with an internal locus of control, adopt a healthier lifestyle and take better care of themselves such as eating a healthy diet, exercising, and not smoking. Second, according to **transactional stress moderation models**, some personality traits, like Neuroticism or sensation seeking, may influence a person's exposure to stressful or dangerous circumstances. For example, recall from Chapter 7 how high sensation seekers seek out situations and behaviors, such as unsafe sexual practices and recreational drug use, that actually place them at an increased risk for injury and illness (Hoyle et al., 2000; Kaestner et al., 1977; Mawson et al., 1988; Zuckerman, 2007).

Constitutional predisposition models suggest that there may be some underlying genetic or constitutional factor that influences both personality and disease. For example, recall Hans Eysenck's Psychoticism-Extraversion-Neuroticism model (Eysenck, 1990) and Jeffrey Gray's reward sensitivity theory (Corr, 2008b) from Chapter 7. Both theories claim that differences in personality come from differences in physiological reactivity and neurology. The constitutional predisposition model suggests that these biological differences may also be related to physical or psychological disorders.

Finally, **interactional stress moderation models** are perhaps the most fascinating of all and the ones we focus on here. These models suggest that personality characteristics modify physiological responses by reducing or increasing them. For example, in Chapter 10 we saw how optimism bolsters the immune system making people less susceptible to damage from long-term stress (Brydon et al., 2009). Are there other personality characteristics that can help us be resilient in the face of adversity?

Characteristics of Resilient People

THINK ABOUT IT

What characteristics of the five-factor model might be related to resilience?

What kind of person is more likely to recover from a stressful event? Personality psychologists have pursued the answer to this question from at least three different lines of research. Resilient people tend to be high in hardiness, trait resilience, and to experience lots of positive emotions. These personality characteristics, along with a healthy dose of positive emotions such as joy, interest, contentment, pride, love, elevation, and happiness, may protect people from the deleterious effects of stress and facilitate recovery from trauma.

THINK ABOUT IT

How might a person high in Neuroticism create more stress for themselves?

Grammy-award winning singer, songwriter, and breast cancer survivor Sheryl Crow as spokesperson for the National Breast Cancer Coalition urging congress to pass legislation to increase funding for breast cancer research.

Hardiness: Control, Commitment, and Challenge

Have you ever noticed that some people seem to catch a cold at the worst time of the semester? Endocrinologist and pioneer researcher on the biology of stress, Hans Selye, recognized over 50 years ago that there must be something unique that allows some people to experience high levels of stress without becoming ill whereas others succumb to illness (Selye, 1956). To find out what personality characteristics distinguished these so-called hardy types from others, researchers embarked on a 12-year-long study of middle and upper managers of the Illinois Bell Telephone Company. At the time, the industry was undergoing deregulation so that the workers experienced high stress, facing both industry and company reorganization.

In the first of many studies, the researchers divided this sample of highly stressed workers into those who experienced a high rate of illness and those with a low rate of illness. Working with a small subset of the entire sample, they identified personality characteristics that distinguished the high and low illness group from each other. They then cross-validated their results from this subset on the rest of the sample. Of course, based on theorizing of the time, the researchers had some idea of what characteristics might be related to hardiness. Hardy executives, those who stayed healthy despite being under high stress, were higher in the three Cs of control, commitment, and challenge (Kobasa, 1979; see Figure 13.3).

First, hardy people believe that they can control their own outcomes and reinforcements. As we saw in Chapter 10, an internal locus of control prevents people from feeling helpless, being passive, and giving up in the face of adversity (Hiroto, 1974). A sense of control makes hardy people dig in and try to change the course of events around them for the better (Maddi, Kahn, & Maddi, 1998).

Second, hardy people are also actively engaged in the social world around them. They are committed to others and to causes greater than themselves. They use their sense of commitment to get involved rather than alienated, to turn their stressful experiences into something interesting or important (Maddi et al., 1998).

Finally, challenge is seeing the negative event as an opportunity rather than as the end of the world. For example, I knew a resilient woman who was about to lose her hair due to the side effects of chemotherapy. Rather than being upset, she decided that this was the perfect time to try out a new hair color, one that she was ordinarily too timid to wear in public.

Even when things are going well, hardy people know how to get the most out of life by reflecting on their experiences and interactions with others, savoring them and learning what they can from them. A person without this sense of challenge would not be able to grow and develop from his or her experiences (Maddi, 2002). In contrast, hardy people seek fulfillment in their lives. They approach life seeking continual growth and challenge rather than routine, security, and ease (Maddi et al., 1998).

Together these three values help a hardy person get involved, take action, and turn a stressful event into something manageable, interesting, important, and a learning experience (Maddi, 2002).

In numerous research studies with different populations, hardiness is related to better health, protection against burnout, greater activity in the elderly, better quality of life among those facing a serious illness, better performance, less stress in the face of life changes, more effective coping, engagement in healthier behaviors, and greater immune response (Maddi et al., 1998). One study found that hardiness provided greater protection

"Stressed" spelled backward is "desserts"!

"Brick walls are there for a reason. The brick walls are not there to keep us out; the brick walls are there to give us a chance to show how badly we want something. The brick walls are there to stop the people who don't want it badly enough. They are there to stop the other people!"

Randy Pausch

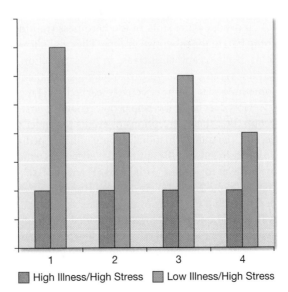

Figure 13.3 Schematic comparing high hardiness and low hardiness groups on four key variables: 1 = Perception of Personal Stress; 2 = Internal Locus of Control; 3 = Commitment to Own Values; 4 = Seeking Out Challenge. *Source:* Based on data from Kobasa (1979).

■ High Illness/High Stress   ■ Low Illness/High Stress

Alexandra "Alex" Scott battled childhood cancer throughout most of her young life. Though she died at age 8, she coped with her illness by raising over $1 million by selling lemonade to help find a cure for cancer. The Alex's Lemonade Stand foundation continues the work she started.

The Chinese symbol for "crisis" is made up of two words, one meaning danger and the other meaning opportunity.

"It's just a speed bump, it's not a dead end."

Dimitrios Diamantaras

THINK ABOUT IT

How is hardiness similar to locus of control, explanatory style, or dispositional optimism discussed in Chapter 10?

against illness than social support or physical exercise (Maddi et al., 1998).

According to Salvatore Maddi and his colleagues (Maddi, 1987; Maddi & Kobasa, 1984), when we face a stressful event, our immediate response is arousal. With more events, or more devastating events, or prolonged stress, the stress and strain on a person may produce physical or mental illness, ineffectiveness, a decreased sense of social support, and decreased job satisfaction. However, people high in hardiness face their problems rather than avoid them. They may appraise their own thoughts and emotions raised by the stressful situation, striving to understand them more fully, putting them in a broader perspective, taking actions to decrease their stressfulness, and creating meaning around the event. Through what Maddi and his colleagues call **transformational coping**, people high in hardiness turn the experience into something less threatening and ultimately even growth enhancing.

In one study, managers at a utility company who volunteered for a stress management course were randomly assigned to one of three treatment conditions (Maddi et al., 1998). Regardless of treatment, participants met in small groups for 1.5 hours once a week for 10 weeks. In the hardiness training condition, participants learned about transformational coping through exercises and discussions. In the relaxation/meditation treatment, a standard treatment for stress, participants learned a combination of muscle relaxation exercises, visualization techniques, and simple meditation. In the passive listening condition, participants related their stressful experiences while the facilitator emphasized the importance of finding one's own solution through discussion and reflection with peers in a supportive setting, just like they were doing during the session. All three groups had homework assignments. Although all three treatments are effective ways of managing stress, the researchers predicted that the hardiness training would be superior to the other two methods.

Indeed, participants in the hardiness training group showed a larger gain in hardiness compared to the other two groups. They also showed a greater reduction in tension and symptoms of illness and an increase in job satisfaction and perceived social support. Not only did hardiness cause these positive outcomes, but the positive attitude associated with hardiness is something that can be effectively learned and taught (Maddi et al., 1998).

How does hardiness help people rebound? First, by finding meaning even under duress, hardy people alter their perceptions of events to render them less stressful (Maddi & Kobasa, 1984). Second, the transformational coping of hardy people is an effective way of coping (Funk, 1992), probably because of the optimism it engenders which, as we saw in Chapter 10, is a very powerful mechanism for coping with stress (Peterson, 2000; Scheier et al., 2001). Also, transformational coping is an active problem-focused strategy rather than a passive emotion-focused strategy for dealing with a traumatic event (Scheier & Carver, 1985). Third, hardy people are more engaged with people, and psychologists know that social support is very important (Cobb, 1976). People low in hardiness do not have these sources of social support (Maddi & Kobasa, 1984). Finally, people high in hardiness—no doubt due to their internal locus of control—live healthier lives and take better care of themselves (Lefcourt, 1982; Selander et al., 2005).

As promising as these findings are, newer research found many problems with the concept of hardiness (Funk, 1992; Funk & Houston, 1987). First, the three components of hardiness—control, commitment, and challenge—appear to be separate components rather than aspects of a single personality type. That is, they don't seem to go together the same way the facets of Neuroticism or Extraversion go together, for example (e.g., Costa & McCrae, 1992). Also, any one of these three components helps buffer people from stress; having all three components doesn't provide any greater advantage than having just one.

A second, and perhaps bigger problem is that hardiness is not a unique concept: it overlaps with other concepts such as dispositional optimism (Scheier & Carver, 1987), locus of control (Hull, Van Treuren, & Virnelli, 1987), and Neuroticism (Funk, 1992). That is, hardiness does not explain or predict outcomes any better than these other variables. In one study, hardy people scored significantly higher on Extraversion, Openness and Conscientiousness and lower on Neuroticism on the NEO Personality Inventory than people low in hardiness (Ramanaiah & Sharpe, 1999; see also Robins, Caspi, Moffitt, & Stouthamer-Loeber, 1996). Further, the effects of hardiness are eliminated when Neuroticism scores are included, suggesting that hardiness overlaps with emotional stability (Funk, 1992).

Finally, like resilience, we know that hardiness is related to lower levels of illness and distress, but we do not know why. This could be due to the usual bias with self-report research, problems with the scales used to measure hardiness, imprecision of the definition of hardiness, or flawed research designs testing for hardiness effects (Funk, 1992; Funk & Houston, 1987). There is not even a standard questionnaire for measuring hardiness, making it difficult to compare and evaluate findings across studies (Funk, 1992).

For example, both people high in Neuroticism and people low in hardiness are more negative in their self-reports. People high in Neuroticism report more physical symptoms and view their life more negatively than people low in Neuroticism, even though there are no differences in objective measures of health or quality of life (Funk, 1992). People low in hardiness share a similar reporting bias, where they report more symptoms and less life satisfaction than people high in hardiness (Rhodewalt & Zone, 1989).

Further, this negativity of hardy/neurotic people may actually create social worlds that are more stressful than those of people without these characteristics (Rhodewalt & Zone, 1989), illustrating the transactional stress moderation model discussed previously. Some have claimed that both lack of control and lack of commitment are stressful. No wonder that people without control or commitment—those low in hardiness—are more distressed than people with these characteristics (Hull et al., 1987)!

The controversy surrounding the concept of hardiness suggests that control, commitment, and challenge may not be the key characteristics that protect people from illness. Instead, variables that are confounded with hardiness—such as negative and positive emotion—may be responsible for the protective effect of hardiness.

> **THINK ABOUT IT**
>
> Is the report bias of people high in Neuroticism due to their traits or their cognitions? Can it be changed?

Trait Resilience

The term *resilience* first appeared in the psychological literature over 60 years ago in dissertations written by psychologists and collaborators Jack and Jeanne Block in the early 1950s. In keeping with the Freudian thinking of the day, the Blocks reasoned that people would either exert more or less control over their own emotions and actions in response to a situational stressor. Some people, those who are better able to roll with the punches say, are better able to respond flexibly to a frustration or a stressor and are quicker to return to their characteristic level of self-control. They termed this **ego-resilience** which is what we might think of as self-regulation today (see Chapter 9). Ego-resiliency referred to the ability to modify one's responses to meet the requirements of a stressful situation and to return to one's characteristic level of self-regulation after a stressor (Block & Kremen, 1996). Researchers today refer to this concept as **trait resilience.** The Ego-Resiliency Scale (Block & Kremen, 1996; see Table 13.1) is one of many scales designed to measure resilience (Ahern, Kiehl, Sole, & Byers, 2006).

"Man never made any material as resilient as the human spirit."
Bern Williams

Table 13.1 Items of the Ego-Resiliency (ER89) Scale

1. I am generous with my friends.
2. I quickly get over and recover from being startled.
3. I enjoy dealing with new and unusual situations.
4. I usually succeed in making a favorable impression on people.
5. I enjoy trying new foods I have never tasted before.
6. I am regarded as a very energetic person.
7. I like to take different paths to familiar places.
8. I am more curious than most people.
9. Most of the people I meet are likable.
10. I usually think carefully about something before acting.
11. I like to do new and different things.
12. My daily life is full of things that keep me interested.
13. I would be willing to describe myself as a pretty "strong" personality.
14. I get over my anger at someone reasonably quickly.

Note: Respond to each item using the following scale: 1 = *Does not apply at all;* 2 = *Applies slightly, if at all;* 3 = *Applies somewhat;* and 4 = *Applies very strongly.* In one sample of college students aged 17 to 40, ER scores ranged from 28 to 54 with a mean of 42 (SD = 6.41) (Tugade & Fredrickson, 2004).

Source: Block and Kremen (1996, Table 1, p. 352); Tugade and Fredrickson (2004). Block, J., & Kremen, A. M. (1996). IQ and ego-resiliency: Conceptual and empirical connections and separateness. *Journal of Personality and Social Psychology,* 70(2), 349–361. Copyright American Psychological Association. Reprinted with permission.

We can think of trait resilience or self-control as occurring on a continuum, where some people may undercontrol their responses, others might overcontrol their responses, but resilient people are able to strike an appropriate balance between these two extremes (Block & Kremen, 1996). In a sample of adolescent boys, the researchers identified three personality types who differed in the extent to which they were able to regulate their own behaviors: overcontrolled, undercontrolled, and resilient (Robins et al., 1996).

Resilients were best able to regulate their own behavior, responding appropriately to frustrations and stressors and returning to their usual state. Caregivers described them as assertive, expressive, energetic, dependable, personable, open-minded, smart, and self-confident. In contrast, overcontrollers were shy, timid, interpersonally sensitive, and dependent. They were also somewhat anxious and withdrawn, yet warm, cooperative, and considerate. Undercontrolled boys were impulsive, self-centered, manipulative, confrontational, and outgoing. However, they showed significantly greater delinquent behaviors, performed worse in school, and scored lower on an intelligence test than boys in the other two groups. In addition, these three groups differed on the five factors of Extraversion, Agreeableness, Conscientiousness, Emotional Stability, and Openness (see Figure 13.4).

Similar results were found in a study of 18-year-old men and women. Those who were high in trait resilience reported being more flexible and adaptable and showed better psychological adjustment than people who were low in trait resilience. Resilients also reported being more confident and experiencing more positive emotions. In contrast, overcontrollers may rigidly overregulate instead of showing flexibility when faced with a stressful experience whereas undercontrollers may underregulate and have no clear strategy for how to manage stress. Neither of these two extremes is adaptive (Block & Kremen, 1996).

Resilient undergraduates were rated by acquaintances as having wide interests, a high aspiration level, and being socially skilled, confident, assertive, and cheerful. They had meaningful lives. Undercontrollers were described as being moody, unpredictable, assertive, rebellious, self-indulgent, and dramatizing. Overcontrollers were rated as more dependable, consistent, calm, and bland (Letzring, Block, & Funder, 2005).

Much research supports the notion that trait resilient people do indeed rebound from stressful experiences faster physiologically (Tugade & Fredrickson, 2004) and emotionally (Ong, Bergeman, Bisconti, & Wallace, 2006; Waugh, Fredrickson, & Taylor, 2008) than people low in resilience (Tugade & Fredrickson, 2007).

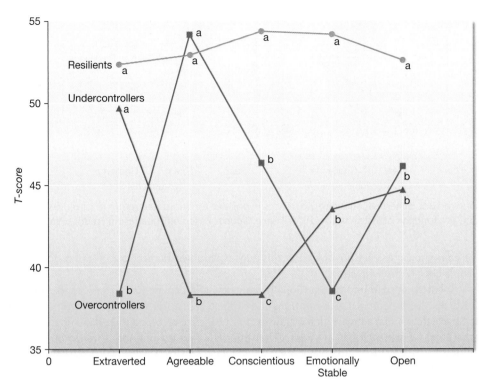

Figure 13.4 Big Five profiles of the three adolescent personality types. Means with different letters differ at $p < .01$. *Source:* From Robins et al. (1996, Figure 1, p. 163). Robins, R. W., Caspi, A., Moffitt, T. E., & Stouthamer-Loeber, M. (1996). Resilient, overcontrolled, and undercontrolled boys: Three replicable personality types. *Journal of Personality and Social Psychology*, 70(1), 157–171. Copyright American Psychological Association. Reprinted with permission.

SEE FOR YOURSELF

The next time you are facing a stressful situation, try viewing it as a challenge or opportunity instead of a threat.

For example, in one experiment undergraduates who were high and low in trait resilience prepared an impromptu speech that they thought would be videotaped and critiqued by other undergraduates. For half of the participants, this task was described as a challenge; for the other half it was described as threatening. While anticipating the speech and then finding out no speech would be given, researchers recorded the cardiovascular reactivity of the participants. They found that the blood pressure and heart rate of people high in trait resilience returned to baseline faster than that of low resilients and that they experienced more positive emotions, especially if they were in the threat condition. However, there was no difference in cardiovascular reactivity or positive emotion between people high and low in resilience in the challenge condition (see Figure 13.5). This suggests that viewing a situation as a challenge, rather than as a threat, induces positive emotions in low-resilient people, providing them with a measure of protection comparable to what highly resilient people are able to do naturally (Tugade & Frederickson, 2004).

Recall that viewing events as a challenge is one of the three Cs of hardiness. This study further suggests that hardiness and trait resilience are similar in that people high in either characteristic experience more positive emotions than those low in hardiness or low in trait resilience. Indeed,

Viewing a situation as a challenge rather than a threat helps protect people during a stressful event.

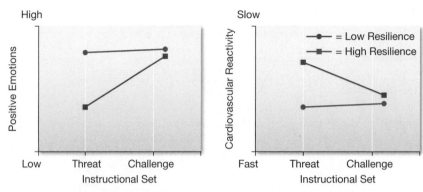

Figure 13.5 Schematic showing differences in positive emotions and return to cardiovascular base rate as a function of instructions and resilience. *Source:* Based on Tugade and Fredrickson (2004).

the ability to experience positive emotions may explain *why* hardiness and trait resilience help people cope better with stress.

What about rebounding emotionally from stressful experiences? Consider the following study on positive and negative emotions and resilience. In a study of men and women aged 62 to 80, participants who were high or low in trait resilience recorded their daily fluctuations in emotions and distress for 30 to 45 days. They found that positive emotions were more common among resilient people (Ong, Bergeman, et al., 2006).

To understand the significance of this finding, we need to first understand a bit about how emotions work. When we are not under stress, positive emotions and negative emotions tend to be separate experiences (Diener & Emmons, 1984). That is, it is *not* the case that the more sadness we feel on a given day the less happiness we feel, or vice versa. We can feel sadness while watching a movie but delight in the experience of watching it with friends while sharing a bowl of popcorn. We can get angry at the driver who cut us off on the way to a restaurant, but then enjoy being out with the gang. The number of positive experiences people have over the course of a typical day is not negatively correlated with the number of negative experiences they report. However, when we are dealing with a stressful event, positive and negative emotions are negatively correlated, so that that the more sadness we feel, the less happiness we feel (Ong, Bergeman, et al., 2006).

In this study of daily moods that's just what the researchers found. People low—but not high—in resilience showed an inverse relationship between negative and positive emotion while under distress: the more negative emotion they reported on a given day the less positive emotion they reported feeling. This was especially true on highly stressful days. However, highly resilient people, even under duress, experienced a fair amount of both negative and positive experiences. In addition, these effects were virtually identical whether hardiness or trait resilience was used to identify resilient people (Ong, Bergeman, et al., 2006).

Remarkably, these findings even held for a sample of women who recently lost their husbands, enduring a particularly stressful time in their lives. Highly resilient widows experienced a range of positive emotions, such as cheerfulness, peacefulness, and happiness, right along with negative emotions such as depression, worry, and anxiety (Ong, Bergeman, et al., 2006; see Figure 13.6).

Together, these two studies suggest that the reason why people high in resilience—defined either as hardiness or as trait resilience—are able to endure and recover from stressful experiences better than people low in resilience has to do with the experiences

---

THINK ABOUT IT

Is it that people low in resilience have fewer opportunities to experience positive emotions or that they are just not uplifted by the opportunities they do have?

Figure 13.6 Relationship between daily positive and negative emotion as a function of trait resilience, on high-stress days in recently widowed women. *Source:* Ong, Bergeman, et al., (2006, Figure 5, p. 742). Ong, A. D., Bergeman, C. S., Bisconti, T. L., & Wallace, K. A. (2006). Psychological resilience, positive emotions, and sucessful adaptation to stress in later life. *Journal of Personality and Social Psychology,* 91(4), 730–749. Copyright American Psychological Association. Reprinted with permission.

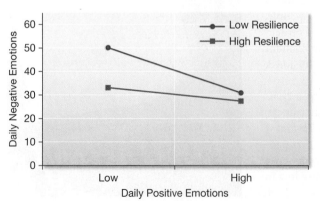

of positive emotions. Positive emotions help people regulate and recover physiologically and emotionally from stress. The key component of resilience may well be the ability to regulate positive emotions (Ong, Bergeman, et al., 2006; Tugade & Fredrickson, 2004, 2007).

Positive Emotions

Positive emotions have proved somewhat of a puzzle to psychologists (Fredrickson, 1998). For one, they don't involve as much physiological arousal as negative emotions do. Second, according to one estimate, negative emotions outnumber positive emotions by a factor of about 3 or 4 to 1. Third, negative emotions seem to have unique facial expressions associated with them whereas many positive emotions share variations of just the one expression: the Duchenne smile or true smile, involving both the mouth and the eyes. For example, there are fewer differences between happiness and joy, interest and wonder, or love and elation than there are between sadness and anger. Fourth, even though it's easy to see how the fight or flight response associated with negative emotions helps preserve our species when faced with life-threatening events, positive emotions don't seem to create the same urgency to take action for self-preservation. Certainly life is more fun with positive emotions, and positive emotions may signal health and well-being, important attributes for mating, but are they truly important for our survival?

> **THINK ABOUT IT**
>
> From an evolutionary perspective, what purpose do positive emotions serve?

Emerging research suggests that positive emotions don't just feel good—they actually do us good (Ong, Bergeman, et al., 2006; see Table 13.2). Positive emotions increase flexibility in thinking and problem solving (Fredrickson & Branigan, 2005; Isen, Daubman, & Nowicki, 1987), undo the physiological effects of negative emotions (Fredrickson & Levenson, 1998; Ong & Allaire, 2005), foster adaptive coping (Folkman & Moskowitz, 2000, 2004), build enduring social connections (Fredrickson & Branigan, 2001; Keltner & Bonanno, 1997), and trigger an upward spiral of increased well-being (Fredrickson, 2000; Fredrickson & Joiner, 2002). Let's take a closer look at some of the research evidence for these conclusions.

Positive Emotions Foster Adaptive Ways of Coping.   The results from the diary study of resilient widows suggest that positive emotions are particularly adaptive when people are under stress or are low in resilience, as they help people recover from adversity (Ong, Bergeman, et al., 2006). This may be because positive emotions interrupt the experience of stress, giving people a much-needed psychological break from their feelings of distress (Folkman & Moskowitz, 2000; Ong, Bergeman, et al., 2006). Positive emotions may also replenish one's ability for self-control, making it easier to adapt to stressors that come along later (c.f., Tangney, Baumeister, & Boone, 2004). For example, adults and elders who were low in Neuroticism (i.e., low in negative emotion), high in Extraversion (high in positive emotion), and high in Openness reported greater well-being and seemed to cope better with stressors in their lives (McCrae & Costa, 1986). Positive emotions help people regulate emotional distress and facilitate the recovery process (Ong, Bergeman, et al., 2006).

> **THINK ABOUT IT**
>
> Is it true that laughter is the best medicine?

In one study of people living with the chronic pain of arthritis or fibromyalgia, feelings of positive affect, such as interest, excitement, enthusiasm, pride, or inspiration, lessened negative feelings like distress, upset, fear, irritability, or nervousness typically experienced along with pain. As pain increased, the buffering effect of positive emotions was even stronger. Positive emotion during a painful episode seemed to interrupt the usual link between pain and

Table 13.2 Don't Worry Be Happy: How Positive Emotions Produce Health and Well-Being

Positive Emotions
1. Foster adaptive ways of coping.
2. Repair the harmful physiological effects of negative emotions.
3. Increase flexibility in thinking.
4. Build enduring social connections.
5. Increase future well-being.

Source: Ong, Bergeman, et al. (2006).

Figure 13.7 The interaction
between weekly positive
affect and pain in women
with arthritis. Positive affect
was related to a weaker link
between pain and negative
affect. Weeks with increased
pain showed less of an
increase in negative affect if
positive affect was also high.
The same pattern of results
was found in women with
fibromyalgia. *Source:* Zautra
(2001, Figure 1, p. 790). Zautra,
A. J., Smith, B., Affleck, G. G., &
Tennen, H. (2001). Examinations
of chronic pain and affect
relationships: Applications of
a dynamic model of affect.
*Journal of Consulting and
Clinical Psychology,* 69(5),
786–795. Copyright American
Psychological Association.
Reprinted with permission.

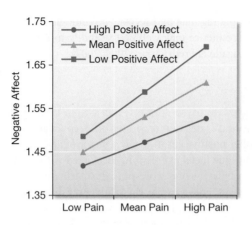

negative affect. Further, the greater the positive affect, the weaker the link between pain and negative affect (Zautra, Smith, Affleck, & Tennen, 2001). In this way, positive emotions lessened the emotional distress people reported feeling (see Figure 13.7).

According to the **broaden-and-build theory**, positive emotions—like elevation (Haidt, 2000), joy, interest, contentment, pride, and love—broaden or expand people's awareness, thoughts, and actions (Fredrickson, 2001). This engagement in new ways of thinking and doing helps build physical, intellectual, social, and psychological resources. Think of it like this: When we are in pain, physical or emotional, we develop a kind of psychological tunnel vision where all we are aware of is our pain. Positive emotions produce the opposite effect, causing us to open up to a wider array of possibilities beyond our immediate situation and ourselves (Fredrickson, 2001). For example, when we are joyful, we feel an urge to play and be creative (Ellsworth & Smith, 1988). When we feel interest, we venture out exploring our world taking in new experiences and information (Csikszentmihalyi, 1990; Ryan & Deci, 2000). When we feel love, we seek out contact and interaction with friends and family (Izard, 1977).

In turn, the expansion of our attention, thoughts, and actions help us build and bank new resources. Through trying new activities we build physical resources, by developing our interests we expand our intellectual resources, by encountering new experiences we build our psychological resources, and by interacting with others we build social resources. No doubt you've heard the advice to "save for a rainy day"? The resources built through the experience of positive emotions act like money in the bank to be drawn on for sustenance during hard times. Taking the metaphor a step further, positive emotions accumulate and compound, much like interest on a savings account, and lead to more positive emotions and better coping in the future (Fredrickson & Joiner, 2002). Essentially, positive emotions help build resilience to future adversities (Fredrickson, 2000; see Figure 13.8).

Figure 13.8 The broaden-and-build theory of positive emotions. *Source:* Frederickson (2002, Figure 9.1, p. 124). Fredrickson, B. L., & Joiner, T. (2002), "Positive emotions trigger upward spirals toward emotional well-being," *Psychological Science,* 13(2), 172–175. Copyright © 2002 by Sage Publications. Reprinted by permission of Sage Publications.

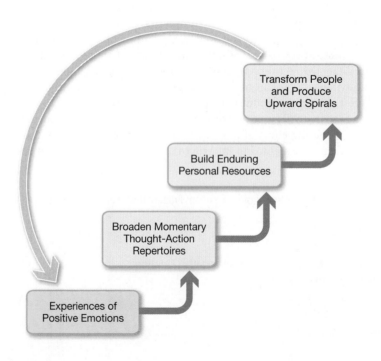

Positive Emotions Repair the Harmful Physiological Effects of Negative Emotions.   The survival benefit of positive emotions may be that they can correct or undo the deleterious physical and psychological effects of prolonged exposure to negative emotions that occur under stress (Fredrickson & Levenson, 1998). Specifically, positive emotions may help the body recover faster from cardiovascular reactivity (Fredrickson, Mancuso, Branigan, & Tugade, 2000).

To test this notion, researchers monitored the blood pressure and heart rate of undergraduate volunteers as they anticipated giving a speech that they believed would be videotaped and later evaluated (Fredrickson et al., 2000). Participants thought that they had a 50–50 chance that a computer would randomly select them to give their speech or that they would watch a film instead. Of course, this manipulation merely served to successfully induce anxiety in the participants. No speeches were actually given and instead, at this point, participants were randomly assigned to view one of three brief film clips. The three films were pretested to be of comparable interest, but to evoke different emotions: waves crashing on a beach (contentment), puppies playing (amusement), or an abstract film of colorful sticks piling up (no emotion).

As you can see in Figure 13.9, participants who watched the contentment and amusement films recovered from the anxiety of anticipating a speech sooner than participants in the neutral film condition. The groups differed in the number of seconds it took to return to their prestress baseline of heart rate and pulse. Positive emotions—whether contentment or amusement—lessened the cardiovascular reactivity associated with anxiety, and they did so even in men and African Americans, groups known to be at particular risk for cardiovascular illness (Fredrickson et al., 2000). In a second study, Fredrickson et al. (2000) ruled out the possibility that positive emotions merely replace negative cardiovascular reactivity with positive reactivity, further supporting the notion that positive emotions counteract the cardiovascular effects of anxiety, fear, and other health-damaging stressors.

Positive Emotions Increase Flexibility in Thinking.   Direct evidence for the broaden-and-build theory comes from an experiment in which undergraduates viewed two emotional film clips and then took a visual processing test or made a list of action tendencies (i.e., things they felt like doing as a result of the emotion elicited by the film). The researchers reasoned that positive emotion would make people think broadly and to imagine many possible actions they could take, whereas negative emotions would make people think more narrowly, focusing on small details and limiting the potential actions they could imagine doing (Fredrickson & Branigan, 2005).

Participants were randomly assigned to view one of five possible clips, varying in the specific positive or negative emotion evoked by the film. Two video clips elicited the positive emotions of amusement (penguins playing) or contentment (a nature film) and two elicited the negative emotions of disgust (bullies taunting Amish passers-by from the movie *Witness*) or anxiety (a prolonged mountain climbing accident from the movie *Cliffhanger*). There was also a neutral film, the same abstract film with colorful sticks used in previous research.

For the visual processing test, participants had to view a series of graphics and judge which of the two arrays was most similar to the target array. Figure 13.10 shows a sample

> **THINK ABOUT IT**
>
> Many hospitals and nursing homes include pet therapy, where dogs visit with the patients. Why might this be an effective treatment?

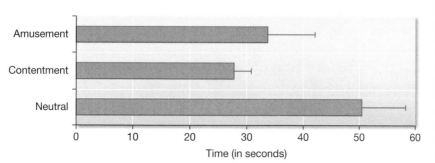

Figure 13.9 Mean duration of cardiovascular reactivity by film. Error bars represent standard errors of the means. *Source:* From Frederickson et al. (2000, Figure 2, p. 248). Frederickson, B. L., Mancuso, R. A., Branigan, C., & Tugade, M. M. (2000). The undoing effect of positive emotions. *Motivation and Emotion,* 24(4), 237–258.

Figure 13.10 An example of stimuli used for the visual processing task. Would participants who felt negative or positive emotions judge similarity based on general characteristics of arrangement and number or on fine details like shape? Test figures at the top shared broad characteristics with the figures below them on the left and narrow characteristics with figures below them on the right. *Source:* From Frederickson and Branigan (2005, Figure 1, p. 317). Fredrickson, B. L., & Branigan, C. (2005), "Positive emotions broaden the scope of attention and throught-action repertoires," *Cognition and Emotion,* 19(3), 313–332. Reprinted by permission of Taylor and Francis.

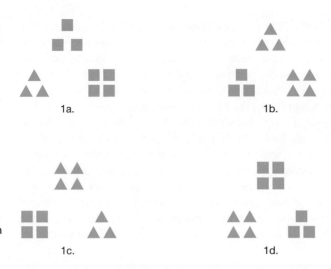

THINK ABOUT IT

If positive emotions make people think more broadly, can they help people think of new solutions to their problems? Can they help them view negative events as challenges rather than threats?

of four stimuli (labeled a–d) used in this experiment. As you can see at the top of the first figure (top left, labeled 1a) participants had to decide whether the three squares (at the very top) were more similar to the three triangles (below them on the left) because they share the same number of items arranged in a triangular format, or if the three squares were more similar to the four squares (below them on the right) because they share the same shape. Previous research had shown that when subjects are anxious or depressed they tend to choose based on the more narrow characteristic of shape, but when they are feeling happy or optimistic they choose similarity based on broader characteristics like number (Fredrickson & Branigan, 2005).

The researchers wondered, how would the emotions of amusement, contentment, disgust, and anxiety, evoked in participants by the film clips, affect their ratings in this task? Viewing either of the two positive films caused participants to think more broadly, judging a visual array based on general characteristics (arrangement, number) rather than on fine details (shape), when compared to the judgment of participants who watched the neutral film (see Figure 13.11). Participants who viewed the negative films tended to make narrower judgments compared to the neutral film, but these did not quite reach statistical significance.

Figure 13.11 Mean number of global choices on the visual processing task by film viewing condition. *Source:* From Frederickson and Branigan (2005, Figure 2, p. 323). Fredrickson, B. L., & Branigan, C. (2005), "Positive emotions broaden the scope of attention and throught-action repertoires," *Cognition and Emotion,* 19(3), 313–332. Reprinted by permission of Taylor and Francis.

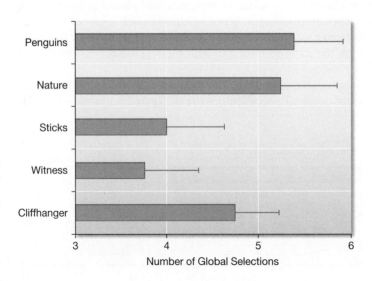

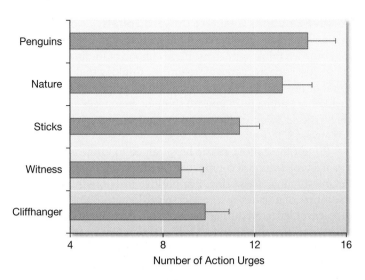

Figure 13.12 Mean number of action tendencies listed by film viewing condition. *Source:* From Frederickson and Branigan (2005, Figure 3, p. 324). Fredrickson, B. L., & Branigan, C. (2005), "Positive emotions broaden the scope of attention and throught-action repertoires," *Cognition and Emotion,* 19(3), 313–332. Reprinted by permission of Taylor and Francis.

Similarly, viewing either of the two positive films gave participants more ideas of what they would like to do than the neutral film. But viewing two negative films produced significantly fewer desires than in participants who viewed the neutral film (see Figure 13.12). In fact, newer research suggests that the intensity of the emotion, which increases the tendency to act, is what causes the broadening and narrowing of attention, not whether the emotion is positive or negative (Gable & Harmon-Jones, 2010).

As you can see, when people are feeling positive emotions they feel more of a desire to act, attend to stimuli in a global way, and think more broadly. Negative emotions decrease the desire to act, and cause a narrowing of attention and thought. Other studies have also found that positive moods make people think in unusually flexible, creative, and receptive ways (Isen, 1987). Further, researchers found that this effect is linked to increases in brain dopamine, the neurotransmitter that responds to pleasure and incentive (Ashby, Isen, & Turken, 1999).

Positive Emotions Build Enduring Social Connections.   Positive emotions function as rewards or reinforcements for behaviors we find rewarding in others and which they find rewarding in us. Positive emotions lead to continued interactions whereas negative emotions deter undesirable behavior and discourage further interaction (Keltner & Haidt, 2001). For example, depressed people often—and alas correctly!—perceive that others are rejecting them; after all, they are no fun to be around (Myers, 2000a). Humor, amusement, smiling, and play—all of which are often expressions of affection and love—are not only forms of communication, but they increase the responsiveness of others, build social bonds, and solidify attachments between and among individuals (Fredrickson & Branigan, 2001). In turn, the social connections built and strengthened through shared positive emotions become sources of support in times of need. In fact, resilient people have a knack for eliciting positive emotions in the people they interact with (Tugade, Fredrickson, & Barrett, 2004).

"Smile and the whole world smiles with you, cry and you cry alone."

Can positive emotions build social connections that can endure even the death of a loved one? Apparently so! Men and women aged 21 to 55 who lost a spouse or partner in the previous 3 to 6 months who could talk about their deceased partners with at least one genuine instance of smiling and laughter remembered their relationships as healthier and more warm than people who did not show a genuine smile and laughter (Keltner & Bonanno, 1997). While talking about their deceased partners to an interviewer, people who laughed expressed less distress, less negative emotions such as anger, distress, fear, or guilt, and greater positive, relative to negative, emotions.

Positive Emotions Generate Upward Spirals. Not only does finding meaning in a traumatic event lead to positive emotions that facilitate coping, but these positive emotions, because they broaden thinking, increase the likelihood of finding meaning in future events (Fredrickson, 2000). Just as depression and pessimistic thinking build on each other and lead to a downward spiral of physical and psychological illness, improved coping and positive emotions build on each other leading to an upward spiral of good feelings, effective coping, increased well-being (Fredrickson & Joiner, 2002), and psychological resilience (Cohn, Fredrickson, Brown, Mikels, & Conway, 2009).

To test these ideas, researchers wanted to know if positive emotions led to an increased use of a broad-minded coping style (Fredrickson, 1998). Undergraduate men and women filled out questionnaires assessing their positive emotions, negative emotions, and coping styles over the course of a semester (Fredrickson & Joiner, 2002). When faced with "the most important problem" they faced during the past year, participants with broad-minded coping were more likely to say that they tried to "think of different ways to deal with the problem" or tried to "step back from the situation and be more objective."

In addition, the more positive emotions participants felt at the beginning of the study, the more broad-minded coping they showed 5 weeks later. Broad-minded coping was the only coping strategy that was related to positive emotions; no coping style was related to negative emotion. In addition, participants who used broad-minded coping showed an increase in positive emotions, but not a decrease in negative emotions, over the course of the study. Finally, the researchers found that broad-minded coping and positive emotions built on each other over time (Fredrickson & Joiner, 2002).

> "The pain passes but beauty endures."
>
> *Auguste Renoir, to Henri Matisse, when asked why he continued to paint with crippling arthritis in his hands*

Interestingly, the key difference between participants who relied on broad-minded coping or another style was not in their experience of negative emotions or the amount of distress they felt, but in their experience of positive emotions. Positive emotions led to a broader way of thinking, which in turn led to a broader way of coping, which led to more positive emotions in the following weeks and an increase in their overall well-being.

A more recent study, using similar methods, took these results a step further and discovered that positive emotions increased trait resilience and life satisfaction in undergraduates over the course of a month (Cohn et al., 2009). Participants who experienced higher average levels of amusement, awe, compassion, contentment, gratitude, hope, interest, joy, love, and pride on a daily basis not only felt better but they became more trait resilient as well. This ability to adapt to change, including recognizing opportunities, adapting to circumstances, and bouncing back from adversity, helped them deal with a range of life's challenges and gave them feelings of satisfaction with the course of their lives (Cohn et al., 2009).

The Seven Habits of Highly Resilient People

> "Live well, love much, laugh often."

If anything, the research just reviewed suggests that, rather than one hardy or resilient personality type, there may be *many* pathways to resilience (Bonanno, 2004). In fact, there is remarkable overlap, as you no doubt noticed, among hardiness, trait resilience, and positive emotions. These three lines of research have suggested at least seven characteristics, experiences, and behaviors that build resilience and buffer against stress (see Table 13.3). Let's take a closer look at some of these.

As we saw, positive emotions produce health and well-being by fostering adaptive coping, repairing the physiological wear-and-tear of negative emotions, increasing cognitive flexibility, building enduring social connections, and generating a store of good feelings for the future. One very big way of building resilience, therefore, is to cultivate positive emotions including joy, playfulness, interest, curiosity, wonder, flow, contentment, and love.

If positive emotions help people physically and mentally cope with adversity, then laughter may indeed be the best medicine. Laughter helps people cope with traumatic events (Keltner & Bonanno, 1997) and enhances immune system functioning in people who are prone to laugh a lot (Dillon, Minchoff, & Baker, 1985–1986). Resilient people use humor as a coping mechanism (Tugade & Fredrickson, 2004, 2007).

Table 13.3 The Seven Habits of Highly Resilient People

1. Positive emotions and laughter: joy, playfulness, interest, curiosity, wonder, flow, contentment, love, etc.

2. Loving relationships with family and friends

3. A meaningful life

4. Optimism and hope

5. Gratitude

6. Relaxation

7. Happiness

An important part of getting through tough times is having loving relationships with family and friends. Resilient people have a network of people they can depend on in times of stress (Cobb, 1976; Maddi & Kobasa, 1984). Recall that according to the self-determination theory, relatedness—or the interest, time, and energy others give to us that lead us to feel connected to and valued by others—is an essential psychological need (Connell, 1990). Without this, people feel unmotivated, disaffected, and disengaged and show poor well-being (Deci & Ryan, 2008b). Similarly, attachment theory also supports the importance of relationships (Ainsworth et al., 1974; Bowlby, 1969, 1973, 1980).

Having meaning in one's life leads to better physical and psychological well-being (Davis, Nolen-Hoeksema, & Larsen, 1998; Taylor, Kemeny, Reed, Bower, & Gruenewald, 2000). Meaning creates positive emotions that help people cope with adversity (Folkman & Moskowitz, 2000; Fredrickson, 2000) and also increases immune system functioning (Epel, McEwen, & Ickovics, 1998). Happy people also have satisfying work that provides them with feelings of flow, a state marked by deep enjoyment, intense concentration, and complete absorption in an activity (Myers & Diener, 1995).

People can find positive meaning through positive reappraisal, where they reframe adverse events in a positive light; by infusing ordinary events with positive value; and by pursuing and attaining realistic goals (Fredrickson, 2000). In a study of people who were caring for a loved one with AIDS/HIV, 22% of caregivers reported that they using positive reappraisal in their daily lives by feeling connected to others and cared about (Folkman, Moskowitz, Ozer, & Park, 1997). Other ways of finding meaning included having an opportunity to be distracted from everyday cares (21%), feeling a sense of achievement, pride, or self-esteem (17%), feeling hope or optimism (13%), and receiving affirmation or validation from others (11%). Religion is yet another way that people can find meaning in their lives (Fredrickson, 2000).

> "Red, hope is a good thing, maybe the best of things, and no good thing ever dies."
> *Andy Dufresne in* The Shawshank Redemption

Like positive emotions, hope appears to help lessen the impact of negative emotions and facilitate recovery from stress (Ong, Edwards, & Bergeman, 2006; Snyder, 2002). The more hope a person felt on a given day, agreeing with statements like "At the present time, I am energetically pursuing my goals" and "There are lots of ways around any problem that I am facing now," the less impact negative emotions had on them and the better able they were to cope with adversity. This effect was even stronger in people who had characteristically high levels of trait hope (Ong, Edwards, & Bergeman, 2006; see Table 13.4).

Did you ever have somebody tell you to count your blessings? This bit of folk wisdom does seem to help people cope with the negative events in their life by helping them focus on the good as well as reflect on how they are better off than others (Emmons & McCullough, 2003). Either way, feelings of gratitude (Emmons & McCullough, 2003), contentment (Fredrickson, 2000), and loving kindness toward others (Fredrickson, Cohn, Coffey, Pek, & Finkel, 2008) increase positive emotions and boost well-being. Undergraduates who kept a weekly gratitude journal reported fewer physical symptoms, exercised more regularly, felt better about their lives, and made more progress toward important academic, interpersonal, or health-related personal

The Viennese psychologist and Holocaust survivor Viktor Frankl took the words of Friedrich Nietzsche to heart that "He who has a why can endure any how," founding his logotherapy school of psychotherapy on the importance of finding meaning in one's life (Frankl, 1959).

goals. Students who listed their daily hassles or merely reported the good and bad events of their week did not reap these psychological and physical benefits (Emmons & McCullough, 2003).

Finally, relaxation through imagery, muscle relaxation, yoga, biofeedback, or meditation practice are also effective ways of dealing with stress (Fredrickson, 2000) and bolstering immune system functioning (Davidson et al., 2003).

Based on this review, you can see how resilient people are better equipped to cope with stressful events. The hardy reservists from the Bartone (1999) study that opened this chapter had a combination of personality traits, cognitions, values, and beliefs that protected them in times of stress, including many of these characteristics of resilient people such as positive emotions, an optimistic outlook, close relationships, and meaning in their lives.

Table 13.4 Items of the State Hope Scale

1. If I should find myself in a jam, I could think of many ways to get out of it.

2. At the present time, I am energetically pursuing my goals.

3. There are lots of ways around any problem that I am facing now.

4. Right now I see myself as being pretty successful.

5. I can think of many ways to reach my current goal.

6. At this time, I am meeting the goals that I have set for myself.

Note: Please take a few moments to focus on yourself and what is going on in your life at this moment. Once you have this *here and now* set, go ahead and answer each item according to the scale. Please select the number that best describes *how you think about yourself right now* and put that number in the blank provided: 1 = *Definitely False;* 2 = *Mostly False;* 3 = *Somewhat False;* 4 = *Slightly False;* 5 = *Slightly True;* 6 = *Somewhat True;* 7 = *Mostly True;* and 8 = *Definitely True.* In one sample of college students, the mean of 444 students was 37 (SD = 6.33).

Source: Snyder, Sympson, Ybasco and Borders (1996, Appendix, p. 335). Snyder, C. R., Sympson, S. C., Ybasco, F. C., & Borders, T. F. (1996). Development and validation of the state hope scale. *Journal of Personality and Social Psychology, 70*(2), 321–335. Copyright American Psychological Association. Reprinted with permission.

The Personality of Everyday Life

Who is happy?

Happy people, in particular, demonstrate a number of habits that help people cope with adversity. Happy people are more successful than unhappy people when it comes to income, career, and health (Lyubomirsky, King, & Diener, 2005), but money cannot buy happiness (Myers, 2000b). Happy people are also more energetic, decisive, creative, and sociable, and report a great deal of positive emotions in their lives (Myers, 2000a). Because people's judgments of life satisfaction come from the balance between positive and negative emotions (Diener & Larsen, 1993), positive emotions may be at the heart of the positive outcomes in life due to happiness (Lyubomirsky et al., 2005).

Happy people also tend to have high self-esteem, an internal locus of control, and to be high in Extraversion (Myers & Diener, 1995) and low in Neuroticism (Lyubomirsky et al., 2005). Extraverts are more engaged in events in their daily lives that have the potential to inspire more positive emotions. In contrast, people who are high in Neuroticism are more sensitive to the negative events in their lives (Zautra, Affleck, Tennen, Reich, & Davis, 2005). Recall that people high in trait resilience were also high in Extraversion and high in emotional stability (Robins et al., 1996).

Happy people also have close, loving relationships with family and friends including people with whom they are comfortable sharing intimate concerns (Myers, 2000b). For example, married people tend to be happier than unmarried people. Happy people are more successful in marriage and friendships (Lyubomirsky et al., 2005).

Finally, happy people tend to be religious and attend services frequently (Myers, 2000b). Religion may increase happiness because it often provides answers to life's deep questions, a sense of meaning and purpose for our existence, hope, and a supportive community (Myers & Diener, 1995). No doubt you recognize that happy people and hardy people share the characteristics of personal control, commitment to others, and imparting meaning on adversity by seeing it as a challenge rather than a threat (Maddi et al., 1998).

As a result, happy people are better able to tolerate frustration and to delay immediate gratification (Myers, 2000a). They are more often lenient, loving, and forgiving, and less often abusive. They are less likely to overreact to slight criticism. They prefer upbeat music, stories, movies, and people, and tend to be more optimistic, focusing on the brighter side of life (Myers, 2000a) and demonstrating an optimistic explanatory style (Fredrickson, 2000).

Chapter Summary

In this chapter we started out with the question of why some people are able to bounce back from adversity and achieve good outcomes in life. Though you may think there is something special about the personality of highly resilient people, resilience is actually more common than many people think and involves characteristics that we all have the ability to cultivate in ourselves.

How does personality impact health? There are four kinds of models that psychologists have proposed to understand the impact of personality on physical and psychological health: health behavior models, transactional stress moderation models, constitutional predisposition models, and interactional stress moderation models.

The elements of what makes people resilient seem to boil down to hardiness (i.e., internal locus of control, commitment, and challenge), trait resilience (i.e., ego resilience or the ability to self-regulate emotional reactions and behaviors; neither overcontrolled nor undercontrolled), and positive emotions. People who are high in hardiness, for example, use transformational

✓⦁ **Study** and **Review**
on **mysearchlab.com**
Go online for more resources to help you review.

coping to turn traumatic experiences into growth-enhancing ones. Despite initially promising research in this area, hardiness may be confounded with other variables that are known to be related to health and well-being (e.g., control, positive affect, Neuroticism).

Researchers are just now appreciating the power of positive emotions to foster adaptive ways of coping, repair the harmful physiological effects of negative emotions, increase flexibility in thinking, build enduring social connections, and generate good feelings as protection against future stressors. Positive emotions function like money in the bank, protecting us in case of emergency and amassing good feelings for the future. Much of the power of positive emotions comes from the broaden-and-build theory that says that positive emotions broaden our attention, thoughts, and range of possible behaviors. These in turn lead to better ways of coping and greater resilience in the face of adversity.

Finally, what does it take to build physical and psychological resilience? Based on research reviewed in this chapter, the answer is positive emotions—including happiness, laughter, love, hope, and gratitude—an optimistic outlook, close relationships, a meaningful life, and relaxation. Indeed, many of these were identified as characteristics of the hardy reservists from the Bartone (1999) study that opened this chapter. Having this combination of personality traits, cognitions, values, and beliefs protects people in times of stress, whether it be giving a speech in front of a class or coping with combat during times of war.

Review Questions

1. Discuss the Bartone (1999) study of military personnel and hardiness. What personality characteristics make up hardiness?
2. What is resilience? What are the four kinds of models proposed by psychologists to understand how personality impacts health?
3. What are the three characteristics of resilient people?
4. What are the three Cs of hardiness? What are some criticisms of the work on hardiness?
5. What is trait resilience? How is it measured? Do people with various levels of trait resilience differ in Extraversion, Agreeableness, Conscientiousness, Emotional Stability, and Openness?
6. How do people high in hardiness or trait resilience experience and regulate positive emotions compared to less resilient people?
7. What are the five ways in which positive emotions produce health and well-being?
8. What are the seven habits of highly resilient people?
9. What makes people happy?

Key Terms

Resilience
Health behavior models
Transactional stress moderation models

Constitutional predisposition models
Interactional stress moderation models

Transformational coping
Ego-resilience
Trait resilience
Broaden-and-build theory

GLOSSARY

Acquiescent responding   A type of response set in which respondents agree with nearly every question.

Active genotype–environment correlation   When people with a certain genotype seek out a specific environment because of their personality.

Actualizing tendency   The motive to actualize, that is, to bring about growth and positive change.

Adult attachment interview   A method for assessing attachment in adults by using open-ended interview questions to probe memories of adults' relationships with their primary caregivers.

Agency   A traditionally masculine way of approaching the social world concerned with actions and accomplishments.

Agreeableness   A personality trait which describes the quality of personal relationships; how much a person feels for and gets along with others. People who are low in Agreeableness tend to be quarrelsome, critical, harsh, blunt, and aloof.

Ah-Q   An indigenous Chinese trait term that means defensiveness; named for Ah-Q, a well-known fictional Chinese character depicted in a classic novel.

Alleles   Alternative forms of the same gene which occur in pairs, one inherited from each birth parent.

Alpha   Part of the two-factor model of personality, being emotionally stable enough to get along with others. Includes the factors of Emotional Stability, Agreeableness, and Conscientiousness.

Amae   An indigenous Japanese trait term describing a state of dependency on another person and the inducing of responsibility for caregiving in that other person.

Amotivation   The state of having no motivation, being neither intrinsically nor extrinsically motivated. Often accompanied by feelings of apathy or alienation.

Anal expulsive personality   A fixation in the early part of the anal stage resulting in inhibition, self-confidence, resistance to authority, lack of sphincter or bowel control, and the symbolic behaviors of generosity and creativity.

Anal retentive personality   A fixation in the later part of the anal stage resulting in rigidity, compulsiveness, living up to the expectations of others, constipation, stinginess, and the symbolic behaviors of orderliness, stubbornness, and perfectionism.

Androgens   Masculine hormones, like testosterone, that regulate sexual behavior and the brain structures that support these behaviors.

Androgynous   Males and females who score high on both the masculinity and femininity scales of the Bem Sex Role Inventory (BSRI).

Anhedonia   The lack of positive emotion; a loss of or inability to experience pleasure that may or may not be accompanied by the presence of negative emotions.

Anxious-ambivalent attachment   An insecure bond children have with their primary caregivers, marked by inconsistent responsiveness at home, little exploration in the strange situation, distress when separated, and seeking out of the mother on reunion, but being unable to be comforted.

Arousability   In physiology, how reactive people are to stimulation; an important difference between extraverts and introverts. In sexuality, the capacity to become aroused to sexual stimuli.

Arrangement techniques   A type of performance-based test in which respondents move objects around or choose their favorites using ambiguous stimuli.

Ascending reticular activating system (ARAS) A pathway transmitting signals from the limbic system and hypothalamus to the cortex. Activation here can make a person alert and mentally sharp.

Association techniques A type of performance-based test, such as the Word Association Test and Rorschach inkblot test, in which respondents report their reactions to ambiguous stimuli.

Assumption of representativeness The assumption that identical twins are typical of the population on the specific characteristic under investigation, an assumption behind the double-the-difference between MZ and DZ twins reared apart measure of heritability.

Attributional Style Questionnaire (ASQ) A 12-item personality test designed to measure explanatory style.

Attributive self-descriptions In the Twenty Statements Test, aspects of the self-concept that refer to psychological or physiological states or traits.

Authentic self-presentation Presenting a true, correct image of the self.

Autonomic nervous system Regulates smooth muscles including inner organs, cardiac muscle, and glands. Includes the sympathetic division and parasympathetic division.

Autonomous orientation The degree to which people interpret a situation as autonomy supportive, providing information to allow them to be self-regulating.

Autonomy One of the three needs according to self-determination theory; feeling free and able to make choices about one's actions.

Avoidant attachment An insecure bond children have with their primary caregivers, marked by little affection at home, exploration in the strange situation, no overt reaction to separation, and no seeking of comfort on reunion.

Avoidant coping Strategies aimed at avoiding problems and not managing the negative emotions associated with stressful events.

Barnum Effect When people falsely believe that invalid personality tests are actually good measures of personality because they contain feedback so general that it applies to many people at the same time.

Behavioral approach system (BAS) The brain system associated with stimuli that are enticing, pleasurable, and rewarding and the personality characteristics of optimism, impulsiveness, addictive behaviors, high-risk impulsive behaviors, and mania. The BAS makes a person more sensitive to rewards.

Behavioral genetics The study of the genetic and environmental contributions to individual differences in personality and behavior.

Behavioral inhibition system (BIS) The brain system associated with conflicts that may cause feelings of anxiety, worry, rumination, risk assessment, vigilance, a sense of possible danger, and a sense of loss. May be related to obsessive-compulsive disorders or a generalized anxiety disorder. When the BIS is activated, people become more sensitive to punishment.

Behavioral residue Physical traces in living spaces left behind by the everyday actions of people.

Beneficence Along with respect for persons and justice, one of the three principles of ethical research with human participants outlined in the Belmont report.

Beta Part of the two-factor model of personality, being open and adapting to new experiences. Includes the factors of Extraversion and Openness.

Big Five A five-factor model of personality based on the lexical approach: Surgency (Extraversion), Agreeableness, Conscientiousness, Emotional Stability, and Culture.

Biopsychosocial model A model of gender differences that suggests gender differences are caused by a combination of biological, psychological, and social forces interacting with one another.

Bipolar scale A scale that measures a single dimension, defined at either end by two contrasting qualities (e.g., masculinity–femininity, active–passive).

Boredom susceptibility The need for change and variety and an aversion to routine and sameness. One of the four subscales of the Sensation Seeking scale.

Broaden-and-build theory The theory that positive emotions like elevation, joy, interest, contentment, pride, and love expand people's awareness, thoughts, and actions and help build physical, intellectual, social, and psychological resources for coping with adversity.

Cardinal trait A single trait that completely dominates a person's entire personality. Most often found in fictional characters than in actual people.

Case study method The in-depth research study of a single individual.

Castration anxiety When a boy lives in fear that his father will castrate him as revenge for loving his mother.

Catharsis The release of built-up id energy.

Causality orientation   People's typical way of regulating their motivation and behavior developed over a lifetime of experiences with internal and external motivation.

CAVE technique   (the content analysis of verbatim explanations technique) A method for measuring explanatory style from any kind of verbal material.

Central nervous system   The brain and the spinal cord.

Central traits   The 5 to 10 traits that best describe a person.

Challenge test   A technique to identify neurotransmitter function in which researchers administer a drug with a known effect on a specific neurotransmitter and monitor the impact of the drug on reactions that are thought to be related to the neurotransmitter.

Change   When a personality trait is different, either increasing or decreasing, over time.

Clear purpose integrity tests   (overt integrity tests) A type of personality assessment, often used during the hiring process, to test the honesty of job candidates in a way that is clearly stated and obvious to the test taker.

Cognitive foundations   One of the building blocks of personality concerned with how people perceive and think about information about themselves and the world.

Cognitive unconscious   The part of the mind that contains nonconscious urges, thoughts, wishes, desires, and memories that may influence our conscious thoughts.

Collectivism   The belief that the views, needs, and goals of the group are more important than those of the individual, emphasizing the interconnectedness of individuals and the group.

Collectivistic cultures   Cultures that emphasize collectivism more than individualism.

Common rule   Regulations about human participant research adopted by all U.S. federal agencies establishing an institutional review board and procedures for obtaining informed consent at all institutions where research is conducted.

Communion   A traditionally feminine way of approaching the social world concerned with nurturing and getting along with others.

Competence   One of the three needs according to self-determination theory; feeling effective in one's actions.

Completion techniques   A type of performance-based test, such as sentence completion tests, in which respondents fill in the blanks with their own responses.

Complex   A pattern of thoughts, memories, and perceptions organized around a theme that signify an important, but often unconscious, concern of a person.

Computer axial tomography (CAT) scan   A high-resolution x-ray picture of thin slices of brain tissue, now called a computerized tomography (CT) scan.

Computerized tomography (CT) scan   A high-resolution x-ray picture of thin slices of brain tissue, formerly called a computer axial tomography (CAT) scan.

Conscience   The part of the superego that contains knowledge of what we should not do, actions we have been punished for in the past, and that punishes us with feelings of guilt, shame, and embarrassment when we do something wrong in the present.

Conscientiousness   A personality trait that describes an individual's degree of physical and mental organization and regulation of impulses like thinking before acting, delaying gratification, or following norms and rules. People who are low in Conscientiousness are described as disorganized and tend to be late, careless, and impulsive.

Consistency   When a personality trait stays the same over time; also called continuity.

Constitutional predisposition models   Models of how personality impacts health that suggest that there may be some underlying genetic or constitutional factor which influences both personality and disease.

Construct validity   When an assessment successfully measures the theoretical concept it was designed to measure.

Construction techniques   A type of performance-based test, such as the Thematic Apperception Test and the Draw-A-Person Test, in which respondents create a story or a piece of artwork in response to an ambiguous stimulus.

Content analysis   Organizing and making sense out of people's verbal responses in a meaningful way.

Continuity   When a personality trait stays the same over time; also called consistency.

Control condition   In an experiment, this refers to the group of participants who receive no treatment or a neutral treatment.

Controlled orientation   The degree to which people interpret a situation as controlling, letting the environment or their own introjects control their behavior.

Convergent validity   Establishes how good an assessment is by comparing the results to other tests of the same construct or to tests of related constructs in order to establish what the test measures.

Conversion reaction   When anxiety is so extreme that it causes a physical symptom.

Correlation coefficient   An estimate of the co-relation between two variables. Correlations can be positive or negative depending on the type of relationship.

Correlational study   A type of research design in which experimenters measure variables to see how they are related. Used when certain variables, like personality, cannot be directly manipulated for practical or ethical reasons.

Counterproductive work behaviors   Actions that make it difficult or impossible for people to function in their jobs, including absenteeism, tardiness, turnover, accidents, and stealing.

Criterion validity   Establishes how good an assessment is by comparing the results to an external standard such as another personality test or some behavioral outcome.

Cronbach's alpha   A measure of internal consistency reliability; the average correlation among all possible combinations of test items taking them half at a time.

Cross sex-typed   A female who scores high on the masculinity scale and low on the femininity scale of the Bem Sex Role Inventory (BSRI); a male who scores high on the femininity scale and low on the masculinity scale of the BSRI.

Defense mechanism   How the ego deals with anxiety caused by an unacceptable impulse by changing the impulse or its desires into something more acceptable in order for the ego to protect itself and minimize anxiety and distress.

Deindividuation   The loosening of social norms and roles that occurs when people are anonymous or part of a large group.

Denial   A defense mechanism in which threatening or traumatic events or emotions are not acknowledged.

Dependent variable   The variable under study, a participant's response, the variable the experimenters measure or observe.

Development   Continuity and change in personality over time.

Dialectic   A way of thinking in which contradictions are seen to be part of a higher truth rather than as opposing forces.

Discriminant validity   Establishes how good an assessment is by comparing the results to tests of theoretically unrelated constructs in order to establish what the test doesn't measure.

Disguised purpose integrity tests   A type of personality assessment, often used during the hiring process, to test the honesty of job candidates in a way that is hidden from the test taker.

Disinhibition   The extent to which people have lowered social inhibitions and enjoy letting loose in the company of others without a thought about decorum, proper behavior, or social norms. Disinhibition often takes the form of alcohol use, partying, and sex. Disinhibition is one of the four subscales of the Sensation Seeking scale.

Disorganized/disoriented   A lack of a clear, consistent bond between children and their primary caregivers marked by a lack of attachment strategy in the Strange Situation, often to a mother who is highly anxious and unable to give comfort to the child at home.

Displacement   A defense mechanism in which the ego substitutes an unacceptable object of an impulse with a more acceptable object.

Dispositional optimism   A general expectation that things will get better, good things will happen in the future, events and circumstances will work out for the best.

Dizygotic (DZ) twins   Fraternal twins, sharing about 50% of their genes with each other. DZ twins are created when two different sperm fertilize two different eggs leading to the development of genetically distinct fetuses.

Double-blind technique   A research method to minimize expectancy effects in which neither the experimenter nor the participant knows which condition a participant is in.

Dream analysis   The detailed examination of the content and symbolism of dreams in order to decipher their hidden, unconscious meaning.

Effect size   A statistic that estimates the average difference between two groups.

Efficacy expectation   In self-efficacy theory, the belief that one is capable of acting in a certain way.

Ego ideal   The part of the superego that contains knowledge of what we should do, actions we have been rewarded for in the past.

Ego resilience   The ability to modify one's responses to meet the requirements of a stressful situation and return to one's characteristic level of self-regulation after a stressor; now called trait resilience.

Eigenvalue   In factor analysis, the amount of variation among participants' answers that a factor accounts for.

Electroencephalogram (EEG)   Identifies electrical activity in the brain through electrodes placed on the scalp.

Electromyography (EMG)   A measure of muscle activity during contraction and relaxation.

Emotion-focused coping   Strategies aimed at reducing distress by managing the negative emotions associated with stressful events.

Emotional attachment system   The biological system that maintains romantic relationships by causing us to fall in love; regulated by pair-bonding that evolutionarily keeps couples together to maximize the chances their offspring will survive.

Environmentality (e^2)   The amount of observed individual differences in a characteristic which can be accounted for by environmental differences.

Epigenetics   The study of how the environment changes the function of genes without changing the genes themselves.

Equal environments assumption   The assumption that identical twins are not treated more alike than fraternal twins, an assumption behind the double-the-difference between MZ and DZ twins reared apart measure of heritability.

Erogenous zone   A part of the body where instincts originate; a part of the body that is a special focus of attention during a psychosexual stage of development.

Eros   The life instincts.

Evoked potential   Electrical activity in a specific brain cell in response to a stimulus.

Evolutionary psychology   The branch of psychology that studies how the need to survive, adapt, and reproduce under various biological and environmental conditions has shaped human personality and behavior.

Exemplification   A self-presentation strategy of projecting a false image of the self as a good example in order to arouse guilt in others.

Exon   That part of the gene which codes for a specific trait.

Exotic becomes erotic (EBE) theory   The theory of Daryl Bem that suggests that cultures that emphasize the difference between men and women end up polarizing the genders, causing the other gender to become foreign, mysterious, and a source of sexual interest.

Experience seeking   The desire for moderate arousal through different kinds of experiences involving both the mind and the senses, perhaps through music, travel, or an unconventional lifestyle. One of the four subscales of the Sensation Seeking scale.

Experimental condition   In an experiment, this refers to the group of participants who receive the treatment the experimenter is testing.

Experimental control   This is when all aspects of an experiment are the same except for the specific variable(s) under study. Along with random assignment, this allows experimenters to draw conclusions about the cause of their results.

Explanatory style   How people explain the good and bad events in their lives using the three dimensions of internal–external, stable–unstable, and global–specific.

Expression techniques   A type of performance-based test in which respondents express their thoughts and feelings through creative play or artwork.

External regulation   A type of self-regulation where behavior is controlled by something or someone outside a person often by rewards and punishments.

Extraversion   A personality trait that describes how much people energetically seek out interactions with others and experience positive emotions. People who are low in Extraversion are described as introverted and tend to be reserved, quiet, and shy.

Extreme responding   A type of response set in which respondents avoid the middle of a scale, choosing answers on either end.

Extrinsic motivation   Engaging in an activity due to reasons outside the activity itself.

Extrinsically motivated   Doing something because of external pressures like rewards and punishments.

Face validity   When an assessment appears to measure the theoretical concept it was designed to measure based on the kinds of questions it contains.

Facets   A set of subtraits for each of the five factors originally based on the subscales of the NEO-PI-R, a questionnaire measure of the five-factor model.

Factor analysis   A statistical technique that mathematically identifies a meaningful underlying structure (that is, factors) among a set of variables (such as questions on a questionnaire).

Factor loadings   An estimate of how strongly each question fits into a given factor in a factor analysis.

Faking bad   Falsely answering a personality assessment to appear worse off in specific ways related to the outcome of the test (e.g., unqualified, in need of help, etc.).

Faking good   Falsely answering a personality assessment to appear better off in specific ways related to the outcome of the test (e.g., appearing more psychologically healthy, more qualified, more experienced, etc.).

Feared self   Negative image of what we do not want to become or dread becoming in the future.

Feminine sex-typed   A female who scores high on the femininity scale and low on the masculinity scale of the Bem Sex Role Inventory (BSRI).

Feminist theory   An explanation of gender differences that studies how men and women are different as a result of differences in social status in society, and that different is not necessarily better or worse.

Field studies   Research that is conducted outside a laboratory.

Field-dependent   An individual difference between people in the way they perceive the world by relying more on visual cues, seeing the big picture rather than details.

Field-independent   An individual difference between people in the way they perceive the world by relying on their own sensations, showing a selective attention to the fine details rather than the big picture.

Fight-flight-freeze system (FFFS)   The brain system associated with fear and reactions to aversive stimuli (for example, fight or flight) and the personality characteristics of fearfulness, avoidance, phobias, and panic disorders.

Filial piety   An indigenous Chinese trait term describing the qualities of caring for the mental and physical well-being of one's elderly parents, continuing the family line, and bringing honor to one's family and ancestors.

Five-factor model   A five-factor model of personality based on the measurement approach: Neuroticism, Extraversion, Openness, Agreeableness, and Conscientiousness.

Fixation   When some psychic energy is devoted to unresolved psychosexual issues of the past; may cause certain personality characteristics, behaviors, and symbolic behaviors in adulthood.

Flow   A positive state of complete absorption, deep enjoyment, and intense concentration in a task.

Fluid sexuality   A sexual orientation that is changeable.

Forced-choice format   A type of self-report test in which respondents must choose their answer from among a limited number of alternatives, typically two or three.

Fraternal birth order effect   The finding that gay men tend to have a larger number of older brothers in their families than do non-gay men.

Free association   A Freudian technique in which patients talk about whatever pops into their heads, following one thought to another, without trying to control, monitor, or censor what they are saying.

Freudian slip   A mistake in speaking caused by unconscious desires.

Fully functioning   The combination of being open to new experiences, trusting in oneself and the world, lacking fear of disapproval or rejection, experiencing thoughts and emotions deeply, being sensitive and responsive to others' needs, and volunteering in the community that marks a healthy, well-adjusted adult, according to Carl Rogers. These characteristics are often shown by securely attached adults.

Functional magnetic resonance imaging (fMRI)   A high-resolution three-dimensional picture of brain activity over time using blood-oxygen levels. Color enhancement is used to identify amount of activity across many regions of the brain.

Galvanic skin response (GSR)   A measure of arousal using sweat.

Gender identity   A psychological sense of our maleness or femaleness apart from our biological gender.

Gender inversion   The early and now discredited belief that same-sex behavior is caused by a biological switch that turns males into females and females into males.

Gender socialization   Teaching children to think and act in ways society says are appropriate for males and females.

Gene   A sequence of DNA that codes for a specific trait.

General Personality Factor (GPF)   A single factor that describes human personality in one dimension of being emotionally stable enough to get along with others and flexible enough to deal with change and demands. People who are high in this factor are altruistic, sociable, able to handle stress, relaxed, open to experience, dependable, and task-focused.

Generalizability   Establishes the limits of an assessment, the conditions, uses, and populations for which the measure is valid.

Genetics   One of the building blocks of personality. The study of how genes and environment affect personality and behavior.

Genotype   The genetic makeup that codes for a specific trait.

Genotype–environment correlation   When a genotype is exposed differently to an environment; when personality affects the environments people find themselves in. Genotype–environment correlations may be passive, reactive, or active.

Genotype–environment interaction   When people respond differently to the same environment due to their differing genetic makeup.

Global self-descriptions   In the Twenty Statements Test, aspects of the self-concept that are so abstract, comprehensive, or vague that they do not distinguish the person from others.

Global versus specific   One of three dimensions of explanatory style; whether the cause of an event will also affect other aspects of a person's life (global) or just the one aspect (specific).

Health behavior models   Models of how personality impacts health that suggest that people with certain personality traits adopt a healthier lifestyle and take better care of themselves than others.

Heritability (h^2)   The amount of observed individual differences in a characteristic that can be accounted for by genetic differences.

Heteronormativity   (normative heterosexuality) The view that heterosexuality is the natural, correct, and normal way for people to be.

HEXACO model   A six-factor model of personality including Honesty-Humility, Emotionality, Extraversion, Agreeableness, Conscientiousness and Openness to experience.

Hoped-for self   A positive image of what we would like to become in the future.

Hopelessness model of depression   The theory that helplessness beliefs generalize to future events leading people to lose hope, stop trying, and feel sadness. If these thoughts last more than 2 weeks, may lead to major depression.

Humanistic tradition   A viewpoint in psychology that emphasizes the importance of responsibility, growth, and actualization.

Hypothesis   An educated guess about what may be causing an observed or predicted effect.

Hysterical character   A fixation of females in the phallic stage resulting in hyperfemininity, flirtatiousness, seductiveness, and the symbolic behaviors of promiscuity and male-bashing.

Identification   When the ego finds an object or event that matches the wishes of the id and so satisfies the id impulse.

Identified regulation   A type of self-regulation where behavior is initiated from within a person, because the person has accepted a goal that is more important or interesting than the task at hand.

Identity   Our place in society; definitions and standards imposed on us by others.

Identity crisis   When a socially ascribed identity does not match our unique self-concept.

Idiographic   An approach to the study of traits in which researchers identify the traits that are important for the understanding of a single individual.

Illusion of control   The belief that one has control over an outcome when in reality one does not.

Impersonal orientation   The degree to which people feel they lack control over important outcomes, often resulting in amotivation.

Implicit Association Test (IAT)   A test administered on the computer that uses reaction times to measure unconscious attitudes.

Impression management   Using self-presentation to convey a specific image of the self to others, for example, as likable, dangerous, competent, a good example, or helpless.

Independent variable   The variable experimenters hypothesize to have an effect on participants' responses. This may be manipulated in a true experiment or measured in correlational and quasi-experimental studies.

Independent view of the self   A self-concept seen in individualistic cultures in which the self is autonomous and independent of others.

Indigenous traits   Words describing personality that are unique to a specific culture or language group and not found in Anglo-Saxon cultures.

Individual change   How an individual person changes over time.

Individualism   The belief in the uniqueness of the individual, emphasizing the separateness of individuals from the group.

Individualistic cultures   Cultures that emphasize individualism more than collectivism.

Informed consent   When potential research subjects willingly agree to participate in a study after being told about the study's procedures, likely risks, and potential benefits of their participation.

Infrequency scale   A scale inserted into a personality assessment to identify people who may be using a response set (e.g., a lie scale).

Ingratiation   A self-presentation strategy of projecting a false image of the self as likable in order to arouse affection in others.

Instincts   Unconscious tension, impulse, or excitation originating in a bodily need.

Institutional review board (IRB)   Reviews all research to ensure that it upholds federal standards of ethical principles of research with human participants as outlined in the Common Rule.

Integrated regulation   A type of self-regulation where behavior is initiated from within a person because the person has internalized the goals and values involved with the task at hand such that it is an expression of his or her personality.

Integration   Combining individual parts into a coherent whole, such as how the building blocks of personality combine to form a whole person greater than the mere sum of the parts.

Integrity tests   Personality assessments, often used during the hiring process, to test the honesty of job candidates. These may be overt or clear purpose.

Intellectualization   A defense mechanism in which the ego keeps emotions separate from thoughts so that one can talk about an event without experiencing disturbing emotions; a form of the defense mechanism isolation.

Interactional stress moderation models   Models of how personality impacts health that suggest that certain personality characteristics modify physiological responses by reducing or increasing them and help people be resilient in the face of adversity.

Interdependent view of the self   A self-concept seen in collectivistic cultures in which the self includes others and cannot be understood apart from clan, family, friends, coworkers, and so on.

Internal consistency reliability   When an assessment gives consistent results across items, demonstrated by parallel forms reliability, split-half reliability, or Cronbach's alpha reliability.

Internal versus external   One of three dimensions of explanatory style; whether an event was caused more by people's own actions (internal) or by outside influences (external).

Internal working models   Internalized expectations of what caregiving relationships are like, based on our early experiences.

Interpersonal relatedness   An indigenous personality factor unique to the Chinese referring to instrumentality of relationships, propriety, avoidance of conflict, support of traditions, and compliance with norms. Includes the traits of Harmony, Ren Qing, Ah-Q, and Face.

Interrater reliability   A measure of rater consistency; when there is agreement among raters.

Intimidation   A self-presentation strategy of projecting a false image of the self as dangerous in order to arouse fear in others.

Intrapsychic foundations   One of the building blocks of personality concerned with our own thoughts, feelings, and motives, both conscious and unconscious.

Intrinsic motivation   Engaging in an activity due to reasons inherent in the activity itself like satisfaction or pleasure.

Intrinsic regulation   Freely choosing to engage in an activity because of the pleasure, satisfaction, or interest inherent in the activity itself.

Intrinsically motivated   Doing something because of the pleasure, satisfaction, and interest in the activity itself.

Introjected regulation   A type of self-regulation where behavior is controlled by something inside a person, often by guilt and anxiety.

Intron   That part of the gene which does not code for a specific trait but may orchestrate the functioning of nearby genes in direct response to the environment.

Isolation   A defense mechanism in which the ego mentally keeps an unacceptable thought or feeling separate from other thoughts and feelings.

Justice   Along with respect for persons and beneficence, one of the three principles of ethical research with human participants outlined in the Belmont report.

L data   See *Life data*.

Latent content   The true meaning of the dream as revealed through free association and dream analysis.

Learned helplessness   A state of lack of motivation, problems in thinking and learning, and negative emotions including depression caused by experiencing a lack of control.

Left–right asymmetries   Individual differences in how strongly the left side of the cortex responds to negative emotion compared to how strongly the right side responds to positive emotions.

Levels   In an experiment, the number of groups in an independent variable.

Lexical approach   Using synonyms within or commonalities across languages to identify the most important traits for understanding personality.

Libido   The energy of the life instincts (eros).

Life data   Called L data, they include information about people that is publically available, such as graduating from college, clubs and organizations, criminal records, marriages, and so forth.

Locus of causality   People's beliefs about the choice to engage in a behavior, feeling autonomous or controlled.

Locus of control   People's beliefs about what determines their outcomes in life, their own efforts (internal) or outside circumstances, such as other people, fate, or luck (external).

Longitudinal study   An experimental design in which research participants are followed over long periods of time, such as from childhood to adulthood, or from early to later adulthood.

Looking-glass self   Seeing our self as others see us.

Magnetic resonance imaging (MRI)   A high-resolution three-dimensional picture of the brain tissue obtained by the use of radio frequency waves.

Manifest content   What people remember seeing in their dreams.

Masculine sex-typed   A man who scores high on the masculinity scale and low on the femininity scale of the Bem Sex Role Inventory (BSRI).

Maternal immune hypothesis   The theory that each male fetus increases the sensitivity of the mother's immune system which increases the chances that later-born male children will be gay.

Maturation   Changes in personality that occur due to the normal process of growing from one period of life (for example, childhood, adolescence, early adulthood, middle adulthood, old age) to another.

Mean-level change   A type of general change that affects nearly all people as they grow from infancy to adulthood.

Measurement approach   Using questionnaires and statistics to identify the most important traits for understanding personality.

Mendelian inheritance   A pattern of inheritance named after Gregor Mendel, in which one trait dominates over another recessive trait that is later manifested in successive generations.

Meta-analysis   A technique in which researchers combine the effects of a specific variable, like gender, from many studies into a single index in order to estimate more accurately the average effect of that variable.

Mirror test   A test to see if an animal or human infant has a sense of self by showing self-directed behaviors while looking in a mirror. Often tested by placing a red spot on the research subject and observing its behavior.

Moderate responding   A type of response set in which respondents avoid the ends of a scale, choosing answers in the middle.

Monozygotic (MZ) twins   Identical twins, exact genetic duplicates of each other. MZ twins are created when a fertilized egg, the zygote, splits into two (or more) identical parts, each of which develops into a fetus.

Monozygotic twins raised apart (MZA)   Identical twins who were separated at birth and raised in different environments.

Motivated unconscious   The part of the mind that contains nonconscious urges, thoughts, wishes, desires, and memories and which strives to make these urges known in our conscious thoughts.

Narrow traits   The subtraits that make up each of the three factors of Eysenck's PEN theory.

Negative genotype–environment correlation   When a genotype is exposed differently to an environment that is unfavorable for developing certain characteristics. For example, an environment may discourage the development of certain personality characteristics.

Neuroscience   One of the building blocks of personality. The study of how our brain and nervous system affect personality and behavior through the study of bodily responses, brain structure, brain activity, and biochemical activity.

Neuroticism   A personality trait that describes how anxious and vulnerable to negative emotions a person is. People who are low in Neuroticism are described as emotionally stable and tend to be calm, relaxed, and able to handle stress well.

Neurotransmitters   Chemicals released by neurons to inhibit or excite the next neuron into action to help transmit signals through the nervous system.

Nomothetic   An approach to the study of traits in which researchers seek to identify human universals (i.e., the key traits that are important for describing the personality of many different people).

Non-shared environment   Aspects of the family or nonfamily environment that are unique to an individual family member and that make him or her different from his or her siblings living in the same household.

Noncontent responding   Any way that people respond to a personality assessment that is not directly related to the questions asked.

Nonindependence error   A flaw in some fMRI studies that occurs when researchers unintentionally bias their results by not independently selecting which brain areas to correlate with personality characteristics or other variables.

Normative change   How people change over time, on average.

O data   See *Observation data.*

Objective self-awareness   Seeing the self as an object of social scrutiny.

Observation data   Called O data, they include information given by friends, family, teachers, trained raters, or others based on watching how people behave in the laboratory or in their daily lives.

Observational study   A type of research design in which scientists observe what people do and generate a hypothesis to explain their findings.

Oedipus complex   When a child falls in love with the other-sex parent and shows hostility to the same-sex parent.

Openness   A personality trait that describes how much people appreciate creativity and the life of the mind as revealed in ideas, thoughts, fantasies, art, and beauty. People who are low in Openness are described as conventional, preferring the concrete and traditional.

Optimal challenge   The point at which an activity is neither too easy, leading to boredom, or too difficult, leading to frustration.

Optimistic explanatory style   A consistent way of explaining good and bad events in which people believe that positive events are explained by causes that tend to be internal, stable, and global and that negative events are explained by events that tend to be external, unstable, and specific.

Oral incorporative personality   A fixation in the early part of the oral stage resulting in dependency, eating, drinking, smoking, kissing, and the symbolic behaviors of collecting things and being a good listener.

Oral sadistic personality   A fixation in the later part of the oral stage resulting in aggression, gum-chewing, nail-biting, overeating, and the symbolic behaviors of sarcasm, cynicism, and ridicule.

Outcome expectation   In self-efficacy theory, the belief that acting in a certain way will produce a certain outcome.

Overjustification effect   When people lose interest in a formerly intrinsically interesting activity as a result of extrinsic control.

Overt integrity tests   (clear purpose integrity tests) A type of personality assessment, often used during the hiring process, to test the honesty of job candidates in a way that is clearly stated and obvious to the test taker.

Parallel-forms reliability   A measure of internal consistency reliability; when two or more versions of a test give consistent results.

Parapraxes   Mistakes in speaking (e.g., slips of the tongue), or acting (e.g., accidents, bungled actions, mistakes, errors) caused by unconscious desires.

Parasympathetic division   Part of the autonomic nervous system; replenishes the body's energy stores through salivation, digestion, and other functions.

Passive genotype–environment correlation   When a genotype is exposed to an environment but has done nothing to obtain the environment.

Path analysis   A technique in which researchers use statistics to test hypotheses about how variables relate to one another.

Path diagram   A visual illustration of the results of a path analysis that shows the significant connections among variables.

Patterned responding   A type of response set in which respondents answer by making patterns on their response sheet.

Penis envy   Feelings of jealousy and inferiority girls feel when they realize that they do not have a penis but boys do.

Performance-based tests   Assessments in which people respond to unstructured stimuli, projecting their own meanings, significances, patterns, feelings, interpretations, concerns, or worldviews; sometimes called projective tests.

Peripheral nervous system   The somatic nervous system and the autonomic nervous system.

Personality assessment   The measurement of individual characteristics of a person, often through personality tests, interviews, and other measures.

Personality coherence   When the level of a personality trait within a person stays the same (e.g. from childhood to adulthood) but the way it is expressed differs.

Personality development   How personality changes or remains the same over time.

Personality psychology   The scientific study of what makes us who we are. The study of individual differences: identifying ways in which people are both similar and different and explaining how they became that way.

Personality questionnaires   Tests in which people answer questions about themselves that identify certain aspects of their personality or personality functioning.

Pessimistic explanatory style   A consistent way of explaining good and bad events in which people believe that negative events are explained by causes that tend to be internal, stable, and global and that positive events are explained by events that tend to be external, unstable, and specific.

Phallic character   A fixation of males in the phallic stage resulting in hypermasculinity, a concern for virility, and the symbolic behaviors of owning and using power tools, big cars and trucks, and large machinery.

Phenotype   The manifestation of the genes; the observable physical or psychological trait which is coded by the genes.

Philotimo   An indigenous Greek trait term describing the qualities of being polite, generous, responsible, respectful, and having a strong sense of honor.

Phrenology   The discredited theory of Joseph Gall from the 1790s that the size, shape, and location of bumps on the scalp was related to particular mental or personality characteristics.

Physical self-descriptions   In the Twenty Statements Test, aspects of the self-concept that refer to physical qualities.

Pleasure principle   How the id operates, wanting what it wants when it wants it, without concern for reality or social standards.

Positional cloning   A possible way of preventing inherited diseases by replacing defective genetic code with corrected code that matches the gene as closely as possible.

Positive genotype–environment correlation   When a genotype is exposed differently to an environment that is favorable for developing certain characteristics. For example, an environment may encourage the development of certain personality characteristics.

Positron emission tomography (PET) scan   A picture of brain activity using a radioactive substance and a special scanner. Color enhancement is used to identify amounts of activity across many regions of the brain.

Possible selves   Images of what we hope, fear, or expect that we may become in the future.

Primary control   A way of exercising control by changing the circumstances.

Primary process thinking   Making decisions based on wants and desires without logical rules and conscious reasoning; used by the id.

Problem-focused coping   Strategies aimed at reducing distress by working directly on remedying the source of the stress and problem solving.

Proceptivity   The motivation to initiate sexual activity; sexual desire.

Projection   A defense mechanism in which the ego attributes its own disturbing or unacceptable impulses onto another person.

Psychosexual stages   The progression from childhood to adulthood, according to Sigmund Freud, in which we move from an immature reflexive expression of sexual impulses involving the id, to a mature, socially acceptable expression of sexual impulses involving ego and superego.

Psychoticism   A personality trait that describes how tough-minded, selfish, and antisocial a person is. People who are low in Psychoticism are high in Agreeableness and Conscientiousness.

Qualitative methods   Research methods that classify, judge, or organize participants' verbal responses into themes or patterns.

Quantitative methods   Research methods that use numerical measures of some sort including questionnaires, rating scales, test scores, and the like.

Quasi-experimental design   A research study in which experimenters, either for practical, logistical, or ethical reasons, do not randomly assign people to experimental conditions.

Random assignment   What experimenters do to make sure every participant has an equal chance of being a part of each experimental condition. Along with experimental control, this allows experimenters to draw conclusions about the cause of their results.

Rater consistency   When an assessment gives consistent results across multiple raters, often demonstrated by interrater reliability.

Rationalization   A defense mechanism in which the ego acknowledges an unacceptable behavior but reinterprets it to make it seem more acceptable.

Reactant responding   A type of response set in which respondents disagree or say no to nearly every question.

Reaction formation   A defense mechanism in which the true unacceptable impulse is expressed by the opposite, acceptable impulse.

Reactive genotype–environment correlation   When the environment responds to certain personalities because of their genotype.

Reality principle   How the ego operates, satisfying id impulses within the confines of what is possible in the social and physical world.

Reflected appraisals   The opinions of significant others that are used as a mirror to evaluate ourselves.

Reflex action   Seeking gratification through immediate physical action; used by the id.

Regulation and motivation   One of the building blocks of personality concerned with how people adjust their responses to the environment, both consciously and unconsciously.

Reinforcement sensitivity theory   The theory that the way people's brain and nervous systems respond to stimuli determines personality. The three hypothetical brain systems thought to be related to personality differences are the fight-flight-freeze system (FFFS), the behavioral approach system (BAS), and the behavioral inhibition system (BIS).

Relatedness   One of the three needs according to self-determination theory; feeling meaningfully connected to others.

Reliability   How consistent a measure is over time, items, or raters.

Ren Qing   An indigenous Chinese trait term that refers to a traditional relationship orientation emphasizing give and take and connectedness.

Repression   A defense mechanism in which the ego unconsciously keeps unacceptable thoughts or urges in the unconscious.

Resilience   The ability to recover from tragedy, adversity, hardship, or to adapt to ongoing life stressors.

Respect for persons   Along with beneficence and justice, one of the three principles of ethical research with human participants outlined in the Belmont report.

Response set   A habitual way of responding to a personality assessment that is not directly related to the questions asked; noncontent responding.

S data   See *Self-report data.*

Safe haven   A primary caregiver to whom the child can turn for comfort when distressed.

Scatterplot or scattergram   A two-dimensional graph that shows the relationship between two variables.

Schema   A pattern of thoughts, memories, and perceptions organized around a concept.

Scientific method   A set of guidelines for making and testing observations about the world in order to build knowledge while minimizing error and bias.

Secondary control   A way of exercising control by changing oneself.

Secondary process thinking   Logical thinking, weighing the costs and rewards of possible actions; used by the ego.

Secondary traits   Traits of lesser importance or less consistently displayed within a person.

Secure base   A primary caregiver with whom the child feels safe enough to explore the environment.

Securely attached   Children are securely attached when they have a positive bond children have with their primary caregivers, marked by responsiveness at home, exploration in the strange situation, distress when separated, and comfort on reunion.

Selective placement   The assumption that adopted families of MZ twins raised apart are different from each other, that the identical twins were not purposely placed in similar environments, an assumption behind the r_{mza} measure of heritability.

Self and identity   One of the building blocks of personality. Our own sense of who we are, including self-concept, self-esteem, and social identity.

Self-concept   The set of ideas and inferences we hold about ourselves.

Self-concept clarity   How well people know themselves; consistency of self-concept.

Self-determination theory   The theory by Edward Deci and Richard Ryan that states that people need autonomy, competence, and relatedness in order to feel intrinsic motivation.

Self-efficacy   The belief that one can be competent and effective at some activity.

Self-esteem   The evaluative component of the self; how we evaluate ourselves.

Self-esteem stability   How consistent people's feelings of self-worth are over time; consistency of self-esteem.

Self-fulfilling prophecy   The tendency for our own beliefs about what we think others are like to come true.

Self-handicapping   Purposely setting oneself up for failure in order to have a ready-made excuse when things go wrong and look particularly good when things go right.

Self-monitoring   A personality trait that describes the extent to which people are aware of and manipulate their self-presentations, expressive behaviors, and nonverbal displays of emotion in order to control the images and impressions others form of them.

Self-presentation   Acting, speaking, or dressing in a certain way in order to convey a specific image of ourselves to our self or others.

Self-promotion   A self-presentation strategy of projecting a false image of the self as competent in order to arouse respect in others.

Self-report data   Called S data, they include any information people respond to directly, such as objective personality tests, interviews, narratives, life stories, and survey questions.

Self-report tests   Assessments in which respondents answer questions about themselves; sometimes called objective tests.

Sensation seeking   The pursuit of varied, novel, complex, or intense experiences and the willingness to take risks to have such experiences.

Sexual attractions   Thoughts, feelings, wants, or desires for sexual relations or to be in a loving sexual relationship with another person; it does not include sexual behavior.

Sexual behavior   Sexual actions people have actually engaged in, including genital contact with sexual excitement, with or without intercourse or orgasm, occurring with mutual consent.

Sexual desire system   The biological system that promotes sexual union; regulated by sexual mating that evolutionarily maximizes the chances of reproduction and survival of the species.

Sexual identity   Labels people associate with their sexuality, whether personally selected or socially ascribed.

Sexual orientation   The prevalence of erotic arousals, feelings, fantasies, and behaviors one has for males, females, or both.

Sexy Seven   Dimensions of personality that describe sexuality and overlap about 80% with the five factors: Sexual Attractiveness, Relationship Exclusivity, Gender Orientation, Sexual Restraint, Erotophilic Disposition, Emotional Investment, and Sexual Orientation.

Shared environment   Aspects of the family environment that are generally the same for all the children living in the same household, including physical, psychological, and social aspects.

Social constructionism   The idea that gender differences are in the eye of the beholder and actively constructed rather than being innate differences between males and females.

Social identity   Who people are when they are with others; the part of the self people present to others.

Socially desirable responding   Falsely answering a personality assessment to appear more cooperative, likable, or socially appropriate, often by not admitting to distasteful, but perfectly human tendencies (e.g., gossiping, jealousy, etc.).

Social role theory   The theory that males and females have different personality and social behavior due to the different roles they hold in society.

Social self-descriptions   In the Twenty Statements Test, aspects of the self-concept that refer to social roles, institutional memberships, or a socially defined status.

Somatic nervous system   Part of the peripheral nervous system; controls muscle movements.

Spiritual transcendence   A dimension of personality separate from the five factors: the ability of individuals to view life from a larger, more objective perspective; a personal search for a greater connection across all of humanity.

Split-half reliability   A measure of internal consistency reliability; when each half of a test gives consistent results.

Stable versus unstable   One of three dimensions of explanatory style; whether the cause of a positive or negative event is likely to reoccur in the future (stable) or not (unstable).

Stereotype   A generalization about a group of people in which attributes are assumed to be true of all members of the group regardless of the actual variation among group members.

Stereotype threat   The distress people feel in a situation where their performance may confirm a stereotype. This distress causes them to perform worse than they are capable of.

Strange Situation   A research technique devised by Mary Ainsworth in which children go through a series of separations and reunions with their primary caregivers and observed to measure the quality of their attachment bonds.

Strategic self-presentation   Presenting a false image of the self to others in order to achieve a goal.

Structural model of personality   The parts of the personality according to Sigmund Freud comprised of the id, ego, and superego.

Sublimation   A defense mechanism in which the ego substitutes an unacceptable impulse with a more acceptable impulse.

Supplication   A self-presentation strategy of projecting a false image of the self as helpless in order to arouse nurturance in others.

Suppression   A coping mechanism in which the ego consciously keeps unacceptable thoughts or urges in the unconscious.

Symbolic behavior   An innocent behavior that actually represents an unconscious desire, often sexual or aggressive.

Sympathetic division   Part of the autonomic nervous system; mobilizes energy for fight or flight.

T data   See *Test data*.

Temperament   A set of personality characteristics that are relatively stable across the life span, present from birth, determined by genetic factors, and develop with maturation and experience.

Temporal consistency reliability   When an assessment gives consistent results across time, often demonstrated by test–retest reliability.

Test data   Called T data, they include information about people's reactions to a structured situation, such as experimental procedures, intelligence tests, performance tests, and projective tests.

Test–retest reliability   A measure of temporal consistency; when a test gives a consistent result from one point in time to a later point in time.

Thanatos   The death instincts.

Theoretical approach   Using theory to identify the most important traits for understanding personality.

Thrill and adventure seeking   Arousal seeking through physical sensations produced by speed, height, falling, danger, like through extreme sports. One of the four subscales of the Sensation Seeking scale.

Topographic model of personality   The location of thoughts, memories, and desires in the mind according to Sigmund Freud, comprised of the unconscious, preconscious, and conscious.

Trait resilience   The ability to modify one's responses to meet the requirements of a stressful situation and return to one's characteristic level of self-regulation after a stressor; once called ego resilience.

Traits   One of the building blocks of personality. A person's typical way of thinking, feeling, and acting in various situations at different times.

Transactional stress moderation models   Models of how personality impacts health that suggest that certain personality traits may influence a person's exposure to stressful or dangerous circumstances.

Transcranial magnetic stimulation (TMS)   Using an electrical current to disrupt or enhance neuron functioning to pinpoint with greater accuracy than other techniques an exact area of brain function.

Transference   The unconscious redirection of feelings for one person onto a different person who resembles the original person in some way, especially from a person who was important in childhood onto a person who is important in the present.

Transformational coping   A way of coping with adversity in which people high in hardiness reinterpret an experience as less of a threat and more of a growth-enhancing experience.

Triadic design   A research method in learned helplessness experiments in which three groups are used to test the controllability of an aversive stimulus.

Triangulation   Using multiple methodologies within a single study.

True experiment   A design in which participants are randomly assigned to conditions which are identical except for the variable(s) under study, which allows experimenters to draw conclusions about the cause of their results.

Twenty Statements Test (TST)   A test of self-concept where participants generate 20 answers to the statement "I am _____."

Undifferentiated   Males and females who score low on both the masculinity and femininity scales of the Bem Sex Role Inventory (BSRI).

Undoing   A defense mechanism in which the ego tries to nullify one action or thought with another.

Unidimensional scale   A scale that measures a single dimension.

Validity   How well a test measures what it was designed to measure.

Wish fulfillment   Seeking gratification through imagining what one wants; used by the id.

Word association method   A technique used to uncover unconscious material and complexes in which participants respond to one word with the first word that comes to their minds.

Yoking   A research technique in which participants in one group are matched to participants in another group so that they receive the same treatment.

REFERENCES

Abela, J. R. Z., & Seligman, M. E. P. (2000). The hopelessness theory of depression: A test of the diathesis-stress component in the interpersonal and achievement domains. *Cognitive Therapy and Research, 24*(4), 361–378.

Abramson, L. Y., Metalsky, G. I., & Alloy, L. B. (1989). Hopelessness depression: A theory-based subtype of depression. *Psychological Review, 96*(2), 358–372.

Abramson, L. Y., Seligman, M. E. P., & Teasdale, J. D. (1978). Learned helplessness in humans: Critique and reformulation. *Journal of Abnormal Psychology, 87*(1), 49–74.

Ackerman, S. J. (2006). *Hard science, hard choices.* New York: Dana Press.

Affleck, G., Tennen, H., & Apter, A. (2001). Optimism, pessimism, and daily life with chronic illness. In E. C. Chang (Ed.), *Optimism & pessimism: Implications for theory, research, and practice* (pp. 147–168). Washington, DC: American Psychological Association.

Ahern, N. R., Kiehl, E. M., Sole, M. L., & Byers, J. (2006). A review of instruments measuring resilience. *Issues in Comprehensive Pediatric Nursing, 29,* 103–125.

Ainsworth, M. D. S., Bell, S. M., & Stayton, S. (1974). Infant–mother attachment and social development. In M. P. Richards (Ed.), *The introduction of the child into a social world* (pp. 99–135). London, England: Cambridge University Press.

Ainsworth, M. D. S., Blehar, M., Waters, E., & Wall, S. (1978). *Patterns of attachment: A psychological study of the strange situation.* Hillsdale, NJ: Erlbaum.

Alexander, G. M. (2003). An evolutionary perspective of sex-typed toy preferences: Pink, blue, and the brain. *Archives of Sexual Behavior, 32*(1), 7–14.

Alexander, G. M., & Evardone, M. (2008). Blocks and bodies: Sex differences in a novel version of the mental rotations test. *Hormones and Behavior, 53,* 177–184.

Alexander, G. M., & Hines, M. (2002). Sex differences in response to children's toys in nonhuman primates (*Cercopithecus aethiops sabaeus*). *Evolution and Human Behavior, 23,* 467–479.

Alexander, G. M., Wilcox, T., & Woods, R. (2009). Sex differences in infants' visual interest in toys. *Archives of Sexual Behavior, 38,* 427–433.

Allen, L. S., & Gorski, R. A. (1992). Sexual orientation and the size of the anterior commissure of the human brain. *Proceedings of the National Academy of Sciences, 89,* 7199–7202.

Alloy, L. B., Abramson, L. Y., Hogan, M. E., Whitehouse, W. G., Rose, D. T., Robinson, M. S., et al. (2000). The Temple-Wisconsin cognitive vulnerability to depression project: Lifetime history of axis I psychopathology in individuals at high and low cognitive risk for depression. *Journal of Abnormal Psychology, 109,* 403–418.

Allport, G. W. (1927). Concepts of trait and personality. *Psychological Bulletin, 24,* 284–293.

Allport, G. W. (1937). *Personality: A psychological interpretation.* New York: Holt.

Allport, G. W. (1937/1961). *Pattern and growth in personality.* New York: Holt, Rinehart and Winston.

Allport, G. W. (1962). The general and the unique in psychological science. *Journal of Personality, 30,* 405–422.

Allport, G. W. (1965). *Letters from Jenny.* New York: Harcourt, Brace and World.

Allport, G. W., & Odbert, H. S. (1936). Trait names: A psycho-lexical study. *Psychological Monographs, 47*(Whole No. 211), 1–171.

Almagor, M., Tellegen, A., & Waller, N. G. (1995). The big seven model: A cross-cultural replication and further exploration of the basic dimensions of natural language trait descriptors. *Journal of Personality and Social Psychology, 69*(2), 300–307.

Alvarez, J. M., Ruble, D. N., & Bolger, N. (2001). Trait understanding or evaluative reasoning: An analysis of children's behavioral predictions. *Child Development, 72*, 1409–1425.

Álvarez, M. S., Balaguer, I., Castillo, I., & Duda, J. L. (2008). Coach autonomy support and quality of sport engagement in young soccer players. *The Spanish Journal of Psychology, 12*(1), 138–148.

American Educational Research Association, American Psychological Association, & National Council on Measurement in Education. (1999). *The standards for educational and psychological testing.* Washington, DC: American Educational Research Association.

American Psychological Association. (2002). Ethical principles of psychologists and code of conduct. *American Psychologist, 57*, 1060–1073.

American Psychological Association. (2010). 2010 amendments to the 2002 "ethical principles of psychologists and code of conduct." *American Psychologist, 65*(5), 493.

Anderegg, D. (2004). Paging Dr. Froid: Teaching psychoanalytic theory to undergraduates. *Psychoanalytic Psychology, 21*(2), 214–221.

Anderson, C. A., & Arnoult, L. H. (1985). Attributional style and everyday problems in living: Depression, loneliness, and shyness. *Social Cognition, 3*(1), 16–35.

Anderson, C. A., Horowitz, L. M., & French, R. D. (1983). Attributional style of lonely and depressed people. *Journal of Personality and Social Psychology, 45*, 127–136.

Anderson, C. R. (1977). Locus of control, coping behaviors, and performance in a stress setting: A longitudinal study. *Journal of Applied Psychology, 62*(4), 446–451.

Anderson, R., Manoogian, S. T., & Reznick, J. S. (1976). The undermining and enhancing of intrinsic motivation in preschool children. *Journal of Personality and Social Psychology, 34*, 915–922.

Anonymous. (1946). Letters from Jenny. *Journal of Abnormal and Social Psychology, 41*, 315–350, 449–480.

Archer, J. (2004). Sex differences in aggression in real world settings: A meta-analytic review. *Review of General Psychology, 8*(4), 291–322.

Ardelt, M. (2000). Still stable after all these years? Personality stability theory revisited. *Social Psychology Quarterly, 63*, 392–405.

Aronson, E. (1968). Dissonance theory: Progress and problems. In R. P. Abelson, E. Aronson, W. J. McGuire, T. M. Newcomb, M. J. Rosenberg, & P. H. Tannenbaum (Eds.), *Theories of cognitive consistency: A sourcebook* (pp. 5–27). Chicago: Rand McNally.

Aronson, E., Ellsworth, P. C., Carlsmith, J. M., & Gonzales, M. H. (1990). *Methods of research in social psychology.* New York: McGraw-Hill.

Aronson, E., Wilson, T. D., & Akert, R. M. (2001). *Social psychology* (7th ed.). Upper Saddle River, NJ: Pearson.

Aronson, J., Lustina, M. J., Good, C., Keough, K., & Steele, C. M. (1999). When White men can't do math: Necessary and sufficient factors in stereotype threat. *Journal of Experimental Social Psychology, 35*(1), 29–46.

Aronson, J., Quinn, D. M., & Spencer, S. J. (1998). Stereotype threat and the academic underperformance of minorities and women. In J. K. Swim & C. Stangor (Eds.), *Prejudice: The target's perspective* (pp. 83–103). San Diego, CA: Academic Press.

Aronson, J., & Rogers, L. (2008). Overcoming stereotype threat. In S. J. Lopez (Ed.), *Positive psychology: Exploring the best in people: Vol. 3. Growing in the face of adversity* (pp. 109–121). Westport, CT: Praeger.

Ashby, F. G., Isen, A. M., & Turken, A. U. (1999). A neuropsychological theory of positive affect and its influence on cognition. *Psychological Review, 106*, 529–550.

Ashton, M. C., & Lee, K. (2005). Honesty-humility, the Big Five, and the five-factor model. *Journal of Personality, 73*(3), 1321–1353.

Ashton, M. C., & Lee, K. (2007). Empirical, theoretical, and practical advantages of the HEXACO model of personality structure. *Personality and Social Psychology Review, 11*(2), 150–166.

Ashton, M. C., Lee, K., & Goldberg, L. R. (2004). A hierarchical analysis of 1710 English personality-descriptive adjectives. *Journal of Personality and Social Psychology, 87*(5), 707–721.

Ashton, M. C., Lee, K., Goldberg, L. R., & de Vries, R. E. (2009). Higher order factors of personality: Do they exist? *Personality and Social Psychology Bulletin, 13*(2), 79–91.

Ashton, M. C., Lee, K., Perugini, M., Szarota, P., de Vries, R. E., DiBlas, L., et al. (2004). A six-factor structure of personality-descriptive adjectives: Solutions from psycholexical studies in seven languages. *Journal of Personality and Social Psychology, 86*(2), 356–366.

Aspinwall, L. G., & Richter, L. (1999). Optimism and self-mastery predict more rapid disengagement from unsolvable tasks in the presence of alternatives. *Motivation and Emotion, 23,* 221–245.

Aspinwall, L. G., Richter, L., & Hoffman, R. R., III. (2001). Understanding how optimism works: An examination of optimists' adaptive moderation of belief and behavior. In E. C. Chang (Ed.),*Optimism & pessimism: Implications for theory, research, and practice* (pp. 217–238). Washington, DC: American Psychological Association.

Auster, C. J., & Ohm, S. C. (2000). Masculinity and femininity in contemporary American society: A reevaluation using the Bem Sex-Role Inventory. *Sex Roles, 43*(7/8), 499–528.

Ávila, C., & Torrubia, R. (2004). Personality, expectations, and response strategies in multiple-choice question examinations in university students: A test of Gray's hypotheses. *European Journal of Personality, 18,* 45–59.

Ávila, C., & Torrubia, R. (2008). Performance and conditioning studies. In P. J. Corr (Ed.), *The reinforcement sensitivity theory of personality* (pp. 228–260). Cambridge, England: Cambridge University Press.

Avtgis, T. (1998). Locus of control and persuasion, social influence and conformity: A meta-analytic review. *Psychological Reports, 83,* 899–903.

Azar, B. (1997, October). Was Freud right? Maybe, maybe not. *APA Monitor on Psychology,* 28, 30.

Baard, P. P., Deci, E. L., & Ryan, R. M. (2004). Intrinsic need satisfaction: A motivational basis of performance and well-being in two work settings. *Journal of Applied Social Psychology, 34,* 2045–2068.

Bailey, J. M. (2003). Biological perspectives on sexual orientation. In L. Garnets & D. C. Kimmel (Eds.), *Psychological perspectives on lesbian, gay, and bisexual experience* (pp. 50–85). New York: Columbia University Press.

Bailey, J. M., & Dawood, K. (1998). Behavioral genetics, sexual orientation, and the family. In C. J. Patterson & A. R. D'Augelli (Eds.), *Lesbian, gay and bisexual identities in families* (pp. 3–18). New York: Oxford University Press.

Bailey, J. M., Dunne, M. P., & Martin, N. G. (2000). Genetic and environmental influences on sexual orientation and its correlates in an Australian twin sample. *Journal of Personality and Social Psychology, 78*(3), 524–536.

Bailey, J. M., & Pillard, R. C. (1991). A genetic study of male sexual orientation. *Archives of General Psychiatry, 48,* 1089–1096.

Bailey, J. M., & Pillard, R. C. (1995). Genetics of human sexual orientation. *Annual Review of Sex Research, 6,* 126–150.

Bailey, J. M., Pillard, R. C., Dawood, K., Miller, M. B., Farrer, L. A., Trivedi, S., et al. (1999). A family history study of male sexual orientation using three independent samples. *Behavior Genetics, 29*(2), 79–86.

Bailey, J. M., Pillard, R. C., Neale, M. C., & Agyei, Y. (1993). Heritable factors influence sexual orientation in women. *Archives of General Psychiatry, 50,* 217–223.

Bailey, J. M., Willerman, L., & Parks, C. (1991). A test of the maternal stress theory of human male homosexuality. *Archives of Sexual Behavior, 20*(3), 277–293.

Bailey, J. M., & Zucker, K. J. (1995). Childhood sex-typed behavior and sexual orientation: A conceptual analysis and quantitative review. *Developmental Psychology, 31*(1), 43–55.

Bakan, D. (1966). *The quality of human existence.* Boston: Beacon Press.

Balaguer, I., Castillo, I., & Duda, J. L. (2007). Propiedades psicométricas de la escala de motivación deportiva en deportistas españoles. *Revista Mexicana de Psicología, 24,* 197–207.

Baldwin, A. L. (1942). Personal structure analysis: A statistical method for investigating the single personality. *Journal of Abnormal and Social Psychology, 37,* 163–183.

Bandura, A. (1977a). Self-efficacy: Toward a unifying theory of behavioral change. *Psychological Review, 84*(2), 191–215.

Bandura, A. (1977b). *Social learning theory.* Englewood Cliffs, NJ: Prentice Hall.

Bandura, A. (1982). Self-efficacy mechanism in human agency. *American Psychologist, 37*(2), 122–147.

Bandura, A. (2000a). Exercise of human agency through collective efficacy. *Current Directions in Psychological Science, 9*(3), 75–78.

Bandura, A. (2000b). Self-efficacy. In A. E. Kazdin (Ed.), *Encyclopedia of psychology* (Vol. 7, pp. 212–213). Washington, DC: American Psychological Association.

Bandura, A. (2001). Social cognitive theory: An agentic perspective. In S. T. Fiske, D. L. Schacter, & C. Zahn-Waxler (Eds.), *Annual Review of Psychology* (Vol. 52, pp. 1–26). Palo Alto, CA: Annual Reviews.

Bandura, A., Adams, N. E., Hardy, A. B., & Howells, G. N. (1980). Tests of the generality of self-efficacy theory. *Cognitive Therapy and Research, 4,* 39–66.

Bandura, A., Barbaranelli, C., Caprara, G. V., & Pastorelli, C. (2001). Self-efficacy beliefs as shapers of children's aspirations and career trajectories. *Child Development, 72*(1), 187–206.

Barahal, H. S. (1940). Testosterone in psychotic male homosexuals. *Psychiatric Quarterly, 14,* 319–329.

Bardeen, M. (2000). Retrieved July 9, 2010, from http://ed.fnal.gov/projects/scientists/amy.html.

Barenbaum, N. B. (1997). The case(s) of Gordon Allport. *Journal of Personality, 65*(3), 743–755.

Barenbaum, N. B., & Winter, D. G. (2008). History of modern personality theory and research. In O. P. John, R. W. Robins, & L. A. Pervin (Eds.), *Handbook of personality: Theory and research.* New York: Guilford Press.

Barrett, L. F. (2009). Understanding the mind by measuring the brain. *Perspectives on Psychological Science, 4*(3), 314–318.

Barrett, P., & Eysenck, S. B. G. (1984). The assessment of personality factors across 25 countries. *Personality and Individual Differences, 5,* 615–632.

Barrick, M. R., & Mount, M. K. (1991). The Big Five personality dimensions and job performance: A meta-analysis. *Personnel Psychology, 44,* 1–26.

Barry, H. I. (2007). Characters named Charles or Charley in novels by Charles Dickens. *Psychological Reports, 101*(2), 497–500.

Bartholomew, K., Henderson, A. J. Z., & Marcia, J. E. (2000). Coded semistructured interviews in social psychological research. In H. T. Reis & C. M. Judd (Eds.), *Handbook of research methods in social and personality psychology* (pp. 286–312). Cambridge, England: Cambridge University Press.

Bartone, P. T. (1999). Hardiness protects against war-related stress in army reserve forces. *Consulting Psychology Journal: Practice and Research, 51*(2), 72–82.

Bartram, D. (2005). The great eight competencies: A criterion-centric approach to validation. *Journal of Applied Psychology, 90*(6), 1185–1203.

Baumeister, R. F. (1982). A self-presentational view of social phenomena. *Psychological Bulletin, 91*(1), 3–26.

Baumeister, R. F. (1986). *Identity: Cultural change and the struggle for self.* New York: Oxford University Press.

Baumeister, R. F. (1987). How the self became a problem: A psychological review of historical research. *Journal of Personality and Social Psychology, 52*(1), 163–176.

Baumeister, R. F. (1997). Identity, self-concept, and self-esteem: The self lost and found. In R. Hogan, J. Johnson, & S. Briggs (Eds.), *Handbook of personality psychology* (pp. 681–710). San Diego, CA: Academic Press.

Baumeister, R. F. (1999). The nature and structure of the self: An overview. In R. F. Baumeister (Ed.), *The self in social psychology* (pp. 1–20). Philadelphia: Taylor and Francis.

Baumeister, R. F. (2000). Gender differences in erotic plasticity: The female sex drive as socially flexible and responsive. *Psychological Bulletin, 126*(3), 347–374.

Baumeister, R. F., Campbell, J. D., Kreuger, J. I., & Vohs, K. D. (2003). Does high self-esteem cause better performance, interpersonal success, happiness, or healthier lifestyles? *Psychological Science in the Public Interest, 4*(1), 1–44.

Baumeister, R. F., Dale, K., & Sommer, K. L. (1998). Freudian defense mechanisms and empirical findings in modern social psychology: Reaction formation, projection, displacement, undoing, isolation, sublimation, and denial. *Journal of Personality, 66*(6), 1081–1124.

Baumeister, R. F., Tice, D. M., & Hutton, D. G. (1989). Self-presentational motivations and personality differences in self-esteem. *Journal of Personality, 57,* 547–579.

Baumgardner, A. H. (1990). To know oneself is to like oneself: Self-certainty and self-affect. *Journal of Personality and Social Psychology, 58,* 1062–1072.

Bazana, P. G., & Stelmack, R. M. (2004). Stability of personality across the life span: A meta-analysis. In *On the psychobiology of personality: Essays in honor of Marvin Zuckerman* (pp. 113–144). Amsterdam, Netherlands: Elsevier.

Beall, A. E. (1993). A social constructionist view of gender. In A. E. Beall & R. J. Sternberg (Eds.), *The psychology of gender* (pp. 127–147). New York: Guilford Press.

Beaver, J. D., Lawrence, A. D., van Ditzhuijzen, J., Davis, M. H., Woods, A., & Calder, A. J. (2006). Individual differences in reward drive predict neural responses to images of food. *The Journal of Neuroscience, 26*(19), 5160–5166.

Beck, A. T. (1976). *Cognitive therapy and the emotional disorders.* New York: International Universities Press.

Beck, A. T., Steer, R. A., & Brown, G. K. (1996). *Manual for the Beck Depression Inventory-II.* San Antonio, TX: Psychological Corporation.

Becker, B. J. (1986). Influence again: An examination of reviews and studies of gender difference in social influence. In J. S. Hyde & M. C. Linn (Eds.), *The psychology of gender: Advances through meta-analysis* (pp. 178–209). Baltimore, MD: Johns Hopkins Press.

Bell, A. P. (1974). Homosexualities: Their range and character. In *Nebraska symposium on motivation 1973* (Vol. 21, pp. 1–26). Lincoln: University of Nebraska Press.

Bell, A. P., Weinberg, M. S., & Hammersmith, S. K. (1981a). *Sexual preference: Its development in men and women.* Bloomington: Indiana University Press.

Bell, A. P., Weinberg, M. S., & Hammersmith, S. K. (1981b). *Sexual preference: Its development in men and women. Statistical appendix.* Bloomington: Indiana University Press.

Bem, D. J. (1967). Self-perception: An alternative interpretation of cognitive dissonance phenomena. *Psychological Review, 74,* 183–200.

Bem, D. J. (1972). Self-perception theory. In L. Berkowitz (Ed.), *Advances in experimental social psychology* (Vol. 6, pp. l–62). New York: Academic Press.

Bem, D. J. (1996). Exotic becomes erotic: A developmental theory of sexual orientation. *Psychological Review, 103*(2), 320–335.

Bem, D. J. (1998). Is EBE theory supported by the evidence? Is it androcentric? A reply to Peplau et al. (1998). *Psychological Review, 105*(2), 395–398.

Bem, D. J. (2000). Exotic becomes erotic: Interpreting the biological correlates of sexual orientation. *Archives of Sexual Behavior, 29*(6), 531–548.

Bem, D. J. (2008). Is there a causal link between childhood gender nonconformity and adult homosexuality? *Journal of Gay and Lesbian Mental Health, 12*(1), 61–79.

Bem, S. L. (1974). The measurement of psychological androgyny. *Journal of Consulting and Clinical Psychology, 42,* 155–162.

Bem, S. L. (1977). On the utility of alternative procedures for assessing psychological androgyny. *Journal of Consulting and Clinical Psychology, 45*(2), 196–205.

Bem, S. L. (1981). Gender schema theory: A cognitive account of sex typing. *Psychological Review, 88,* 354–364.

Bem, S. L. (1984). Androgyny and gender schema theory: A conceptual and empirical integration. In *Nebraska symposium on motivation* (Vol. 32, pp. 179–226). Lincoln: University of Nebraska Press.

Bem, S. L. (1989). Genital knowledge and gender constancy in preschool children. *Child Development, 60,* 649–662.

Bem, S. L. (1993). *The lenses of gender: Transforming the debate on sexual inequality.* New Haven, CT: Yale University Press.

Bem, S. L. (1995). Dismantling gender polarization and compulsory heterosexuality: Should we turn the volume down or up? *The Journal of Sex Research, 32*(4), 329–334.

Benassi, V. A., Sweeney, P. D., & Dufour, C. L. (1988). Is there a relationship between locus of control orientation and depression? *Journal of Abnormal Psychology, 97,* 357–367.

Benet, V., & Waller, N. G. (1995). The big seven factor model of personality description: Evidence for its cross-cultural generality in a Spanish sample. *Journal of Personality and Social Psychology, 69*(4), 701–718.

Benet-Martínez, V., & Oishi, S. (2008). Culture and personality. In O. P. John, R. W. Robins, & L. A. Pervin (Eds.), *Handbook of personality: Theory and research* (pp. 542–567). New York: Guilford Press.

Benet-Martínez, V., & Waller, N. G. (2002). From adorable to worthless: Implict and self-report structure of highly evaluative personality descriptors. *European Journal of Personality, 16,* 1–41.

Benjamin, L. T., Jr. (2009). Psychoanalysis, American style. *APA Monitor on Psychology, 40*(8), 24.

Bennett, D. S., & Bates, J. E. (1995). Prospective models of depressive symptoms in early adolescence: Attributional style, stress and support. *Journal of Early Adolescence, 15,* 299–315.

Berenbaum, S. A., & Snyder, E. (1995). Early hormonal influences on childhood sex-typed activity and playmate preferences: Implications for the development of sexual orientation. *Developmental Psychology, 31*(1), 31–42.

Berlant, L., & Warner, M. (1998). Sex in public. *Critical Inquiry, 24*(2), 547–566.

Bernstein, I. H. (1980). Security guards' MMPI profiles: Some normative data. *Journal of Personality Assessment, 44*(4), 377–380.

Berry, C. M., Sackett, P. R., & Wiemann, S. (2007). A review of recent developments in integrity test research. *Personnel Psychology, 60,* 271–301.

Berry, J. W., Poortinga, Y. H., Segall, M. H., & Dasen, P. R. (1992). *Cross-cultural psychology: Research and applications.* Cambridge, England: Cambridge University Press.

Best, D. L., & Williams, J. E. (1993). A cross-cultural viewpoint. In A. E. Beall & R. J. Sternberg (Eds.), *The psychology of gender* (pp. 215–248). New York: Guilford Press.

Best, D. L., & Williams, J. E. (2001). Gender and culture. In D. Matsumoto (Ed.), *The handbook of culture and psychology* (pp. 195–219). Cambridge, MA: Oxford University Press.

Bettencourt, B. A., & Miller, N. (1996). Gender differences in aggression as a function of provocation: A meta-analysis. *Psychological Bulletin, 119*(3), 422–447.

Beyer, S. (1999). Gender differences in the accuracy of grade expectations and evaluations. *Sex Roles, 41,* 279–296.

Bhanot, R., & Jovanovic, J. (2005). Do parents' academic gender stereotypes influence whether they intrude on their children's homework? *Sex Roles, 52,* 597–607.

Billieux, J., Linden, M. V. D., D'Acremont, M., Ceschi, G., & Zermatten, A. (2006). Does impulsivity relate to perceived dependence on and actual use of the mobile phone? *Applied Cognitive Psychology, 21,* 527–537.

Blackburn, R., Renwick, S. J. D., Donnelly, J. P., & Logan, C. (2004). Big five or big two? Superordinate factors in the NEO five factor inventory and the antisocial personality questionnaire. *Personality and Individual Differences, 37,* 957–970.

Blackwood, E. (1984). Sexuality and gender in certain native American tribes: The case of cross-gender females. *SIGNS: Journal of Women in Culture and Society, 10*(1), 27–42.

Blackwood, E. (2000). Culture and women's sexualities. *Journal of Social Issues, 56*(2), 223–238.

Blanchard, R. (1997). Birth order and sibling sex ratio in homosexual versus heterosexual males and females. *Annual Review of Sex Research, 8,* 27–67.

Blanchard, R. (2001). Fraternal birth order and the maternal immune hypothesis of male homosexuality. *Hormones and Behavior, 40,* 105–114.

Blanchard, R., & Bogaert, A. F. (1996). Homosexuality in men and number of older brothers. *American Journal of Psychiatry, 153,* 27–31.

Blanchard, R., & Klassen, P. (1997). H-Y antigen and homosexuality in men. *Journal of Theoretical Biology, 185,* 373–378.

Blanchard, R., & Sheridan, P. M. (1992). Sibship size, sibling sex ratio, birth order, and parental age in homosexual and nonhomosexual gender dysphorics. *Journal of Nervous and Mental Disease, 180,* 40–47.

Blanchard, R., & Zucker, K. J. (1994). Reanalysis of Bell, Weinberg, and Hammersmith's data on birth order, sibling sex ratio, and parental age in homosexual men. *American Journal of Psychiatry, 151,* 1375–1376.

Blanchard, R., Zucker, K. J., Bradley, S. J., & Hume, C. S. (1995). Birth order and sibling sex ratio in homosexual male adolescents and probably prehomosexual feminine boys. *Developmental Psychology, 31,* 22–30.

Block, J. (1961). *The Q-sort methodology in personality assessment.* Springfield, IL: Thomas.

Block, J. (1995). A contrarian view of the five-factor approach to personality description. *Psychological Bulletin, 117,* 187–215.

Block, J. (2001). Millennial contrarianism: The five-factor approach to personality description 5 years later. *Journal of Research in Personality, 35,* 98–107.

Block, J. (2010). The five-factor framing of personality and beyond: Some ruminations. *Psychological Inquiry, 21*(2), 2–25.

Block, J., & Kremen, A. M. (1996). IQ and ego-resiliency: Conceptual and empirical connections and separateness. *Journal of Personality and Social Psychology, 70*(2), 349–361.

Bobrow, D., & Bailey, J. M. (2001). Is male homosexuality maintained via kin selection? *Evolution and Human Behavior, 22,* 361–368.

Boden, J. M. (2006). Motive and consequence in repression. *Behavioral and Brain Sciences, 29*(5), 514–515.

Bohan, J. S. (1996). *Psychology and sexual orientation.* New York: Routledge.

Bolger, N., & Schilling, E. A. (1991). Personality and the problems of everyday life: The role of neuroticism in exposure and reactivity to daily stressors. *Journal of Personality, 59*(3), 255–386.

Bonanno, G. A. (2004). Loss, trauma, and human resilience: Have we underestimated the human capacity to thrive after extremely aversive events? *American Psychologist, 58*(1), 20–28.

Bond, M. H. (1994). Trait theory and cross-cultural studies of person perception. *Psychological Inquiry, 5*(2), 114–168.

Boomsma, D. I., de Geus, E. J. C., van Baal, G. C. M., & Koopmans, J. R. (1999). A religious upbringing reduces the influence of genetic factors on disinhibition: Evidence for interaction between genotype and environment on personality. *Twin Research, 2,* 115–125.

Borgatta, E. F. (1964). The structure of personality characteristics. *Behavioral Science, 9*(1), 8–17.

Borman, W. C., Hanson, M. A., & Hedge, J. W. (1997). Personnel selection. *Annual Review of Psychology, 48,* 299–337.

Bouchard, T. J., & McGue, M. (2003). Genetic and environmental influences on human psychological differences. *Journal of Neurobiology, 54,* 4–45.

Bowlby, J. (1969). *Attachment and loss: Vol. 1. Attachment.* New York, Basic Books.

Bowlby, J. (1973). *Attachment and loss: Vol. 2. Separation: Anxiety and anger.* New York: Basic Books.

Bowlby, J. (1980). *Attachment and loss: Vol. 3. Loss, sadness, and depression.* New York: Basic Books.

Bradley, R. H., Stuck, G. B., Coop, R. H., & White, K. P. (1977). A new scale to assess locus of control in three achievement domains. *Psychological Reports, 41*(2), 656–661.

Brandt, A. C., & Vonk, R. (2006). Who do you think you are? On the link between self-knowledge and self-esteem. In M. H. Kernis (Ed.), *Self-esteem issues and answers* (pp. 224–228). New York: Psychology Press.

Brannigan, G. G., Hauk, P. A., & Guay, J. A. (1991). Locus of control and daydreaming. *The Journal of Genetic Psychology, 152*(1), 29–33.

Brebner, J. (2003). Gender and emotions. *Personality and Individual Differences, 34,* 387–394.

Brennan, F. X., & Charnetski, C. J. (2000). Explanatory style and immunoglobulin A (IgA). *Integrative Physiological and Behavioral Science, 35*(4), 251–255.

Brennan, K. A., & Shaver, P. R. (1993). Attachment styles and parental divorce. *Journal of Divorce & Remarriage, 21*(1–2), 161–175.

Brenner, C. (1982). *The mind in conflict.* Madison, CT: International Universities Press.

Brenner, C. (2003). Is the structural model still useful? *International Journal of Psychoanalysis, 84,* 1093–1103.

Bretherton, I. (1990). Open communication and internal working models: Their role in the development of attachment relationships. In R. A. Thompson (Ed.), *Nebraska symposium on motivation 1988* (Vol. 36, pp. 57–113). Lincoln, NB: University of Nebraska Press.

Breur, J., & Freud, S. (1893/1955). On the psychical mechanisms of hysterical phenomena: Preliminary communication. In *Standard edition* (Vol. 2, pp. 1–17). London: Hogarth Press. (Original work published 1893).

Brewer, M. B. (1991). The social self: On being the same and different at the same time. *Personality and Social Psychology Bulletin, 17,* 475–482.

Brewer, M. B. (2000). Research design and issues of validity. In H. T. Reis & C. M. Judd (Eds.), *Handbook of research methods in social and personality psychology* (pp. 3–84). Cambridge, England: Cambridge University Press.

Brewer, M. B., & Chen, Y. (2007). Where (who) are collectives in collectivism? Toward conceptual clarification of individualism and collectivism. *Psychological Review, 114*(1), 133–151.

Brewin, C. R. (2003). *Post-traumatic stress disorder: Malady or myth?* New Haven, CT: Yale University Press.

Brilleslijper-Kater, S. N., & Baartman, H. E. M. (2000). What do young children know about sex? Research on the sexual knowledge of children between the ages of 2 and 6 years. *Child Abuse Review, 9,* 166–182.

Brockner, J. (1984). Low self-esteem and behavioral plasticity: Some implications for personality and social psychology. In L. Wheeler (Ed.), *Review of personality and social psychology* (Vol. 4, pp. 237–271). Beverly Hills, CA: Sage.

Brockner, J. (1988). *Self-esteem at work: Research, theory, and practice. Issues in organization and management series.* Lexington, MA: Lexington Books.

Brody, L. R. (1993). On understanding gender differences in the expression of emotion: Gender roles, socialization, and language. In S. Ablong, D. Brown, E. Khantzian, & J. Mack (Eds.), *Human feelings: Explorations in affect development and meaning* (pp. 89–121). Hillsdale, NJ: Analytic Press.

Brody, L. R. (1999). *Gender, emotion, and the family.* Cambridge, MA: Cambridge University Press.

Brody, L. R. (2000). The socialization of gender differences in emotional expression: Display rules, infant temperament, and differentiation. In A. H. Fischer (Ed.), *Gender and emotion: Social psychological perspectives* (pp. 24–47). Cambridge, England: Cambridge University Press.

Brody, L. R., & Hall, J. A. (2008). Gender and emotion in context. In M. Lewis, J. M. Haviland-Jones, & L. F. Barrett (Eds.), *The handbook of emotions* (3rd ed., pp. 395–408). New York: Guilford Press.

Bromberger, J. T., & Matthews, K. A. (1996). A longitudinal study of the effects of pessimism, trait anxiety, and life stress on depressive symptoms in middle-aged women. *Psychology and Aging, 11,* 207–211.

Brown, H. D. (1994). *Principles of language learning and teaching.* Englewood Cliffs, NJ: Prentice Hall.

Brown, J. C., & Strickland, B. R. (1972). Belief in internal–external control of reinforcement and participation in college activities. *Journal of Consulting and Clinical Psychology, 38*(1), 148.

Brown, J. D. (1993). Motivational conflict and the self: The double-bind of low self-esteem. In R. F. Baumeister (Ed.), *Self-esteem: The puzzle of low self-regard* (pp. 117–130). New York: Plenum Press.

Brown, J. D., & Marshall, M. A. (2001). Great expectations: Optimism and pessimism in achievement settings. In *Optimism & pessimism: Implications for theory, research, and practice* (pp. 239–255). Washington, DC: American Psychological Association.

Brown, J. D., & McGill, K. L. (1989). The cost of good fortune: When positive life events produce negative health consequences. *Journal of Personality and Social Psychology, 57,* 1103–1110.

Brown, W. L., McDowell, A. A., & Robinson, E. M. (1965). Discrimination learning of mirrored cues by rhesus monkeys. *Journal of Genetic Psychology, 106,* 123–128.

Brumbaugh, C. C., & Fraley, R. C. (2006). Transference and attachment: How do attachment patterns get carried forward from one relationship to the next? *Personality and Social Psychology Bulletin, 32*(4), 552–560.

Brunwasser, S. M., Gillham, J. E., & Kim, E. S. (2009). A meta-analytic review of the Penn resiliency program's effect on depressive symptoms. *Journal of Consulting and Clinical Psychology, 77*(6), 1042–1054.

Brydon, L., Walker, C., Wawrzyniak, A. J., Chart, H., & Steptoe, A. (2009). Dispositional optimism and stress-induced changes in immunity and negative mood. *Brain, Behavior, and Immunity, 23,* 810–816.

Buchanan, G. M. (1995). Explanatory style and coronary heart disease. In G. M. Buchanan & M. E. P. Seligman (Eds.), *Explanatory style* (pp. 225–232). Hillsdale, NJ: Erlbaum.

Buchanan, G. M., & Seligman, M. E. P. (1995). *Explanatory style.* Hillsdale, NJ: Erlbaum.

Buckman, A. (2010, June 21). Reap rewards of good grades [Television broadcast]. Philadelphia: WPVI TV.

Burger, J. M., & Burns, L. (1988). The illusion of unique invulnerability and the use of effective contraception. *Personality and Social Psychology Bulletin, 14*(2), 264–270.

Burt, S. A. (2008). Genes and popularity: Evidence of an evocative gene–environment correlation. *Psychological Science, 19*(2), 112–113.

Burt, S. A. (2009). A mechanistic explanation of popularity: Genes, rule breaking, and evocative gene–environment correlations. *Journal of Personality and Social Psychology, 96*(4), 783–794.

Bushman, B. J., & Baumeister, R. F. (1998). Threatened egotism, narcissism, self-esteem, and direct and displaced aggression: Does self-love or self-hate lead to violence? *Journal of Personality and Social Psychology, 75,* 219–229.

Bushman, B. J., Baumeister, R. F., & Stack, A. D. (1999). Catharsis, aggression, and persuasive influence: Self-fulfilling or self-defeating prophecies? *Journal of Personality and Social Psychology, 76*(3), 367–376.

Buss, A., & Plomin, R. (1994). *Temperament: Early developing personality traits.* New York: Erlbaum.

Buss, D. M. (1995a). Evolutionary psychology: A new paradigm for psychological science. *Psychological Inquiry, 6,* 1–30.

Buss, D. M. (1995b). Psychological sex differences: Origins through sexual selection. *American Psychologist, 50,* 164–168.

Buss, D. M. (1996). Social adaptation and five major factors of personality. In J. S. Wiggings (Ed.) *The five-factor model of personality: Theoretical perspectives* (pp. 180–207). New York: Guilford Press.

Buss, D. M. (2003). *The evolution of desire: Strategies of human mating.* New York: Basic Books.

Buss, D. M. (2004). *Evolutionary psychology: The new science of the mind.* Boston: Allyn & Bacon.

Buss, D. M. (2005). *The handbook of evolutionary psychology.* New York: Wiley.

Buss, D. M., Larsen, R. J., & Westen, D. (1992). Sex differences in jealousy: Evolution, physiology, and psychology. *Psychological Science, 3*(4), 251–255.

Buss, D. M., Larsen, R. J., & Westen, D. (1996). Sex differences in jealousy: Not gone, not forgotten, and not explained by alternative hypotheses. *Psychological Science, 7*(6), 373–375.

Busseri, M. A., Choma, B. L., & Sadava, S. W. (2009). "As good as it gets" or "The best is yet to come"? How optimists and pessimists view their past, present, and anticipated future life satisfaction. *Personality and Individual Differences, 47,* 352–356.

Bussey, K., & Bandura, A. (1999). Social cognitive theory of gender development and differentiation. *Psychological Review, 106,* 676–713.

Butcher, J. N. (1994). Psychological assessment of airline pilot applicants with the MMPI-2. *Journal of Personality Assessment, 62*(1), 31–44.

Butcher, J. N., Dahlstrom, W. G., Graham, J. R., Tellegen, A., & Kaemmer, B. (1989). *The Minnesota Multiphasic Personality Inventory-2 (MMPI-2): Manual for administration and scoring.* Minneapolis: University of Minnesota Press.

Butler, B., & Moran, G. (2007). The impact of death qualification, belief in a just world, legal authoritarianism, and locus of control on venirepersons' evaluations of aggravating and mitigating circumstances in capital trials. *Behavioral Sciences & the Law, 25*(1), 57–68.

Bybee, J. A., & Wells, Y. V. (2006). Body themes in descriptions of possible selves: Diverse perspectives across the life span. *Journal of Adult Development, 13*(2), 95–101.

Byne, W. (1995). Science and belief: Psychobiological research on asexual orientation. *Journal of Homosexuality, 25*(3/4), 303–344.

Byne, W., Tobet, S., Mattiace, L., Lasco, M. S., Kemether, E., Edgar, M. A., et al. (2001). The interstitial nuclei of the human anterior hypothalamus: An investigation of variation within sex, sexual orientation and HIV status. *Hormones and Behavior, 40,* 86–92.

Byrnes, J. P., Miller, D. C., & Schafer, W. D. (1999). Gender differences in risk taking: A meta-analysis. *Psychological Bulletin, 125*(3), 367–383.

Cacioppo, J. T., & Patrick, W. (2008). *Loneliness: Human nature and the need for social connection.* New York: Norton.

Cacioppo, J. T., & Petty, R. E. (1982). The need for cognition. *Journal of Personality and Social Psychology, 42,* 116–131.

Cacioppo, J. T., Petty, R. E., & Kao, C. F. (1984). The efficient assessment of need for cognition. *Journal of Personality Assessment, 48*(3), 306–307.

Campbell, D. T., & Fiske, D. W. (1959). Convergent and discriminant validation by the multitrait-multimethod matrix. *Psychological Bulletin, 56*(2), 81–105.

Campbell, D. T., & Stanley, J. C. (1966). *Experimental and quasi-experimental designs for research.* Chicago: Rand McNally.

Campbell, J. B., & Hawley, C. W. (1982). Study habits and Eysenck's theory of extraversion-introversion. *Journal of Research in Personality, 16,* 139–146.

Campbell, J. D. (1990). Self-esteem and clarity of the self-concept. *Journal of Personality and Social Psychology, 59,* 538–549.

Campbell, J. D., Chew, B., & Scratchley, L. S. (1991). Cognitive and emotional reactions to daily events: The effects of self-esteem and self-complexity. *Journal of Personality, 59,* 473–505.

Campbell, J. D., & Lavallee, L. F. (1993). Who am I? the role of self-concept confusion in understanding the behavior of people with low self-esteem. In R. F. Baumeister (Ed.), *Self-esteem: The puzzle of low self-regard* (pp. 3–20). New York: Plenum Press.

Campbell, J. D., Trapnell, P. D., Heine, S. J., Katz, I. M., Lavallee, L. F., & Lehman, D. R. (1996). Self-concept clarity: Measurement, personality correlates, and cultural boundaries. *Journal of Personality and Social Psychology, 70,* 141–156.

Canli, T. (2006). Genomic imaging of extraversion. In T. Canli (Ed.), *Biology of personality and individual differences* (pp. 93–115). New York: Guilford Press.

Canli, T. (2008). Toward a "molecular psychology" of personality. In O. P. John, R. W. Robins, & L. A. Pervin (Eds.), *Handbook of personality: Theory and research* (pp. 311–327). New York: Guilford Press.

Canli, T., & Lesch, K. P. (2007). Long story short: The serotonin transporter in emotion regulation and social cognition. *Nature Neuroscience, 10*(9), 1103–1109.

Canli, T., Sievers, H., Whitfield, S. L., Gotlib, I. H., & Gabrieli, J. D. E. (2002). Amygdala response to happy faces as a function of extraversion. *Science, 296*(5576), 2191.

Canli, T., Zhao, Z., Desmond, J. E., Kang, E., Gross, J., & Gabrieli, J. D. E. (2001). An fMRI study of personality influences on brain reactivity to emotional stimuli. *Behavioral Neuroscience, 115,* 33–42.

Cantor, J. M., Blanchard, R., Paterson, A. D., & Bogaert, A. F. (2002). How many gay men owe their homosexual orientation to fraternal birth order? *Archives of Sexual Behavior, 31,* 57–65.

Cardno, A., & McGuffin, P. (2002). Quantitative genetics. In P. McGuffin, M. J. Owen, & I. R. Gottesman (Eds.), *Psychiatric genetics and genomics* (pp. 31–53). Oxford, England: Oxford University Press.

Carey, G. (2003). *Human genetics for the social sciences.* Thousand Oaks, CA: Sage.

Carlson, N. R. (2010). *Physiology of behavior.* Boston: Allyn & Bacon.

Carlson, R. (1988). Exemplary lives: The uses of psychobiography for theory development. *Journal of Personality, 56,* 105–138.

Carter, S., & Snow, C. (2004, May). Helping singles enter better marriages using predictive models of marital success. *Paper presented at the 16th Annual Convention of the American Psychological Society,* Chicago, IL.

Carver, C. S. (1998). Resilience and thriving: Issues, models and linkages. *Journal of Social Issues, 54*(2), 245–266.

Carver, C. S. (2004). Negative affects deriving from the behavioral approach system. *Emotion, 4,* 3–22.

Carver, C. S. (2005). Impulse and constraint: Perspectives from personality psychology, convergence with theory in other areas, and potential for integration. *Personality and Social Psychology Review, 9,* 312–333.

Carver, C. S. (2008). Two distinct bases of inhibition of behavior: Viewing biological phenomena through the lens of psychological theory. *European Journal of Personality, 22,* 388–390.

Carver, C. S., & Baird, E. (1998). The American dream revisited: Is it what you want or why you want it that matters? *Psychological Science, 9*(4), 289–292.

Carver, C. S., & Gaines, J. G. (1987). Optimism, pessimism, and postpartum depression. *Cognitive Therapy and Research, 11*(4), 449–462.

Carver, C. S., Lehman, J. M., & Antoni, M. H. (2003). Dispositional pessimism predicts illness-related disruption of social and recreational activities among breast cancer patients. *Journal of Personality and Social Psychology, 84*(4), 813–821.

Carver, C. S., Pozo, C., Harris, S. D., Noriega, V., Scheier, M. F., Robinson, D. S., et al. (1993). How coping mediates the effect of optimism on distress: A study of women with early stage breast cancer. *Journal of Personality and Social Psychology, 65,* 375–390.

Carver, C. S., Pozo-Kaderman, C., Harris, S. D., Noriega, V., Scheier, M. F., Robinson, D. S., et al. (1994). Optimism versus pessimism predicts the quality of women's adjustment to early stage breast cancer. *Cancer, 73,* 1213–1220.

Carver, C. S., & Scheier, M. F. (1990). Origins and functions of positive and negative affect: A control process view. *Psychological Review, 97,* 19–35.

Carver, C. S., & Scheier, M. F. (1998). *On the self-regulation of behavior.* New York: Cambridge University Press.

Carver, C. S., & Scheier, M. F. (2001). Optimism, pessimism, and self-regulation. In E. C. Chang (Ed.), *Optimism & pessimism: Implications for theory, research, and practice* (pp. 31–51). Washington, DC: American Psychological Association.

Carver, C. S., & Scheier, M. F. (2002). Optimism. In C. R. Snyder & S. J. Lopez (Eds.), *Handbook of positive psychology* (pp. 231–243). New York: Oxford University Press.

Carver, C. S., & Scheier, M. F. (2003a). Optimism. In S. J. Lopez & C. R. Snyder (Eds.), *Positive psychological assessment: A handbook of models and measures* (pp. 75–89). Washington, DC: American Psychological Association.

Carver, C. S., & Scheier, M. F. (2003b). Three human strengths. In L. G. Aspinwall & U. M. Staudinger (Eds.), *A psychology of human strengths: Fundamental questions and future directions for a positive psychology* (pp. 87–102). Washington, DC: American Psychological Association.

Carver, C. S., Scheier, M. F., & Weintraub, J. K. (1989). Assessing coping strategies: A theoretically based approach. *Journal of Personality and Social Psychology, 56*(2), 267–283.

Carver, C. S., Smith, R. G., Antoni, M. H., Petronis, V. M., Weiss, S., & Derhagopian, R. P. (2005). Optimistic personality and psychosocial well-being during treatment predict psychosocial well-being among long-term survivors of breast cancer. *Health Psychology, 24*(5), 508–516.

Carver, C. S., & White, T. L. (1994). Behavioral inhibition, behavioral activation, and affective responses to impending reward and punishment: The BIS/BAS scales. *Journal of Personality and Social Psychology, 67*(2), 319–333.

Carver, P. R., Yunger, J. L., & Perry, D. G. (2003). Gender identity and adjustment in middle childhood. *Sex Roles, 49*(3/4), 95–109.

Caspi, A., Elder, G. H., & Bem, D. J. (1988). Moving away from the world: Life-course patterns of shy children. *Developmental Psychology, 24*(6), 824–831.

Caspi, A., Harrington, H., Milne, B., Amell, J. W., Theodore, R. F., & Moffitt, T. E. (2003). Children's behavioral styles at age 3 are linked to their adult personality traits at age 26. *Journal of Personality, 71*, 495–513.

Caspi, A., McClay, J., Moffitt, T., Mill, J., Martin, J., Craig, I. W., et al. (2005). Role of genotype in the cycle of violence in maltreated children. *Science, 297*, 851–854.

Caspi, A., & Moffitt, T. E. (1993). When do individual differences matter? A paradoxical theory of personality coherence. *Psychological Inquiry, 4*(4), 247–271.

Caspi, A., & Roberts, B. W. (2001). Personality development across the life course: The argument for change and continuity. *Psychological Inquiry, 12*(2), 49–66.

Caspi, A., Roberts, B. W., & Shiner, R. L. (2005). Personality development: Stability and change. *Annual Review of Psychology, 56*, 453–484.

Caspi, A., & Shiner, R. L. (2006). Personality development. In W. Damon & R. M. Lerner (Eds.), *Handbook of child psychology: Social, emotional, and personality development* (Vol. 3, pp. 300–365). Hoboken, NJ: Wiley.

Caspi, A., & Silva, P. A. (1995). Temperamental qualities at age three predict personality traits in young adulthood: Longitudinal evidence from a birth cohort. *Child Development, 66*, 486–498.

Caspi, A., Sugden, K., Moffitt, T. E., Taylor, A., Craig, I. W., Harrington, H., et al. (2003). Influence of life stress on depression: Moderation by a polymorphism in the 5-HTT gene. *Science, 301*(5631), 386–389.

Cass, V. C. (1979). Homosexual identity formation: A theoretical approach. *Journal of Homosexuality, 4*, 219–235.

Cattell, R. B. (1946). *Description and measurement of personality.* Yonkers, NY: World Book.

Cattell, R. B., & Anderson, J. C. (1953). *The I.P.A.T. music preference test of personality.* Champaign, IL: Institute for Personality and Ability Testing.

Cattell, R. B., Eber, H. W., & Tatsuoka, M. M. (1970). *Handbook for the sixteen personality factor questionnaire (16PF).* Champaign, IL: Institute for Personality and Ability Testing.

Cattell, R. B., & Saunders, D. R. (1954). Musical preferences and personality diagnosis: A factorization of one hundred and twenty themes. *Journal of Social Psychology, 39*, 3–24.

CBS3 News. (2008). *Drexel students create 'mind control' video games.* Retrieved July 27, 2009, from http://cbs3.com/topstories/Drexel.University.Games.2.762554.html.

Ceci, S. J., & Williams, W. M. (2010). Sex differences in math-intensive fields. *Current Directions in Psychological Science, 19*(5), 275–279.

Cha, A. E. (2005, March 27). Employers relying on personality tests to screen applicants. *Washington Post*, p. A01.

Chamorro-Premuzic, T., & Furnham, A. (2007). Personality and music: Can traits explain how people use music in everyday life? *British Journal of Psychology, 98*, 175–185.

Chan, D., Schmitt, N., DeShon, R. P., Clause, C. S., & Delbridge, K. (1997). Reactions to cognitive ability tests: The relationships between race, test performance, face validity perceptions, and test-taking motivation. *Journal of Applied Psychology, 82*(2), 300–310.

Chang, E. C. (2001). Cultural influences on optimism and pessimism: Differences in Western and Eastern construals of the self. In E. C. Chang (Ed.), *Optimism & pessimism: Implications for theory, research, and practice* (pp. 257–280). Washington, DC: American Psychological Association.

Chaplin, W. F., Phillips, J. B., Brown, J. D., Clanton, N. R., & Stein, J. I. (2000). Handshaking, gender, personality, and first impressions. *Journal of Personality and Social Psychology, 79*(1), 110–117.

Chavanon, M. L., Stemmler, G., & Wacker, J. (2008). A cognitive-affective extension to reinforcement sensitivity. *European Journal of Personality, 22*, 391–393.

Chemers, M. M., Hu, L., & Garcia, B. F. (2001). Academic self-efficacy and first-year college student performance and adjustment. *Journal of Educational Psychology, 93*(1), 55–64.

Chen, C., Lee, S., & Stevenson, H. W. (1995). Response style and cross-cultural comparisons of rating scales among East Asian and North American students. *Psychological Science, 6*(3), 170–175.

Cherkas, L., Hochberg, F., MacGregor, A. J., Sneider, H., & Spector, T. D. (2000). Happy families: A twin study of humor. *Twin Research, 3*, 17–22.

Cheryan, S., Plaut, V. C., Davies, P. G., & Steele, C. M. (2010). Ambient belonging: How stereotypical cues impact gender participation in computer science. *Journal of Personality and Social Psychology, 97*(6), 1045–1060.

Cheung, F. M., & Leung, K. (1998). Indigenous personality measures: Chinese examples. *Journal of Cross-Cultural Psychology, 29*(1), 233–248.

Cheung, F. M., Leung, K., Fan, R. M., Song, W., Zhang, J., & Zhang, J. (1996). Development of the Chinese personality assessment inventory. *Journal of Cross-Cultural Psychology, 27*(2), 181–199.

Cheung, F. M., Leung, K., Zhang, J., Sun, H., Gan, Y., Song, W., et al. (2001). Indigenous Chinese personality constructs: Is the five-factor model complete? *Journal of Cross-Cultural Psychology, 32*(4), 407–433.

Chivers, M. L. (2005). A brief review and discussion of sex differences in the specificity of sexual arousal. *Sexual and Relationship Therapy, 20*(4), 377–390.

Choi, S. C., Kim, U., & Choi, S. H. (1993). Indigenous analysis of collective representations: A Korean perspective. In U. Kim & J. W. Berry (Eds.), *Indigenous psychologies: Research and experience in cultural context* (pp. 193–210). Belmont, CA: Sage.

Christie, R., & Geis, F. L. (1970). *Studies in Machiavellianism.* New York: Academic Press.

Church, A. T., & Ortiz, F. A. (2005). Culture and personality. In V. J. Derlega, B. A. Winstead, & W. H. Jones (Eds.), *Personality: Contemporary theory and research* (pp. 420–456). Belmont, CA: Wadsworth.

Ciani, A. C., Corna, F., & Capiluppi, C. (2004). Evidence for maternally inherited factors favouring male homosexuality and promoting female fecundity. *Proceedings of the Royal Society of London, Series B: Biological Sciences, 271,* 2217–2221.

Clark, A. J. (1998). *Defense mechanisms in the counseling process.* New York: Sage.

Clark, L. A., & Watson, D. (1995). Constructing validity: Basic issues in objective scale development. *Psychological Assessment, 7*(3), 309–319.

Clark, L. A., & Watson, D. (2008). Temperament: An organizing paradigm for trait psychology. In O. P. John, R. W. Robins, & L. A. Pervin (Eds.), *Handbook of personality: Theory and research* (3rd ed., pp. 265–286). New York: Guilford Press.

Clausen, J. A., & Gilens, M. (1990). Personality and labor force participation across the life course: A longitudinal study of women's careers. *Sociological Forum, 5*(4), 595–618.

Cleveland, H. H., Udry, J. R., & Chantala, K. (2001). Environmental and genetic influences on sex-typed behaviors and attitudes of male and female adolescents. *Personality and Social Psychology Bulletin, 27*(12), 1587–1598.

Cloninger, C. R. (1998). The genetics and psychobiology of the seven-factor model of personality. In K. R. Silk (Ed.), *Biology of personality disorders* (pp. 63–92). Washington, DC: American Psychiatric Press.

Cloninger, C. R. (2008). Psychobiological research is crucial for understanding human personality. *European Journal of Personality, 22,* 393–396.

Cobb, S. (1976). Social support as a moderator of life stress. *Psychosomatic Medicine, 38,* 300–314.

Cohen, J. (1988). *Statistical power analysis for the behavioral sciences* (2nd ed.). Hillsdale, NJ: Erlbaum.

Cohn, M. A., Fredrickson, B. L., Brown, S. L., Mikels, J. A., & Conway, A. M. (2009). Happiness unpacked: Positive emotions increase life satisfaction by building resilience. *Emotion, 9*(3), 361–368.

Cole, S. W., Hawkley, L. C., Arevalo, J. M., Sung, C. Y., Rose, R. M., & Cacioppo, J. T. (2007). Social regulation of gene expression in human leukocytes. *Genome Biology, 8,* R189 (doi:10.1186/gb-2007-8-9-r189).

Collins, H., & Vedantam, S. (1999, December). Penn denies therapy lapse killed teen the FDA found 2 violations in the gene test. *Philadelphia Inquirer,* p. A01.

Condry, J. C., & Condry, S. (1976). Sex differences: A study of the eye of the beholder. *Child Development, 47,* 812–819.

Condry, J. C., & Ross, D. F. (1985). Sex and aggression: The influence of gender label on the perception of aggression in children. *Child Development, 56*(1), 225–233.

Confer, J. C., Easton, J. A., Fleischman, D. S., Goetz, C. D., Lewis, D. M. G., Perilloux, C., et al. (2010). Evolutionary psychology: Controversies, questions, prospects, and limitations. *American Psychologist, 65*(2), 110–126.

Connell, J. P. (1990). Context, self, and action: A motivational analysis of self-system processes across the life span. In D. Cicchetti (Ed.), *The self in transition: Infancy to childhood* (pp. 61–97). Chicago: University of Chicago Press.

Connell, J. P., & Wellborn, J. G. (1990). Competence, autonomy, and relatedness: A motivational analysis of self-system processes. In M. Gunnar & L. A. Sroufe (Eds.), *The Minnesota symposia on child psychology* (Vol. 22, pp. 43–77). Minneapolis: University of Minnesota Press.

Constantinople, A. (1973). Masculinity-femininity: An exception to a famous dictum? *Psychological Bulletin, 80*(5), 389–407.

Cooley, C. H. (1902). *Human nature and the social order.* New York: Scribner's.

Cools, R., Calder, A. J., Lawrence, A. D., Clark, L., Bullmore, E., & Robbins, T. W. (2005). Individual differences in threat sensitivity predict serotonergic modulation of amygdala response to fearful faces. *Psychopharmacology, 180*(4), 670–679.

Corr, P. J. (2001). Testing problems in J. A. Gray's personality theory: Commentary on Matthews and Gilliland. *Personality and Individual Differences, 30,* 333–352.

Corr, P. J. (2002). J. A. Gray's reinforcement sensitivity theory: Tests of the joint subsystems hypothesis of anxiety and impulsivity. *Personality and Individual Differences, 33,* 511–532.

Corr, P. J. (2004). Reinforcement sensitivity theory and personality. *Neuroscience and the Biobehavioral Reviews, 28,* 317–322.

Corr, P. J. (2006). *Understanding biological psychology.* Malden, MA: Blackwell.

Corr, P. J. (2008a). An intermediate-level approach to personality: Dissolving the bottom-up and top-down dilemma. *European Journal of Personality, 22,* 396–398.

Corr, P. J. (2008b). The reinforcement sensitivity theory (RST): An introduction. In P. J. Corr (Ed.), *The reinforcement sensitivity theory of personality* (pp. 1–43). Cambridge, England: Cambridge University Press.

Corr, P. J., & McNaughton, N. (2008). Reinforcement sensitivity theory and personality. In P. J. Corr (Ed.), *The reinforcement sensitivity theory of personality* (pp. 155–187). Cambridge, England: Cambridge University Press.

Cortina, J. M. (1993). What is coefficient alpha? An examination of theory and applications. *Journal of Applied Psychology, 78*(1), 98–104.

Costa, P. T., & McCrae, R. R. (1976). Age differences in personality structure: A cluster analysis approach. *Journal of Gerontology, 31,* 564–570.

Costa, P. T., & McCrae, R. R. (1980). Influence of extraversion and neuroticism on subjective well-being: Happy and unhappy people. *Journal of Personality and Social Psychology, 38,* 668–678.

Costa, P. T., & McCrae, R. R. (1985). *The NEO personality inventory manual.* Odessa, FL: Psychological Assessment Resources.

Costa, P. T., & McCrae, R. R. (1992). *Revised NEO personality inventory (NEO-PI-R) and NEO five-factor inventory (NEO-FFI) professional manual.* Odessa, FL: Psychological Assessment Resources.

Costa, P. T., & McCrae, R. R. (1994). Set like plaster: Evidence for the stability of adult personality. In T. F. Heatherton & J. L. Weinberger (Eds.), *Can personality change?* (pp. 21–40). Washington, DC: American Psychological Association.

Costa, P. T., McCrae, R. R., & Dye, D. A. (1991). Facet scales for agreeableness and conscientiousness: A revision of the NEO personality inventory. *Personality and Individual Differences, 12*(9), 887–898.

Costa, P. T., Terracciano, A., & McCrae, R. R. (2001). Gender differences in personality traits across cultures. *Journal of Personality and Social Psychology, 81*(2), 322–331.

Cousins, S. D. (1989). Culture and self-perception in Japan and the United States. *Journal of Personality and Social Psychology, 56*(1), 124–131.

Cowey, A. (2001). Functional localisation in the brain: From ancient to modern. *The Psychologist, 14*(5), 250–254.

Cramer, P. (2000). Defense mechanisms in psychology today. *American Psychologist, 55*(6), 637–646.

Cramer, P. (2006). *Protecting the self: Defense mechanisms in action.* New York: Guilford Press.

Creed, P. A., Patton, W., & Bartrum, E. (2002). Multidimensional properties of the LOT-R: Effects of optimism and pessimism on career and well-being related variables in adolescents. *Journal of Career Assessment, 10*(1), 42–61.

Crews, F. C. (1996). The verdict on Freud. *Psychological Science, 7*(2), 63–68.

Crews, F. C. (1998). *Unauthorized Freud.* New York: Viking.

Crews, F. C. (2006). What Erdelyi has repressed. *Behavioral and Brain Sciences, 29*(5), 516–517.

Crocker, J., & Knight, K. M. (2005). Contingencies of self-worth. *Current Directions in Psychological Science, 14*(4), 200–203.

Cronbach, L. J. (1947). Test "reliability": Its meaning and determination. *Psychometrika, 12,* 1–16.

Cronbach, L. J. (1950). Further evidence on response sets and test design. *Educational and Psychological Measurement, 10,* 3–31.

Cronbach, L. J. (1951). Coefficient alpha and the internal structure of tests. *Psychometrika, 16,* 297–334.

Cronbach, L. J. (1957). The two disciplines of scientific psychology. *American Psychologist, 12,* 671–684.

Cronbach, L. J. (1960). *Essentials of psychological testing* (2nd ed.). New York: Harper & Row.

Cronbach, L. J., Rajaratnam, N., & Gleser, G. C. (1963). Theory of generalizability: A liberalization of reliability theory. *The British Journal of Statistical Psychology, 16*(2), 137–163.

Cross, S., & Markus, H. R. (1991). Possible selves across the life span. *Human Development, 34,* 230–255.

Cross, S. E., & Markus, H. R. (1999). The cultural constitution of personality. In L. A. Pervin & O. P. John (Eds.), *Handbook of personality: Theory and research* (2nd ed., pp. 378–396). New York: Guilford Press.

Cross, W. E., & Cross, T. B. (2008). Theory, research, and models. In S. M. Quintana & C. McKown (Eds.), *Handbook of race, racism, and the developing child* (pp. 154–181). Hoboken, NJ: Wiley.

Crowell, J. A., Fraley, R. C., & Shaver, P. R. (2008). Measurement of individual differences in adolescent and adult attachment. In J. Cassidy & P. R. Shaver (Eds.), *Handbook of attachment* (pp. 599–634). New York, NY: Guilford Press.

Crowne, D. P., & Liverant, S. (1963). Conformity under varying conditions of personal commitment. *Journal of Abnormal and Social Psychology, 66,* 547–555.

Crowne, D. P., & Marlow, D. (1960). A new scale of social desirability independent of psychopathology. *Journal of Consulting Psychology, 24*(4), 349–354.

Csikszentmihalyi, M. (1975). *Beyond boredom and anxiety.* San Francisco, CA: Jossey-Bass.

Csikszentmihalyi, M. (1990). *Flow: The psychology of optimal experience.* New York: Harper Perennial.

Csikszentmihalyi, M. (1997). *Finding flow: The psychology of engagement with everyday life.* New York, NY: Basic Books.

Daly, M., & Wilson, M. (1988). *Homicide.* New York: Aldine de Gruyter.

Damasio, A. R. (1999). Commentary by Antonio R. Damasio. *Neuro-Psychoanalysis, 1*(1), 38–39.

Darlington, R. B. (2009). *Factor analysis.* Retrieved February 23, 2009, from http://www.psych.cornell.edu/Darlington/factor.htm.

Davidson, R. J. (1992). Emotion and affective style. *Psychological Science, 3*(1), 39–43.

Davidson, R. J. (2004). What does the prefrontal cortex "do" in affect: Perspectives on frontal EEG asymmetry research. *Biological Psychology, 67,* 219–233.

Davidson, R. J. (2009). *Lab for affective neuroscience.* Retrieved July 17 from http://psyphz.psych.wisc.edu/web/news.html.

Davidson, R. J., Kabat-Zinn, J., Schumacher, J., Rosenkranz, M., Muller, D., Santorelli, S. F., et al. (2003). Alterations in brain and immune function produced by mindfulness meditation. *Psychosomatic Medicine, 65,* 564–570.

Davis, C. G., Nolen-Hoeksema, S., & Larsen, J. (1998). Making sense of loss and benefitting from experience: Two construals of meaning. *Journal of Personality and Social Psychology, 75,* 561–574.

Davis, D., Shaver, P. R., & Vernon, M. L. (2003). Physical, emotional, and behavioral reactions to breaking up: The roles of gender, age, emotional involvement, and attachment style. *Personality and Social Psychology Bulletin, 29*(7), 871–884.

Davis, J. A., Smith, T. W., & Marsden, P. V. (2010). *General social surveys, 1972–2008.* Storrs, CT: Roper Center for Public Opinion Research, University of Connecticut/Ann Arbor, MI: Interuniversity Consortium for Political and Social Research. Available from http://www.icpsr.umich.edu/icpsrweb/ICPSR/series/00028/studies/25962/detail.

Day, D. V., & Schleicher, D. J. (2006). Self-monitoring at work: A motive-based perspective. *Journal of Personality, 74,* 685–713.

Deb, M. (1983). Sales effectiveness and personality characteristics. *Psychological Research Journal, 7*(2), 59–67.

DeBono, K. G. (1987). Investigating the social adjustive and value expressive functions of attitudes: Implications for persuasion processes. *Journal of Personality and Social Psychology, 52,* 279–287.

DeBono, K. G. (2006). Self-monitoring and consumer psychology. *Journal of Personality, 74*(3), 715–737.

DeCharms, R. (1981). Personal causation and locus of control: Two different traditions and two uncorrelated constructs. In H. M. Lefcourt (Ed.), *Research with the locus of control construct: Vol. 1. Assessment methods* (pp. 337–358). San Diego, CA: Academic Press.

Deci, E. L. (1971). Effects of externally mediated rewards on intrinsic motivation. *Journal of Personality and Social Psychology, 18*(1), 105–115.

Deci, E. L. (1975). *Intrinsic motivation.* New York: Plenum Press.

Deci, E. L. (1980). *The psychology of self-determination.* Lexington, MA: Lexington Books.

Deci, E. L., Connell, J. P., & Ryan, R. M. (1989). Self-determination in a work organization. *Journal of Applied Psychology, 74*(4), 580–590.

Deci, E. L., Koestner, R., & Ryan, R. M. (1999). A meta-analytic review of experiments examining the effects of extrinsic rewards on intrinsic motivation. *Psychological Bulletin, 125*(6), 627–668.

Deci, E. L., & Ryan, R. M. (1985a). The general causality orientations scale: Self-determination in personality. *Journal of Research in Personality, 19,* 109–134.

Deci, E. L., & Ryan, R. M. (1985b). *Intrinsic motivation and self-determination in human behavior.* New York: Plenum Press.

Deci, E. L., & Ryan, R. M. (1991). A motivational approach to self: Integration in personality. In R. Dienstbier (Ed.), *Nebraska symposium on motivation: Vol. 38. Perspectives on motivation* (pp. 237–288). Lincoln: University of Nebraska Press.

Deci, E. L., & Ryan, R. M. (1995). Human autonomy: The basis for true self-esteem. In M. H. Kernis (Ed.), *Efficacy, agency, and self-esteem* (pp. 31–49). New York: Plenum Press.

Deci, E. L., & Ryan, R. M. (2008). Self-determination theory: A macrotheory of human motivation, development and health. *Canadian Psychology, 49*(3), 182–185.

Deci, E. L., Ryan, R. M., Gagné, M., Leone, D. R., Usunov, J., & Kornazheva, B. P. (2001). Need satisfaction, motivation, and well-being in the work organizations of a former Eastern bloc country. *Personality and Social Psychology Bulletin, 27,* 930–942.

De Fruyt, F., Bartels, M., Van Leeuwen, K. G., De Clercq, B., Decuyper, M., & Mervielde, I. (2006). Five types of personality continuity in childhood and adolescence. *Journal of Personality and Social Psychology, 91*(3), 538–552.

Delfour, F., & Marten, K. (2001). Mirror image processing in three marine mammal species: Killer whales (*orcinus orca*), false killer whales (*pseudorca crassidens*) and california sea lions (*zalophus californianus*). *Behavioural Processes, 53,* 181–190.

Delsing, M. J. M. H., TerBogt, T. F. M., Engels, R. C. M. E., & Meeus, W. H. J. (2008). Adolescents' music preferences and personality characteristics. *European Journal of Personality, 22,* 109–130.

Department of Health and Human Services. (1979). *The Belmont report: Ethical principles and guidelines for the protection of human subjects of research* (DHEW Publication No. 1983, 381-132, 3205). Washington, DC: Government Printing Office.

De Pascalis, V. (2004). On the psychophysiology of extraversion. In R. M. Stelmack (Ed.), *On the psychobiology of personality: Essays in honor of Marvin Zuckerman* (pp. 295–327). New York: Elsevier.

DePaulo, B. M. (1992). Nonverbal behavior and self-presentation. *Psychological Bulletin, 111*(2), 203–243.

Depue, R. A., & Collins, P. F. (1999). Neurobiology of the structure of personality: Dopamine, facilitation of incentive motivation, and extraversion. *Behavioral and Brain Sciences, 22,* 491–569.

Depue, R. A., Luciano, M., Arbisi, P., Collins, P., & Leon, A. (1994). Dopamine and the structure of personality: Relation of agonist-induced dopamine activity to positive emotionality. *Journal of Personality and Social Psychology, 67*(3), 485–498.

DeRubeis, R. J., & Hollon, S. D. (1995). Explanatory style in the treatment of depression. In G. M. Buchanan & M. E. P. Seligman (Eds.), *Explanatory style* (pp. 99–112). Hillsdale, NJ: Erlbaum.

Development Dimensions International Inc. (2005). *Research results: Predicting employee engagement.* Pittsburgh, PA: Author.

DeVries, A. C., Johnson, C. L., & Carter, C. S. (1997). Familiarity and gender influence social preferences in prairie voles (*Microtus ochrogaster*). *Canadian Journal of Zoology, 75,* 295–301.

DeYoung, C. G. (2006). Higher-order factors of the Big Five in a multi-informant sample. *Journal of Personality and Social Psychology, 91*(6), 1138–1151.

DeYoung, C. G., Peterson, J. B., & Higgins, D. M. (2002). Higher-order factors of the Big Five predict conformity: Are there neuroses of health? *Personality and Individual Differences, 33*(4), 533–552.

Diamond, L. M. (2003a). Was it a phase? Young women's relinquishment of lesbian/bisexual identities over a 5-year period. *Journal of Personality and Social Psychology, 84*(2), 352–364.

Diamond, L. M. (2003b). What does sexual orientation orient? A biobehavioral model distinguishing romantic love and sexual desire. *Psychological Review, 110*(1), 173–192.

Diamond, L. M. (2004). Emerging perspectives on distinctions between romantic love and sexual desire. *Current Directions in Psychological Science, 13*(3), 116–119.

Diamond, L. M. (2005). A new view of lesbian subtypes: Stable versus fluid identity trajectories over an 8-year period. *Psychology of Women Quarterly, 29,* 119–128.

Diamond, L. M. (2006a). The evolution of plasticity in female–female desire. In M. R. Kauth (Ed.), *Handbook of the evolution of human sexuality* (pp. 245–274). London: Haworth Press.

Diamond, L. M. (2006b). What we got wrong about sexual identity development: Unexpected findings from a longitudinal study of young women. In A. M. Omoto & H. S. Kurtzman (Eds.), *Sexual orientation and mental health: Examining identity and development in lesbian, gay, and bisexual people* (pp. 73–94). Washington, DC: American Psychological Association.

Diamond, L. M. (2007). A dynamic systems approach to the development and expression of female same-sex sexuality. *Perspectives on Psychological Science, 2*(2), 142–161.

Diamond, L. M. (2008a). Female bisexuality from adolescence to adulthood: Results from a 10-year longitudinal study. *Developmental Psychology, 44*(1), 5–14.

Diamond, L. M. (2008b). *Sexual fluidity: Understanding women's love and desire.* Cambridge, MA: Harvard University Press.

Dickerson, C. A., Thibodeau, R., Aronson, E., & Miller, D. (1992). Using cognitive dissonance to encourage water conservation. *Journal of Applied Social Psychology, 22*(1), 841–854.

Diener, E. (2009). Editor's introduction to Vul et al. (2009) and comments. *Perspectives on Psychological Science, 4*(3), 272–273.

Diener, E. (2010). Neuroimaging: Voodoo, new phrenology, or scientific breakthrough? Introduction to special section on fMRI. *Perspectives on Psychological Science, 5*(6), 714–715.

Diener, E., & Emmons, R. A. (1984). The independence of positive and negative affect. *Journal of Personality and Social Psychology, 47,* 1105–1117.

Diener, E., & Larsen, R. J. (1993). The experience of emotional well-being. In M. Lewis & J. M. Haviland (Eds.), *Handbook of emotions* (pp. 405–415). New York: Guilford Press.

Digman, J. M. (1989). Five robust trait dimensions: Development, stability, and utility. *Journal of Personality, 57,* 195–214.

Digman, J. M. (1990). Personality structure: Emergence of the five-factor model. *Annual review of psychology, 41,* 417–440.

Digman, J. M. (1996). The curious history of the five-factor model. In J. S. Wiggins (Ed.), *The five-factor model of personality: Theoretical perspectives* (pp. 1–20). New York: Guilford Press.

Digman, J. M. (1997). Higher-order factors of the Big Five. *Journal of Personality and Social Psychology, 73*(6), 1246–1256.

DiLalla, L. F. (2004). Behavioral genetics: Background, current research, and goals for the future. In L. F. DiLalla (Ed.), *Behavioral genetics principles: Perspectives in development, personality, and psychopathology* (pp. 3–15). Washington, DC: American Psychological Association.

Dillon, K., Minchoff, B., & Baker, K. H. (1985–1986). Positive emotional states and enhancement of the immune system. *International Journal of Psychiatry in Medicine, 15,* 13–18.

Doherty, K. T. (2004). *Society for teaching of psychology discussion list archives.* Available from http://list .kennesaw.edu/archives/psychteacher.html.

Doherty, R. W. (1997). The emotional contagion scale: A measure of individual differences. *Journal of Nonverbal Behavior, 21*(2), 131–154.

Doi, T. (1973). *The anatomy of dependence.* New York: Harper Row.

Dollinger, S. J. (1993). Research note: Personality and music preference: Extraversion and excitement seeking or openness to experience? *Psychology of Music, 21,* 73–77.

Domes, G., Heinrichs, M., Michel, A., Berger, C., & Herpertz, S. C. (2007). Oxytocin improves "mind-reading" in humans. *Biological Psychiatry, 61,* 731–733.

Dondi, M., Simion, F., & Caltran, G. (1999). Can newborns discriminate between their own cry and the cry of another newborn infant? *Developmental Psychology, 35*(2), 418–426.

Donnellan, M. B., Conger, R. D., & Burzette, R. (2007). Personality development from late adolescence to young adulthood: Differential stability, normative maturity, and evidence for the maturity-stability hypothesis. *Journal of Personality, 75,* 237–263.

Donnellan, M. B., Trzesniewski, K. H., Robins, R. W., Moffitt, T. E., & Caspi, A. (2005). Low self-esteem is related to aggression, antisocial behavior, and delinquency. *Psychological Science, 16*(4), 328–335.

Donovan, D. M., & O'Leary, M. R. (1978). The drinking-related locus of control scale: Reliability, factor structure and validity. *Journal of Studies on Alcohol, 39*(5), 759–784.

Downey, J. I., & Friedman, R. C. (1998). Female homosexuality: Classical psychoanalytic theory reconsidered. *Journal of the American Psychoanalytic Association, 46,* 471–506.

Drexel University Replay Lab. (2009). Retrieved July 27, 2009, from http://www.replay.drexel.edu/.

Dumit, J. (2004). *Picturing personhood: Brain scans and biomedical identity.* Princeton, NJ: Princeton University Press.

Dunkel, C. S., Kelts, D., & Coon, B. (2006). Possible selves as mechanisms of change in therapy. In C. Dunkel & J. Kerpelman (Eds.), *Possible selves: Theory, research and application* (pp. 187–204). New York: Nova Science Publishers.

Dunn, D. S. (1999). *The practical researcher: A student guide to conducting psychological research.* Boston: McGraw-Hill.

Dunn, D. S., & Dougherty, S. B. (2005). Teaching Freud by reading Freud: Controversy as pedagogy. *Teaching of Psychology, 32*(2), 114–116.

Dunn, E. W., Biesanz, J. C., Human, L. J., & Finn, S. (2007). Misunderstanding the affective consequences of everyday social interactions: The hidden benefits of putting one's best face forward. *Journal of Personality and Social Psychology, 92*(6), 990–1005.

Dunning, D., Heath, C., & Suls, J. M. (2004). Flawed self-assessment: Implications for health, education, and the workplace. *Psychological Science in the Public Interest, 5*(3), 69–106.

Durand, D. E., & Shea, D. (1974). Entrepreneurial activity as a function of achievement motivation and reinforcement control. *The Journal of Psychology, 88,* 57–63.

Durrett, C., & Trull, T. J. (2005). An evaluation of evaluative personality terms: A comparison of the big seven and five-factor model in predicting psychopathology. *Psychological Assessment, 17*(3), 359–368.

Duval, S., & Wicklund, R. A. (1972). *A theory of objective self awareness.* New York: Academic Press.

Dwairy, M. (2002). Foundations of psychosocial dynamic personality theory of collective people. *Clinical Psychology Review, 22,* 343–360.

Dweck, C. S. (1999). *Self-theories: Their role in motivation, personality, and development.* Philadelphia: Psychology Press.

Eagly, A. H. (1978). Sex differences in influenceability. *Psychological Bulletin, 85,* 86–116.

Eagly, A. H. (1987). *Sex differences in social behavior: A social-role interpretation.* Hillsdale, NJ: Erlbaum.

Eagly, A. H. (2009a). The his and hers of prosocial behavior: An examination of the social psychology of gender. *American Psychologist, 64*(8), 644–658.

Eagly, A. H. (2009b). Possible selves in marital roles: The impact of the anticipated division of labor on the mate preferences of women and men. *Personality and Social Psychology Bulletin, 35*(4), 403–414.

Eagly, A. H., & Carli, L. L. (1981). Sex of researchers and sex-typed communications as determinants of sex differences in influenceability: A meta-analysis of social influence studies. *Psychological Bulletin, 90*(1), 1–20.

Eagly, A. H., & Crowley, M. (1986). Gender and helping behavior: A meta-analytic review of the social psychological literature. *Psychological Bulletin, 100,* 283–308.

Eagly, A. H., & Johannesen-Schmidt, M. C. (2001). The leadership styles of women and men. *Journal of Social Issues, 57*(4), 781–797.

Eagly, A. H., Johannesen-Schmidt, M. C., & van Engen, M. L. (2003). Transformational, transactional, and laissez-faire leadership styles: A meta-analysis comparing women and men. *Psychological Bulletin, 129*(4), 569–591.

Eagly, A. H., & Johnson, B. T. (1990). Gender and leadership style: A meta-anlaysis. *Psychological Bulletin, 108*(2), 233–256.

Eagly, A. H., & Karau, S. J. (1991). Gender and the emergence of leaders: A meta-analysis. *Journal of Personality and Social Psychology, 60*(5), 685–710.

Eagly, A. H., Karau, S. J., & Makhijani, M. G. (1995). Gender and the effectiveness of leaders: A meta-analysis. *Psychological Bulletin, 117*(1), 125–145.

Eagly, A. H., Makhijani, M. G., & Klonsky, B. G. (1992). Gender and the evaluation of leaders: A meta-analysis. *Psychological Bulletin, 111,* 3–22.

Eagly, A. H., & Sczesny, S. (2009). Stereotypes about women, men, and leaders: Have times changed? In M. Barrento, M. K. Ryan, & M. T. Schmitt (Eds.), *The glass ceiling in the 21st century: Understanding barriers to gender equality* (pp. 21–47). Washington, DC: American Psychological Association.

Eagly, A. H., & Steffen, V. J. (1986). Gender and aggressive behavior: A meta-analytic review of the social psychological literature. *Psychological Bulletin, 100*(3), 309–330.

Eagly, A. H., & Wood, W. (1999). A social role interpretation of sex differences in human mate preferences. *American Psychologist, 54,* 408–423.

Easton, W. O., & Enns, L. R. (1986). Sex differences in human motor activity level. *Psychological Bulletin, 100,* 19–28.

Eaves, L., Eysenck, H. J., & Martin, N. (1989). *Genes, culture and personality: An empirical approach.* New York: Academic Press.

Egan, S. K., & Perry, D. G. (2001). Gender identity: A multidimensional analysis with implications for psychosocial adjustment. *Developmental Psychology, 37*(4), 451–463.

Egloff, B., & Schmukle, S. C. (2002). Predictive validity of an implicit association test for assessing anxiety. *Journal of Personality and Social Psychology, 83*(6), 1441–1455.

Eisenberg, N., & Lennon, R. (1983). Sex differences in empathy and related capacities. *Psychological Bulletin, 94*(1), 100–131.

Eisenberger, R., Pierce, W. D., & Cameron, J. (1999). Effects of reward on intrinsic motivation—negative, neutral, and positive: Comment on Deci, Koestner, and Ryan (1999). *Psychological Bulletin, 125*(6), 677–691.

Elder, G. H. (1969). Occupational mobility, life patterns, and personality. *Journal of Health and Social Behavior, 10*(4), 308–323.

Elliot, A. J., & Reis, H. T. (2003). Attachment and exploration in adulthood. *Journal of Personality and Social Psychology, 85*(2), 317–331.

Elliot, A. J., & Thrash, T. M. (2008). Approach and avoidance temperaments. In G. J. Boyle, G. Matthews, & D. H. Saklofske (Eds.), *The SAGE handbook of personality theory and assessment: Vol. 1. Personality theories and models* (pp. 315–333). Los Angeles: Sage.

Ellis, A. (1962). *Reason and emotion in psycholherapy.* Secaucus, NJ: Lyle Stuart.

Ellis, H. (1928). *Studies in the psychology of sex: Vol. 2. Sexual inversion.* Philadelphia: F. A. Davis.

Ellis, L. (1996). Theories of homosexuality. In R. C. Savin-Williams & K. M. Cohen (Eds.), *The lives of lesbians, gay, and bisexuals: Children to adults* (pp. 11–70). Fort Worth, TX: Harcourt Brace College.

Ellis, L., & Ames, M. A. (1987). Neurohormonal functioning and sexual orientation: A theory of homosexuality/heterosexuality. *Psychological Bulletin, 101,* 233–258.

Ellis, L., Ames, M. A., Peckham, W., & Burke, D. (1988). Sexual orientation of human offspring may be altered by severe maternal stress during pregnancy. *The Journal of Sex Research, 25*(1), 152–157.

Ellis, L., & Cole-Harding, S. (2001). The effects of prenatal stress, and of prenatal alcohol and nicotine exposure, on human sexual orientation. *Physiology & Behavior, 74,* 213–226.

Ellison, N. B., Steinfield, C., & Lampe, C. (2007). The benefits of Facebook "friends": Social capital and college students' use of online social network sites. *Journal of Computer-Mediated Communication, 12*(4), article 1.

Ellsworth, P. C., & Smith, C. A. (1988). Shades of joy: Patterns of appraisal differentiating pleasant emotions. *Cognition and Emotion, 2,* 301–331.

Elms, A. C. (2007). Psychobiography and case study methods. In R. W. Robins, R. C. Fraley, & R. F. Krueger (Eds.), *Handbook of research methods in personality psychology* (pp. 97–113). New York: Guilford Press.

Else-Quest, N. M., Hyde, J. S., Goldsmith, H. H., & Van Hulle, C. A. (2006). Gender differences in temperament: A meta-analysis. *Psychological Bulletin, 132*(1), 33–72.

Else-Quest, N. M., Hyde, J. S., & Linn, M. C. (2010). Cross-national patterns of gender differences in mathematics: A meta-analysis. *Psychological Bulletin, 136*(1), 103–127.

Emmons, R. A., Barrett, J. L., & Schnitker, S. A. (2008). Personality and the capacity for religious and spiritual experience. In O. P. John, R. W. Robins, & L. A. Pervin (Eds.), *Handbook of personality: Theory and research.* New York: Guilford Press.

Emmons, R. A., & McCullough, M. E. (2003). Counting blessings versus burdens: An experimental investigation of gratitude and subjective well-being in daily life. *Journal of Personality and Social Psychology, 84*(2), 377–389.

Enriquez, V. G. (1994). *From colonial to liberation psychology: The Philippine experience.* Manila, Philippines: De La Salle University Press.

Epel, E. S., McEwen, B. S., & Ickovics, J. R. (1998). Embodying psychological thriving: Physical thriving in response to stress. *Journal of Social Issues, 54*(2), 301–322.

Epping-Jordan, J. E., Compas, B. E., Osowiecki, D. M., Oppedisano, G., Gerhardt, C., Primo, K., et al. (1999). Psychological adjustment in breast cancer: Processes of emotional distress. *Health Psychology, 18*, 315–326.

Equal Employment Opportunity Commission, Civil Service Commission, Department of Labor, & Department of Justice. (1978). Adoption by four agencies of uniform guidelines on employee selection procedures. *Federal Register, 43*, 38290–38315.

Erdelyi, M. H. (2000). Repression. In A. E. Kazdin (Ed.), *Encyclopedia of psychology* (Vol. 7, pp. 69–71). Washington, DC: American Psychological Association.

Erdelyi, M. H. (2006a). The return of the repressed [Author's Response]. *Behavioral and Brain Sciences, 29*(5), 535–543.

Erdelyi, M. H. (2006b). The unified theory of repression. *Behavioral and Brain Sciences, 29*, 499–551.

Erikson, E. H. (1950). *Childhood and society.* New York: Norton.

Erikson, E. H. (1968). *Identity: Youth and crisis.* New York: Norton.

Esterson, A. (1993). *Seductive mirage: An exploration of the work of Sigmund Freud.* Chicago: Open Court.

Esterson, A. (1998). Jeffrey Masson and Freud's seduction theory: A new fable based on old myths. *History of the Human Sciences, 11*(1), 1–21.

Esterson, A. (2001). The mythologizing of psychoanlytic history: Deception and self-deception in Freud's accounts of the seduction theory episode. *History of Psychiatry, 12*, 329–352.

Esterson, A. (2002a). Freud's seduction theory: A reply to Gleaves and Hernandez. *History of Psychology, 5*, 85–91.

Esterson, A. (2002b). The myth of Freud's ostracism by the medical community in 1896–1905: Jeffrey Masson's assault on truth. *History of Psychology, 5*, 115–134.

Evans, D. C., Gosling, S. D., & Carroll, A. (2008, March 31–April 2). What elements of an online social networking profile predict target-rater agreement in personality impressions? In *Proceedings of the international conference on weblogs and social media.* Seattle, WA.

Evans, W. P., Owens, P., & Marsh, S. C. (2005). Environmental factors, locus of control, and adolescent suicide risk. *Child and Adolescent Social Work Journal, 22*(3–4), 301–319.

Eysenck, H. J. (1952). *The scientific study of personality.* London: Routledge and Kegan Paul.

Eysenck, H. J. (1967). *The biological basis of personality.* Springfield, IL: Charles C. Thomas.

Eysenck, H. J. (1990). Biological dimensions of personality. In L. A. Pervin (Ed.), *Handbook of personality: Theory and research* (pp. 244–276). New York: Guilford Press.

Eysenck, H. J. (1991). Dimensions of personality: 16, 5, or 3?—criteria for a taxonomic paradigm. *Personality and Individual Differences, 12*(8), 773–790.

Eysenck, H. J. (1997). Personality and experimental psychology. *Journal of Personality and Social Psychology, 73*(6), 1224–1237.

Eysenck, H. J. (1998). *Dimensions of personality.* New Brunswick, NJ: Transaction.

Eysenck, H. J., & Eysenck, M. W. (1985). *Personality and individual differences.* New York: Plenum Press.

Eysenck, H. J., & Eysenck, S. B. G. (1975). *Manual of the Eysenck personality inventory.* San Diego, CA: Educational and Industrial Testing Service.

Eysenck, H. J., & Eysenck, S. B. G. (1976). *Psychoticism as a dimension of personality.* London: Hodder and Stoughton.

Fabrigar, L. R., Wegener, D. T., MacCallum, R. C., & Strahan, E. J. (1999). Evaluating the use of exploratory factor analysis in psychological research. *Psychological Methods, 4*(3), 272–299.

Feingold, A. (1992). Gender differences in mate selection preferences: A test of the parental investment model. *Psychological Bulletin, 112*.

Feingold, A. (1994). Gender differences in personality: A meta-analysis. *Psychological Bulletin, 116*(3), 429–456.

Feng, J., Spence, I., & Pratt, J. (2007). Playing an action video game reduces gender differences in spatial cognition. *Psychological Science, 18*(10), 850–855.

Fenichel, O. (1945/1995). *The psychoanalytic theory of neurosis.* New York: Norton. (Original work published 1945)

Festinger, L. (1957). *A theory of cognitive dissonance.* Evanston, IL: Row, Peterson.

Fincham, F. D., & Bradbury, T. N. (1993). Marital satisfaction, depression, and attributions: A longitudinal analysis. *Journal of Personality and Social Psychology, 64*, 442–452.

Finn, R. (2004, March 25). This Queer Eye takes design to the masses. *New York Times*, p. B2.

Fischer, A. H., & Manstead, A. S. R. (2000). The relation between gender and emotion in different cultures. In A. H. Fischer (Ed.), *Gender and emotion: Social psychological perspectives* (pp. 71–98). New York: Cambridge University Press.

Fisher, H. E. (1998). Lust, attraction, and attachment in mammalian reproduction. *Human Nature, 9*, 23–52.

Fisher, S., & Greenberg, R. P. (1996). *Freud scientifically reappraised: Testing the theories and therapy.* New York: Wiley.

Fiske, D. W. (1949). Consistency of the factorial structures of personality ratings from different sources. *Journal of Abnormal and Social Psychology, 44*(3), 329–344.

Fleeson, W. (2007). Studying personality processes: Explaining change in between-persons longitudinal and within-person multilevel models. In R. W. Robins, R. C. Fraley & R. F. Krueger (Eds.), *Handbook of research methods in personality psychology* (pp. 523–542). New York: Guilford Press.

Flouri, E. (2006). Parental interest in children's education, children's self-esteem and locus of control, and later educational attainment: Twenty-six-year follow-up of the 1970 British birth cohort. *British Journal of Educational Psychology, 76*(1), 41–55.

Foa, E. B., Riggs, D. S., Massie, E. D., & Yarczower, M. (1995). The impact of fear activation and anger on the efficacy of exposure treatment for PTSD. *Behavioral Therapy, 26*, 487–499.

Folkman, S., & Moskowitz, J. T. (2000). Positive affect and the other side of coping. *American Psychologist, 55*(6), 647–654.

Folkman, S., & Moskowitz, J. T. (2004). Coping: Pitfalls and promise. *Annual Review of Psychology, 55*, 745–774.

Folkman, S., Moskowitz, J. T., Ozer, E. M., & Park, C. L. (1997). Positive meaningful events and coping in the context of HIV/AIDS. In B. H. Gottlieb (Ed.), *Coping with chronic stress* (pp. 293–314). New York: Plenum Press.

Fonagy, P., Gergely, G., & Target, M. (2008). Psychoanalytic constructs and attachment theory and research. In J. Cassidy & P. R. Shaver (Eds.), *Handbook of attachment* (2nd ed., pp. 783–810). New York: Guilford Press.

Forer, B. R. (1949). The fallacy of personal validation: A classroom demonstration of gullibility. *The Journal of Abnormal and Social Psychology, 44*(1), 118–123.

Forsyth, D. R., Lawrence, N. K., Burnette, J. L., & Baumeister, R. F. (2007). Attempting to improve the academic performance of struggling college students by bolstering their self-esteem: An intervention that backfired. *Journal of Social and Clinical Psychology, 26*(4), 447–459.

Foster, J. D., Kernis, M. H., & Goldman, B. M. (2007). Linking adult attachment to self-esteem stability. *Self and identity, 6*, 64–73.

Fox, K. R., & Corbin, C. B. (1989). The physical self-perception profile: Development and preliminary validation. *Journal of Sport & Exercise Psychology, 11*(4), 408–430.

Fraley, R. C. (2002). Attachment stability from infancy to adulthood: Meta-analysis and dynamic modeling of developmental mechanisms. *Personality and Social Psychology Review, 6*(2), 123–151.

Fraley, R. C., Brumbaugh, C. C., & Marks, M. J. (2005). The evolution and function of adult attachment: A comparative and phylogenetic analysis. *Journal of Personality and Social Psychology, 89*(5), 731–746.

Fraley, R. C., & Shaver, P. R. (1998). Airport separations: A naturalistic study of adult attachment dynamics in separating couples. *Journal of Personality and Social Psychology, 75*(5), 1198–1212.

Fraley, R. C., & Shaver, P. R. (2008). Attachment theory and its place in contemporary personality theory and research. In O. P. John, R. W. Robins, & L. A. Pervin (Eds.), *Handbook of personality: Theory and research* (pp. 518–541). New York: Guilford Press.

Frankl, V. E. (1959). *Man's search for meaning.* Boston: Beacon Press.

Franzoi, S. L., & Shields, S. A. (1984). The body esteem scale: Multidimensional structure and sex differences in a college population. *Journal of Personality Assessment, 48*(2), 173–178.

Fredrickson, B. L. (1998). What good are positive emotions? *Review of General Psychology, 2*(3), 300–319.

Fredrickson, B. L. (2000). Cultivating positive emotions to optimize health and well-being. *Prevention & Treatment, 3*(1), ArtID 1.

Fredrickson, B. L. (2001). The role of positive emotions in positive psychology: The broaden-and-build theory of positive emotions. *American Psychologist, 56*(3), 218–226.

Fredrickson, B. L. (2002). Positive emotions. In C. R. Snyder & S. J. Lopez (Eds.), *Handbook of positive psychology* (pp. 120–134). New York: Oxford University Press.

Fredrickson, B. L., & Branigan, C. (2001). Positive emotions. In G. A. Bonanno & T. J. Mayne (Eds.), *Emotions: Current issues and future directions* (pp. 123–151). New York: Guilford Press.

Fredrickson, B. L., & Branigan, C. (2005). Positive emotions broaden the scope of attention and thought-action repertoires. *Cognition and Emotion, 19*(3), 313–332.

Fredrickson, B. L., Cohn, M. A., Coffey, K. A., Pek, J., & Finkel, S. M. (2008). Open hearts build lives: Positive emotions, induced through loving-kindness meditation, build consequential personal resources. *Journal of Personality and Social Psychology, 95*(5), 1045–1062.

Fredrickson, B. L., & Joiner, T. (2002). Positive emotions trigger upward spirals toward emotional well-being. *Psychological Science, 13*(2), 172–175.

Fredrickson, B. L., & Levenson, R. W. (1998). Positive emotions speed recovery from the cardiovascular sequelae of negative emotions. *Cognition and Emotion, 12*(2), 191–220.

Fredrickson, B. L., Mancuso, R. A., Branigan, C., & Tugade, M. M. (2000). The undoing effect of positive emotions. *Motivation and Emotion, 24*(4), 237–258.

Frei, R. L., & McDaniel, M. A. (1998). Validity of customer service measures in personnel selection: A review of criterion and construct evidence. *Human Performance, 11*(1), 1–27.

Freud, A. (1937/1966). *The ego and the mechanisms of defense.* Madison, CT: International Universities Press. (Original work published 1937)

Freud, E. L. (Ed.). (1960/1992). Letter to his fiancée Martha Bernays (27 June 1882). In E. L. Freud (Ed.), *Letters of Sigmund Freud* (pp.10-12). Mineola, NY: Dover Publications.

Freud, S. (1900/1953). The interpretation of dreams. In J. Strachey (Ed. and Trans.), *Standard edition* (Vols. 4 & 5). London: Hogarth Press. (Original work published 1900)

Freud, S. (1901/1960). The psychopathology of everyday life. In J. Strachey (Ed. and Trans.), *Standard edition* (Vol. 6). London: Hogarth Press. (Original work published 1901)

Freud, S. (1905/1959). Fragment of an analysis of a case of hysteria. In A. Strachey & J. Strachey (Eds.), *Collected papers* (Vol. 3, pp. 13–136). New York: Basic Books.

Freud, S. (1905/1960). Jokes and their relation to the unconscious. In J. Strachey (Ed. and Trans.), *Standard edition* (Vol. 8). London: Hogarth Press. (Original work published 1905)

Freud, S. (1908/1959). Character and anal eroticism. In J. Strachey (Ed. and Trans.), *Standard edition* (Vol. 9, pp. 167–175). London: Hogarth Press. (Original work published 1908)

Freud, S. (1909a/1955). Analysis of a phobia in a five-year-old boy. In J. Strachey (Ed. and Trans.), *Standard edition* (Vol. 10, pp. 5–149). London: Hogarth Press. (Original work published 1909)

Freud, S. (1909b/1955). Notes upon a case of obsessional neurosis. In J. Strachey (Ed. and Trans.), *Standard edition* (Vol. 10, pp. 153–320). London: Hogarth Press. (Original work published 1909)

Freud, S. (1910/1964). *Leonardo Da Vinci and a memory of his childhood* (A. Tyson, Trans.). New York: Norton.

Freud, S. (1911/1958). Formulations on the two principles of mental functioning. In J. Strachey (Ed. and Trans.), *Standard edition* (Vol. 12, pp. 215–226). London: Hogarth Press. (Original work published 1911)

Freud, S. (1914/1957). On narcissism. In J. Strachey (Ed. and Trans.), *Standard edition* (Vol. 14, pp. 67–102). London: Hogarth Press. (Original work published 1914)

Freud, S. (1915a/1957). Instincts and their vicissitudes. In J. Strachey (Ed. and Trans.), *Standard edition* (Vol. 14, pp. 111–140). London: Hogarth Press. (Original work published 1915)

Freud, S. (1915b/1957). Repression. In J. Strachey (Ed. and Trans.), *Standard edition* Vol. 14, pp. (141–158). London: Hogarth Press. (Original work published 1915)

Freud, S. (1915/2000). *Three essays on the theory of sexuality* (J. Strachey, Ed. and Trans.). New York: Basic Books. (Original work published 1915)

Freud, S. (1920/1955). Beyond the pleasure principle. In J. Strachey (Ed. and Trans.), *Standard edition* (Vol. 18, pp. 3–64). London: Hogarth Press. (Original work published 1920)

Freud, S. (1923a/1961). The ego and the id. In J. Strachey (Ed. and Trans.), *Standard edition* (Vol. 19, pp. 12–66). London: Hogarth Press. (Original work published 1923)

Freud, S. (1923b/1961). The infantile genital organization: An interpolation into the theory of sexuality. In J. Strachey (Ed. and Trans.), *Standard edition* (Vol. 19). London: Hogarth Press. (Original work published 1923)

Freud, S. (1925/1959). Inhibitions, symptoms and anxiety. In J. Strachey (Ed. and Trans.), *Standard edition* (Vol. 20, pp. 77–175). London: Hogarth Press. (Original work published 1925)

Freud, S. (1925/1961). Some psychical consequences of the anatomical distinction between the sexes. In J. Strachey (Ed. and Trans.), *Standard edition* (Vol. 19, pp. 248–258). London: Hogarth Press. (Original work published 1925)

Freud, S. (1929/1989). *Civilization and its discontents.* New York: Norton. (Original work published 1929)

Freud, S. (1933/1990). The anatomy of the mental personality (Lecture 31). In *New introductory lectures on psychoanalysis.* New York: Norton. (Original work published 1933)

Freud, S. (1955). Two encyclopedia articles. In J. Strachey (Ed. and Trans.), *Standard edition* (Vol. 18, pp. 235–259). London: Hogarth Press. (Original work published 1923)

Freud, S. (1967). *Woodrow Wilson: A psychological study.* London: Hogarth Press.

Freyd, J. J. (2006). The social psychology of cognitive repression. *Behavioral and Brain Sciences, 29*(5), 518–519.

Fung, H. H., & Ng, S. (2006). Age differences in the sixth personality factor: Age differences in interpersonal relatedness among Canadians and Hong Kong Chinese. *Psychology and Aging, 21*(4), 810–814.

Funk, S. C. (1992). Hardiness: A review of theory and research. *Health Psychology, 11*(5), 335–345.

Funk, S. C., & Houston, B. K. (1987). A critical analysis of the hardiness scale's validity and utility. *Journal of Personality and Social Psychology, 53*(3), 572–578.

Furnham, A. (1986). Economic locus of control. *Human Relations, 39*, 29–43.

Furnham, A., & Fudge, C. (2008). The five factor model of personality and sales performance. *Journal of Individual Differences, 29*(1), 11–16.

Furnham, A., Sadka, V., & Brewin, C. R. (1992). The development of an occupational attributional style questionnaire. *Journal of Organizational Behavior, 13*, 27–39.

Gable, P., & Harmon-Jones, E. (2010). The blues broaden, but the nasty narrows: Attentional consequences of negative affects low and high in motivational intensity. *Psychological Science, 21*, 211–215.

Gabriel, M. T., Critelli, J. W., & Ee, J. S. (1994). Narcissistic illusions in self-evaluations of intelligence and attractiveness. *Journal of Personality, 62*, 143–155.

Gagné, M., & Deci, E. L. (2005). Self-determination theory and work motivation. *Journal of Organizational Behavior, 26*, 331–362.

Gagné, M., Ryan, R. M., & Bargmann, K. (2003). Autonomy support and need satisfaction in the motivation and well-being of gymnasts. *Journal of Applied Sport Psychology, 15*, 372–390.

Gale, C. R., Batty, G. D., & Deary, I. J. (2008). Locus of control at age 10 years and health outcomes and behaviors at age 30 years: The 1970 British cohort study. *Psychosomatic Medicine, 70*, 397–403.

Gale, S. F. (2002, April). Three companies cut turnover with tests. *Workforce,* 66–69.

Gallup, G. G. (1977). Self-recognition in primates: A comparative approach to the bidirectional properties of consciousness. *American Psychologist, 32*(5), 329–338.

Garnets, L. D. (2002). Sexual orientations in perspective. *Cultural Diversity and Ethnic Minority Psychology, 8*(2), 115–129.

Gay, P. (1988). *Freud: A life for our time.* New York: Norton.

Ge, X., Conger, R. D., Cadoret, R. J., Neiderhiser, J. M., Yates, W., Troughton, E., et al. (1996). The developmental interface between nature and nurture: A mutual influence model of child antisocial behavior and parent behaviors. *Developmental Psychology, 32*(4), 574–589.

Geen, R. G. (1984). Preferred stimulation levels in introverts and extraverts: Effects on arousal and performance. *Journal of Personality and Social Psychology, 46*(6), 1303–1312.

Geen, R. G. (1997). Psychophysiological approaches to personality. In R. Hogan, J. Johnson, & S. Briggs (Eds.), *Handbook of personality psychology* (pp. 387–414). San Diego, CA: Academic Press.

Geher, G. (2000). Perceived and actual characteristics of parents and partners: A test of the Freudian model of mate selection. *Current Psychology, 19*(3), 194–214.

Geis, F. L. (1978). Machiavellianism. In H. London & J. Exner (Eds.), *Dimensions of personality* (pp. 285–313). New York: Wiley.

George, M. S., & Bellmaker, R. H. (2000). *Transcranial magnetic stimulation in neuropsychiatry.* Washington, DC: American Psychological Association.

Gergen, K. J. (1985). The social constructionist movement in modern psychology. *American Psychologist, 40*(3), 266–275.

Gergen, K. J. (1991). *The saturated self.* New York: Basic Books.

Getzels, J. W., & Csikszentmihalyi, M. (1976). *The creative vision.* New York: Wiley.

Gibb, B. E., Beevers, C. G., Andover, M. S., & Holleran, K. (2006). The hopelessness theory of depression: A prospective multi-wave test of the vulnerability-stress hypothesis. *Cognitive Therapy and Research, 30*, 763–772.

Gibran, K. (1947/2006). *The Kahlil Gibran reader.* New York: Kensington Publishing (Original work published 1947)

Gillespie, W., & Myors, B. (2000). Personality of rock musicians. *Psychology of Music, 28,* 154–165.

Gillham, J. E., Brunwasser, S. M., & Freres, D. R. (2007). Preventing depression in early adolescence. In J. R. Z. Abela & B. L. Hankin (Eds.), *Handbook of depression in children and adolescents* (pp. 309–332). New York: Guilford Press.

Gillham, J. E., Reivich, K. J., Jaycox, L. H., & Seligman, M. E. P. (1995). Prevention of depressive symptoms in schoolchildren: Two year follow-up. *Psychological Science, 6,* 343–351.

Gillham, J. E., Shatté, A. J., Reivich, K. J., & Seligman, M. E. P. (2001). Optimism, pessimism, and explanatory style. In E. C. Chang (Ed.), *Optimism & pessimism: Implications for theory, research, and practice* (pp. 53–75). Washington, DC: American Psychological Association.

Gilmor, T. M., & Reid, D. W. (1978). Locus of control, prediction, and performance on university examinations. *Journal of Consulting and Clinical Psychology, 46*(3), 565–566.

Gladstone, T. R. G., & Kaslow, N. J. (1995). Depression and attributions in children and adolescents: A meta-analytic review. *Journal of Abnormal Child Psychology, 23,* 597–606.

Glaser, J., & Kihlstrom, J. F. (2005). Compensatory automaticity: Unconscious volition is not an oxymoron. In R. R. Hassin, J. R. Uleman, & J. A. Bargh (Eds.), *The new unconscious* (pp. 171–195). New York: Oxford University Press.

Gleaves, D. H., & Hernandez, E. (1999). Recent reformulations of Freud's development and abandonment of his seduction theory: Historical/scientific clarification or a continued assault on truth? *History of Psychology, 2*(4), 324–354.

Goffman, E. (1959). *The presentation of self in everyday life.* Garden City, NY: Doubleday.

Goldberg, L. R. (1981). Language and individual differences: The search for universals in personality lexicons. In L. Wheeler (Ed.), *Review of personality and social psychology* (Vol. 2, pp. 141–165). Beverly Hills, CA: Sage.

Goldberg, L. R. (1990). An alternative "description of personality": The Big Five factor structure. *Journal of Personality and Social Psychology, 59,* 1216–1229.

Goldman, D., Kohn, P. M., & Hunt, R. W. (1983). Sensation seeking, augmenting, reducing, and absolute auditory threshold: A strength of the nervous system perspective. *Journal of Personality and Social Psychology, 45*(2), 405–411.

Goldstein, S. (2000). *Cross-cultural explorations: Activities in culture and psychology.* Needham Heights, MA: Allyn & Bacon.

Goleman, D. (1995). *Emotional intelligence.* New York: Bantam Books.

Golombok, S., Spencer, A., & Rutter, M. (1983). Children in lesbian and single-parent households: Psychosexual and psychiatric appraisal. *Journal of Child Psychology and Psychiatry, 4,* 551–572.

Gonzales, F., & Espin, O. (1996). Latino men, Latina women, and homosexuality. In R. Cabaj & T. Stein (Eds.), *Textbook of homosexuality and mental health* (pp. 583–601). Washington, DC: American Psychiatric Press.

Gordon, R. A. (2008). Attributional style and athletic performance: Strategic optimism and defensive pessimism. *Psychology of Sport and Exercise, 9*(3), 336–350.

Gore, P. M., & Rotter, J. B. (1963). A personality correlate of social action. *Journal of Personality, 31*(1), 58–64.

Gosling, S. D. (2008). *Snoop: What your stuff says about you.* New York: Basic Books.

Gosling, S. D., Ko, S. J., Mannarelli, T., & Morris, M. E. (2002). A room with a cue: Personality judgments based on offices and bedrooms. *Journal of Personality and Social Psychology, 82*(3), 379–398.

Gosling, S. D., Rentfrow, P. J., & Swann, W. B. (2003). A very brief measure of the big-five personality domains. *Journal of Research in Personality, 37,* 504–528.

Gottesman, I. I. (1991). *Schizophrenia genesis: The origins of madness.* San Francisco: W. H. Freeman.

Gottlieb, L. (2006). How do I love thee? *The Atlantic Monthly, 297*(3), 58–70.

Gottman, J. M. (1993). *What predicts divorce? The relationship between marital processes and marital outcomes.* New York: Psychology Press.

Gough, H. G. (1979). A creative personality scale for the adjective check list. *Journal of Personality and Social Psychology, 37*(8), 1398–1405.

Gough, H. G., & Heilbrun, A. B. (1983). *Adjective Check List manual.* Palo Alto, CA: Consulting Psychologists Press.

Gray, J. A. (1970). The psychophysiological basis of introversion-extraversion. *Behaviour Research and Therapy, 8*, 249–266.

Gray, J. A. (1976). The behavioural inhibition system: A possible substrate for anxiety. In M. P. Feldman & A. Broadhurst (Eds.), *Theoretical and experimental bases of behaviour modification* (pp. 3–41). London: Wiley.

Gray, J. A. (1982). *The neuropsychology of anxiety: An enquiry into the functions of the septo-hippocampal system.* Oxford, England: Oxford University Press.

Gray, J. A., & McNaughton, N. (2000). *The neuropsychology of anxiety: An enquiry into the functions of the septo-hippocampal system.* Oxford, England: Oxford University Press.

Gray, P. O. (2001). *Psychology* (4th ed.). New York: MacMillian.

Graziano, W. G., & Eisenberg, N. H. (1997). Agreeableness: A dimension of personality. In R. Hogan, J. Johnson & S. Briggs (Eds.), *Handbook of personality psychology* (pp. 795–824). San Diego, CA: Academic Press.

Green, R. (1978). Sexual identity of 37 children raised by homosexual or transsexual parents. *American Journal of Psychiatry, 135*, 692–697.

Green, R. (1987). *The "sissy boy syndrome" and the development of homosexuality.* New Haven, CT: Yale University Press.

Greenberg, J. R., & Mitchell, S. (1993). *Object relations in psychoanalytic theory.* Cambridge, MA: Harvard University Press.

Greene, B. (2000). African American lesbian and bisexual women. *Journal of Social Issues, 56*, 239–250.

Greenwald, A. G., & Farnham, S. D. (2000). Using the Implicit Association Test to measure self-esteem and self-concept. *Journal of Personality and Social Psychology, 79*, 1022–1038.

Greenwald, A. G., McGhee, D. E., & Schwartz, J. L. K. (1998). Measuring individual differences in implicit cognition: The implicit association test. *Journal of Personality and Social Psychology, 74*, 1464–1480.

Greenwald, A. G., Nosek, B. A., & Banaji, M. R. (2003). Understanding and using the implicit association test: I. An improved scoring algorithm. *Journal of Personality and Social Psychology, 85*(2), 197–216.

Greenwald, A. G., Poehlman, T. A., Uhlmann, E. L., & Banaji, M. R. (2009). Understanding and using the implicit association test: III. Meta-analysis of predictive validity. *Journal of Personality and Social Psychology, 97*(1), 17–41.

Grolnick, W. S., & Ryan, R. M. (1987). Autonomy support in education: Creating the facilitating environment. In N. Hastings & J. Schwieso (Eds.), *New directions in educational psychology: Vol. 2. Behaviour and motivation* (pp. 213–232). London: Falmer Press.

Grolnick, W. S., & Ryan, R. M. (1989). Parent-styles associated with children's self-regulation and competence in school. *Educational Psychology, 81*, 143–154.

Gross, J. J. (2008). Emotion and emotion regulation: Personality processes and individual differences. In O. P. John, R. W. Robins, & L. A. Pervin (Eds.), *Handbook of personality: Theory and research* (pp. 701–724). New York: Guilford Press.

Gross, J. J., Sutton, S. K., & Ketelaar, T. (1998). Relations between affect and personality: Support for the affect-level and affective-reactivity view. *Personality and Social Psychology Bulletin, 24*(3), 279–288.

Guadagno, R. E., Okdie, B. M., & Eno, C. A. (2008). Who blogs? Personality predictors of blogging. *Computers in Human Behavior, 24*, 1993–2004.

Guiffrida, D., Gouveia, A., Wall, A., & Seward, D. (2008). Development and validation of the need for relatedness at college questionnaire (NRC-Q). *Journal of Diversity in Higher Education, 1*(4), 251–261.

Guimond, S. (2008). Psychological similarities and differences between women and men across cultures. *Social and Personality Psychology Compass, 2*(1), 494–510.

Guterl, F. (2002, November 11). What Freud got right. *Newsweek, 140*(20), 50–51.

Haeffel, G. J., Getchell, M., Koposov, R. A., Yrigollen, C. M., DeYoung, C. G., af Klinteberg, B., et al. (2008). Association between polymorphisms in the dopamine transporter gene and depression. *Psychological Science, 19*(1), 62–69.

Haeffel, G. J., Gibb, B. E., Metalsky, G. I., Alloy, L. B., Abramson, L. Y., Hankin, B. L., et al. (2008). Measuring cognitive vulnerability to depression: Development and validation of the cognitive style questionnaire. *Clinical Psychology Review, 28*(5), 824–836.

Haidt, J. (2000). The positive emotion of elevation. *Prevention & Treatment, 3*(3), ArtID 3c.

Hall, C., Smith, K., & Chia, R. (2008). Cognitive and personality factors in relation to timely completion of a college degree. *College Student Journal, 42*(4), 1087–1098.

Hall, J. A. (1978). Gender effects in decoding nonverbal cues. *Psychological Bulletin, 85*(4), 845–857.

Hall, J. A. (1984). *Nonverbal sex differences: Communication accuracy and expressive style.* Baltimore: Johns Hopkins University Press.

Hall, J. A. (2006a). Nonverbal behavior, status, and gender: How do we understand their relations? *Psychology of Women Quarterly, 30,* 384–391.

Hall, J. A. (2006b). Women's and men's nonverbal communication: Similarities, differences, stereotypes, and origins. In V. Manusov & M. L. Patterson (Eds.), *The SAGE handbook of nonverbal communication* (pp. 201–218). Thousand Oaks, CA: Sage.

Halpern, D. F. (1997). Sex differences in intelligence: Implications for education. *American Psychologist, 52,* 1091–1102.

Halpern, D. F. (2000). *Sex differences in cognitive abilities.* Mahwah, NJ: Erlbaum.

Halpern, D. F. (2004). A cognitive-process taxonomy for sex differences in cognitive abilities. *Current Directions in Psychological Science, 13*(4), 135–139.

Halpern, D. F., Benbow, C. P., Geary, D. C., Gur, R. C., Hyde, J. S., & Gernsbacher, M. A. (2007). The science of sex differences in science and mathematics. *Psychological Science in the Public Interest, 8*(1), 1–51.

Halpern, D. F., & LaMay, M. L. (2000). The smarter sex: A critical review of sex differences in intelligence. *Educational Psychology Review, 12*(2), 229–246.

Halvari, A. E. M., & Halvari, H. (2006). Motivational predictors of change in oral health: An experimental test of self-determination theory. *Motivation and Emotion, 30,* 295–306.

Hammen, C. L., Adrian, C., & Hiroto, D. (1988). A longitudinal test of the attributional vulnerability model in children at risk for depression. *British Journal of Clinical Psychology, 27,* 37–46.

Hammer, D. H., Hu, S., Magnuson, V. L., Hu, N., & Pattatucci, A. M. (1993). A linkage between DNA markers on the X chromosome and male sexual orientation. *Science, 261,* 321–327.

Hargrave, G. E., & Hiatt, D. (1989). Use of the California psychological inventory in law enforcement officer selection. *Journal of Personality Assessment, 53*(2), 267–277.

Harker, L., & Keltner, D. (2001). Expressions of positive emotions in women's college yearbook pictures and their relationship to personality and life outcomes across adulthood. *Journal of Personality and Social Psychology, 80,* 112–124.

Harlow, H. F. (1958). The nature of love. *American Psychologist, 13,* 673–685.

Harris, K. J., Kacmar, K. M., Zivnuska, S., & Shaw, J. D. (2007). The impact of political skill on impression management effectiveness. *Journal of Applied Psychology, 92*(1), 278–285.

Harter, S. (1983). Developmental perspectives on the self-system. In P. H. Müssen (Ed.), *Handbook of child psychology: Vol. 4. Socialization, personality and social development* (pp. 275–386). New York: Wiley.

Harter, S. (1998). The development of self-representations. In W. Damon & N. Eisenberg (Eds.), *Handbook of child psychology: Vol. 3. Social, emotional, and personality development* (pp. 553–617). New York: Wiley.

Harter, S. (1999). *The construction of the self: A developmental perspective.* New York: Guilford Press.

Harter, S. (2003). The development of self-representations during childhood and adolescence. In M. R. Leary & J. P. Tangney (Eds.), *Handbook of self and identity* (pp. 610–642). New York: Guilford Press.

Harter, S. (2005). Self-concepts and self-esteem, children and adolescents. In C. B. Fisher & R. M. Lerner (Eds.), *Encyclopedia of applied developmental science* (Vol. 2, pp. 972–977). Thousand Oaks, CA: Sage.

Hartung, C. M., & Widiger, T. A. (1998). Gender differences in the diagnosis of mental disorders: Conclusions and controversies of the DSM-IV. *Psychological Bulletin, 123,* 260–278.

Hassett, J. M., Siebertand, E. R., & Wallen, K. (2008). Sex differences in rhesus monkey toy preferences parallel those of children. *Hormones and Behavior, 54,* 359–364.

Hathaway, S. R., & McKinley, J. C. (1940). A multiphasic personality schedule (Minnesota): I. Construction of the schedule. *Journal of Psychology, 10,* 249–254.

Hayne, H., Garry, M., & Loftus, E. F. (2006). On the continuing lack of scientific evidence for repression. *Behavioral and Brain Sciences, 29*(5), 521–522.

Hazan, C., & Shaver, P. R. (1987). Romantic love conceptualized as an attachment process. *Journal of Personality and Social Psychology, 52*(3), 511–524.

Hazan, C., & Shaver, P. R. (1990). Love and work: An attachment-theoretical perspective. *Journal of Personality and Social Psychology, 59*(2), 270–280.

Hazan, C., & Zeifman, D. (1994). Sex and the psychological tether. In *Advances in personal relationships: A research annual* (Vol. 5, pp. 151–177). London: Jessica Kingsley.

Healy, W., Bronner, A. F., & Bowers, A. M. (1931). *The struture and meaning of psychoanalysis.* New York: Alfred A. Knopf.

Heatherington, L., Daubman, K. A., Bates, C., Ahn, A., Brown, H., & Preston, C. (1993). Two investigations of "female modesty" in achievement situations. *Sex Roles, 29,* 739–754.

Hebb, D. O. (1955). Drives and the CNS (conceptual nervous system). *Psychological Review, 62,* 243–259.

Hedges, L. V., & Nowell, A. (1995). Sex differences in mental test scores, variability, and numbers of high-scoring individuals. *Science, 269,* 41–45.

Heine, S. J., & Lehman, D. R. (1995). Cultural variation in unrealistic optimism: Does the West feel more invulnerable than the East? *Journal of Personality and Social Psychology, 68,* 595–607.

Helms, J. E. (1990). *Black and White racial identity: Theory, research, and practice.* New York: Greenwood Press.

Helson, R. (1967). Personality characteristics and developmental history of creative college women. *Genetic Psychologic Monographs, 76,* 205–256.

Helson, R., & Wink, P. (1992). Personality change in women from the early 40s to the early 50s. *Psychology and Aging, 7,* 46–55.

Henry, P. C. (2005). Life stresses, explanatory style, hopelessness, and occupational class. *International Journal of Stress Management, 12*(3), 241–256.

Herek, G. M. (2010). Sexual orientation differences as deficits: Science and stigma in the history of American psychology. *Perspectives on Psychological Science, 5*(6), 693–699.

Hesse, E. (2008). The adult attachment interview: Historical and current perspectives. In J. Cassidy & P. R. Shaver (Eds.), *The handbook of attachment: Theory, research, and clinical applications* (pp. 552–598). New York: Guilford Press.

Hetherington, E. M., & Clingempeel, W. G. (1992). Coping with marital transitions: A family systems perspective. *Monographs of the Society for Research in Child Development, 57*(2–3, Serial No. 227).

Hiers, J. M., & Heckel, R. V. (1977). Seating choice, leadership, and locus of control. *The Journal of Social Psychology, 103,* 313–314.

Hilgard, E. R. (1977). *Divided consciousness.* New York: Wiley.

Hill, C., Corbett, C., & St. Rose, A. (2010). *Why so few? Women and girls in science, technology, engineering and mathematics.* Washington, DC: American Association of University Women.

Hiroto, D. S. (1974). Locus of control and learned helplessness. *Journal of Experimental Psychology, 102*(2), 187–193.

Hiroto, D. S., & Seligman, M. E. P. (1975). Generality of learned helplessness in man. *Journal of Personality and Social Psychology, 31*(2), 311–327.

Ho, D. Y. F. (1996). Filial piety and its psychological consequences. In M. H. Bond (Ed.), *The handbook of Chinese psychology.* Hong Kong: Oxford University Press.

Ho, D. Y. F. (1998). Indigenous psychologies: Asian perspectives. *Journal of Cross-Cultural Psychology, 29*(1), 88–103.

Hock, M. F., Deshler, D. D., & Schumaker, J. B. (2006). Enhancing student motivation through the persuit of possible selves. In C. Dunkel & J. Kerpelman (Eds.), *Possible selves: Theory, research and application* (pp. 205–221). New York: Nova Science Publishers.

Hofhansl, A., Voracek, M., & Vitouch, O. (2004). Sex differences in jealousy: A meta-analytical reconsideration. *Paper presented at the 16th annual meeting of the Human Behavior and Evolution Society,* July 21–25, Berlin, Germany.

Hogan, R. (1996). A socioanalytic perspective on the five-factor model. In J. S. Wiggins (Ed.), *The five-factor model of personality: Theoretical perspectives* (pp. 163–179). New York: Guilford Press.

Hogan, R., Hogan, J., & Roberts, B. W. (1996). Personality measurement and employment decisions. *American Psychologist, 51*(5), 469–477.

Hojat, M., Callahan, C. A., & Gonnella, J. S. (2004). Students' personality and rating of clinical competence in medical school clerkships: A longitudinal study. *Psychology, Health & Medicine, 9*(2), 247–252.

Holahan, C. K., & Sears, R. R. (1995). *The gifted group in later maturity.* Palo Alto, CA: Stanford University Press.

Holden, R. R., & Jackson, D. N. (1979). Item subtlety and face validity in personality assessment. *Journal of Consulting and Clinical Psychology, 47*(3), 459–468.

Holmes, D. S. (1995). The evidence for repression: An examination of sixty years of research. In J. Singer (Ed.), *Repression and dissociation: Implications for personality theory, psychopathology and health* (pp. 85–102). Chicago: University of Chicago Press.

Hong, T. B., Oddone, E. Z., Dudley, T. K., & Bosworth, H. B. (2006). Medication barriers and anti-hypertensive medication adherence: The moderating role of locus of control. *Psychology, Health & Medicine, 11*(1), 20–28.

Hooker, C. I., Verosky, S. C., Miyakawa, A., Knight, R. T., & D'Esposito, M. (2008). The influence of personality on neural mechanisms of observational fear and reward learning. *Neuropsychologia, 46*, 2709–2724.

Horgan, J. (1996). Why Freud isn't dead. *Scientific American, 275*(6), 106–111.

Hörmann, H., & Maschke, P. (1996). On the relations between personality and job performance of airline pilots. *The International Journal of Aviation Psychology, 6*(2), 171–178.

Hough, L. M., Eaton, N. K., Dunnette, M. D., Kamp, J. D., & McCloy, R. A. (1990). Criterion-related validities of personality constructs as the effect of response distortion on those validities. *Journal of Applied Psychology, 75*, 581–595.

Houran, J., Lange, R., Rentfrow, P. J., & Bruckner, K. H. (2004). Do online matchmaking tests work? An assessment of preliminary evidence for a publicized "predictive model of marital success." *North American Journal of Psychology, 6*(3), 507–526.

Houston, D. M., McKee, K. J., & Wilson, J. (2000). Attributional style, efficacy, and the enhancement of well-being among housebound older people. *Basic and Applied Social Psychology, 22*(4), 309–317.

Hoyle, R. H. (2006). Self-knowledge and self-esteem. In M. H. Kernis (Ed.), *Self-esteem issues and answers* (pp. 208–215). New York: Psychology Press.

Hoyle, R. H., Fejfar, M. C., & Miller, J. D. (2000). Personality and sexual risk-taking. a quantitative review. *Journal of Personality, 68*(6), 1203–1231.

Hoyle, R. H., Stephenson, M. T., Palmgreen, P., Lorch, E. P., & Donohew, R. L. (2002). Reliability and validity of a brief measure of sensation seeking. *Personality and Individual Differences, 32*, 401–414.

Hoyt, M. F. (1973). Internal–external control and beliefs about automobile travel. *Journal of Research in Personality, 7*(3), 288–293.

Huesmann, L. R., Eron, L. D., Lefkowitz, M. M., & Walder, L. O. (1984). Stability of aggression over time and generations. *Developmental Psychology, 20*, 1120–1134.

Hull, J. G., Van Treuren, R. R., & Virnelli, S. (1987). Hardiness and health: A critique and alternative approach. *Journal of Personality and Social Psychology, 53*(3), 518–530.

Hurlburt, A. C., & Ling, Y. (2007). Biological components of sex differences in color preference. *Current Biology, 17*, 623–625.

Hyde, J. S. (1984). How large are gender differences in aggression? A developmental meta-analysis. *Developmental Psychology, 20*(4), 722–736.

Hyde, J. S. (1986). Gender differences in aggression. In J. S. Hyde & M. C. Linn (Eds.), *The psychology of gender: Advances through meta-analysis* (pp. 51–66). Baltimore: Johns Hopkins University Press.

Hyde, J. S. (1993). Gender differences in mathematics ability, anxiety, and attitudes: What do meta-analyses tell us? In L. A. Penner, G. M. Batsche, H. M. Knoff, D. L. Nelson, & C. D. Spielberger (Eds.), *The challenge in mathematics and science education: Psychology's response* (pp. 237–249). Washington, DC: American Psychological Association.

Hyde, J. S. (2004). *Half the human experience: The psychology of women.* Boston: Houghton Mifflin.

Hyde, J. S. (2005). The gender similarities hypothesis. *American Psychologist, 60*, 581–592.

Hyde, J. S. (2007). New directions in the study of gender similarities and differences. *Current Directions in Psychological Science, 16*(5), 259–263.

Hyde, J. S., & DeLamater, J. D. (2006). *Understanding human sexuality.* Boston: McGraw-Hill.

Hyde, J. S., & Durik, A. M. (2000). Gender differences in erotic plasticity—Evolutionary or sociocultural forces? Comment on Baumeister (2000). *Psychological Bulletin, 126*(3), 375–379.

Hyde, J. S., Fennema, E., & Lamon, S. J. (1990). Gender differences in mathematics performance: A meta-analysis. *Psychological Bulletin, 107*, 139–155.

Hyde, J. S., & Jaffee, S. R. (2000). Becoming a heterosexual adult: The experiences of young women. *Journal of Social Issues, 56*(2), 283–296.

Hyde, J. S., & Linn, M. C. (1988). Gender differences in verbal ability: A meta-analysis. *Psychological Bulletin, 104,* 53–69.

Hyde, J. S., & Linn, M. C. (2006). Gender similarities in mathematics and science. *Science, 314*(5799), 599–600.

Hyde, J. S., & Oliver, M. B. (2000). Gender differences in sexuality: Results from meta-analysis. In C. B. Travis & J. W. White (Eds.), *Sexuality, society, and feminism* (pp. 57–77). Washington, DC: American Psychological Association.

Icard, L. D. (1996). Assessing the psychosocial well-being of African American gays. In J. F. Longres (Ed.), *Men of color: A context for service to homosexually active men* (pp. 25–50). London: Haworth Press.

Ickes, W., Gesn, P. R., & Graham, T. (2000). Gender differences in empathic accuracy: Differential ability or differential motivation? *Personal Relationships, 7,* 95–109.

Ickes, W., Holloway, R., Stinson, L. L., & Hoodenpyle, T. G. (2006). Self-monitoring in social interaction: The centrality of self-affect. *Journal of Personality, 74*(3), 659–684.

Iemmola, F., & Ciani, A. C. (2009). New evidence of genetic factors influencing sexual orientation in men: Female fecundity increase in the maternal line. *Archives of Sexual Behavior, 38,* 393–399.

Ilardi, S. S., Craighead, E. W., & Evans, D. D. (1997). Modeling relapse in unipolar depression: The effects of dysfunctional cognitions and personality disorders. *Journal of Consulting and Clinical Psychology, 65,* 381–391.

Irwin, M. R., & Miller, A. H. (2007). Depressive disorders and immunity: 20 years of progress and discovery. *Brain Behavior and Immunity, 21,* 374–383.

Isaacowitz, D. M., & Seligman, M. E. P. (2001). Is pessimism a risk factor for depressive mood among community-dwelling older adults? *Behaviour Research and Therapy, 39,* 255–272.

Isaacowitz, D. M., & Seligman, M. E. P. (2003). Cognitive styles and well-being in adulthood and old age. In M. H. Bornstein, L. Davidson, C. L. M. Keyes, K. A. Moore, & The Center for Child Well-being (Eds.), *Well-being: Positive development across the life course* (pp. 449–475). Mahwah, NJ: Erlbaum.

Isen, A. M. (1987). Positive affect, cognitive processes, and social behavior. *Advances in Experimental Social Psychology, 20,* 203–253.

Isen, A. M., Daubman, K. A., & Nowicki, G. P. (1987). Positive affect facilitates creative problem solving. *Journal of Personality and Social Psychology, 52*(6), 1122–1131.

Izard, C. E. (1977). *Human emotions.* New York: Plenum Press.

Jackson, D. N. (1984). *Personality research form manual.* Port Huron, MI: Research Psychologists Press.

Jaffee, S. R., Caspi, A., Moffitt, T., Polo-Thomas, M., Price, T. S., & Taylor, A. (2004). The limits of child effects: Evidence for genetically mediated child effects on corporal punishment but not on physical maltreatment. *Developmental Psychology, 40,* 1047–1058.

James, W. (1890). *The principles of psychology.* New York: Holt.

Jang, K. L., Dick, D. M., Wolf, H., Livesley, W. J., & Paris, J. (2005). Psychosocial adversity and emotional instability: An application of gene–environmental interaction models. *European Journal of Personality, 19,* 359–372.

Jang, K. L., McCrae, R. R., Angleitner, A., Riemann, R., & Livesley, W. J. (1998). Heritability of facet-level traits in a cross-cultural twin sample: Support for a hierarchical model of personality. *Journal of Personality and Social Psychology, 74,* 1556–1565.

Janoff-Bullman, R. (1992). *Shattered assumptions: Towards a new psychology of trauma.* New York: Free Press.

Jaycox, L. H., Reivich, K. J., Gillham, J., & Seligman, M. E. P. (1994). Prevention of depressive symptoms in schoolchildren. *Behaviour Research and Therapy, 32*(8), 801–816.

Jenkins, J. M. (1993). Self-monitoring and turnover: The impact of personality on intent to leave. *Journal of Organizational Behavior, 14*(1), 83–91.

John, O. P. (1989). Towards a taxonomy of personality descriptors. In D. M. Buss & N. Cantor (Eds.), *Personality psychology: Recent trends and emerging directions* (pp. 260–271). New York: Springer-Verlag.

John, O. P. (1990). The "Big Five" factor taxonomy: Dimensions of personality in the natural language and in questionnaires. In L. A. Pervin (Ed.), *Handbook of personality: Theory and research* (pp. 66–100). New York: Guilford Press.

John, O. P., & Benet-Martínez, V. (2000). Measurement: Reliability, construct validation, and scale construction. In H. T. Reis & C. M. Judd (Eds.), *Handbook of research methods in social and personality psychology* (pp. 339–369). Cambridge, England: Cambridge University Press.

John, O. P., Naumann, L. P., & Soto, C. J. (2008). Paradigm shift to the integrative Big Five trait taxonomy: History, measurement, and conceptual issues. In O. P. John, R. W. Robins, & L. A. Pervin (Eds.), *Handbook of personality: Theory and research.* New York: Guilford Press.

John, O. P., & Robins, R. W. (1993). Gordon Allport: Father and critic of the five-factor model. In K. H. Craik, R. Hogan, & R. N. Wolfe (Eds.), *Fifty years of personality psychology* (pp. 215–236). New York: Plenum Press.

John, O. P., Robins, R. W., & Pervin, L. A. (Eds.). (2008). *The handbook of personality psychology: Theory and research.* New York: Guilford Press.

John, O. P., & Soto, C. J. (2007). The importance of being valid. In R. W. Robins, R. C. Fraley & R. F. Krueger (Eds.), *Handbook of research methods in personality psychology* (pp. 461–494). New York: Guilford Press.

John, O. P., & Srivastava, S. (1999). The Big Five trait taxonomy: History, measurement, and theoretical perspectives. In L. A. Pervin & O. P. John (Eds.), *Handbook of personality: Theory and research* (2nd ed., pp. 102–138). New York: Guilford Press.

Johnson, A. M., Vernon, P. A., & Feiler, A. R. (2008). Behavioral genetic studies of personality: An introduction and review of the results of 50+ years of research. In G. J. Boyle, G. Matthews, & D. H. Saklofske (Eds.), *The Sage handbook of personality theory and assessment* (Vol. 1, pp. 145–173). Los Angeles: Sage.

Johnson, B. T., & Boynton, M. H. (2008). Cumulating evidence about the social animal: Meta-analysis in social-personality psychology. *Social and Personality Psychology Compass, 2*(2), 816–841.

Johnson, W., & Deary, V. (2008). Is RST the Newtonian mechanics of personality psychology? *European Journal of Personality, 22,* 398–400.

Johnson, W., & Krueger, R. F. (2006). How money buys happiness: Genetic and environmental processes linking finances and life satisfaction. *Journal of Personality and Social Psychology, 90*(4), 680–691.

Joiner, T. E., & Wagner, K. D. (1995). Attribution style and depression in children and adolescents: A meta-analytic review. *Clinical Psychology Review, 15,* 777–798.

Jones, E. E., & Pittman, T. S. (1982). Toward a theory of strategic self-presentation. In J. Suls (Ed.), *Psychological perspectives on the self* (pp. 231–262). Hillsdale, NJ: Erlbaum.

Jones, M. (1993). Influence of self-monitoring on dating motivations. *Journal of Research in Personality, 27,* 197–206.

Jordan, C. H., Spencer, S. J., & Zanna, M. P. (2005). Types of high self-esteem and prejudice: How implicit self-esteem relates to ethnic discrimination among high explicit self-esteem individuals. *Personality and Social Psychology Bulletin, 31*(5), 693–702.

Joseph, J. E., Liu, X., Jiang, Y., Lynam, D., & Kelly, T. H. (2009). Neural correlates of emotional reactivity in sensation seeking. *Psychological Science, 20*(2), 215–223.

Joussemet, M., Landry, R., & Koestner, R. (2008). A self-determination theory perspective on parenting. *Canadian Psychology, 49,* 194–200.

Joyce, N., & Baker, D. B. (2008, May). Husbands, rate your wives. *Monitor on Psychology, 39*(5), 18.

Judge, T. A., & Bono, J. E. (2001). Relationship of core self-evaluations traits—self-esteem, generalized self-efficacy, locus of control, and emotional stability—with job satisfaction and job performance: A meta analysis. *Journal of Applied Psychology, 86,* 80–92.

Jung, C. G. (1910). The association method. *The American Journal of Psychology, 21*(2), 219–269.

Jung, C. G. (1921/1971). *Psychological types* (R.F.C. Hull, trans.). Princeton, NJ: Princeton University Press, Bollingen Series XX (Vol. 6). (Original work published 1921)

Jung, C. G. (1934/1960). A review of the complex theory. In *The structure and dynamics of the psyche* (pp. 92–104). Princeton, NJ: Princeton University Press, Bollingen Series XX (Vol. 8). (Original work published 1934)

Jussim, L. (1986). Self-fulfilling prophecies: A theoretical and integrative review. *Psychological Review, 93,* 429–445.

Jussim, L., & Eccles, J. S. (1992). Teacher expectations: II. Construction and reflection of student achievement. *Journal of Personality and Social Psychology, 63,* 947–961.

Kabat-Zinn, J. (1990). *Full catastrophe living.* New York: Random House.

Kaestner, E., Rosen, L., & Apel, P. (1977). Patterns of drug abuse: Relationships with ethnicity, sensation seeking, and anxiety. *Journal of Consulting and Clinical psychology, 45*(3), 462–468.

Kamen-Siegel, L., Rodin, J., Seligman, M. E. P., & Dwyer, J. (1991). Explanatory style and cell-mediated immunity in elderly men and women. *Health Psychology, 10*(4), 229–235.

Kao, E. M., Nagata, D. K., & Peterson, C. (1997). Explanatory style, family expressiveness, and self-esteem among Asian American and European American college students. *The Journal of Social Psychology, 137*(4), 435–444.

Karen, R. (1994). *Becoming attached: First relationships and how they shape our capacity to love.* New York: Oxford University Press.

Kasen, S., Chen, H., Sneed, J., Crawford, T., & Cohen, P. (2006). Social role and birth cohort influences on gender-linked personality traits in women: A 20-year longitudinal analysis. *Journal of Personality and Social Psychology, 91*(5), 944–958.

Kashy, D. A., & DePaulo, B. M. (1996). Who lies? *Journal of Personality and Social Psychology, 70*(5), 1037–1051.

Kasser, T., & Ryan, R. M. (1993). A dark side of the American dream: Correlates of financial success as a central life aspiration. *Journal of Personality and Social Psychology, 65*(2), 410–422.

Kasser, T., & Ryan, R. M. (1996). Further examining the American dream: Differential correlates of intrinsic and extrinsic goals. *Personality and Social Psychology Bulletin, 22*(3), 280–297.

Katcher, A. (1955). The discrimination of sex differences by young children. *The Journal of Genetic Psychology, 87,* 131–143.

Kay, A. C., Jimenez, M. C., & Jost, J. T. (2002). Sour grapes, sweet lemons, and the anticipatory rationalization of the status quo. *Personality and Social Psychology Bulletin, 28*(9), 1300–1312.

Kelly, G. (1955). *The psychology of personal constructs.* New York: Norton.

Keltner, D., & Bonanno, G. A. (1997). A study of laughter and dissociation: Distinct correlates of laughter and smiling during bereavement. *Journal of Personality and Social Psychology, 73*(4), 687–702.

Keltner, D., & Haidt, J. (2001). Social functions of emotions. In T. J. Mayne & G. A. Bonanno (Eds.), *Emotions: Current issues and future directions* (pp. 192–213). New York: Guilford Press.

Kendler, K. S., Thorton, L. M., Gilman, S. E., & Kessler, R. C. (2000). Sexual orientation in a U.S. national sample of twin and nontwin sibling pairs. *American Journal of Psychiatry, 157,* 1843–1846.

Kenrick, D. T., & Trost, M. R. (1993). The evolutionary perspective. In A. E. Beall & R. J. Sternberg (Eds.), *The psychology of gender* (pp. 148–172). New York: Guilford Press.

Kernberg, O. (1975). *Borderline conditions and pathological narcissism.* New York: Jason Aronson.

Kernberg, O. (1984). *Severe personality disorders: Psychotherapeutic strategies.* New Haven, CT: Yale University Press.

Kernis, M. H., & Goldman, B. M. (2003). Stability and variability in self-concept and self-esteem. In M. R. Leary & J. P. Tangney (Eds.), *Handbook of self and identity* (pp. 106–127). New York: Guilford Press.

Kernis, M. H., Grannemann, B. D., & Barclay, L. C. (1989). Stability and level of self-esteem as predictors of anger arousal and hostility. *Journal of Personality and Social Psychology, 56,* 1013–1023.

Kernis, M. H., Grannemann, B. D., & Barclay, L. C. (1992). Stability of self-esteem: Assessment correlates. *Journal of Personality, 60,* 621–644.

Kernis, M. H., Greenier, K. D., Herlocker, C. E., Whisenhunt, C. R., & Abend, T. (1997). Self-perception of reactions to positive and negative outcomes: The roles of stability and level of self-esteem. *Personality and Social Psychology Bulletin, 22,* 845–854.

Kernis, M. H., Lakey, C. E., & Heppner, W. L. (2008). Secure versus fragile high self-esteem as a predictor of verbal defensiveness: Converging findings across three different markers. *Journal of Personality, 76*(3), 477–512.

Kihlstrom, J. F. (2006). Repression: A unified theory of a will-o'-the-wisp. *Behavioral and Brain Sciences, 29*(5), 523.

King, L. A., & Smith, N. G. (2004). Gay and straight possible development. *Journal of Personality, 72*(5), 967–994.

Kinsey, A. C., Pomeroy, W. B., & Martin, C. E. (1948). *Sexual behavior in the human male.* Bloomington: Indiana University Press.

Kinsey, A. C., Pomeroy, W. B., Martin, C. E., & Gebhard, P. H. (1953). *Sexual behavior in the human female.* Bloomington: Indiana University Press.

Kirk, K. M., Bailey, J. M., Dunne, M. P., & Martin, N. G. (2000). Measurement models for sexual orientation in a community twin sample. *Behavior Genetics, 30*(4), 345–356.

Kirkpatrick, M., Smith, C., & Roy, R. (1981). Lesbian mothers and their children: A comparative survey. *American Journal of Orthopsychiatry, 51,* 545–551.

Kite, M. E., Deaux, K., & Haines, E. L. (2008). Gender stereotypes. In F. L. Denmark & M. A. Paludi (Eds.), *Psychology of women: A handbook of issues and theories* (2nd ed., pp. 205–236). Westport, CT: Praeger/Greenwood.

Klein, F., Sepekoff, B., & Wolf, T. J. (1985). Sexual orientation: A multi-variable dynamic process. *Journal of Homosexuality, 11*(1/2), 35–49.

Kling, K. C., Hyde, J. S., Showers, C. J., & Buswell, B. N. (1999). Gender differences in self-esteem: A meta-analysis. *Psychological Bulletin, 125*(4), 470–500.

Kluckhohn, C., & Murray, H. A. (1948). Personality formation: The determinants. In C. Kluckhohn & H. A. Murray (Eds.), *Personality in nature, society and culture.* New York: Alfred A. Knopf.

Knight, G. P., Fabes, R. A., & Higgins, D. A. (1996). Concerns about drawing causal inferences from meta-analyses: An example in the study of gender differences in aggression. *Psychological Bulletin, 119*(3), 410–421.

Knight, R. T. (2007). Neural networks debunk phrenology. *Science, 316*(5831), 1578–1579.

Knutson, B., & Bhanji, J. (2006). Neural substrates for emotional traits? The case of extraversion. In T. Canli (Ed.), *Biology of personality and individual differences* (pp. 116–132). New York: Guilford Press.

Knutson, B., Momenan, R., Rawlings, R. R., Fong, G. W., & Hommer, D. (2001). Negative association of neuroticism with brain volume ratio in healthy humans. *Biological Psychiatry, 50,* 685–690.

Kobasa, S. C. (1979). Stressful life events, personality, and health: An inquiry into hardiness. *Journal of Personality and Social Psychology, 37*(1), 1–11.

Koestner, R., Ryan, R. M., Bernieri, F., & Holt, K. (1984). Setting limits on children's behavior: The differential effects of controlling vs. informational styles on intrinsic motivation and creativity. *Journal of Personality, 52*(3), 233–248.

Kohn, P. M., Hunt, R. W., & Hoffman, F. M. (1982). Aspects of experience seeking. *Canadian Journal of Behavioral Science, 14*(1), 13–23.

Kohut, H. (1966). Forms and transformations of narcissism. *Journal of the American Psychoanalytic Association, 14,* 243–272.

Kohut, H. (1971). *The analysis of the self: A systematic psychoanalytic approach to the treatment of narcissistic personality disorders.* New Haven, CT: Yale University Press.

Kohut, H. (1977). *The restoration of the self.* New York: International Universities Press.

Kohut, H. (1984). *How does analysis cure?* Chicago: University of Chicago Press.

Koop, C. E. (1995). Editorial: A personal role in health-care reform. *American Journal of Public Health, 85*(6), 759–760.

Koppitz, E. M. (1968). *Psychological evaluation of children's human figure drawing.* New York: Grune & Stratton.

Kowert, P. A. (1996). Where does the buck stop?: Assessing the impact of presidential personality. *Political Psychology, 17,* 421–452.

Krafft-Ebing, R. (1908/1986). *Psychopathia sexualis* (F. J. Rebman, trans.). Brooklyn, NY: Physicians and Surgeons Book Co. (Original work published 1908)

Krämer, N. C., & Winter, S. (2008). Impression management 2.0: The relationship of self-esteem, extraversion, self-efficacy, and self-presentation within social networking sites. *Journal of Media Psychology, 20*(3), 106–116.

Krueger, R. F., & Johnson, W. (2008). Behavior genetics and personality: A new look at the integration of nature and nurture. In O. P. John, R. W. Robins, & L. A. Pervin (Eds.), *Handbook of personality: Theory and research* (pp. 287–310). New York: Guilford Press.

Krueger, R. F., Markon, K. E., & Bouchard, T. J. (2003). The extended genotype: The heritability of personality accounts for the heritability of recalled family environments in twins reared apart. *Journal of Personality, 71*(5), 809–833.

Krueger, R. F., & Tackett, J. L. (2003). Personality and psychopathology: Working toward the bigger picture. *Journal of Personality Disorders, 17*(2), 109–128.

Krug, S. E., & Johns, E. F. (1986). A large-scale cross-validation of second-order personality structure defined by the 16PF. *Psychological Reports, 46,* 509–522.

Kuhn, M., & McPartland, T. S. (1954). An empirical investigation of self-attitudes. *American Sociological Review, 19,* 68–76.

La Guardia, J. G., & Patrick, H. (2008). Self-determination theory as a fundamental theory of close relationships. *Canadian Psychology, 49,* 201–209.

Långström, N., Rahman, Q., Carlström, E., & Lichtenstein, P. (2010). Genetic and environmental effects on same-sex sexual behavior: A population study of twins in Sweden. *Archives of Sexual Behavior, 39,* 75–80.

LaForge, M. C., & Cantrell, S. (2003). Explanatory style and academic performance among college students beginning a major course of study. *Psychological Reports, 92,* 861–865.

LaFrance, M., & Banaji, M. (1992). Towards a reconsideration of the gender-emotion relationship. In M. S. Clark (Ed.), *Emotion and social behavior* (pp. 178–201). Newbury Park, CA: Sage.

Lahey, B. J. (2009). Public health significance of neuroticism. *American Psychologist, 64*(4), 241–256.

Lai, C. (2006, December 11). *How much of human height is genetic and how much is due to nutrition?* Retrieved April 9, 2009, from http://www.sciam.com/article.cfm?id=how-much-of-human-height.

Lambird, K. H., & Mann, T. (2006). When do ego threats lead to self-regulation failure? Negative consequences of defensive high self-esteem. *Personality and Social Psychology Bulletin, 32*(9), 1177–1187.

Langer, E. J., & Rodin, J. (1976). The effects of choice and enhanced personal responsibility for the aged: A field experiment in an institutional setting. *Journal of Personality and Social Psychology, 34*(2), 191–198.

Larsen, R. J., & Ketelaar, T. (1989). Extraversion, neuroticism and susceptibility to positive and negative mood induction procedures. *Personality and Individual Differences, 10*(12), 1221–1228.

Larsen, R. J., & Ketelaar, T. (1991). Personality and susceptibility to positive and negative emotional states. *Journal of Personality and Social Psychology, 61*(1), 132–140.

Laumann, E. O., Gagnon, J. H., Michael, R. T., & Michaels, S. (1994). *The social organization of sexuality: Sexual practices in the United States.* Chicago: University of Chicago Press.

Lazar, N. A. (2009). Discussion of "puzzlingly high correlations in fMRI studies of emotion, personality, and social cognition" by Vul et al. (2009). *Perspectives on Psychological Science, 4*(3), 308–309.

Leary, M. R. (2004). *The curse of the self: Self-awareness, egotism, and the quality of human life.* Cambridge, MA: Oxford University Press.

Leary, M. R., Tchividjian, L. R., & Kraxberger, B. E. (1994). Self-presentation can be hazardous to your health: Impression management and health risk. *Health Psychology, 13*(6), 461–470.

Lee, K., & Ashton, M. C. (2004). Psychometric properties of the HEXACO personality inventory. *Multivariate Behavioral Research, 39*(2), 329–358.

Lee, K., & Ashton, M. C. (2007). Factor analysis in personality research. In R. W. Robins, R. C. Fraley, & R. F. Krueger (Eds.), *Handbook of research methods in personality psychology* (pp. 424–443). New York: Guilford Press.

Lee, K., Ogunfowora, B., & Ashton, M. C. (2005). Personality traits beyond the Big Five: Are they within the HEXACO space? *Journal of Personality, 73*(5), 1437–1463.

Lee, S. J., & Oyserman, D. (2009). Expecting to work, fearing homelessness: The possible selves of low-income mothers. *Journal of Applied Social Psychology, 39*(6), 1334–1355.

Lee, S. J., Quigley, B. M., Nesler, M. S., Corbet, A. B., & Tedeschi, J. T. (1999). Development of a self-presentation tactics scale. *Personality and Individual Differences, 26,* 701–722.

Lee, Y., & Seligman, M. E. P. (1997). Are Americans more optimistic than the Chinese? *Personality and Social Psychology Bulletin, 23*(1), 32–40.

Lefcourt, H. M. (1979). Locus of control for specific goals. In L. C. Perlmutter & R. A. Monty (Eds.), *Choice and perceived control* (pp. 209–220). Hillsdale, NJ: Erlbaum.

Lefcourt, H. M. (1981). The construction and development of the multidimensional-multiattributional causality scales. In H. M. Lefcourt (Ed.), *Research with the locus of control construct: Vol. 1. Assessment methods* (pp. 245–277). New York: Academic Press.

Lefcourt, H. M. (1982). *Locus of control: Current trends in theory and research.* Hillsdale, NJ: Erlbaum.

Lefcourt, H. M. (1983). The locus of control as a moderator variable: Stress. In H. M. Lefcourt (Ed.), *Research with the locus of control construct: Vol. 2. Developments and social problems* (pp. 253–268). San Diego, CA: Academic Press.

Lefcourt, H. M. (1991). Locus of control. In J. P. Robinson, P. R. Shaver, & L. S. Wrightsman (Eds.), *Measures of personality and social psychological attitudes* (pp. 413–499). San Diego, CA: Academic Press.

Lefcourt, H. M., Martin, R. A., Fick, C. M., & Saleh, W. E. (1985). Locus of control for affiliation and behavior in social interactions. *Journal of Personality and Social Psychology, 48*(3), 755–759.

Legerstee, M., Anderson, D., & Schaffer, A. (1998). Five- and eight-month-old infants recognize their faces and voices as familiar social stimuli. *Child Development, 69,* 37–50.

Lehman, D. R., & Taylor, S. E. (1987). Date with an earthquake: Coping with a probable, unpredictable disaster. *Personality and Social Psychology Bulletin, 13*(4), 546–555.

Lehnart, J., & Neyer, F. J. (2006). Should I stay or should I go? Attachment and personality in stable and instable romantic relationships. *European Journal of Personality, 20,* 475–495.

Lenney, E. (1977). Women's self-confidence in achievement settings. *Psychological Bulletin, 84*(1), 1–13.

Leone, C. (2006). Self-monitoring: Individual differences in orientations to the social world. *Journal of Personality, 74*(3), 633–657.

Leone, C., & Hawkins, L. B. (2006). Self-monitoring and close relationships. *Journal of Personality, 74*(3), 739–778.

Lepper, M. R., Corpus, J. H., & Iyengar, S. S. (2005). Intrinsic and extrinsic motivational orientations in the classroom: Age differences and academic correlates. *Journal of Educational Psychology, 97*(2), 184–196.

Lepper, M. R., Greene, D., & Nisbett, R. E. (1973). Undermining children's intrinsic interest with extrinsic reward: A test of the "overjustification" hypothesis. *Journal of Personality and Social Psychology, 28*(1), 129–137.

Lesch, K. P. (2007). Linking emotion to the social brain. The role of the serotonin transporter in human social behaviour. *EMBO Reports, 8*(S1), S24–S29.

Lesch, K. P., Bengel, D., Heils, A., Sabol, S. Z., Greenberg, B. D., Petri, S., et al. (1996). Association of anxiety-related traits with a polymorphism in the serotonin transporter gene regulatory region. *Science, 274*(5292), 1527–1531.

Letzring, T. D., Block, J., & Funder, D. C. (2005). Ego-control and ego-resiliency: Generalization of self-report scales based on personality descriptions from acquaintances, clinicians and the self. *Journal of Research in Personality, 39*(4), 395–422.

LeVay, S. (1991). A difference in hypothalamic structure between heterosexual and homosexual men. *Science, 253*(5023), 1034–1037.

Lewis, M., & Brooks-Gunn, J. (1979). *Social cognition and the acquisition of self.* New York: Plenum Press.

Lewis, M., & Ramsay, D. (2004). Development of self-recognition, personal pronoun use, and pretend play during the 2nd year. *Child Development, 75,* 1821–1831.

Lewis, P., Cheney, T., & Dawes, S. A. (1977). Locus of control of interpersonal relationships questionnaire. *Psychological Reports, 41*(2), 507–510.

Liberman, A., & Chaiken, S. (1992). Defensive processing of personally relevant health messages. *Personality and Social Psychology Bulletin, 18,* 669–679.

Lieberman, M. D., Berkman, E. T., & Wager, T. D. (2009). Correlations in social neuroscience aren't voodoo. *Perspectives on Psychological Science, 4*(3), 299–307.

Lifton, R. J. (1986). *The Nazi doctors: Medical killing and the psychology of genocide.* New York: Basic Books.

Lightdale, J. R., & Prentice, D. A. (1994). Rethinking sex differences in aggression: Aggressive behavior in the absence of social roles. *Personality and Social Psychology Bulletin, 20*(1), 34–44.

Lilienfeld, S. O., Wood, J. M., & Garb, H. N. (2000). The scientific status of projective techniques. *Psychological Science in the Public Interest, 1*(2), 27–66.

Lindquist, M. A., & Gelman, A. (2009). Correlations and multiple comparisons in functions imaging: A statistical perspective (commentary on Vul et al., 2009). *Perspectives on Psychological Science, 4*(3), 310–313.

Lindzey, G. (1959). On the classification of projective techniques. *Psychological Bulletin, 56,* 158–168.

Linn, M. C., & Petersen, A. C. (1985). Emergence and characterization of sex differences in spatial ability: A meta-analysis. *Child Development, 56,* 1479–1498.

Lippa, R. A. (2000). Gender-related traits in gay men, women, and heterosexual men and women. *Journal of Personality, 68,* 899–926.

Lippa, R. A. (2002). Gender-related traits of heterosexual and homosexual men and women. *Archives of Sexual Behavior, 31,* 83–98.

Lippa, R. A. (2003). Are 2D:4D finger-length ratios related to sexual orientation? Yes for men, no for women. *Journal of Personality and Social Psychology, 85*(1), 179–188.

Lippa, R. A. (2005a). *Gender, nature, and nurture.* Mahwah, NJ: Erlbaum.

Lippa, R. A. (2005b). Sexual orientation and personality. *Annual Review of Sex Research, 16,* 119–153.

Lippa, R. A. (2006a). The gender reality hypothesis. *American Psychologist, 61,* 639–640.

Lippa, R. A. (2006b). Is high sex drive associated with increased sexual attraction to both sexes? *Psychological Science, 17*(1), 46–52.

Litle, P., & Zuckerman, M. (1986). Sensation seeking and music preferences. *Personality and Individual Differences, 7*(4), 575–577.

Loehlin, J. C. (1992). *Genes and environment in personality development.* Newbury Park, CA: Sage.

Loevinger, J. (1957). Objective tests as instruments of psychological theory. *Psychological Reports, 3,* 635–694.

Loftus, E. F., & Bernstein, D. M. (2005). Rich false memories. In A. F. Healy (Ed.), *Experimental cognitive psychology and its applications* (pp. 103–113). Washington, DC: American Psychological Association.

Loftus, E. F., Garry, M., & Feldman, J. (1994). Forgetting sexual trauma: What does it mean when 38% forget? *Journal of Consulting and Clinical Psychology, 62,* 1177–1181.

Luhtanen, R., & Crocker, J. (1992). A collective self-esteem scale: Self-evaluation of one's social identity. *Personality and Social Psychology Bulletin, 18*(3), 302–318.

Lummis, M., & Stevenson, H. W. (1990). Gender differences in beliefs and achievement: A cross-cultural study. *Developmental Psychology, 26,* 254–263.

Lumsden, M. A., Bore, M., Millar, K., Jack, R., & Powis, D. (2005). Assessment of personal qualities in relation to admission to medical school. *Medical Education, 39,* 258–265.

Lyubomirsky, S., King, L., & Diener, E. (2005). The benefits of frequent positive affect: Does happiness lead to success? *Psychological Bulletin, 131*(6), 803–855.

Maccoby, E. E., & Jacklin, C. N. (1974). *The psychology of sex differences.* Palo Alto, CA: Stanford University Press.

MacDonald, A. P. (1970). Internal–external locus of control and the practice of birth control. *Psychological Reports, 27*(1), 206.

MacDonald, D. A. (2000). Spirituality: Description, measurement, and relation to the five factor model. *Journal of Personality, 68*(1), 153–197.

Machiavelli, N. (1532/1940). *The prince.* New York: The Modern Library.

Machover, K. (1949). *Personality projection in the drawing of the human figure.* Springfield, IL: Charles C. Thomas.

Macmillan, M. (1991). *Freud evaluated: The completed arc.* Amsterdam, Netherlands: North-Holland.

Maddi, S. R. (1987). Hardiness training at Illinois Bell Telephone. In J. Opatz (Ed.), *Health promotion evaluation* (pp. 101–115). Stephens Point, WI: National Wellness Institute.

Maddi, S. R. (2002). The story of hardiness: Twenty years of theorizing, research, and practice. *Consulting Psychology Journal: Practice and Research, 54*(3), 173–185.

Maddi, S. R., Kahn, S., & Maddi, K. L. (1998). The effectiveness of hardiness training. *Consulting Psychology Journal: Practice and Research, 50*(2), 78–86.

Maddi, S. R., & Kobasa, S. C. (1984). *The hardy executive.* Homewood, IL: Jones-Irwin.

Madrid, G. A., MacMurray, J., Lee, J. W., Anderson, B. A., & Comings, D. E. (2001). Stress as a mediating factor in the association between the DRD2 Taq I polymorphism and alcoholism. *Alcoholism, 23,* 117–122.

Magaña, J. R., & Carrier, J. M. (1991). Mexican and Mexican-American male sexual behavior and spread of AIDS in California. *Journal of Sex Research, 28,* 425–441.

Magee, M., & Miller, D. C. (1997). *Lesbian lives: Psychoanalytic narratives old and new.* Hillsdale, NJ: Analytic Press.

Maier, S. F. (1970). Failure to escape traumatic shock: Incompatible skeletal motor response or learned helplessness? *Learning and Motivation, 1,* 157–170.

Maier, S. F., & Seligman, M. E. P. (1976). Learned helplessness: Theory and evidence. *Journal of Experimental Psychology: General, 105*(1), 3–46.

Main, M. (1996). Introduction to the special section on attachment and psychopathology: 2. Overview of the field of attachment. *Journal of Consulting and Clinical Psychology, 64*(2), 237–243.

Main, M., Kaplan, N., & Cassidy, J. (1985). Security in infancy, childhood, and adulthood: A move to the level of representation. *Monographs of the Society for Research in Child Development, 50*(1–2), 66–104.

Main, M., & Solomon, J. (1990). Procedures for identifying infants as disorganized/disoriented during the Ainsworth Strange Situation. In M. T. Greenberg, D. Cicchetti, & E. M. Cummings (Eds.), *Attachment in the preschool years* (pp. 121–160). Chicago: University of Chicago Press.

Malcolm, J. (1994). *Psychoanalysis: The impossible profession.* New York: Jason Aronson.

Markon, K. E., Krueger, R. F., & Watson, D. (2005). Delineating the structure of normal and abnormal personality: An integrative hierarchical approach. *Journal of Personality and Social Psychology, 88*(1), 139–157.

Markus, H. R., & Kitayama, S. (1991). Culture and the self: Implications for cognition, emotion and motivation. *Psychological Review, 98*(2), 224–253.

Markus, H. R., & Nurius, P. (1986). Possible selves. *American Psychologist, 41*(9), 954–969.

Marsh, H. W. (1993). Academic self-concept: Theory, measurement, and research. In J. Suls (Ed.), *Psychological perspectives on the self* (pp. 59–98). Hillsdale, NJ: Erlbaum.

Marshall, E. (1995). NIH's "gay gene" study questioned. *Science, 268,* 1841.

Marshall, J. C. (1984). Multiple perspectives on modularity. *Cognition, 17,* 209–242.

Martin, N. J., Holroyd, K. A., & Penzien, D. B. (1990). The headache-specific locus of control scale: Adaptation to recurrent headaches. *Headache: The Journal of Head and Face Pain, 30*(11), 729–734.

Maslow, A. (1954). *Motivation and personality.* New York: Harper & Row.

Masson, J. M. (1984a). *The assault on truth: Freud's suppression of the seduction theory.* New York: Farrar, Straus & Giroux.

Masson, J. M. (1984b, February). Freud and the seduction theory. *The Atlantic Monthly,* 33–60.

Masten, A. S. (2001). Ordinary magic: Resilience processes in development. *American Psychologist, 56*(3), 227–238.

Matthews, G. (2008). Challenges to personality neuroscience: Measurement, complexity and adaptation. *European Journal of Personality, 22,* 400–403.

Mawer, S. (2006). *Gregor Mendel: Planting the seeds of genetics.* New York: Abrams.

Mawson, A. R., Jacobs, K. W., Winchester, Y., & Biundo, J. J. (1988). Sensation-seeking and traumatic spinal cord injury: Case-control study. *Archives of Physical Medicine and Rehabilitation, 69*(12), 1039–1043.

McAdams, D. P. (1988). Biography, narrative, and lives: An introduction. *Journal of Personality, 56*(1), 1–18.

McAdams, D. P. (1992). The five-factor model in personality: A critical appraisal. *Journal of Personality, 60*(2), 229–361.

McAdams, D. P. (2009). *The person: An introduction to the science of personality psychology* (5th ed.). New York: Wiley.

McClelland, D. C., Atkinson, J. W., Clark, R. A., & Lowell, F. L. (1953). *The achievement motive.* New York: Appleton-Century-Crofts.

McCown, W., Keiser, R., Mulhearn, S., & Williamson, D. (1997). The role of personality and gender in preferences for exaggerated bass in music. *Personality and Individual Differences, 23*(4), 543–547.

McCrae, R. R. (1989). Why I advocate the five-factor model: Joint factor analyses of the NEO-PI with other instruments. In D. M. Buss & N. Cantor (Eds.), *Personality psychology: Recent trends and emerging directions* (pp. 237–245). New York: Springer-Verlag.

McCrae, R. R. (1990). Traits and trait names: How well is Openness represented in natural languages? *European Journal of Personality, 4,* 119–129.

McCrae, R. R. (2001). Trait psychology and culture: Exploring intercultural comparisons. *Journal of Personality, 69,* 819–846.

McCrae, R. R. (2002). NEO-PI-R data from 36 cultures: Further intercultural comparisons. In R. R. McCrae & J. Allik (Eds.), *The five-factor model of personality across cultures* (pp. 105–125). New York: Kluwer Academic/Plenum.

McCrae, R. R. (2007). Aesthetic chills as a universal marker of openness to experience. *Motivation and Emotion, 31,* 5–11.

McCrae, R. R., & Costa, P. T. (1983). Joint factors in self-reports and ratings: Neuroticism, extraversion and openness to experience. *Personality and Individual Differences, 4*(3), 245–255.

McCrae, R. R., & Costa, P. T. (1985). Updating Norman's "adequate taxonomy": Intelligence and personality dimensions in natural language and questionnaires. *Journal of Personality and Social Psychology, 49,* 710–721.

McCrae, R. R., & Costa, P. T. (1986). Personality, coping, and coping effectiveness in an adult sample. *Journal of Personality, 54*(2), 385–405.

McCrae, R. R., & Costa, P. T. (1987). Validation of the five-factor model of personality across instruments and observers. *Journal of Personality and Social Psychology, 52,* 81–90.

McCrae, R. R., & Costa, P. T. (1989). Rotation to maximize the construct validity of factors in the NEO Personality Inventory. *Multivariate Behavioral Research, 24,* 107–124.

McCrae, R. R., & Costa, P. T. (1996). Towards a new generation of personality theories: Theoretical contexts for the five-factor model. In J. S. Wiggins (Ed.), *The five-factor model of personality: Theoretical perspectives* (pp. 51–87). New York: Guilford Press.

McCrae, R. R., & Costa, P. T. (1997a). Conceptions and correlates of openness to experience. In R. Hogan, J. Johnson, & S. Briggs (Eds.), *Handbook of personality psychology* (pp. 825–847). New York: Academic Press.

McCrae, R. R., & Costa, P. T. (1997b). Personality trait structure as a human universal. *American Psychologist, 52*(5), 509–516.

McCrae, R. R., & Costa, P. T. (2008). The five-factor theory of personality. In O. P. John, R. W. Robins, & L. A. Pervin (Eds.), *Handbook of personality: Theory and research* (pp. 159–181). New York: Guilford Press.

McCrae, R. R., Costa, P. T., Pedroso de Lima, M., Simões, A., Ostendorf, F., Angleitner, A., et al. (1999). Age differences in personality across the adult life span: Parallels in five cultures. *Developmental Psychology, 35*(2), 466–477.

McCrae, R. R., Costa, P. T., & Yik, M. S. M. (1996). Universal aspects of Chinese personality structure. In M. H. Bond (Ed.), *The handbook of Chinese psychology.* Hong Kong: Oxford University Press.

McCrae, R. R., & John, O. P. (1992). An introduction to the five-factor model and its applications. *Journal of Personality, 60,* 175–215.

McCrae, R. R., Terracciano, A., & 78 Members of the Personality Profiles of Cultures Project. (2005a). Universal features of personality traits from the observer's perspective: Data from 50 cultures. *Journal of Personality and Social Psychology, 88,* 547–561.

McCrae, R. R., Terracciano, A., & 79 Members of the Personality Profiles of Cultures Project. (2005b). Personality profiles of cultures: Aggregate personality traits. *Journal of Personality and Social Psychology, 89*(3), 407–425.

McCrae, R. R., Yamagata, S., Jang, K. L., Riemann, R., Ando, J., Ono, Y., et al. (2008). Substance and artifact in the higher-order factors of the Big Five. *Journal of Personality and Social Psychology, 95*(2), 442–455.

McGuffin, P. (2004). Behavioral genomics: Where molecular genetics is taking psychiatry and psychology. In L. F. DiLalla (Ed.), *Behavioral genetics principles: Perspectives in development, personality, and psychopathology* (pp. 191–204). Washington, DC: American Psychological Association.

McGuire, W. J. (1967). Some impending reorientation in social psychology. *Journal of Experimental Social Psychology, 3*(2), 124–139.

McKnight, J., & Malcolm, J. (2000). Is male homosexuality maternally linked? *Psychology, Evolution, & Gender, 2,* 229–239.

McNally, R. J. (2003a). Recovering memories of trauma: A view from the laboratory. *Current Directions in Psychological Science, 12*(1), 32–35.

McNally, R. J. (2003b). *Remembering trauma.* Cambridge, MA: Belknap Press/Harvard University Press.

McNamara, L., & Ballard, M. E. (1999). Resting arousal, sensation seeking, and music preference. *Genetic, social, and general psychology monographs, 125*(3), 229–250.

McNaughton, N. (2008). Unscrambling the personality omelet. *European Journal of Personality, 22,* 403–405.

McNaughton, N., & Corr, P. J. (2004). A two-dimensional neuropsychology of defense: Fear/anxiety and defensive distance. *Neuroscience and the Biobehavioral Reviews, 28*(3), 285–305.

McNaughton, N., & Corr, P. J. (2008). The neuropsychology of fear and anxiety: A foundation for reinforcement sensitivity theory. In P. J. Corr (Ed.), *The reinforcement sensitivity theory of personality* (pp. 44–94). Cambridge, England: Cambridge University Press.

Mead, G. H. (1925). The genesis of the self and social control. *International Journal of Ethics, 35,* 251–273.

Mednick, M. T., & Thomas, V. G. (1993). Women and the psychology of achievement: A view from the eighties. In F. L. Denmark & M. A. Paludi (Eds.), *Psychology of women: A handbook of issues and theories.* Westport, CT: Greenwood Press.

Medvec, V. H., Madey, S. F., & Gilovich, T. (1995). When less is more: Counterfactual thinking and satisfaction among Olympic medalists. *Journal of Personality and Social Psychology, 69*(4), 603–610.

Meehl, P. E. (1956). Wanted—a good cookbook. *American Psychologist, 11,* 263–272.

Meek, R. (2007). The parenting possible selves of young fathers in prison. *Psychology, Crime and Law, 13*(4), 371–382.

Meltzhoff, A. N. (1990). Foundations for developing a concept of self: The role of imitation in relating self to other and the value of social mirroring, social modeling, and self-practice in infancy. In D. Cicchetti & M. Beeghly (Eds.), *The self in transition: Infancy to childhood* (pp. 139–164). Chicago: University of Chicago Press.

Metalsky, G. I., Abramson, L. Y., Seligman, M. E. P., Semmel, A., & Peterson, C. (1982). Attributional styles and life events in the classroom: Vulnerability and invulnerability to depressive mood reactions. *Journal of Personality and Social Psychology, 43,* 612–617.

Metalsky, G. I., Halberstadt, L. J., & Abramson, L. Y. (1987). Vulnerability to depressive mood reactions: Toward a more powerful test of the diathesis-stress and causal mediation components of the reformulated theory of depression. *Journal of Personality and Social Psychology, 52,* 386–393.

Metalsky, G. I., Joiner, T. E., Hardin, T. S., & Abramson, L. Y. (1993). Depressive reactions to failure in a naturalistic setting: A test of the hopelessness and self-esteem theories of depression. *Journal of Abnormal Psychology, 102,* 101–109.

Meyer, G. J., Finn, S. E., Eyde, L. D., Kay, G. G., Moreland, K. L., Dies, R. R., et al. (2001). Psychological testing and psychological assessment: A review of evidence and issues. *American Psychologist, 56*(2), 128–165.

Meyer, I. H. (2003). Prejudice, social stress, and mental health in lesbian, gay, and bisexual populations: Conceptual issues and research evidence. *Psychological Bulletin, 129,* 674–697.

Meyer, M. (1926). Review of handbuch der vergleichenden psychologie. *Psychological Bulletin, 23*(5), 261–276.

Meyer-Bahlburg, H. F. L. (1984). Psychoendocrine research on sexual orientation. current status and future options. *Progress in Brain Research, 61,* 375–398.

Meyer-Bahlburg, H. F. L. (1997). The role of prenatal estrogens in sexual orientation. In L. Ellis & L. Ebertz (Eds.), *Sexual orientation: Toward biological understanding* (pp. 41–51). Westport, CT: Praeger.

Meyer-Bahlburg, H. F. L., Ehrhardt, A. A., Rosen, L. R., Gruen, R. S., Veridiano, N. P., Vann, F. H., et al. (1995). Prenatal estrogens and the development of homosexual orientation. *Developmental Psychology, 31,* 12–21.

Mikulincer, M., & Shaver, P. R. (2007). *Attachment in adulthood.* New York: Guilford Press.

Milam, J. E., Richardson, J. L., Marks, G., Kemper, C. A., & McCutchan, A. J. (2004). The roles of dispositional optimism and pessimism in HIV disease progression. *Psychology and Health, 19*(2), 167–181.

Millar, R., & Shevlin, M. (2007). The development and factor structure of a career locus of control scale for use with school pupils. *Journal of Career Development, 33*(3), 224–249.

Miller, N. (1992). *Out in the world: Gay and lesbian life from Buenos Aires to Bangkok.* New York: Random House.

Miller, P. C., Lefcourt, H. M., & Ware, E. E. (1983). The construction and development of the Miller marital locus of control scale. *Canadian Journal of Behavioural Science/Revue canadienne des sciences du comportement, 15*(3), 266–279.

Mills, J. (1976). A procedure for explaining experiments involving deception. *Personality and Social Psychology Bulletin, 2*(1), 3–13.

Mischel, W. (1966). A social-learning view of sex differences in behavior. In E. E. Maccoby (Ed.), *The development of sex differences* (pp. 56–81). Palo Alto, CA: Stanford University Press.

Mischel, W., & Shoda, Y. (1995). A cognitive-affective system theory of personality: Reconceptualizing situations, dispositions, dynamics, and invariance in personality structure. *Psychological Review, 102*(2), 246–268.

Miserandino, M. (1996). Children who do well in school: Individual differences in perceived competence and autonomy in above-average children. *Journal of Educational Psychology, 88,* 203–214.

Miserandino, M. (1998). Attributional retraining as a method of improving athletic performance. *Journal of Sport Behavior, 21,* 286–297.

Missuz J. (n.d.). *I am from . . .* Retrieved August 29, 2009, from http://www.missuzj.com/mjblog/2005/11/index.html.

Mitchell, S. A. (1988). *Relational concepts in psychoanalysis: An integration.* Cambridge, MA: Harvard University Press.

Mitchell, S. A. (1993). *Hope and dread in psychoanalysis.* New York: Basic Books.

Mitchell, S. A. (1997). *Autonomy and influence in psychoanalysis.* Hillsdale, NJ: Analytic Press.

Miyake, A., Kost-Smith, L. E., Finkelstein, N. D., Pollock, S. J., Cohen, G. L., & Ito, T. A. (2010). Reducing the gender achievement gap in college science: A classroom study of values affirmation. *Science, 330*(6008), 1234–1237.

Moffitt, T. E., Caspi, A., & Rutter, M. (2006). Measured gene-environment interactions in psychopathology. *Perspectives on Psychological Science, 1*(1), 5–27.

Mohr, J. J. (2008). Same-sex romantic attachment. In J. Cassidy & P. R. Shaver (Eds.), *Handbook of attachment* (2nd ed., pp. 482–502). New York: Guilford Press.

Monroe, S. M., & Reid, M. W. (2008). Gene–environment interactions in depression research. *Psychological Science, 19*(10), 947–956.

Montemayor, R., & Eisen, M. (1977). The development of self-conceptions from childhood to adolescence. *Developmental Psychology, 13*(4), 314–319.

Moore, D. S., & Johnson, S. P. (2008). Mental rotation in human infants. *Psychological Science, 19*(11), 1063–1066.

Morgan, C. D., & Murray, H. A. (1935). A method of investigating fantasies: The thematic apperception test. *Archives of Neurology and Psychiatry, 34,* 289–306.

Morgan, W. G. (1995). Origin and history of the thematic apperception test images. *Journal of Personality Assessment, 65*(2), 237–254.

Moskowitz, D. S., Suh, E. J., & Desaulniers, J. (1994). Situational influences on gender differences in agency and communion. *Journal of Personality and Social Psychology, 66,* 753–761.

Motley, M. T. (1985). Slips of the tongue. *Scientific American, 253*(3), 116–127.

Motley, M. T., & Baars, B. (1979). Effects of cognitive set upon laboratory induced verbal (Freudian) slips. *Journal of Speech and Hearing Research, 22*(3), 421–432.

Mroczek, D. K. (2007). The analysis of longitudinal data in personality research. In R. W. Robins, R. C. Fraley, & R. F. Krueger (Eds.), *Handbook of research methods in personality psychology* (pp. 543–556). New York: Guilford Press.

Mroczek, D. K., & Spiro, A. (2003). Modeling intraindividual change in personality traits: Findings from the normative aging study. *Journal of Gerontology, 58B*(3), P153–P165.

Mroczek, D. K., & Spiro, A. (2007). Personality change influences mortality in older men. *Psychological Science, 18*(5), 371–376.

Munafò, M. R., & Flint, J. (2009). Replication and heterogeneity in gene x environment interaction studies. *International Journal of Neuropsychopharmacology, 12,* 727–729.

Munsey, C. (2009, July/August). Frisky, but more risky: High sensation-seekers' quest for new experiences leads some to the high-stress jobs society needs done but makes others vulnerable to reckless behavior. *APA Monitor on Psychology, 37*(7), 40.

Muris, P. (2006). Freud was right . . . about the origins of abnormal behavior. *Journal of Child and Family Studies, 15*(1), 1–12.

Murray, H. A. (1938). *Explorations in personality.* New York: Oxford University Press.

Muscarella, F. (2006). The evolution of male–male sexual behavior in humans: The alliance theory. In M. R. Kauth (Ed.), *Handbook of the evolution of human sexuality* (pp. 275–311). London: Haworth Press.

Musek, J. (2007). A general factor of personality: Evidence for the Big One in the five-factor model. *Journal of Research in Personality, 41,* 1213–1233.

Musson, D. M., & Helmreich, R. L. (2004). Personality characteristics and trait clusters in final stage astronaut selection. *Aviation, Space, and Environmental Medicine, 75*(4), 342–349.

Mustanski, B. S., & Bailey, J. M. (2003). A therapist's guide to the genetics of human sexual orientation. *Sexual and Relationship Therapy, 18*(4), 429–436.

Mustanski, B. S., Chivers, M. L., & Bailey, J. M. (2002). A critical review of recent biological research on human sexual orientation. *Annual Review of Sex Research, 13,* 89–140.

Mutch, C. (2005). Higher-order factors of the Big Five model of personality: A reanalysis of Digman (1947). *Psychological Reports, 96*(1), 167–177.

Myers, D. G. (2000a). Feeling good about Fredrickson's positive emotions. *Prevention & Treatment, 3*(1), ArtID 2c.

Myers, D. G. (2000b). The funds, friends, and faith of happy people. *American Psychologist, 55*(1), 56–67.

Myers, D. G., & Diener, E. (1995). Who is happy? *Psychological Science, 6*(1), 10–17.

Myers, I. B., & McCauley, M. H. (1985). *Manual: A guide to the development and use of the Myers-Briggs type indicator.* Palo Alto, CA: Consulting Psychologists Press.

Najmi, S., & Wegner, D. M. (2006). The united states of repression. *Behavioral and Brain Sciences, 29*(5), 528–529.

Nakamura, J., & Csikszentmihalyi, M. (2009). Flow theory and research. In S. J. Lopez & C. R. Snyder (Eds.), *Oxford handbook of positive psychology research* (pp. 195–206). Oxford, England: Oxford University Press.

Narusyte, J., Andershed, A., Neiderhiser, J. M., & Lichtenstein, P. (2007). Aggression as a mediator of genetic contributions to the association between negative parent–child relationships and adolescent antisocial behavior. *European Child and Adolescent Psychiatry, 16,* 128–137.

Nasby, W., & Read, N. W. (1997). The life voyage of a solo circumnavigator: integrating theoretical and methodological perspectives. *Journal of Personality, 65,* 785–1068.

Needles, D. J., & Abramson, L. Y. (1990). Positive life events, attributional style, and hopefulness: Testing a model of recovery from depression. *Journal of Abnormal Psychology, 99*(2), 156–165.

Nettle, D. (2007). *Personality: What makes you the way you are?* Oxford, England: Oxford University Press.

Neuman, W. L. (1997). *Social research methods: Qualitative and quantitative approaches.* Boston: Allyn & Bacon.

Newman, L. S., Duff, K. J., & Baumeister, R. F. (1997). A new look at defensive projection: Thought suppression, accessibility, and biased person perception. *Journal of Personality and Social Psychology, 72*(5), 980–1001.

Newman, L. S., Duff, K. J., Hedberg, D. A., & Blitstein, J. (1996). Rebound effects in impression formation: Assimilation and contrast effects following thought suppression. *Journal of Experimental Social Psychology, 32,* 460–483.

Newman, R. (2005). APA's resilience initiative. *Professional psychology: Research and practice, 36*(3), 227–229.

Ng, T. W. H., Sorensen, K. L., & Eby, L. T. (2006). Locus of control at work: A meta-analysis. *Journal of Organizational Behavior, 27*(8), 1057–1087.

Ng, W., & Diener, E. (2009). Feeling bad? The "power" of positive thinking may not apply to everyone. *Journal of Research in Personality, 43,* 455–463.

Nichols, T. E., & Poline, J. (2009). Commentary on Vul et al.'s (2009) "Puzzlingly high correlations in fMRI studies of emotion, personality and social cognition." *Perspectives on Psychological Science,4*(3), 291–293.

Nix, G., Ryan, R. M., Manly, J. B., & Deci, E. L. (1999). Revitalization through self-regulation: The effects of autonomous and controlled motivation on happiness and vitality. *Journal of Experimental Social Psychology, 35,* 266–284.

Nolen-Hoeksema, S., Girgus, J. S., & Seligman, M. E. P. (1986). Learned helplessness in children: A longitudinal study of depression, achievement, and explanatory style. *Journal of Personality and Social Psychology, 51*(2), 435–442.

Nolen-Hoeksema, S., & Hilt, L. M. (2009). Gender differences in depression. In I. H. Gotlib & C. L. Hammen (Eds.), *Handbook of depression* (2nd ed., pp. 386–404). New York: Guilford Press.

Nord, W. R., Connelly, F., & Daignault, G. (1974). Locus of control and aptitude test scores as predictors of academic achievement. *Journal of Educational Psychology, 66*(6), 956–961.

Norem, J. N. (2003). Pessimism: Accentuating the positive possibilities. In E. E. C. Chang & L. L. J. Sanna (Eds.), *Virtue, vice, and personality: The complexity of behavior* (pp. 91–104). Washington, DC: American Psychological Association.

Norman, P., Bennett, P., Smith, C., & Murphy, S. (1997). Health locus of control and leisure-time exercise. *Personality and Individual Differences, 23*(5), 769–774.

Norman, W. T. (1963). Toward an adequate taxonomy of personality attributes: Replicated factor structure in peer nomination personality ratings. *Journal of Abnormal and Social Psychology, 66,* 574–583.

Nosek, B. A., Greenwald, A. G., & Banaji, M. R. (2005). Understanding and using the implicit association test: 2. Method variables and construct validity. *Personality and Social Psychology Bulletin, 31*(2), 166–180.

NPR. (2004). *Google entices job-searchers with math puzzle.* Retrieved May 27, 2010, from http://www.npr.org/templates/story/story.php?storyId=3916173.

Nunnally, J. C., & Bernstein, I. H. (1994). *Psychometric theory* (3rd ed.). New York: McGraw-Hill.

Nurius, P. S., Casey, E., Lindhorst, T. P., & Macy, R. J. (2006). Identity health, stress, and support: Profiles of transition to motherhood among high risk adolescent girls. In C. Dunkel & J. Kerpelman (Eds.), *Possible selves: Theory, research and application* (pp. 97–121). New York: Nova Science Publishers.

Oda, M. (1983). Predicting sales performance of car salesmen by personality traits. *Japanese Journal of Psychology, 54*(2), 73–80.

Oliver, M. B., & Hyde, J. S. (1993). Gender differences in sexuality: A meta-anlaysis. *Psychological Bulletin, 114,* 29–51.

Omura, K., Constable, R. T., & Canli, T. (2005). Amygdala gray matter concentration is associated with extraversion and neuroticism. *Cognitive Neuroscience and Neuropsychology, 16,* 1905–1908.

Ones, D. S., Dilchert, S., Viswesvaran, C., & Judge, T. A. (2007). In support of personality assessment in organizational settings. *Personnel Psychology, 60,* 995–1027.

Ones, D. S., Viswesvaran, C., & Schmidt, F. L. (1993). Comprehensive meta-analysis of integrity test validity: Findings and implications for personnel selection and theories of job performance. *Journal of Applied Psychology Monograph, 787*(4), 679–703.

Ong, A. D., & Allaire, J. C. (2005). Cardiovascular intraindividual variability in later life: The influence of social connectedness and positive emotions. *Psychology and Aging, 20*(3), 476–485.

Ong, A. D., Bergeman, C. S., Bisconti, T. L., & Wallace, K. A. (2006). Psychological resilience, positive emotions, and successful adaptation to stress in later life. *Journal of Personality and Social Psychology, 91*(4), 730–749.

Ong, A. D., Edwards, L. M., & Bergeman, C. S. (2006). Hope as a source of resilience in later adulthood. *Personality and Individual Differences, 41,* 1263–1273.

OSS Assessment Staff (1948). *Assessment of men: Selection of personnel for the Office of Strategic Service.* New York: Rinehart & Company.

Overmier, J. B., & Seligman, M. E. P. (1967). Effects of inescapable shock upon subsequent escape and avoidance responding. *Journal of Comparative and Physiological Psychology, 63*(1), 28–33.

Oyserman, D. (1993). The lens of personhood: Viewing the self and others in a multicultural society. *Journal of Personality and Social Psychology, 65*(5), 993–1009.

Oyserman, D., Coon, H. M., & Kemmelmeier, M. (2002). Rethinking individualism and collectivism: Evaluation of theoretical assumptions and meta-analyses. *Psychological Bulletin, 128*(1), 3–72.

Oyserman, D., & Lee, S. W. S. (2008). Does culture influence what and how we think? Effects of priming individualism and collectivism. *Psychological Bulletin, 134*(2), 311–342.

Oyserman, D., & Markus, H. R. (1990). Possible selves and delinquency. *Journal of Personality and Social Psychology, 59*(1), 112–125.

Oyserman, D., Terry, K., & Bybee, D. (2002). A possible selves intervention to enhance school involvement. *Journal of Adolescence, 25,* 313–326.

Ozer, D. J. (2007). Evaluating effect size in personality research. In R. W. Robins, R. C. Fraley, & R. F. Krueger (Eds.), *Handbook of research methods in personality psychology* (pp. 495–501). New York: Guilford Press.

Ozer, D. J., & Reise, S. P. (1994). Personality assessment. In L. W. Porter & M. R. Rosenzweig (Eds.), *Annual review of psychology* (Vol. 45, pp. 357–388). Palo Alto, CA: Annual Reviews.

Paradise, A. W., & Kernis, M. H. (2002). Self-esteem and psychological well-being: Implications of fragile self-esteem. *Journal of Social and Clinical Psychology, 21*(4), 345–361.

Pardo, Y., Aguilar, R., Molinuevo, B., & Torrubia, R. (2007). Alcohol use as a behavioural sign of disinhibition: Evidence from J. A. Gray's model of personality. *Addictive Behaviors, 32,* 2398–2403.

Patrick, B. C., Skinner, E. A., & Connell, J. P. (1993). What motivates children's behavior and emotion? Joint effects of perceived control and autonomy in the academic domain. *Journal of Personality and Social Psychology, 65*(4), 781–791.

Patterson, C. J. (1997). Children of lesbian and gay parents. In T. H. Ollendick & R. J. Prinz (Eds.), *Advances in clinical child psychology* (Vol. 19, pp. 235–282). New York: Plenum Press.

Paulhus, D. L. (1991). Measurement and control of response bias. In J. P. Robinson, P. R. Shaver, & L. S. Wrightsman (Eds.), *Measures of personality and social psychological attitudes* (pp 17–59). San Diego, CA: Academic Press.

Paulhus, D. L., & Trapnell, P. D. (2008). Self-presentation of personality: An agency-communion framework. In O. P. John, R. W. Robins, & L. A. Pervin (Eds.), *Handbook of personality: Theory and research* (pp. 492–517). New York: Guilford Press.

Paulhus, D. L., & Vazire, S. (2007). The self-report method. In R. W. Robins, R. C. Fraley, & R. F. Krueger (Eds.), *Handbook of research methods in personality psychology* (pp. 224–258). New York: Guilford Press.

Paunonen, S. V. (2002). *Design and construction of the supernumerary personality inventory* (Research Bulletin 763). London, Ontario: University of Western Ontario.

Paunonen, S. V., & Jackson, D. N. (2000). What is beyond the Big Five? Plenty! *Journal of Personality, 68*(5), 821–835.

Pavlov, I. P. (1928). *Lectures on conditioned reflexes.* London: Martin Lawrence.

Pelham, B. W. (1993). The ideographic nature of human personality: Examples of the idiographic self-concept. *Journal of Personality and Social Psychology, 64*(4), 665–677.

Pelletier, L. G., Fortier, M. S., Vallerand, R. J., Tuson, K. M., Brière, N. M., & Blais, M. R. (1995). Toward a new measure of intrinsic motivation, extrinsic motivation, and amotivation in sports: The sport motivation scale (SMS). *Journal of Sport and Exercise Psychology, 17,* 35–53.

Peltonen, L., & McKusick, V. A. (2001). Genomics and medicine: Dissecting human disease in the post-genomic era. *Science, 291*(5507), 1224–1229.

Peplau, L. A. (2001). Rethinking women's sexual orientation: An interdisciplinary, relationship-focused approach. *Personal Relationships, 8,* 1–19.

Peplau, L. A. (2003). Human sexuality: How do men and women differ? *Current Directions in Psychological Science, 12*(2), 37–40.

Peplau, L. A., & Garnets, L. D. (2000). A new paradigm for understanding women's sexuality and sexual orientation. *Journal of Social Issues, 56*(2), 329–350.

Peplau, L. A., Garnets, L. D., Spalding, L. R., Conley, T. D., & Veniegas, R. C. (1998). A critique of Bem's "exotic becomes erotic" theory of sexual orientation. *Psychological Review, 105*(2), 387–394.

Peplau, L. A., & Huppin, M. (2008). Masculinity, femininity and the development of sexual orientations in women. *Journal of Gay and Lesbian Mental Health, 12*(1/2), 145–165.

Peplau, L. A., Spalding, L. R., Conley, T. D., & Veniegas, R. C. (1999). The development of sexual orientation in women. *Annual Review of Sex Research, 10,* 70–99.

Perry, V. G. (2008). Giving credit where credit is due: The psychology of credit ratings. *The Journal of Behavioral Finance, 9,* 15–21.

Petersen, J. L., & Hyde, J. S. (2010). A meta-analytic review of research on gender differences in sexuality, 1993–2007. *Psychological Bulletin, 136*(1), 21–38.

Peterson, C. (1988). Explanatory style as a risk factor for illness. *Cognitive Therapy and Research, 12,* 117–130.

Peterson, C. (2000). The future of optimism. *American Psychologist, 55*(1), 44–55.

Peterson, C., & Barett, L. C. (1987). Explanatory style and academic performance among university freshmen. *Journal of Personality and Social Psychology, 53*(3), 603–607.

Peterson, C., & Bossio, L. M. (2001). Optimism and physical well-being. In E. C. Chang (Ed.), *Optimism & pessimism: Implications for theory, research, and practice* (pp. 127–145). Washington, DC: American Psychological Association.

Peterson, C., & Chang, E. C. (2003). Optimism and flourishing. In C. L. M. Keyes & J. Haidt (Eds.), *Flourishing: Positive psychology and the life well-lived* (pp. 55–79). Washington, DC: American Psychological Association.

Peterson, C., & De Avila, M. (1995). Optimistic explanatory style and the perception of health problems. *Journal of Clinical Psychology, 51,* 128–132.

Peterson, C., Luborsky, L., & Seligman, M. E. P. (1983). Attributions and depressive mood shifts: A case study using the symptom-context method. *Journal of Abnormal Psychology, 92,* 96–103.

Peterson, C., Maier, S. F., & Seligman, M. E. P. (1993). *Learned helplessness: A theory for the age of personal control.* New York: Oxford University Press.

Peterson, C., & Seligman, M. E. P. (1984). Causal explanations as a risk factor for depression: Theory and evidence. *Psychological Review, 91,* 347–374.

Peterson, C., Seligman, M. E. P., & Vaillant, G. E. (1988). Pessimistic explanatory style is a risk factor for physical illness: A thirty-five year longitudinal study. *Journal of Personality and Social Psychology, 55,* 23–27.

Peterson, C., Semmel, A., von Baeyer, C., Abramson, L. Y., Metalsky, G. I., & Seligman, M. E. P. (1982). The attributional style questionnaire. *Cognitive Therapy and Research, 6*(3), 287–300.

Peterson, C., & Steen, T. A. (2002). Optimistic explanatory style. In C. R. Snyder & S. J. Lopez (Eds.), *Handbook of positive psychology* (pp. 244–256). London: Oxford University Press.

Peterson, C., & Villanova, P. (1988). An expanded attributional style questionnaire. *Journal of Abnormal Psychology, 97*(1), 87–89.

Phares, E. J., & Wilson, K. G. (1972). Responsibility attribution: Role of outcome severity, situational ambiguity, and internal–external control. *Journal of Personality, 40*(3), 392–406.

Pickering, A. D., & Corr, P. J. (2008). J. A. Gray's reinforcement sensitivity theory (RST) of personality. In G. J. Boyle, G. Matthews, & D. H. Saklofske (Eds.), *The SAGE handbook of personality theory and assessment: Vol 1. Personality theories and models* (pp. 238–256). Los Angeles: Sage.

Pickering, A. D., Corr, P. J., Powell, J. H., Kumari, V., Thornton, J. C., & Gray, J. A. (1997). Individual differences in reactions to reinforcing stimuli are neither black nor white: To what extent are they gray? In H. Nyborg (Ed.), *The scientific study of personality: Tribute to Hans J. Eysenck at eighty* (pp. 36–67). London: Elsevier.

Pickering, A. D., & Gray, J. A. (1999). The neuroscience of personality. In L. A. Pervin & O. P. John (Eds.), *Handbook of personality: Theory and research* (pp. 277–299). New York: Guilford Press.

Piedmont, R. L. (1999). Does spirituality represent the sixth factor of personality? Spiritual transcendence and the five-factor model. *Journal of Personality, 67*(6), 985–1013.

Piedmont, R. L., & Leach, M. M. (2002). Cross-cultural generalizability of the spiritual transcendence scale in India. *American Behavioral Scientist, 45*(12), 1888–1901.

Pines, H. A., & Julian, J. W. (1972). Effects of task and social demands on locus of control differences in information processing. *Journal of Personality, 40,* 407–416.

Piotrowski, C., & Armstrong, T. (2006). Current recruitment and selection practices: A national survey of Fortune 1000 firms. *North American Journal of Psychology, 8*(3), 489–496.

Plomin, R., Asbury, K., & Dunn, J. (2001). Why are children in the same family so different? Non-shared environment a decade later. *Canadian Journal of Psychiatry, 46,* 225–233.

Plomin, R., & Caspi, A. (1999). Behavioral genetics and personality. In L. A. Pervin & O. P. John (Eds.), *Handbook of personality: Theory and research* (2nd ed., pp. 251–276). New York: Guilford Press.

Plomin, R., & Daniels, D. (1987). Why are children in the same family so different from one another? *Behavioral and Brain Sciences, 10,* 1–60.

Plomin, R., DeFries, J. C., Craig, I. W., & McGuffin, P. (2003). Behavioral genetics. In R. Plomin, J. C. DeFries, I. W. Craig, & P. McGuffin (Eds.), *Behavioral genetics in the postgenomic era* (pp. 3–15). Washington, DC: American Psychological Association.

Plomin, R., DeFries, J. C., & Loehlin, J. C. (1977). Genotype–environment interaction and correlation in the analysis of human behavior. *Psychological Bulletin, 84*(2), 309–322.

Plomin, R., DeFries, J. C., McClearn, G. E., & McGuffin, P. (2008). *Behavioral genetics.* New York: Worth.

Plomin, R., Happé, F., & Caspi, A. (2002). Personality and cognitive abilities. In P. McGuffin, M. J. Owen, & I. R. Gottesman (Eds.), *Psychiatric genetics and genomics* (pp. 77–112). Oxford, England: Oxford University Press.

Plotnik, J. M., de Waal, F. B. M., & Reiss, D. (2006). Self-recognition in an Asian elephant. *Proceedings of the National Academy of Sciences, 103*(45), 17053–17057.

Pomeroy, W. B. (1972). *Dr. Kinsey and the Institute for Sex Research.* New York: Harper & Row.

Pontius, A. A. (1997). Lack of sex differences among east Ecuadorian school children on geometric figure rotation and face drawings. *Perceptual and Motor Skills, 85,* 72–74.

Pope, H. G., Oliva, P. S., & Hudson, J. I. (1999). Repressed memories: The scientific status. In D. L. Faigman, D. H. Kaye, M. J. Saks, & J. Sanders (Eds.), *Modern scientific evidence: The law and science of expert testimony* (Vol. 1, pp. 115–155). Eagan, MN: West.

Posada, G., Gao, Y., Wu, F., Posada, R., Tascon, M., Schoelmerich, A., et al. (1995). The secure-base phenomenon across cultures: Children's behavior, mothers' preferences, and experts' concepts. *Monographs of the Society for Research in Child Development, 60*(2–3), 27–48.

Prior, H., Schwarz, A., & Güntürkün, O. (2008). Mirror-induced behavior in the magpie (*Pica pica*): Evidence of self-recognition. *PLoS Biology, 6*(8), e202.

Prociuk, T. J., & Breen, L. J. (1974). Locus of control, study habits and attitudes, and college academic performance. *Journal of Psychology: Interdisciplinary and Applied, 88*(1), 91–95.

Proudfoot, J. G., Corr, P. J., Guest, D. E., & Dunn, G. (2009). Cognitive-behavioural training to change attributional style improves employee well-being, job satisfaction, productivity, and turnover. *Personality and Individual Differences, 46,* 147–153.

Pullman, H., Raudsepp, L., & Allik, J. (2006). Stability and change in adolescents' personality: A longitudinal study. *European Journal of Personality, 20,* 447–459.

Pyszczynski, T., Greenberg, J., & Holt, K. (1985). Maintaining consistency between self-serving beliefs and available data: A bias in information processing. *Personality and Social Psychology Bulletin, 11,* 179–190.

Quinn, P. C., & Liben, L. S. (2008). A sex difference in mental rotation in young infants. *Psychological Science, 19*(11), 1067–1070.

Rahim, M. A. (1997). Relationships of stress, locus of control, and social support to psychiatric symptoms and propensity to leave a job: A field study with managers. *Journal of Business and Psychology, 12*(2), 159–174.

Rajecki, D. W., Ickes, W., & Tanford, S. (1981). Locus of control and reactions to strangers. *Personality and Social Psychology Bulletin, 7*(2), 282–289.

Ramanaiah, N. V., & Sharpe, J. P. (1999). Hardiness and major personality factors. *Psychological Reports, 84,* 497–500.

Ramchand, R., Karney, B. R., Osilla, K. C., Burns, R. M., & Caldarone, L. B. (2008). Prevalence of PTSD, depression, and TBI among returning service members. In T. Tanielian & L. H. Jaycox (Eds.), *Invisible wounds of war: Psychological and cognitive injuries, their consequences, and services to assist recovery* (pp. 35–85). Santa Monica, CA: Rand Corporation.

Rawlings, D., & Ciancarelli, V. (1997). Music preferences and the five-factor model of the NEO personality inventory. *Psychology of Music, 25,* 120–132.

Rawlings, D., & Dawe, S. (2008). Psychoticism and impulsivity. In G. J. Boyle, G. Matthews, & D. H. Saklofske (Eds.), *The SAGE handbook of personality theory and assessment: Vol. 1. Personality theories and modules* (pp. 357–378). Los Angeles: Sage.

Reeve, J., & Deci, E. L. (1996). Elements of the competitive situation that affect intrinsic motivation. *Personality and Social Psychology Bulletin, 22*(1), 24–33.

Reeve, J., & Jang, H. (2006). What teachers say and do to support students' autonomy during a learning activity. *Journal of Educational Psychology, 98*(1), 209–218.

Reeves, E. G. (2009). *Can I wear my nose ring to the interview?: A crash course in finding, landing, and keeping your first real job.* New York: Workman.

Regan, P. C., & Berscheid, E. (1995). Gender differences in beliefs about the causes of male and female sexual desire. *Personal Relationships, 2,* 345–358.

Regan, P. C., & Berscheid, E. (1996). Beliefs about the state, goals, and objects of sexual desire. *Journal of Sex and Marital Therapy, 22,* 110–120.

Reilly, P. R. (2006). *The strongest boy in the world.* Cold Spring Harbor, NY: Cold Spring Harbor Laboratory Press.

Reis, H. T., & Patrick, B. P. (1996). Attachment and intimacy: Component processes. In E. T. Higgins & A. W. Kruglanski (Eds.), *Social psychology: Handbook of basic principles* (pp. 523–563). New York: Guilford Press.

Reiss, D., & Marino, L. (2001). Mirror self-recognition in the bottlenose dolphin: A case of cognitive convergence. *Proceedings of the National Academy of Sciences, 98*(10), 5937–5942.

Reitz, H. J., & Jewell, L. N. (1979). Sex, locus of control, and job involvement: A six-country investigation. *Academy of Management Journal, 22*(1), 72–80.

Rentfrow, P. J., & Gosling, S. D. (2003). The do re mi's of everyday life: The structure and personality correlates of music preferences. *Journal of Personality and Social Psychology, 84*(6), 1236–1256.

Rettew, D., & Reivich, K. (1995). Sports and explanatory style. In G. M. Buchanan & M. E. P. Seligman (Eds.), *Explanatory style* (pp. 173–185). Hillsdale, NJ: Erlbaum.

Reuter, M., & Montag, C. (2008). Switching the perspective from neuroscience to personality. *European Journal of Personality, 22,* 405–407.

Revelle, W. (2007). Experimental approaches to the study of personality. In R. W. Robins, R. C. Fraley, & R. F. Krueger (Eds.), *Handbook of research methods in personality psychology* (pp. 37–61). New York: Guilford Press.

Revelle, W., & Wilt, J. (2008). Personality is more than reinforcement sensitivity. *European Journal of Personality, 22,* 407–409.

Reverby, S. M. (2009). *The infamous syphilis study and its legacy.* Chapel Hill: University of North Carolina Press.

Rhodewalt, F., & Zone, J. B. (1989). Appraisal of life change, depression, and illness in hardy and nonhardy women. *Journal of Personality and Social Psychology, 56*(1), 81–88.

Rice, G., Anderson, C., Risch, N., & Ebers, G. (1999). Male homosexuality: Absence of linkage to microsatellite markers at Xq28. *Science, 284,* 665–667.

Riemann, R., Angleitner, A., & Strelau, J. (1997). Genetic and environmental influences on personality: A study of twins reared together using the self- and peer report NEO-FFI scales. *Journal of Personality, 65,* 449–476.

Riketta, M., & Ziegler, R. (2006). Self-ambivalence and self-esteem. *Current Psychology: Developmental, Learning, Personality, Social, 25*(3), 192–211.

Roberts, B. W. (1997). Plaster or plasticity: Are adult work experiences associated with personality change in women? *Journal of Personality, 65*(2), 205–232.

Roberts, B. W. (2010, Winter). Personality, continuity, and change. In C. Berger (Ed.), *Psychology times* (pp. 1, 4–5). Champaign: Psychology Department, University of Illinois at Urbana–Champaign.

Roberts, B. W., & Bogg, T. (2004). A longitudinal study of the relationships between conscientiousness and the social-environmental factors and substance-use behaviors that influence health. *Journal of Personality, 72*(2), 325–353.

Roberts, B. W., Caspi, A., & Moffitt, T. E. (2003). Work experiences and personality development in young adulthood. *Journal of Personality and Social Psychology, 84*(3), 582–593.

Roberts, B. W., & Chapman, C. N. (2000). Change in dispositional well-being and its relation to role quality: A 30-year longitudinal study. *Journal of Research in Personality, 34,* 26–41.

Roberts, B. W., & DelVecchio, W. F. (2000). The rank-order consistency of personality traits from childhood to old age: A quantitative review of longitudinal studies. *Psychological Bulletin, 126*(1), 3–25.

Roberts, B. W., & Helson, R. (1997). Changes in culture, changes in personality: The influence of individualism in a longitudinal study of women. *Journal of Personality and Social Psychology, 72,* 641–651.

Roberts, B. W., Kuncel, N. R., & Viechtbauer, W. (2007). Meta-analysis in personality psychology. In R. W. Robins, R. C. Fraley, & R. F. Krueger (Eds.), *Handbook of research methods in personality psychology* (pp. 652–672). New York: Guilford Press.

Roberts, B. W., & Mroczek, D. (2008). Personality trait change in adulthood. *Current Directions in Psychological Science, 17*(1), 31–35.

Roberts, B. W., Walton, K.E., Bogg, T., & Caspi, A. (2006). De-investment in work and non-normative personality trait change in young adulthood. *European Journal of Personality, 20,* 461–474.

Roberts, B. W., Walton, K. E., & Viechtbauer, W. (2006). Patterns of mean-level change in personality traits across the life course: A meta-analysis of longitudinal studies. *Psychological Bulletin, 132*(1), 1–25.

Roberts, B. W., Wood, D., & Caspi, A. (2008). The development of personality traits in adulthood. In O. P. John, R. W. Robins, & L. A. Pervin (Eds.), *Handbook of personality: Theory and research* (pp. 375–398). New York: Guilford Press.

Robins, C. J., & Hayes, A. M. (1995). The role of causal attributions in the prediction of depression. In G. M. Buchanan & M. E. P. Seligman (Eds.), *Explanatory style* (pp. 71–98). Hillsdale, NJ: Erlbaum.

Robins, R. W., Caspi, A., & Moffitt, T. E. (2002). It's not just who you're with, it's who you are: Personality and relationship experiences across multiple relationships. *Journal of Personality, 70*(6), 925–964.

Robins, R. W., Caspi, A., Moffitt, T. E., & Stouthamer-Loeber, M. (1996). Resilient, overcontrolled, and undercontrolled boys: Three replicable personality types. *Journal of Personality and Social Psychology, 70*(1), 157–171.

Robins, R. W., Fraley, R. C., & Krueger, R. F. (Eds.). (2007). *Handbook of research methods in personality psychology.* New York: Guilford Press.

Robins, R. W., Tracy, J. L., & Sherman, J. W. (2007). What kinds of methods do personality psychologists use? A survey of journal editors and editorial board members. In R. W. Robins, R. C. Fraley, & R. F. Krueger (Eds.), *Handbook of research methods in personality psychology* (pp. 673–678). New York: Guilford Press.

Robinson-Whelen, S., Kim, C., MacCallum, R. C., & Kiecolt-Glaser, J. K. (1997). Distinguishing optimism from pessimism in older adults: Is it more important to be optimistic or not to be pessimistic? *Journal of Personality and Social Psychology, 73*(6), 1345–1353.

Rodin, J., & Langer, E. J. (1977). Long-term effects of a control-relevant intervention with the institutionalized aged. *Journal of Personality and Social Psychology, 35*(12), 897–902.

Roese, N. J., Sanna, L. J., & Galinsky, A. D. (2005). The mechanics of imagination: Automaticity and control in counterfactual thinking. In R. R. Hassin, J. R. Uleman, & J. A. Bargh (Eds.), *The new unconscious* (pp. 138–170). New York: Oxford University Press.

Rofé, Y. (2008). Does repression exist? Memory, pathogenic unconscious and clinical evidence. *Review of General Psychology, 12*(1), 63–85.

Rogers, C. R. (1951). *Client-centered therapy: Its current practice, implications, and theory.* Boston: Houghton Mifflin.

Rogers, C. R. (1968). *On becoming a person: A therapist's view of psychotherapy.* Boston: Houghton Mifflin.

Rorschach, H. (1921). *Psychodiagnostics: A diagnostic test based on perception.* New York: Grune & Stratton.

Rose, R. J., & Dick, D. M. (2004/2005). Gene–environment interplay in adolescent drinking behavior. *Alcohol Research and Health, 28*(4), 222–229.

Rose, R. J., Viken, R. J., Dick, D. M., Bates, J. E., Pulkkinen, L., & Kaprio, J. (2003). It *does* take a village: Nonfamilial environments and children's behavior. *Psychological Science, 14*(3), 271–277.

Rosenberg, M. (1965). *Society and the adolescent self-image.* Princeton, NJ: Princeton University Press.

Rosenberg, S. (1989). A study of personality in literary autobiography: An analysis of Thomas Wolfe's Look Homeward Angel. *Journal of Personality and Social Psychology, 56*(3), 416–430.

Rosenthal, R., & Jacobson, L. (1968). *Pygmalion in the classroom: Teacher expectations and student intellectual development.* New York: Holt, Rinehart and Winston.

Ross, T. P., Calhoun, E., Cox, T., Wenner, C., Kono, W., & Pleasant, M. (2007). The reliability and validity of qualitative scores for the Controlled Oral Word Association Test. *Archives of Clinical Neuropsychology, 22*(4), 475–488.

Rosse, J. G., Stecher, M. D., Miller, J. L., & Levin, R. A. (1998). The impact of response distortion on preemployment personality testing and hiring decisions. *Journal of Applied Psychology, 83,* 634–644.

Rothstein, M. G., & Goffin, R. D. (2006). The use of personality measures in personnel selection: What does current research support? *Human Resource Management Review, 16,* 155–180.

Rotter, J. B. (1966). Generalized expectancies for internal versus external control of reinforcement. *Psychological Monographs: General and Applied, 80*(1), 1–28.

Rotter, J. B. (1975). Some problems and misconceptions related to the construct of internal versus external control of reinforcement. *Journal of Consulting and Clinical Psychology, 43*(1), 56–67.

Rotter, J. B., Chance, J. E., & Phares, E. J. (1972). *Applications of social learning theory of personality.* New York: Holt, Rinehart and Winston.

Rowatt, W. C., Cunningham, M. R., & Druen, P. B. (1998). Deception to get a date. *Personality and Social Psychology Bulletin, 24,* 1228–1242.

Rowe, J. L., Montgomery, G. H., Duberstein, P. R., & Bovbjerg, D. H. (2005). Health locus of control and perceived risk for breast cancer in healthy women. *Behavioral Medicine, 31,* 33–40.

Rowling, J. K. (1999). *Harry Potter and the chamber of secrets.* New York: Scholastic.

Rubenzer, S. J., Faschingbauer, T. R., & Ones, D. S. (2000). Assessing the U.S. presidents using the revised NEO Personality Inventory. *Assessment, 7*(4), 403–420.

Rubinstein, G., & Strul, S. (2007). The five factor model (FFM) among four groups of male and female professionals. *Journal of Research in Personality, 41,* 931–937.

Ruble, D. (1983). The development of social comparison processes and their role in achievement-related self-socialization. In E. T. Higgins, D. Ruble, & W. Hartup (Eds.), *Social cognition and social behavior* (pp. 134–157). New York: Cambridge University Press.

Ruchkin, V., Koposov, R. A., af Klinteberg, B., Oreland, L., & Grigorenko, E. L. (2005). Platelet MAO-B, personality, and psychopathology. *Journal of Abnormal Psychology, 114,* 477–482.

Rudman, L. A., & Glick, P. (1999). Feminized management and backlash toward agentic women: The hidden costs to women of a kinder, gentler image of middle managers. *Journal of Personality and Social Psychology, 77,* 1004–1010.

Rushton, J. P., Bons, T. A., & Hur, Y. (2008). The genetics and evolution of the general factor of personality. *Journal of Research in Personality, 42,* 1173–1185.

Rushton, J. P., & Irwing, P. (2008). A general factor of personality (GFP) from two meta-analyses of the Big Five: Digman (1997) and Mount, Barrick, Scullen, and Rounds (2005). *Personality and Individual Differences, 45,* 679–683.

Rushton, J. P., & Irwing, P. (2009). A general factor of personality in the Comrey Personality Scales, the Minnesota Multiphasic Personality Inventory-2, and the Multicultural Personality Questionnaire. *Personality and Individual Differences, 46,* 437–442.

Rutter, M. (2008). Implications of attachment theory and research for child care policies. In J. Cassidy & P. R. Shaver (Eds.), *Handbook of attachment* (pp. 958–974). New York: Guilford Press.

Ryan, R. M., Chirkov, V. I., Little, T. D., Sheldon, K. M., Timoshina, E., & Deci, E. L. (1999). The American dream in Russia: Extrinsic aspirations and well-being in two cultures. *Personality and Social Psychology Bulletin, 25*(12), 1509–1524.

Ryan, R. M., & Deci, E. L. (2000). Self-determination theory and the facilitation of intrinsic motivation, social development, and well-being. *American Psychologist, 55,* 68–78.

Ryan, R. M., & Deci, E. L. (2008a). Self-determination theory and the role of basic psychological needs in personality and the organization of behavior. In O. P. John, R. W. Robins, & L. A. Pervin (Eds.), *Handbook of personality: Theory and research* (pp. 654–678). New York: Guilford Press.

Ryan, R. M., & Deci, E. L. (2008b). A self-determination theory approach to psychotherapy: The motivational basis for effective change. *Canadian Psychology, 49*(3), 186–193.

Ryan, R. M., Deci, E. L., & Grolnick, W. S. (1995). Autonomy, relatedness, and the self: Their relation to development and psychopathology. In D. Cicchetti & D. J. Cohen (Eds.), *Developmental psychopathology: Theory and methods* (pp. 618–655). New York: Wiley.

Ryan, R. M., Patrick, H., Deci, E. L., & Williams, G. C. (2008). Facilitating health behaviour change and its maintenance: Interventions based on self-determination theory. *The European Health Psychologist, 10,* 2–5.

Sackett, P. R., Burris, L. R., & Callahan, C. (1989). Integrity testing for personnel selection: An update. *Personnel Psychology, 42,* 491–529.

Sackett, P. R., & Wanek, J. E. (1996). New developments in the use of measures of honesty, integrity, conscientiousness, dependability, trustworthiness, and reliability for personnel selection. *Personnel Psychology, 49,* 787–829.

Salovey, P., & Mayer, J. D. (1994). Emotional intelligence. *Imagination, Cognition, and Personality, 9,* 185–211.

Saltzer, E. B. (1982). The Weight Locus of Control (WLOC) scale: A specific measure for obesity research. *Journal of Personality Assessment, 46,* 620–628.

Sampson, S. M. (2006). Slow-frequency rTMS reduces fibromyalgia pain. *Pain Medicine, 7*(2), 115–118.

Santana, M. A. (2005). The girl. In Arts Council of Princeton (Ed.), *Under age* (Vol. 17, pp. 16–17). Princeton, NJ: Arts Council of Princeton.

Satterfield, J. M., Monahan, M., & Seligman, M. E. P. (1997). Law school performance predicted by explanatory style. *Behavioral Sciences & the Law, 15,* 95–105.

Satterfield, J. M., & Seligman, M. E. P. (1994). Military aggression and risk predicted by explanatory style. *Psychological Science, 5,* 77–82.

Saucier, G. (1992). Openness versus intellect: Much ado about nothing? *European Journal of Personality, 6,* 381–386.

Saucier, G. (1997). Effects of variable selection on the factor structure of person descriptors. *Journal of Personality and Social Psychology, 73*(6), 1296–1312.

Saucier, G. (2003). Factor structure of English-language personality type-nouns. *Journal of Personality and Social Psychology, 85*(4), 695–708.

Saucier, G., Georgiades, S., Tsaousis, I., & Goldberg, L. R. (2005). The factor structure of Greek personality adjectives. *Journal of Personality and Social Psychology, 88*(5), 856–875.

Saucier, G., & Goldberg, L. R. (1996). The language of personality: Lexical perspectives on the five-factor model. In J. S. Wiggins (Ed.), *The five-factor model of personality: Theoretical perspectives* (pp. 21–50). New York: Guilford Press.

Saucier, G., & Goldberg, L. R. (1998). What is beyond the Big Five? *Journal of Personality, 66*(4), 495–524.

Saucier, G., & Goldberg, L. R. (2001). Lexical studies of indigenous personality factors: Premises, products, and prospects. *Journal of Personality, 69,* 847–879.

Sauser, W. I. (2007). Employee theft: Who, how, why, and what can be done. *SAM Advanced Management Journal, 72*(3), 13–25.

Savin-Williams, R. C. (1998). ". . . And then I became gay": Young men's stories. New York: Routledge.

Savin-Williams, R. C. (2006). Who's gay? Does it matter? *Current Directions in Psychological Science, 15*(1), 40–44.

Savin-Williams, R. C. (2007). *The new gay teenager.* Cambridge, MA: Harvard University Press.

Savory, E. (2004). *Indepth: Meditation in depth meditation: The pursuit of happiness.* Retrieved July 17, 2009 from http://www.cbc.ca/news/background/meditation/.

Scarr, S., & McCartney, K. (1983). How people make their own environments: A theory of genotype environment effects. *Child Development, 54,* 424–435.

Schacter, D. L. (1987). Implicit memory: History and current status. *Journal of Experimental Psychology: Learning, Memory and Cognition, 13,* 501–518.

Scheier, M. F., & Carver, C. S. (1985). Optimism, coping and health: Assessment and implications of generalized outcome expectancies. *Health Psychology, 4,* 219–247.

Scheier, M. F., & Carver, C. S. (1987). Dispositional optimism and physical well-being: The influence of generalized outcome expectancies on health. *Journal of Personality, 55,* 169–210.

Scheier, M. F., & Carver, C. S. (1988). A model of behavioral self-regulation: Translating intention into action. In L. Berkowitz (Ed.), *Advances in experimental social psychology* (Vol. 21, pp. 303–346). San Diego, CA: Academic Press.

Scheier, M. F., & Carver, C. S. (1992). Effects of optimism on psychological and physical well-being: Theoretical overview and empirical update. *Cognitive Therapy and Research, 16,* 201–228.

Scheier, M. F., & Carver, C. S. (1993). On the power of positive thinking: The benefits of being optimistic. *Current Directions in Psychological Science, 2*(1), 26–30.

Scheier, M. F., Carver, C. S., & Bridges, M. W. (1994). Distinguishing optimism from neuroticism (and trait anxiety, self-mastery, and self-esteem): A reevaluation of the Life Orientation Test. *Journal of Personality and Social Psychology, 67,* 1063–1078.

Scheier, M. F., Carver, C. S., & Bridges, M. W. (2001). Optimism, pessimism, and psychological well-being. In E. C. Chang (Ed.), *Optimism & pessimism: Implications for theory, research, and practice* (pp. 189–216). Washington, DC: American Psychological Association.

Scheier, M. F., Matthews, K. A., Owens, J. F., Magovern, G. J., Lefebvre, R. C., Abbot, A. R., et al. (1989). Dispositional optimism and recovery from coronary artery bypass surgery: The beneficial effects on physical and psychological well-being. *Journal of Personality and Social Psychology, 57*(6), 1024–1040.

Scheier, M. F., Weintraub, J. K., & Carver, C. S. (1986). Coping with stress divergent strategies of optimists and pessimists. *Journal of Personality and Social Psychology, 51,* 1257–1264.

Schein, E., & Bernstein, P. (2008). *Identical strangers: A memoir of twins separated and reunited.* New York: Random House.

Schlenker, B. R., & Pontari, B. A. (2000). The strategic control of information: Impression management and self-presentation in daily life. In A. Tesser, R. B. Felson, & J. M. Suls (Eds.), *Psychological perspectives on self and identity.* Washington, DC: American Psychological Association.

Schmitt, D. P., & Allik, J. (2005). Simultaneous administration of the Rosenberg self-esteem scale in 53 nations: Exploring the universal and culture-specific features of global self-esteem. *Journal of Personality and Social Psychology, 89*(4), 623–642.

Schmitt, D. P., & Buss, D. M. (2000). Sexual dimensions of person description: Beyond or subsumed by the Big Five? *Journal of Research in Personality, 34,* 141–177.

Schmitt, D. P., Realo, A., Voracek, M., & Allik, J. (2008). Why can't a man be more like a woman? Sex differences in Big Five personality traits across 55 cultures. *Journal of Personality and Social Psychology, 94*(1), 168–182.

Schmitz, N., Neumann, W., & Oppermann, R. (2000). Stress, burnout and locus of control in German nurses. *International Journal of Nursing Studies, 37,* 95–99.

Schroth, M. L. (1991). Dyadic adjustment and sensation seeking compatibility. *Personality and Individual Differences, 12*(5), 467–471.

Schuerger, J. M., Zarrella, K. L., & Hotz, A. S. (1989). Factors that influence the temporal stability of personality by questionnaire. *Journal of Personality and Social Psychology, 56,* 777–783.

Schulman, P. (1995). Explanatory style and achievement in school and work. In G. M. Buchanan & M. E. P. Seligman (Eds.), *Explanatory style* (pp. 159–171). Hillsdale, NJ: Erlbaum.

Schulman, P. (1999). Applying learned optimism to increase sales productivity. *Journal of Personal Selling and Sales Management, 19*(1), 31–37.

Schultz, R., Heckhausen, J., & Locher, J. L. (1991). Adult development, control, and adaptive functioning. *Journal of Social Issues, 47,* 177–196.

Schultz, T. (2006). *File:dti-sagittal-fibers.jpg.* Retrieved July 27, 2009, from http://en.wikipedia.org/wiki/File:DTI-sagittal-fibers.jpg.

Schultz, W. T. (2005). *Handbook of psychobiography.* New York: Oxford University Press.

Schutter, D. J. L. G. (2009). Transcranial magnetic stimulation. In E. Harmon-Jones & J. S. Beer (Eds.), *Methods in social neuroscience* (pp. 233–260). New York: Guilford Press.

Scollon, C. N., & Diener, E. (2006). Love, work, and changes in extraversion and neuroticism over time. *Journal of Personality and Social Psychology, 91*(6), 1152–1165.

Seashore, C. E. (1912). Review of Charles H. Olin's *Phrenology. Journal of Educational Psychology, 3*(4), 227.

Seavey, C. A., Katz, P. A., & Zalk, S. R. (1975). Baby X: The effect of gender labels on adult responses to infants. *Sex Roles, 1*(2), 103–109.

Sedikides, C., & Green, J. D. (2006). The mnemic neglect model: Experimental demonstrations of inhibitory repression in normal adults. *Behavioral and Brain Sciences, 29*(5), 532–533.

Seeman, M. (1963). Alienation and social learning in a reformatory. *American Journal of Sociology, 69,* 270–284.

Seeman, M., & Evans, J. (1962). Alienation and learning in a hospital setting. *American Sociological Review, 27,* 772–782.

Segall, M., & Wynd, C. A. (1990). Health conception, health locus of control, and power as predictors of smoking behavior change. *American Journal of Health Promotion, 4,* 338–344.

Segerstrom, S. C. (2001). Optimism, goal conflict, and stressor-related immune change. *Journal of Behavioral Medicine, 24,* 441–467.

Segerstrom, S. C. (2005). Optimism and immunity: Do positive thoughts always lead to positive effects? *Brain Behavior and Immunity, 19,* 195–200.

Segerstrom, S. C., Taylor, S. E., Kemeny, M. E., & Fahey, J. L. (1998). Optimism is associated with mood, coping, and immune change in response to stress. *Journal of Personality and Social Psychology, 74,* 1646–1655.

Selander, J., Marnetoft, S., Åkerström, B., & Asplund, R. (2005). Locus of control and regional differences in sickness absence in Sweden. *Disability and Rehabilitation: An International, Multidisciplinary Journal, 27*(16), 925–928.

Seligman, M. E. P. (1975). *Helplessness: On depression, development, and death.* San Francisco: Freeman.

Seligman, M. E. P. (1990). *Learned optimism.* New York: Simon & Schuster.

Seligman, M. E. P. (1995). *The optimistic child.* Boston: Houghton Mifflin.

Seligman, M. E. P., Castellon, C., Cacciola, J., Schulman, P., Luborsky, L., Ollove, M., et al. (1988). Explanatory style change during cognitive therapy for unipolar depression. *Journal of Abnormal Psychology, 97,* 13–18.

Seligman, M. E. P., & Maier, S. F. (1967). Failure to escape traumatic shock. *Journal of Experimental Psychology, 74*(1), 1–9.

Seligman, M. E. P., Nolen-Hoeksema, S., Thornton, K. M., & Thornton, N. (1990). Explanatory style as a mechanism of disappointing athletic performance. *Psychological Science, 1,* 143–146.

Seligman, M. E. P., & Schulman, P. (1986). Explanatory style as a predictor of productivity and quitting among life insurance sales agents. *Journal of Personality and Social Psychology, 50,* 832–838.

Seligman, M. E. P., Schulman, P., DeRubeis, R. J., & Hollon, S. D. (1999). The prevention of depression and anxiety. *Prevention & Treatment, 2,* ArtID8.

Seligman, M. E. P., Steen, T. A., Park, N., & Peterson, C. (2005). Positive psychology progress: Empirical validation of interventions. *American Psychologist, 60*(5), 410–421.

Selye, H. (1956). *The stress of life.* New York: McGraw-Hill.

Shaffer, D. R. (2009). *Social and personality development* (6th ed.). Belmont, CA: Wadsworth.

Sharps, M. J., Price, J. L., & Williams, J. K. (1994). Spatial cognition and gender: Instructional and stimulus influences on mental image rotation performance. *Psychology of Women Quarterly, 18,* 413–425.

Sharps, M. J., Welton, A. L., & Price, J. L. (1993). Gender and task in the determination of spatial cognitive performance. *Psychology of Women Quarterly, 17,* 7183.

Shaver, P. R., & Clark, C. L. (1994). The psychodynamics of adult romantic attachment. In J. M. Masling & R. F. Bornstein (Eds.), *Empirical perspectives on object relations theory* (pp. 105–156). Washington, DC: American Psychological Association.

Shaver, P. R., & Mikulincer, M. (2005). Attachment theory and research: Resurrection of the psychodynamic approach to personality. *Journal of Research in Personality, 39,* 22–45.

Shaver, P. R., & Mikulincer, M. (2007). Attachment theory and research. In A. W. Kruglanski & E. T. Higgins (Eds.), *Social psychology: Handbook of basic principles* (pp. 650–677). New York: Guilford Press.

Sheldon, K. M., Elliot, A. J., Kim, Y., & Kasser, T. (2001). What is satisfying about satisfying events? Testing 10 candidate psychological needs. *Journal of Personality and Social Psychology, 80*(2), 325–339.

Sheldon, K. M., Ryan, R. M., Deci, E. L., & Kasser, T. (2004). The independent effects of goal contents and motives on well-being: It's both what you pursue and why you pursue it. *Personality and Social Psychology Bulletin, 30*(4), 475–486.

Sheldon, K. M., Ryan, R. M., Rawsthorne, L., & Ilardi, B. (1997). Trait self and true self: Cross-role variation in the Big Five traits and its relations with authenticity and subjective well-being. *Journal of Personality and Social Psychology, 73,* 1380–1393.

Shelley, M., & Pakenham, K. I. (2004). External health locus of control and general self-efficacy: Moderators of emotional distress among university students. *Australian Journal of Psychology, 56*(3), 191–199.

Shenk, J. W. (2009, June). What makes us happy? *The Atlantic,* 36–53.

Shernoff, D. J., Csikszentmihalyi, M., Schneider, B., & Shernoff, E. S. (2003). Student engagement in high school classrooms from the perspective of flow theory. *School Psychology Quarterly, 18*(2), 158–176.

Shields, S. A. (1995). The role of emotion beliefs and values in gender development. In N. Eisenberg (Ed.), *Review of personality and social psychology* (Vol. 15, pp. 212–232). Thousand Oaks, CA: Sage.

Shiner, R., & Caspi, A. (2003). Personality differences in childhood and adolescence: Measurement, development, and consequences. *Journal of Child Psychology and Psychiatry, 44*(1), 2–32.

Showers, C. J. (1992). Compartmentalization of positive and negative self-knowledge: Keeping bad apples out of the bunch. *Journal of Personality and Social Psychology, 62,* 1036–1049.

Showers, C. J., & Zeigler-Hill, V. (2006). Pathways among self-knowledge and self-esteem: How are self-esteem and self-knowledge linked? Are these links direct or indirect? In M. H. Kernis (Ed.), *Self-esteem issues and answers* (pp. 216–223). New York: Psychology Press.

Showers, C. J., & Zeigler-Hill, V. (2007). Compartmentalization and integration: The evaluative organization of contextualized selves. *Journal of Personality, 75*(6), 1181–1204.

Shrauger, J. S., & Rosenberg, S. E. (1970). Self-esteem and the effects of success and failure feedback on performance. *Journal of Personality, 38,* 404–417.

Shrauger, J. S., & Sorman, P. B. (1977). Self-evaluations, initial success and failure, and improvement as determinants of persistence. *Journal of Consulting and Clinical Psychology, 45,* 784–795.

Sidorowicz, L. S., & Lunney, G. S. (1980). Baby X revisited. *Sex Roles, 6*(1), 67–73.

Siegler, I. C., Costa, P. T., Brummett, B. H., Helms, M. J., Barefoot, J. C., Williams, R. B., et al. (2003). Patterns of change in hostility from college to midlife in the UNC alumni heart study predict high-risk status. *Psychosomatic Medicine, 65,* 738–745.

Silverberg, N. D., Hanks, R. A., Buchanan, L., Fichtenberg, N., & Mills, S. R. (2008). Detecting response bias with performance patterns on an expanded version of the controlled oral word association test. *The Clinical Neuropsychologist, 22*(1), 140–157.

Silvetoinen, K., Sammalisto, S., Perola, M., Boomsma, D. I., Cornes, B. K., Davis, C., et al. (2003). Heritability of adult body height: A comparative study of twin cohorts in eight countries. *Twin Research, 6*(5), 399–408.

Simms, L. J., & Watson, D. (2007). The construct validation approach to personality scale construction. In R. W. Robins, R. C. Fraley, & R. F. Krueger (Eds.), *Handbook of research methods in personality psychology* (pp. 240–258). New York: Guilford Press.

Simonton, D. K. (1986). Presidential personality: Biographical use of the Gough adjective checklist. *Journal of Personality and Social Psychology, 51,* 149–160.

Simonton, D. K. (1999). Significant samples: The psychological study of eminent individuals. *Psychological Methods, 4*(4), 425–451.

Sinha, D. (1993). Indigenization of psychology in India and its relevance. In U. Kim & J. W. Berry (Eds.), *Indigenous psychologies: Research and experience in cultural context* (pp. 30–43). Newbury Park, CA: Sage.

Skinner, E., Furrer, C., Marchand, G., & Kindermann, T. (2008). Engagement and disaffection in the classroom: Part of a larger motivational dynamic? *Journal of Educational Psychology, 100*(4), 765–781.

Smedley, B. D., Myers, H. F., & Harrell, S. P. (1993). Minority-status stresses and the college adjustment of ethnic minority freshmen. *Journal of Higher Education, 64,* 434–452.

Smillie, L. D. (2008). What is reinforcement sensitivity? Neuroscience paradigms for approach-avoidance process theories of personality. *European Journal of Personality, 22,* 359–384.

Smillie, L. D., Pickering, A. D., & Jackson, C. J. (2006). The new reinforcement sensitivity theory: Implications for personality measurement. *Personality and Social Psychology Review, 10*(4), 320–335.

Smith, C. P. (2000). Content analysis and narrative analysis. In H. T. Reis & C. M. Judd (Eds.), *Handbook of research methods in social and personality psychology* (pp. 313–335). New York: Cambridge University Press.

Smith, E. R. (2000). Research design. In H. T. Reis & C. M. Judd (Eds.), *Handbook of research methods in social and personality psychology* (pp. 17–39). Cambridge, England: Cambridge University Press.

Smith, G. (2005). *The genomics age.* New York: American Management Association.

Smith, S. R., & Archer, R. P. (2008). Introducing personality assessment. In R. P. Archer & S. R. Smith (Eds.), *Introducing personality assessment* (pp. 1–36). New York: Taylor and Francis.

Smith, T. W. (2006a). *American sexual behavior: Trends, socio-demographic differences, and risk behavior.* Chicago: National Opinion Research Center, University of Chicago.

Smith, T. W. (2006b). Personality as risk and resilience in physical health. *Current Directions in Psychological Science, 15*(5), 227–231.

Smither, J. W., Reilly, R. R., Millsap, R. E., Perlman, K., & Stoffey, R. W. (1993). Applicant reactions to selection procedures. *Personnel psychology, 46,* 49–76.

Smits, D. J. M., & Boeck, P. D. (2006). From BIS/BAS to the Big Five. *European Journal of Personality, 20,* 255–270.

Snyder, C. R. (2002). Hope theory: Rainbows in the mind. *Psychological Inquiry, 13,* 249–275.

Snyder, C. R., Shenkel, R. J., & Lowery, C. R. (1977). Acceptance of personality interpretations: The "Barnum Effect" and beyond. *Journal of Consulting and Clinical Psychology, 45*(1), 104–114.

Snyder, C. R., Sympson, S. C., Ybasco, F. C., & Borders, T. F. (1996). Development and validation of the state hope scale. *Journal of Personality and Social Psychology, 70*(2), 321–335.

Snyder, M. (1974). Self-monitoring of expressive behavior. *Journal of Personality and Social Psychology, 30,* 526–537.

Snyder, M. (1979). Self-monitoring processes. *Advances in experimental social psychology, 12,* 85–128.

Snyder, M. (1987). *Public appearances/private realities.* New York: W. H. Freeman.

Snyder, M., & DeBono, K. G. (1985). Appeals to image and claim about quality: Understanding the psychology of advertising. *Journal of Personality and Social Psychology, 49,* 586–597.

Snyder, M., & Gangestad, S. W. (1986). On the nature of self-monitoring: Matters of assessment, matters of validity. *Journal of Personality and Social Psychology, 51*(1), 125–139.

Snyder, M., Gangestad, S. W., & Simpson, J. A. (1983). Choosing friends as activity partners: The role of self-monitoring. *Journal of Personality and Social Psychology, 45*(5), 1061–1072.

Society for Industrial and Organizational Psychology. (2010). *How many U.S. companies use employment tests?* Retrieved May 27, 2010, from http://www.siop.org/workplace/employment%20testing/usingoftests.aspx.

Soldz, S., & Vaillant, G. E. (1999). The Big Five personality traits and the life course: A 45-year longitudinal study. *Journal of Research in Personality, 33,* 208–232.

Sosis, R. H., Strickland, B. R., & Haley, W. E. (1980). Perceived locus of control and beliefs about astrology. *The Journal of Social Psychology, 110,* 65–71.

Spangler, G., & Grossmann, K. E. (1993). Biobehavioral organization of securely and insecurely attached infants. *Child Development, 64,* 1439–1450.

Spanier, G. B. (1976). Measuring dyadic adjustment: New scales for assessing the quality of marriage and similar dyads. *Journal of Marriage and the Family, 38,* 15–28.

Spector, P. E. (1982). Behavior in organizations as a function of employee's locus of control. *Psychological Bulletin, 9*(13), 482–497.

Spector, P. E. (1988). Development of the Work Locus of Control Scale. *Journal of Occupational Psychology, 61*(4), 335–340.

Spence, J. T. (1991). Do the BSRI and the PAQ measure the same or different concepts? *Psychology of Women Quarterly, 15,* 141–165.

Spence, J. T. (1993). Gender-related traits and gender idiology: Evidence for a multifactorial theory. *Journal of Personality and Social Psychology, 64*(4), 624–635.

Spence, J. T., Helmreich, R., & Stapp, J. (1974). The personal attributes questionnaire: A measure of sex role stereotypes and masculinity–femininity. *Journal Supplement Abstract Service Catalog of Selected Documents in Psychology, 4,* 43–44 (Ms. 617).

Spence, J. T., Helmreich, R., & Stapp, J. (1975). Ratings of self and peers on sex-role attributes and their relation to self-esteem and conceptions of masculinity and femininity. *Journal of Personality and Social Psychology, 32*(1), 29–39.

Spence, J. T., & Helmreich, R. L. (1978). *Masculinity and femininity: Their psychological dimensions, correlates and antecedents.* Austin: University of Texas Press.

Spence, J. T., & Helmreich, R. L. (1979). On assessing "Androgyny." *Sex Roles, 5*(6), 721–738.

Spence, J. T., & Sawin, L. L. (1985). Images of masculinity and femininity: A reconceptualization. In V. O'Leary, R. Unger, & B. Wallston (Eds.), *Sex, gender, and social psychology* (pp. 35–66). Hillsdale, NJ: Erlbaum.

Spencer, S. J., Steele, C. M., & Quinn, D. M. (1999). Stereotype threat and women's math performance. *Journal of Experimental Social Psychology, 35,* 4–28.

Sprecher, S., Sullivan, Q., & Hatfield, E. (1994). Mate selection preferences: Gender differences examined in a national sample. *Journal of Personality and Social Psychology, 66,* 1074–1080.

Srivastava, S., John, O. P., Gosling, S. D., & Potter, J. (2003). Development of personality in early and middle adulthood: Set like plaster or persistent change? *Journal of Personality and Social Psychology, 84*(5), 1041–1053.

Stacy, A. W., Leigh, B. C., & Weingardt, K. (1997). An individual-difference perspective applied to word association. *Personality and Social Psychology Bulletin, 23*(3), 229–237.

Stanton, A. L., & Snider, P. R. (1993). Coping with a breast cancer diagnosis: A prospective study. *Health Psychology, 12,* 16–23.

Steed, L., & Symes, M. (2009). The role of perceived wealth competence, wealth values, and internal wealth locus of control in predicting wealth creation behavior. *Journal of Applied Social Psychology, 39*(10), 2525–2540.

Steele, C. M., & Aronson, J. (1995). Stereotype threat and the intellectual test performance of African Americans. *Journal of Personality and Social Psychology, 69*(5), 797–811.

Steele, C. M., Spencer, S. J., & Aronson, J. (2002). Contending with group image: The psychology of stereotype and social identity threat. In M. P. Zanna (Ed.), *Advances in experimental social psychology* (Vol. 34, pp. 379–440). San Diego, CA: Academic Press.

Stelmack, R. M., & Rammsayer, T. H. (2008). Psychophysiological and biochemical correlates of personality. In G. J. Boyle, G. Matthews, & D. H. Saklofske (Eds.), *The SAGE handbook of personality theory and assessment: Vol. 1. Personality theories and models* (pp. 33–55). Los Angeles: Sage.

Sternberg, R. J. (1993). What is the relation of gender to biology and environment: An evolutionary model of how what you answer depends on just what you ask. In A. E. Beall & R. J. Sternberg (Eds.), *The psychology of gender* (pp. 1–6). New York: Guilford Press.

Sternberg, R. J., Conway, B. E., Ketron, J. L., & Bernstein, M. (1981). People's conceptions of intelligence. *Journal of Personality and Social Psychology, 41*(1), 37–55.

Steunenberg, B., Twisk, J. W., Beekman, A. T., Deeg, D. J., & Kerkhof, A. J. (2005). Stability and change in neuroticism in aging. *Journal of Gerontology: Psychological Sciences, 60,* 27–33.

Stinson, D. A., Wood, J. V., & Doxey, J. R. (2008). In search of clarity: Self-esteem and domains of confidence and confusion. *Personality and Social Psychology Bulletin, 34*(11), 1541–1555.

Stipek, D., Gralinski, H., & Kopp, C. (1990). Self-concept development in the toddler years. *Developmental Psychology, 26,* 972–977.

Stone, D., Deci, E. L., & Ryan, R. M. (2009). Beyond talk: Creating autonomous motivation through self-determination theory. *Journal of General Management, 34,* 75–91.

Stone, J., Aronson, E., Crain, L. A., Winslow, M. P., & Fried, C. B. (1994). Inducing hypocrisy as a means of encouraging young adults to use condoms. *Personality and Social Psychology Bulletin, 20*(1), 116–128.

Story, A. L. (2004). Self-esteem and self-certainty: A mediational analysis. *European Journal of Personality, 18,* 115–125.

Strelau, J. (1998). *Temperament: A psychological perspective.* New York: Plenum Press.

Strickland, B. R. (1965). The prediction of social action from a dimension of internal–external control. *The Journal of Social Psychology, 66*(2), 353–358.

Strickland, B. R. (1973). Delay of gratification and internal locus of control in children. *Journal of Consulting and Clinical Psychology, 40*(2), 338.

Stürmer, T., Hasselbach, P., & Amelang, M. (2006). Personality, lifestyle, and risk of cardiovascular disease and cancer: Follow-up of population based cohort. *British Medical Journal, 332*(7554), 1359.

Suls, J., & Fletcher, B. (1985). The relative efficacy of avoidant and nonavoidant coping strategies: A meta-analysis. *Health Psychology, 4,* 249–288.

Swaab, D. F. (2005). The role of the hypothalamus and endocrine system in sexuality. In J. S. Hyde (Ed.), *Biological substrates of human sexuality* (pp. 21–74). Washington, DC: American Psychological Association.

Swaab, D. F., & Hofman, M. A. (1990). An enlarged suprachiasmatic nucleus in homosexual men. *Brain Research, 537,* 141–148.

Swann, W. B., Chang-Schneider, C., & McClarty, K. L. (2007). Do people's self-views matter? Self-concept and self-esteem in everyday life. *American Psychologist, 62*(2), 84–94.

Swann, W. B., Pelham, B. W., & Krull, D. S. (1989). Agreeable fancy or disagreeable truth?: Reconciling self-enhancement and self-verification. *Journal of Personality and Social Psychology, 57,* 782–791.

Swanson, D. P., Cunningham, M., Youngblood, II, J., & Spencer, M. B. (2009). Racial identity development during childhood. In H. A. Neville, B. M. Tynes, & S. O. Utsey (Eds.), *Handbook of African American psychology* (pp. 269–281). Thousand Oaks, CA: Sage.

Swartz, S. J. (2008). Self and identity in early adolescence: Some reflections and an introduction to the special issue. *The Journal of Early Adolescence, 28*(1), 5–15.

Swede, S. W., & Tetlock, P. E. (1986). Henry Kissinger's implicit theory of personality: A quantitative case study. *Journal of Personality, 54,* 617–646.

Sweeney, P. D., Anderson, K., & Bailey, S. (1986). Attributional style in depression: A meta-analytic review. *Journal of Personality and Social Psychology, 50,* 974–991.

Tafoya, T. (1997). Native gay and lesbian issues: The two-spirited. In B. Greene (Ed.), *Ethnic and cultural diversity among lesbians and gay men* (p. 109). Thousand Oaks, CA: Sage.

Tangney, J. P., Baumeister, R. F., & Boone, A. L. (2004). High self-control predicts good adjustment, less pathology, better grades, and interpersonal success. *Journal of Personality, 72*(2), 271–324.

Taylor, S. E., & Brown, J. (1988). Illusion and well-being: A social psychological perspective on mental health. *Psychological Bulletin, 103,* 193–210.

Taylor, S. E., Kemeny, M. E., Reed, G. M., Bower, J. E., & Gruenewald, T. L. (2000). Psychological resources, positive illusions, and health. *American Psychologist, 55*(1), 99–109.

Taylor, S. E., Klein, L. C., Lewis, B. P., Gruenewald, T. L., Gurung, R. A. R., & Updegraff, J. A. (2000). Biobehavioral responses to stress in females: Tend-and-befriend, not fight-or-flight. *Psychological Review, 107,* 411–429.

Terman, L. M. (1926). *Mental and physical traits of a thousand gifted children: Vol. 1. Genetic studies of genius.* Palo Alto, CA: Stanford University Press.

Tett, R. P., Anderson, M. G., Ho, C., Yang, T. S., Huang, L., & Hanvongse, A. (2006). Seven nested questions about faking on personality tests. In R. L. Griffith & M. H. Peterson (Eds.), *A closer examination of applicant faking behavior* (pp. 43–84). Scottsdale, AZ: Information Age.

Thayer, C. R. (1973). The relationship between clinical judgements of missionary fitness and subsequent ratings of actual field adjustment. *Review of Religious Research, 14*(2), 112–116.

Thomas, J. R., & French, K. E. (1985). Gender differences across age in motor performance: A meta-analysis. *Psychological Bulletin, 98,* 260–282.

Thomas, M. D., Henley, T. B., & Snell, C. M. (2006). The draw a scientist test: A different population and a somewhat different story. *College Student Journal, 40*(1), 140–148.

Thorn, B. E., & Lokken, K. L. (2006). Biological influences. In F. Andrasik (Ed.), *Comprehensive handbook of personality and psychopathology: Vol. 2. Adult psychopathology* (pp. 85–98). Hoboken, NJ: Wiley.

Tice, D. M. (1991). Esteem protection or enhancement? Self-handicapping motives and attributions differ by trait self-esteem. *Journal of Personality and Social Psychology, 60,* 711–725.

Tice, D. M. (1993). The social motives of people with low self-esteem. In R. F. Baumeister (Ed.), *Self-esteem: The puzzle of low self-regard* (pp. 37–53). New York: Plenum Press.

Tice, D. M. (1995). When modesty prevails: Differential favorability of self-presentation to friends and strangers. *Journal of Personality and Social Psychology, 69*(6), 1120–1138.

Tice, D. M., & Baumeister, R. F. (1997). Longitudinal study of procrastinaion, performance, stress and health: The costs and benefits of dawdling. *Psychological Science, 8*(6), 454–458.

Tiggemann, M., Winefield, A. H., Winefield, H. R., & Goldney, R. D. (1991). The prediction of psychological distress from attributional style: A test of the hopelessness model of depression. *Australian Journal of Psychology, 43*, 125–127.

Toma, C. L., Hancock, J. T., & Eillison, N. B. (2008). Separating fact from fiction: An examination of deceptive self-presentation in online dating profiles. *Personality and Social Psychology Bulletin, 34*(8), 1023–1036.

Tomarken, A. J., Davidson, R. J., Wheeler, R. E., & Doss, R. C. (1992). Individual differences in anterior brain asymmetry and fundamental dimensions of emotion. *Journal of Personality and Social Psychology, 62*(4), 676–687.

Torrubia, R., Ávila, C., Moltó, J., & Caseras, X. (2001). The sensitivity to punishment and sensitivity to reward questionnaire (SPSRQ) as a measure of Gray's anxiety and impulsivity dimensions. *Personality and Individual Differences, 29*, 837–862.

Torrubia, R., Ávila, C., Moltó, J., & Grande, I. (1995). Testing for stress and happiness: The role of the behavioral inhibition system. In C. D. Spielberger, I. G. Sarason, J. Brebner, E. Greenglass, P. Langani, & A. M. O'Roark (Eds.), *Stress and emotion: Anxiety, anger, and curiosity* (Vol. 15, pp. 189–211). Washington, DC: Taylor and Francis.

Trafimow, D., Triandis, H. C., & Goto, S. G. (1991). Some tests of the distinction between the private self and the collective self. *Journal of Personality and Social Psychology, 60*(5), 649–655.

Triandis, H. C. (1990). Cross-cultural studies of individualism and collectivism. In J. J. Berman (Ed.), *Nebraska symposium on motivation 1989* (Vol. 49, pp. 41–133). Lincoln: University of Nebraska Press.

Triandis, H. C., Marin, G., Lisansky, J., & Betancourt, H. (1984). *Símpatica* as a cultural script of Hispanics. *Journal of Personality and Social Psychology, 47*, 1363–1375.

Trochim, W. M. K. (2006). *Research methods knowledge base* (3rd ed.). Cincinnati, OH: Atomic Dog.

Tugade, M. M., & Fredrickson, B. L. (2004). Resilient individuals use positive emotions to bounce back from negative emotional experiences. *Journal of Personality and Social Psychology, 86*(2), 320–333.

Tugade, M. M., & Fredrickson, B. L. (2007). Regulation of positive emotions: Emotion regulation strategies that promote resilience. *Journal of Happiness Studies, 8*, 311–333.

Tugade, M. M., Fredrickson, B. L., & Barrett, L. F. (2004). Psychological resilience and positive emotional granularity: Examining the benefits of positive emotions on coping and health. *Journal of Personality, 72*(6), 1161–1190.

Turkheimer, E. (2000). Three laws of behavior genetics and what they mean. *Current Directions in Psychological Science, 9*, 160–164.

Turkheimer, E. (2004). Spinach and ice cream: Why social science is so different. In L. F. DiLalla (Ed.), *Behavioral genetics principles: Perspectives in development, personality, and psychopathology* (pp. 161–189). Washington, DC: American Psychological Association.

Turkheimer, E., & Waldron, M. (2000). Nonshared environment: A theoretical, methodological, and quantitative review. *Psychological Bulletin, 126*(1), 78–108.

Turnley, W. H., & Bolino, M. C. (2001). Achieving desired images while avoiding undesired images: Exploring the role of self-monitoring in impression management. *Journal of Applied Psychology, 86*(2), 351–360.

Twenge, J. M. (1997). Changes in masculine and feminine traits over time: A meta-analysis. *Sex Roles, 36*, 305–325.

Twenge, J. M. (1999). Mapping gender: The multifactorial approach and the organization of gender-related attributes. *Psychology of Women Quarterly, 23*, 85–502.

Twenge, J. M., Zhang, L., & Im, C. (2004). It's beyond my control: A cross-temporal meta-analysis of increasing externality in locus of control, 1960–2002. *Personality and Social Psychology Review, 8*(3), 308–319.

Tyssen, R., Dolatowski, F. C., Røvik, J. O., Thorkildsen, R. F., Ekeberg, O., & Hem, E. (2007). Personality traits and types predict medical school stress: A six-year longitudinal and nationwide study. *Medical Education, 41*, 781–787.

U. S. Department of Labor Employment and Training Administration. (2006). *Testing and assessment: A guide to good practices for work force investment professionals.* Washington, DC: U. S. Department of Labor.

Uleman, J. S. (2005). Introduction: Becoming aware of the new unconscious. In R. R. Hassin, J. R. Uleman, & J. A. Bargh (Eds.), *The new unconscious* (pp. 3–15). New York: Oxford University Press.

Unemori, P., Omoregie, H., & Markus, H. R. (2004). Self-portraits: Possible selves in European-American, Chilean, Japanese and Japanese-American cultural contexts. *Self and Identity, 3,* 321–338.

Unger, R. K. (1979). Toward a redefinition of sex and gender. *American Psychologist, 34*(11), 1085–1094.

Urlings-Strop, L. C., Stijnen, T., Themmen, A. P. N., & Splinter, T. A. W. (2009). Selection of medical students: A controlled experiment. *Medical Education, 43,* 175–183.

Uttal, W. (2001). *The new phrenology: The limits of localizing cognitive processes in the brain.* Cambridge, MA: MIT Press/Bradford Books.

Uziel, L. (2010). Rethinking social desirability scales: From impression management to interpersonally oriented self-control. *Perspectives on Psychological Science, 5*(3), 243–262.

Vaidya, J. G., Gray, E. K., Haig, J., & Watson, D. (2002). On the temporal stability of personality: Evidence for differential stability and the role of life experiences. *Journal of Personality and Social Psychology, 83*(6), 1469–1484.

Vaillant, G. E. (1977). *Adaptation to life.* Boston: Little, Brown.

Vaillant, G. E. (1995a). *Natural history of alcoholism revisited.* Cambridge, MA: Harvard University Press.

Vaillant, G. E. (1995b). *The wisdom of the ego.* Cambridge, MA: Harvard University Press.

Vaillant, G. E. (1998). Where do we go from here? *Journal of Personality [Special Issue], 66,* 1147–1157.

Vaillant, G. E. (2002a). *Aging well.* Boston: Little, Brown.

Vaillant, G. E. (2002b). The study of adult development. In E. Phelps, F. F. Furstenberg, & A. Colby (Eds.), *American longitudinal studies of the twentieth century* (pp. 116–132). New York: Russell Sage Foundation.

Vaillant, G. E., & Vaillant, C. O. (1990). Determinants and consequences of creativity in a cohort of gifted women. *Psychology of Women Quarterly, 14,* 607–616.

Valentine, J. C., DuBois, D. L., & Cooper, H. (2004). The relation between self-beliefs and academic achievement: A meta-analytic review. *Educational Psychologist, 39*(2), 111–133.

Vallerand, R. J., & Bissonnette, R. (1992). Intrinsic, extrinsic, and amotivational styles as predictors of behavior: A prospective study. *Journal of Personality, 60,* 599–620.

Van Aken, M. A. G., Denissen, J. J. A., Branje, S. J. T., Dubas, J. S., & Goossens, L. (2006). Midlife concerns and short-term personality change in middle adulthood. *European Journal of Personality, 20,* 497–513.

van der Linden, D., te Nijenhuis, J., & Bakker, A. B. (2010). The general factor of personality: A meta-analysis of Big Five intercorrelations and a criterion-related validity study. *Journal of Research in Personality, 44,* 315–327.

Vandello, J. A., & Cohen, D. (1999). Patterns of individualism and collectivism across the United States. *Journal of Personality and Social Psychology, 77*(2), 279–292.

Vansteenkiste, M., Simons, J., Soenens, B., & Lens, W. (2004). How to become a persevering exerciser? Providing a clear, future intrinsic goal in an autonomy-supportive way. *Journal of Sport & Exercise Psychology, 26,* 232–249.

Vasey, P. L., & VanderLaan, D. P. (2010). An adaptive cognitive dissociation between willingness to help kin and nonkin in Samoan Fa'afafine. *Psychological Science, 21*(2), 292–297.

Vazire, S., & Gosling, S. D. (2004). E-perceptions: Personality impressions based on personal websites. *Journal of Personality and Social Psychology, 87*(1), 123–132.

Venkatapathy, R. (1984). Locus of control among entrepreneurs: A review. *Psychological Studies, 29*(1), 97–100.

Venter, J. C., Adams, M. D., Myers, E. W., Li, P. W., Mural, R. J., Sutton, G. G., et al. (2001). The sequence of the human genome. *Science, 291,* 1304–1351.

Vincent, N., Sande, G., Read, C., & Giannuzzi, T. (2004). Sleep locus of control: Report on a new scale. *Behavioral Sleep Medicine, 2*(2), 79–93.

Vogel, D. A., Lake, M. A., Evans, S., & Karraker, K. H. (1991). Children's and adults' sex-stereotyped perceptions of infants. *Sex Roles, 24*(9/10), 605–616.

Von Ah, D., Kang, D. H., & Carpenter, J. S. (2007). Stress, optimism, and social support: Impact on immune responses in breast cancer. *Research in Nursing & Health, 30,* 72–83.

Vox, M. (2004). *Mysterious billboard may be Google recruitment ad.* Retrieved May 27, 2010, from http://www.marketingvox.com/mysterious_billboard_may_be_google_recruitment_ad-016350/.

Voyer, D., Voyer, S., & Bryden, M. P. (1995). Magnitude of sex differences in spatial abilities: A meta-analysis and consideration of critical variables. *Psychological Bulletin, 117,* 250–270.

Vul, E., Harris, C., Winkielman, P., & Pashler, H. (2009a). Puzzlingly high correlations in fMRI studies of emotion, personality, and social cognition. *Perspectives on Psychological Science, 4*(3), 271–290.

Vul, E., Harris, C., Winkielman, P., & Pashler, H. (2009b). Reply to comments on "Puzzlingly high correlations in fMRI studies of emotion, personality, and social cognition." *Perspectives on Psychological Science, 4*(3), 319–324.

Wade, C. (2006). Some cautions about jumping on the brain-scan bandwagon. *APS Observer, 19*(9), 24.

Wade, E., George, W. M., & Atkinson, M. (2009). A randomized controlled trial of brief interventions for body dissatisfaction. *Journal of Consulting and Clinical Psychology, 77*(5), 845–854.

Wallston, K. A. (2001). Conceptualization and operationalization of perceived control. In A. Baum, T. A. Revenson, & J. E. Singer (Eds.), *Handbook of health psychology* (pp. 49–58). Mahwah, NJ: Erlbaum.

Wallston, K. A., Wallston, B. S., & DeVellis, R. (1978). Development of the Multidimensional Health Locus of Control (MHLC) scales. *Health Education Monographs, 62*(2), 160–170.

Walsh, V., & Cowey, A. (2000). Transcranial magnetic stimulation and cognitive neuroscience. *Nature Reviews, 1*(1), 73–79.

Walton, G. M., & Spencer, S. J. (2009). Latent ability: Grades and test scores systematically underestimate the intellectual ability of negatively stereotyped students. *Psychological Science, 20*(9), 1132–1139.

Wanek, J. E. (1999). Integrity and honesty testing: What do we know? How do we use it? *International Review of Selection and Assessment, 1,* 183–195.

Waugh, C. E., Fredrickson, B. L., & Taylor, S. F. (2008). Adapting to life's slings and arrows: Individual differences in resilience when recovering from an anticipated threat. *Journal of Research in Personality, 42,* 1031–1046.

Webb, E. J., Campbell, D. T., Schwartz, R. D., Sechrest, L., & Grove, J. B. (1981). *Nonreactive measures in the social sciences.* Boston: Houghton Mifflin.

Webster, R. (1995). *Why Freud was wrong: Sin, science, and psychoanalysis.* New York: Basic Books.

Wegner, D. M. (1989). *White bears and other unwanted thoughts.* New York: Vintage.

Wegner, D. M. (1994). Ironic processes of mental control. *Psychological Review, 101,* 34–52.

Wegner, D. M., & Erber, R. (1992). The hyperaccessibility of suppressed thoughts. *Journal of Personality and Social Psychology, 63,* 903–912.

Wegner, D. M., Schneider, D. J., Carter, S. R., & White, T. L. (1987). Paradoxical effects of thought suppression. *Journal of Personality and Social Psychology, 53,* 5–13.

Wegner, D. M., Wenzlaff, R. M., & Kozak, M. (2004). Dream rebound: The return of suppressed thoughts in dreams. *Psychological Science, 15*(4), 232–236.

Weinberg, M. S., Williams, C. J., & Pryor, D. W. (1994). *Dual attraction: Understanding bisexuality.* New York: Oxford University Press.

Weinberger, J., & Westen, D. (2001). Science and psychodynamics: From arguments about Freud to data. *Psychological Inquiry, 12*(3), 129–166.

Weinstein, N. D. (1980). Unrealistic optimism about future life events. *Journal of Personality and Social Psychology, 39,* 806–820.

Weisz, J. R., Eastman, K. L., & McCarty, C. A. (1996). Primary and secondary control in East Asia: Comments on Oerter et al. *Culture and Psychology, 2,* 63–76.

Weisz, J. R., Rothbaum, F. M., & Blackburn, T. C. (1984). Standing out and standing in: The psychology of control in America and Japan. *American Psychologist, 39,* 955–969.

Westen, D. (1998a). The scientific legacy of Sigmund Freud: Toward a psychodynamically informed psychological science. *Psychological Bulletin, 124*(3), 333–371.

Westen, D. (1998b). Unconscious thought, feeling, and motivation: The end of a century-long debate. In R. F. Bornstein & J. M. Masling (Eds.), *Empirical perspectives on the psychoanalytic unconscious* (pp. 1–43). Washington, DC: American Psychological Association.

Westen, D. (2000). Psychoanalysis: Theories. In A. E. Kazdin (Ed.), *Encyclopedia of psychology* (Vol. 6, pp. 344–349). Washington, DC: American Psychological Association.

Westen, D., Gabbard, G. O., & Ortigo, K. M. (2008). Psychoanalytic approaches to personality. In O. P. John, R. W. Robins, & L. A. Pervin (Eds.), *Handbook of personality: Theory and research* (pp. 61–113). New York: Guilford Press.

Wester, S. R., Vogel, D. L., Pressly, P. K., & Heesacker, M. (2002). Sex differences in emotion: A critical review of the literature and implications for counseling psychology. *The Counseling Psychologist, 30*(4), 630–652.

Whitam, F. L., & Mathy, R. M. (1991). Childhood cross-gender behavior of homosexual females in Brazil, Peru, the Philippines, and the United States. *Archives of Sexual Behavior, 20*(2), 151–170.

Whittle, S., Allen, N. B., Lubman, D. I., & Yücel, M. (2006). The neurobiological basis of temperament: Towards a better understanding of psychopathology. *Neuroscience and Biobehavioral Reviews, 30,* 511–525.

Whittle, S., Yücel, M., Fornito, A., Barrett, A., Wood, S. J., Lubman, D. I., et al. (2008). Neuroanatomical correlates of temperament in early adolescents. *The Journal of the American Academy of Child and Adolescent Psychiatry, 47*(6), 682–693.

Widiger, T. A., & Smith, G. T. (1999). Personality and psychopathology. In L. A. Pervin & O. P. John (Eds.), *Handbook of personality: Theory and research.* New York: Guilford Press.

Wiggins, J. S. (1968). Personality structure. *Annual Review of Psychology, 19,* 293–350.

Wiggins, J. S. (1973). *Personality and prediction: Principles of personality assessment.* Reading, MA: Addison-Wesley.

Wiggins, J. S. (2003). *Paradigms of personality assessment.* New York: Guilford Press.

Williams, G. C., Grow, V. M., Freedman, Z. R., Ryan, R. M., & Deci, E. L. (1996). Motivational predictors of weight loss and weight-loss maintenance. *Journal of Personality and Social Psychology, 70,* 115–126.

Williams, G. C., McGregor, H. A., Sharp, D., Levesque, C., Kouides, R. W., Ryan, R. M., et al. (2006). Testing a self-determination theory intervention for motivating tobacco cessation: Supporting autonomy and competence in a clinical trial. *Health Psychology, 25*(1), 91–101.

Williams, G. C., Patrick, H., Niemiec, C. P., Williams, L. K., Devine, G., Lafata, J. E., et al. (2009). Reducing the health risks of diabetes: How self-determination theory may help improve medication adherence and quality of life. *Diabetes Educator, 35,* 484–492.

Williams, J. E., & Best, D. L. (1990). *Measuring sex stereotypes: A multination study.* Newbury Park, CA: Sage.

Wills, G. I. (1984). A personality study of musicians working in the popular field. *Personality and Individual Differences, 5*(3), 359–360.

Wilson, E. O. (1978). *Human nature.* Cambridge, MA: Harvard University Press.

Wilson, P. M., Mack, D. E., & Grattan, K. P. (2008). Understanding motivation for exercise: A self-determination theory perspective. *Canadian Psychology, 49*(3), 250–256.

Winter, D. G. (1997). Allport's life and Allport's psychology. *Journal of Personality, 65*(3), 723–731.

Winter, D. G. (2005). Things I've learned about personality from studying political leaders at a distance. *Journal of Personality, 73*(3), 557–584.

Winter, D. G., & Carlson, L. A. (1988). Using motive scores in the psychobiographical study of an individual: The case of Richard Nixon. *Journal of Personality, 56,* 75–103.

Wise, D., & Rosqvist, J. (2006). Explanatory style and well-being. In J. C. Thomas & D. L. Segal (Eds.), *Comprehensive handbook of personality and psychopathology: Vol. 1. Personality and everyday functioning* (pp. 285–305). Hoboken, NJ: Wiley.

Witkin, H. A., Moore, C. A., Goodenough, D. R., & Cox, P. W. (1977). Field-dependent and field-independent cognitive styles and their educational implications. *Review of Educational Research, 47*(1), 1–64.

Woike, B. A. (2007). Content coding of open-ended responses. In R. W. Robins, R. C. Fraley, & R. F. Krueger (Eds.), *Handbook of research methods in personality psychology* (pp. 292–307). New York: Guilford Press.

Wolitzky, D. L. (2006). Psychodynamic theories. In J. C. Thomas & D. L. Segal (Eds.), *Comprehensive handbook of personality and psychopathology: Vol. 1. Personality and everyday functioning* (pp. 65–95). Hoboken, NJ: Wiley.

Wood, W., & Eagly, A. H. (2002). A cross-cultural analysis of the behavior of women and men: Implications for the origins of sex differences. *Psychological Bulletin, 128*(5), 609–727.

Wood, W., & Eagly, A. H. (2009). Gender identity. In M. R. Leary & R. H. Hoyle (Eds.), *Handbook of individual differences in social behavior* (pp. 109–125). New York: Guilford Press.

Wood, W., & Eagly, A. H. (2010). Gender. In S. T. Fiske, D. T. Gilbert, & G. Lindzey (Eds.), *The handbook of social psychology* (5th ed., Vol. 1, pp. 629–667). New York: Wiley.

Wright, C. I., Williams, D., Feczko, E., Barrett, L. F., Dickerson, B. C., Schwartz, C. E., et al. (2006). Neuroanatomical correlates of extraversion and neuroticism. *Cerebral Cortex, 16*(12), 1809–1819.

Wright, R. (2001). Self-certainty and self-esteem. In T. J. Owens, S. Stryker, & N. Goodman (Eds.), *Extending self-esteem theory and research: Sociological and psychological currents* (pp. 101–134). Cambridge, MA: Cambridge University Press.

Wrightsman, L. S. (1991). Interpersonal trust and attitudes towards human nature. In J. P. Robinson, P. R. Shaver, & L. S. Wrightsman (Eds.), *Measures of personality and social psychological attitudes* (pp. 373–412). San Diego, CA: Academic Press.

Wundt, W. (1894). Old and new phrenology. In J. E. Creighton & E. B. Titchner (Eds.), *Lectures on human and animal psychology* (trans. from German, 2nd ed., pp. 437–454). New York: Swan Sonnenschein & Co.

Xenikou, A. (2005). The interactive effect of positive and negative occupational attributional styles on job motivation. *European Journal of Work and Organizational Psychology, 14*(1), 43–48.

Yarkoni, T. (2009). Big correlations in little studies: Inflated fMRI correlations reflect low statistical power—commentary on Vul et al. (2009). *Perspectives on Psychological Science, 4*(3), 294–298.

Yarkoni, T. (2010). Personality in 100,000 words: A large-scale analysis of personality and word use among bloggers. *Journal of Research in Personality, 44*(3), 363–373.

Yavari, C. (2002). *Self-conceptions from childhood to adolescence: A brief experiment.* Retrieved August 24, 2009, from http://www.psychology.sbc.edu/yavari.htm.

Ye, M., She, Y., & Wu, R. (2007). The relationship between graduated students' subjective well-being and locus of control. *Chinese Journal of Clinical Psychology, 15*(1), 63–65.

Yee, D., & Eccles, J. S. (1988). Parent perceptions and attributions for children's math achievement. *Sex Roles, 19,* 317–333.

Yoder, J. D., & Kahn, A. S. (2003). Making gender comparisons more meaningful: A call for more attention to social context. *Psychology of Women Quarterly, 27,* 281–290.

Young, T. J., & French, L. A. (1996). Judged political extroversion-introversion and perceived competence of U.S. presidents. *Perceptual and Motor Skills, 83*(2), 578.

Yu, D. L., & Seligman, M. E. P. (2002). Preventing depressive symptoms in Chinese children. *Prevention & Treatment, 5,* ArtID9.

Zautra, A. J., Affleck, G. G., Tennen, H., Reich, J. W., & Davis, M. C. (2005). Dynamic approaches to emotions and stress in everyday life: Bolger and Zuckerman reloaded with positive as well as negative affects. *Journal of Personality, 73*(6), 1–28.

Zautra, A. J., Smith, B., Affleck, G. G., & Tennen, H. (2001). Examinations of chronic pain and affect relationships: Applications of a dynamic model of affect. *Journal of Consulting and Clinical Psychology, 69*(5), 786–795.

Zeidner, M. (1993). Coping with disaster: The case of Israeli adolescents under threat of missile attack. *Journal of Youth and Adolescents, 22*(1), 89–108.

Zeigler-Hill, V., & Showers, C. J. (2007). Self-structure and self-esteem stability: The hidden vulnerability of compartmentalization. *Personality and Social Psychology Bulletin, 33*(2), 143–159.

Zhang, J., & Bond, M. H. (1998). Personality and filial piety among college students in two Chinese societies. *Journal of Cross-Cultural Psychology, 29*(3), 402–417.

Zimbardo, P. G. (1969). The human choice: Individualism, reason and order versus deindividuation, impulse and chaos. In W. J. Arnold & D. Levine (Eds.), *Nebraska symposium on motivation* (Vol. 17, pp. 237–307). Lincoln: University of Nebraska Press.

Zinbarg, R. E., & Mohlman, J. (1998). Individual differences in the acquisition of affectively valenced associations. *Journal of Personality and Social Psychology, 74*(4), 1024–1040.

Zucker, K. J. (1990). Gender identity disorders in children: Clinical descriptions and natural history. In R. Blanchard & B. W. Steiner (Eds.), *Clinical management of gender identity disorders in children and adults* (pp. 1–23). Washington, DC: American Psychiatric Press.

Zuckerman, M. (1969). Theoretical formulations. In J. P. Zubek (Ed.), *Sensory deprivation: Fifteen years of research* (pp. 407–432). New York: Appleton-Century-Crofts.

Zuckerman, M. (1971). Dimensions of sensation seeking. *Journal of Consulting and Clinical Psychology, 36*(1), 45–52.

Zuckerman, M. (1979). *Sensation seeking: Beyond the optimal level of arousal.* Hillsdale, NJ: Erlbaum.

Zuckerman, M. (1984). Sensation seeking: A comparative approach to a human trait. *Behavioral and Brain Sciences, 7,* 413–434.

Zuckerman, M. (1993a). A comparison of three structural models for personality: The big three, the Big Five, and the alternative five. *Journal of Personality and Social Psychology, 65,* 757–768.

Zuckerman, M. (1993b). P-impulsive sensation seeking and its behavioural, psychophysiological and biochemical correlates. *Neuropsychobiology, 28*(1–2), 30–36.

Zuckerman, M. (1994). *Behavioral expressions and biosocial bases of sensation seeking.* New York: Cambridge University Press.

Zuckerman, M. (1995). Good and bad humors: Biochemical bases of personality and its disorders. *Psychological Science, 6*(6), 325–332.

Zuckerman, M. (2002). Zuckerman-Kuhlman Personality Questionnaire (ZKPQ): An alternative five-factorial model. In B. DeRaad & M. Peraigini (Eds.), *Big Five assessment* (pp. 377–396). Seattle, WA: Hogrefe & Huber.

Zuckerman, M. (2005). *Psychobiology of personality.* New York: Cambridge University Press.

Zuckerman, M. (2006). Biosocial bases of sensation seeking. In T. Canli (Ed.), *Biology of personality and individual differences* (pp. 37–59). New York: Guilford Press.

Zuckerman, M. (2007). *Sensation seeking and risky behavior.* Washington, DC: American Psychological Association.

Zuckerman, M. (2008). Personality and sensation seeking. In G. J. Boyle, G. Matthews, & D. H. Saklofske (Eds.), *The SAGE handbook of personality theory and assessment: Vol. 1. Personality theories and models* (pp. 379–398). Los Angeles: Sage.

Zuckerman, M., & Kuhlman, D. M. (2000). Personality and risk-taking: Common biosocial factors. *Journal of Personality, 68*(6), 999–1029.

Zuckerman, M., & Neeb, M. (1980). Demographic influences in sensation seeking and expressions of sensation seeking in religion, smoking, and driving habits. *Personality and Individual Differences, 1*(3), 197–206.

Zuckerman, M., Persky, H., Link, K. E., & Basu, G. K. (1968). Experimental and subject factors determining responses to sensory deprivation, social isolation, and confinement. *Journal of Abnormal and Social Psychology, 73*(3), 183–194.

Zuckerman, M., Simons, R. F., & Como, P. G. (1988). Sensation seeking and stimulus intensity as modulators of cortical, cardiovascular, and electrodermal response: A cross-modality study. *Personality and Individual Differences, 9,* 361–372.

Zullow, H. M. (1995). Pessimistic rumination in American politics and society. In G. M. Buchanan & M. E. P. Seligman (Eds.), *Explanatory style* (pp. 21–48). Hillsdale, NJ: Erlbaum.

Zullow, H. M., Oettingen, G., Peterson, C., & Seligman, M. E. P. (1988). Pessimistic explanatory style in the historical record. *American Psychologist, 43*(9), 673–682.

Zullow, H. M., & Seligman, M. E. P. (1990). Pessimistic rumination predicts defeat of presidential candidates, 1900 to 1984. *Psychological Inquiry, 1*(1), 52–61.

Zurbriggen, E. L., & Sherman, A. M. (2007). Reconsidering "sex" and "gender": Two steps forward, one step back. *Feminism & Psychology, 17*(4), 475–480.

Zurcher, L. A. (1977). *The mutable self: A self-concept for social change.* Beverly Hills, CA: Sage.

Zweigenhaft, R. L. (2008). A do re mi encore: A closer look at personality correlates of music preference. *Journal of Individual Differences, 29*(1), 45–5.

PHOTO CREDITS

Chapter 7

Page 167: © DocCheck Medical Services GmbH/Alamy; **page 168:** © marcstock/Shutterstock; **page 170:** © Simon Fraser/Newcastle General Hospital/Photo Researchers, Inc.; **page 171:** © Monkey Business Images/Dreamstime.com; **page 172 (top):** © AJPhoto/Photo Researchers, Inc.; **page 172 (bottom):** © CARY WOLINSKY/National Geographic Image Collection; **page 177:** © AISPIX/Shutterstock; **page 179 (right):** © Rushour/Dreamstime.com; **page 179 (left):** © Robert Kneschke/Shutterstock; **page 182:** © laurent hamels/Fotolia; **page 185:** © Andrew Brown/Fotolia; **page 186:** © Forgiss/Dreamstime.com; **page 189 (top):** © World History Archive/Alamy; **page 189 (bottom):** © TOM BARRICK, CHRIS CLARK, SGHMS/Photo Researchers, Inc.; **page 191:** © Mind2concept/Dreamstime.com; **page 194:** © Boudikka/Shutterstock; **page 195 (top):** © Jeff Miller/University of Wisconsin-Madison; **page 198:** © Vitalii Nesterchuk/Shutterstock.

Chapter 8

Page 203: © akg-images/Newscom; **page 205:** © World History Archive/Alamy; **page 207:** © SuperStock/SuperStock; **page 210:** © CORBIS; **page 214:** © k09/ZUMA Press/Newscom; **page 215 (left):** Jupiter Images/© Getty Images/Thinkstock; **page 215 (right):** © Robepco/Fotolia; **page 216:** © Aflo Foto Agency/Alamy; **page 218:** © Aguaviva/Fotolia; **page 219:** © Zhiltsov Alexandr/Shutterstock; **page 224:** © Digitalpress/Dreamstime.com; **page 227:** © The Granger Collection, NYC; **page 228:** © Bettmann/CORBIS; **page 231:** © Jaspe/Dreamstime.com; **page 232:** © niv koren/Fotolia; **page 235:** © microimages/Fotolia; **page 236:** © Otnaydur/Dreamstime.com.

Chapter 9

Page 241: © charles taylor/Shutterstock; **page 242:** © FotoliaXIV/Fotolia; **page 244:** © PhotostoGO; **page 246:** © Beckyabell/Dreamstime.com; **page 247:** © Alena Ozerova/Fotolia; **page 249:** © Marcito/Fotolia; **page 250:** © Deanm1974/Dreamstime.com; **page 253:** © Monkey Business/Fotolia; **page 255:** © Checco/Dreamstime.com; **page 259:** © Shutterstock; **page 263:** © Deklofenak/Dreamstime.com; **page 264:** ©Photographerlondon/Dreamstime.com; **page 267:** © Savoi67/Dreamstime.com.

Chapter 10

Page 271: © Derek Gordon/Shutterstock; **page 272:** © Lisa F. Young/Fotolia; **page 277:** © Polina Nefidova/Fotolia; **page 278:** © winni/Fotolia; **page 279 (left):** © H. ARMSTRONG ROBERTS/CLASSICSTOCK/Everett Collection; **page 279 (right):** © Andres Rodriquez/Fotolia; **page 280:** © Aleksan/Dreamstime.com; **page 282:** © Chad McDermott/Fotolia; **page 283:** © Goodshoot/Thinkstock; **page 285:** © Jupiterimages/Thinkstock; **page 287:** Photo by Clyde Wills, Metropolis Planet (Illinois) Editor Emeritus; **page 289:** © moodboard/Fotolia; **page 292:** © Jack Hollingsworth/Thinkstock; **page 295:** © Paylessimages/Fotolia; **page 297:** © Nyul/Dreamstime.com; **page 299:** © Lana Langlois/Shutterstock; **page 304:** © Nikitta/Dreamstime.com.

Chapter 11

Page 311: © Danita Delimont/Alamy; **page 313:** © Wavebreakmediamicro/Dreamstime.com; **page 314:** © Vishakha27/Dreamstime.com; **page 325:** © Lovrencg/Fotolia; **page 326:** © BananaStock/Thinkstock; **page 329:** © AP Photo/Sergei Karpukhin; **page 332:** © Image Source/Alamy; **page 335:** © Melissa Schalke/Fotolia; **page 338:** © joshhhab/Shutterstock; **page 343:** © Bruce2/Dreamstime.com.

Chapter 12

Page 349: © Xinhua/Jiang Xintong/Newscom; **page 353:** © Purmar/Dreamstime.com; **page 355:** © Karimala/Dreamstime.com; **page 359:** © pshek/Fotolia; **page 362:** © Monkey Business Images/Dreamstime.com; **page 363:** © Tiburon Studios/iStockphoto; **page 367:** © Galina Barskaya/Fotolia; **page 369 (left):** © vgstudio/Fotolia; **page 369 (right):** ©MAXFX/Fotolia; **page 370 (left):** © Yuri Arcurs/Fotolia; **page 370 (right):** © .shock/Dreamstime.com.

Chapter 13

Page 373: © Joel Calheiros/Shutterstock; **page 375:** © Rich Beauchesne photo 2010; **page 376:** © Aurora Photos/Alamy; **page 378:** © Handout/MCT/Newscom; **page 381:** © Endostock/Dreamstime.com; **page 390:** © AP Photo/Ronald Zak.

AUTHOR INDEX

SUBJECT INDEX

What's new in Psychology?

Abnormal Psychology
Beidel, Bulik & Stanley Abnormal Psychology, 2/e ©2012
9780205205011 / 0205205011

Oltmanns & Emery Abnormal Psychology, 7/e ©2012
9780205037438 / 0205037437

Meyer & Chapman & Weaver Case Studies in Abnormal Behavior, 9/e ©2012
9780205036998 / 0205036996

Adjustment
Duffy, Kirsh & Atwater Psychology for Living: Adjustment, Growth and Behavior, 10/e ©2011
9780205790364 / 0205790364

Adolescent Development
Arnett Adolescence and Emerging Adulthood: A Cultural Approach, 4/e ©2010
9780138144586 / 0138144583

Dolgin The Adolescent, 13/e ©2011
9780205731367 / 0205731368

Garrod, Smulyan, Powers & Kilkenny Adolescent Portraits: Identity, Relationships, and Challenges, 7/e ©2012
9780205036233 / 0205036236

Adulthood & Aging
Bjorklund Journey of Adulthood, 7/e ©2011
9780205018055 / 020501805X

Mason Adulthood and Aging ©2011
9780205433513 / 0205433510

Behavior Modification
Martin & Pear Behavior Modification, 9/e ©2011
9780205792726 / 0205792723

Biopsychology / Behavioral Neuroscience
Pinel Biopsychology, 8/e ©2011
9780205832569 / 0205832563

Child Development (Chronological Approach)
Feldman Child Development, 6/e ©2012
9780205253548 / 0205253547

Child Development (Topical Approach)
Kail Children and Their Development, 6/e ©2012
9780205034949 / 0205034942

Boyd The Developing Child, 13/e ©2012
9780205256020 / 0205256023

Clinical Psychology
Lilienfeld & O'Donohue Great Readings in Clinical Science ©2012
9780205698035 / 0205698034

Linden & Hewitt Clinical Psychology, ©2012
9780132397278 / 0132397277

Close Relationships / Interpersonal
Erber & Erber Intimate Relationships: Issues, Theories, and Research, 2/e ©2011
9780205454464 / 0205454461

Cognition
Levitin Foundations of Cognitive Psychology: Core Readings, 2/e ©2011
9780205711475 / 0205711472

Robinson-Riegler Cognitive Psychology: Applying The Science of the Mind, 3/e ©2012
9780205033645 / 0205033644

Cross-Cultural / Multicultural Psychology
Parham, Ajamu & White Psychology of Blacks, 4/e ©2011
9780131827738 / 0131827731

Drugs and Behavior
Ettinger Psychopharmacology ©2011
9780136013068 / 0136013066

Levinthal Drugs, Behavior, and Modern Society, 7/e ©2012
9780205037261 / 0205037267

Grilly Drugs and Human Behavior, 6/e ©2012
9780205750528 / 0205750524

Gender
Helgeson Psychology of Gender, 4/e ©2012
9780205050185 / 0205050182

Health Psychology
Ragin Health Psychology ©2011
9780131962972 / 0131962973

Human Sexuality
King Human Sexuality Today, 7/e ©2012
9780205015672 / 0205015670

Hock Human Sexuality, 3/e ©2012
9780205225682 / 0205225683

Infant Development
Gross Infancy: From Birth to Age 3, 2/e ©2011
9780205734191 / 0205734197

Introductory Psychology
Ciccarelli & White Psychology, 3/e ©2012
9780205832576 / 0205832571

Wade & Tavris Psychology, 10/e ©2011
9780205711468 / 0205711464

Zimbardo The World of Psychology, 7/e ©2011
9780205215133 / 0205215130

Introductory Psychology Brief
Krause & Corts Psychological Science: Modeling Scientific Literacy ©2012
9780131739857 / 0131739859

Internship / Introduction to Counseling and Psychotherapy
Baird The Internship, Practicum, and Field Placement Handbook, 6/e ©2011
9780205804962 / 0205804969

Lifespan Development (Chronological Approach)
Arnett Human Development: A Cultural Approach, ©2012
9780205595266 / 020559526X